THE ROYAL TOUCH

THE
ROYAL TOUCH

Sacred Monarchy and Scrofula
in England and France

Marc Bloch

Translated by
J. E. Anderson

ROUTLEDGE & KEGAN PAUL
LONDON
McGILL-QUEEN'S UNIVERSITY PRESS
MONTREAL

English edition first published in 1973
by Routledge & Kegan Paul Ltd
and McGill–Queen's University Press
Printed in Great Britain
by W & J Mackay Limited, Chatham
Translated from
Les Rois thaumaturges
© 1961 Max Leclerc et Cie, Proprietors of
Librairie Armand Colin
© this edition Routledge & Kegan Paul and
McGill–Queen's University Press 1973

RKP ISBN 0 7100 7355 0

McGill–Queen's ISBN 0 7735 0071 5

Library of Congress Catalog Card Number 72-91245
Legal deposit 1st quarter 1973

Contents

v

CONTENTS

Plates

Preface

Few books can have deserved as much as this one to be called the work of friendship; for have I not indeed the right to give the name of friends to all those generous collaborators who have been good enough to help me? Some of them showed a kindness that was all the more admirable in that it was not addressed to me personally, since they had never met me. The extremely scattered nature of the source material, and the complexity of the problems I was forced to deal with, would have made my task downright impossible if I had not had so many invaluable helpers. I blush at the thought of all the professors or colleagues in Strasbourg, Paris, London, Tournai, Bologna, Washington and elsewhere whom I have troubled with requests for information or suggestions, and who have always been ready and eager with a prompt reply. If I attempted to thank them all here one by one, I should try the reader's patience with an almost endless list of names. Moreover, they have shown such a disinterested kindness that they will not take it amiss if I do not mention them by name, at any rate in this foreword. Yet I should really not be doing my duty if I did not straight away express my special gratitude to the librarians and archivists who have been kind enough to give me their guidance among their respective collections of records: Mr Hilary Jenkinson, in the Public Record Office; MM. Henri Girard, André Martin and Henri Moncel at the Bibliothèque Nationale, M. Gaston Robert at the Rheims archives. I must likewise acknowledge forthwith the enormous amount of useful information I owe to the unwearying kindness of Miss Helen Farquhar and the Rev. E. W. Williamson. Finally, I must not omit to acknowledge the help given me by Dr Wickersheimer in avoiding innumerable errors in a territory that I felt to be thoroughly treacherous ground. It was invaluable to have the ready and almost daily help of such a particularly competent historian of medicine. I should also like to express my respectful gratitude to the Institut de France, which gave me access to its London branch and thus afforded me a ready entry into the libraries and records of England.

But our own Faculté des Lettres is the place where I have felt myself above all surrounded by lively and active sympathy, for its constitution and habits of life are specially favourable to work pursued in common. More particularly my colleagues Lucien Febvre and Charles Blondel will discover so much of their own in some of the following pages that I can thank them only by pointing out how much I have borrowed in all friendship from their ideas.[1]

It would be presumptuous, when publishing a work of this nature, to talk of a second edition. But it is at least legitimate to envisage the possibility of some further supplementary material. The principal advantage that I hope will result from my labours is to draw attention to a kind of question which has hitherto been too much neglected. Many of my readers will no doubt be shocked by my errors, and particularly by the omissions. I can only say that there are some works which would remain for ever unfinished if one were insistent upon avoiding not only unforeseen but also foreseeable gaps, without however being able to fill them in; and the work I am now making public is certainly one of this kind. I shall always be profoundly grateful if my readers will bring to my notice any errors or omissions in whatever way suits them best. Nothing would give me greater pleasure than to see the continuance in this way of a collaboration to which this book in its present form already owes so much.

Marlotte, 4 October 1923

As I correct the proofs and re-read these few lines of thanks, I cannot be content to leave them as they stand. There are two names missing, which I was prevented from including through a kind of sentimental modesty—perhaps unnecessarily delicate; but I can no longer let them be passed over in silence. There is no doubt at all that I should never have thought of undertaking these researches without the long-standing interchange of ideas that took place between my brother and myself. As a doctor with a passionate interest in his profession, he helped me to reflect upon the case of the royal healers. He was attracted towards comparative ethnography and religious psychology, and his lively interest in this field—his favourite among all the many subjects over which his tireless curiosity was wont to range for enjoyment—helped me to realize the interest of the great problems which I have hardly done more than touch upon here. Then I owe to my father the best part of my training as a historian. The lessons he gave me, starting in childhood and continuing all down the years, have left on me what I believe to be a permanent impression. My brother only knew this book when it was scarcely more than a rough outline. My father read it in manuscript, but did not live to see it in print. I should be lacking in filial and fraternal affection if I did not recall the memory of these two dear ones, though in the years to come I shall only have their examples and the thought of them to guide me on my way.

28 December 1923

Note on quotations from manuscripts and on the chronology

I have indicated the sources from which my information has come by the following abbreviations:

Arch. Nat.   Archives Nationales, Paris
Bibl. Nat.   Bibliothèque Nationale, Paris
B.M.   British Museum, London
E.A.   Exchequer Accounts in the Public Record Office, London
P.R.O.   Public Record Office, London (material other than the Exchequer Accounts)

Unless otherwise indicated, all the dates have been given in the new style, starting the year on 1 January. English dates before 14 September 1752 and French dates before 20 December 1582 are given according to the Julian calendar.

Introduction

'Ce roi est un grand magicien.' (Montesquieu, *Lettres Persanes*, 24.)

'Le seul miracle qui est demeuré perpetuel en la religion des Chrestiens et en la maison de France . . .' (Pierre Mathieu, *Histoire de Louys XI, roi de France*, 1610, p. 472.)

On 27 April 1340 Brother Francis, of the Order of Preachers, Bishop of Bisaccia in the province of Naples, chaplain to King Robert of Anjou and for the time being ambassador of Edward III, King of England, appeared before the Doge of Venice.[1] This was just after the outbreak of the dynastic struggle between England and France, which was destined to become the Hundred Years' War. Hostilities had already begun, but the diplomatic campaign was still continuing. Everywhere in Europe the two rival monarchs were seeking alliances. Brother Francis had been commissioned by his master to seek the support of the Venetians, and request their friendly intervention with the Genoese. We still possess a summary of what he said.[2] As was only fitting, he made much of the peaceful inclinations of the English sovereign. 'His Serene Highness Prince Edward' was, so he said, ardently desirous of avoiding the slaughter of a mass of innocent Christians. He had written to 'Philip of Valois, who calls himself King of France', proposing three possible methods of deciding the great matter at issue between them without a war; first, combat in the lists, true judgment of God, either in the form of a duel between the two claimants themselves, or a contest on a larger scale between two groups of from six to eight loyal supporters; alternatively, one or other of the following trials: 'If Philip of Valois is—as he affirms—the true king of France, let him prove the fact by exposing himself to hungry lions; for lions never attack a true king; or let him perform the miraculous healing of he sick, as all other true kings are wont to do'—meaning, no doubt, the

I

other true kings of France. 'If he should fail, he would own himself to be unworthy of the kingdom.' But Philip—so Brother Francis affirmed—had 'in his pride' rejected these suggestions.[3]

We may well wonder if Edward III had ever really made them. The documents covering the Anglo–French negotiations have come down to us in fairly good condition, but they do not reveal a single trace of the letter summarized by the Bishop of Bisaccia. It may well be that, in his desire to dazzle the Venetians, he imagined it in its entirety. But even supposing that it really had been sent, there is no need to take the trial by lions or by miracle any more seriously than the invitation to a duel. This was a classic challenge which monarchs who observed the rules of good form were accustomed to exchange in those days before entering into a state of war; yet never within human memory had any man seen a king enter the lists. It was simply a diplomatic formality; or rather, in the present case, the airy talk of a somewhat garrulous diplomat.

Nevertheless, these idle words should give the historian cause for thought. In spite of their apparent insignificance, they throw a vivid light upon some very deep questions. Compare them with what a plenipotentiary placed in a similar position today might say. The difference reveals the gulf that separates these two outlooks; for such protestations meant for the gallery are obviously a reflection of the collective consciousness. Brother Francis did not succeed in persuading the Venetians to abandon the neutrality which they considered advantageous to their trade. Neither were they swayed by the display of Edward III's peaceful intentions, of which—so they were told—he had given proof up to the last moment, or by the more specific promises in the later part of the speech. But the so-called offers said to have been made by the king of England to his French rival were perhaps not met with as much incredulity as we might imagine. Doubtless the Venetians did not expect to see Philip of Valois enter the lions' den; but the idea, 'K'enfant de roys ne peut lyons menger' (That the royal seed no lion will devour), was familiar enough to them in all the contemporary literature of adventure. They were well aware that Edward III was not disposed to give up the kingdom of France to his rival, even if the latter were to succeed in effecting miraculous cures. But even the most sceptical in the fourteenth century were hardly inclined to doubt what was known from experience—that every true king of France—or of England, for that matter—was capable of such marvels. In Venice and throughout Italy, the reality of this strange power was believed in, and if need be, it was resorted to. A document, saved by chance from destruction, has preserved the memory of four worthy Venetians who visited France in 1307—thirty-three years before Brother Francis' mission—to obtain healing from Philip the Fair.[4]

Thus the speech of a somewhat boastful diplomat is a timely reminder that our ancestors in the Middle Ages and even into more recent times had a picture of royalty very different from our own. In every country, in those days, kings were considered sacred, and in some countries at least they were held to possess miraculous powers of healing. For many centuries, the kings of France and the kings of England used to 'touch for scrofula'—to use the classical expression of the time. That is to say, they claimed to be able, simply by their touch, to cure people suffering from this disease, and their subjects shared a common belief in their medicinal powers. Over an almost equally long period, the kings of England used to distribute to their subjects, and even beyond the boundaries of their own State, the so-called cramp rings which, by virtue of their consecration at the hands of the king, were held to have acquired the power to restore health to the epileptic, and to assuage all kinds of muscular pain. These facts—or at least a general outline of them—are well known to all who have studied or who are interested in such matters. Yet it must be admitted that they are peculiarly repugnant to the modern mind, since they are usually passed over in silence. Historians have written massive tomes on the idea of royalty without ever mentioning them. The chief purpose of the following pages is therefore to fill in this gap.

The idea of studying these healing rites and—more generally—the concept of royalty implied by them came to me a few years ago when I was reading in the Godefroy *Ceremonial* the documents referring to the anointing of the French kings. At that time I was very far from realizing the true extent of the task I was undertaking. The magnitude and complexity of the research into which I have been drawn has far exceeded my expectations. Was I nevertheless right to persevere in the attempt? I am afraid that the people to whom I confided my intentions must have more than once considered me to be the victim of a strange and, on the whole, rather idle curiosity. What out-of-the-way exploration was I embarking on? A kindly Englishman, in fact, called it 'this curious by-path of yours'. Nevertheless this little-trodden track seemed to be worth following, and experience seemed to suggest that it was leading somewhere worth while. I found that what had so far been merely anecdotal could be turned into history. This introduction is not the place to attempt a detailed justification of my project. A book should justify itself. I simply want to indicate briefly here how I conceived my task and what leading ideas guided me.

There could be no question of considering the healing rites in isolation, leaving aside the whole group of superstitions and legends which form the 'marvellous' element in the monarchical idea. That would have condemned me in advance to see in them nothing but a ridiculous anomaly, quite unconnected with the general tendencies of the collective consciousness. I have used them as a guide-line for studying—particularly in France and England—the supernatural character that was long attributed to the royal power. Using a term the sociologists have slightly twisted from its original meaning, one might call this the 'mystique' of royalty. Royalty! Its history dominates the whole evolution of European institutions. Almost all the peoples of Western Europe down to our own times have been ruled by kings. The political development of human societies in our countries could for a long period be summed up almost entirely in the vicissitudes of power of the great dynasties. Now in order to understand what the monarchies were in former times, and above all to understand their long-lasting hold upon the human spirit, it will not be enough to enter into the most minute details of the workings of the administrative, judicial and financial organization which they imposed upon their subjects. Neither will it be enough to conduct an abstract analysis, nor to attempt to extract from a few great theories the concepts of absolutism or divine right. We must also fathom the beliefs and fables that grew up around the princely houses. On a good many points, this folklore tells us more than any doctrinal treatise. As Claude d'Albon, 'jurisconsult and poet of Dauphiné', writing in 1575, justly observed in his treatise *De la Maiesté royalle*, 'what has caused the kings to be so venerated has been chiefly the divine virtues and powers seen in them alone, and not in other men'. [5]

Of course, Claude d'Albon did not believe that those 'divine virtues and powers' were the only *raison d'être* for the royal power. And it should scarcely be necessary to declare that I do not believe this either. Nothing would be more ridiculous than to treat kings as nothing more than sorcerers on the grounds that the kings of the past, including the greatest among them—such as St Louis, Edward I and Louis XIV—all claimed, like our 'secret healers' in the countryside today, to cure illnesses simply by their touch. They were heads of State, judges and leaders in war. The institution of monarchy served to satisfy certain eternal needs in the societies of old, needs which were entirely real and essentially human. The societies of today are equally aware of them, yet are usually content to satisfy them in other ways. But in the eyes of his faithful subjects a king was, after all, something very different from a mere high official. He was surrounded by a 'veneration' which did not simply originate in the services he performed. How can we understand this feeling of loyalty which was so strong and so specific at certain periods in our history if, from the outset, we refuse to see the supernatural aura which surrounded these crowned heads?

We shall not have to examine this 'mystical' royalty in its germinal stage, or go back to first principles. Its origins elude the historian of mediaeval and modern Europe; in fact, they elude the historian altogether, and only comparative ethnography seems able to cast a certain degree of light upon them. The civilizations from which our own is directly descended received this heritage from still older civilizations, lost in the shadows of prehistory. Could it be, then, that we shall find as our object of study only what is sometimes a little disdainfully called 'a relic'?

We shall have occasion later on to observe that this word cannot in any way be legitimately applied to the healing rites considered in themselves. Indeed, the touch for scrofula will appear as the creation of the first Capetians in France and the Normans in England. As for the blessing of rings by the English sovereigns, we shall see that this occurs only later in the evolution of miraculous royalty. There remains the intrinsic notion of the sacred and miraculous character of kings, an essentially psychological feature, and the rites we are considering constituted only one among many of its manifestations. This notion is much older than the most ancient historical dynasties of France or England, and might be said to have long outlived the social environment which had first conditioned its birth—an environment of which we know practically nothing. But if we are to understand 'relic' in the usual sense, that is to say, an institution or belief from which all real life has disappeared, the continued existence of which can only be justified by its having once upon a time corresponded to some reality—in fact a kind of fossil bearing witness to ages that have long since passed away—then in this sense the idea we are considering had nothing about it, in the Middle Ages and right up to the seventeenth century at least, which would authorize the use of this term. Its longevity involved no degeneration. On the contrary, it retained a profound vitality; it continued to be endowed with a power of feeling that remained constantly active; it adapted itself to new political, and, more particularly, new religious conditions; and it assumed forms that had hitherto been unknown, among which healing rites are a case in point. We shall not explain its origins, for that would take us out of our proper field of study; but we shall have to explain its continuance and its evolution, both of which are a part—and a very important part—of the total explanation. In biology, to give an account of an organism's existence is not simply to search for its parental forms; it is equally important to determine the character of the environment which allows it to live, yet forces it to undergo certain modifications. The same is true—*mutatis mutandis*—for occurrences in society.

In short, what I have attempted here is essentially a contribution to the political history of Europe, in the widest and truest sense of those words.

By the very nature of the material, this essay in political history has had to take on the form of an essay in comparative history; for France and England both possessed kings with healing powers, and the idea of royalty as something miraculous and sacred was common to the whole of Western Europe. This is a fortunate necessity, if it is true, as I believe, that the evolution of the civilizations we have inherited will become fairly clear to us only when we are able to consider it outside the very limited framework of national traditions.[6]

But there is more to be said. If I had not been afraid of adding to a title that was already too lengthy, I should have given this book a second subtitle: *The history of a miracle*. As the Bishop of Bisaccia reminded the Venetians, the healing of scrofula or of epilepsy by the royal touch was indeed a 'miracle': in truth, a great miracle, which must be reckoned among the most renowned, and certainly among the most continuous, miracles presented by the past. Countless witnesses have testified to it, and its fame died out only after seven centuries of sustained popularity and almost unclouded glory. Surely a critical history of such a supernatural manifestation cannot be a matter of indifference to religious psychology, or rather, to our knowledge of the human mind?

The greatest difficulty I have met with in the course of my research has come from the condition of the source material. Not that testimonies relating to the miraculous healing-power of kings, taken as a whole and with the necessary reservations about the beginnings, are lacking in number; but they are extremely scattered, and enormously diverse in kind. A single example will illustrate the point. Our oldest information on the touch for scrofula by the kings of France occurs in a little work of religious polemics entitled *De Pignoribus Sanctorum*. In England, the first certain testimony to the same rite comes in a private letter, which is perhaps nothing more than an exercise in style. The first known mention of healing rings consecrated by the English kings is to be found in a royal prescription. For the rest of the story, I have had to draw upon a mass of documents of various kinds—account books, administrative material of every sort, narrative literature, political and theological writings, medical treatises, liturgical texts, figured monuments—and many more I will not mention. The reader will even find himself faced with a game of cards. The royal accounts, both French and English, could not be put to full use without a critical examination, and I have devoted a special study to them. But it would have overloaded the Introduction, so I have consigned it to the end of the book. The iconographical material was fairly scanty, and relatively easy to list; I have tried to draw up an accurate inventory of it, which will also be found in an Appendix. The other sources seemed to be too numerous and disparate to warrant any attempt at a complete list; it will be enough to quote them and comment upon them as they are used. Besides, with material like this, what is the good of attempting any nomenclature for the sources? It could be no more than a list of random soundings. With very few of the documents could one venture to predict with any certainty that it would or would not provide useful information about the royal miracles. It is a matter of groping one's way, trusting to good luck or instinct, and wasting a great deal of time for a very meagre return. If only all collections of texts were provided with an index—an index of subject matter! But it is scarcely necessary to point out that in many cases this is totally lacking. These indispensable tools seem to grow even rarer as the documents become more recent in date. Their too frequent absence constitutes one of the most shocking deficiencies in our present method of publication. I feel perhaps a little sore on this point, for this vexatious omission has often made things extremely difficult for me. Moreover, even when there is an index, it often happens that its author has systematically omitted all mention of the healing rites, judging such practices as futile and beneath the dignity of history. Many a time I have felt like a man placed in the middle of a large number of closed coffers, some of them containing gold and others nothing but stones, with no directions to help distinguish between the treasure and the pebbles. In other words, I make no claim at all to completeness: I can only hope that this book may encourage researchers to make new discoveries!

Fortunately, I was by no means exploring entirely new ground. As far as I knew, there was no historical work in existence on the subject in hand with the breadth and critical character I have endeavoured to embody in mine. Yet the 'literature' on the royal healings is fairly rich. It is in fact of a dual kind. There are two literatures with different origins, moving side by side and mostly ignoring each other. One is the work of professional scholars, and the other—more extensive—is the work of doctors. I have done my best to study and use them both. The reader will find in this book a bibliographical list which will no doubt seem tolerably lengthy. But I should not like certain particularly distinguished works, which I have constantly drawn upon, to remain lost in the crowd; and I must make a point of naming my principal guides here. The studies by Law Hussey and Waterton, both of them published some time ago, have been of great service to me. Among authors still living, I owe more than I can express to M. François-Delaborde, Dr Crawfurd, and Miss Helen Farquhar.

I also owe a large debt of gratitude to my predecessors of another age. Much was written from the sixteenth to the eighteenth century on the healing rites, and in this literature of the *ancien régime* even the lumber is interesting, for it often provides information of an out-of-the-way kind on the state of mind of that age. But it does not contain merely lumber. The seventeenth century in particular did produce, alongside some works or pamphlets of a peculiarly inept kind some remarkable works, such as the pages devoted to scrofula by du Peyrat in his *Histoire ecclésiastique de la Cour*. Outstanding above all are two academic treatises, by Daniel Georges Morhof and Jean Joachim Zentgraff respectively. They have furnished an abundance of useful references such as I have not found elsewhere. I am particularly happy to recall here all that I owe to the second of these dissertations, for I can address myself to its author as a colleague. Jean Joachim Zentgraff was a native of Strasbourg. He was born in the free city, became a subject of Louis XIV, delivered the eulogy on Henry of Navarre,[7] and carved out a brilliant university career in his native city, which had then become French. The present book figures among the publications of our revived Faculté des Lettres; and I am delighted thus to be able to continue in some measure—though with full awareness of the difference between

7

the spirit of our respective times—the work begun in former days by a Rector of the ancient University of Strasbourg.

BOOK 1

THE ORIGINS

I

The beginnings of
the touch for scrofula

1 *Scrofula*

The two words 'écrouelles', or more often 'scrofula', which is only a learned form of the first (both of them coming from the Latin *scrofula*), are used by doctors today to signify tuberculous adenitis, that is to say inflammation of the lymph nodes due to the bacillus of tuberculosis. It is obvious that before the advent of bacteriology, such specialization of these two names, which go back to the medicine of antiquity, was quite impossible. It was not possible to distinguish between the various infections of the ganglia; or at any rate the tentative scientific efforts at classification —which were bound to be abortive—did not leave any traces in current medical language. All these infections were uniformly called 'écrouelles' in French and *scrofula* or *strumae* in Latin; these last two words were generally synonymous. It should be added that by far the greater number of inflammations of the ganglia are tuberculous in origin; so that the majority of cases classed as scrofula by the doctors in the Middle Ages would also be diagnosed as such by our doctors today. But popular language was less precise than technical language. The ganglia most easily attacked by tuberculosis are those of the neck; and when the disease goes untreated, and suppurations occur, the face may easily appear to be affected. Hence a confusion, apparent in many of the documents, between scrofula and various other affections of the face or even the eyes.[1] Tubercular adenitis is very widespread, even nowadays; so what must it have been like in conditions of hygiene notably inferior to our own? If we mentally add the other kinds of adenitis, and all the vague crop of miscellaneous diseases popularly confused with them, we shall have some idea of the ravages attributable to what Europe of old used to include under the name of 'scrofula'. In certain regions, as both mediaeval and modern doctors testify, these diseases were virtually endemic.[2] This is hardly ever a fatal disease; but especially where there is a failure to give the appropriate treatment, it is very trying and disfiguring. The frequent suppurations had something repulsive about them, and the horror they engendered is naïvely expressed in more than one ancient account. The face became 'putrid' and the sores gave forth a 'foetid odour'. The background picture, then, which the historian of the royal miracle should keep in mind, is that of countless sufferers longing for healing, and ready to have recourse to any remedies they might hear of through common report.

I have already reminded the reader of what this miracle was. In France of old it was called 'mal le roi'; in England, the King's Evil. The kings of France and of England claimed that a simple touch of their hands, made according to the traditional rites, was able to cure the scrofulous. When did they begin to exercise this miraculous power? How were they led to make this claim? And how did their subjects come to acknowledge it? These are delicate problems, which I shall try to resolve. The rest of this study will be based upon reliable testimony; but here, in this first book devoted to origins, we are touching on a very obscure past, and we shall have to resign ourselves in advance to giving considerable place to hypotheses. The historian may legitimately make use of them, provided he does not put them forward as certainties. Let us then start by bringing together the most ancient texts relating to the 'physician princes', as they used to be called, beginning with France.

2 *The beginnings of the French rite*

We owe the first document, in which without a shadow of doubt the French 'touch' appears, to the chance fact of an unusual controversy.[3] About the beginning of the twelfth century the monastery of St-Médard of Soissons claimed to possess a most outstanding relic—a tooth belonging to Our Saviour, a milk-tooth, so it was said.[4] In order to spread the news of their glorious treasure, the monks had a short treatise put together, which has since disappeared; but thanks to numerous other examples, it is not difficult to guess what it was like. It must have been a fairly crude production—a small booklet for the use of pilgrims, containing a collection of miracles.[5] Now at this time there lived not far from Soissons a certain Guibert, the abbot of Nogent-sous-Coucy, one of the best writers of the period. Nature had endowed him with a mind that was both judicious and subtle; moreover, there may have been some obscure quarrel which has now passed into oblivion spurring him on against his 'neighbours' of Soissons,[6] one of those bitter Church rivalries that abound in the history of the time. This may well have helped to sharpen his love of truth in the matter at issue. He did not believe in the authenticity of the famous tooth; and when the document referred to above appeared, he in his turn determined to open the eyes of the faithful who had been deluded by the 'falsifiers' of St-Médard.[7] That was the origin of this curious treatise *De Pignoribus Sanctorum*, which seems to have aroused little interest in the Middle Ages. In fact, there remains only one manuscript, copied perhaps under the eyes of Guibert himself;[8] today, however, scholars have been delighted to discover, among a great deal of rubbish, evidence of a quite unfettered critical sense—something extremely rare in the twelfth century. It is a rather disconnected work, containing alongside amusing anecdotes a quantity of rather unrelated observations on the subject of relics, visions, and miraculous manifestations in general.[9] Let us look at Book I, in which Guibert, in perfect conformity with the most orthodox doctrine, develops the idea that miracles are not by themselves any indication of holiness. God alone is their author; and in His Divine Wisdom chooses as instruments or 'channels' those men who are fitted to His purposes even if they are ungodly. Then there follow some examples from the Bible, or from the historians of antiquity, who were looked upon by the scholars of that time with almost as blind a faith as the Sacred Book itself. He mentions Balaam's prophecy, and Caiaphas', Vespasian's healing of a lame man, the sea at Pamphylia parting in front of Alexander the Great, and finally the signs that so often announced the birth or the death of princes.[10] To which Guibert adds:

But what am I saying? Have we not seen our Lord King Louis performing a customary marvel? With my own eyes I have seen people suffering from scrofula on the neck or other parts of the body crowd round the king in order to be touched by him—and to his touch he added also the sign of the cross. I was there quite near him, and even helped to keep the crowds from pressing too close upon him. The king, however, showed his innate generosity towards them, drawing them to himself with his serene hand and humbly making the sign of the cross over them. His father Philip had also zealously applied himself to the exercise of this glorious and miraculous power; and I do not know what sins he committed to make him lose it.[11]

Such are the few lines that have been quoted again and again since the seventeenth century by the historians of scrofula. The two princes mentioned in them are clearly Louis VI and his father Philip I. What conclusions can we draw?

In the first place Louis VI (who reigned from 1108 to 1137) was considered to possess the power of healing scrofula; crowds were wont to press round him, and the king, himself fully persuaded of the power given to him from above, acceded to their prayers. And not only once, on some random occasion, in a moment of exceptional popular enthusiasm; no, we are already confronted with a 'customary' practice, a regular rite clothed in the forms that were to belong to it throughout the course of the French monarchy. The king touches the sufferers and makes the sign of the cross over them—these were the two successive gestures destined to remain a permanent part of the tradition. Guibert was an eye-witness, whose testimony cannot be put in doubt; he met Louis VI at Laon, and perhaps on other occasions; his office as abbot meant that he would have regular close access to his sovereign.[12]

But there is more to be said. This miraculous power was not considered as belonging personally to King Louis. It was recalled that his father and predecessor Philip I (1060–1108), whose long reign takes us back almost to the middle of the eleventh century, had exercised this power before him; and it was said that he had subsequently lost it because of 'I do not know what sins', as Guibert delicately puts it, for he was greatly attached to the Capetian family, and disposed to cover up their faults. There can be no doubt that it was a question of the doubly adulterous union between Philip and Bertrade de Montfort. The king was excommunicated for this crime, and it was thought that the divine wrath had struck him with various 'shameful' diseases.[13] No wonder, then, that he had at the same time lost his healing power. This ecclesiastical legend is of little consequence for us here. But it does indicate that Philip I is the first French king of whom we can say with certainty that he touched the scrofulous.

It should also be observed that this invaluable text remains absolutely unique for its period. As we pass down the ages step by step, in search of healings carried out by the kings of France, we have to travel on as far as the reign of St-Louis (1226–70), about whom, incidentally, we have fairly full information,[14] before we arrive at any new document. If the monks of St-Médard had not claimed to possess a tooth of Christ, and if Guibert had not taken it into his head to hold forth against them, or if his treatise—like so many others of the same kind—had been lost, we should no doubt have been tempted to see St-Louis as the first healing monarch. There is in actual fact no reason to suppose that between 1137 and 1226 any interruption took place in the exercise of the miraculous gift. The texts dealing with St-Louis demonstrate clearly his powers as traditional and hereditary. Yet the continuous silence of the documents over almost a century demands an explanation, which we shall attempt later on. For the moment, however, we must concentrate upon determining when the rite began, and need only remember what has just been said by way of prudent counsel. By fortunate chance, we still have a few sentences from a twelfth-century writer who recalls in passing that his sovereign used to heal the scrofulous; and other less fortunate hazards may well have deprived us of similar references to previous kings. If without more ado we were to affirm that Philip I was the first to 'touch for scrofula', we should be in danger of making the same kind of mistake as if—supposing the only manuscript of the *De Pignoribus Sanctorum* to have been lost—we had concluded in the absence of any mention earlier than St-Louis that this king had initiated the rite.

Can we hope to go further back than Philip I?

It is no new question, whether the first two royal lines already possessed the medicinal powers claimed by the Capetians. It was thrashed out again and again by the scholars of the sixteenth and seventeenth centuries, in controversies whose echoes even reached the royal table.

One Easter Day at Fontainebleau Henry IV, after touching for scrofula, thought it good to enliven his dinner by a novel kind of joust. He selected as the combatants certain scholars—André du Laurens, his senior physician, Pierre Mathieu, his historiographer, and Guillaume du Peyrat, his almoner. The doctor and historiographer maintained that the power of which their master had just given fresh proof went back to Clovis; the almoner denied that the Merovingians or Carolingians had ever exercised this power.[15] Let us then also enter the lists and try to form an opinion. It is a complicated problem, but it may be split up into a number of simpler questions which must be examined one by one.

First, is there any documentary trace suggesting that any king of the first two dynasties may perhaps have claimed to heal the scrofulous? On this point, we shall have no difficulty in siding with the negative opinion, often expressed forcibly by du Peyrat, by Scipion Dupleix, and by all the learned minds of the seventeenth century. No document of that kind has ever been produced. But we should go further than this. Our knowledge of the High Middle Ages is based upon sources that are scanty, and therefore easy to explore. They have been conscientiously sifted over several centuries by the scholars of all nations. If such a source has never been discovered, it may safely be concluded that it does not exist. Later on, we shall have occasion to see how the story arose in the sixteenth century of the healing by Clovis of his squire Lanicet; and we shall then see that this tradition is without any real foundation. It is a younger sister of the legends about the Holy Phial or the heavenly origin of the fleur-de-lis, and must be consigned, along with its elder sisters, to the department of outworn historical accessories—as all serious historians long ago agreed.

We must now put our problem in a more comprehensive form. Neither the Merovingians nor the Carolingians, as far as documentary evidence goes, possessed this special form of healing power for the specific illness of scrofula. But may they not have been considered capable of healing either some other particular disease, or even diseases in general? Let us see what Gregory of Tours has to say. In Book IX, with reference to King Guntram, the son of Clotaire I, there occurs the following passage:

It was commonly related among the faithful that a certain woman
whose son lay stretched upon a bed of pain, suffering from a quaternary
fever, made her way through the crowd from behind the king,
and without his noting it, managed to pull off a part of the fringe of
the royal cloak. She soaked it in water, and then gave this water to

15

her son to drink. The fever immediately abated, and the disease was cured. For my part, I do not doubt this matter; for indeed I myself have often seen demons who inhabit the bodies of those possessed cry out the name of this king, and, being unmasked by the virtue proceeding from him, confess their crimes.[16]

So it would seem that Guntram possessed among his subjects and advisers—of whom Gregory of Tours was avowedly one—the reputation of being a healer. There was a miraculous power inherent in the clothes that had touched his person. His mere presence—or perhaps simply the invocation of his name (the text is not very clear on this point)—could deliver the possessed. The whole question is to know if he shared this miraculous capacity with those of his line, or whether it was simply a personal gift. His memory would not appear to have been the object of any officially recognized cult, although the Italian hagiographer Pietro Natali thought him worthy of a place in his *Catalogus Sanctorum*.[17] But there is no doubt that many of his contemporaries, and first and foremost the bishop of Tours, considered him to be a saint. Not that his manners were particularly pure or gentle; but he was so pious!—for, says Gregory, a little before the passage quoted above, 'you would have taken him for a bishop rather than a king'. Moreover, this same Gregory gives us a host of details about Guntram's ancestors and uncles and brothers. Veriantius Fortunatus sang the praises of several Merovingian monarchs, but nowhere does it appear that any of those princes, though praised as more or less pious or generous or brave, had healed anyone. For the Carolingians, the verdict is the same. The Carolingian renaissance has left us a relatively abundant literature containing in particular some treatises of a semi-political and semi-moralistic character on the subject of royalty, and some biographies or collections of anecdotes about certain sovereigns; but it would be impossible to discover anything in them relating to the healing power of kings. If we were to rely on a single passage in Gregory of Tours and decide that the early Merovingians possessed medicinal powers, we should also have to assume that these powers had suffered an eclipse under the Carolingians. There would thus be no possibility of establishing continuity between Guntram and Philip I, between a king of the sixth century and one of the eleventh. It is simpler to admit that these miracles were attributed to Guntram by common belief, not as a royal attribute, but as a seemingly necessary consequence of the saintly character ascribed to him by his faithful. For in the eyes of his contemporaries, what was a saint but —first and foremost—a worker of beneficent miracles? Moreover, as we shall see later on, it was all the easier for Guntram to appear saintly because he was a king, and belonged to a dynasty the Franks had long been accustomed to consider holy. But if he partly at least owed his sanctity—and consequently his miraculous powers—to his royal origin, this gift nevertheless constituted a personal grace not possessed by his immediate forefathers, ancestors or successors. The uninterrupted series of physician-kings in mediaeval France does not begin with the pious sovereign so dear to the heart of Gregory of Tours.

But at this point I shall perhaps be interrupted with an objection. No doubt, it will be said, the Merovingian or Carolingian texts—at least in the form in which they have come down to us—nowhere show us a king healing scrofula, and except for the passage just studied from Gregory of Tours, never mention royal healings of any imaginable kind whatsoever. This cannot be denied. But our sources—as we recalled above—are very scanty; and are we justified in taking their silence as anything more than an admission of ignorance? Is it not possible, although we know nothing about it, that the sovereigns of the first two lines did in fact lay hands upon the sick? To be sure, in all scientific matters negative proof is dangerous; and, in historical criticism more especially, the argument from silence is always full of pitfalls. Nevertheless, we should not let ourselves be led astray by this formidable word 'negative'. On this very subject du Peyrat writes quite admirably as follows:

> Someone may say to me, perchance, that the argument from negative authority cannot be conclusive; but I would answer him as Coeffeteau answers Plessis Mornay, namely that this is a logic that does not apply to history; on the contrary, it is in truth an affirmative argument; for all those authors—St-Remy, Gregory of Tours, Hincmar and others who followed them during the second royal line—were in duty bound, as faithful historians, to mention such a memorable thing in their writings, if it had indeed been practised in their time . . . and in as much as they did not write of such a miracle, they did in fact affirm that it was unknown in their century.[18]

In other words, it is all a question of knowing whether the documents contemporary with the Merovingian and Carolingian dynasties are of such a kind that if the practice of royal healing had existed, they could have passed it over in silence. And that is something which will appear very unlikely, particularly where the sixth century—the period of Fortunatus and Gregory of Tours—is concerned, and more so still for the splendid age of the next dynasty. If Charlemagne or Louis the Pious had laid hands upon the sick, is it conceivable that the monk of St-Gall or the Astronomer would not have mentioned this miraculous feat? Is it likely that any of those writers at the royal court, who formed the brilliant constellation of the 'Carolingian renaissance', could fail to make some passing allusion to such a notable fact? No doubt—as I recalled above—there is an equal documentary silence from Louis VI to St-Louis; but later on I shall offer an explanation of this silence, which after all only lasted three reigns. I shall show how this originated in a movement of political thought arising from the Gregorian reforms, whose ruling ideas were as different as possible from those inspiring the authors mentioned above. The incomparably much longer silence of Merovingian and Carolingian literature would be absolutely inexplicable on any other assumption than the absence of the very rite we are searching for, but in vain. There is no reason to believe that the descendants of Clovis or Pepin ever claimed to heal anyone in their capacity as king.

We will now go on to the early Capetians. As we all know, the life of the second prince of this line, Robert the Pious, was written by one of his protégés, a monk called Helgaud. It is, frankly, a panegyric: Robert is adorned with all the virtues, especially those calculated to appeal to the monks. Helgaud particularly vaunts his kindness to lepers, and adds:

> The divine virtue granted to this perfect man a very great grace, to wit, the power of healing men's bodies; for by touching with his most pious hand the sores of the suffering and signing them with the holy cross, he was wont to deliver them from their pains and diseases.[19]

This short passage has been much discussed. Excellent scholars have refused to see it as the earliest reference to the healing power of the French kings. Let us look at the reasons they put forward.

What precisely does the *Life* of King Robert say? It says that this king used to heal the sick; but was this by special grace, or by virtue of an hereditary vocation belonging to him in common with all his line? The text is silent on this point. It may well be wondered whether Helgaud, full of admiration for the king whose mighty deeds he recounted, and perhaps with an eye to his future canonization, may not have considered the miraculous power attributed to his hero as a strictly individual manifestation of sanctity. Let us come back a moment to the passage quoted above from Gregory of Tours. Our conclusion was that King Guntram was personally considered to have been a saint, rather than that the Merovingians as a whole were considered to have possessed miraculous powers of healing. Surely the testimony of Helgaud should carry the same interpretation. Yet closer consideration shows this analogy to be thoroughly superficial. The text by Gregory of Tours stood out as an absolutely isolated witness in the midst of a prolonged and universal documentary silence. In order to link the healing powers of the son of Clotaire and the authentic beginnings of the touch for scrofula in the reign of Philip I, we should have to leap five centuries and three dynasties; we should have to assume complete silence about the past by a mass of authors who had no motive at all for silence. But in this later case, there is no difficulty of this nature. Between Robert II and his grandson Philip I there is only a short interval of twenty-nine years—a single generation, a single reign, that of Henry I, which happens to be the least well-known of all the reigns in this period. We know practically nothing about this prince. He may well have laid hands on the sick without any memory of this gesture coming down to us; and we even have no right to be surprised at our ignorance on this matter. Let us assume for the moment that Robert II initiated the famous rite the history of which we are attempting to trace, and see what may have happened. His faithful followers believed him capable of healing, for this is testified by the mouth of his biographer. They may after all have considered this a gift peculiar to their lord. But after him his descendants and successors claimed the paternal privilege as their prescriptive inheritance. We do not know if Helgaud survived his hero for any considerable time; but he may have been ignorant of their claims, or, being aware of them, he may have preferred for one reason or another to be silent. But for us, there is really no cause for doubt, since we have irrefutable textual evidence that his grandson Robert exercised the same power only a few years later. In truth, nothing could be more natural than to imagine, between two generations that lay so close to one another, the continuity of one and the same miraculous tradition, or rather the same rite,—the touch, followed by the sign of the cross—whether it be Robert or Louis VI, for the healing gestures would seem to have been exactly the same. On this point, so far as Philip I is concerned, the documents are silent. Helgaud does not appear to have viewed the 'great grace' granted to his king as a heritage from his ancestors. We may thus conclude, with a fair chance of being right, that Robert II was the first of the wonder-working kings, the original link in this glorious chain; but not that no subsequent king accomplished healings, for this would be contradicted by the facts.

There is a further difficulty. We know that Philip I touched the scrofulous; now in Helgaud's account there is no mention of scrofula. Helgaud's 'great grace' occurs after he has been describing the behaviour of the king towards the lepers, though his act would not appear to have particular reference to lepers. It is not any special disease as such, scrofula or leprosy or anything else, but rather all diseases in general that Robert could cure, according to his admirers. 'It should be noted', writes Delaborde, 'that scrofula is not mentioned in the passage from this biography which has been taken as the earliest reference to our kings' particular gift; the reference is purely to the general power to heal disease common to all the saints.'[20] I agree. But is it certain that the gift recognized as belonging to the king was in the first place thought of as 'particular' to him? We are so accustomed to seeing the miraculous power of the French princes attached solely to the healing of scrofula that we are no longer surprised at its having taken this strictly limited form. But it would be an unjustifiable postulate to assume from the outset that such was indeed the case, and this can be shown by a comparison. The majority of the really popular saints also have their own special talent. People call on one of them for help in eye diseases, another for stomach affections, and so on. But, as far as we can see, these specializations are seldom recognized at the beginning: the best proof of this is the variations sometimes to be found. In the popular mind, every saint is considered a physician, and gradually, through an association of ideas that is often obscure, and sometimes merely through a play upon words, the faithful become accustomed to ascribing to their saint the gift of alleviating such and such a disease with a specific name. Then time completes the work. After a certain number of years, belief in this very specific power has become a genuine article of faith among the unfortunate sufferers from this disease. Later on we shall come across one of these great pilgrimage saints, St-Marcoul of Corbeny. Like the kings of France, he was a healer of scrofula, and as such he acquired a notable fame, though very late in time. Earlier, for several centuries, he had only been one saint among many others, whom people called upon indiscriminately for any kind of disease. We know his story fairly well; and it would seem probable that it was only a repetition—though at some centuries' remove—of the story of the French kings, which is more imperfectly known to us. Like the saint of Corbeny, the kings no doubt began by healing a number of diseases, and only secondarily came to specialize in one. The collective notions giving rise to the idea of a medical power residing in royalty are a delicate matter to pursue in all their ramifications, but they are not impossible to understand. A little later I shall try to reconstruct them, and show that they are connected to a whole cycle of beliefs relating to the sacred character of royalty which we are just beginning to uncover. What would be really inconceivable is that the French should suddenly have got it into their heads that their sovereigns could cure scrofula and the scrofulous only, rather than diseases and illnesses in general.

Let us assume, on the contrary, that events took the same course as with St-Marcoul. Let us suppose that the early Capetians—say from Robert the Pious onwards—'touched' and 'signed with the cross' all the poor sufferers from various diseases who flocked around them, attracted by their wonder-working reputation. This crowd would certainly have included some scrofulous sufferers, for in Europe at that period scrofula was a very frequent and much-dreaded illness. But basically it was a fairly benign affection, more repulsive to look at than really dangerous, and above all subject to remissions, at least of an apparent or temporary kind.[21] Among the scrofulous over whom the royal hand had passed, some would get well, and many others would appear to do so; in the course of nature, as we should say nowadays, by virtue of the royal touch, as they said in the eleventh century. It can easily be conceived that some cases of this kind happened to occur, for one reason or another, in conditions particularly calculated to strike the imagination. People would then be naturally inclined to contrast the sufferers thus relieved with others suffering from different diseases, who had been touched by the king without success, and that would be quite enough to instil into the popular mind the belief that the Capetian princes specialized in the healing of scrofula. No doubt, in reconstructing a sequence of events of this sort, there is necessarily a large element of hypothesis. It will always be difficult to follow out in detail the process by which a healer in general becomes a specialized healer, because it comes about as the result of a multitude of small occurrences, very diverse in kind, which are effective solely in their cumulative weight. Taken separately, they would be too insignificant for mention in the documents; and this is what historians call 'chance'. But the possibility of such a process is abundantly demonstrated by the cults of the saints. Here we possess a solid support for our argument, since we have a specific text. There is no reason to reject Helgaud's testimony, and there is nothing contrary to probability in the development it enables us to trace. It should therefore be accepted.

We can feel sure, therefore, that we are on solid ground if we sum up as follows: Robert the Pious, the second Capetian, was held by his faithful admirers to possess the gift of healing the sick. His successors inherited his power; but as it passed down the generations, this dynastic virtue became gradually modified or rather grew more precise. The idea arose that the royal touch was a sovereign remedy, not for all diseases indiscriminately, but in particular for one extremely widespread disease, scrofula; and by the time of Philip I, Robert's grandson, this transformation had been accomplished.

We have thus been able to fix with some probability the genesis of touching for scrofula in France. It remains to search out the origins, in the proper sense of the word; that is, to understand how it came about that the kings were looked upon as such prodigious physicians. But for the moment, this is not something that can be undertaken with a full measure of success. For the royal miracle was just as much English as French, and in any explanatory study of its origins, the two countries must not be treated separately. If it is a question of determining why the healing rite made its appearance in France at one particular moment rather than at another, the attempt cannot be made without having fixed the time when the same rite first saw the light of day in England. Without this indispensable precaution, there would be no means of knowing whether the French kings did not simply imitate their English rivals. Again, if it is a question of analysing the concept of royalty embodied in this rite, the same collective ideas will be found at the source in these two neighbouring nations. So we must first of all undertake the same critical enquiry for England as we have carried out on the French documents.

3 The beginnings of the rite in England

Towards the end of the twelfth century there was at the court of Henry II, king of England, a cleric of French origin, Peter of Blois. He was one of those ecclesiastic scholars of whom the brilliant Plantagenet court produced so many—men far more spiritual, according to Hauréau,[22] than those assembled at the same period round the king of France. Among other works by him we possess an invaluable collection of letters, well worth perusing. In it, we shall find two letters closely connected with each other, both being addressed to clerics of the royal entourage. In the first, Peter says everything bad he can think of about the court and its courtiers; in the second, he sings its praises.[23] Was he forced to make this retraction—as certain historians have believed[24]—by his sovereign's displeasure? For my part, I admit that it goes against the grain to take these two letters seriously: I find it hard to see in them any more than two exercises in rhetoric or sophistry, a *sic et non* thoroughly in keeping with the taste of the period. Not that this really matters, however. The second letter contains the following passage:

> I would have you know that to attend upon the king is [for a cleric] something sacred, for the king himself is holy; he is the Anointed of the Lord; it is not in vain that he has received the sacrament of royal unction, whose efficacy—if someone should chance to be ignorant of it or doubt it—would be amply proved by the disappearance of that plague affecting the groin and by the healing of scrofula.[25]

So Henry II used to heal the scrofulous. The disappearance (*defectus*) of a plague attacking the groin (*inguinariae pestis*) was likewise attributed to his royal power. We do not know precisely to what these words refer. Perhaps it was some bubonic plague epidemic which was believed to have yielded to the miraculous influence of the king. It was quite possible, as that excellent historian of medicine, Dr Crawfurd, points out, for a man of that time[26] to confuse certain forms of bubonic plague with adenitis of the groin. Peter of Blois was not a doctor and he shared in the popular errors of his day; he probably considered the bubonic plague, which he, like most of his associates, believed Henry II to have miraculously cured, as a particular case of the huge group of those affections of the ganglia which the Middle Ages lumped together under the name of scrofula. In short, scrofula was Henry II's speciality. His healing power was not personal, but belonged to his function, for it was as king that he had this wonder-working gift. Henry died in 1189. For the following century, we have a series of documents, increasing in number as we approach the year 1300, indicating that his successors inherited the same gift.[27] In the history of this royal miracle, he occupies the same place for England as Philip I does for France, namely that of the first sovereign of whom it may be said with certainty that he touched for scrofula. But there is no reason why we should not, if need be, use a certain amount of conjecture and go further back in time than Henry II.

We have seen that, according to certain learned Frenchmen of the *ancien régime*, the initiator of the rite on the French side of the Channel was Clovis. An English clergyman of the sixteenth century, William Tooker, conferred the same honour upon King Lucius, who was supposed to be the first Christian to reign over Great Britain.[28] This story did not find much support, and deserves none at all. Clovis at least was a real person; the good Lucius never existed except in the imagination of scholars. In solid history, during the greater part of the Anglo-Saxon period, we do not come across any mention of healing power attributed to the kings.[29] Not till the period immediately preceding the Norman conquest do we find a prince who was—rightly or wrongly—credited with being the first of a line of healing kings. Edward the Confessor is still almost universally considered today as the founder of the English rite. This tradition is all the weightier because Shakespeare, drawing as usual upon Holinshed, made it his own, in one of his most famous and most widely-read plays. In *Macbeth*,[30] Malcolm and Macduff, fleeing from the hatred of the Scottish tyrant, take refuge in the court of Edward the Confessor, where Malcolm becomes the astonished witness of the miracle, which he reports to his companion:

> strangely visited people,
> All sworn and ulcerous, pitiful to the eye,
> The mere despair of surgery, he cures,
> Hanging a golden stamp about their necks,
> Put on with holy prayers; and 'tis spoken,
> To the succeeding royalty he leaves
> The healing benediction.

(Macbeth, IV, iii)

Are we to support this opinion of Shakespeare?

The life and, more especially, the supernatural virtues of Edward the Confessor are known to us in particular from four documents: some passages in William of Malmesbury's *Historia Regum*, and three biographies, the first anonymous, and the two others respectively by Osbert of Clare and Ailred of Rievaulx. Ailred was writing in 1163, under Henry II, Osbert in 1138, in the time of Stephen of Blois. William is a little earlier, the first edition of his *Historia* falling in the second half of Henry I's reign in 1124 or 1125. Lastly, the anonymous *Life* is usually considered to be roughly contemporary with its hero. It was probably put together after Edward's death, about 1067, and certainly before 1076. Such at least was the general opinion up till now. I have attempted elsewhere to show that it is not well founded, and that the *Life*, too, dates from the reign of Henry I, but from the first part of it, between 1103 and 1120. I shall here assume this to be so.[31]

Edward the Confessor was soon held to be a saint; his veneration, though as yet without any official sanction, was already flourishing under Henry I.

Osbert espoused the cause of his canonization, which had just taken place when Ailred began his work. Consequently, it is not surprising that the four works enumerated above ascribe a good number of miraculous healings to him, for, being a saint, it was only to be expected that he would be a wonder-worker. Among the various anecdotes, only one has been traditionally preserved by historians of the 'touch', and it is to be found in almost the same form in all these four authors. Here, as elsewhere, Ailred does little more than put into good shape the confused and wordy account given by Osbert, who clearly knew the anonymous *Life*. As for the two earlier authors, William and the unknown author of the *Life*, commonly called the Biographer, they seem both to have drawn upon a collection of miracles, no doubt composed at Westminster, and also quoted by Osbert. We can briefly summarize this famous episode as follows.[32]

There was at this time in England a young woman suffering from an appalling disease, a swelling in the glands of the neck which gave out a foetid odour. She was told in a dream to seek healing at the hands of the king. The king sent for a vase of water, dipped his fingers in it, then touched the affected parts, signing them several times with the cross. Immediately blood and pus came out under the pressure of the royal hand, and the disease appeared to abate. The patient was kept at court, but the treatment does not seem to have been repeated. Nevertheless, after scarcely a week, the woman was overjoyed to find herself completely healed; and not only healed of this illness, but also of a stubborn sterility which was a great source of grief to her; and that same year she presented her husband with a son.

Such is the general outline of the story. Our authors add certain comments, which concern us as much as or even more than the text.

Here, to begin with, is a comment peculiar to William of Malmesbury:

> In our day, some have used these miracles [the miracle of the young
> woman and others like it, ascribed—as we shall see—to Edward before
> he was grown up] to support a false idea. They have claimed that
> the king possessed the power to heal this illness, not by virtue of
> his holiness, but by hereditary title, as a privilege of the royal
> line.[33]

This is a doubly valuable observation, because it informs us both of William's ideas, and of the very different ones held by many of his contemporaries. The monk of Malmesbury holds that only saints perform miracles; kings may perform them if they are saints, but not by virtue of their royalty. There is no such thing as a wonder-working dynasty. We shall come across this concept later on, a concept which, as we remember Gregory VII, we may well call Gregorian. For the moment, what particularly interests us is the opposite opinion; for in combating it, William has provided us with irrefutable testimony.

We are in England, in the year 1124 or 1125. Edward the Confessor, who died some sixty years before, is thought to have relieved many sufferers. Were those healings all of the same kind? Clearly not everyone thinks so. Some consider that the scrofula healings should be set in a special class; for it was by reason of his royal origin, and not his religious virtues, that Edward must have been able to perform them. The upholders of this view evidently have reason to believe that kings do heal scrofula; where can such an idea have come from? No doubt, from the facts they have before their eyes. Their king is Henry I; could this mean that Henry I was already claiming the miraculous gift we know his grandson Henry II was to claim? It is difficult to avoid this conclusion.

There is another document more or less contemporary with the *Historia Regum*, which must also be taken into account. I quoted above the famous passage from Guibert de Nogent constituting our earliest testimony to the rite in France; but I deliberately omitted the final words. Let us fill in the gap:

> What is the practice of other kings on the subject of healing the scrofula? I will keep silent on this matter; yet as far as I know, no English king has ever presumed to attempt it.[34]

French historians have long used these short sentences to prove that when the *De Pignoribus Sanctorum* was written—during the reign of Henry I—the English kings had as yet no share in the splendid privilege already belonging to the Capetians.[35] This interpretation would have delighted Guibert, for it is what he wanted posterity to believe. But it is perhaps rather over-simplified. There is something a little suspect about the zeal with which the Abbot of Nogent—whose exaggerated patriotism is well known—defends the French dynasty's prerogative, for he surely had no need to choose out this Norman prince from among all the sovereigns of Europe, and expressly deny him the gift of medicinal healing. It looks very much as though 'some rumour of usurpation'—as Dr Crawfurd so delightfully puts it—had reached him from England.[36] Taken by itself, his evidence would not perhaps have proved anything one way or the other; but when put alongside William of Malmesbury's it is an indirect and involuntary confirmation of what we arrived at by induction above. In all probability, Henry I did touch for scrofula.

The passage from William of Malmesbury just discussed is not the only gloss in our various sources accompanying the healing of the scrofulous woman. I must now quote a sentence occurring in very similar form in three different authors, the Biographer, William and Osbert. It would seem probable that it already existed in the primitive collection of miracles drawn upon by the first two writers. I will give it in the words of the Biographer, who is the earliest of the three. In order to understand it, we should remember that Edward had been driven from his country by the Danish invasion, and had spent his youth at the court of his family, the Norman Dukes.

> Now, strange though it may seem to us, the French say that he often did the same thing in his young days when he was in Neustria, which is now called Normandy.[37]

What an astonishing remark. Certainly, no man is a prophet in his own country. All the same, it is difficult to see why Edward as a young exile should have exercised for the benefit of foreigners a wonder-working power which was later to fail him in his own kingdom. Or rather, it is hard to understand how the notion that this had happened could have taken root in the minds of his hagiographers. Besides, what is the point of this appeal to people on the other side of the Channel, namely the French, in reference to a specifically English saint? A closer look at the history of Henry I's reign will provide us with the key to this mystery.[38]

Although a sovereign whose title was far from legitimate, Henry I was an extremely adroit politician. He made a point of flattering the feelings of his native subjects. Despite the gibes of the Norman nobility, he married a lady belonging to the island's ancient royal family. A son was born to him from this union, and he put about a prophecy according to which the young prince represented the national aspirations, offering him as the new green shoot from the old dynastic tree cut down in days gone by, by Harold's usurpation and by the Norman conquest. Since this vision needed a prophet, Henry and his advisers chose Edward the Confessor; and the last of the Anglo-Saxon kings was made to announce on his deathbed the advent of the predestined child. This episode occurred in the lives of the saint, and we come across it in the works enumerated above, in all of them under the same, or almost the same, form. Their common basis—made up, as we know, in all probability, from a collection of miracles that has not survived—had thus been influenced by Henry I's own political ideas.

In the light of these facts, let us now try to interpret the little story of the woman suffering from scrofula. It is mentioned in all the lives of St Edward, though naturally their testimony cannot be taken to mean that the Confessor really healed—or thought he healed—adenitis of the neck. It simply proves that at the time when the earliest of these lives was put together, this miracle was commonly being recounted; and this was during the reign of Henry I. We have weighty reasons for thinking that Henry did actually touch for scrofula. Upon what did he base his claims? William of Malmesbury has seen to it that we are aware of the conclusions respecting the miracle popularly attributed to St Edward, drawn by certain zealous persons anxious to find a precedent for their prince's beneficial action; and this was no doubt the official interpretation. What finer origin could be found for the royal prerogative than to link it up with the memory of that most pious monarch, dear to the hearts of Englishmen, whose heir William the Conqueror himself had always claimed to be? The saint's biography thus reconstituted in the twelfth century bears very clear marks, as we have seen, of a governmental stamp. A prophecy having been introduced into it, would it not also have been quite natural to slip in a miraculous cure? Yet it is not likely that the story of the young English woman was invented just as it stands by unscrupulous redactors. The deliverance of a sufferer from scrofula was as natural, and—if we may so put it—as classic an exploit as to restore sight to the blind or the use of his limbs to a paralytic; and the hagiographers did not fail to attribute such mighty acts to St Edward. But when Henry I's advisers came across this miracle as part of the legend in its formative stage, along with many other similar manifestations, they were quite naturally led to give it a special place and use it to justify the wonder-working virtues of their master. Only there was one difficulty: this miracle was unique. Once only in his reign had Edward 'touched' for scrofula; and this was a very fragile basis for the special healing power claimed by King Henry as part of his royal heritage. On this point, the legend was already firmly established; it may well have seemed inconvenient, and perhaps even sacrilegious, to make any alterations. But before he came to the throne, Edward had lived in Normandy, though the English tradition paid no heed to this stay; so the idea was invented that there, at any rate, in the very court of Henry I's direct ancestors, Edward had healed numerous cases of scrofula. This emendation came into the primitive hagiological version, and is to be found in all the early lives.[39] William of Malmesbury rejected the conclusions being drawn from the Norman miracles by those about him; but he did not venture to reject a piece of information coming from his sources. Like everyone else, he believed in these prodigies performed on foreign soil. Today, we may rightly be more sceptical, or rather, more critical; and we must consider these prodigies too as 'a work of falsehood'.[40]

There is no reason, therefore, to believe that the Anglo-Saxon kings ever claimed by virtue of their royalty to heal the scrofulous—and Edward the Confessor was no more likely to have done so than his predecessors. It is certain that Henry II exercised this power, and probable that Henry I had already appropriated it. Working to justify it, he gave it the support of a great name, that of St Edward. So far then as our knowledge goes, such would seem to be the beginnings of the rite in England.[41]

The origins of the royal healing power: the sacred aspects of royalty in the early centuries of the Middle Ages

1 *The evolution of royalty in its sacred aspects: the anointing*

The problem confronting us now is a double one. The royal miracle stands out above all as the expression of a certain concept of supreme political power. From this point of view, to explain it would be to link it with the whole body of ideas and beliefs of which it was one of the most characteristic expressions. Moreover, does not all scientific 'explanation' rely on the principle of bringing a particular case within the compass of some more general phenomenon? But having brought our research this far, we shall not yet have completed our task, for if we were to stop at this point, we should be letting precisely the particular case slip through our fingers. We shall still have to see why the healing rite, begotten by a movement of thought and feeling common to a whole region of Europe, first saw the light at one particular moment rather than another, both in France and in England, but not elsewhere. In short, we must enquire into the deeper causes on the one hand, and on the other into the exact occasion, the quirk of history which brought into actual being an institution that had long held sway in people's minds.

But, it may perhaps be objected, do we really need a long investigation in order to discover the collective elements which are at the origin of touching for scrofula? Surely it is obvious from the outset that this apparently singular rite was only the last echo in mediaeval and modern society of those 'primitive' beliefs which science today has managed to reconstruct by studying the savage races. To understand this practice, it will surely be enough to run through the great catalogues of facts so carefully and ingeniously collected by Sir James Frazer in *The Golden Bough* and *The Magic Art and the Evolution of Kings*. 'What would Louis XIV have said', writes Salomon Reinach, 'if it had been demonstrated to him that in touching for scrofula he was imitating a Polynesian chieftain?'[1] And already Montesquieu, under the mask of the Persian Usbeck, had written of this same prince: 'This king is a great magician: he rules even over the minds of his subjects . . . He even goes so far as to make them believe he can heal them of all sorts of evils by touching them, so great is the strength and the power he has over their spirits.'[2] In Montesquieu's thought, the word magician was no more than a verbal sally: but nowadays we can readily give it its full meaning. I have placed this short quotation at the beginning of the Introduction of this book; but it might more fittingly still have stood on the first page of those splendid works by Sir James Frazer, which have taught us how to see links, which long remained un-known, between certain ancient concepts of the nature of things and the earliest political institutions of the human race. Yes, the miracle of scrofula is incontestably bound up with a whole psychological system which may on two counts be called 'primitive'; first, because it bears the marks of an undeveloped way of thinking still steeped in the irrational; and secondly, because it is found in a particularly pure state in those societies we are agreed to call 'primitive'. But in so saying, we have done no more than give an approximate indication of the kind of mental pictures to which our research should be directed. Historical reality is less simple and very much richer than any such formulae.

Sir James Frazer writes in *The Golden Bough*:

Royal personages in the Pacific and elsewhere have been supposed to live in a sort of atmosphere highly charged with what we may call spiritual electricity, which, if it blasts all who intrude into its charmed circle, has happily also the gift of making whole again by a touch.

We may conjecture that similar views prevailed in ancient times as to the predecessors of our English monarchs and *that accordingly scrofula received its name of the King's Evil from the belief that it was caused as well as cured by contact with a king*.[3]

Let us make certain that we understand. Sir James Frazer does not claim that the English or French sovereigns in the eleventh or twelfth centuries were thought capable of spreading scrofula all round them, as well as relieving it; he is simply imagining that, long ago in the dawn of history, their ancestors had used this double-edged weapon. Then gradually the deadly side of the royal gift had been forgotten, and only the beneficial side retained. In actual fact, as we already know, the wonder-working kings of the eleventh or twelfth centuries did not have to reject part of the ancestral heritage, since nothing in their miraculous powers came to them from a very remote past. This argument would seem then to be sufficient; yet, putting it on one side for the moment, let us suppose, if you like, that the healing powers of the Norman or Capetian princes went back to very distant origins. Would Sir James Frazer's hypothesis then be strengthened? I do not think so. It is based upon the case of the Tonga Islands in Polynesia, where certain chiefs are said to exercise a power of this kind. But what is this argument from analogy really worth? The comparative method is extremely fertile, provided it is confined to general proportions: it cannot be used to reconstruct details.

Certain collective ideas affecting the whole social life are met with among a large number of peoples, showing great similarities in their broad outlines, and apparently symptomatic of specific states of civilization, for they vary in accordance with these. In other societies known to us only by relatively recent or incomplete documentation, there is no historical testimony to such ideas. Does this mean that no such ideas existed? Probably not; and comparative sociology allows us to reconstruct them with considerable likelihood. But these broad notions common to more or less the whole of humanity have clearly received varying applications in different places and circumstances. A study of the tribes of Oceania throws light upon the idea of a sacrosanct royalty as it existed under other skies in ancient or even mediaeval Europe; but one cannot expect to rediscover in Europe all the institutions of Oceania. In a Polynesian archipelago—the only example quoted—the chieftains are both the agents of disease and doctors: that is the form ascribed to the supernatual power residing in them. But elsewhere, the same power may have manifested itself in a different way, beneficially, for instance, and without any adverse counterpart. Many of the early missionaries thought they could descry among the 'savages' faint surviving traces of all sorts of Christian ideas. We should beware of making the opposite mistake by transporting the Antipodes to Paris or to London.

Let us then try to reconstruct in all its complexity the movement of beliefs and sentiments which made it possible for the rite of touching to come into existence in two countries of Europe.

The French and English kings were able to become miraculous physicians because they had already long been considered sacred persons. 'He is holy and the Anointed of the Lord,' as Peter of Blois said of his master Henry II, in order to justify his wonder-working powers. We must therefore show first of all how the sacred character of royalty came to be recognized, before going on to explain how by a natural association of ideas their healing power was deduced from this character as an almost self-evident conclusion.[4]

The Capetians always maintained themselves to be the authentic heirs of the Carolingian dynasty, and the Carolingians likewise of Clovis and his descendants; and the Norman kings of England claimed as their own patrimony the succession to the Anglo-Saxon princes. There are direct and continuous links between the chieftains of the ancient Franks, Angles and Saxons and the French or English kings of the twelfth century. So it is to the ancient Germanic royal lines that we must look in the first place, for through them we make contact with a deposit of extremely ancient ideas and institutions.

Unfortunately, our knowledge of them is very imperfect. In the absence of any written literature, the whole of pre-Christian Germany will always remain irremediably obscure. All that we can glimpse is a few gleams of light; but enough to make us certain that the concept of royalty among the Teutons, as with all peoples at the same stage of civilization, was deeply impressed with a religious character.[5] Tacitus had already observed that among the Teutons there was a distinction between the temporary leaders in warfare, freely chosen for their personal valour, and the kings, who were taken solely from certain noble families; that is to say, no doubt, certain families hereditarily endowed with a sacred virtue.[6] The kings were considered divine beings, or at the very least descended from the gods. 'Since the Goths', as Jordanes tells us in so many words, 'used to attribute their victories to the blessed influence emanating from their princes, they did not wish to look upon them as simple men; so they gave them the name of *Ases*, that is, demi-gods'.[7] The word *Ases* recurs in the ancient Scandinavian languages, where it served to designate the gods, or certain categories of them. We still possess several Anglo-Saxon royal genealogies, which all go back to Woden.[8] From this faith in the supernatural origin of kings there sprang a feeling of loyalty. It was not attached to a particular individual, for primogeniture did not exist, and hereditary rights within a dynasty were uncertain. The sovereign could be changed, provided that he was always taken from the same dynasty. As Athalaric wrote to the Roman Senate: 'Just as anyone born from among you is said to be of senatorial origin, so he who comes of the Amal family—to which all nobility gives first place—is worthy to reign.' And elsewhere, this same prince, with a blend of Germanic ideas and Roman vocabulary, spoke of 'the blood of the Amal family, destined for the purple'.[9] Only these predestined families were capable of providing really efficient masters, for they alone were the possessors of that mysterious blessing, *quasi fortuna* as Jordanes calls it, to which the people attributed their triumphs much more than to the military talent of a particular captain. The notion of personal legitimacy was weak, but that of dynastic legitimacy very strong.[10] In the sixth century, a detached group of the Heruli had settled in the region of the Danube; it had been followed there by a branch of the traditional line, which provided it with chiefs. But the day came when this line died out completely. The last of the line, like so many princes in those violent times, fell victim to assassination by his own subjects. But these barbarians, who had murdered their king, did not resign themselves to being without royal blood. They decided to go and bring back a representative of the ancient line from the distant country of their origins—'from Thule', as Procopius says—meaning no doubt the Scandinavian peninsula. Their first choice died on the journey; the ambassadors than retraced their steps and came back with a second. Meanwhile, the Heruli, tired of waiting, had finally chosen a new head, one of their own company, picked out solely on his individual merit. Not daring, maybe, to elect him themselves, they had asked for a nomination by the Byzantine Emperor. But when the lawful heir arrived, in the course of a single night he gained the support of almost the whole people, although he was a complete stranger.[11]

These kings were in their divine capacity considered to possess a certain power over nature. In accordance with a notion met with in many other peoples, and particularly strong in Chinese societies, they were held responsible for the general order of things. A legend recorded in the thirteenth-century *Heimskringla* relates that Halfdan the Black, king of Norway, had been 'of all kings the one who had brought most success to the harvests'. When he died, instead of burying his corpse entire and in one single place, his subjects cut it into four pieces, and buried each portion under a mound in each of the four principal districts of the country; for 'the possession of the body'—or one of its fragments—'seemed to those who obtained it to give hope of further good harvests'.[12] It was also believed among the Danes of the eleventh century that by touching children and crops, a worthy prince could ensure a man fine offspring and fine harvests.[13] Now and again, when the harvest happened to fail, the king would be deposed. In a like case, the same fate used to befall the Burgundian kings, according to the testimony of Ammianus Marcellinus; and the Roman historian, with his customary intelligence, himself invites the reader to compare this custom with the traditions of ancient Egypt, the classic country of sacred royalty. The same practice seems to have flourished in pagan Sweden.[14]

Did the Teutonic kings with their mastery over the fertile seasons also extend their power to the healing of disease? The *Heimskringla* attributes some healings to King Olaf, the son of Harold, who reigned in Norway at the beginning of the eleventh century;[15] but, as we recalled above, this text was not written in Iceland until the thirteenth century, by a priest called Snorri Sturlason. Moreover, Olaf—St Olaf—was a Christian saint, and the miracles attributed to him by the Icelandic saga may be no more than the echo of a theme in hagiography. Our documents are no doubt too meagre to assert that no Germanic people ever viewed their king as a physician; and prudent wisdom suggests we had better leave this an open question. In the absence of documents, it is always tempting to have recourse to comparative sociology. Yet here too there is no obligation to maintain that kings in ancient Germany, just because they were endowed with divine power, were all or even mostly healers, for healing kings would seem to have been at all times and in all places distinctly rare. That at least is the impression given by Sir James Frazer's works. For examples of this form of royal magic recorded in these great collections are not very numerous. The Oualo chieftains of Senegal and the Polynesians of the Tonga Islands are quoted again and again, and their constant reappearances remind one of those figures in the theatre who walk round and round the same 'sets' to represent an army marching past on the stage.[16] Indeed, there is nothing surprising about this dearth of examples. The miraculous power attributed to their kings by the 'primitives' is generally conceived as employed for collective ends which are intended to serve the well being of the whole group, and not as directed towards individual benefits. Their role is to call down rain or assure that the harvests are regular rather than to relieve the sufferings of individuals. Indeed, it would be easy to fill pages with examples of the 'rain-making' chiefs who appear in ethnographical records. This may perhaps explain why the rite of touching, with which we are here concerned, developed more readily in societies where religion prevented men from ascribing to their kings any influence over the great cosmic phenomena that rule the lives of nations.

A revolution in religion did, in fact, strike a deadly blow at the ancient concept of sacred royalty as it had flourished among the Teutons. The advent of Christianity stripped it of its natural support, the national paganism. The kings continued to exist as heads of State, and for a short while after the invasions their political power was even stronger than ever before; but they ceased—at least officially—to be considered divine persons. No doubt the old ideas did not die out all at once. They probably continued to live on more or less obscurely in the popular consciousness. Our documents show traces of this now and again, and we should probably discover many more if our sources were not all ecclesiastical in origin, and as a result hostile to the past[17] on this particular point. The long hair constituting the traditional attribute of the Frankish dynasty (all other freemen wore their hair short as soon as they were adult) had certainly been at the beginning a symbol of a supernatural nature. Or rather, hair that had never been cut must have been thought of originally as the seat of the miraculous power resident in the sons of the chosen race. The *reges criniti* were so many Samsons. This custom, which is supported by very ancient testimony, lasted as long as the Merovingians themselves, though we have no means of knowing whether it continued up to the end to have magic significance, at any rate among the common people.[18] Many persons belonging to the Anglo-Saxon royal houses were venerated as saints after their death, and the same is true, though in smaller numbers, of the Merovingians. Not that these lines were particularly fertile in religious or private virtues—far from it; but it was a favourite practice to canonize at the altar the members of families customarily considered holy.[19] From Dagobert onwards, the Merovingian dynasty sank into a state of impotence; yet these kings, who were simply marionettes, continued in office for more than a century and a half. The first *coup d'état* attempted against them—by Grimoald—was a miserable failure. Charles Martel himself thought he had sufficient power to suppress royalty for a time, though not in order to usurp the title himself. This failure and this prudent abstention can be partly explained by the rivalries among the great—but only in part; for we must believe that the legitimate line preserved a kind of prestige through this time of abasement.

A comparison has sometimes been drawn between the descendants of Clovis, reduced by the Mayors of the Palace to a purely representative existence, and the lives of the Mikados in ancient Japan under the Shoguns. Without getting this matter out of proportion, it would in fact seem probable that the Frankish princes, like the Japanese emperors, were protected over a long period if not exactly by their sacred character, at least by the dim memory in men's minds of their role in ancient times. Yet if we confine ourselves to official appearances, until the eighth century the Frankish or English kings do not seem to have been more than ordinary Christians—mere laymen, we might say. Their coming to the throne was not celebrated by any ecclesiastical ceremony, but only by rituals regulated by somewhat uncertain custom. They did not receive upon their foreheads any special religious impress.[20]

To those of the Germanic sovereigns who—like the Merovingians—found themselves reigning after the invasions over a profoundly romanized country, the traditions of the conquered people offered all the splendours of the imperial religion. Here too, no doubt, Christianity had exercised a passing influence; but although it had gradually changed some of the forms, it had scarcely affected the underlying foundations. In Byzantium, the imperial religion was destined to survive almost as long as the Empire.[21] We only know its official splendours, but cannot really enter into the hold it must have exercised on men's spirits. Some of the emperors were held to have wonder-working powers. Vespasian, who was proclaimed emperor in the East, in a milieu charged with messianic hopes, performed some healings; but this was at Alexandria, a place accustomed for thousands of years to venerating its chiefs as divine. Moreover, there were suspicions that the priests of Serapeum, whose skill was generally acknowledged, had engineered these miraculous manifestations. Hadrian, too, was said to have healed a blind woman.[22] But these are isolated instances. We shall never know whether the belief in the divinity of the emperors was strong enough for the masses to hold their miraculous powers as genuinely efficacious. Yet there can be no doubt that emperor-worship was a marvellously effective instrument of government, which was allowed to lapse with the coming of the barbarians.[23] Besides, the Merovingians did not pose as successors to the Empire. True, if we are to accept the testimony of Gregory of Tours—and I see no reason to reject it—Clovis did accept office at the hands of the sovereign of Byzantium, and by a sort of usurpation adopted the title of Augustus.[24] But his descendants did not continue to use this title. Nevertheless, they may well have felt freer than he did in relation to the Augustus on the shores of the Bosphorus; for the conquests of Justinian, reintroducing 'Roman' arms into the West, had led the Frankish kings to break free finally from all dependence upon the ancient masters of the world. Up till then, they had been willing to accept the rather vague supremacy of a distant emperor; now, they did not wish to remain attached by any links of subjection, however vague, to a neighbour who was only too close and too menacing. They asserted their autonomy, notably by minting money in their own name; but whether from a remaining vestige of respect, or from mere indifference, they stopped short at assuming any of those ancient titles which recalled the sacred character of princes. The imperial cult disappeared from Gaul at the same time as the Roman domination. The most we can suppose is that with it the old habits of thought, and a certain tendency to confuse the categories of politics and divinity, did not completely perish.

Later on, Charlemagne renewed the links with the Roman tradition. The Empire came to life again.[25] But it was now an entirely Christian Empire. The imperial religion, which had been essentially pagan, and moreover interrupted by a long period of proscription, could not join in this revival. At Byzantium, the emperors had continued to call themselves divine; Charlemagne, or the particular counsellor who drew up in his name the preface to the *Libri Carolini*, could not refrain from reproaching them for their pride from the lofty security of his own orthodox position.[26] Nevertheless, this period saw the reintroduction of some more inoffensive expressions derived from the obsequious language of the Byzantine Empire, such as the sacred Emperors, the most sacred Augustus, and the sacred palace.[27] Did not Hincmar himself, for all his scrupulous denial of any sacerdotal character to the temporal sovereigns, so far forget himself one day as to write: 'the sacred eyes' of the Emperor?[28] But this term should not leave us under any illusion. In France, at any rate, it hardly survived beyond the Carolingian era.[29] Already in Rome it had been progressively divested of its original meaning. These pious formulae had become more or less simply expressions of politeness. With the writers of the ninth century, in short, they indicate no more than a verbal acquaintance with the Latin texts. Or if these apparently ancient words did sometimes carry a full sense with the first Frankish emperors' contemporaries, it meant that they were no longer thinking of the old outworn cult which had formerly used such terms, but of a new and authentically Christian ceremonial. Thanks to a new institution, the sovereigns of the West had once more become officially sacred; for they now received ecclesiastical consecration, and more particularly unction, the fundamental part of this rite, when they came to the throne. As we shall see, unction made its appearance in the barbarian kingdoms of the seventh and eighth centuries. In Byzantium, on the other hand, it was only introduced quite late in the day, and in obvious imitation of foreign customs. In Charlemagne's time, the people of those parts were apt to jeer at this gesture they did not understand. They said—probably in derision—that the Pope had anointed the Frankish emperor 'from head to foot'.[30] Historians have sometimes wondered what was the origin of the differences between the royal ceremonies of the West and the East. I think the reason is clear. The imperial religion was still very much alive in the Rome of the East, and so made the new rite superfluous.

To sum up, it may be said that in the kingdoms which had arisen from the invasions, a multitude of memories with various origins, Germanic or Romano-oriental, surrounded royalty with a quasi-religious atmosphere of veneration; but there was no regular institution to embody this vague sentiment. In the end, it was the Bible that provided the means of reintroducing into the lawful ceremonies of Christianity the sacred royalty of past ages. To begin with, it provided some useful comparisons. In chapter 14 of Genesis there was the account of Abraham receiving the bread and wine at the hands of Melchisedech, who was both King of Salem and priest of the most High God[31]—a mysterious episode which the exegetes of today still have some difficulty in explaining. The early commentators got out of the difficulty by giving it a symbolical meaning. Melchisedech was a figure of Christ; and it is by virtue of this that he can be seen represented on so many cathedrals. But such an enigmatic personage was also calculated to tempt the apologists of royalty, for to those who attributed a superhuman character to kings this priest-king took the ideal back into a mysteriously distant past. At the time of the great controversy between the sacerdotal and the imperial power in the eleventh and twelfth centuries, Melchisedech —St Melchisedech, as the Carolingian sacramentary of St-Amand calls him[32]—was distinctly in the fashion. He was presented as a model as early as the Merovingian period. Fortunatus says of Childebert: 'Our Melchisedech [who is] justly [called] king and priest, though a layman, has carried out the work that pertains to religion.'[33]

But the Old Testament was not only a source of symbols; it also provided the model for a very concrete institution. In the ancient world of the East, kings were as a matter of course considered to be sacred persons. Among a good many peoples, their supernatural character was marked by a ceremony whose significance was clear. On their accession, they were anointed on certain parts of their body with oil that had previously been blessed and hallowed. The Tell-el-Amarna tablets have preserved a letter that a dynast of Syria, Addu-nirari by name, addressed to the Pharaoh Amenophis IV about the year 1500 B.C., to remind him of the day when 'Manahbiria, the King of Egypt, your grandfather, made my grandfather Taku king in Nuhasse, and poured oil upon his head.' The day when the documents bearing on the anointing of our kings are finally collected, the transcription of this venerable clay fragment might well stand at the head of the work. For it is from those ancient Syrian or Canaanite civilizations, which had become so strangely familiar to the Christians of the seventh and eighth centuries through their reading of the Bible, that royal unction has come down to us. The sons of Israel were amongst those who practised it. Moreover, with them, and probably with the surrounding peoples, too, unction was not confined to their kings. It was a primary element in all

Hebrew ceremonial, and constituted the normal procedure for transferring a person or an object from the profane to the sacred category.[34] In this general application it was borrowed by Christianity from the Ancient Law, and soon began to play an important part in the ritual of the new religion, particularly in the West, and more especially in the countries of the Gallican Rite, Spain, Gaul, Great Britain and northern Italy. Here it was used more particularly in the confirmation of catechumens, and in the ordination of priests and bishops.[35] The idea of resuming these ancient Israelite customs in their entirety, and transferring them from the unction of catechumens or priests to the anointing of kings, must have been quite a natural development. The examples of David and Solomon provided a way of restoring to kings in a Christian setting the sacred character that belonged to them.[36]

The new institution first took shape in the Visigothic kingdom of Spain. Here, after the disappearance of Arianism, the Church and the royal dynasty enjoyed a particularly intimate union, and the institution came in as early as the seventh century. It was next introduced into the Frankish State.

It was never by virtue of their kingship that the Merovingians had received unction; and this applies, as we need hardly be reminded, to Clovis, no less than to the others. The only anointing he received was the one prescribed by the Gallican Rite for all catechumens. As we shall be seeing, legend much later in the day converted the ceremony carried out by St-Rémi at Rheims into the first royal consecration, though it was in truth no more than simple baptism. But in 751 Pepin, boldly risking the step his father Charles Martel had not dared to take, decided to consign to a convent the last descendants of Clovis, and to claim royal honours as well as royal power. He then felt the need to colour his usurpation with a sort of religious prestige. There is no doubt that the kings of old had always been considered by their faithful supporters far superior to the rest of the people; but the vague aura of mysticism surrounding them was solely due to the influence upon the collective consciousness of obscure memories dating from pagan times. The new dynasty, on the other hand, possessing an authentic sacrosanctity, were to owe their consecration to a definite act justified by the Bible, and fully Christian. The theologians in Gaul were quite prepared to accept this revival of Jewish practice, for the trend among them at that time was favourable to the Old Testament; and partly as a result of Irish influence, the Laws of Moses were penetrating into the discipline of the Church.[37] Thus Pepin became the first of the French kings to receive unction from the hands of priests, after the manner of the Hebrew chiefs. 'It is manifest to all men', he announced proudly in one of his proclamations, 'that, by anointing, Divine Providence has raised us to this throne.'[38] His successors were not slow to follow his example; and it was likewise towards the end of the eighth century that the same rite took root in England, probably in imitation of what had just taken place in

France. Before long, it had become a general practice throughout almost the whole of Western Europe.

At the same time a second rite with a different origin was being joined to it. On 25 December 800, in the basilica of St Peter, Pope Leo III had placed a 'crown' on the head of Charlemagne, and proclaimed him emperor. This was no doubt a golden circle, like the one that had for many centuries on the heads of the Byzantine sovereigns replaced the diadem formerly worn by Constantine and his immediate successors—a band of material ornamented with pearls and precious stones. Crown and diadem had both been borrowed by the emperors from the Eastern monarchs; the diadem probably from Persia. Originally, no doubt, they had possessed a religious virtue; but in the eyes of Christians contemporary with Charlemagne, the only sacred character of the crown came from the hands that set it upon the prince's head, namely the Patriarch in Byzantium and the Pope in Rome, and from the ecclesiastical ritual surrounding the prelate at that moment. Having once been anointed king, Charlemagne was not re-anointed emperor. For the first time at Rheims in 816, his son, Louis the Pious, received from Pope Stephen IV, along with the imperial title, the anointing with holy oil as well as the crown. From that time onwards, the two actions became more or less inseparable. For the consecration of an emperor, both became necessary; and this was soon the case for the consecration of a king. From the time of Charles the Bald in France, and from the ninth century in England, we see the kings being successively anointed and crowned. Around these two fundamental rites there rapidly grew up in every country a full and rich ceremonial. In a very short time there was a multiplication of the royal insignia handed to the new sovereign. Already in Charles the Bald's time the sceptre had made its appearance along with the crown; and the same thing took place in England, according to the old English liturgical texts. The emblems were mostly ancient; the novelty was to give them a place in the religious ceremonies of the enthronement. In short, there was always something of a double element in these solemnities: on the one hand, the handing over of the insignia, among which the crown remained the main element; on the other, the anointing, which remained up to the end the particular act of sanctification. This was how consecration came into being.[39]

And so, to use the biblical expression, kings had become the 'Lord's Anointed', protected from all the machinations of the wicked by the divine word, for God himself had said: 'Touch not mine anointed'. This commandment was recalled in 787 at the Council of Chelsea, in the course of which the first royal anointing in England probably took place.[40] The effect was to transform the enemies of royalty into apparently sacrilegious persons; though this provided a rather illusory protection, to judge by the violent history of those troubled times.[41] For all we know, however, princes may well have set more store by it than we should imagine today, and the desire to claim the benefit of this divine word from the Sacred Book may have influenced more than one of them to seek the consecration offered by the Church.

By the holy oil, sovereigns were exalted far above the common crowd, for did they not share this privilege with priests and bishops? Yet there was a reverse side of the coin. In the course of the ceremony, the officiating priest carrying out the unction seemed for a moment superior to the monarch who was devoutly receiving it. It might well have been thought from henceforth that a priest was necessary for the making of a king, an obvious sign of the superiority of the spiritual over the temporal. Very soon after the time of Charlemagne, ideas of this kind were already being upheld by some prelates. For instance, there was Hincmar of Rheims: no one attached more value to royal consecration than he did. Although this ceremony only had a fairly short history behind it, Hincmar—as we shall see later on—managed to find a famous and miraculous precedent for it, either by invention, or by the ingenious adaptation of a legend. How was it that this man, pre-eminently capable of vast designs, should have been so interested in these liturgical actions? All we need do in order to understand the reasons for his attitude is to set side by side two passages selected from his works. In 868 he wrote to Charles the Bald: 'It is to your anointing, an episcopal and spiritual act, and to the blessing that flows from it, much more than to your temporal power, that you owe your royal dignity.' So there could be no true king without consecration, whatever his 'terrestrial' claims to the throne might be. Certain ecclesiastical circles had already reached this conclusion within less than a hundred years after the first Frankish consecration. And in another passage from the proceedings of the Council of Ste-Macre, drawn up by Hincmar, who presided over the assembly: 'The dignity of pontiffs is above that of kings; for kings are consecrated kings by pontiffs, whereas pontiffs cannot be consecrated by kings.'[42] Nothing could really be clearer. Perhaps it was fear of a similar interpretation that led the king of Germany, Henry I, in the following century, to be the only one of his time and his line to refuse both the anointing and the crown at the hands of the Archbishop of Mainz, and to reign 'without the blessing of the pontiffs'[43]—to quote the reproach levelled at him by the author of a certain life of a saint, who puts the words into the mouth of the apostle St Peter. The new rite was clearly a two-edged weapon.

Yet it was only to be seen quite openly as such some few centuries later, when the great Gregorian controversy had opened. For the first two or three centuries, it would seem above all to have helped confirm in the minds of the people—with the exception of a few of the Church's theorists —the notion of the sacred character, or better still, the quasi-priestly character, of royalty. Of course, some discerning minds were quickly aware of the dangers for the Church, and even for Christianity, in this confusion between an essentially temporal dignity and the priesthood as such. And here we once again come across Hincmar. He never tired of repeating that since the advent of Christ, no man could be both priest and king.[44] But his very insistence proves how widespread was the idea he wished to combat. The ancient liturgy of consecration will show us better than any other document that it had assumed an official colouring.

For a moment, then, let us examine these ancient texts. We shall have no difficulty in noting that a special point has been made of putting into them everything that could possibly favour a confusion between these two very similar rites, one the gateway to the priesthood, the other to royalty. In general, the necessary formulae are taken from the Old Law: 'May thy hands be anointed with the holy oil, which anointed the kings and *the prophets*'—so runs a very ancient ritual, contemporary with the early days of the Carolingian dynasty. The same thought is developed with more precision in a doubtless later prayer. We do not know its exact date of composition, but it appears for the first time in history at the crowing of Charles the Bald as king of Lorraine. By a strange chance, it was Hincmar in person who carried out the act of consecration that day; and he was no doubt bound by already established tradition to use the following words: 'May God crown thee with the crown of glory . . . and make thee king by this anointing given with oil by the grace of the Holy Spirit, who anointed the priests and kings and prophets and martyrs.' And here is the ancient Anglo–Saxon ceremonial wording: 'O God . . . Thou who by the anointing with oil didst consecrate thy servant Aaron to be priest, and didst in later days with the self-same oil of anointing make priests and kings and prophets to reign over Israel . . . we pray Thee, Almighty Father, that Thou wilt vouchsafe to sanctify with thy blessing, by means of this oil taken from one of thy creatures, thy servant here present before Thee . . . and grant him the power to be a faithful follower of the example of Aaron in thy service.'[45] Clearly, the vision conjured up before the English or Frankish sovereigns on this consecration-day was not simply a picture of the Jewish kings, but also the priests and the prophets, and the great figure of Aaron, founder of the Hebrew priesthood—all, so to speak, their ancestors. It is hardly surprising to find that a poet of the time, celebrating the consecration of an emperor—a pretty poor emperor, Berengar of Frinli, but what does that matter here?—ventures to say of his hero, as he shows him advancing towards the church where the ceremony will take place: 'soon he would be a priest', *mox quippe sacerdos futurus erat*.[46]

Moreover, the leaders of the clergy had not always spoken in the language of Hincmar. At the period when he was so crisply setting forth the incompatibility under the New Law of combining the dignities of priest and king, the growing weakness of the dynasty was encouraging the prelates to claim the position of mentors to the king; whereas during the flourishing days of the Carolingian State, this tone would have been quite out of place. In 794, the bishops of northern Italy present at the Synod of Frankfurt published a defence of orthodox doctrine against the Spanish Adoptionists. At the end of this theological declaration there was an appeal to the sovereign, as protector of the faith. In it, Charlemagne was called not only 'lord and father' and 'most prudent governor of all Christians', but also—in so many words—'king and priest'.[47] And some years earlier, Pope Stephen III himself, wishing to flatter Charles and Carloman, whose services he needed, had had the idea of seeking out from the First Epistle of Peter an expression applied by the apostle to the elect, and by slightly diverting it from its original meaning, using it in honour of the Frankish dynasty: 'you are a holy race, and royal priesthood.'[48] In spite of all that could subsequently be said by all the Hincmars in the world, such expressions were never forgotten.

Thus the monarchies of Western Europe, already heirs to long years of veneration, found themselves definitively stamped with a divine seal, which they were to bear for ever. On this point, tradition was not denied either by Capetian France, or Norman England, or for that matter by the Saxon or Salic emperors of Germany. It was quite the contrary. For in the eleventh century, a whole party made it their business to bring the royal dignity closer to the priesthood, in a more outright manner than ever before. We shall have a word or two to say later on about those efforts, but they do not concern us for the moment. It is enough to know that, quite independently of any exact assimilation to the priesthood, the kings in the two countries specially concerning us continued to be considered sacred beings. Of this, the documents do not leave us in the slightest doubt. We still have certain letters addressed to Robert the Pious by one of the highly respected prelates of his time, Fulbert, Bishop of Chartres, in which the bishop does not scruple to give the king the titles of 'Holy Father' and 'Your Holiness', reserved by Catholics today for the supreme head of their Church.[49] And we already saw above how Peter of Blois deduced the 'holiness' of kings from their anointing; a subject on which, no doubt, most of his subjects were of this same opinion.

But Peter of Blois went further. My master, he said in effect, is a sacred person: so he can heal the sick. This would appear at first sight to be a strange deduction; but as we shall see, to a mind of normal breadth of outlook in the twelfth century, there would have been nothing astonishing about this idea.

2 *The healing power of the sacred person*

The men of the Middle Ages—or the vast majority of them at all events—were accustomed to picture the things of religion in an extremely rational

and down-to-earth fashion. And it is difficult to see how this could have
been otherwise. The miraculous world to which the Christian rites gave
access did not appear to them to be separated from the world they lived in
by an impassable abyss, for the two worlds interpenetrated one another.
How could it be possible for actions affecting the life beyond not to have
an effect also on this life here below? Of course, the idea of this kind of
intervention did not shock anyone, since no one had any accurate conception of natural laws. Sacred actions, objects or individuals were thus
thought of not only as reservoirs of powers available beyond this present
life, but also as sources of energy capable of exerting an immediate influence on this earth too. Moreover, they pictured this energy in such
concrete terms that they sometimes even represented it as possessing a
certain weight. Gregory of Tours tells us that a piece of material placed
upon the altar of a great saint—such as St Peter or St Martin—would
become heavier than before, provided always that the saint was willing to
display his power.[50]

The priest, thought to be possessed of sacred powers, was considered by
many as a kind of magician, and as such was sometimes venerated and
sometimes hated. In certain places, people would cross themselves as he
passed by, since meeting him was considered a bad omen.[51] In eleventh-
century Denmark, the priests were held responsible for disturbances in the
weather and for infections in the same way as witches, and they were sometimes persecuted as the agents of such evils, and with such bitterness that
Gregory VII had to make a protest.[52] Besides, there is no need for us to
look so far north; for there is no doubt at all that the following instructive
anecdote belongs to thirteenth-century France. Jacques de Vitry, the
popular writer who relates it, says that he had it 'on very reliable authority'.
An epidemic broke out in a certain village, and to put an end to it, the
villagers could think of nothing better than to sacrifice their curé. One day,
when he was wearing his robes and conducting a funeral, they threw him
headlong into the grave alongside the corpse.[53] And similar insensate
practices—though in rather milder forms—still survive today.

Thus the power commonly ascribed by public opinion to a sacred person
could sometimes take on formidable or adverse shapes; but, more often
than not, it was of course regarded as beneficent. Now is there any greater
and more perceptible benefit than health? It was an easy step to attribute
healing power to everything that in some measure formed part of the consecration rite.[54] The Host, the communion wine, the baptismal water, the
ablution water in which the officiant had dipped his hands after touching
the sacred elements, the very fingers of the priest—all these were regarded
as so many remedies. And even today, in certain provinces, the dust from a
church and the moss growing on its walls are held to partake of the same
properties.[55] This kind of idea sometimes led uneducated minds into
strange aberrations. Gregory of Tours tells the story of some barbarian

chieftains who, suffering pains in their feet, bathed them in a paten[56] which was used to hold the sacred host. The clergy naturally condemned such excesses; but they allowed the continuance of those practices which they did not consider harmful to the due dignity of worship. Moreover, popular beliefs were largely out of their control. Among all the sacramentals, the holy oils, being the normal vehicle of consecrations, seemed to be particularly rich in supernatural virtues. The parties to a trial by ordeal would swallow some in order to ensure a favourable result for themselves. Above all, the holy oils were held to be marvellously effective against all bodily ills, and it proved necessary to safeguard the vessels containing them against the indiscreet attentions of the faithful.[57] In truth, in those days the word 'consecrated' implied the possession of power to heal.

Let us remember, then, what kings were at this period. Almost everyone believed, in the words of Peter of Blois, in their 'holiness'. But this notion went even further. Whence came this 'holiness'? Largely, no doubt, in the eyes of the people, from this family predestination in which the masses, holding on to ancient ideas, had certainly not lost faith; but also since Carolingian times, more specifically and from a more Christian sentiment, from the religious rite of unction—in other words, from the consecrated oil which likewise seemed the most effective remedy for so many illnesses. Thus kings were doubly marked out for the role of beneficent wonder-workers—first by their sacred character *per se*, and then more particularly by the most apparent and venerable of its origins, through which this sacred character was held to act. Sooner or later, it would seem, they were bound to figure as healers.

Yet they did not become healers straight away, that is, not immediately after the introduction of anointing for kings in the States of Western Europe, nor in all countries. So the general considerations just put forward are not enough to explain the appearance of the royal touch in France and in England; they can do no more than show how men's minds were prepared to conceive or to admit such a practice. In order to account for its birth at a specific date and in a particular environment, we shall have to appeal to facts of a different and more fortuitous order, since they imply to a higher degree the interplay of individual wills.

3 The dynastic policy of the early Capetians and of Henry I (Beauclerc)

The first French sovereign thought to have healed the sick was Robert the Pious. Now Robert was the second representative of a new dynasty. He received the royal title and anointing in his father Hugh's lifetime, in 987, that is to say in the very year of the usurpation. The Capetians were successful, and that is why it is not easy for us to imagine how frail their power must have seemed in those early years. Yet we know that it was in fact contested. There was great prestige attached to the Carolingians, and since 936 no one had dared to dispute their right to the crown. It needed a hunting accident (causing the death of Louis V) and an international intrigue to make their fall a possibility. In 987, and even later, who could have been certain that they had fallen for good? For many, no doubt, this association of father and son together on the throne was only an interim measure: as Gerbert wrote in 989 or 990, they were only 'kings provisionally' (*inter-reges*).[58] For a long time there were centres of opposition, notably at Sens, and in the South. As a matter of fact, a lucky stroke on Palm Sunday 991, which delivered the pretender of Charlemagne's line into Hugh's hands, was to make ineffectual any efforts that might have been made by the partisans of his line, since its head was henceforward a prisoner, and its last descendants were destined to disappear into oblivion. But this un-looked-for success was no guarantee for the future. The continuing loyalty towards the descendants of their former masters shown by some legitimists had perhaps never been a very serious threat to the Capetian house. The real menace lay elsewhere, in the sharp blow that these same events of 987, to which the new kings owed their throne, had administered to the loyalty of their subjects and above all to the principle of hereditary monarchy. The decisions of the assembly at Senlis looked dangerously like a triumph for the elective principle. To be sure, this was no new principle. In the ancient Germanic people, at least, as we have seen, it had been balanced by the obligation to choose the king always from the sacred line. But now it looked as though the right of free choice might become quite unfettered. The historian Richer puts into the mouth of Archbishop Adalberon, as part of his harangue to the notables in favour in Hugh Capet, the following formidable phrase: 'Royalty is not a matter of hereditary right'[59] and in a work dedicated to King Hugh and King Robert themselves, Abbo wrote these words: 'We recognize three kinds of general election—that of a king or emperor, that of a bishop, and that of an abbot'.[60] This latter statement should be noted as outstandingly significant. The clergy, used to considering election as the sole canonical source of the bishop's or the abbot's power, were naturally tempted to see it also as the most laudable origin of supreme political power. What had been brought about by one election however, could be undone by another, if need be without waiting for the death of the first elected person, and in any case without regard for the claims of his children. People had certainly not forgotten what had happened during the fifty years that had followed the deposition of Charles the Fat. And whatever might be the origin of the fortunate candidate, there was always unction to sanctify the choice. In short, the most urgent task confronting the Capetians was to re-establish the legitimacy of their line to their own advantage. They had only to be conscious of the perils surrounding them, and the dangers bound to fall upon their descendants' heads, to feel the necessity for some fresh manifestation calculated to increase the splendour of their name. In very similar conditions, the Carolingians had fallen back upon a biblical rite, royal unction. It is surely very possible for the appearance of the healing power under Robert II to be explained as the result of the same kind of solicitude as had formerly prompted Pepin to imitate the example of the Hebrew princes. To affirm this would be presumptuous; but it is certainly a tempting supposition.

Of course, it was not simply a matter of cold calculation. Robert enjoyed a great reputation for personal piety, which probably explains why the Capetian miracle began with him and not with his father Hugh. The saintly character attributed to the king as a human being, together with the sanctity inherent in royalty, must quite naturally have led his subjects to credit him with wonder-working gifts of healing. We can if we like suppose that the first people who asked for the royal touch—at a date we are never likely to know—did so of their own accord. It is even quite possible after all that other similar deeds had already been performed, here and there, in the previous reigns, as formerly in the time of Guntram. But when we see these beliefs, hitherto rather insubstantial, taking shape at such an opportune moment for this still rather insecure dynasty, it seems hard to think that there was not some ulterior political motive at work in their crystallization, though not of course in their original formation. Moreover, there is no doubt that Robert and his advisers had faith in the marvellous powers emanating from his person. The history of religions gives abundant proof that there is no need to be a sceptic in order to exploit a miracle. The court probably did its utmost to attract sufferers and to spread abroad the good news of any cures that took place. To start with, it cannot have seemed of much importance to know whether the power to heal was personal to the master of the moment, or inherent in the Capetian blood. In fact, as we have already noted, Robert's successors took good care not to let such a splendid gift fall into disuse. They too proceeded to heal, and soon came to specialize in the specific disease of scrofula.

It may be wondered whether each of them, as he claimed his share in this glorious privilege, was looking any further than his own personal interest. Nevertheless, unconsciously perhaps, their united efforts had the ultimate effect of endowing their whole house with a supernatural character. Besides, up to the reign of Henry Beauclerc, who—as we know—instituted the rite in England, that is to say, up to, at the earliest, the year 1100, Robert II and his descendants were the only European kings to touch the sick; the other kings, although 'the Lord's anointed', did not attempt to heal. It would seem then that something else besides unction was needed to convey this wonderful talent. To make a real king, a really saintly king, something else was required beyond an election followed by consecration: ancestral virtue was still an element that counted for something. The persistence of the claims to miraculous healing-powers in the

Capetian line certainly did not by itself create that faith in the legitimacy of their family which was to prove one of the best supports of the French crown. Precisely the opposite was the case: the idea of this inherited miracle was only accepted because there still lingered on in men's hearts some trace of the ancient notions concerning hereditarily sacred families. Yet it cannot be doubted that the spectacle of these royal healings served to strengthen this feeling, and somehow renew its youth. The second Capetian had begun these wonders; his descendants—much to the benefit of the monarchy—made it no longer the prerogative of a particular king, but of the whole dynasty.

Let us pass on now to England. There too we shall find physician-kings. So we are confronted by the eternal problem facing historians when they meet with similar institutions in neighbouring States; is this coincidence, or a case of interaction? And if we incline to the latter hypothesis, in which dynasty are we to look for the models, and in which for the imitators? It was formerly a burning question, for patriotism was long interested in its solution. The early scholars of the sixteenth or seventeenth century who took it up never failed to come down on the side of France or England according to whether they were French or English themselves. Today, it will not be difficult for us to face the question more dispassionately. Of course, the collective beliefs that originated the healing rites and made possible their success were the fruits of a political and religious state common to the whole of Western Europe. They had blossomed of their own accord in England no less than in France, and then likewise faded away; but a day came when they took concrete shape on both sides of the Channel in a precise and regular institution—the royal 'touch'; and it was in the birth of this institution that the influence of one of the countries on the other made itself felt.

Let us take a look at the dates. Henry Beauclerc, the first of his line known to have touched the sick, came to the throne in the year 1100. By this time Robert II, who certainly seems to have been the initiator in France, had been dead sixty-nine years. The Capetians were not plagiarists: but were they themselves plagiarized? If the royal miracle had developed in England independently of all foreign imitation, it would probably have evolved in the same manner as in France: first the appearance of wonder-working virtue applied to all diseases indiscriminately, then—by a random development that will always remain mysterious—a progressive specialization towards one specific disease; and it would be puzzling to think that scrofula too had been chosen purely by chance. True, scrofula is a disease lending itself particularly to the miraculous, because, as we have already seen, it can easily give the illusion of having been cured. But there are many other affections to which this applies. There were saints known to specialize in the healing of scrofula; but how many other illnesses are there in which such-and-such a particular saint is invoked? Now, the English kings would never appear to have claimed even at the beginning any healing power of an indeterminate character. From the very start, the disease they claimed to be able to relieve was precisely the one their neighbours in France had taken upon them to heal as a result of a perfectly natural development. Remember that Henry I was more than half French: he could scarcely be unaware of the cures performed by the Capetian who was his feudal lord and rival. He must have envied their prestige, and must surely have wanted to imitate them.[61]

But he did not admit to any imitation. He had the happy idea of placing his miraculous power under the patronage of a great national figure. As his patron and guarantor he took Edward the Confessor, the last representative of the Anglo-Saxon dynasty to which he had striven to link himself in marriage. What could have been a better choice than this virtuous sovereign who was soon to become the official saint of the monarchy? Did he perhaps experience some difficulties with the religious opinions of his country? At the time when Robert the Pious had begun to touch those who were suffering from disease in France, the Gregorian reforms had not yet come into being. We shall return to them later, and shall see how little sympathy they had for the prerogatives of kings, and especially how hostile they were to anything that smacked of usurpation in respect of any priestly privileges. When the healing rite crossed the Channel, the reform was at the height of its activity; and its leading ideas were expressed, as we have seen, in William of Malmesbury's scornful phrase in protest against the 'falsification' undertaken by the faithful supporters of royalty. But William's attitude must not be taken as typical of all English Churchmen. About the time when Henry I began to use his miraculous powers, a cleric attached to York Minster was writing his thirty-five treatises, representing the quintessence of all the anti-Gregorian ideas, and displaying the most absolute and unyielding faith in the virtues of royal anointing, and in the sacerdotal and quasi-divine character of royalty.[62] Henry I himself, at least throughout the first part of his reign, was in a delicate situation as regards the reformers. It was probably members of his entourage who drew up a false papal bull, defying all these new principles, and recognizing that the kings of England possessed 'the patronage and right of protection . . . of all the churches in England' and a kind of perpetual pontifical power of legation.[63] It is not to be wondered at that this was the moment doubtless chosen by Henry to establish the wonder-working practice in his dominions, seeing that it represented the apotheosis of belief in the sacred power of kings. Nor is it surprising that this practice flourished from that time onwards in a thoroughly favourable soil.

This rite, then, would seem to have originated in France towards the year 1000, and about a century later in England. Thus the royal touch made its appearance in dynasties where, in contrast to the ancient Germanic custom, primogeniture was beginning to prevail. In Moslem countries during the early days of Islam, it was thought that the royal blood could cure rabies; but among the mass of believers the reigning monarch, the Caliph, was not the sole possessor of this virtue, for every member of the family from which the Caliph had to be chosen had the same miraculous powers attributed to the blood which flowed in his veins.[64] The fact is that the whole royal race was considered sacred; Islamic States have never, in fact, recognized the privileges of the first-born in any political matter. On the other hand in France and in England, the healing of scrofula was always held to be a prerogative strictly reserved to the sovereign. The king's descendants did not share in it, unless they themselves were kings.[65] No longer, as among the early Germanic peoples, did the sacred character extend to a whole line; it had become definitively concentrated in a single person, the head of the eldest branch, the sole lawful heir to the crown, who alone possessed the right to work miracles.

For all religious phenomena, there are two traditional explanations. One—call it Voltairian, if you like—prefers to see the fact under study as the conscious work of an individual thought very sure of what it is doing. The other, on the contrary, looks rather for the expression of social forces of an obscure and profound nature; this might well be called the romantic approach. For has not one of the great services of Romanticism been its vigorous accentuation of the spontaneous in human affairs? These two kinds of interpretation are only apparently in contradiction. If an institution marked out for particular ends chosen by an individual will is to take hold upon an entire nation, it must also be borne along by the deeper currents of the collective consciousness. The reverse is perhaps also true: for a rather vague belief to become crystallized in a regular rite, it is of some importance that clearly expressed personal wills should help it to take shape. If the hypotheses put forward above are acceptable, the history of the royal touch will deserve to be numbered among the already plentiful examples from the past in which a dual action of this kind has been at work.

BOOK 2

THE GRANDEUR AND VICISSITUDES OF THE ROYAL HEALERS

I

Touching for scrofula and
its popularity up to the end of
the fifteenth century

1 *The French and English rites*

We have seen how the practice of touching made its appearance in Capetian France and Norman England. We shall now watch its expansion during the course of the closing centuries of the Middle Ages, up to the great moral crisis towards the end of the fifteenth century, which shook, among so many other old ideas, men's belief in the healing power of kings. But first let us try to trace the outward forms in which the rite was embodied during this period.

At first, the French and English rites were exactly the same. It could hardly have been otherwise, since the second had been copied from the first. In any case, they were both very rudimentary. But all ritual possesses a certain internal power of development, and the ceremony of the touch did not escape this common law. Gradually the ceremony became more complicated, and at the same time fairly profound differences between the two countries began to develop. This evolution falls to a large extent outside the present chapter, for it only became clearly evident in modern times, when the royal miracle had come to rank as one of those minutely regulated and splendid ceremonies surrounding the absolute monarchies. For the moment, we shall only be concerned with forms that were both fairly simple and unstabilized, of which our knowledge is far from complete, at least in matters of detail; for the courts of the Middle Ages, just because their etiquette was not at all strict, have hardly left us any documents dealing with ceremonial.

In fact, those primitive forms had nothing original about them. The physician-kings were naturally inclined to reproduce the unchanging actions that long tradition popularized by the lives of the saints attributed to miracle-workers. Like the pious healers whose stories were familiar to them, they used to touch the sufferers with their hand, most often, it would seem, on the affected parts themselves. They were thus unconsciously repeating a very ancient custom, going right back to the oldest beliefs of the human race. The contact of two bodies, made in one way or another and more particularly through the agency of the hand, had always seemed the most effective method of transmitting invisible forces from one individual to another. To this ancient magical gesture they added another, likewise traditional in their time, but specifically Christian—the sign of the cross, made upon the patients or on their sores. By the use of this sacred sign, it was said, the saints had triumphed over diseases in many different circumstances. The kings proceeded to follow their example, from the time of Robert II onwards in France, and in England, it would seem, from the beginning. Besides, religious people were accustomed to use this sacred sign in all the important actions of life; and it would have been strange indeed if it had not been used to sanctify the rite of healing.[1] Thereby the king made it evident to the eyes of all that he was exercising his miraculous power in the name of God. The expression frequently used in the English accounts of the thirteenth century is very characteristic: in order to indicate that the king touched the sufferers from disease, they often say quite simply that he 'signed' them.[2]

The ancient Lives of Edward the Confessor contain a curious piece of information. When a scrofulous woman was told in a dream to go and find her king, so the hagiographers tell us, it was revealed to her that she would be delivered from her evil 'if she caused herself to be washed in water by the king'. And later on in the story, we see the saint—to use the peculiar expression of the anonymous Life—anointing the affected parts with the tip of his fingers moistened with water. Here, too, we recognize an old procedure, a heritage from magic in the remote past. The liquid in which the healer had dipped his hands was considered to have then acquired miraculous properties. Is this an indication, then, that kings generally used this recipe? I do not think so. All the authoritative descriptions of both the French and English rites attribute the healing power to the direct touch of the hands.[3] It would not be possible to extract from the Lives of St Edward any precise information about the ritual followed at the English court during the twelfth century or later; for the scrofula episode, utilized by Henry I's advisers as the prototype of the royal miracle, was clearly not invented by them altogether. It must have formed part of the Confessor's traditional cycle before their master came to the throne. Other stories alongside it in the same biographies also attribute an important role to water. So it would seem that we are dealing here with a theme in saint-lore of which there are many examples in the literature of legend, particularly in works written in Great Britain, and not with a constituent of the healing ceremonial as actually practised by the kings of England.[4]

Yet in the ceremonial on both sides of the Channel, water did occupy a certain place, at any rate in principle, though a much more modest one. It was only right and proper that after having touched so many repulsive tumours, kings should wash their hands. This gesture arose from the most elementary needs of cleanliness, and did not originally have any wonder-working character. But it would have been unnatural for the people not to have credited the water from the royal washing-basins with a certain healing virtue. By virtue of its contact with a healing hand, it seemed likely itself to have become a means of healing. Etienne de Conty, a monk of Corbie, who composed a little treatise on royalty in France about the beginning of Charles VI's reign, described the rite of healing for scrofula. He tells us that after having touched, the king washes himself, and the water he has used is collected by the sufferers, who drink it for nine days, fasting most devoutly; after which, they are cured 'without any other medicine'.[5] This strange superstition would seem never to have crossed the Channel; and even in France there was no trace left of it in modern times. But in England, as we shall see, the coin given to the scrofulous became the subject of an essentially similar belief. In both cases, the healing fluid was thought to have been transferred from the royal hand to the object it had touched. A whole folklore was bound to spring up and flourish round the primitive nucleus of the official rite.

The kings were not silent as they accomplished the wondrous act of healing. Very early on, the French kings were accustomed to accompany the traditional double gesture with certain hallowed words. Geoffroi de Beaulieu tells us that St-Louis used to pronounce certain words as he touched the sick, words 'appropriate to the circumstances and sanctioned by custom, words that were altogether holy and Catholic'.[6] They were the same 'holy and devout' words taught by Philip the Fair on his deathbed, it was said, to Prince Louis his successor; or rather, words of which he reminded him, for there cannot have been anything very secret about them.[7] What were these words? We must be content to remain in ignorance. There is no testimony earlier than the sixteenth century for the sterotyped formula adopted by the French monarchs later on: 'The king toucheth thee, God healeth thee'. This phrase seems never to have been used on the other side of the Channel, nor anything like it. Not that the English kings remained silent; but they said nothing more than prayers.

It need hardly be added that religion also came into the French rite. It entered into this rite by the sign of the cross, and in other ways as well. Etienne de Conty relates that before going to heal the sick, the king would give himself to prayer. This was no doubt an ancient custom, but did it involve anything more than silent prayer? In the sixteenth century, we shall see the appearance of special forms of prayer for this occasion; but they are very short, and bear the marks of late legend.[8] By contrast with this poverty, England offers us an extremely rich supply, for in England the ceremony of the royal touch turned into a veritable liturgical service, in which the king, assisted by his chaplain, almost played the part of officiant. Unfortunately, the English liturgy for scrofula has not left any surviving examples earlier than modern times. The earliest 'service for healing the sick' in our possession dates from Henry VIII, or perhaps Henry VII. There is however no doubt that it incorporates much older material; and it is quite certain that this very specific ritual development goes back a long way. In a philosophical treatise written in 1344, Edward III's chaplain, Thomas Bradwardine, was already noting that before going to heal, his king would 'remain a good while in prayer'.[9] Better still, in the previous century, there is the evidence of the English Royal Household accounts. The expression they use for the royal touch is not only—as I have already mentioned—that he 'signs' them, but also, and more often, that he 'blesses' them, a term which had become more or less classic. It is found in Bradwardine, and in the writing of a doctor called John of Gaddesden.[10] To be sure, we shall see later on that the value attributed to the royal blessing in itself was not at this period confined to England. The sacred power ascribed to the sovereign's hand was exhibited as much in a protecting gesture of this kind, as in the gesture that was supposed to be able to dispel disease. There must, it seems, have been a natural tendency to confuse the two. Yet the French documents never assimilate them. In England, on the contrary, the two were constantly confused. This was because the English had in front of their eyes a healing ceremonial which seemed obliged to make use of a word borrowed from the Church's vocabulary.

What were the reasons for this striking contrast between the two rites? They are wrapped in obscurity. One possible hypothesis would be to look for them in the environment in which the English rite first came into being. The notion of the sacred character of royalty had been heightened by the controversies aroused in connection with the Gregorian reforms. If Henry's entourage contained many clerics like the anonymous priest at York, it would not be surprising to find that he was easily persuaded to adopt a more or less sacerdotal attitude, subsequently imitated by his successors.

In early times, kings would seem to have exercised their miraculous powers somewhat at random on behalf of any sick people who presented themselves. The crowd pressing round Louis VI, shown us by Guibert de Nogent, was a pretty disorderly affair. Gradually, as the great Western monarchies became better policed in general and the regular habits of bureaucracy and routine even penetrated the life at court, a certain discipline came into the external forms of the royal miracle. Louis VI would seem to have 'touched' the sick every day, or at least every day when there was a demand, but only at a specified time, after he had attended Mass. Late-comers would have to spend the night at the palace, where they were given food and lodging, and would then come before the king at the proper time the next day. The habit of practising the rite at irregular times still existed in France under Philip the Fair, and likewise in England under the three Edwards, where it continued in this way up to the end of the fifteenth century. Henry VII does not seem to have had any fixed dates for touching the sick. In France, on the other hand, in Louis XI's reign, the sick were only brought before the king in groups, once a week, which must certainly have meant a great saving in time for a busy and active monarch.[11]

It also became the custom in France, from the fifteenth century at latest, to select suitable candidates from the poor folk who came to their sovereign for the relief of their various ills. For from that time onwards, the august royal doctor's speciality was well established: he healed scrofula and nothing else. It was therefore right and proper to admit to his presence only those who suffered from that disease. To have opened the doors to the others would have wasted the prince's time, and perhaps also risked compromising his prestige. It would not have looked well to ask him to perform the healing gestures in cases where they were thought bound to fail. And so a rough and ready preliminary diagnosis was carried out, no doubt from this time onwards by the court physician; and all who desired the favour of the royal touch had first of all to submit to this examination. This was not always accepted without angry protests. One day when Charles VII happened to be at Langres, a certain Henri Payot, a blacksmith living near the town, wanted to bring his sister before the king, for she was said to have scrofula. But the king's officials refused to admit her, giving out that she was not suffering from it. Henri Payot, who was already embittered by the losses he had sustained through war, took his revenge for this final disappointment by indulging in some strong language. He called down the curse of God upon his sovereign and the queen, and said the royal pair must be out of their senses. These remarks, and others equally unpleasant in tone, were repeated; with the result that the unfortunate man had subsequently to procure a letter of pardon, for which, no doubt, he had to pay in hard cash.[12]

Generosity towards this world's poor was a duty that the conscience of the Middle Ages imposed with considerable moral force upon sovereigns in general. And they were not at all niggardly in fulfilling it. In France, documents dealing with royal expenses are unfortunately extremely rare; in England, they have been infinitely better preserved. But anyone who has gone through the accounts of expenditure in the royal households knows that alms were no small part of it.[13] Now among the sick who came to the king to ask for healing, there were many in a state of poverty, and the habit of giving them some money soon became established. In France under Philip the Fair, money was only given as a rule, it would seem, to those who came from afar, either foreigners or nationals from the remotest parts of the kingdom; and the value of the gift varied from twenty sous— the usual amount, at any rate in 1307 and 1308—to six or even twelve livres.[14] I cannot say anything about the following reigns, for from Philip IV to Charles VIII there is a complete lack of any information on this subject. In England during the reigns of Edward I, Edward II and Edward III, the alms given to the scrofulous were always the same, namely one penny.[15] The alms were much smaller than in France, because much more widely distributed. Indeed, all or nearly all the sick had a share in them, though it may perhaps be supposed that in the early days some of the nobler and wealthier may have chosen not to accept the alms. Yet those exceptions must have been extremely rare, otherwise the totals of disbursement would not have reached the formidable figures I shall quote in a moment. These exceptions no doubt soon disappeared; and in modern times there are none at all. The piece of money had by then become an essential feature of the rite in the eyes of the public: not to receive it at the hands of the king would have been to miss at least half the miracle. I shall examine this superstition in more detail later on, but I must not fail to mention it here and now. It is of interest for the Middle Ages by reason of its distant origins, since its genesis can only be explained by the early and widespread custom in the English court of always accompanying the royal gesture of healing with alms.

We have seen, then, some of the rites and the ceremonial accompanying the exercise of this marvellous royal power. It remains to enquire how convincing these claims seemed to the public at large. The kings posed as wonder-workers: who believed in them? They posed as doctors: who were their patients?

2 *The popularity of the royal touch*

It will be remembered that in the three successive reigns of Edward I, Edward II and Edward III (1272–1377), the sick—or nearly all of them— when they had been touched by the king, used to receive alms, a small coin invariably fixed at one penny. We still have some accounts giving for various periods the total amounts, either for the whole exercise as a lump sum, or—better still—by the day, or week, or fortnight. First, then, let us allow the figures to speak for themselves. There is a kind of rough eloquence about them. It will then be time enough to comment upon them.[16]

Of the three sovereigns mentioned above, the first would appear according to our sources to have held the 'record' for miraculous healing—though the records are too incomplete to allow for exact comparisons. Edward I 'blessed' 983 individuals during the twenty-eighth year of his reign; 1219 during the thirty-second year; 1736 during the eighteenth. Some rather less spectacular years were as follows: in the twenty-fifth year, 725; in the fifth, 627; in the seventeenth, 519; in the twelfth, 197.[17]

Going on now to Edward II, we find that the one complete year's figure in our possession is low—79 persons touched in the fourteenth year of his reign (8 July 1320 – 7 July 1321). But other information not falling within the same chronological framework gives a rather less unfavourable picture of his medical activity. In 1320, from 20 March to 7 July—a period of four months—he received 93 sick persons; in 1316, from 27 July to 30 November —a slightly longer period of time—214.[18]

Edward III performed 136 healings between 10 July 1337 and 10 July 1338; but this was a comparatively poor year, and must not be taken as typical. Between 12 July 1338 and 28 May 1340—slightly over 22 months— the number reached 885, an average of very nearly 500 a year. On the other hand, between 25 January 1336 and 30 August 1337—19 months—it did not rise above 108.[19]

These figures, taken as a whole, are impressive. They give an imposing idea of the healing prestige enjoyed by the Plantagenets. Thomas Bradwardine, who died as Archbishop of Canterbury in 1349, tells us in a work composed when he was still Edward III's chaplain, that the miracles performed by his master were testified to 'by the sick persons who had been cured, by those present when the cures took place, or who had seen the results of them, by the people of many nations, and by their universal renown'.[20] Was he exaggerating the popularity of the English rite? One might be tempted to think so if the accounts did not invite us to take his affirmations seriously. The renown invoked by him was no mere figure of rhetoric: it was real enough to send people thronging into the presence of the English kings, sometimes more than a thousand a year.

There is no document giving us precise figures about the medical activities of the kings of France. It would seem likely, however, that their reputation at this same period was no less than their neighbours'. There were similar beliefs in the two countries, and they formed the basis of a similar rite. Philip the Fair, as we shall see in a moment, was not only approached by his immediate subjects. On the days when he administered the royal touch, he would receive Spaniards and Italians, and among the French, people from distant and unruly fiefs. These foreigners or half-foreigners seem to have had just as strong a faith in him as the people of his own domains. Bradwardine recognizes that the French princes, as well as the Plantagenets, possessed this healing power. He says that the royal miracle was proclaimed 'in both kingdoms, with unanimous voice'. As far as England is concerned, the documents confirm his testimony at every point; and the picture would no doubt be the same for France, if only our source-material were more complete.

Yet the English figures, although impressive as a whole, are extremely variable in their details. The differences do not seem to arise from any variations in the way the information has come down to us. The accounts of the Royal Household upon which we have drawn were no less carefully kept under Edward III than under Edward I; and for the twelfth year of the latter's reign they were just as accurate as for the eighteenth. The smaller figures are no less worthy of credence than the higher. Why are there these irregularities?

For certain years, the reason is simple enough: the king was at the wars, or travelling. He was therefore unable to carry out, except on rare occasions, this peaceful rite, which only took place very exceptionally elsewhere than on English soil. Sometimes he was totally unable to perform it for several months on end. From 20 November 1283 to 19 November 1284 (the twelfth year of his reign), Edward I only touched, as we have seen, 197 people. But if we take a closer look at our accounts, we notice that they give 185 as presenting themselves before 15 March.[21] Now it was precisely on this date that the king entered Wales in order to complete its submission; and he was still there on 19 November. Of the twelve remaining individuals, three came to him during a brief stay he made in between whiles in the county of Chester, which lay on the frontier.[22] The other nine were no doubt soldiers or Welsh deserters. The 983 sick entered on the list between 28 November 1299 and 19 November 1300 (the twenty-eighth year of his reign) by the Royal Household account-books should not be attributed in actual fact to these twelve months. In the registers, all mention of the royal touch ceases abruptly on 12 December. This is explained by the fact that, on the 13, the king and his army entered Scotland, which was still in full revolt. The entries begin again from 3 January: on 1 January, Edward was back on English soil. Then the entries break off once again on 24 June: on 5 July the court was again in Scotland. The 725 sick persons we have assigned to the twenty-fifth year of the reign (20 November 1296 to 19 November 1297) were in fact blessed in a space of slightly less than nine months ending on 18 August. Between 22 and 27 of that month, Edward crossed the sea to Flanders, and remained there till the end of his financial enterprises, during which there was no question of healing anyone.

For Edward III, we have less information. The figures are only given in summary form covering large periods of time. It is immediately obvious, however, that the number of 885 given for the space of almost two years stretching from 12 July 1338 to 17 May 1340 cannot represent the regular average. Nearly all those cures, as we shall see later, were performed on the continent.

There were other periods, it would seem, when the kings could give little time to the healing rite because more urgent occupations only left them scanty leisure. From 25 January 1336 to 19 July 1338, Edward III carried out rather less than 244 cures.[23] This period of minimal healing activity coincided notably with a period of extreme diplomatic and military activity, entirely occupied by the preliminaries to war against France. Similarly in the year of his reign 1283–4, Edward I blessed only 187 people in four months, a much lower figure than usual. At this time, his days were no doubt employed in discussing or arranging the important measures leading up to the submission of the ancient country of Wales.

But these travels and wars and preparations for war, those chance events providing the reason for certain of our lowest figures, in no way affected

belief in the virtues of the royal hand. We cannot boast of complete knowledge of the facts: other causes of the same kind, such as illness on the part
of the king, court festivities, epidemics, famine, unsafe roads, may at other
times have prevented the august doctors from carrying out their healing
task, or momentarily checked the crowds of the faithful. It would be futile
to claim as an explanation of all the irregularities in our statistics, or even
the greater part of them, some indeterminate fluctuations of men's faith
in the miraculous healing of scrofula. The three account registers of
Edward III that have come down to us all contain figures notably lower
than those for Edward I. Should this be regarded as proof of a decline in
faith? We have no right to do so, for none of these documents refers to a
period that could be regarded as normal. Nevertheless, the statistics of the
royal touch should interest the historian attempting to trace the evolution
of loyalty to the monarchy in all its subtle variations. Literary texts and
official documents often present us with nothing but a distorted picture,
which is always suspect; whereas our accounts, in England and even in
France, give us the thing in action, in one of its most characteristic and
spontaneous manifestations; and sometimes—exceptionally—they can even
register its variations.

Consider first of all the reign of Edward II. All the chronicles, and most
modern historians, agree in giving us the impression that he was an unpopular sovereign.[24] He seems to have been a prince of second-rate character and intelligence, with bad advisers; suspected or repugnant vices,
betrayed by his close friends, and destined to come to a miserable end.
But their testimony may be dubious: we are afraid it may simply reflect the
hatred of a few great lords. What did the common people think? Let us
enquire of our accounts. The three figures they give for this reign are all
rather low, and there is no journeying beyond the frontiers or military
preparation to explain this paucity.[25] And it is particularly significant that
they go down progressively. In 1316, there were 214 sick persons blessed
in about four months; between 20 March 1320 and 7 July of the same year
—about the same length of time—no more than 93; from 8 July 1320 to
7 July 1321—a year—the figure drops to 79. Now 1320 and 1321 were the
years when there loomed up before the feeble king the figure of his nephew,
Thomas of Lancaster. He too was a person of little worth, but to the
popular mind he was a hero; and when on 22 March 1322 he was beheaded,
miracles were popularly ascribed to him.[26] There can be no doubt that
from 1320 onwards Edward's popularity was paling before the ever-
increasing glory of his rival. Hardly anyone continued to come for healing
to a monarch lacking in prestige.

We saw just now that in 1299–1300 Edward I's healing power seemed
to come suddenly to a halt when this prince set foot in Scotland. This was a
time when Scotland was almost entirely in a state of revolt against the
English invaders. But if we now transport ourselves to this same country

in the thirty-second year of the reign (1303–4), we find that the conquest of the country is drawing to an end. Many former enemies are rallying to the English side; in February, the Regent himself and a majority of the nobility come and make their submission, and annexation becomes the order of the day. Until 25 August 1304 Edward stays north of the Tweed, and there, from 20 November onwards, he blesses no less than 995 sick persons. It is not to be supposed that all these supplicants were English people in his entourage; there must certainly have been a good many Scots as well. Many of the inhabitants of this formerly rebellious country were beginning to recognize this Plantagenet as their lawful king, and were begging for miracles from him.

The kings of France and of England both claimed the power to heal, Now the English king owned lands on the continent held in fief from the king of France. In these half-French, half-English regions, to which of the rival healers did the sufferers from scrofula go? We possess the very detailed accounts showing the cures carried out by Edward I in the course of a journey in his possessions in Aquitaine. He touched some sick persons there, at Condom, at Condat near Libourne and at other places, but only very few: 124 in about seven months. But after 12 August, when he was back in England, some 395 appear to have come to him.[27] Apparently the prestige attaching to the lord of the fief was damaging to his vassals in the eyes of the inhabitants of Bordeaux and the Gascons. As we shall be seeing later on, even in Bordeaux itself, the inhabitants did not disdain to go and seek for health at the hands of a Capetian.

The situation must have changed when the Plantagenets assumed the title of kings of France. In 1297, when Edward I reached Flanders, he at once ceased to heal. This was because in this nominally French country not linked in any way to the English crown he was only a foreign sovereign.[28]

But now let us pass on to Edward III. It will be remembered that the summary accounts of his Household expenses for the period from 12 July 1338 to 27 May 1340 give the figure of 885 sick people blessed. Now during these twenty-two months, Edward was only twice resident in England, and that for less than four months.[29] All the rest of this period was spent on the other side of the Channel, making war against Philip of Valois or negotiating with the lords and citizens of the Low Countries. In particular, he traversed Flanders and those regions of the north that were in effect French; in fact, he hardly went outside this Capetian kingdom that he was claiming as his heritage. It is difficult to believe that the 885 miraculous cures can all be set down to a period of less than four months, or that they all belonged to the king's immediate followers; the majority of them were most probably people from the continent. A prince who received the homage of the inhabitants of Ghent on 26 January 1340 as king of France might well exercise his tremendous powers on French soil.

The English accounts have taken us onto French soil, and there we will remain for the moment. Let us go back some years to the period when the Capetians' lawful claims were not contested, and examine the wax tablets which served as a register of expenses for the accountants of the Royal Household under Philip the Fair. Such as we have of them stretch from 18 January to 28 June 1307, and from 1 July to 30 December 1308, and were kept by Renaud de Roye. He seems to have been a most meticulous official, not satisfied with showing precisely the destination of all sums given to 'sufferers from the royal evil' (his predecessors had lumped them together among the other alms), but making a positive point of each time noting the name and home address of the patient. This is immensely valuable information for the historian, although, apart from Abbé Lebeuf,[30] no one seems hitherto to have realized its interest. It will be recalled that not all the scrofulous received money at this time, but only those who came from afar. The French Household tablets do not therefore allow us to draw up complete statistics, as we can from the English documents. But thanks to the precise character of Renaud de Roye, they bring the people who were miraculously healed to life in a more striking manner.[31]

As a rule, the social status of those touched is not indicated. All the same there is not much difficulty in discovering that all classes were represented in the crowd of sufferers who thronged round the king. That demoiselle Jeanne de la Tour, who after having received the royal touch at Poitiers on 12 May 1307, accepted 60 sous from the hands of Vivien, the porter, must certainly have been a noble lady.[32] The religious orders, too, were not afraid to appear before the royal healer. During these twelve months approximately, between 1307 and 1308, and solely from among foreigners or French natives from distant provinces, there was one Augustinian, two Friars Minor, and one Franciscan nun.[33]

As a general rule, we do not possess the names of the sick living near the court, that is, in the years 1307 and 1308 when Philip the Fair did not go farther south than Poitiers, but remained mostly in the north; the reason being that they did not normally receive alms. Nevertheless Normandy (Elbeuf), Artois (Montreuil-sur-Mer), and Champagne (Hans near Sainte-Menehould) appear exceptionally among the places of origin noted by Renaud de Roye. No doubt Agnes of Elbeuf, Gilette the Châtelaine of Montreuil and Marguerite de Hans were all poor women, who could not be refused some money.[34] The mention of more distant districts is of particular interest. It shows that the Capetians' healing powers had supporters in the provinces of central France, so much off the beaten track, and in the region of Toulouse, which had not long been attached to the French crown; in Bigorra, a distant Pyrenean valley sequestrated by the king not even twenty years earlier; and on the lands of the great vassals, in Burgundy, in Brittany (more than half of which was independent), at Montpellier, owing allegiance to the king of Majorca, and at Bordeaux, the continental capital of the Plantagenets.[35]

Let us ponder these facts for a moment. We are in 1307 and 1308—tragic years during which the ever more pressing need for money was to drive the Capetians into the scandalous business of the Templars. Without a doubt, the fiscal demands of the crown were beginning to press upon the people with almost unbearable weight. Yet, despite all the difficulties, sick persons seem to have made their way towards the king from all corners of the kingdom. When poor people living at Guingamp, in the heart of the most Breton part of Brittany, and in the villages near Toulouse—the *langue d'oc* country, once the home of the Albigenses—feel that they are suffering from scrofula, they take up their staff and, walking by difficult and sometimes dangerous ways, they reach the château in the Île de France or the valley of the Loire, where their sovereign sojourns; and they come to beseech him for a miracle. On 13 December 1307, in mid-winter, when the court was at Nemours on the Loing, a man called Guilhelm arrived, having come all the way from Hauban in Bigorra, where the high banks overhang the Adour; and he had made this long journey in order to obtain the favour of the royal touch.[36] Does not the story of this humble believer speak more eloquently than all the books that have been written about the prestige and the sacred role of kings?

However far from Paris they lived—Languedoc, Bordeaux, the heart of Brittany—they were all of them French; and it was from their king that they hoped for healing. In the same way the Scots blessed by Edward I, whose side they had joined, and the Flemings blessed by Edward III, whom they accepted as authentic inheritor of the French crown, only expected miracles from these monarchs because they considered them their lawful masters. In the groups of sufferers lined up around the physician-kings, were there on either side of the Channel any genuine foreigners? Bradwardine relates that crowds flocked to his sovereign, 'from England, *from Germany, from France*, and from everywhere'.[37] The English accounts do not allow us to check his statement, as they contain only figures; but it would seem that we ought to have some confidence in this royal chaplain, seeing that it was part of his duty to assist his master in the miraculous rite. Besides, up till now we have found him accurate in all his statements. Among the thousands who sought the royal touch, there must no doubt have been some who were not the Plantagenets' subjects. And as for the Capetians, the Household tablets in Philip the Fair's time give a vivid picture of their European reputation.

First come the imperial territories. All along France's western frontier there stretched a strip of land from north to south, the former share of Lothair in the Carolingian partitions. Nominally, it was dependent on the German sovereigns, but in actual fact French influence had from the start disputed the claim made by the imperial powers. Philip the Fair in particular was very active in this direction. His 'policy of expansion' has often been described;[38] but the only impression retained by the ordinary reader is the one given by the chronicles and diplomatic documents, namely the treaties with towns or overlords, judicial procedures, or association in dominion. Yet one would like to go a little deeper, and discover what the crowd in the regions where Capetian power was gradually infiltrating thought of the French king with the fleur-de-lis. But how is this to be done? At least we know, thanks to Renaud de Roye, that on occasions they could turn to him as to a worker of miracles. There was belief in the royal touch in Lorraine, particularly in the town of Metz, whose bishops had several times in the course of recent years been sought as allies by the government of France. It was likewise believed in farther south, at Lausanne, in Savoy, and, on the banks of the Rhône, at Tarascon near Arles.[39]

The same faith flourished farther afield, in even more purely foreign countries, such as the little kingdom of Navarre, brought as dowry to her husband by the Queen of France, as well as in Spain proper, and especially beyond the Alps. In those single years 1307 and 1308, the royal suppliants included at least sixteen Italians—Lombards (in particular people from Milan, Parma and Piacenza), Giovanni from Verona, four Venetians, a Tuscan, people from the Romagna, a woman from Urbino, and a friar from the district of Perugia.[40] This was about the time when Dante wrote of the Capetian dynasty that 'this evil plant' was casting its shadow everywhere,[41] This invasive monarchy had its weapons—not least, the weapon of miracle.

What splendid propagandists they must have been, if by chance they found themselves healed after being touched—Brother Gregory, of the Augustine Order, or dame Chiara, at Bologna 'Grassa' her home town.[42]

The ecclesiastical policy of Philip the Fair has sometimes seemed a kind of historical paradox. This prince, who inflicted such a blow on the papacy, was without doubt a profoundly religious man, devout and almost an ascetic.[43] There was nothing of the Frederick II Hohenstaufen about him. How is his attitude to be explained? The enigma is not perhaps as difficult to solve as it might seem at first sight. We are too liable to forget who Boniface VIII was. He was a pope of dubious legitimacy, owing the tiara solely to the 'great refusal' made by his predecessor, an abdication of doubtful validity in itself, and obtained under suspicious circumstances; and as a persecutor of the Spirituals, he was an object of scandal to many faithful Christians. It needed the efforts of Sciarra Colonna and Nogaret to turn him into a martyr. In spite of everything, there remains something obscure about the state of soul of this very pious monarch who could authorize or allow, and then cover up with his name, this notorious deed; not to mention the mentality of his servants, mostly good Catholics, who were nearly always more implacable even than their master. Our study of touching for scrofula may perhaps throw some light on this psychological problem. In a memoir written to justify the deed in 1310, Nogaret and Plaisians end a long eulogy of their master with these words, which are to some extent its climax: 'Through the king's hands, God most evidently performs miracles on behalf of the sick'.[44] We must not take this sentence as nothing more than the empty quibble of an advocate. For contemporaries, these words expressed an incontestable fact which was the source of a whole way of feeling. The same hope that sent pilgrims forth along the roads leading to the great sanctuaries urged crowds thirsting for healing towards this Capetian king. Perugia and Urbino, two towns theoretically belonging to the patrimony of St Peter, were still sending their scrofula sufferers to him in 1308—the date is worth noting—five years after Anagni. The king of France was no mere temporal sovereign, either in his own eyes or in those of his subjects. He was an instrument chosen by the grace from on high, a marvellous physician whose help was sought like a saint's throughout almost all the Catholic world. There was too much of the divine in him to make him feel constrained to bow his head to Rome. Who can say what secret pride in the heart of Philip the Fair could maintain the consciousness of his wonder-working power? Or what comfort his faithful followers may not have drawn in times of difficulty from the sight of sufferers from all nations pressing round the royal doors?

The second half of the fourteenth century and almost the whole of the fifteenth were a period of crisis for the monarchies, first in France and then in England too. In France, there was the rivalry between the Valois and the Plantagenets, foreign invasion, political and social disorders of every kind; in England, dynastic revolutions and civil war shook the fabric of the State. Through all this upheaval, did the royal miracle remain intact? We should indeed like to know. But unfortunately there is a lack of exact information. The French accounts have perished. The books of English accounts from the Royal Household have in part survived, but they give no information on the subject of our enquiry. For this period, they no longer give the sum-total of alms doled out to the sufferers from scrofula. Sometimes this has been taken to prove that the kings were no longer performing their healings, or at least less frequently than before. But such an inference is, I think, unwarrantable. It may be more simply explained by a change in the recording methods. The almoner, no doubt, still continued to give the sick money, as in the past; but in the daily record of expenditure, payments made by him on this account were now lumped together with his other disbursements. We still have the overall figure for royal alms, but no longer the details. Moreover, it can scarcely be doubted that in England and in France during the Hundred Years' War and the Wars of the Roses the kings went on touching for scrofula; for there are a good many documents of various kinds—chronicles, medical works and political polemics[45]—which assure us that they did, though not enabling us to judge the degree of popularity enjoyed by the rite.

It would seem highly probable, however, that the struggle taking place between the different branches of the royal family in England did have a disturbing effect on popular sentiment. Besides, this is not merely a matter of conjecture. Sir John Fortescue, a partisan of Henry VI, has given us some striking evidence. Exiled to Scotland between 1461 and 1463, he wrote at that time various treatises in support of his master, which are still in our possession. In these writings he denies to Edward IV, who was then in possession of the throne, any wonder-working power; in his opinion, this belongs solely to Henry VI.

> At the touch of his most pure hands . . . you can see even today sufferers from the King's Evil, including those despaired of by physicians, recovering their longed-for health by divine intervention; and this redounds to the praise of the Almighty, for it is from divine grace that the grace of health proceeds. Those who witness these deeds are strengthened in their loyalty to the king, and this monarch's undoubted title to the throne is thus confirmed by divine approval.[46]

Thus the Lancastrians refused to admit that the House of York could possess this miraculous gift. And their political adversaries, no doubt, responded in the same vein. Each side sought to discredit the rite as practised by the other party. And it is only too likely that some of this discredit overflowed onto the rite in general. The common opinion was that the lawful king could heal; but who was the lawful king? The uncertainty on this delicate point, which was constantly in debate, could hardly fail to dry up to some extent the stream of sufferers who had in times past thronged so eagerly to receive the royal touch on the appointed day. As we saw above, it is not possible to give decisive numerical proof of this decline in faith; but we have some indications of it, which we will now examine.

Not long after the Wars of the Roses, there is a reappearance in Henry VII's and Henry VIII's accounts of certain references to the royal touch. They are infrequent, because they are in all probability incomplete. The majority of sick persons were no doubt included in the general budget for alms, of which we still possess no details. We only know of certain exceptional payments made by persons outside the regular service of the royal charities, and therefore entered in the Household cash-books, which we still possess in part. And so for the early Tudor period, as for the immediately preceding one, we must give up any attempt to draw up annual figures comparable to those for Edward I, Edward II and Edward III. But instead of comparing totals, let us make a separate examination of the various articles concerned with 'healings' in the accounts of Henry VII. Those on whom the king laid hands each received the sum of six shillings and eight pence. As we have already noted, in the days of the three Edwards, it was also a fixed sum, but much smaller—only one penny. Of course, the difference in value cannot be established by a simple numerical comparison. It is no use simply saying that six shillings and eight pence are equal to eighty pence, for in Henry VII's time this same word penny denoted a much smaller precious metal content than at the end of the thirteenth century, for instance; for the constant fall in the value of the coinage is one of the fundamental economic facts of the Middle Ages. Yet there is no doubt that the alms given by Henry VII had a much higher value than those which sufficed for the patients of Edward I, or even Edward III. In the latter's reign, a penny was a small silver coin weighing rather less than $1\frac{1}{2}$ grammes.[47] Under Henry VII and during the early years of Henry VIII, six shillings and eight pence was the equivalent of a gold coin weighing slightly more than five grammes.[48] It was called an *angel*, because it bore the image of St Michael the Archangel. The *angel* became the coin specially used under the Tudors for giving to those who received the royal touch, and continued to be so used under the Stuarts. Its value as money of account varied, like that of the other metal coins, according to the financial policy of the moment. In 1526, Henry VIII raised it to seven shillings and eight pence. This was 'debasing' the coinage; but the sufferers did not lose by this operation, since from then onwards they received the precise amount of seven shillings and eight pence. In other words, they continued to receive the same gold coin as in the past, so indispensable did it seem not to deprive them of a definite quantity, always more or less fixed, of the precious metal.[49] As regards the purchasing power of money at different periods, the present state of our knowledge does not allow us to measure it at all accurately. Nevertheless we know that before the Black Death a penny was the usual daily wage of a reaper—that is, a rather poorly-paid worker—and at the beginning of the sixteenth century, the *angel* was the normal consultation-fee of a doctor in great repute: the contrast between these two is obvious.[50] To sum up, it may be said that from Edward III to Henry VII the alms given to scrofula sufferers changed from silver to gold, and at the same time its economic value rose steeply. When did the change take place—under Henry VII or before his time? All at once, or in stages? We do not know. Edward IV seems to have been the first king to mint *angels*; but we have no means of knowing whether he was also the first to use them for the needs of the healing rite. One thing however is certain: this strange transformation, which ended by turning the alms given to the sick into something of a prize, a lure to those who might have hesitated to come forward for the royal touch, took place during a period of crisis, when rivals for the throne were mutually denying each other the power to work healing miracles. Was this pure coincidence? It is difficult to think so. Each of the claimants must have sought to attract to himself by all possible means those who were suffering from scrofula and seeking to be cured; for—in Fortescue's words—there was no more signal 'confirmation' of an 'indubitable title' than the gift of miraculous healing. In France, where no such internal struggles took place, the sum handed to the beneficiaries of the royal touch remained fairly small; under Louis XII and Francis I, it was two shillings, a figure equivalent to two very small silver coins.[51] Surely the astonishing rise in the rate of alms in England must have been the result of this competitive bidding between the rival houses.

In spite of everything, faith in the royal miracle victoriously survived the vicissitudes of politics. We shall see later on some of the deep psychological factors which gave it the power to resist destruction. But at the period we have now reached, this faith still had other supports than these half-unconscious psychic tendencies; for medical science, theology and political philosophy had all seized upon it and given it the sanction of the written word. So let us turn to the writers of books, beginning with the doctors.

3   *The royal touch for scrofula in the medical literature of the Middle Ages*

For a long time, it would seem, medical writers avoided any allusion to the wonder-working powers of kings. In truth, a large number of them confined themselves to copying, or commenting more or less slavishly upon either the classical writers or the Arabs. Their silence can largely and quite naturally be explained by that of their models. But there would seem to be another reason, which we shall easily discover when we see when this silence was first broken.

A compendium of medicine, *Compendium Medicinae*, enjoying some renown in the Middle Ages has come down to us under the name of Gilbert the Englishman, Gilbertus Anglicus. Nothing certain is known about him. His surname shows that he was somehow linked with England, perhaps by nationality, or family origins, or a stay in that country— we cannot say which. As to the date of composition, that can be definitely fixed in the first half of the thirteenth century; but greater precision is not possible. This rather mysterious work is, as far as I know, the first of its kind to refer to the royal touch. In Book III, we read the following words: 'Scrofula . . . also called the King's Evil, because kings can heal it'.[52] This is, as one can see, a simple allusion, more or less in passing, and more concerned with linguistic usage than with any method of treatment specifically recommended by the author. The writers who really admitted the royal miracle to science were Frenchmen and subjects of Philip the Fair, namely Bernard Gordon,[53] the four anonymous authors who wrote glosses on the surgical treatises of Roger and Roland de Parma,[54] and Henri de Mondeville, the king's own surgeon, who was so proud of finding in his master a professional colleague. We find him naïvely exclaiming: 'Just as Our Lord and Saviour Jesus Christ exercised the power of surgery with his hands and in so doing honoured all surgeons, so and in the same manner our Most Serene Sovereign King of France does honour both to them and to their profession by healing the scrofula through the mere touch of his hands'.[55] But not everyone shared this enthusiasm. About 1325 there lived at Ypres a surgeon called Jan Yperman, who has left us a treatise on his art. It seems that he had taken part in the political struggles then rending Flanders, and was one of the opponents of the fleur-de-lis; hence, no doubt, his scepticism with respect to the healing gift attributed to the Capetians by French medical opinion. 'It will now be said', he writes, 'that many people believe God to have given the king of France the power to heal suppurating scrofula simply by laying on of hands; and it is commonly believed that many of those so touched are cured. But sometimes they are not cured'.[56] Clearly, in Yperman's eyes, the idea of including the royal touch among the remedies listed in the classical pharmacopoeia still had an air of novelty about it. But it soon ceased to rank as such. Indeed, the writers of the following period fell in without more ado with the lead given by the French group round about the year 1300. Such were Guy de Chauliac in France, in his *Chirurgia Magna*, drawn up in 1363, destined to remain a favourite work among practitioners right down to modern times;[57] and in England, John of Gaddesden, under Edward III,[58] and John Mirfield under Richard II.[59] Now it is extremely remarkable that the healing rite should thus have obtained a kind of scientific ratification at the same time as the doctrine of the Church put an end to the almost unanimous ostracism which had previously existed—and in much the same circles. In the silence they had maintained over so many years on this subject, doctors had no doubt only been following the prudent example set them by theology, for reasons which will be explained later.

Moreover, not all of them changed their behaviour. Only French and English doctors sometimes gave the healing rite a place in their writings, for they were by virtue of their nationality directly interested in the glory surrounding it. But they were not followed by their foreign colleagues, though these did not usually go as far as to throw doubt upon the healing virtue of the royal touch. The case of Jan Yperman, inspired by his vigorous hatred for the Capetians, of a kind so often engendered by municipal strife in Flanders, is quite exceptional. For the most part, they were content to say nothing. How is their silence to be explained? Mostly through ignorance, or routine indifference; but with some it would certainly seem to have been a deliberate attitude. Take for instance Arnold of Villanova, one of the greatest doctors of the fourteenth century. Though a native of Aragon, he lived in France and at Avignon. It is hard to believe that he never heard of the cures performed by the Valois; yet one looks in vain for any mention of them in the chapter *De scrophula* of his *Breviarium Medicinae*.[60] His was an independent mind, capable of a sort of originality even where he is being credulous, and he certainly did not share the blind faith of his contemporaries. As far as I can see, the idea of kings possessing healing powers did not enter into the international literature of medicine until the sixteenth century.[61]

Besides, it must not be thought that the doctors of the Middle Ages, even if English or French, went out of their way to be enthusiastic about these healing rites. Miracles whether worked by temporal princes or by the saints were quite familiar things to them, in no way contradicting their system of the world. They believed in them, but in a placid and dispassionate manner. Moreover, they were hazy about the distinction between natural remedies, which they generally looked upon as utterly mysterious, and supernatural ones, and normally set them side by side in all good faith. Most of the time, they would send on to the king scrofula cases who proved refractory to every other form of treatment. 'As a last resort,' says Bernard Gordon in his *Lilium Medicinae*, 'recourse must be had to the surgeon; or if not, we must approach the king.'[62] John of Gaddesden inverts this order. As we read in his *Rosa Anglica*: 'If all remedies prove ineffective, let the patient go to the king and be touched and blessed by him . . . in the very last resort, if everything else has proved ineffective, let him hand himself over to the surgeon.'[63] We must not read any irony into this advice: Gaddesden does not think that the surgeon is bound to do better than the king; on the contrary, he believes that this dangerous operation should be avoided at all costs. Recourse to it should be had only after all other possibilities have been exhausted—including miraculous healing. Kings are not always successful in healing, any more than the saints; yet this does not throw doubt upon the virtues of either. The apologists for royal healing in the sixteenth and seventeenth centuries were to speak in quite a different tone; and this because they were not living in the same atmosphere, and had to raise their voices more to get a hearing from a public that was then much less trusting. A simple faith expresses itself quite simply and naïvely.

Thus the touch for scrofula in England and in France had become a medical commonplace, and the technical manuals served in their own way to glorify the monarchy. No doubt many a practitioner who had derived his own knowledge and skill from them would give his patients the classical advice to 'go to the king'. Let us now try to discover what the doctors of the Church used to say to their faithful flock.

4 *The ecclesiastical view of the touch for scrofula*

In the eleventh century, soon after the establishment of the first healing rite in France, a great doctrinal movement shook the life of Catholic Europe to its very foundations. Historians have made Pope Gregory VII its eponymous hero and therefore usually call it the Gregorian Movement. I shall conform to this customary usage; but it will be as well to recall that this religious awakening, born of deep feelings, was first and foremost a collective phenomenon. A group of monks and prelates revolutionized the Church. These men, whose actions were so powerful, were in no sense inventors: the themes they kept repeating *ad nauseam* had been advanced by others before them. Their originality lay elsewhere, in the implacable sense of logic which impelled them to go to extremes in the application of the principles handed down by tradition and somewhat blunted by long use. What was new was the astringent sincerity that gave the most well-worn theories, when enunciated by them, a novel accent; and above all the heroic efforts they made to transform into rules of practical conduct ideas that were mostly as old as Christianity, but which men had become accustomed to imprison innocuously within the world of the moral and theological treatise. The influence of these men was to decide for many years the attitude to be adopted by ecclesiastical literature towards the royal miracle; and we shall see the direction in which it took effect.[64]

In order to understand this school's political ideas, it is important to form an accurate notion of what they were opposing—though this point is sometimes forgotten. The temporal power they attacked so relentlessly had nothing in common with the Lay State destined much later on to be attacked in its turn by other Catholic thinkers. Far from seeking to break off all links with religion, lay power claimed on the contrary to be endowed with a highly religious character; for it was no less than sacred royalty, that legacy of past ages, to which the Church had—imprudently perhaps—given her sanction in the eighth and ninth centuries. Since its introduction into Western Europe, the rite of royal unction had steadily grown in importance and in prestige. As we shall be seeing at our leisure later on, the quasi-sacerdotal character of sovereigns was, in certain circles at any rate, being deduced from it with ever-increasing zeal. Emperors and kings drew conclusions from the holy oil of unction in order to acquire a hold over their clergy, and even over the papacy itself.

Now, it was the primary aim of the reformers to deprive these secular princes, who believed themselves to be sacred persons, of their supernatural impress. They wanted to reduce them to the level of ordinary human beings whose empire was confined to things of this world—whatever might be the opinion of their loyal adherents. This is why we come across the apparent paradox that the partisans of the popular origin of the State, whose theories supported some kind of social contract, are to be found at this period among the most fanatical supporters of authority in matters of religion. In the days of Gregory VII, an Alsatian monk called Manegold of Lautenbach, in a treatise devoted to a defence of papal policy, explained how kings were chosen in order that they might frustrate the designs of the wicked and protect the good. But if a king failed to fulfil those conditions, he would forfeit his high office, 'for in that case he himself is quite evidently breaking the pact by which he became king'. This pact between the people and their ruler was essentially revocable; and a few lines further on, Manegold did not hesitate to compare it to the agreement a man makes 'for a fair wage' with the shepherd he employs to look after his pigs.[65] These statements were particularly categorical; the author himself did not perhaps grasp their immense significance, though they certainly belonged to the deep logic of the movement of thought from which they had sprung. Historians have often presented this movement as an attempt to subject the temporal to the spiritual. This is indeed an accurate interpretation, but it is incomplete. In the first place, it was a vigorous attempt in the political domain to destroy the ancient confusion between the temporal and the spiritual.

Moreover, we have Gregory VII's own opinion about monarchical power in the famous letter he addressed on 15 March 1081 to Hermann, Bishop of Metz. He had just excommunicated the Emperor Henry IV for the second time; he knew that he had entered upon a struggle from which there could be no drawing back, and he no longer needed to go gently. In his brilliant manifesto, he lays bare his thought, perhaps with a certain forced emphasis, for he ordinarily expressed himself more mildly. Yet the exaggerations—if such there are—only serve to underline the essential features of a doctrine that is perfectly firm and coherent as a whole. There is a kind of fury in the way he humiliates royalty before the priesthood, and ranks it so low that it is presented almost as a diabolical institution. What was the reason, as he saw it, for the flagrant inferiority of the princes of this world? It was because, being laymen, they had no share in the super-natural graces. For what was an emperor or a king, however powerful he might seem on this earth, in comparison with a priest who 'by a simple spoken word' could transform the bread and the wine 'into the body and blood of Our Lord'?—or even compared with an exorcist (that is to say, a cleric possessing the third of the minor orders). The emperor or king is only in command over men, whereas the exorcist (and here Gregory conveniently remembers the actual wording of the ordinal) is 'a spiritual emperor empowered to expel demons'.[66] And the pope adds these memorable words:

> Where shall we find among the emperors or kings a man who has equalled the miracles of St Martin or St Benedict, not to mention the apostles and martyrs? What emperor or king has ever brought the dead to life, restored health to the lepers and sight to the blind? Look at Constantine of pious memory, Theodosius and Honorius, Charles and Louis, all of them lovers of justice, propagators of the Christian religion, protectors of the Church. The Holy Church praises them and reveres them, but does not invest them with the glory of any such miracles.[67]

Thus Gregory VII expressly denied to the temporal sovereigns, even the most pious of them, any miraculous gifts. In so doing, was he thinking of the wonder-working powers the French monarchs had already been claiming for two generations? The very general form in which he cast his thoughts hardly allows us to read into them any such specific allusion; besides, his eyes were turning at that time towards the Empire, rather than towards the little kingdom of the Capetians. His only intention, no doubt, was to draw a perfectly natural conclusion from the ideas he had formed about the nature of political power, without regard to any particular case. But the same ideas, necessarily following from the principles of the Gregorian School, occurred to others besides him; and they did not fail to apply them to the French or English kings. The Church has doubtless always taught that miracles are no proof of holiness: they come from God, who chooses his instruments where he will.[68] To conciliatory spirits like Guibert de Nogent, this seemed a way of accepting royal miracles without a direct collision with orthodoxy; but to the stricter Doctors, this could appear nothing but an unworthy way of getting out of a difficulty, for they were well aware that this did not reflect the lines of popular thought. To have admitted that a lay prince was capable as such of accomplishing supernatural cures would have been, willy-nilly, to strengthen in men's minds the very notion of sacred royalty they were so zealously attempting to destroy.

Their state of mind was perfectly expressed, in the very early days of the royal touch, by William of Malmesbury. We shall remember how he denounced 'the work of falsehood' perpetrated by those who claimed that Edward the Confessor 'possessed the power to heal, not by virtue of his holiness, but by virtue of hereditary title, and as a privilege of the royal race'.[69] The strange thing is that no one repeated this explicit protest. Other writers announcing the same doctrine did indeed protest in their own several ways, but without any blowing of trumpets. For almost two centuries in France, all the ecclesiastical literature—that is, for this period, all historical and didactic literature—observed an almost unanimous silence on the subject of the healing rite. It was the same in England, and for an even longer period. Was this pure chance, or casual neglect? It is hard to think so. For instance, take the letter sent between 1235 and 1253 by the Bishop of Lincoln, Robert Grosseteste, to Henry III, his lord, explaining to him, by request, the nature and effects of royal unction.[70] You will look in vain for any allusion to the marvellous virtues which the popular mind considered to be imparted by the holy oil; and mere forgetfulness would hardly cover the case: it must surely be a deliberate omission. Two authors only are an exception—Guibert de Nogent in France and Peter of Blois at the English court; but their attitude should not surprise us, for they showed no more than a very moderate enthusiasm for all the ideas that came from the Gregorian School. Guibert, who was contemporary with the formidable pope, had no sympathy for the persecution of the married priests.[71] And Peter of Blois, who was intimate with Henry II, does not seem to have disapproved of his master's ecclesiastical policy, which is well known to have been unfavourable to the 'liberties' of the clergy.[72] Only men who were as indifferent as this to the notions dear to the hearts of the reformers could find a place in their writings for the royal miracle; the rest were silent, in obedience to a more or less tacit command from on high, which was none the less binding upon their consciences. I have already had occasion to refer, in connection with the French rite, to the long silence of the documents in the face of all the historians' enquiries. We can now see the reason for it—the influence of the great eleventh-century revival, which extended its effects in successive waves, as it were, over the two following centuries. Nor should one be too surprised that this influence should have had an equal effect on all contemporary writers, not only on theologians or monastic chroniclers, but also on authors writing in the popular tongue, the troubadours. Never, it would seem, in any of their epics or adventurous romances, did they attribute to their legendary kings the marvellous cures that were being daily accomplished, close at hand, by sovereigns of more real and solid substance. We know nowadays that all that world was much more under ecclesiastical authority than was formerly supposed.[73]

But—it will no doubt be objected—why did the supporters of Gregorian ideas choose this policy of silence? Why did these bold fanatics not directly attack the rite that they held in such abhorrence? Besides, they were not after all the only masters: they must have encountered many able and eloquent opponents, even among the clergy themselves: why did none of them come forward explicitly in defence of the royal miracle? A whole polemical system grew up round the Gregorian movement, of decisive importance for the political education of the mediaeval world: why did the touch for scrofula have no place at all in it? The answer is simple: this great battle of ideas left France and England almost entirely outside its field of operations. The mysterious English or Norman writer whom—for want of a better name—we call the Anonymous of York, may be said to constitute an almost unique exception. He can hardly be reproached for silence on the subject of a rite that was then in its earliest infancy, if indeed it had by then actually come into being. Apart from this author, the men who carried on the battle in books and in pamphlets were Germans or Italians, hardly conscious of anything but the Empire, and ignoring the kingdoms of the West. This does not mean that in these latter countries the great quarrel between King and Priesthood did not disturb the State as much as elsewhere; but for a long time it hardly did more than bear upon matters of fact concerned with nomination to ecclesiastical dignities or upon the fiscal or judicial liberties of the clergy. These bitter disputes, although fought out on the territory of practical matters, did indeed presuppose a background of opposing rival conceptions and sentiments. Only here, this deep antagonism remained mostly unconscious, or at least unexpressed. There were a few rare exceptions to this rule, and we shall see later on that the most glaring one can be explained by circumstances that were in themselves quite exceptional. But in general, in the two countries we are considering, there was always a tendency to avoid raising difficulties of principle. This may have been through prudence, for neither in France nor in England did the struggle ever take on the same implacable

character as in the Empire; or it may have been due to a dislike of theoretical speculations. At any rate, these matters of principle were avoided in
France until the Capetian monarchy under Philip the Fair became a great
European power and seemed likely to inherit the role left vacant by the disappearance of the Hohenstaufen. Then the French king in his turn posed
as defender of this temporal power, and the French polemical writers
entered the arena in support of their master. As we shall see in a moment,
they took good care not to forget the gift of miraculous healing.

In France, moreover, the conspiracy of silence had already begun to
flag by the middle of the thirteenth century. There were two obscure
ecclesiastical writers, the anonymous author of the miracles of the Saints of
Savigny (composed between 1242 and 1244)[74] and a certain Clement, who
drew up about 1260 a life of a Norman priest called Thomas de Biville. The
former incidentally mentions 'the King's Evil',[75] the latter more explicitly
'the disease of scrofula which the king of France through divine grace
heals with his hands'.[76] But it was only after the death of St-Louis, and
with regard to his works, that any really prominent priests ventured to
break the old ban of silence. The pious king seemed to sanctify all that
concerned him. Note, however, the circumspection with which his
biographers venture on to this dangerous ground. Guillaume de St-Pathus
only makes passing mention of the royal touch.[77] Geoffroi de Beaulieu, on
the other hand, develops the subject at some length, and with a definite
intention to bring out the religious character of this disputed practice. He is
not content to stress that the words spoken on this occasion are 'truly holy
and Catholic'; he goes so far as to claim that his hero was the first to introduce the sign of the cross into the rite, 'so that healing might be ascribed
rather to the virtues of the cross than to the action of his Royal Majesty'.[78]
This statement can hardly be accepted as true, for we know through Helgaud and Guibert de Nogent that Robert II and Louis VI were already
using this same gesture, and it is difficult to see why tradition should have
been broken off on this particular point. Geoffroi's statement is inaccurate:
whether intentionally or not, there is no means of knowing. The point is not
really important, for whichever hypothesis is adopted, the explanation
remains the same. The intention was to show that the pious sovereign had
been at pains to exercise his healing powers in full conformity with the
strictest orthodoxy. Nothing could be stronger evidence of the scrupulous
demands of ecclesiastical opinion.[79]

This takes us on to Philip the Fair. As we saw above, it was during
the great struggle with the curia that the apologists of the French monarchy appealed for the first time to the royal miracle of healing. We have
already heard the evidence of Nogaret and Plaisians.[80] The same thesis
is developed with a certain fullness in the little treatise generally known as
Quaestio in utramque partem. It enjoyed enough reputation to be copied,
about the same time as it was composed, in one of the registers kept by the

Chancery; and in the following century Charles V still thought highly enough of it to have it translated into French by his accredited translator, Raoul de Presles. The anonymous author enumerates the proof of the French king's 'just claim':

> Secondly, the same thing is proved by these obvious miracles, which are manifest to all the world, and notoriously manifest. Of which our lord the King may say in support of his just claim the self-same words used in the Gospel of Our Lord Jesus Christ in answer to the calumnies of the Jews: 'If ye will not believe in me, believe for the very works' sake'. For just as the son succeeds the father by way of inheritance, so also by a manner of inheritance our king succeeds another in the like power of performing these same miracles, which God accomplishes through them, as through his ministers.[81]

The historians then followed the line of the publicists. Laymen like Guillaume Guiart under Philip the Fair, [82] ecclesiastics like the monk Ivo of St-Denis, under Philip V, who was a kind of official historiographer,[83] were no longer afraid to give the 'miracle' of the royal touch a place in their writings. But things went even further. Even sacred eloquence put itself at this time in the service of the Capetians' healing prestige. There is an interesting sermon by a Norman Dominican friar, Brother Guillaume de Sauqueville, on the theme 'Hosanna to the son of David',[84] preached about the year 1300. It shows the preacher to be full of an extremely vigorous national pride. He proclaims the independence of France against the Empire, and holds the Empire up to ridicule by means of a deplorable pun (empire: en pire—'going from bad to worse'). That was the time when the great controversy of the French writers with the papacy was reinforced by polemics against the imperial pretensions to universal hegemony.[85] The king of France, says Brother William, deserves the name of Son of David because David means 'valiant hand' (*manu fortis*); and the royal hand is valiant in healing the sick: 'Every prince who inherits the kingdom of France, as soon as he is anointed and crowned, receives from God the special grace and peculiar virtue of healing the sick by laying on of hands; and so we see sufferers from the King's Evil coming to the king from many places and divers territories'. Those are the very opening words of the sermon.[86] Polemical pleadings scarcely reached the crowds; but what must have been the effect on the crowds of words like those delivered from the pulpit!

About the same time there lived in Italy a writer whose attitude to the healing rites was destined in due course to exercise a really powerful influence on the whole of ecclesiastical opinion. Fra Tolomeo, a Dominican friar, a native of Lucca, died as Bishop of Torcello about the year 1327. He was an extremely prolific historian and political theorist. It would not be easy to extract any very definite doctrine from his works, for this voluble writer was not a thinker with any great range of knowledge. He was un-doubtedly hostile to the Empire and favourable to the papal supremacy; but he should no doubt be considered not so much a faithful papal supporter as a devoted partisan of the House of Anjou. At this time, there was a strong community of interests between this House and the head of the Church on a number of points, though by no means on all. Nothing could have been more natural in a native of Lucca, for Lucca was one of the strongest supporters of Angevin policy in the north of Italy. Charles of Anjou, who was Imperial Vicar in Tuscany, was much respected there; and Tolomeo twice calls him his lord and king. When this great Guelph con-queror was dead, the attachment our Dominican had sworn to him seems to have been transferred to his line. For in 1315, when Prince Charles of Taranto, nephew of Robert of Naples, fell on the battlefield of Montecatini, it was Tolomeo—then prior of Santa Maria Novella in Florence—who took it upon himself to go and seek his body from the victorious forces of Pisa.[87] Now Charles of Anjou, the brother of St-Louis, was a Capetian; and as such he must have believed in the royal miracle, and all the more firmly because when he became king in Italy, he too claimed—as we shall see—to possess the gift of healing. These consi-derations explain the favour accorded by Tolomeo to the royal touch for scrofula. He expressed himself on this subject in two of his works. First, in a pamphlet of political polemics called *Determinatio compendiosa de jurisdictione imperii* written about the year 1280, expressly to serve the interests of the King of Naples against the King of the Romans and the pope himself. In chapter XVIII, where he is intent upon proving that royalty comes from God, he produces—among others—the following argument. He claims this theory to be proved 'by the example of certain princes of our time, good Catholics and members of the Church; for by virtue of a special divine influence and a participation greater than that of ordinary men in the Absolute Being, they possess a singular power over the sick. Such are the kings of France, and Charles our lord and king' (note the Angevin touch); 'and also, they say, the kings of England'.[88] If Tolomeo had only spoken of this 'singular power' in the *Determinatio*, which was much read in his time, but was forgotten after the fourteenth century, his name would not deserve more than a minor place in the history that now concerns us. But about the same period he composed another work that was to have much greater success. He had been a disciple of St Thomas Aquinas, and he found among his master's works a *Treatise on the Government of Princes* which had been left unfinished; he took it upon himself to finish it. In one of the chapters thus added by him to the original, he devoted some lines to unction, especially as received by the kings of France, where we read these words: 'The kings who are the successors of Clovis are anointed [with an oil once brought down from heaven by a dove]; and as a result of this unction, divers signs, prodigies and healings appear in them'.[89] This is a much less explicit phrase than the one quoted above; yet it was destined to enjoy a far wider renown. For the *Treatise on the Government of Princes* shared in the vogue generally enjoyed by the works of St Thomas; and no clear distinction was made between the portions belonging to his pen and the additions made by his continuator. Under the *ancien régime* in particular, apologists of the royal touch readily appealed to the authority of St Thomas.[90] In reality, they had no right to claim more than Fra Tolomeo's authority; but even for more circumspect historians, the text of the *Treatise* posed a difficult problem, even up to recent times: why was it that this author from Lucca, with his vigorous defence of the Church and the Papacy, had been almost the first to acknowledge the 'prodigies' and the 'healings' which up till then neither the Church nor the popes had professed to favour? The fairly recent publication of the *Determinatio* has solved the riddle. It was the Angevin claims that made Tolomeo such a staunch supporter of the royal touch, and indirectly obtained for the wonder-working rites the apocryphal, but none the less invaluable, support of Thomas Aquinas.

The first French publicists putting forward arguments for this miracle had shown a certain audacity; their successors had only to gather what they had sown.

It was especially in Charles V's entourage, and in the fourteenth century, that the widest use was made of this support in France. Consider first a solemn charter given in 1380 to the Chapter of Rheims by the king himself. At the head of the document are the two royal initials, K and A, decorated with small elegant ornamental drawings; and alongside the classic scene of the granting of the charter—the sovereign handing to the canons the parchment that will make them lords of the domains of Vauclerc—there is a picture of the miraculous baptism of Clovis. The preamble does indeed recall the legend of the Holy Phial; but it also directly links it with the gift of healing:

In the holy church of the illustrous city of Rheims, Clovis, at that time king of France, heard a sermon from that most glorious confessor of happy memory, Rémi, bishop of this famous town. And there, as the bishop was baptizing the said king and his people, the Holy Spirit, or it may be an angel, appearing in the form of a dove, came down from Heaven, bearing a phial full of the oil of holy chrism; and it is from this chrism that the king himself, and all the kings of France our predecessors, and I myself in due course, have by God's grace on the day of our consecration and coronation received unction; by which unction, and by the influence of the divine mercy, such virtue and such grace have been imparted to the kings of France that merely by the laying on of their hands they protect the sick against the evil of scrofula; which thing is clearly testified by the facts, and the witness of innumerable persons.[91]

This is the first time a Christian monarch explicitly put himself forward as a worker of miracles. As for the orators and writers whose learned eloquence flourished at the court of this wise king, they vied with one another in vaunting the power of the royal touch. The author of the *Somnium Viridarii* sings its praises through the lips of his knight, asserting over against the priesthood the divine character of the temporal power.[92] We have already mentioned Raoul de Presles, and his translation from Latin into French of the *Quaestio in utramque partem*. And in the preface to his translation of St Augustine's *City of God*, likewise undertaken on his master's orders, he sounds a pompous eulogy of the French monarchy in which he does not fail to make mention of this miraculous royal privilege.[93] As we shall see later on in more detail, so did Jean Golein, in his translation of Guillaume Durand's *Rationale Divinorum Officiorum*; and Master Anseau Choquart, towards the end of April 1367, haranguing Pope Urban V in the king's name in order to dissuade him from returning to Rome.[94]

Let us make no mistake, however. The exaltation of the royal healing power in these circles was only one among many manifestations of a general tendency whose meaning is clear enough. For among Charles V's advisers and entourage you can distinctly see the most energetic attempts to reinforce by every possible means the religious and supernatural prestige of the Capetians. As Noël Valois has demonstrated, that was the time when the idea arose at the French court of reserving to their kings, as the peculiar honour of their House, the title of 'Most Christian', which had up till then been quite commonplace.[95] Never was there more resounding praise of the miraculous traditions of which the monarchy of the fleur-de-lis was so proud. What is more—as we shall presently note—it would seem that, in these small loyalist circles centring on the royal *scriptorium*, they even ventured to add a little enrichment to the legendary heritage handed down by their ancestors.[96] In general opinion, it was from the ceremonies of anointing that the kings received their divine impress; and Charles V certainly showed a particular interest in them. His library contained no less than seven volumes relating to the French rite; and to these should be added a work on the imperial anointing, and a psalter containing the English consecration rite.[97] Moreover, it was through his direct encouragement that one of his paid writers, the Carmelite Jean Golein, composed a little treatise on the anointing of the kings and queens of France, which we shall be studying later in more detail. What then was the origin of the zeal displayed by the Sovereign and his entourage for everything that had to do with sacred royalty? Something, no doubt, must be set down to Charles V's own personal bent. Naturally very pious, and profoundly convinced of the grandeur of his office, he was bound to stress the religious character of 'the royal estate'. Moreover, his mind was drawn towards theological speculation. In the words of Jean Golein, he had 'put his subtle mind to study these matters', in so far as he understood the terms of theology.[98] Hence his natural inclination towards mystical and symbolical theories of royalty and consecration, which the literary men of his time were more than ready to offer him. Yet it would be somewhat ingenuous to see all the stir created at this time by the official or unofficial writers on the subject of the miraculous elements in monarchy as no more than the product of their desire to flatter a prince's disinterested inclinations. We shall see the regular recurrence of a certain phenomenon in the course of the history we are studying: whenever it was a question of repairing the breaches made in the French and English dynasties' popularity by the serious crises which repeatedly shook them, the favourite theme of the loyal propagandists was nearly always that of the cycle of sacred royalty, and especially of the power to work miraculous cures. To take no more than a couple of clear and relatively recent examples—the reign of Henry IV in France and that of Charles II in England—this was the string on which the servants of legitimacy preferred above all to harp.

Now under Charles V, the State was emerging from a truly formidable crisis, touched off throughout the kingdom by the battle of Poitiers. Certain historians of our day have sought to minimize the dangers then confronting the Valois dynasty and the monarchy itself. Yet the danger seems to have been genuine, and really grave, not only from the efforts of certain intelligent men to subject the government to a kind of national control, but more still because of the violent movement of hatred and revolt which then roused a whole part of the common people against the nobility. The rich merchant classes took part in it also, for they had not yet succeeded, as they did in the following centuries, in making a forcible mass entry into the privileged class. For a short while, the monarchy itself seemed to be enveloped in the discredit which had descended upon a caste with whom royalty appeared to have made common cause. Anyone who is in doubt about the strength of the feelings which troubled men's minds during these few tragic years should read the three letters from Étienne Marcel, which have chanced to come down to us. This is not the place to go into the ways by which the Valois triumphed over these vicissitudes; but there can be no doubt that the memory of these events, which we know to have had a very powerful and enduring effect on Charles V's outlook, spurred him on to strengthen by every possible means the hold of the monarchy over the minds of his subjects. It should not surprise us that a prince who, as it has been rightly observed, was quick to appreciate the true value of 'the power of public opinion', should have taken good care not to neglect the weapon of the miraculous.[99]

But this subtle politician was at the same time a most devout man. It certainly seems as though the sometimes indiscreet praise of his miraculous power by those who surrounded him inspired him at a certain moment with some scruples. He was anxious to confine his apologists within the limits set by sound orthodoxy. We have an interesting testimony to his anxieties in a document that has been more or less ignored up till now, which it will be helpful to describe in some detail. Among the numerous works Charles V had had translated at his own expense from Latin into French was one of the most important Liturgical treatises of the Middle Ages, the *Rationale Divinorum Officiorum* composed by the Bishop of Mende, Guillaume Durand, around the year 1285. The translation, which had been entrusted to the Carmelite Jean Golein, was presented to the king by its author in 1372. It is a well-known work and was even printed in 1503, at a time when the didactic literature from Charles V's *Scriptorium* was providing the presses of certain enterprising publishers with splendid material. But what has usually not been noticed is that this work was something more and better than a translation. At the end of the chapter in which the Bishop of Mende had given the theory of unction in general, without applying it particularly to royal unction, Jean Golein, 'out of reverence' for his most venerable sovereign lord, who had been consecrated king of France on 19 May 1364, thought good to add material of his own. This was a 'little treatise on the consecration of princes', which in the original manuscript bearing the royal book-plate fills no less than twenty-five pages in double column, written in a rather fine hand. This is not so much a treatise on the consecration of princes in general as a study and description of the French rite of consecration in particular. Along with a rather heavy-handed development of the symbolic meaning, the 'mystical interpretation' of the Rheims ritual, there is a mass of invaluable details on French public law—particularly on the legendary foundations of the right of succession—and on the concept of sacred royalty and its miraculous aspects; several of these will be utilized later on in the present work. But there is something more useful still. On one point at least, the healing power, which specially interests us for the moment, Jean Golein explicitly proclaims himself to be the authorized interpreter of his master's own thought. Raoul de Presles, addressing himself to Charles V in his preface to the *City of God*, had written: 'you have such virtue and power—given and attributed to you by God—that you work miracles in the course of your life'. Several of the previously quoted texts show this language to be perfectly in keeping with current usage. Nevertheless it seems to have shocked the pious monarch. 'He would neither be made a saint nor a worker of miracles', Jean Golein insists; such things are said without his 'consent'; and the good Carmelite goes on to explain most learnedly that only God works miracles. Perfectly true, no doubt; but do not let us get an exaggerated idea of this prince's humility, or that of his mouth-piece. For Golein takes good care to remind us that this incontestable theological fact is true of the saints as well as of the wonder-working kings. In both cases, the prodigies they perform are the work of divine power. And that is why those who are ignorant of 'theological language' say in either case that they perform miracles or heal such and such diseases. The comparison was probably enough to satisfy the royal pride. And so Charles V and his Doctors managed to reconcile their cravings for orthodoxy with their just desire that 'the royal estate' should not be 'less held in honour than it should be by right reason'.[100]

The impetus had first of all been given by the entourage of Philip the Fair, and then by that of Charles V. From this point onwards, miraculous healings became a necessary part of any eulogy of the French crown. Under Charles VI, a monk called Étienne de Conty ranks them among the splendid privileges he attributes to his kings.[101] On at least two occasions—under Charles VII and Louis XI—these same gifts were invoked by the French ambassadors at the papal court in order to prove the special holiness of the House of France, and consequently the lawfulness of the power their masters exercised over the Church.[102]

These last examples are particularly significant. As we shall be seeing later on, there was a whole complex of ideas and sentiments, expressed in doctrinal form as Gallicanism, in which the ancient notion of sacred royalty played its part, including what was most real and evident to the ordinary mind, namely the gift of healing. One must therefore not be surprised to find the argument from miracle employed even by lawyers pleading in cases of an ecclesiastical nature. At the beginning of 1493 a lawsuit involving the deepest political and religious interests came before Parliament. The contestants were two clerics who both claimed the title of Bishop of Paris. They were Girard Gobaille, elected by the Chapter, and Jean Simon, nominated by the king and confirmed by the Pope. Jean Simon's counsel, Master Olivier, naturally thought fit to defend the king's right to intervene in ecclesiastical nominations, for one of its most striking applications was the *régale spirituelle*. This was a right traditionally exercised by the French monarchy to provide for benefices in the gift of certain bishoprics while the see was vacant. In the course of his pleading, counsel exclaimed (in a mixture of Latin and French, which was then the custom):

> In the same way, the king is not purely a lay person, for he is not only crowned and anointed like other kings, but also consecrated. But more than this: as Giovanni Andrea [an Italian canonist whom we shall meet later on] writes in his treatise upon the Decretals, in the chapter entitled *licet*, the king heals the sick simply by the contact of his hand; and therefore it is no marvel that he should possess the *droit de régale*.[103]

In England, writers do not seem to have made much use of this kind of argument. Perhaps this was because during the fourteenth and fifteenth centuries they had less occasion than France to cross swords with Rome.

Nevertheless, a writer from this nation, in a resounding piece of polemics against the papacy, did make use of the wonder-working weapon. But though an Englishman, he was in the service of the Empire. At this time, about the year 1340, a German sovereign, Ludwig of Bavaria, had revived the old quarrel that had been almost dormant since the end of the Hohenstaufen period. He gathered round him a number of literary men, some of them the most vigorous thinkers of that age, one of whom was William of Occam. Among other works composed on this occasion by the famous philosopher was one entitled *Octo Quaestiones de Potestate et Dignitate Papali*. In the eighth chapter of the fifth question, Occam claims to demonstrate that through unction kings receive 'the grace of spiritual gifts'; and among his proofs he quotes the healing of scrofula by the kings of France and of England.[104] His tone could hardly be less Gregorian.

Thus during the fourteenth and fifteenth centuries, the royal miracle was widely used by the apologists of royalty. At this same time, what were the views of those who championed papal supremacy? The Portuguese bishop Alvarez Pelayo, a contemporary of Occam, and one of the most violent pamphleteers on the papal side, described it as all 'lies and dreams'.[105] Much later on, Pope Pius II expressed in his *Commentaries* a discreet scepticism on the subject of the cures said to have been performed by Charles VII. This was perhaps principally a reflection of his annoyance at the constantly repeated arguments of the Gallican polemical writers and orators, for whom he had no liking. Moreover, the *Commentaries* were not destined to be published during their author's lifetime.[106] But such declarations would seem to have been quite exceptional. The publicists in French pay had ceased to remain silent on the healing rites; instead, they made a point of putting them forward. But their opponents did not follow them in this field. And this was not only so from the moment when the Great Schism turned the thoughts of ecclesiastical pamphleteers in other directions. Even in Philip the Fair's reign there is no evidence that the writers on the papal side ever took up the challenge thrown down by Nogaret or the author of the *Quaestio in utramque partem*. One gets the impression that towards the beginning of the fourteenth century the cures performed by the Capetians or the English sovereigns had taken firm hold upon everybody, even upon the stubbornest religious opinion, and had been accepted as a sort of experimental truth. A general free discussion of these things began, no doubt because no one was any longer offended by them. In England, they were quoted by Thomas Gradwardine, a very orthodox philosopher and a future archbishop, in Edward III's time, in the course of a general disquisition on miracles, without the slightest sinister intent.[107] Then there were the Italian canonists Giovanni Andrea —the Jean André of our old authors—in the first half of the fourteenth century, and Felino Sandei at the end of the following century; both of them make passing mention of the 'miracles' worked by the king of France, as though they were a well-known fact. True, Sandei attributes them to '*vi parentelae*', that is to say, to a kind of hereditary physiological predisposition, rather than a divine grace reserved for monarchs. But he obviously believes in them, and never dreams of taking offence.[108] The miraculous powers of the two dynasties become one of the commonplaces of diplomacy. Brother Francis with a suit to the doge of Venice from Edward III,[109] Louis XI's envoys addressing the Duke of Milan,[110] a Scottish ambassador haranguing Louis XI himself,[111] all allude to them quite naturally. Should this be reckoned one of the clearest signs of victory for a long-contested belief, that it has passed into the realm of the commonplace?

It would seem that the end of the fifteenth century was also the time when the royal healings first made their appearance in the world of art. Mediaeval iconography was entirely religious; and as far as we know, it had never dared to represent this prodigy, which might almost be called profane; for a miniature of the thirteenth century depicting Edward the Confessor laying hands on the scrofulous woman should certainly be reckoned as a piece of hagiography. But in 1488, André Laure had some splendid stained glass made for the abbey of Mont St-Michel. Ever since the closing years of the war with England, and especially since the creation, on 1 August 1469, of the Order of St Michael, a Royal Order of Chivalry, this abbey had really become a national and dynastic sanctuary. One of these stained glass windows, in the rectangular chapel then known as St-Michel du Circuit, depicted the anointing of the French kings. There you could see divided into several compartments the essential features of the ceremony; and the wonder-working gift, which the abbot no doubt considered a consequence of the unction, was not forgotten, but was included in one of the upper medallions. This is how Abbé Pigeon, the author of a *Nouveau Guide historique et descriptif du Mont Saint-Michel* (1864), describes it: 'The second medallion represents the king, who, having taken Communion in both kinds, has gone to a park where a considerable number of sick persons are assembled. He touches them one after the other with his right hand, from forehead to chin and from one cheek to the other.' Alas! we can no longer compare this only moderately precise description with the original. Among many other crimes against art, the Prison Administration, who had control of Mont St-Michel for much longer than they should have, allowed the oldest of its monuments to be destroyed or fall into decay—a monument raised by faithful subjects to the glory of the royal miracle. No trace remains of the stained glass depicting the consecration of the kings of France.[112] But what an honour this was for the royal miracle, to be thus set side by side with the miracles of the saints among the pictures this church offered for the veneration of the faithful! It would seem, then, that the ancient belief in the wonder-working powers of princes had definitively triumphed not only, as we saw above, over political rivalries, but even over the violent or covert hostility which the most active elements in ecclesiastical opinion had for a long time displayed against it.

5 *The touch for scrofula and national rivalries; attempts at imitation*

In the eleventh and twelfth centuries, only two royal families had begun to practise the touch for scrofula—the Capetians in France, and the Norman princes and their successors, the Plantagenets, in England. There was something of a competition between them; besides, they could not fail to arouse envy on the part of the other sovereigns. It will be worth while studying the reactions of national or dynastic pride provoked by their mutual rivalries, which tended also to stir up rivalries against them in common.

It is rather surprising to find that the majority of French or English writers in the Middle Ages were disposed to accept the cures performed by a foreign king on the other side of the Channel without any acrimony. Guibert de Nogent did not find any imitators to repeat his denial of all healing power to Henry I. Even the strongest chauvinists were usually content to draw a veil of silence over the marvels accomplished on the other side of the Channel. Sometimes they merely claimed, without further detail, that their king alone possessed the healing power:

> For he healed scrofula
> Solely by touching it,
> Without placing plasters on it;
> No other king could do this,[113]

as the poet-soldier Guillaume Guiart sang of Philip the Fair. But no writer —even the most zealous of them—went as far as to indulge in real polemics on this subject. But the more conciliatory spirits, like the doctor Bernard Gordon,[114] did not hesitate to recognize that both dynasties possessed the same miraculous healing power. This moderation is all the more striking in its contrast with the very different attitude—as we shall see—adopted in modern times by the patriots of both countries. In truth from the sixteenth century onwards, it was rather religious hatred than national passions that prevented the French or English, as the case might be, from recognizing the miraculous in the other royal line. Before the Reformation, there was nothing of this kind. Besides, there was too deep a faith in the miraculous during the Middle Ages for anyone to be too critical about one more evidence of the supernatural. The attitude of the French towards the English rite and vice versa was not unlike that of those devout pagans who, whilst faithful to their own city's god, and persuaded of his superior powers and benevolence, did not feel bound to deny all existence to the gods of the neighbouring nations:

I have my God whom I serve, and you have yours.
They are both powerful Gods.

Outside the two great western kingdoms, public opinion seems likewise to have been quite ready to admit the touch for scrofula. Its efficacy was never openly questioned except by the very few writers who, as it happened, were not complying with national prejudice. Such were the Portuguese bishop Alvarez Pelayo and Pope Pius II, who voiced ecclesiastical orthodoxy or hatred of Gallicanism; or the Flemish doctor Jan Yperman, whose opposition to the fleur-de-lis was based upon what we might almost call internal policy. Above all, as we are already aware, the Capetians and perhaps also the Plantagenets had been visited ever since the beginning of the fourteenth century by crowds of sick people from foreign countries; and this is the most striking proof that their renown had spread beyond the bounds of national frontiers.

Thus more or less everywhere people could hardly refuse to recognize the wonder-working powers of the French and English kings. Yet in various countries, attempts were sometimes made to raise up competition. By whom?—or, to put the problem more generally, were there in Europe (apart from France and England) physician-princes exercising their art either in imitation of French or English practice, or by virtue of an independent tradition—for this is a possibility that cannot be ruled out *a priori*? This is what we must now examine.

The right to answer this question with certainty could only belong to a historian who had undertaken the almost impossible task of sifting all existing documents on the subject, whatever their source. My own research has necessarily been limited. Fortunately, I have received invaluable help from the labours of experts in the *ancien régime*, particularly French and Spanish scholars. Although the conclusions I am about to put forward must be provisional, I think they can be considered distinctly probable. I shall begin by examining the problem as a whole, while holding myself free to step now and again outside the chronological framework of this chapter. Some of the testimony we shall be considering is indeed later than the Middle Ages. But there could have been no serious successful attempt in the direction indicated later than the beginning of the sixteenth century; and the failures—for as far as I have been able to ascertain, all the attempts were unsuccessful—are a kind of counter-proof, leading to important conclusions about the reasons for the rise and expansion of the healing rites in the Capetian kingdom and in England during the mediaeval period.

Let us first take a quick look at some of the unfounded assertions about the different European States. At the beginning of the seventeenth century, two French polemical writers, Jérôme Bignon and Arroy, intent upon reserving for the Bourbons a kind of privileged position in miraculous healing, pointed out the contrast between France and Denmark. In France, the king effected the cure through simple laying on of hands; in Denmark, the kings were said to heal falling sickness, that is to say, epilepsy, but only thanks to a 'secret remedy'.[115] No doubt this was an attempt to answer some argument put forward by a publicist from the opposite camp, whom I have not been able to identify. But there would not appear to be any historical justification for such a statement. From the sixteenth century onwards, some writers devoted to the Hapsburgs credited the kings of Hungary (a title inherited, as we know, by the heads of the House of Austria) with the power to cure icterus, or jaundice. The choice of this illness can be explained by reference to ancient classical scientific terms. For reasons unknown, it often gave jaundice the name of *morbus regius*, the royal disease. It would seem, however, that the miraculous talent attributed to the kings of Hungary was nothing more than a learned fable; at least, there is no evidence that they ever put it into action. We cannot do better than repeat the wise words written by an anonymous author in 1736, in the *Bibliothèque raisonée des ouvrages des savants de l'Europe*: 'They were very lacking in charity if they really possessed this gift, but did not use it'.[116]

There was certainly a widespread belief in Germany in the curative powers of kings or princes. Luther's *Table-talk* contains an interesting echo of this idea:

There is something miraculous in seeing certain remedies—and I know what I am talking about—effective when applied through the hands of great princes or lords, though they have no effect when given by a doctor. I have heard that the two Electors of Saxony, Duke Frederick and Duke John, possess an eye-water which works when administered by them in person, whether the trouble is caused by heat or by cold. But no doctor would dare to give it. It is the same in theology, where it is a question of spiritual counsel. One particular preacher has more grace in instruction or consolation of men's consciences than another one.[117]

But these elusive notions do not ever seem to have taken solid shape. Certain lords, like the Electors of Saxony, did certainly possess some family remedies. The library at Gotha still possesses three manuscript volumes— unpublished, as far as I can ascertain—in which the Elector John (the man Luther mentions) had set down certain medical or pharmaceutical information. Perhaps one could still read in its pages the recipe for the eye-water, with its wonderfully efficacious properties.[118] When administered by the princes themselves, it was thought to be a particularly powerful remedy. But laying on of hands was not enough. Above all, there was nowhere any systematic development of a regular and permanent ritual.

Certain authors, however, have claimed that the Hapsburgs possessed a true wonder-working power. The oldest of these, and no doubt the original source for all the others, was a Swabian monk, Felix Fabri, who composed towards the end of the fifteenth century a *Description of Germany, Swabia and the town of Ulm*, where we read as follows:

> The chronicles of the Counts of Hapsburg tell us that these noblemen have freely received such grace that any scrofulous or gouty person who receives his drink from the hands of one of them soon finds his throat once more perfectly healthy and sound. This was often witnessed in Albrechstal in Upper Alsace, where there are people congenitally suffering from scrofula; for they came and were healed as I have just said, in the days when the valley belonged to the Counts of Hapsburg or the Dukes of Austria. Moreover, it is a notorious and often demonstrated fact that any stammerer who is embraced by these princes, even without asking, soon finds he can speak quite easily, at least in so far as his years permit.[119]

Splendid tales, to be sure, and worthy of such a great traveller as Felix Fabri. But it is difficult to take them seriously. In particular, the reference to the Albrechtstal is suspicious; for this territory, known nowadays as the Val de Villé, which came to Rudolf of Hapsburg as his wife's dowry in about 1254, went out of the hands of the Austrian House in 1314, and never came back to them.[120] We should have more confidence in the monk of Ulm if he had placed the most striking of the Hapsburg cures anywhere else but in a country where they had ceased to exercise power more than a century and a half before his time. To be sure, he would never have thought of telling these tales unless everyone around him had been accustomed to consider kings as beings endowed with all kinds of miraculous virtues. He was embroidering a popular theme, but the work seems to be his own invention. At least, there is no other testimony in confirmation of his, for all that subsequent historians do is to repeat it, with even less precision.[121] If the Hapsburgs had practised a healing rite with any regularity, like their rivals in France and England, it is highly unlikely that we should be reduced to this single piece of information about it coming from the hearsay stories of an obscure Swabian chronicler, and to the vague affirmations of a few publicists in the pay of Austria or Spain.

Alvarez Pelayo we have met already. It will be recalled that on one occasion he called the French and English claims so many 'lies and dreams'. He was not always as hard on the wonder-working powers of royalty. His protectors' interests, and no doubt also his own patriotism, were at least once strong enough to silence his orthodoxy. Born perhaps in the Kingdom of Castile, and certainly brought up at the Castilian court, he wrote not long after 1340 on behalf of this country's sovereign, Alphonso XI, a work entitled *Speculum regum*. Its purpose was to prove that although the temporal power was the outcome of human sin, it nevertheless subsequently received divine sanction. Here is one of his proofs:

It is said that the kings of France and of England possess a [healing] power; likewise the most pious kings of Spain, from whom you are descended, possess a power which acts on the demoniacs and certain sick persons suffering from divers ills. When a small child, I myself saw your grandfather king Sancho [Sancho II, 1284–95], who brought me up, place his foot upon the throat of a demoniac who proceeded to heap insults upon him; and then, by reading words taken from a little book, drive out the demon from this woman, and leave her perfectly healed.[122]

As far as I know, this is the oldest testimony we have to the exorcizing gifts claimed by the House of Castile. It will be noticed that, unlike Felix Fabri, Alvarez relates a precise fact which he may well have actually witnessed. The same tradition recurs in various authors of the seventeenth century,[123] and we have no right to cast doubts upon it. In all probability, the people of Castile did really credit their kings with the power of healing the nervous diseases which in those days were commonly thought to be diabolical in origin. Besides, there is no type of affection more amenable to miraculous healing, which was a primitive form of psychotherapy. There were probably a certain number of isolated cures, like the one reported of Don Sancho by Alvarez; but there, too, the belief in them does not seem to have ever given rise to a regular rite, nor does it appear to have possessed much lasting vitality. By the seventeenth century it had become no more than a memory, exploited by the apologists of the dynasty, but lacking any popular support, and encountering avowed sceptics, even in Spain itself. A doctor of this nation, Don Sebastian de Soto, denied the miraculous cures in a work with the rather strange title *Of the illnesses which make it lawful for nuns to break their strict enclosure*. Another doctor, Don Gutier-rez, who was more faithful to the monarchical tradition, answered him as follows:

His [Don Sebastian's] arguments are valueless. He concludes from the absence of any acts of healing that the power does not exist; but that is as though he were to say that God, because he has not produced and will not produce every possible creature, is incapable of producing them. In the same way, our kings possess this power, but out of humility they do not exercise it . . .[124]

Thus both the adversaries and the defenders of this power over demons ascribed to the kings of Castile were at this time agreed on one point at any rate, namely that this power had never been put to the test. In other words, no one any longer believed in it.

Thus in the seventeenth century the Spanish kings, heirs of the kings of Castile, were reckoned to have at least an honorary title to heal the possessed. And sometimes their partisans considered them also able, like the kings of France, to heal the scrofulous; and this, as the learned explained, because they were the successors of that other great Iberian dynasty, the House of Aragon. In fact, we know of at least one prince of Aragon at the end of the Middle Ages, Don Carlos de Viana, to whom—among other miraculous cures—the healing of scrofula was attributed. Popular super- stition, cleverly exploited by a political party, attributed this power to him after his death and perhaps even—though this is less certain—during his lifetime. When on 23 September 1461 this Infante of Aragon and Navarre ended his adventurous and tragic career, his faithful supporters, who had tried during his lifetime to make him the standard-bearer of Catalan independence, attempted to make him into a saint, since they had now only his memory to work upon. Miracles were attributed to his dead body; and Louis XI, in a letter of condolence addressed to the deputies of Cata- lonia as early as 13 October, slipped in a deliberate allusion to these timely miracles. In particular, a woman suffering from scrofula was healed at the saint's tomb, as a contemporary enquiry relates: 'A woman who had not had the opportunity to appear before the prince during his lifetime said: "I wasn't able to see him and be healed by him while he was alive, but I am sure that he will hear my prayers after he is dead".' It is difficult to know how much importance to attach to these words. We should need more reliable testimonies to come to a firm conclusion that Don Carlos, even while still alive, had played the part of a doctor. But there can be no doubt that his mortal remains were really considered to possess the bene- ficent gift of relieving illness, and especially the scrofula. Although his cult never received the Church's official sanction, it was very flourishing right up to the sixteenth and seventeenth centuries. His principal sanctuary was the Abbey of Poblet, near Barcelona, where the miraculous body had its resting-place. Among the relics, a hand was the object of peculiar veneration; and its touch was said to heal the sufferers from scrofula.[125]

The case of Don Carlos is a curious one. He can be regarded as an example of a tendency which we shall find increasingly familiar as our research proceeds. In every country collective opinion was inclined to represent persons of noble blood and destined for the crown as essentially wonder-workers, especially when their lives rose above the ordinary. There was stronger reason still for this attitude where notorious but undeserved misfortunes gave them something of a martyr's crown, as in the case of the unfortunate Prince of Viana. Moreover, it is probable that in countries bordering on France, and—like Catalonia—permeated by French in- fluences, the royal miracles quite naturally took on in popular imagination the classical form of the Capetian example. This infectious imitation was all the easier through Don Carlos' descent on his mother's side from the Capetian dynasty of Navarre. But there is no trace of any regular rite of touching ever having developed at the Aragonese court.

As for the pretensions of the polemical writers in the seventeenth century who had leanings towards Spain,[126] and their claims for the gift of relieving scrofula inherent in their royal masters, they can only be viewed as a rather empty attempt to enhance the Spanish Hapsburgs' prestige at the expense of the French monarchy. There are plenty of reliable testimonies that at this time, and even a century earlier, many Spaniards travelled to France especially to receive the royal touch, and others pressed round Francis I for the same purpose when he had been taken prisoner after Pavia and landed on the coast of Aragon.[127] This zeal can only be explained by the assumption that no similar ceremony ever took place in Madrid or at the Escorial.

So we come finally to Italy, where in the last decades of the thirteenth century, a sovereign attempted to pose as a healer of scrofula—or at least his supporters tried to represent him as such. This was Charles of Anjou, whom we have already come across, and he belonged to the Capetian line.[128] The French blood in his veins was no doubt his strongest title to the role of healer. Our only information about this attempt comes from the very brief mention already referred to by Tolomeo of Lucca. There is no evidence that the Angevin kings of Naples ever seriously persevered in it.

Thus the French and English kings may very well, in the course of time, have evoked the jealousy of certain publicists and induced them to claim a similar power for their own sovereigns; but they never had any serious imitators. Even where a belief like that which flourished on either side of the Channel did seem to have an independent life for a certain period—as in Castile—it lacked the necessary vigour to give birth to a regular and deep-rooted institution. Why was it that France and England retained the monopoly of royal healings?

This is an infinitely delicate and indeed almost insoluble problem. The historian already has his work cut out to explain the genesis of positive phenomena; what must his difficulties be when it comes to producing the reasons for something non-existent! In such cases, he must usually be content with doing no more than putting forward probabilities. The following considerations seem to me the least unsatisfactory in accounting for the lack of healing power displayed by most of the European dynasties.

When we were studying the origins of the royal touch, we seemed to descry both deep-down causes and circumstantial causes. The deep-down cause was the belief in the supernatural character of royalty. The circumstantial causes, as far as France was concerned, seemed to lie in the politics of the Capetian dynasty in its early years; in England, in the ambition and ability of King Henry I. The belief itself was common to the whole of Western Europe. What was lacking in countries other than France or England was merely the particular circumstances. In these two kingdoms, there must have been conditions that allowed a hitherto rather vague idea to crystallize in the eleventh and twelfth centuries into a precise and stable institution. In Germany, it may be conjectured that the Saxon and

Swabian dynasties enjoyed too great a measure of glory from the imperial crown to dream of playing the part of doctors. In the other countries, no doubt, the sovereigns lacked the necessary astuteness to conceive such a design, or the necessary boldness, perseverance or personal prestige to carry it through. An element of chance, or, if you will, individual genius, must have contributed to the rise of the French or English rites. And it would seem that elsewhere, too, chance—understood in the same sense— was responsible for the absence of any similar manifestations.

About the end of the thirteenth century, when the fame of the cures performed by the Capetians and Plantagenets had spread far and wide throughout the Catholic world, one may well believe that more than one prince felt envious of them. But it was probably too late to attempt to imitate them with much likelihood of success. The French and English rites had the support of tradition, the strongest force of those days. No one would seriously have ventured to deny a miracle vouched for down the generations. To create a new miracle, however, which the teaching of the Church, with its dislike on principle of royal miraculous healing, would certainly have attacked, was a dangerous undertaking. Perhaps it was never attempted; or if an attempt was made by certain rash individuals—which is something outside our knowledge—it was almost bound to fail. France and England did not lose the privilege assured to them by long custom and habit.

The concept of sacred and miraculous royalty helped by fortuitous circumstances had given birth to the touch for scrofula. Being firmly anchored in the popular mind and soul, it was able to survive all storms and all attacks. Moreover it is probable that royalty in turn derived new strength from the touching. To begin with, people had said, with Peter of Blois: 'Kings are holy persons; let us go to them, for they have doubtless received, along with countless other graces, the power of healing'. Then they came to say, with the author of *Quaestio in utramque partem*, at the time of Philip the Fair: 'My king can heal; so he is not a mere man like others.' But it is not enough to have demonstrated the vitality and even the expansion of these primitive practices during the closing centuries of the Middle Ages. In England at any rate during this period a second healing rite made its appearance, entirely different from the old one—the blessing of medicinal rings, held to be a sovereign cure for epilepsy. This will be a convenient place to examine the flowering of the old beliefs in a new form.

II

The second miracle of English royalty: cramp rings

1 *The rite in the fourteenth century*

Every year on Good Friday in the Middle Ages the kings of England, like all other good Christians, used to adore the cross. In the chapel of the castle where they happened to be staying at that time, it was the custom—at least in the fourteenth century—to set up a cross, the 'Cross of Gyneth'. This was the name given to a miraculous relic taken, it would seem, by Edward I from the Welsh. It was believed to contain a fragment of the very wood to which Christ had been nailed.[1] The king would place himself at a little distance, prostrate himself, and then—without getting up——slowly approach the symbol of the crucifixion. That was the posture prescribed for this act by all the liturgiologists: 'In this act of adoration', says Jean d'Avranches, 'the belly must touch the ground, for St Augustine, in his commentary on Psalm 43, tells us that genuflexion is not a complete humiliation; but for the man who humiliates himself by prostrating himself completely on the ground, there is nothing else in him that he can further humiliate.'[2] In an interesting miniature of a manuscript in the Bibliothèque Nationale containing the life of St-Louis by Guillaume de St-Pathus,[3] the pious king is shown most conscientiously carrying out this rite. Quite early on the English texts gave this the characteristic name of 'creeping to the cross'.[4] Up till that point, then, there was nothing to distinguish the practice of the English court from the customs universally observed by the Catholic Church.

But under the Plantagenets—certainly not later than Edward II's time —the Good Friday ceremonial acquired as far as the king was concerned an additional complication, by the addition of a strange practice not belonging to the current ritual. What used to take place on that day in the royal chapel in the time of Edward II and his successors, up to and including the reign of Henry V, is this:

Once he had finished his prostrations, the English king would go up to the altar and place upon it an offering consisting of a certain quantity of gold and silver in good new coin, florins, nobles, or sterlings. Then he would take up these coins again—'redeem' them, as it was called—and replace them by an equivalent sum in any ordinary coin. Out of this precious metal, offered one moment and redeemed the next, he would have a number of rings made. It must be understood that these rings, the final result of rather complicated operations, were no ordinary rings. They were considered capable of curing those who wore them of certain diseases. The oldest documents do not precisely specify what diseases. A prescription of Edward II's time calls them '*anulx a doner pour medicine as divers gentz*'; the Royal Household accounts merely call them *anuli medicinales*. But in the fifteenth century, there are some more explicit textual references, making it clear that these talismans were reckoned to relieve muscular pains or spasms, and more especially epilepsy: hence the name cramp rings, given to them from this time onwards, and still in common use by English historians today. As we shall see in a moment, the comparative study of popular medicine tends to show that from the outset these rings were considered as specially effective in this kind of miraculous cure.[5]

Such was this strange rite, more or less complementary to the royal touch, but different in its being confined to English royalty: there was nothing of the kind in France. What explanation can we give of its origins?

2 *Legendary explanations*

When faith in the miraculous powers of the cramp rings had reached its peak, it was only natural to look for the support of legendary patrons. The lofty figure of Joseph of Arimathea dominates the poetical history of English Christianity. He was a disciple of Christ, to whom the honour had fallen—according to the Gospel—of burying the body taken down from the cross. Pious authors affirmed him to have been the first to preach the Gospel to the island of Britain, a flattering belief for a Church in search of quasi-apostolic origins; and from the beginning of the Middle Ages, the legends of the Round Table had made it familiar to a very wide public. This wonder-worker was also supposed to have brought to England, among several deep secrets culled from the books of Solomon, the art of healing epileptics by means of rings. That at least is the tradition—probably of English origin—re-echoed by Jacques Valdes, the Spanish historian who set it down in the year 1602.[6] The reader will no doubt consider it unnecessary to discuss the legend here.

Considerably earlier, at any rate by the early years of the sixteenth century, another interpretation had seen the light. Its aim was to place the Good Friday ceremonial under the patronage of Edward the Confessor. Strangely enough, this theory still finds a kind of support among English historians. Not that anyone today seriously maintains that Edward really possessed a healing ring; but it is readily believed that from the very beginning of the rite, wherever that may be placed, the English kings thought that they were in some sort imitating the example of their pious predecessor.

A ring does indeed play the principal part in a particularly famous episode in the legends of Edward the Confessor. Here is a brief summary of the story told for the first time in the *Life* written by St-Ailred of Rievaulx in 1163.[7] Edward was one day approached by a beggar, and wanted to give him alms. But his purse happened to be empty, so he gave him his ring instead. Now, the rags of this poor man concealed no less a person than St John the Evangelist. Some time later—seven years, according to some accounts—two English pilgrims travelling in Palestine met a handsome old man. Once again, it was St John. He gave them back the ring, asking them to return it to their master and to tell him at the same time that it would not be long before he was called to join the company of the elect. This poetic little story, further embroidered by attractive additions on the part of certain hagiographers well versed in the secrets of the next world,[8] became extremely popular. Sculptors, miniaturists, painters, glass-makers, ornamentalists of all kinds vied with each other in reproducing it, on the continent as well as in England.[9] Henry III, who was particularly devoted to the last of the Anglo-Saxon kings, gave his eldest son the name of Edward, which had not so far figured among the list of names given by the Norman and Angevin dynasties. He also had this scene of the meeting between these two saints painted on the walls of the Chapel of St John in the Tower of London. Then Edward II, on his consecration day, presented two gold statuettes to Westminster Abbey, one depicting the prince offering his ring, and the other the beggar in disguise receiving it.[10] Westminster was indeed the fitting place for such a gift. Not only did it contain the much-venerated shrine of St Edward, but the monks still showed the faithful a ring taken from the holy body when it had been transferred to a new reliquary in 1163.[11] This was commonly held to be the self-same ring once accepted by the Evangelist and then given back by him to the king. 'If anyone would have proof that these things are so', said the popular preacher John Mirk about the year 1400, after having told his audience the famous story, 'let him go to Westminster, where he will see the ring which was for the space of seven years in Paradise'.[12] But the fact is that among the fairly numerous texts mentioning this precious relic, none down to relatively recent times indicates that any particular healing power was ascribed to it. Moreover, there is absolutely nothing in the royal ceremonial for Good Friday referring to St Edward or St John. In order to find some mention of the Confessor in connection with the cramp rings, we have to come down to the time of the Italian humanist Polydore Virgil. He was in the service of Henry VII and Henry VIII, and wrote at their request a *History of England* first published in 1534. The obvious intention of their official historiographer was to find an authoritative prototype for the miraculous rings distributed by his masters. That was why he was pleased to consider the rings preserved in the 'temple' of Westminster as also endowed with sovereign power against epilepsy. His book enjoyed great success, and was largely responsible for spreading what henceforward became the common opinion, that the healing of epilepsy by means of the cramp rings, like the touch for scrofula, had been instituted by Edward the Confessor.[13] But the idea had certainly not been invented by this Italian. It would seem that he must have picked it up ready-made in his protectors' entourage. After all, what could have been more natural than to credit the great saint of this dynasty with having fathered both of these dynastic miracles? The famous ring, which had been 'in Paradise', provided an easy link between the stories of the saint and the rite itself; and by virtue of a sort of retrospective action, he was credited rather late in the day with having possessed the medical power necessary to establish his claim to be the ancestor of the cramp rings. It would probably have become an object of pilgrimage for the sick if the Reformation coming so soon after the appearance of a belief which was so favourable to the interests of Westminster Abbey had not put an end to the cult of relics in England. But the true origins of the Good Friday rite have no connection either with Edward the Confessor or with the monarchical legend in general. We must search for its secret in the comparative history of superstitious practices in general.

3 *The magical origins of the cramp ring rite*

From the earliest times, rings have been among the favourite instruments of magic, and more especially the magic of medicine.[14] This was so in the Middle Ages, as in previous centuries. There was a suspicion of sorcery attaching to the more innocent of these practices. The rings worn by Joan of Arc were closely scrutinized by her judges; and the poor girl had to protest—though probably without convincing the court—that she had never used them for anybody's healing.[15] These almost universal talismans were used to relieve certain kinds of disease, preferably muscular cramps and epilepsy. The latter, with its violent fits, was calculated to evoke a natural superstitious terror, and was ordinarily considered to have a diabolical origin.[16] It was therefore more amenable than any other disease to supernatural means of healing. Of course for these purposes people did not simply use any kind of metal circles, but special rings, on which exceptional powers had been conferred by particular religious or magical rites of consecration. The learned name for them was *anuli vertuosi*. A German prescription of the fifteenth century to cure gout gives substantially the following instructions: go out and beg in the name of Our Lord's sacrifice and his Sacred Blood, until you have collected thirty-two deniers. Then take sixteen of them and use them for the making of a ring; with the other sixteen, you will pay the smith. You must then wear the ring continuously and recite five Our Fathers and five Hail Marys every day in memory of Our Lord's death and His Sacred Blood.[17] Elsewhere, the prescriptions have a distinctly macabre flavour: the advice is to use metal taken from old coffins, or a nail on which a man has hanged himself.[18] In the county of Berkshire, about the year 1800, experienced persons were recommending a recipe that looks more innocuous, but also more complicated. In order to make a ring for a sovereign remedy against cramp, it was necessary, they said, to collect five sixpenny pieces, each from a different bachelor; and the donors must not know the object for which they are making this gift. Then the money so collected must be taken by another bachelor to a blacksmith who must himself be a bachelor . . .[19] Examples of this kind could easily be multiplied. The rings consecrated by royalty were only a particular case of a very general class of remedy.

Let us take a closer look now at the royal rite, and first at its date. This was most rigorously fixed by custom. The king only placed the gold and silver pieces on the altar once a year, on Good Friday, after the adoration of the cross, that is to say, on a day of solemn commemoration of our Redeemer's supreme sacrifice. Was it mere chance that this was the chosen day? Far from it. The memory of the Passion recurs as a kind of *leitmotiv* in the recipes for curing muscular pains or epilepsy, and particularly in the making of medicinal rings. At the beginning of the fifteenth century, St Bernardino of Siena, preaching against popular superstitions in Italy, criticized those 'who to cure the cramp wear rings made while the Passion of Christ is being read . . .'[20] And even in England about the same time a medical treatise contained the following advice: 'To cure the cramp, go on Good Friday into five parish churches, and in each of them take the first penny that is given as an offering at the Adoration of the Cross. Then gather them all together, go up to the cross, and there say five Our Fathers in honour of the five wounds and carry them with you for five days, each day saying the same prayer in the same manner. After this, have a ring made out of these coins, without any other alloy; write on the inside *Gaspar, Balthazar, Attrapa*, and on the outside *Ihc. Nazarenus*; then go and fetch it from the goldsmith's on a Friday, and say five Our Fathers as before; and then wear it continuously.'[21]

It would take a long time to make a detailed analysis of this prescription, which is a veritable potpourri of magical notions, with a diversity of origins. The names of the Magi—frequently invoked against epilepsy—figure alongside the divine name; or rather, two of the Magi only, for the third has been replaced by a mysterious word, *Attrapa*, reminiscent of the *Abrazas* used by the adepts of hermetical science. But the Passion remains constantly in the forefront. The figure five was often used: we have already come across it in the German prescription. It stands for the five wounds of Our Saviour.[22] Above all, the desire to place oneself under the protection of the cross accounts for the dates fixed for the essential actions and the supplementary one—Good Friday, and a subsequent Friday. We find the same thing in France. A *curé* in La Beauce, Jean-Baptiste Thiers, writing in 1679, has preserved the memory of a practice used in his day for curing epileptics. We shall describe it in detail a little later on. For the moment, we will simply note the day and time chosen for carrying out these 'ceremonies', as Thiers calls them,—namely, Good Friday, at the very moment of the Adoration of the Cross.[23] And surely ideas of the same nature must have been responsible for King Charles V wearing on Fridays, and Fridays only, a special ring engraved with two crosses in black, and a cameo representing the scene of Calvary.[24] There can be no doubt about it: magical medicine made a somewhat sacrilegious comparison between the sufferings due to 'cramp' and the agony of Christ upon the cross. It was therefore considered that religious anniversaries and prayers recalling the tortures of Christ crucified were particularly suitable for conveying to the rings the power to heal pains in the muscles.[25] First and foremost, the royal cramp rings owed their power to the particular day set apart for the consecration of the metal of which they were made, and to the miraculous influence emanating from the cross adored by the king in a 'creeping' posture before going up to the altar.

Yet this was not the real essence of the rite. The centre of the action was a sort of juridical procedure, the offering of the gold and silver coins and their redemption by means of an equivalent sum. Nor was this feature itself really original. For it was then, and still is in our time, a widespread opinion among the superstitious that money received as a gift by churches was specially suitable for making healing rings. We have already noted an example of this idea above, in a treatise composed in England in the fourteenth century. And it is said that even today [1924] in the English countryside peasants will seek out pence and shillings given in the collection at Holy Communion in order to use them for making rings against epilepsy and rheumatism.[26] In such cases, indeed, the element of redemption is not present. But it comes in elsewhere, along with the offering, just as it does in the royal Good Friday ceremony.

Here to begin with is an instance of magic from France, vouched for in the seventeenth century, in the words of Jean-Baptiste Thiers: 'Those who say they belong to the family of St Martin claim to be able to heal the falling-sickness'—that is, epilepsy—'by observing the following ceremonies: On a Good Friday, one of these doctors takes a patient, brings him along to the Adoration of the Cross, kisses it in the presence of the priests and other ecclesiastics, and throws a coin into the collection-bowl. The patient kisses the cross after him, takes back the coin and replaces it by two others. Then he returns home, pierces a hole through the coin and wears it round his neck.'[27]

Let us now look at the German-speaking countries. A manuscript of the fifteenth century, which used to be kept in the monks' library at St-Gall, contains the following prescription against epilepsy. The action must take place on Christmas Eve, when—as everyone knows—three Masses are celebrated one after the other. At the beginning of the first Mass, the patient makes an offering of three silver pieces—the figure three being in honour of the Holy Trinity. The priest takes them, and places them beside, or even under, the corporal, so that the canonical signs of the cross he makes will be just above them. At the end of the first Mass, our patient redeems his three coins with six. Then the second Mass begins, and the three coins are offered once more. At its conclusion, they are once again redeemed, this time by twelve. The same ceremony takes place at the third Mass, the final redemption-price being twenty-four coins. All that remains to be done is to make from the metal thus consecrated by a threefold gift a ring which will guarantee the epileptic against any recurrence of his illness, provided he wears it constantly on his finger.[28]

So we have looked at a French prescription, one from St-Gall, and the royal rite as practised in England. A comparison between the three shows resemblances, but differences as well. In France, the coin—elsewhere transformed into a ring—is worn just as it is. At St-Gall, the chosen day is Christmas, and no longer Good Friday. Again, the redemption appears, if we may so put it, to be raised to the power of three. In France, there is only one redemption, but the price is double the first offering; at the English court, there is one redemption only, equal in value to the original . . . It is worth pointing out these divergences, because they clearly prove that the three practices were not simply copied from one another. Yet they are after all no more than subsidiary details. There is not the slightest doubt that we are dealing with three applications of the same fundamental idea, differing only from one time to another, or one place to another. The fundamental idea behind them all is clear enough. The aim is naturally to sanctify the metals of which the healing talisman is to be made. To that end, it would have been possible to be satisfied with simply placing them upon the altar; but this commonplace procedure did not appear adequate, and something better was desired. So the idea was conceived of giving them to the altar. For a brief space, however short it might be, they were the Church's property. But we can go even further, and say that when the ceremony took place on Good Friday, they became the property of the cross of adoration that stood above the collection-plate. But the handing over could only be figurative, since it was necessary to recover the material that had thus become suitable for the beneficent purposes intended. Yet in order to make the offering serious, and so efficacious, the gift could only be redeemed by a payment, just as when something is bought from its legitimate owner. Thus the gold or silver, having been for a short while truly and juridically the property of the Church or the Cross, would share to the full in the miraculous power of things sacred.

It will now be realized that in the conservation of medicinal rings, the kings only played a minor part. This is true at least in so far as the ceremony followed the lines I have just traced out. The actions accomplished by them, the offering and the redemption, effected the consecration; but it was not through the touch of the royal hands that the precious metals acquired their supernatural power. This came about through their brief transfer to the property of the altar, in the course of a solemn ceremony considered peculiarly appropriate for relieving muscular pains. In short, the ceremony that so often took place on the anniversary of the Passion in the Plantagenet castle was fundamentally no more than a magical prescription, lacking in originality and analogous to other prescriptions commonly practised on the Continent by people who had nothing princely about them. Nevertheless this action, although purely popular in other places, took on a genuinely royal character in England. How did this come about? This is the whole problem of the history of cramp rings. We must now come face to face with it. We shall see, as we go along, that the fourteenth-century ritual, analysed at the beginning of this chapter, represents only one stage in a long evolution.

4   *How the royal miracle was victorious over the magical prescription*

Who was the first king to place upon the altar the silver and gold that were to be forged into medicinal rings? This is something we shall doubtless never know. But it may be conjectured that whoever this prince was, he was on this occasion simply imitating a widespread custom, with no thought of monopolizing it. The humblest faithful Christians, particularly in England, always thought they possessed the power to make from the coins offered in church talismans of well-tried virtue. It was natural enough for it to occur to them, as well as to the French sorcerers or the remedy-seekers of St-Gall, that they could offer the coins themselves and then redeem them. True, we do not possess any text indicating that in England this simulated offering ever took place anywhere than in the royal chapel; but we have such scanty information about the popular customs of the old days that there is nothing surprising about this silence.

Yet kings were not like other men; they were held to be sacred persons, or rather—at least in England and in France—they ranked as wonder-workers. It would indeed have been strange if before long people had not contrived to credit them with some active part in adding medicinal virtue to this healing rite. Because they had long been regarded as healers of scrofula, people came to imagine that the marvellous force emanating from them also played a part in the transmission of supernatural power to the rings. It was not forgotten, to be sure, for many a year to come, that the real source of this power lay in certain gestures calculated to transfer the metal to the category of the sacred; but these gestures were thought to be specially efficacious when carried out by the same mighty hand that could by its touch restore health to the scrofulous. Public opinion gradually came to reserve this privilege to kings as born to combat disease.

To begin with, kings probably did not consecrate these rings at all regularly. The day came, however, when they began to consider it, along with the touch for scrofula, as one of the normal functions of their royal state, and made a point of practising it more or less regularly on each Good Friday. This is the state of affairs we first get a glimpse of in regulations governing the administration of the Royal Household promulgated by Edward II in York in the course of June 1323.[29] This is our oldest documentary reference to the cramp rings. Thanks to it, the royal rite, which up to this point has only been a matter of conjecture, now steps out into the full light of day. From then onwards, up to the death of Mary Tudor, no sovereign seems to have failed to lay the florins, nobles or sterlings at the foot of the cross on the prescribed days. For two reigns only the evidence is lacking—those of Edward V and Richard III; but the former was so short that it did not even include one Holy Week, and is thus only an apparent exception; and as for the latter, which was just long enough to include two of the propitious seasons for these solemnities, our ignorance about it can probably be explained by sheer chance. Usually, the Royal Household accounts, drawn up at the end of the ceremonies, give us our information about the Good Friday offerings; but those from Richard III's reign seem to have been lost or destroyed.[30] From Edward II to Mary Tudor, as I shall try to show in a moment, certain details of the ceremony varied; but it did not undergo any notable interruption.

To start with, then, we may suppose this to have been no more than an occasional practice. But from 1323 at the latest it became incorporated in the unvarying ceremonial of the Royal Household. This meant a big step towards the final annexation of the ancient magical prescriptions by wonder-working royalty. Are there any grounds for believing that Edward II had something to do with this transformation? I am inclined to think so. Not, of course, that we can base any certain conclusions on the silence of our sources before the Household Ordinance of York. Nevertheless, it is striking. I have broken down a fair number of the Household accounts for Edward I's reign, and I have been able to see three for Edward II's reign, all before 1323; but none of them mentions the consecration of the rings, which the documents of the same kind from Edward III to Mary Tudor so faithfully record in the section dealing with alms.[31] Yet one cannot be sure *a priori* that some simple method of entry—for instance, lumping together all the offerings under a total figure—may not be responsible for hiding from our eyes the thing we are looking for. The case of the royal touch for scrofula, which disappeared from the accounts at a time when we can be sure that it was still being practised, would be reason enough to remind us that negative proofs can in themselves carry very little weight. On the other hand, they may take on an unexpected value when confirmed by other historical probabilities. All we know about the sovereign who issued the Household Ordinance of York in 1323—about his mentality, his misfortunes, his efforts to buttress his tottering authority—gives a certain plausibility to the idea of ascribing some part to him in the adoption by the English monarchy of a new healing rite.

From the very beginning of his reign, Edward II was decidedly unpopular. He could not fail to be aware of the dangers surrounding him—or at least his entourage must have taken note of them on his behalf. Surely he may well have had the idea—directly or indirectly, it does not much matter—of remedying this disfavour that attached to him individually by reinforcing the sacred character of his person, derived from his royal office, which was his strongest title to respect on the part of the masses. And sure enough, this idea did occur to him. Later on, we shall be studying the cycle of legends attaching to the dynasties of the West; and we shall then see how in 1318 Edward II attempted to give new splendour to his line's prestige, and his own in particular, by having himself anointed in imitation of the Capetians with a holy oil said to have been brought down from heaven. The attempt failed; but it throws a flood of light upon the policy of this prince in search of a borrowed lustre for his name.[32] Surely he would not have neglected the possibilities of miraculous healing. No doubt he was already touching for scrofula; but as we know, because of his unpopularity his success had been mediocre, and was steadily diminishing. It is natural enough to conjecture that he sought to avenge himself by adding a new attribute to his wonder-working crown. To be sure, he would not have invented the rite of the cramp rings: he had no need to do so. Tradition, perhaps already of a long-standing nature, offered it him ready-made as a gift from the national folklore. We may readily believe, as I suggested above, that even before Edward II's accession, some of his predecessors had practised this double gesture of consecration after the Adoration of the Cross. But it was to him apparently that the honour fell of converting this hitherto ill-defined ceremony into one of the institutions of the monarchy. The miraculous healing of scrofula would probably never have reached the magnificent proportions it possessed without the anxieties arising from the slender claims to the throne of a Robert the Pious or a Henry Beauclerc. And later on this same miracle owed much to the deliberate designs of a Henry IV in France and a Charles II in England. We may well believe that Edward II's misfortunes and anxieties had some connection with the fortunes of the cramp rings. But, of course, the actions we have suggested as likely for this king or his advisers could only be conceived or realized because of the belief in the supernatural character of kings. In England the almost daily spectacle of the touch for scrofula, which was born of this belief, had become its firmest and richest support; and it had penetrated to the very depths of the collective consciousness.

Moreover, the Europe of old was sincerely credulous, and it was thus easy for clever persons to exploit the general credulity. It was no doubt not uncommon for a magic procedure, which by its very nature seemed likely to remain open to everybody, to be taken over in the end and monopolized by hereditary healers. The very history of the rites we have just compared with the consecration of the cramp rings is a striking example of this kind of victory. It will be recalled that at St-Gall, the successive gift and redemption of the coins on the altar could be performed by any person; but in the days of Jean-Baptiste Thiers, things were not the same in France. The redemption was still performed by the patient himself, but the gift had to be made by a man belonging to 'the race of St-Martin'. That was the name given to a huge tribe of magicians who were said to derive their powers from a supposed relationship with the great wonder-worker of Tours. Throughout the world at that period there was more than one family of charlatans who boasted in the same way of a sacred origin. In Italy, there were those who claimed relationship with St Paul. By virtue of the incident recorded in the Acts of the Apostles, when the apostle to the gentiles was stung by a viper in Malta, and yet suffered no harm, they posed as healers of poisonous bites. In Spain, the *Saludadors*, who possessed so many fine secret remedies for illness, liked to claim relationship with St Catherine of Alexandria. More or less everywhere, and more especially in France, those who claimed relationship with St-Roch were said to be proof against all attacks of the plague, and sometimes able even to cure it. The followers of St-Hubert, who were particularly famous, were said to be able to protect their patients from hydrophobia or rabies simply by a touch.[33] We shall never know how the descendants of St-Martin managed to persuade the people that the offering of a silver coin on Good Friday was efficacious only if it was made by their own hand. But the fact remains that in France and in England this commonplace prescription became the perquisite of a special class. In France, it was appropriated by quacks; in England, by the royal line.

Yet it must not be imagined that its evolution in England had reached the final stage by 1323. Even in the palace chapel on Good Friday, the kings did not as yet possess a complete monopoly over the consecrating rite; for it would seem that the queens shared this privilege with them. We know on reliable authority that at Windsor on 30 March 1369 Philippa, the wife of Edward III, followed her husband in repeating the traditional gestures after him. She too placed upon the altar a certain sum of money—not gold, for the most precious of metal was no doubt reserved for the king—and then redeemed it for the making of medicinal rings.[34] True, this is the only case of the kind of which we have knowledge; but we are in general much less well informed about the queens' private expenditure than about their husbands'. In all probability, if their Household accounts had been better preserved, we should come across—at least for the four-teenth century—more than one mention like the one preserved by chance from the Household accounts of 1369. To be sure, Philippa was not a person of humble condition, for she wore a crown. But it should be emphasized that although she was a queen, she did not, like Mary Tudor, Elizabeth or Victoria, reign by hereditary right. As the daughter of a plain Count of Hainault, she owed her status purely to her union with a king. No queen of this kind ever touched for scrofula: for the healing of scrofula, only a genuinely royal hand, in the full sense of the word, would suffice. But there was more to it that this. For as we shall see presently, when about the middle of the fifteenth century the ceremony of the cramp rings had assumed a new character, and the king's role had become much more important than in the past, it was completely forgotten that once upon a time queens had been able fully to perform the ceremony with success. This point had not yet been reached under Edward III, for santifi-cation by means of the altar and the cross continued to be looked upon as the essential action; and why should not a woman of exalted birth and rank have been capable of performing it?

Moreover, at this time the cures effected by the cramp rings were not placed to the credit of the king's wonder-working powers. In this very reign of Edward III, Archbishop Bradwardine gave us as one of the most notable examples of miracles the miracle of royal healing, and discoursed upon it at great length; but he only took account of the touch for scrofula.[35] He did not make the slightest allusion to the cramp rings, which only began to be reckoned among the manifestations of royal supernatural power about a century later. But by that time, the rite had been transformed.

As far as I know, the first writer to give full acceptance to the consecra-tion of the rings as one of the divine graces imparted to the English mon-archy was the self-same Sir John Fortescue, whose name and work on the subject of scrofula we have already encountered. Among the treatises against the princes of York written by him during his Scottish exile, between April 1461 and July 1463, there is one entitled *A Defence of the Rights of the House of Lancaster*. In it, he is at pains to show that descent through the female line does not transmit the privileges of the royal blood. He says in effect that a woman—even a queen—does not receive unction upon the hands; and such was in fact the English rule for the spouses of kings. But it should be noted that subsequently it was not observed for princesses who succeeded to the throne by hereditary right—Mary Tudor, Elizabeth, Mary the daughter of James II, Anne and Victoria.[36] And so, continues our writer, a queen's hands do not possess the miraculous power possessed by those of a king; and no queen can heal the scrofulous simply by her touch. Then Fortescue adds: 'In the same way, gold and silver that have been devoutly touched and offered up by the anointed hands of the English kings on Good Friday, according to the yearly custom of the Kings of England, are able to heal spasms and epilepsy, just as the power of the rings made from this gold and silver and placed on the sufferers' fingers has been proved by frequent use in a great many parts of the world. This grace is not granted to queens, for they are not anointed on the hands.'[37] It is clear from these words that the times of Philippa of Hainault already lie well in the past. To Fortescue's mind, consecration on the altar, the giving and the redemption, no longer occupy more than a quite secondary place in the rite. The metal owes its remedial power to the 'sacred' hands that have handled it; or rather, in the final analysis, to the holy oil poured upon these august hands. For the oil had long been considered the agent which conferred on them the gift of healing for scrofula. All the rest had become absorbed by the royal miracle.

From this time onwards, moreover, the evolution of ideas had taken concrete shape in a considerable alteration of the ceremonial forms themselves. Usually, as we have seen, the rings were only made after the silver and gold coins offered on the altar in the course of the Good Friday ceremonies had been subsequently melted down. In the end, however, it was found more convenient to make them in advance and bring them all ready-made on the appointed day. Henceforward, it was the rings themselves, instead of the former coins, that were placed for a moment at the foot of the cross and then redeemed by means of a sum fixed once and for all at twenty-five shillings. By carefully scrutinizing the royal accounts we can ascertain that this change took place between 1413 and 1441, probably during the early years of Henry VI's reign.[38] This modified procedure continued in use under the Tudors. Under Henry VIII, as we learn from an account of court ceremonial, the highest-ranking lord present[39] had the privilege of presenting the plate containing the rings to the king before the offering. A little later, in the missal belonging to Mary Tudor, there is an interesting miniature immediately before the text of the liturgical office for the blessing of the rings. It depicts the queen kneeling before the altar; and on either side, resting on the top of the railings round the kind of rectangular enclosure where she is kneeling, there are two flat golden dishes, in which the artist has depicted in a formalized, though recognizable, fashion some small metal circles.[40]

The first Master of Ceremonies to make this change in the traditional customs, probably at the beginning of Henry VI's reign, certainly did so for purely practical reasons. His intention was to cut out what seemed to him a useless complication. But in simplifying the old rite, he profoundly altered it. For the juridical fiction which was at the heart of it only made sense if the material used for making the rings had really been offered in a manner no wise different from the normal offerings. It must not, so to speak, seem to have been made on purpose, so that the gold and silver could still rightly be considered to have really belonged for a brief while to the altar and the cross. What is the normal offering during a religious service? Coins: hence the use of florins, nobles and sterlings for the royal cramp rings, or—more modestly—deniers, or nowadays shillings, taken from the collection, whether genuine or fictitious, for so many other healing rings. To start by placing ready-made rings on the altar was to recognize it as only a simulated offering; and this very fact took away the essential meaning of the simulacrum. It is probable that by the beginning of the fifteenth century, the old practice of the simulated gift and redemption had almost lost its meaning. Fortescue and Henry VIII's ceremonial account simply say that the king 'offers' the rings—meaning, no doubt, that he places them momentarily upon the altar; once this has been done, the ceremony seems to them to be complete. It was of little importance that some coins should then be placed more or less in the same place as the metal rings had been. Nobody remembered that this commonplace act of generosity, apparently quite unconnected with the consecration rite that had just taken place, had at one time been its central feature.[41]

In the same way, even the offering of the rings on the altar ceased in time to be the centre of the rite. It would certainly seem to be implied by Fortescue's account that already in his time the king used to touch the rings in order to impregnate them with the mysterious virtue proceeding from his hands. Such at any rate is the gesture that comes clearly to light in the ordered ceremonial of Mary Tudor's reign. As ill-luck would have it, we do not possess much detailed information about the consecration ritual for the cramp rings except for this reign, which was the last to practise the ancient custom. That is no doubt unfortunate, but need not disturb us overmuch, for we cannot imagine that this princess, with all her faithfulness to the old beliefs, would have suppressed any specifically religious feature in the customs of the court. Nor would she have continued any of the innovations that may have been introduced by her two Protestant predecessors. We shall certainly not be wrong in assuming that the rules observed by her had already been followed by the last Catholic kings before the Reformation. Here, then, according to the liturgy in her private missal,[42] and according to the account of an eye-witness, the Venetian Faitta,[43] is the Good Friday ceremony in all the royal pomp followed by the pious Mary, and no doubt long before her time.

When the adoration of the Cross was finished, the queen took her place in a square enclosure at the foot of the altar, formed by four benches draped with material or carpets. She knelt down, and the plates containing the rings were placed beside her—as shown in the picture in her missal referred to above. First of all she said a fairly long prayer, the only noteworthy passage being a kind of exaltation of sacred royalty:

Almighty and Eternal God, . . . who hast vouchsafed to pour upon those whom Thou hast raised up to the heights of royal dignity the adornment of singular graces, and hast made them instruments and channels of Thy gifts, so that even as they reign and rule by Thy power, so also by Thy will they are serviceable to others and transmit Thy benefits to their peoples . . .

Then follows another prayer, said this time over the rings, and two special blessings, in which there is a clear reference to epilepsy as a diabolical disease:

O God, . . . vouchsafe to bless and sanctify these rings [so runs the second blessing, which is particularly explicit in this respect] so that those who wear them may be protected from the snares of Satan . . . and may be preserved from all nervous spasms and the perils of epilepsy.

Then follows a psalm, no doubt sung by the clergy present, and another prayer, showing signs of a rather curious concern lest there should be an appeal to forbidden magic, that 'all superstition may be far removed, and all suspicions of diabolical deception'!

Then comes the essential action. The queen takes the rings and rubs them, one at a time no doubt, with her hands, saying the following words, which indicate more clearly than any commentary the significance of this gesture:

O Lord, sanctify these rings, sprinkle them with the goodness of Thy heavenly dew and benediction, and *consecrate them by the rubbing of our hands which Thou hast deigned to bless, according to the order of our ministry, through the anointing of the holy oil,* so that what the natural metal cannot effect may be accomplished by the greatness of Thy grace . . .[44]

Finally, there is a specifically religious procedure. The rings are sprinkled with holy water—we do not know whether by the queen herself or a priest of her chapel—while she, and the others present no doubt, say some further liturgical prayers.

Thus it is evident that the prestige of the supernatural force emanating from royalty has obliterated everything else. The holy water only figures in the ceremony as a commonplace piece of piety, like the sign of the cross in the touch for scrofula. Neither the missal, nor the Venetian's account, makes any mention of redeeming the rings, or even of placing them upon the altar. It is probable, however, that this latter part of the traditional ceremony was still carried out under Mary Tudor. It was still practised, we may be sure, under Henry VIII; and there is no reason why Mary should have abolished it. No doubt it took place after the prayers, which would explain why it is not mentioned in the missal, but no one any longer considered this important: hence the silence of Faitta on this point. The climax of the rite now lay elsewhere, in the liturgy where, as in the service for scrofula, the monarch's personal action was all-important. Above all, it lay in the rubbing of the rings in the royal hands 'sanctified' by unction. Henceforward, as the terms of the official prayer clearly show, this was the essence of the consecrating act.

The evolution begun by the beginning of the fourteenth century, perhaps under the influence of Edward II's personal designs, had now reached its term. The old magical prescription had undergone a definitive mutation into a specifically royal miracle. The final transformation must no doubt be dated in the years leading up to 1500. As we have seen, the early years of the sixteenth century were the time when an attempt was made to link up the cramp rings with the great memory of Edward the Confessor, who was already the patron of the touch for scrofula; and so they had in any case become incorporated into the cycle of miraculous royalty. As we shall note later on, this was also the moment when this new form of the wonder-working gift attributed to the English kings appeared to reach its highest popularity. There is in truth no finer example of the strength still residing in the ancient conception of sacred royalty on the eve of the Renaissance than this complete usurpation of the healing power that had hitherto been ascribed to the influence of the cross and the altar.

III

The sacred and miraculous aspects of royalty
from the beginning of the touch for scrofula
up to the Renaissance

1 *Priestly royalty*

The healing rites originated, as we have seen, in ancient ideas of the super-natural character of kings. If these beliefs had disappeared soon after the birth of these rites, the rites themselves would probably not have survived, or would at any rate have declined in popularity. But far from dying out, they put up a solid resistance, and in certain points expanded as they were involved in new superstitions. How shall we attempt to explain the per-sisting success of the touch for scrofula, or the transformation of ancient magic into the truly royal ceremony of the cramp rings? The first require-ment is to place both these practices in their ancient atmosphere of religious veneration, and see them once more in the environment of marvel which surrounded princes during the last four or five hundred years of the Middle Ages.

In a Catholic society, familiarity with the supernatural is in principle reserved to a very strictly limited class of the faithful—to priests, ministers duly consecrated to the service of God, or at least ordained clerics. As compared with these official intermediaries between this world and the next, did not the wonder-working kings, who were simple laymen, risk being considered usurpers? As we already know, this was certainly the opinion of them held by the Gregorians and their successors; but not by most of the people of the time. The point is that in common opinion, kings were not simple laymen. The very dignity belonging to them was generally believed to endow them with an almost priestly character.

We must emphasize the word *almost*, for the assimilation never had been, and never could be, complete. In the eyes of a Catholic, the priest-hood carries clearly defined privileges of a supra-terrestrial order, con-ferred solely by ordination. No monarch in the Middle Ages, however arrogant or powerful, ever considered he was capable of celebrating the holy sacrifice of the Mass and, by consecrating the bread and wine, bringing God down upon the altar. Gregory VII had given the emperors a sharp reminder that since they could not expel demons, they must consider themselves distinctly inferior to the exorcists. Other civilizations, such as primitive Germany or Greece in the Homeric age, may have had priest-kings in the full sense of the word; but in the Christian Middle Ages, such a hybrid dignity was inconceivable. Those who sided with Gregory VII understood this perfectly. One of the shrewdest of the writers in this camp was a mysterious author whom we must needs call by his Latin name Honorius Augustodunensis, since we do not know his precise nationality. He denounced the pretensions of contemporary sovereigns on this score not only as sacrilegious, but also as betraying a certain confusion of ideas. In a treatise composed shortly after 1123, he says in effect that a man can only be a clerk, or a layman, or possibly a monk. (Monks, although many of them were not ordained, were nevertheless considered as part of the clergy.) Now a king cannot be a clerk, since he has not received Holy Orders; 'and his wife and sword prevent him from being considered a monk'; so he must be a layman.[1] As a logical argument, this was irrefutable; but logic does not ordinarily govern the feelings, especially when they bear the marks of ancient beliefs, and when their roots go down deep into outworn religions and ways of thought which have left behind them particular modes of feeling, like a kind of deposit. Besides, not everyone in those days possessed the implacable precision of an Honorius Augustodunensis—far from it. In practice, as can be seen from jurisprudence, and even in theory, there was a less clear-cut distinction in the Middle Ages between the clergy and the ordinary Christian than after the Council of Trent, and a 'mixed' state was quite conceivable.[2] Kings knew perfectly well that they were not altogether priests, but they did not consider themselves as laymen either, and many of their faithful subjects shared this feeling.[3]

Moreover, this ancient and basically pagan idea had long flourished in Christian lands.[4] We saw this in the lines written by Veriantius Fortunatus under the early Merovingians, thinly veiled by a Biblical allegory. More particularly, we saw its renewed vigour in Carolingian times, drawn from royal unction; we noted how loyalist opinion soon began to interpret this rite common to kings and priests in a sense extremely favourable to monarchy, to the great indignation of Hincmar of Rheims and his party. Now since Pepin's time, the consecration ceremonies had continually increased in fullness and splendour. Let us listen to the famous dialogue between Wazo, Bishop of Liège, and the Emperor Henry III, as reported by Anselm, canon of St-Lambert, about the year 1050. In 1046, Wazo had failed to send contingents to the imperial army. He was therefore summoned before the imperial court; and on the day when the case was heard, he had to remain standing, since no one would offer a chair to this prelate in disgrace. He complained to the prince that even if there was no respect for his old age, there should at least be more consideration for a priest, anointed with the holy oil. To which the Emperor replied: 'I, who have received the right of command over all, I too was anointed with the holy oil'. Whereupon—as the historian tells us—Wazo roundly made answer by proclaiming the superiority of priestly unction over royal unction: 'there is as much difference between these two as between life and death'.[5]

Were these words really spoken in the form given us by Anselm? There may well be some doubt about this. But after all, it does not really matter, for these doubts do not undermine their psychological truth. The fact that a contemporary chronicler chose them as a fitting and precise expression of the opposing outlooks of an emperor and a prelate makes them highly significant. 'I too was anointed with the holy oil' . . . It was assuredly this memory of the divine impress received on the day of the consecration that enabled a monarch, even a very pious one, to feel reassured as to his proper rights when he was attempting—as Anselm says in so many words of Henry III—'to arrogate to himself all power over the bishops in his firm intention to exercise a carnal domination'.

It was more especially around the year 1100 that the thesis of the royal supporters began to take specific shape, for the great Gregorian controversy had forced the contending parties to put their case without further equivocation. Honorius Augustodunensis speaks somewhere of those 'chatterboxes swollen with pride who claim that kings, just because they are anointed with the oil of priesthood, should not be reckoned among the laymen' . . .[6] We are already familiar with the language of some of these 'chatterboxes'. Its clarity leaves nothing to be desired. Here for instance is Guy of Osnabrück, who wrote in 1084 or 1085 a treatise entitled *On the controversy between Hildebrand and the Emperor Henry*—that is of course Henry IV—'The king must be set apart from the general run of laymen; for, being anointed with the holy oil, he participates in the priestly ministry'.[7] And a little later, in England, the Anonymous of York wrote as follows: 'The king, being the Lord's Anointed, cannot be called a layman'.[8]

To be sure, the majority of the polemical writers making these positive affirmations were subjects of the Empire. The daring claims of the anonymous writer of York do not appear ever to have been repeated in his native country. The fact is, as we have already noted, that the apologists of the temporal power (at least at this period) belonged almost entirely to the imperial camp. In France and in England, as elsewhere, the kings were bent upon dominating the Church, and were even fairly successful in their efforts; but up to the ecclesiastical crisis of the last two centuries of the Middle Ages, they refrained as a general rule from openly basing their claims upon the quasi-sacerdotal character of royalty. This long period of silence must be set side by side with the contemporary silence of literature about the touch for scrofula. It was not, however, so absolute a silence as to preclude a periodical breakthrough of the other ruling idea which underlay so many actions, without being overtly expressed; nor in all probability, without being consciously formulated in everybody's mind. In France for instance, Abbot Suger, a semi-official historian, represents Louis VI on the day of his consecration as girding on 'the sword of the Church'. [9] Above all, in Louis VII's reign, there is the famous preamble to the edict of 1143 in favour of the bishops of Paris: 'We know full well that in accordance with the ordinances of the Old Testament and in our own time with the law of the Church, only kings and priests are consecrated by anointing with holy oil. It is meet and right that those who are unique by their common participation in the sacrosanctity of chrism and their headship over the people of God should duly provide for their subjects both temporal and spiritual goods, and should also furnish them mutually to each other.'[10] The complete text given above is perhaps a little less striking than when the final phrase is omitted, as in Luchaire's version;[11] for the 'mutually' would seem to imply that the spiritual gifts were reserved to priests alone, who provide them to kings, just as the temporal goods were the special preserve of lay princes. The principle of the separation of the two powers is thus fully safeguarded. Yet this kind of equivalence—one might almost say alliance—between the two unctions, the royal and the priestly, is still highly significant. So significant, in fact, that it would be difficult to find anything equally emphatic in any other contemporary French documents. Up till now, historians do not appear to have noticed that this document originated from a most peculiar conjunction of circumstances. In 1143, a very serious quarrel had broken out between Rome and the court of France. Innocent II, in spite of the king's opposition, had taken it upon himself to consecrate as Archbishop of Bourges Pierre de Châtre, who had been elected by the canons; and the kingdom was under an interdict. But our information goes further than this. We know the name of the chancellor who countersigned the mandate and must be held responsible for it: it was the self-same Cadurc, who had been the unfortunate competitor of the pontifical candidate for the see of Bourges.[12] This bold intriguing cleric had now no reason at all to spare the Curia: on the contrary, he had now every interest in extolling to the uttermost the privilege of unction, which raised kings almost to the same level as priests, and seemed to give them a right to intervene in ecclesiastical elections. The designs or the grudges of an ambitious man who had been supplanted explain why the Capetian government emerged on this occasion from its customary reserve.

Let us now pass on to England. I do not know whether more learned scholars than myself might extract from the official documents anything comparable to the malign motives of a Cadurc and their fortuitous effect upon the chancery of Louis VII. But it is certain that the train of ideas inspiring the preamble of 1143 was as familiar to the English as to their neighbours. There is testimony to this in the middle of the thirteenth century by an orthodox theologian who was concerned to oppose these views. In a letter to Henry III, already referred to, Robert Grosseteste, Bishop of Lincoln, gives his master an exposition of the true nature of royal unction, and accords it a very lofty status. Yet he feels bound to point out that 'its effect is in no wise to make the royal dignity superior, or even equal, to that of the priest, and does not confer power to perform any of the offices of priesthood'.[13] Robert would clearly not have taken such trouble to guard against what seemed to him such a scandalous confusion unless he had had cause to believe that it was current with regard to the king he was intent upon instructing. No doubt, in England as in France, this was a mental tendency, rather than an explicitly expressed opinion.

Even in the imperial territory, after the extinction of the Salian dynasty it would seem that the priestly character of the temporal princes also ceased to be proclaimed by the partisans of the *regnum* with as much fervour as heretofore. The Concordat of Worms abolished investiture with the crozier and ring, but still allowed the sovereign great influence in the election of the German bishops. Its value to the Gregorians had been rather in the realm of theory. In the same way, their polemics did at least result in muting the declarations of principle on the part of their opponents. Here and there, the old notion still continued to show through. Towards 1158, the famous canonist Rufinus of Bologna wrote a justification of the oath of fidelity taken by bishops to the Emperor—an oath that was contrary to the rule forbidding clerics to bind themselves in this way to a layman: 'It may be said in answer, either that the canons do not allow all that custom has accepted; or that the Emperor, having been consecrated by holy unction, is not altogether a layman'.[14] But it is a far cry from this scholastic argument, presented casually for the reader to take or leave, and almost buried in a huge juridical *Summa*, to the resounding polemics of the preceding ages. Besides, these publicists in the pay of the Hohenstaufen were more intent upon exploiting the imperial idea than on elaborating a doctrine of royalty. That might have given support to the pretensions of 'the provincial kings', as Barbarossa called them[15]—that is to say, the heads of any other nation but Germany, as well as those of Caesar's heir. Not till the advent of the Gallican Movement, as we shall see later on, would there be forthcoming—and that in a different country—any affirmations as categorical as those so lavishly put out by the entourage of Henry IV and Henry V.

But the history of political ideas or sentiments must not be sought in the works of the theorists only; for certain ways of thought and feeling are more clearly brought out by the facts of everyday life than by books. Over a long period, the notion of the wonder-working power of kings, although it did not have free course in literature, served to inspire the healing rites of royalty. In the same way, the conception of royal priesthood, though more or less ignored by French and English writers, and abandoned by the imperial supporters, continued nevertheless to show through clearly and continuously in a large number of practices, modes of speech and traits in common custom.

Let us look first at the ceremony of consecration.

Unction was the royal act *par excellence*. In France, it was so intimately linked to the royal title that the great vassals, who sometimes tried to imitate the other actions in the consecration, never dared to appropriate this particular act. A Duke of Normandy or Aquitaine might well be invested in the course of a religious ceremony at Rouen or Limoges with the sword or the ring, the gonfalon or the ducal crown, but the use of the holy oil remained for ever forbidden.[16] This marvellous rite was securely protected by an ancient and highly respectable tradition; and even the most zealous protagonists of the ideas we have called, for short, Gregorian, would not have dreamt of abolishing it.[17] At any rate they did their best to prevent too close a similarity between the anointing of priests or bishops and that of kings. This was a task in which theologians and liturgiologists vied with one another; but they were no more than partially successful.

In the whole of Catholic dogma, sacramental doctrine was one of the latest to be developed. It only became crystallized under the influence of scholastic philosophy. For a long time, the word sacrament was applied indiscriminately to any act bringing a man or an object into the category of the sacred.[18] It was therefore natural to give this name to royal unction, and theologians were not slow to do so. Learned doctors, like Ivo of Chartres, and champions of Church reform like Peter Damian, or prelates zealously defending the prerogatives of the clergy, like Thomas à Becket, did not scruple to use this word for it.[19] Thus it was currently called by the same name as the ordination of priests. Then in the course of the thirteenth century Church theory became more rigid in this matter, and from now onwards only seven sacraments were recognized. Amongst these was ordination; royal unction, however, was excluded. And so a gulf was created between the act which made a priest and the one which made a king. Yet current language was in no hurry to abandon the ancient usage. Robert Grosseteste, philosopher and theologian, writing between 1235 and 1253,[20] and the papal chancery itself, in the Bulls of 1259 and 1260,[21] were still faithful to the former use. Above all, as was only natural, it lingered on much later in lay works written in popular language. Take for instance the romance of *Charles le Chauve*, composed in the fourteenth century:

> Seigneur pour ceste cause dont je vous voy parlant
> Fut adont acorde en France le vaillant
> C'on ne tenroit a roy jamais homme vivant
> S'en la cité de Rains n'avoit le *sacrement*.[22]

Was this a mere dispute as to the meaning of a word? Certainly not. For however ill-defined the term sacrament remained over a long period, it always carried with it the idea of supernatural action: 'visible signs of things divine', as St Augustine called it.[23] No writer with any pretensions to theological learning could interpret it otherwise. To apply it to royal unction was to state explicitly that consecration with holy oil effected a profound change in the spiritual being of a king; and this, in fact, was commonly believed to be so. As we read in the Book of Samuel, Samuel, after pouring the cruse of oil over Saul's head, said to him: 'Thou . . . shalt be changed into another man'—*mutaberis in virum alienum*.[24] Now the anointing of Saul prefigured the unction of Christian kings; and it was hardly possible not to make use of these words from the Bible to characterize the effects of anointing. In the eleventh century, the German priest Wipo places them in the mouth of the Archbishop of Mainz as part of his address to King Conrad II on the day of his coronation. Later on, Peter of Blois reminds the king of Sicily of them, and Pope Alexander IV recalls them for the benefit of the king of Bohemia.[25] There is no doubt that they were taken in a literal sense. Moreover, if we want to know the usual meaning given to the term sacrament, as applied to royal unction, we have only to turn to Robert Grosseteste. According to this very orthodox and learned prelate, the king receives with his anointing 'the sevenfold gift of the Holy Spirit'—clearly an echo of the theory, and even the ritual, of the sacrament of confirmation.[26] In short, by virtue of sacramental unction, kings seemed to be born into a new kind of mystical life. It was this deeper conception, just as much as the purely verbal approximation to the ordination of priests, which a stricter theology claimed to prohibit by refusing to give the monarchical rite the title hallowed by long custom.

Yet the old idea survived, and was destined to take on a particularly daring form among the entourage of Charles V, king of France. Let us look at the *Traité du sacre* composed, as we know, for the prince himself, and under his inspiration, by the Carmelite Jean Golein. In it, the author follows the ceremony step by step, duly giving each episode its symbolic meaning, until he reaches the moment when the king takes off the clothes he has so far been wearing and puts on specifically royal dress. Here is his mystical interpretation of this fairly simple action:

> Now when the king disrobes, it signifies that he puts aside his former worldly state and takes on a royal religious state; and if he does so with all due devotion, I hold that he is as much cleansed of all his sins as one who enters newly upon the religious life. Of the which, St Bernard says in his book *de precepto et dispensacione*, towards the end, that as at baptism a man's sins are forgiven, so also when he becomes a religious.[27]

There is a wealth of suggestion in these lines, for they compare the royal dignity to a 'religion'—that is, to the monastic state—and they attribute to unction the same regenerative power as entry into the religious life, and even as that of baptism; whereby the king, providing he is in the right spiritual state, is 'cleansed' of all his sins. Strangely enough, this latter undeniably bold theory had already been advanced well before Jean Golein's day, but outside France, and in a written work that could not have been known by the French Carmelite. Shortly before the year 1200, a high dignitary of the Eastern Church, Theodore Balsamon by name, composed a commentary on the decisions of the principal Councils. In connection with the twelfth canon of the Council of Ancyra, he relates how in 969 the Patriarch Polyeuctes first of all excommunicated the Emperor John Tzimisces for having gained the throne by assassination, and then relented of his severity. Here is the explanation of his change of attitude given by our commentator:

> In accordance with the synodical decision of the Holy Synod, which
> was then promulgated, the text of which has been preserved in the
> archives, the Patriarch declared that since the unction of holy
> baptism wipes out all sins previously committed, however great or
> many they may be, so, in precisely the same manner, royal unction
> had wiped out the murder of which Tzimisces had been guilty before
> receiving it.[28]

I do not know whether Polyeuctes and the synod really pronounced this opinion; but Balsamon certainly made it his own. Thus the loyalist priests of both Churches had come to be in agreement about this same astonishing idea, although not as a result of mutual influence. About the beginning of the seventeenth century, this passage from the Greek author caught the attention of a certain doctor of the Sorbonne, Jean Filesac, the author of a rather confused treatise that came out in 1615, entitled *Sur l'Idolâtrie politique et le culte légitime dû au prince*. Filesac, brought up on a more vigorous theology stemming from the Council of Trent, thought such a doctrine thoroughly scandalous. How—he asks in effect—can royal unction wash away a mortal sin since it is not a sacrament?[29] He would no doubt have been greatly astonished to learn that in France an identical notion had been supported by a monk in a document written for one of the most pious of his kings.

The temporal princes aspired to rule the Church; and they were tempted to claim equality with the leaders of the Church. Many details of the consecration ceremonial suggest the intention to affirm steadily, and more and more clearly as the Middle Ages proceed, a kind of parallelism between the monarchical ritual and the one used, not for the ordination of simple priests, but for the consecration of bishops.[30] This, more than anything else, must have seemed dangerous to those who were the self-constituted guardians of spiritual autonomy; and they made up their minds to oppose this tendency with all their power.

Kings were anointed on various parts of their body; and by ancient custom, attested by the early rituals, this included the head. And to be sure, was it not on Saul's head that Samuel had poured the contents of the cruse of oil mentioned in the Bible? The same practice was observed in the consecration of bishops; but in the ordination of priests, they only had the right to be anointed on the hands. The liturgiologists one day came to the conclusion that these practices constituted an intolerable parity between kings and bishops. They decided that henceforth kings should only be anointed on their arms, or at the most on the shoulders or hands. A celebrated Bull of Innocent III, addressed to the Bulgarian Archbishop of Trnovo in 1204 and later included in the *Decretals*, gives the most authoritative summary of the orthodox teaching on unction. A very clear distinction is made between the modes of the episcopal and the royal rites. We find the same distinction in Guillaume Durand's *Rationale divinorum officiorum*, which condenses the whole liturgical science of the thirteenth century.[31] But these efforts proved fruitless. In spite of the authority of Popes and Doctors, the kings of France and England continued as a matter of fact to receive the holy oil upon their heads, after the manner of the apostles' successors.[32]

There was however a difference between bishops and priests. Bishops were not anointed with ordinary holy oil, called the oil of the catechumens, but with a special oil mixed with balm, the oil of chrism. Efforts were made to restrict kings to the simple oil. This was the aim of Innocent III and the Curia in subsequent years; and that was the theory held by Durand. But in spite of all this, the kings of France and England kept the privilege of chrism.[33]

Truth to tell, the quasi-sacerdotal character which the anointing ceremony aimed at imprinting upon royalty was of such a clear-cut kind that in the end liturgical doctrine had to resign itself to toning it down and making it harmless, rather than flatly denying it. Nothing is more characteristic in this respect than the history of the imperial coronation. During the heyday of the Saxon dynasty, and even under the Salians, the official documents regulating this ceremony brought out most clearly the change of states effected in the prince. In the description they contain of the handing to the future Emperor of the tunic, the dalmatic, the cope, the mitre, the hose and the sandals—which were almost priestly garments—they add this simple comment: 'Here the Pope makes him a Clerk', *Ibique facit eum clericum*. This comment disappeared in the twelfth century. But the ceremony of handing over the robes continued, and was to do so as long as there were Emperors crowned by Popes. The interpretation put upon it, however, changed. Henceforward, the king of the Romans was deemed to have been received as a member of the Canons of St Peter. There was no longer any question of entering Holy Orders in the general meaning of the term; instead, there was simply the conferring of a particular dignity. True, it was of an ecclesiastical kind, but clearly conferred here as an honorary title, in accordance with the canonical practice of the period, which could be granted to persons who had barely attained even lower clerical rank. In the various cathedral chapters of the Catholic Church, not all the canons, by any means, were priests or even in orders. Thus the action taking place before the consecration proper, in the little church of Sancta Maria in Turri, though not quite losing its original meaning, was stripped of any significance that could threaten the papal party.[34]

But these efforts were pushed still further. After all, it could hardly be denied that the Emperor was something more than a layman; yet as he was not capable of offering the sacrifice of the Mass, he was clearly not endowed with priesthood. So the authorities decided to give him a more definite position in the hierarchy. From the thirteenth century onwards, the *ordines* for the coronation give clear evidence of an attempt to assimilate the ecclesiastical position of the temporal head of Christendom to that of a deacon, or more often a sub-deacon. The head of the Cardinal deacons read over him the litany used in the ordination of sub-deacons; and the Pope gave him the kiss of peace 'as to one of the Cardinal deacons'. At the end of the ceremony, the new Emperor served Mass for the sovereign pontiff, handing him 'the chalice and the water as the sub-deacons were accustomed to do'.[35] From all these practices, certain scholars deduced a certain doctrine, according to which the Emperor had really assumed 'the order of the sub-diaconate'. And as it was necessary at that time to support every opinion by a more or less forced documentary reference, they continued in addition to buttress their conclusions by a canon from the *Decretum of Gratian*, which represents Valentinian as saying to St Ambrose: 'As befits my order, I shall always be your helper or defender'. Now, was not the sub-deacon essentially the 'helper' of priests and bishops? Guillaume Durand, who mentions this theory, does not himself support it; but he is quite prepared to acknowledge that the Emperor at his consecration did indeed fulfil the functions of this 'order'.[36]

Thus it could no longer be said, as in Gregory VII's time, that any prince of this world, however great he might be, was lower in status than the simple exorcist. But the Emperor, although superior to clerks in minor orders, was in this way explicitly placed below the level of the priest, let alone the bishop. And that was the heart of the matter. Strangely enough, the historian is confronted by a similar feature in Byzantium. There, the *basileus* was the direct heir to the ancient sacred monarchy of the Late Roman Empire, which was permeated, even after Constantine, with pagan traditions. In the fifth century, it was still common to apply to him the word ἱερεύς, that is priest, and ἀρχιερεύς, that is bishop. In the fourteenth and fifteenth centuries, official writers desirous of explaining certain privileges of worship which were granted him, particularly the Emperor's right to communicate at his consecration in the same way as the clergy, did not grant him more than the rank of deacon or even δεποτάτος, an ecclesiastical officer of still lower standing.[37] And so in both halves of the European world similar circumstances had led the Doctors to invent a similar fiction, though probably not through mutual influence.

In the same way, from the fourteenth century onwards, the Western Emperors would seem to have taken this strange idea extremely seriously. Seeing that there had been such insistence upon making them deacons and sub-deacons, they wanted to exercise the functions of a deacon, at least at one of the chief festivals of the year. Thus Charles IV, wearing his crown and carrying his sword, read the seventh lesson for Matins on Christmas Day. It was particularly appropriate for imperial lips, because it begins with the words taken from the Gospel at the Midnight Mass (Luke 2:1): 'And it came to pass in those days that there went out a decree from Caesar Augustus that all the world should be taxed'. On 25 December 1414, Sigismund, Charles IV's son, appeared in the same role before the Fathers at the Council of Constance. In this way the sovereigns continued ingeniously to convert to their own glory a theory that had formerly been elaborated with quite a different intention. Their imposing appearance at the lectern, adorned in all the imperial finery, in the splendid setting of a great liturgical occasion, did more than could have been done by any other gesture to underline their participation in things ecclesiastical in the eyes of the common people. The prestige derived from this privilege seemed so striking that other countries easily took offence at it. In 1378, when Charles IV came to France to visit his nephew Charles V, he had to postpone his journey slightly in order to celebrate Christmas on imperial territory, since he had been informed by the French government that he would not be authorized to say Matins in their country. They would not have allowed the Emperor to perform in public a religious office that could not be carried out by the king of France.[38]

For the French kings were indeed never deacons or sub-deacons. It is true that the *ordines* for the anointing at Rheims from the thirteenth century onwards contained these words about the cotta put on by kings after the unction: 'it must be fashioned after the manner of the tunic worn by the deacons at Mass'. But there was no further attempt to draw out the parallel. Further on in the same documents, the royal surcoat is compared to the priest's chasuble.[39] And Charles V's ceremonial was to introduce a new element into the dress, suggestive of other analogies. It says that the king may, if he likes, put on after unction close-fitting gloves such as bishops are accustomed to wear at their consecration. Thus although there was no precise assimilation, everything was more and more calculated to conjure up the idea of priestly or pontifical adornment in connection with the dress worn by the sovereign on the day when he received holy unction and his crown. Moreover, the practice continued of saying the old prayers in which every line bore testimony to the desire to set up a kind of equivalence between the two unctions, the royal and the sacerdotal.[40]

In the English ritual, the official descriptions of the dress worn, and the liturgical texts, do not evoke any such clear suggestions of the different kinds of ecclesiastical ordination as are contained in their French counterparts. But if we wish to get some idea of the impression made upon the public by the splendours of these royal ceremonies, we have only to read an account of Henry VI's consecration, in which the contemporary author speaks quite naturally of the 'episcopal garment' worn by the king.[41]

The consecration was not the only act to throw light upon the quasi-sacerdotal character of royalty. Towards the end of the thirteenth century, the custom had grown up of strictly reserving to priests Holy Communion in both kinds, thus strongly underlining the distinction between clergy and laity; but the new rule did not apply to all sovereigns. At the Emperor's consecration he continued to receive the wine as well as the bread. In France in 1344, Philip of Valois obtained recognition from Pope Clement VI of a similar prerogative. It was not even limited, like the Emperor's, to a particular occasion, but was quite unrestricted. And it was granted at the same time and with the same conditions to the Queen, and to the Duke of Normandy, heir presumptive to the kingdom, the future John II, and to his wife the duchess. This was in the form of personal authorizations; yet either through an explicit renewal of the privilege in subsequent reigns, or more probably through a kind of tacit toleration, the custom seems to have gradually acquired the force of law, and the French kings continued from this time onwards over many centuries to make use of this glorious privilege. Not till the religious troubles that disturbed Christianity from the fifteenth century onwards, and the discussions then centring round eucharistic discipline, were princes constrained to renounce Communion in both kinds, at least partially or temporarily. Frederick III, who was consecrated Emperor on 19 March 1452, only received the Host in Communion on that occasion. Observation of the ancient custom would have seemed to risk an appearance of compromise with Hussite doctrines. Yet the tradition was only interrupted, for it was later renewed—at least by the seventeenth century—and subsequently extended to solemnities other than consecration. Even in our own time, the Emperor of Austria, the last heir to the sacred monarchies of the past, used to communicate in both kinds on Maundy Thursday. In France, from Henry IV's day onwards, kings were allowed to receive the chalice only at their consecration. It was not thought fitting that Henry of Navarre, on becoming a Catholic, should continue to observe the same Communion rite as he had in his heretical days. His subjects might well have doubted, in their ignorance, the genuineness of his conversion. At least up to the end of the *ancien régime*, the consecration ceremonial remained in this respect unaltered.[42]

No doubt it should be remembered that Communion under both kinds has been reserved to priests only by a disciplinary law which can be and on certain occasion is relaxed. It is said that popes, even in our time, have sometimes allowed this privilege to certain eminent laymen, who certainly had no pretensions to any kind of priestly character. This is perfectly true. But where the eucharistic privileges of kings are concerned, there can be no doubt that they originated in the conception of sacred monarchy—a supra-lay status, we might almost call it—whose vigour is attested by so many other facts. It made its appearance at, or very near, the precise moment when ordinary Christians found themselves excluded once and for all from the chalice. Temporal sovereigns, it would seem—or at least some of them, for the English kings never obtained, and perhaps never sought, the same favours as their French neighbours—refused to let themselves be lumped together with the common crowd. In the Bulls of Clement VI, this permission is accompanied by an authorization of deep significance to handle sacred objects, except the Body of the Lord, which was still restricted to priests; and this is not at all surprising, because it is obvious that the assimilation between royalty and priesthood was never complete, because it never could be. Yet this did not prevent a considerable *rapprochement* between the two. There was a similar development at Byzantium, where the Communion rite, though very different from the Latin customs, likewise made a distinction between laymen and clerks. Only the latter were allowed to consume the bread and the wine separately. But on his consecration day, the *basileus* communicated like the priests, ὥσπερ καὶ οἱ ἱερεῖς';[43] for he too was not 'a pure layman'. Besides, even if the original reason for granting this singular honour to the Western sovereigns had not been the one I have suggested, public sentiment would soon have come to give it that interpretation. In his treatise on consecration, Jean Golein first notes that the king and queen receive the wine and the Host from the Archbishop, and then he goes on to say that such a rite can only signify one or other of the two 'dignities', the 'royal' or the 'priestly'. This was a rather guarded statement; but one can scarcely believe that the common people failed to conclude that the first of these two dignities had a share in the second. Further on, we shall find an explicit statement of this conclusion by weighty authors of the seventeenth century; and common opinion had no doubt come to this conclusion a good deal earlier.[44]

A great poet, the author of the *Chanson de Roland*, portrays in his verse, under the magic name of Charlemagne, the ideal image of the Christian sovereign as conceived by those around him. If we take note of the behaviour attributed to this great Emperor, it is that of a king-priest. When Ganelon sets out for the perilous embassy which the hatred of Roland has thrust upon him, Charles makes the sign of the cross over him and gives him absolution. Later on, when the Franks are preparing for battle against the Emir Baligant, the sixth corps, consisting of men from Poitou and barons from Auvergne, come before the supreme head of the army, who raises the right hand and gives a blessing to the troops: 'Sis beneïst Carles de sa main destre'.[45]

It is true that nowadays, in reaction against theories that have been condemned for good and all, people are apt to modernize this ancient poem somewhat too much. Yet in its author's ecclesiastical attitudes, it bears the stamp of a fairly archaic outlook. More than one priest who had been converted to more vigorous doctrines concerning the distinction between the profane and the sacred must formerly have found occasions for scandal in it. There was Archbishop Turpin, who, not content with fighting as zealously as any layman, and justifying his conduct in theory, boldly contrasted his admiration for warriors with his contempt for monks. He must certainly have been deposed, just like his successor Manasses at Rheims, by the legates of the great reforming popes.[46] One can sense that the Gregorian movement had not yet exercised any serious influence in that direction. On the other hand, its influence was felt later on by one of those who refurbished the *Chanson*. About the beginning of the thirteenth century, when a versifier took up the ancient version and replaced its assonance by rhyme, he also felt obliged to bring its religious ideas up to date. He omitted the absolution given to Ganelon, but allowed the blessing to the troops,[47] which was in complete conformity with contemporary custom, to remain unchanged. About the same time, an actual prince witnessed, like the Emperor in the legend, the spectacle of his soldiers bowing their heads beneath his protecting hand before they rushed into the fray. At Bouvines, before battle was joined, we are told by the chaplain of Philip Augustus, Guillaume le Breton, who was at his side that day, that the prince blessed his soldiers.[48] Philip had no doubt heard the *Chanson de Roland* recited; moreover, Carolingian traditions were highly popular with those around him, and his clerics were wont to compare him to Charlemagne. They even contrived by some strange genealogical device to trace his descent from that great king.[49] On the battlefield where he was about to play such a decisive part he may well have recalled the gesture attributed by the troubadours to his so-called ancestor and deliberately copied it. There would have been nothing surprising about such an imitation. The mediaeval epics were to the period, which was considerably more 'literary' than we are inclined to believe, what Plutarch had been to the ancient world; and it was from them that the men of action often drew their splendid examples. In particular, they did much to maintain and strengthen in men's minds a certain ideal of the State and of royalty. But whether or not its inspiration was some model from poetry, this blessing of the warriors was certainly an eloquent expression of the sacred and quasi-sacerdotal power belonging to the hand of royalty. We need hardly remind ourselves that in England this same word 'bless' was currently used for the royal touch given to the sick in order to dispel their diseases.

It is clear then that in the eyes of their subjects the kings in the Middle Ages never ceased to share more or less vaguely in the glory of priesthood. Fundamentally, it was a truth recognized by almost everyone, though it was not considered salutary to express it. In Philip the Fair's reign, we still find considerable hesitation in the way Cardinal Jean le Moine, who could not be considered a supporter of theocratic ideas, states, with regard to the right of patronage in ecclesiastical affairs exercised by the kings of France and England, that 'anointed kings do not appear to occupy the role of pure laymen, but would seem on the contrary to go somewhat beyond it'.[50] About the middle of the fourteenth century, however, people began once again to speak more freely on this subject. In England, Wyclif, in one of his youthful works, *On the office of King* (1379), made a clear distinction between the two powers, the temporal and the spiritual, and classed royalty as an Order of the Church, *ordo in ecclesia*.[51] In France, Charles V's entourage made an assiduous collection of all the rites and traditions calculated to bring out the sacred aspects of royalty. Jean Golein, who would seem to have been a faithful interpreter of his master's thought, was at pains to keep to the orthodox position. He expressly declares that unction does not make the king into a priest any more than it turns him into a saint 'working miracles'; but he does not conceal his opinion that unction comes 'very near' to 'the priestly order'. And he is not afraid to discourse to us about 'the religious order of royalty'.[52]

Then came the Great Schism, and the long troublous period that ensued, not only in the Church's discipline but, partly at least in consequence, though the crisis was due to a variety of causes, also in the religious life itself. At this point tongues were entirely loosened. The English canonist Lyndwood, in his *Provinciale*, composed in 1430, indicates that it was a widespread opinion—though he does not associate himself with it—'that an anointed king is not a purely lay person, but rather a person of mixed status'.[53] And it was to an English sovereign, Henry V, that the famous humanist Nicolas de Clamanges of Champagne wrote these words, which lay bare the ancient almost prehistoric notion of the priest-king: 'The Lord laid down that royalty should be priestly, for through the holy unction of chrism Christian kings must be considered holy, after the likeness of priests'.[54] Here, there is no hiding, as there was among the theorists mentioned by Lyndwood, under the mask of an indeterminate 'mixed' being.

Truth to tell, it was no good Nicolas de Clamanges addressing himself to an English king, for he was speaking above all as a French cleric, and reflecting the ideas of French circles. Such conceptions were indeed commonly current in France at that time, and were being quite freely expressed. If we are looking for examples, we shall be presented with an almost embarrassing choice. In 1380, the Bishop of Arras, Pierre Masuyer, pleaded his case before Parliament against his Metropolitan, the Archbishop of Rheims, and against the Chapter of that town. It was an important matter. The bishop, who had been recently raised to the episcopate, refused to take the customary oath of obedience to his superior and to offer him as an enthronement gift the cope prescribed by immemorial custom—at least, in the view of the Rheims authorities. The case was thus one concerning ecclesiastical discipline; and that was why the archbishop wished to try it before his own court, and therefore refused to recognize any right of jurisdiction by Parliament in a matter he judged to be purely spiritual. The bishop, on the other hand, required the court, which represented the king, to declare its own competence. Here is one of his arguments: 'our Lord the King does not only possess the temporalities, but also divinity, for he is *inunctus*, and bestows benefices by right of patronage'.[55] We should specially note the last phrase. The right of providing for ecclesiastical benefices during the vacancy of bishoprics subject to his patronage appears in the documents of this period sometimes as the proof, and sometimes as the logical consequence, of the priestly character attributed to royalty. We have already come across the plea advanced in 1493, in a case raising incidentally the question of the royal right of patronage. A lawyer, thinking it was necessary to show that the king was not a 'pure layman', even went as far as to invoke the argument from miracles.[56] As early as 1477, Master Framberge, speaking before Parliament and in the same kind of debate, built a large part of his argument upon the theme of sacred royalty. True, he did not refer to the miraculous healings; but he made due reference to the legends concerning the heavenly origins of unction, which we shall be studying later on; and as the climax of his argument, he reached the following conclusion: 'As has already been remarked, the king is not a purely lay person'.[57]

And now, leaving the lawcourts, let us turn to Jean Jouvenel des Ursins, successively Bishop of Beauvais and Laon, and then Archbishop of Rheims. In the reigns of Charles VII and Louis XI he was one of the great clerical figures in the French Church. In his speeches and in his memoirs he constantly reverts to the same idea, namely that the king is not 'simply a lay person'. By virtue of unction, he is 'an ecclesiastical person', 'an ecclesiastical prelate', as Jean Jouvenel one day said to his 'sovereign lord' Charles VII.[58] As these pleaders were intent upon getting weapons from all sides with which to defend their cause, namely to confine the active policy of the popes within strict limits, we may be afraid that when it came to the question of sounding contemporary religious opinion, they would be witnesses of very doubtful reliability. So, let us listen to one of the great doctors honoured by the French Church, one of the princes of Christian mysticism, Jean Gerson. On the day of Epiphany 1390, he preached before Charles VI and the assembled princes; and nothing could well be more significant than the terms in which he addressed the youthful sovereign: 'Most Christian king, miraculously consecrated, king both spiritual and priestly'.[59]

Some of the texts just quoted are well enough known. Jean Jouvenel's words in particular have been reproduced by nearly all the historians who have tried to throw light upon the sacred character of the French monarchy. But insufficient attention has been paid perhaps to their date. Two centuries earlier, there would be great difficulty in finding any such statements. Even the polemical writers in the service of Philip the Fair did not speak in this tone. After long years of silence, the French clerics of the fourteenth and fifteenth centuries, with their bold praise of priestly royalty, were rejoining the company of the imperial publicists from the days of the Gregorian dispute. This however was an incidental encounter without any direct influence; for Nicolas de Clamanges would hardly have read the forgotten pamphlets of Guy of Osnabrück or the Anonymous of York. Or rather, it was a continuance of the same idea, which had never ceased to be embodied in a whole host of rites and customs, and had therefore never sunk into complete oblivion, but remained always ready to find its voice once again wherever circumstances should allow.

I have already suggested above what these circumstances were. The crisis in the Church and more particularly in the Papacy turned men's minds, even the most pious and orthodox, towards ideas that had long stood condemned. In France, there are clear signs about the same period of a changed attitude of a very characteristic kind in the transformation of an ancient abuse, hitherto prudently consigned to obscurity, into a privilege that was proudly blazed abroad. In spite of the reforms of the eleventh and twelfth centuries, the kings had always kept within their own hands the titles to certain monastic dignities, inherited from remote ancestors even before their dynasty rose to power. For instance, there was the title to the abbacy of St-Martin of Tours or of St-Aignan of Orleans. But since the apparent triumph of the reformers, they had taken good care not to boast of what was a blatant breach of the most venerable monastic rules. Now, however, they could begin to pride themselves on this situation; both they and their faithful adherents could use it as an argument to prove their ecclesiastical character, and therefore their right to rule with a more or less high hand over their kingdoms.[60] In those troublous times, any supporters of the papal supremacy would only regard the kings as laymen; on the other hand, anyone claiming for the Councils the chief share in governing the Church, and a kind of ecclesiastical autonomy for the different Estates of the realm, was inclined towards an approximate equation of the royal dignity and the priesthood. Lyndwood's reluctance to recognize the kings as 'mixed' beings—that is, half way towards the priesthood—was due to his fear of anything that might sap the papal power.[61] Apart from France and England, one of the most powerful opponents of the view rejected by Lyndwood was a certain Italian jurist, Nicolo Tedeschi, known as Panormitanus. This doctor, who was one of the greatest fifteenth century canonists, considered kings to be 'pure laymen', on whom 'coronation and unction do not confer any ecclesiastical Order'. It is not surprising to find that at least when he was composing the gloss from which this quotation comes, Panormitanus was among the most resolute enemies of the conciliar theory.[62] This question could indeed be taken as the touchstone of the two great parties then dividing the Catholic world.

We have now reached the moment when the real birth of the so-called Gallican Movement took place in France. It was an extremely diversified movement, both in its origins, which were an inextricable blend of the noblest aspirations towards suppressing the gravest religious abuses, and the most down-to-earth financial interests, as well as in its very nature. Indeed, Gallicanism presents itself sometimes as an impetus towards at least relative independence for the Church of France, and sometimes as an attempt to subject this Church to the power of the king, once he had finally cut free from the fetters imposed upon him by the papacy. This represents an equivocal dualism, which has often astonished, and sometimes shocked, modern writers. Yet it would appear less surprising if we remembered that among the ideas or feelings appearing or reappearing in the open light of consciousness there was always present this ancient conception of priestly royalty, in which principles that now appear sharply contradictory were easily reconciled.[63]

2 *The problem of unction*

Whence then did kings draw, in the eyes of their subjects, this sacred character, which ranked them almost alongside the priest? Let us at this point leave on one side all we know about the remote origins of monarchical religion. The consciousness of the Middle Ages was completely ignorant of the ancient things from which it had emerged. But it felt the need to find a reason borrowed from the present to justify a sentiment that owed all its strength to the remoteness of its orgins in an extremely ancient past. In the texts cited above, such as Guy of Osnabrück or Nicolas de Clamanges, or in the speeches made by Gallican advocates, there is the obstinate recurrence of one particular word, namely unction. This rite usually provided the requisite reason. Nevertheless, we should beware of imagining that it always and everywhere bore the same significance, in all periods and in every environment. The fluctuations of opinion with regard to it are all the more interesting to us in that they are primarily concerned with the history of miraculous healings.

As we have already seen, it belonged to the very nature of unction to serve as a weapon, now for one party, now for another. It was useful to the monarchists, because it marked kings with a divine impress; and to the defenders of the Church, because it equally much made kings appear to receive their authority from the hands of priests. And this duality never ceased to be felt. According as they belonged to one or the other of these camps, authors would stress one or other of the two divergent aspects of this two-faced institution. Look again, for instance, at the thinkers inspired by the theocratic concept, such as Hincmar in the ninth century, Ratherius of Verona in the tenth, Hugh of St-Victor and John of Salisbury in the twelfth, Innocent III at the beginning of the thirteenth, Egidio Colonna in the time of Philip the Fair and Boniface VIII. From generation to generation they faithfully handed down, like a schoolmen's commonplace, this argument for the consecration: 'the man who receives unction is inferior to the man who bestows it'; or, to borrow the language of St Paul in the Epistle to the Hebrews: 'Without all contradiction, the less is blessed of the better'.[64] As for the sovereigns and their entourage—with some rare exceptions, such as Henry I of Germany, who refused 'to be blessed by pontiffs'—they seem to have gone out of their way over a long period to extol the virtues of the holy oil, without taking too much notice of the clerical interpretations that could be put upon this monarchical rite *par excellence*. Throughout the great Gregorian controversy, this was the almost unanimous attitude of the polemical writers on the imperial side. In one of the most eloquent of his treatises, the Anonymous of York does little more than paraphrase the consecration ritual.

Nevertheless, a time came when the champions of temporal power became more clearly aware than formerly of the possible dangers to royalty in seeming to depend too exclusively on sanctions administered by the Church. There is an interesting expression of these anxieties in a picturesque historical legend coming from Italian circles in the middle of the thirteenth century favourable to the Hohenstaufens. It suggested that the coronation of Frederick Barbarossa had been a purely lay ceremony. On the day in question, the basilica of St Peter had been strictly closed to all members of the clergy.[65] But what was more serious, the theorists of this persuasion set about reducing consecration, as far as the common law was concerned, to no more than the simple recognition of an accomplished fact. According to this thesis, the king's title was purely hereditary, or—as far as Germany was concerned—elective. He was king from the moment of his predecessor's death, or from the moment of his designation by the duly qualified Electors. The pious solemnities that followed served only to adorn him after the real event with a religious consecration which was indeed venerable and striking, but not in the least indispensable. It was in the Empire, the classical scene of the struggle between the two powers, that this doctrine seems first to have seen the light. Under Frederick Barbarossa, Gerhoh of Reichersberg, though he belonged to the moderate party, wrote these words: 'It is clear that the blessing of the priest does not make kings or princes; but . . . once they have been made by election . . . they receive a blessing from the priest'.[66] He obviously considers consecration necessary, in some way or other, for the perfection of the royal state; but a king is a king without it, and before he receives it. Later on, the French writers got hold of the same theme. In the reign of Philip the Fair, Jean de Paris developed it with considerable vigour. The author of the *Somnium Viridarii* and Jean Gerson both took it up too.[67] It was not long before the various chanceries were being inspired by similar ideas. It was no mere chance that from 1270 onwards in France, and from 1272 in England, the royal notaries ceased to calculate the years of the king's reign from the date of his consecration, and from then onwards chose instead the date of his accession, which was usually the day after the death of his predecessor, or the day of his burial. The cry, 'the king is dead, long live the king', was used to our certain knowledge for the first time at the funeral of Francis I; but already on 10 November 1423 the heralds had proclaimed, over the tomb where Charles VI had just been buried, Henry VI of England as king of France. And there can be no doubt that this ceremonial was henceforward fixed by tradition. More ancient still, it would seem, was the conception it embodied, destined later on to find such striking expression in the famous cry mentioned above. In countries ruled by the law of heredity, the demise of one king instantly made the legitimate heir his successor. From the end of the thirteenth century, this thesis was officially professed more or less everywhere.[68] The apologists of royalty had not given up proclaiming the virtues of unction when it was a question of finding a reasoned basis for their theory of the sacrosanctity of princes. But they had stripped this rite of any effective part in the transmission of supreme power, and had more or less refused to admit its capacity to constitute legitimacy. They no doubt thought they had deprived their adversaries of any chance of using this argument, while themselves retaining it as a useful weapon for their own ends.

Truth to tell, the popular mind was hardly concerned with these subtleties. In 1310, when the Emperor Henry of Luxembourg complained to Clement V that 'simple people' were too ready to believe, in spite of the juridical truth, 'that there was no duty of obedience' to a king of the Romans 'before his coronation', he was no doubt concerned first and foremost to lay his hands on every possible argument calculated to persuade the Pope to crown him in person, and as soon as possible. But this argument showed a pretty accurate knowledge of the minds of 'simple people'.[69] Common opinion in every country was reluctant to admit that a king was truly king, or an Emperor Elect truly head of the Empire, before the religious act had been performed. That was the act referred to so eloquently in a letter written by some French noblemen in Joan of Arc's time as 'this splendid mystery' of consecration.[70] As we shall be seeing more fully in a moment, unction was held in France to have had a miraculous origin; and in France, more than anywhere else, this idea had become firmly rooted in the common mind. I have already quoted those significant lines from the romance *Charles le Chauve*. Here is an instructive anecdote current in Paris about the year 1314, handed down to us by the chronicler Jean de St-Victor.

When Enguerran de Marigny was thrown into prison by the young King Louis X, shortly after Philip the Fair's death, it was said that he called up his familiar spirit; and the evil spirit appeared to him, and said:

I had told thee long ago that on the day when the Church would be without a pope, the kingdom of France without king or queen, the Empire without an Emperor, then thy life would have reached its end. And now, as thou seest, these conditions are fulfilled. For him whom thou considerest king of France has not yet been either anointed or crowned; and before these have come to pass, he should not be called king.[71]

There can be no doubt that among the Parisian bourgeoisie, faithfully represented as a rule by Jean de St-Victor, people did not commonly share the opinion, on this latter point, of the evil spirit. In the following century, Aeneas Piccolomini wrote as follows: 'The French deny that any man can be a true king who has not been anointed with this oil,' that is to say, the heavenly oil kept at Rheims.[72] On this point there are indeed some very clear examples to show that the public did not think in the same way as the official theologians. In Charles V's time, the author of the *Grandes Chroniques*, a work directly inspired by the court, attributes the name of king to the prince immediately after the burial of his predecessor John the Good; but Froissart, reflecting popular usage, only gives him this title after the ceremony at Rheims. Less than a century later, Charles VII took the royal title nine days after his father's death; but as long as he had not been consecrated, Joan of Arc preferred to call him Dauphin.[73]

In the countries where the miraculous healing of scrofula flourished, a particularly serious problem arose concerning unction and its effects. Were kings able to cure the sick as soon as they came to the throne? Or did their hands become fully effective only from the moment when the holy oil had made them 'the Lord's Anointed'? In other words, what was the real source of the supernatural character that made them able to work miracles? Was it full-grown in them from the moment of their succession to the throne, or did it only reach perfection after the accomplishment of the religious rites?

Our documents are too inadequate to determine how this question was in practice resolved during the Middle Ages. In seventeenth century England, kings certainly exercised the touch from the moment of their accession, and before they had been consecrated.[74] But how are we to know whether this practice was older than the Reformation, or on the other hand whether it was not simply its product? For Protestantism tended throughout to minimize the importance of sacramental acts. In France, the practice followed from the end of the fifteenth century onwards was very different: no healings took place before the coronation solemnities. But the reason for this delay was not in the anointing. Among these solemn ceremonies, there was a pilgrimage made by the king to the reliquary of a pious abbot of Merovingian times, St-Marcoul, who had gradually become the accredited patron of the royal miracle. It was not at Rheims immediately after receiving the heavenly oil that the new king used to essay his wonder-working powers for the first time, but later, at Corbeny, where he came to venerate the relics of St-Marcoul. Before daring to exercise his wonderful talent, he was accustomed to wait, not for consecration, but rather for the intercession of the saint.[75] We may well wonder—but we are never likely to know—what the French kings did before St-Marcoul became the patron saint of scrofula.

One thing, however, is certain. Towards the close of the Middle Ages, there arose a publicist, an intransigent champion of monarchy, who refused to admit that unction was in any way the source of the king's miraculous power. This was the author of the *Somnium Viridarii*. This work, composed in the entourage of Charles V, is generally recognized to possess little originality. Most of the time its author is closely following the lines of William of Occam's *Octo Quaestiones de Potestate et Dignitate Papali*.Occam had said a little about the royal touch. Influenced as he was by the old imperialist notions, and therefore inclined to hold a high opinion of the virtues of unction, he saw it as the source of the astonishing cures performed by princes. And to his mind, only the fiercest partisans of the Church could think otherwise. The author of the *Somnium Viridarii* draws his inspiration from this discussion, but reverses its terms. He introduces into the dialogue two traditional figures, the cleric, the derogator of the temporal power, whom he exhorts to claim for the holy oil the glory of being the cause for the wonder-working gift; and the knight, who rejects this proposition, which he holds to be derogatory to the dignity of the French monarchy, for he considers that this 'grace' given by God to the kings of France goes back to a source concealed from the eyes of men, and in no way connected with unction; for otherwise many another king who has been anointed would also possess this gift.[76] The strict loyalists, then, were no more willing to admit that unction possessed any creative power in the realm of miracle than in the realm of politics. In their eyes, the royal person was intrinsically endowed with a superhuman character, and the Church could do no more than give it sanction.

After all, this was the historical truth. The notion of sacred royalty had existed in men's minds before being recognized by the Church. But here too common opinion was doubtless never in the least concerned with these over-subtle doctrines. As in Peter of Blois' time, it continued to believe in a more or less vague connection of cause and effect between the 'sacrament' of chrism and the healing actions accomplished by its recipients. For did not the ritual for consecrating the cramp rings, in its latest form, proclaim that the oil poured upon the hands of the English kings enabled them to give an effective blessing to the medicinal rings?[77] Even in Queen

Elizabeth's reign, Tooker considered that at his coronation a sovereign received 'the gift of healing';[78] and this view would appear to echo ancient tradition. Frenchmen could scarcely have avoided attributing to the heavenly oil of Rheims a power to produce miracles. And the attribution was in fact constantly made: witness Tolomeo of Lucca, who had probably drawn his ideas of this subject from the Angevin court, and the edict of Charles V, from which I have quoted the essential passage. The moderate monarchists elaborated a doctrine clearly expressed at a century's interval, in France by Jean Golein, and in England by Sir John Fortescue, namely that unction is necessary for a king to be able to heal, but is not all-sufficient: in addition, it must operate upon a fit person, that is to say, one of legitimate blood. Edward of York, says Fortescue, wrongly claims to enjoy this wonderful privilege. Wrongly, you say? reply the partisans of the House of York; but has he not been anointed, just like his rival Henry VI? Certainly, replies the Lancastrian publicist; but this unction is power-less, because Edward had no right to receive it. Would a woman who received ordination thereby become a priest? And Jean Golein tells us that in France 'if anyone presumed to touch the sick who was not king by right and had been wrongly anointed, he would fall victim to the *mal St-Rémy*' (that is, the plague), 'as has been seen in former times'. So St-Rémi, in a day of just anger, had struck the usurper down with his 'evil', and had thus avenged both the honour of the Holy Phial, which he was bound to hold in special regard, and the rights of the dynasty, which had been so odiously violated. I do not know who was the unworthy sovereign to whom legend ascribed such disasters, and it is of little consequence. The important point is that a legend should have existed denouncing the intervention of an idea more popular than learned; for jurists do not ordinarily invent such stories. Public opinion was not stirred by the antitheses that excited the theoretical thinkers. Everyone knew that to make a king, and to give him wonder-working powers, two conditions were required, which Jean Golein appo-sitely calls 'consecration', and the 'sacred line'.[79] Heirs both to Christian tradition and ancient pagan ideas, the peoples of the Middle Ages were united in showing an equal veneration for the religious rites of accession and the prerogatives of the royal race.

3   *Some legends; the monarchical cycle in France; the miraculous oil
in the English consecration ceremony*

Around the royal line in France there developed a whole cycle of legend suggesting that in its origins it was directly connected with divine powers. Let us recall them one after the other.

First comes the oldest and most famous of them all, the legend of the Holy Phial. Everyone knows how it runs. According to the old story, on the day when Clovis was baptized, the priest whose duty it was to bring the sacred oil was prevented by the crowds from arriving punctually. So a dove,[80] coming down from heaven, brought to St-Rémi in an *ampoule*, that is, a little phial, the balm with which the Frankish prince was to be anointed. This was a supernatural unction; and it was popularly regarded, in spite of history, not only as an act of baptism, but also as the first of the royal anointings. The heavenly *liqueur*, preserved in its original flask at Rheims in the Abbey of St-Rémi, was thenceforward to be used for all the consecrations of kings in France. When and how did this story originate?

Hincmar of Rheims is the earliest author to give us the story. He tells it at full length in his *Vita Remigii*, composed in 877 or 878; and this account, which has been much read and paraphrased, contributed more than any other to spread the legend; yet it was not the first in which this lively prelate gave the story a place, nor indeed the only one. As early as 8 September 869, in the official report drawn up by him of Charles the Bald's coronation as king of Lorraine at Metz, he expressly mentions it; he tells us he had used this miraculous oil for the consecration of his master.[81] Had he invented this edifying story, complete with all its detail? He has sometimes been accused of doing so.[82] It must be admitted that this archbishop, denounced in downright terms by Pope Nicholas I as a forger, and with notorious falsifications to his credit, has no very strong claims to respect from scholars.[83] Yet I should be reluctant to believe that Hincmar, whatever his audacity, one day suddenly produced before the eyes of his clergy and faithful flock a phial full of oil, and decreed that it should henceforth be deemed divine. It would at least have been necessary to provide some setting, and work up some revelation or discovery; and there is no hint of any such thing in the documents. A good while ago, one of the acutest scholars of the seventeenth century, Jean Jacques Chiflet, recognized an iconographical origin in the theme of the Holy Phial legend.[84] I will indicate how I think one may fill in Chiflet's rather summary suggestions and arrive at a possible genesis of the legend.

It would be very surprising if there had not been preserved at Rheims from quite early times some traces, whether authentic or not, of the famous act that transformed the pagan Franks into a Christian nation. There could hardly have been anything more in keeping with the habits of the time than to exhibit to pilgrims, for instance, the *ampoule* in which Rémi had collected the oil destined to serve for the baptism of Clovis, and perhaps even some drops of the oil itself. There is a wealth of documentary evidence that sacred objects or relics were often kept in receptacles made in the shape of a dove, ordinarily hanging above the altar. Moreover, in pictures of Christ's baptism, or more rarely the baptism of ordinary Christians, there is often a dove represented above the person being baptized, symbolizing the Holy Spirit.[85] Popular thought has always liked to see in symbolical pictures a reminder of some actual event. Perhaps a reliquary in the usual shape containing some souvenirs of Clovis and Rémi, and near by a mosaic or sarcophagus depicting a baptismal scene, may well have been enough to suggest the descent of a miraculous bird. Hincmar, no doubt, had only to search out the story in local folklore. But it was indubitably his own idea, carried out for the first time in 869, to use Clovis' balm for the anointing of kings. This happy thought had a touch of genius about it, for it served to adapt a commonplace story to the interests of the metropolitan city under his pastoral care, to the dynasty to whom he had sworn fealty, and to the Church universal which he longed to see predominant over the temporal powers. Secure in their possession of the heavenly oil, the archbishops of Rheims were destined to become the accredited consecrators of their lawful sovereigns. Henceforward, as the only princes of the Frankish race to be anointed with this heaven-sent oil, the kings of Western France were destined to shine with a miraculous splendour which raised them above all other Christian kings. And finally, as it seemed to Hincmar, the rites of anointing, which were a pledge and sign of the subordination of royalty to priesthood, having been introduced into Gaul in comparatively recent times, might well have seemed so far to lack that eminently respectable character that pious gestures can only acquire from a long history behind them. So Hincmar set about creating a tradition.

After his time, the legend spread rapidly in literature and took firm hold in the popular mind. Nevertheless its fortunes were closely linked up with the pretensions set forth by the archbishops of Rheims. Not without difficulty did they win the exclusive right to anoint kings. Fortunately for them, just when the Capetian dynasty was finally assured of the throne, in 987, their great rival, the archbishop of Sens, ranged himself with the opposition. This stroke of fortune was responsible for their triumph. Their privilege was solemnly recognized by Pope Urban II in 1089, and was only to be infringed twice up to the end of the monarchy—in 1110 by Louis VI, and in 1594 by Henry IV. In both cases, the circumstances were quite exceptional.[86] And their victory was also the victory of the Holy Phial.

Naturally enough, in an age that loved the miraculous, the imagination wove new fantasies around the original theme. As early as the thirteenth century it was reported that in the flagon once brought by the dove, the level of the liquid never changed, although some drops were taken from it for every anointing.[87] Later on, the contrary was maintained, namely that after the unction had been accomplished, this amazing phial would suddenly empty, only to refill itself, without the intervention of any human hand, immediately before the next consecration.[88] Or another version would have it that the level was constantly changing, rising or falling according to the good or bad health of the reigning prince.[89] The substance in the phial was of an unknown kind, like nothing else on this earth, and it spread a deliciously fragrant perfume . . .[90] True, all these marvellous features were no more than popular hearsay. They were no part of the authentic legend, which centred entirely round the heavenly origin of the balm. Richier, a thirteenth century poet, the author of a *Vita Remigii*, describes in picturesque fashion the incomparable privilege belonging to the kings of France. 'In all other places', he says, kings must 'buy their unction from the merchants'; but in France, which alone possesses the oil for royal consecration directly sent down from heaven, things are very different:

> onques coçons ne regratiers
> N'i gaaingna denier a vendre
> L'oncion.[91]

It was left to the fourteenth century to add a stone or two to the legendary building. About the middle of the century the traditions relating to the 'invention' of the fleur-de-lis made their appearance.[92] For a long while already, heraldic fleur-de-lis had adorned the escutcheons of the Capetian kings; and from Philip Augustus' time, they figure on their seal.[93] But it would appear to have been a long time before anyone thought of attributing to them a supernatural origin. It was in fact during Philip Augustus' reign that Giraldus Cambrensis, in his book *De principis instructione*, sang the praises of these 'simple little flowers', *simplicibus tantum gladioli flosculis*, which he had seen put to flight the leopard and the lion, proud emblems of the Plantagenets and the Guelphs. If he had known of any miraculous past history, he would certainly have entertained us with it.[94] There is the same silence about a century later in two French poems, both devoted to the praises of the royal armorial bearings: the *Chapel des trois fleurs de lis*, by Philippe de Vitry, composed shortly before 1335, and the *Dict de la fleur de lys*, dating apparently from 1338 or thereabouts.[95] But soon after this, the legend in its new form saw the light.

It seems to have found its first literary expression in a short Latin poem, in very rough rhyming verse, written by a monk of the Abbey of Joyenval, in the diocese of Chartres. It is difficult to be precise about the date, but it must have been round about the year 1350. Joyenval was a monastery of the Premonstratensian Order, founded in 1221 by one of the greatest figures at the French Court, the Chamberlain Barthélemi de Roye. The monastery lay at the foot of the heights above the forest of Marly, on the slopes of a small valley, and near a spring. Not far from there, and a little to the north, was the confluence of the Seine and the Oise, with the village of Conflans Ste-Honorine and a tower called Montjoie on a hill. This seems to have been a sort of common name for any building or pile of stones situated on an eminence, which might serve as a landmark for travellers. It is in this small canton of the Île de France that the author places his simple story, the substance of which is as follows. In pagan times there were two great kings in France, one called Conflatus, who lived at the castle of Conflans, and the other, Clovis, at Montjoie. Although they were both worshippers of Jupiter and Mercury, they waged ceaseless war upon each other; but Clovis was the weaker of the two. He had married a Christian, Clothilda by name, who tried for a long time to convert him, but in vain. One day Conflatus sent him a challenge. Clovis, though he was sure of being defeated, did not want to refuse battle. When the appointed time came, he sent for his weapons and armour; but when his squire brought them, he found to his great astonishment that instead of his usual coat-of-arms bearing the crescent, it figured three golden fleurs-de-lis on an azure background. He sent them back, and demanded fresh ones; but when they came, they too bore the same emblems. This happened four times in succession, until the king gave up the struggle and decided to put on the coat of mail decorated with these mysterious flowers. What had come to pass? In the Joyenval valley, near the spring, there lived at that time a pious hermit often visited by Queen Clothilda. She had gone to see him only a little while before the day fixed for combat, and she and he had prayed together. Then an angel appeared to the holy man, holding an azure buckler ornamented with golden fleurs-de-lis. 'These armorial bearings'—so the heavenly messenger said in effect—'will, if worn by Clovis, bring him victory.' When she reached home, the queen, taking advantage of her husband's absence, arranged for the removal of the ill-fated crescents from his equipment, and replaced them by fleurs-de-lis after the pattern of the marvellous escutcheon. We already know how surprised Clovis was at the results of this piece of deception arranged by his wife. It need hardly be added that, contrary to all expectations, he was victorious at the self-same Montjoie—whence the war-cry *Montjoie St-Denis*;[96] and that, when finally let into the secret by his wife, he became a Christian and an extremely powerful monarch . . .[97] This little story is disconcertingly childish, and the thinness of the material is only equalled by the lameness of the style. Where did it come from? Were its essential features already formed before Joyenval got hold of it? And was the share of the Premonstratensians in the genesis of the legend simply the attachment of its essential episodes to the setting of their own house? Or had the story really been born in the little community near Montjoie, perhaps first of all as a tale told to pilgrims? We cannot say. Yet the fact remains that it spread rapidly across the world.

Charles V's entourage was constantly on the look-out for everything that could strengthen the supernatural prestige of royalty; and they must be accorded the chief honour of having spread this legend. The account of it given by Raoul de Presles in his preface to the *Cité de Dieu* is clearly inspired by the Joyenval tradition.[98] This valley hermit seemed in a fair way of becoming one of the godfathers of monarchy. Nevertheless, he had a formidable rival for some time in the person of St-Denis. Indeed, this great saint, rather than an obscure anchorite, seemed to certain minds the more fitting recipient for the revelation of the royal escutcheon. It seems highly probable that this new form of the anecdote was born in the monastery of St-Denis itself. The proof that it should only be regarded as a secondary form, a transposition of the original theme, lies in the fact that it too places one of the essential elements in the story—the appearance of the angel—'in Montjoie castle, six leagues from Paris', that is, in this very same castle near Joyenval. A story that had grown up entirely at St-Denis had been set in the framework of the abbey or its immediate surroundings. Among those who frequented Charles V's *scriptorium*, or the next generation apologists for royalty, Jean Golein, Étienne de Conty, and the author of a very short Latin poem in praise of lilies, usually attributed to Gerson, were all supporters of St-Denis. Jean Corbechon, the translator and adapter of the famous book by Bartholomew the Englishman entitled *De Proprietatibus Rerum* and the author of the *Somnium Viridarii* remained neutral in their opinions. In the end, the hermit was destined to win the day. He had indeed always had his partisans. We still possess the actual copy of the *Traité du Sacre* by Jean Golein presented to Charles V. It contains some marginal notes by a contemporary reader, which we may perhaps imagine to be the work of the king himself, dictated to his secretary—though we must beware of mistaking this attractive hypothesis for a certainty. Opposite the passage by Golein attributing the fleur-de-lis miracle to St-Denis, the annotator—whoever he may have been—expressed his preference for the Joyenval tradition. And from the fifteenth century onwards, it was this version that definitely prevailed.[99]

Yet it received a certain alteration. The primitive version, as happened so often in the Middle Ages, equated Islam with paganism, and credited Clovis before his conversion with armorial bearings consisting of the crescent. In the *Somnium Viridarii*, a variant appears which was destined to triumph over its rivals: on the French escutcheon, the fleurs-de-lis are preceded by three toads. Why these toads? Should we follow President Fauchet of the seventeenth century, who explained these as an iconographical confusion? On ancient armorial bearings, he suggested, very crudely drawn lilies could well have been mistaken for a rather simplified picture of 'this kind of Animal'. This hypothesis, supported by our author with a diagram, is certainly more ingenious than convincing. There is no doubt, however, that the story of the toads, spread in the first place by writers working for the glory of the French monarchy, ended by providing the dynasty's enemies with a theme for facile jests. 'The Flemings and men of the Low Countries,' says Fauchet, 'therefore despise us and call us French Toads.'[100]

But after all, these jokes were of little importance. The legend of the fleur-de-lis took on its definitive form about 1400, and became one of the finest elements in the cycle of monarchy. On Christmas Day 1429 at Windsor, in the presence of the youthful king Henry VI, wearing the two crowns of France and England, the poet Lydgate pictured this story, along with the legend of the Holy Phial; and from then onwards, the two became permanently associated.[101] From this time onwards, the artists borrowed this motif from the politicians. It figures as the principal episode in a Book of Hours made for the Duke of Bedford,[102] and Flemish tapestries of the fifteenth century also display it.[103] Didactic works, pictures and poems all gave the people the message of the miraculous origin of their kings' coat-of-arms.[104]

After the escutcheon, it was the turn of the flag. The most famous of the royal standards was the oriflamme, the 'banner of the Red Standard' which the Capetians would go and fetch from St-Denis before embarking on a new campaign.[105] There was nothing very mysterious about its past. From being the banner of St-Denis Abbey, it had quite naturally become the royal banner since Philip I acquired the county of Vexin, and the kings had thus become simultaneously the vassals, liegemen and standard-bearers of the saint.[106] But men could hardly have remained content with such an unassuming history for such an exciting object, especially when the second of the royal insignia, the fleur-de-lis banner, used to appear beside it in the fourteenth century at the consecration, recalling to everyone's eyes the miracle of the lilies. Very early on people delighted to refer the origin of the oriflamme to the great princes of former days, to Dagobert, the founder of St-Denis,[107] and above all to Charlemagne. The author of the *Chanson de Roland* was already confusing it with the Roman *vexillum* given to Charles by Pope Leo III, as recorded in the chronicles and depicted in a celebrated mosaic in the Lateran Palace at Rome, certainly familiar to pilgrims.[108] But up to that point, there was no element of the supernatural. It was the authors in the pay of Charles V who took it upon them to supply this. We find the same story in Raoul de Presles and in Jean Golein. The Emperor of Constantinople was said to have seen in a dream a knight standing by his bedside, holding in his hand a lance from which flames issued forth. Then he was told by an angel that none other than this knight would deliver his realm from the Saracens. At length the Greek Emperor recognized Charlemagne as his deliverer, and the flaming lance became the oriflamme.[109] Yet this form of the tradition did not succeed in winning its way. The consecration oil and the royal armorial bearings had been sent down to Clovis from on high. So it was through a natural association of ideas that men came to attribute likewise to Clovis the revelation of the oriflamme. Such would seem to have been the most widespread belief at the end of the fifteenth century.[110]

Add to the Holy Phial, the heaven-sent fleurs-de-lis and the oriflamme of celestial origin, the gift of healing, and we shall have that marvellous cluster which the apologists for Capetian royalty offered ceaselessly from henceforth to the admiration of Europe. Thus, for instance, Charles VII's ambassadors, addressing Pope Pius II on 30 November 1459.[111] Even in the days when the legend of the Holy Phial was the sole constituent of the monarchical cycle, the French dynasty derived from it a great renown. In a semi-official document of the early thirteenth century, an *ordo* of the consecration, a French king boasted of being 'the only one of all the kings of the earth to have the resplendent and glorious privilege of being anointed with an oil sent down from heaven'.[112] A few years later an English chronicler, Matthew Paris, did not hesitate to acknowledge that the French kings possessed a sort of supremacy, based upon this divine origin of their power.[113] Such sentiments, uttered even by the lips of their subjects, could not fail to arouse the Plantagenets' jealousy, for they were the Capetians' rivals in all things. So they in their turn sought for a miraculous balm. The story of this attempt has been hitherto neglected by historians, but it deserves to be set out in some detail.

The first episode takes place under Edward II. In 1318, a Dominican, Friar Nicholas of Stratton, was sent upon a secret mission by the prince to Pope John XXII at Avignon. He gave the sovereign pontiff a fairly long account, of which the substance is as follows.[114]

Let us go back in thought to the time when Henry II Plantagenet was reigning in England. While Thomas à Becket was in France as an exile, he had a vision. Our Lady appeared to him, foretold his death in the near future, and told him of God's designs. The fifth king to reign over England after Henry II would be a 'a man of integrity and champion of the Church'. A very simple calculation will show that, as one might expect, Edward II was the king referred to. This prince, no doubt because of his special merits, would be anointed with a particularly holy oil, whose essential virtue would give him the power to 'reconquer the Holy Land from its pagan inhabitants'. This was a prophecy—or, if you like, a promise in prophetic form—which the English court expected to have a specially happy effect on a pope known at that moment to be busy with plans for a crusade. And the successors of this valiant monarch would also be anointed with the same precious liquid. Whereupon, the Virgin gave the saintly archbishop an *ampoule* containing, of course, the predestined oil. It would take too long to tell in detail how this phial was passed on by Thomas à Becket to a monk of the Abbey of St-Cyprian of Poitiers, was hidden under a stone in the church of St George in this town, thus escaping the covetous eyes of 'the great prince of the pagans', and finally came into the hands of Duke John II of Brabant, the husband of Edward II's sister. According to the English ambassador's version, when John II went to London for his brother-in-law's coronation in 1307, he took the miraculous oil with him, and urged the new king to have it used for his anointing. On the advice of his court, Edward II refused, not wishing to make any changes in the customary ceremonial. But then numerous misfortunes fell upon his kingdom. Might not these be due to the neglect of the oil once given by the Virgin to St Thomas? And might they not come to an end if it was used? This idea was all the more natural because there had recently been proof of the oil's miraculous virtues. It had been instrumental in curing the Countess of Luxembourg, the future Empress, after a serious wound. In short, it was a question of repeating the ceremony of unction, using this time the liquid prescribed in the prophecy. But was it not suggestive of superstition to attach importance to a special oil at the expense of the Church's duly consecrated oil which had been in use since 1307? Above all, did they possess the right to repeat such a serious rite? Would it not be sinful? There were no doubt precedents to turn to in these perplexities, at any rate, one at least: Charlemagne, so Nicholas assured the Pope, was anointed a second time by Archbishop Turpin with oil sent by Leo the Great. This was not generally known, for the act had been kept secret; but it had been recorded on two bronze tablets kept at Aix-la-Chapelle. But it would seem that in spite of this traditional authority—for which Nicholas or his master are our sole guarantees—the conscience of Edward II was not reassured; and he insisted upon obtaining for his plans the explicit approval of the spiritual head of Christendom. Hence the mission of this Dominican, empowered to ask for the Pope's consent to the repetition of the anointing. After this first delegate's return, he sent a second embassy, headed by the Bishop of Hereford, who took with him the further information demanded by the sovereign pontiff, and requested a speedy reply.

The reply was finally forthcoming. We still have its text. The prudent ambiguity of its form barely conceals an obvious scepticism. Did Edward II, for his part, really believe in the clumsy fable related to the Pope by Nicholas of Stratton? We shall never know. But not all his counsellors, one may be sure, were equally naïve. In any case, John XXII was not deceived. Yet while taking good care not to accept such a dubious story as worthy of outright credence, he thought it advisable not to reject it openly. He merely confined himself to a careful avoidance of any opinion about its authenticity. What is more, he seized the opportunity offered by the English king to affirm the official Church theory on unction ,which 'left no impress upon the soul' —that is, was not a sacrament—and so could be repeated without sacrilege. As for giving any practical advice recommending or disapproving Edward II's plan, he categorically refused to do so. Intent likewise upon not compromising the papacy in any way over this matter, he refused, in spite of the king's request, to appoint personally the prelate who should undertake the repetition of the rite. He only gave one piece of advice, or rather, one order. If the king decided to repeat the anointing, he must—in order to avoid possible scandal—have it carried out in secret. The Pope ended with some moral recommendations, rather in the tone of a teacher lecturing a pupil, which this imperious pontiff was fond of using towards temporal princes and more especially the sad-faced king of England. Did Edward II accept being anointed like this *sub rosa*? We do not know. In any case, he must have been singularly disappointed by John XXII's reply, for he had certainly dreamed of striking his people's imagination by a public ceremony sanctioned by the presence of a legate.[115] Friar Nicholas referred to the 'misfortunes which have descended upon the kingdom'—that is, the difficulties encountered since the beginning of his reign by an awkward prince who rapidly became unpopular as well. This gives us the key to the plan in the unfortunate king's mind, namely to reinforce his tottering prestige by an appeal to the miraculous. About the same time, or perhaps a little later, it was probably the same reason that led him to turn the consecration ceremony for the cramp rings into a really royal ceremonial. John XXII's refusal meant that he was unable to realize the hopes based upon a new anointing.[116]

What was the subsequent fate of the marvellous phial? There is no further mention of it for nearly a century. Are we to believe the later story, that it was genuinely lost among the coffers in the Tower? At any rate we know for certain that it fell to the usurper Henry IV of Lancaster to succeed where Edward II had failed. At his coronation on 13 October 1399 Henry had himself anointed with Thomas à Becket's oil, thus covering up his lack of right to the throne by using a rite in which the miraculous was involved. On this occasion, the version made public was a slightly altered edition of the first legend, which ran as follows. The Duke of Lancaster—Henry IV's real father—had discovered this phial when campaigning in Poitou in Edward III's time, enclosed in a receptacle shaped like an eagle, and had handed it over to his brother, the Black Price, for his consecration. But the prince had died before reaching the throne. The relic had then been lost, and had only been rediscovered by Richard II long after his accession. As he could not obtain permission from his clergy for a second anointing, he had had to be satisfied with using the golden eagle as a talisman. He had worn it continuously until his rival Henry of Lancaster had taken it away from him. This account is a medley of certain falsehoods and probable truths which the critical historian must admit himself unable to unravel. Moreover, the essential thing was the prophecy, and a discreet patriotic allusion was slipped into it, to the effect that the first king to be anointed with the sacred balm would reconquer Normandy and Aquitaine, and applied—as was only right and proper—to Henry IV.[117] From then onwards, the English consecration also had its legend, for the kings who succeeded Henry IV, whether Lancastrian, Yorkist or Tudor, continued to insist upon using the oil once given to St Thomas by Our Lady. The tradition seems to have persisted even in spite of the Reformation until the day when James I, who had been brought up in Scottish Calvinism, refused to accept a practice so reminiscent of the abhorred cult of the Virgin and the saints.[118]

Nor was the phial of St Thomas the only miraculous object connected with the English kings' coronation. One can still see today at Westminster, beneath the coronation throne, a lump of reddish sandstone, known as the Stone of Scone or the 'Stone of Destiny', on which the patriarch Jacob was said to have rested his head during that mysterious night when, between Beersheba and Haran he had a dream of the angels ascending and descending on the ladder to heaven. But this relic is in fact no more than a trophy. Edward I brought it to Westminster after he had taken it from the Scots, among whom it had been used in early times at the crowning of a new king. In the town of Scone, it served as a seat for the new monarch. There can be little doubt that long before it was endowed with Biblical status—about A.D. 1300 at the latest— it had simply been a sacred stone, the use of which at the coronation solemnities was probably to be explained at the beginning by purely pagan beliefs that were widespread in Celtic lands. In Ireland, there was a similar stone at Tara which used to be placed beneath the new prince's feet, and which, if he was of pure royal race, would give a booming sound beneath his footsteps.[119]

To sum up, it may be said that the English monarchy's legendary patrimony was and remained extremely poor. The Stone of Scone was only English by conquest, and rather late in the day; and St Thomas' oil was only a second-rate imitation of the Holy Phial, originating four hundred years after Hincmar from the anxious fears of unpopular or illegitimate princes. Neither of these two legends, even in England, let alone on the continent, ever had the fame and splendour of the French cycle. Why was there such a poor showing in face of such a rich display? Was it merely through the chance conjunction in France, just at the right moment, of men capable of creating or adapting such fine stories, and circumstances favourable to their spread, whereas such a coincidence never took place in England? Or was it on the other hand a case of deep collective psychological differences between the two nations? The historian may well pose such questions, but he cannot answer them.

In France, at all events, these traditions surrounded the dynasty with a peculiarly intense atmosphere of veneration. Added to which, there was the reputation for outstanding piety that had surrounded the Capetians since the time of Louis VII, and especially since St-Louis and his imme-diate successors.[120] It is not difficult to understand how, from the thirteenth century onwards, this family was considered pre-eminently holy. As early as 1230, we find the poet Robert Sainceriaux writing of the deceased monarch's four sons in a funeral oration on Louis VIII: 'From St-Louis are they come, and therefore will they do good'.[121] Likewise Jean Golein, in the reign of Charles V, speaks of the 'holy and sacred line' from which his master is descended.[122] But nothing is more instructive on this subject than to compare the three different dedications at the head of three of Egidio Colonna's works in Philip the Fair's reign—remembering that he was hostile to the religious ideas inspiring the French court. For the Count of Flanders' son he wrote: 'to the Lord Philip, born of an illustrious line'; for the King of Naples—a Capetian, but belonging to a younger branch: 'A splendid prince, King Robert, who is my own particular lord'; for Prince Philip, heir to the French throne, the future Philip the Fair: 'to my own particular lord, the Lord Philip, born of a royal and *most holy* line'.[123]

This feeling, based as it was on these legends—especially that of the Holy Phial—gave an almost religious value to dynastic loyalty in France. In his *Vita Remigii*, Richier wrote that the memory of the miraculous unction received by Clovis is an admonition to Frenchmen to love and adore 'the crown' as much as any 'corsain'—that is to say, as much as the most precious relic. The man who dies on its behalf—unless he is a heretic or has previously committed a sin so appalling that he is already damned—will by this very death be saved.[124] These last words are worth thinking over. They irresistibly remind one of other more ancient texts apparently almost the same, and yet profoundly different. In 1301, in the century after the troubadour to whom we owe the romance of *Garin le Lorrain*, the Fathers assembled in Council at Limoges were also ready to promise the glory of martyrdom to heroes who had fallen in defence of an entirely secular cause; but those to whom they so generously offered the reward of Paradise were vassals killed in the service of their lords.[125] At the end of the thirteenth century, the poet who wrote the *Vita Remigii* thinks of the soldiers who fell fighting on behalf of 'the crown'. This shows the difference between these two periods. The development of the faith in the monarchy had kept pace with the material progress of royalty, and tended gradually to supplant the loyalty of vassal to lord. The political and moral transformation had gone on side by side, without its being possible to distinguish cause from effect in this continuous interaction. Thus it was that the 'religion of Rheims' grew up, which, Renan says, Joan of Arc 'lived to the letter'.[126] And who would deny that French patriotism has still preserved something of this mystical touch?

There is a further aspect of these marvellous stories—which created such a brilliant past for the Capetians—of special psychological interest. They all of them possess in common a certain contradiction. Though largely originating from interested parties, they nevertheless enjoyed great popular success, stirring the emotions of crowds and moving men to action. But the combination of the artificial and the spontaneous should not surprise us, least of all when considering the history of the healing rites.

4 Some superstitions: the royal birthmark; kings and lions

In the miraculous concept of royalty held by the popular mind, there were certain elements alongside the pious anecdotes just related with nothing particularly Christian about them. This will be a convenient place to consider them.

In common opinion, kings, being sacred persons, were by that very fact the workers of wonders. It was currently believed that the French and English kings performed marvels during their lifetime; and other marvels were ascribed to them when they were dead. The case of Philip Augustus is particularly typical. It cannot be maintained that he had been a pattern of private virtue during his lifetime, nor of perfect submission to the leaders of the Church; but he had been a great king, whose actions had made a great impression on men's minds. So his corpse was held to perform miracles.[127] By the eleventh century, the process of canonization had been regularized by Rome. That is why it became much rarer from this time onwards for temporal sovereigns to be raised to the altar, i.e. canonized. But their subjects went on considering them to be endowed with powers similar to those of the saints.

Moreover, they were considered to such an extent supernatural that they were often thought to have a mysterious mark upon their bodies, denoting their royal state. Belief in the royal birthmark was one of the most lively superstitions in the Middle Ages. It will give us a deep insight into the popular mind.[128]

Texts of a literary kind are where we shall find its most frequent expression. It appears in the French adventure romances about the middle of the thirteenth century, and remains one of the most well-worn and commonplace themes until the end of the Middle Ages. This is how it quite naturally found its way into them. Many of these romances are built round the old theme of the child lost by chance or through some fearful machinations, and then rediscovered. For example, Richard the Fair, grandson of the King of Frisia,[129] the twins Florentius and Octavian, sons of the Roman Emperor,[130] Orthonet, son of Florentius,[131] Macarius or Louis, son of Charlemagne,[132] Beves of Hamtoun, whose ancestor was king of Scotland,[133] Hugh, son of the Duke of St-Giles and future king of Hungary,[134] John Tristan, son of St-Louis, stolen from his cot by the Saracens,[135] Deusdedit, son of King Philip of Hungary,[136] Lion, Son of Duke Herpin of Bourges . . .[137] This list could probably be prolonged without much difficulty, if the interminable works of fiction in prose and in verse bequeathed to us by the declining years of the Middle Ages had not for the most part been destined to remain for ever unpublished. Now, in order that the poor lost child can be recognized by his family—the necessary *dénouement* for this kind of adventure—he must obviously possess a means of establishing his identity. In the stories just enumerated, this is provided by a skin-blemish or *naevus* in the form of a cross, nearly always on the child's right shoulder, and much more rarely on the chest. Usually, it is red, 'redder than the rose in summer',[138] and sometimes—but rarely—white. This cross serves essentially as a mark of recognition. But make no mistake about it—this is no commonplace individual mark, such as might be borne by anyone, no matter what his family or destiny. It has a particular significance known to everyone, for this is the 'royal cross', a proof of royal blood, a certain pledge of future accession to the throne. Those who discover it, even before they can assign the predestined hero a precise genealogy, do not hesitate to exclaim, like the countess who rescues Richard le Beau, abandoned soon after birth in the forest:

'O God, said she, he shall be king!'[139]

The story-tellers, moreover, take good care not to assign this mark to any of their characters except to those they know will eventually reign. Nothing is more instructive on this count than the Beves of Hamtoun. This poem exists in an Anglo-Norman redaction, and three other versions composed on the Continent. In all of these, Beves figures as a lost child, the grandson—though no one suspects it—of the Scottish king. But only the continental versions make him conquer a kingdom at the end of the story— England, according to one version, Jerusalem according to the two others. Thus three versions—but not the Anglo-Norman one—credit him with the fateful sign.[140] These old authors would have taken good care not to assign it to anyone at random; they were well aware that for whoever bore it

'This signifies that he will be a crowned king.'[141]

This superstition is not peculiar to French literature. It is also found in foreign works. Certain of these, indeed, are an obvious imitation of the French romances. In Spain, for instance, you have the *Historia de la reyna Sebilla*;[142] in Italy, there are stories relating to Beves of Hamtoun, and especially the great collection of the *Reali di Francia*, an adaptation of the Carolingian legend drawn up about the year 1400 by Andrea di Barberino. His was a subtle mind, which delighted to reason about the *Niello* and the *Croce di Sangue*.[143] But the same theme also occurs beyond our frontiers, and in more original compositions. In England, at the beginning of the fourteenth century, there is the *Lay of Havelock the Dane*. Havelock was also the hero of stories in French, or rather Anglo-Norman; but he is only given the 'royal mark, a shining and very beautiful cross' in the English lay, which is generally recognized as following an independent tradition.[144] In Germany, we must note a version of the *Wolfdietrich* dating from the middle of the thirteenth century,[145] and particularly the *Kudrun*, which goes back to about 1210, and seems to be the oldest document in which a king's son is shown as bearing this famous cross.[146] These poems were neither translated from nor directly inspired by French models; but it must not therefore be assumed that the widespread influence of French literature at this time throughout Europe may not have had some influence in the choice of the theme. But whatever the country where belief in the royal sign sprang up for the first time, it put down deep roots, as we shall presently see, in France and likewise beyond her borders.

If it was known to us only through romances, we might be tempted to treat it as a mere literary device, what I might almost call a romantic gambit. But documents of different periods prove that public sentiment applied the theme to persons who had nothing legendary about them. To be sure, there are not a great many of these supporting texts; but what point of mediaeval folklore is illuminated by more than an occasional flash, throwing light now and again on collective ideas which were once no doubt full of vitality, though now shrouded in obscurity?

In France, as early as the thirteenth century, the troubadour Adam de la Halle, singing the praises of Charles of Anjou, a Capetian and King of Sicily, affirms that 'at birth he bore the royal cross'.[147] Adam de la Halle was a literary writer, and may therefore perhaps appear suspect as an interpreter of popular conceptions. But Antoine Thomas has unearthed a letter of remission dated two centuries later, which can hardly be rejected. It relates the following facts.[148] The scene is the village of le Bialon, an out-of-the-way spot in one of the wildest corners of the Massif Central, on 18 or 19 June of the year 1457. Six peasants are sitting round the table in the village inn, among whom is an old man of eighty, Jean Batiffol by name. They are talking politics and discussing taxation. The parish was labouring under a strong sense of grievance, holding that the collector was asking too much and abusing his rights of seizure. If the king knew this, said one of the drinkers, the collector 'would be censured for it', whereupon old Batiffol replied—I quote his actual words, because they are so astonishing—'le roi est roy, mais il ne lui appartenoit pas que fusse roy, car il n'est pas du lieu, car quant le roy nasquit, il n'apporta pas enseigne de roy, et n'avoit pas la flour de flour de liz comme vray roy'. This was what he meant: the king (Charles VII) is nothing but a bastard (we know that Isabella of Bavaria's behaviour had given rise to all kinds of imputations and the enemies of the king of Bourges had not failed to take advantage of them); and what proves that he is not a king's son is that he did not bear the royal mark when he was born. This is no longer the red cross, but has changed its form. The fleur-de-lis, which had long adorned the Capetian coat-of-arms, had no doubt finally replaced the cross in popular imagination, when it was a question of the French royal blood, the cross having come to seem too commonplace. Nothing could have been more natural than to attribute to the child of a chosen race the distinctive mark of his own dynasty's armorial bearings. And so the words of an old and probably illiterate man, when he had had his drink in a country tavern, preserved by sheer chance, throw a vivid light on the marvellous tales that the country people of the fifteenth century used to tell each other about their kings.[149]

Stories of the same kind were also widespread in Germany, where the various claimants or families contending for the Empire made repeated use of the fateful cross. About the year 1260, people imagined they saw it between the shoulders of Frederick de Misnie, grandson on his mother's side of the Emperor Frederick II who was for a short while chosen by the last supporters of the Hohenstaufen in Germany and Italy as the heir of all their hopes.[150] This was the time when Adam de la Halle was singing of Charles of Anjou; and in different countries, the two rival princes, the

Guelph king from Sicily and his Ghibelline competitor, witnessed the same prophetic mark being attributed to them with equal zeal. The heads of the House of Hapsburg, the imperial line, all had this mark on their backs at birth, 'in the form of white hairs in the shape of a cross'; that at least was the contention of the Swabian monk Felix Fabri at the end of the fifteenth century, who was one of their supporters.[151] And finally, later still, at the time of the religious wars, some Lutherans thought they discerned it imprinted on the back of John Frederick, Elector of Saxony. Before his ambitions crumbled to dust on the battlefield of Mühlberg, he had for a moment dreamt of wresting the imperial crown from Charles V himself.[152]

If we are to believe the contemporary evidence of the German historian Philip Kammerer (Camerarius), such rumours even reached England in the early seventeenth century. As we know, James I seemed to be destined by birth for the Scottish throne, but not, at that time, for that of England; yet he was said to have borne on his body from earliest infancy marks which heralded his high destiny: a lion and a crown, to which some added a sword.[153]

To sum up, we may say that there is widespread testimony to belief in the royal birthmark. The aspects it assumed varied with the time and the place. In France, towards the end of the fifteenth century, the belief had been reached, so it would seem, that every legitimate king ought to bear on his skin the mark of his ancestry. In primitive times it was thought to take the shape of a cross, but it had ended by assuming the form of a fleur-de-lis. There was a preference in Germany, and perhaps also in England, for attributing the miraculous birthmark to princes cut off from the throne at birth through some misfortune, but nevertheless destined to occupy it in the future. These were the real heroes of romance and tales so much beloved by the people. German tradition remained faithful to the cross, and saw it mostly as a golden cross, not a red one, as in France. That was the form in which it figured on Hagen of Ireland in the *Kudrun*, and in which Frederick de Misnie's adherents, and those of John Frederick of Saxony and the Counts of Hapsburg, thought they saw it on their masters' bodies.[154] The very variety observable in the different traditions proves their native vigour.

To the eyes of the folklore student, there is nothing very exceptional about the superstition just related. Ancient Greece also had her legends about the 'marks of race', τοῦ γένους τὰ γνωρίσματα: such was the lance-shaped impress said to belong to certain noble Theban families, who were supposed to have sprung from the warriors—the Σπαρτοί—who had once upon a time been born from the dragon's teeth sown by Cadmus. Sometimes, as in the West during the Middle Ages, these distinctive families were of the royal line. The Seleucids were all said to have borne the mark of an anchor on their thigh at birth, testifying to their divine origin; for

Seleucus the Great, who was the first to bear it, was said to have received it from his father Apollo. The same emblem is to be found on certain Seleucid coins, and on two votive vases, called σελευκίδες offered by one of Seleucus IV's ministers at the Apollonian sanctuary of Delos. Like the Valois fleur-de-lis, it was therefore both a bodily 'sign' and a kind of coat-of-arms.[155] Marco Polo tells us that in Georgia 'in olden days all the kings were born with an eagle marked upon their right shoulder'.[156] But according to a missionary who visited these regions in the seventeenth century, the sign had changed its form, and was now said to look like a cross.[157] Even in modern Europe, as we shall presently see, certain sorcerers, claiming to be hereditary healers of various diseases, used to display on their skins certain marks which were a kind of armorial bearing to prove their authentic descent.[158] Thus the idea of a royal or racial sign would seem to belong to nearly all periods and countries. It was born spontaneously in different civilizations, from similar ideas concerning the miraculous character of certain lines, in particular those from which the rulers of a nation were descended. We are obviously confronted at this point with an almost universal theme; but this does not absolve us from the duty of enquiring when the particular application of it favoured by the Middle Ages took shape, or why it should have taken the form of a cross in this particular setting. Moreover, the red or white cross of these legends is not quite the same conception as the Theban lance or the Seleucid anchor, for it is as much a sign of destiny as of origin, heralding a royal future which usually finds its justification in the privileges of blood. It derives from the common motif, but constitutes a variant of it which requires further explanation.

We are indebted to Pio Rajna for the first comprehensive study of the cross in connection with royalty in France. The subject was suggested to him by reading certain French and German poems, especially the *Reali di Francia*. He was struck by the apparently very archaic character of this motif, in which he thought he discerned the survival of certain extremely ancient Germanic notions; and he used them as an argument for his favourite theory concerning the French epic, namely that it was derived from the Merovingian 'Songs'. He was answered by Ferdinand Lot in the periodical *Romania*. In view of this decisive reply, and the general trend of the theories concerning our ancient literary history, I need not dwell at length upon an ingenious hypothesis which has no solid foundations. It has sometimes been thought that some heroes who bore the mark represented certain Merovingian princes, more or less distorted by poetic tradition. But this filiation has been disputed. For us, however, the truth or falsehood of this suggestion is of little importance: these heroes are only characters in a series of romances. We know the superstition embodied in them, not through the texts of the Frankish period, but solely through works of fiction relatively recent in date, none of them earlier than the thirteenth century. The ancient texts of the epics show no trace of this superstition. No doubt it may have been alive in men's minds some time before finding literary expression; but it seems unlikely that the authors of adventurous romances would have been slow to see the splendid themes offered them by the popular imagination, or have failed to take prompt advantage of them. Nothing authorizes us to date the origin of belief in the royal sign much earlier than the earliest testimony to it. To be on the safe side, we may say that it appears to have originated about the twelfth century. We shall never know whether its earliest beginnings were in France or in Germany, or independently in both these countries at the same time. But one thing is certain: it must be taken as a particularly striking sign, along with the healing rites, of the powers of resistance and capacity for development shown at this period by the conception of royalty as something miraculous and sacred, in spite of all the influences in a contrary direction.

But why did the men of that time picture the mark on the body of kings as a cross, and why did they usually place it upon the shoulder, or more accurately, the right shoulder? We are bound to ask this question, but it is impossible to give it a certain answer, for nothing is more obscure than the beginnings of a collective idea like this. But it is allowable to offer some conjectures; and the following seems to me the least improbable. There is a passage in Isaiah, who was the most familiar of all the Old Testament prophets in the Middle Ages, Chapter 9, verse 5, which Christians have interpreted as a promise of the Messiah. No one could be unaware of it, for then, as now, it was sung as part of the Mass for Christians. It contains these words relating to the Son who is destined to come: 'the government shall be upon his shoulder' (*factus est principatus super humerum ejus*).[159] It is a mysterious passage, which modern exegetes are at a loss to explain at all precisely. Theologians saw it as an allusion to the cross which would weigh down the Redeemer's shoulders. May it not well have been the effect of this verse, with its striking obscurity, and the commentaries on it given to the faithful in which the word cross must have constantly recurred, that established an association of ideas leading to the notion that the mark of a royal future was imprinted on the shoulder, and took the form of a cross? This would explain both the particular form of the sign and its role as the herald of destiny. Judged as one supposition against another, I certainly prefer this one to Pio Rajna's hypothesis; for in the eleventh and thirteenth centuries the Merovingian traditions—in which, moreover, there is nothing to recall the cross in reference to prospective kings—were well and truly forgotten, whereas everyone was present at Mass on Christmas Day.[160]

The belief in this royal sign was soon employed as a motif in romances. Incidentally, there cannot be much doubt that works of fiction were largely instrumental in spreading the belief. Yet there is no reason to think that it was properly speaking of literary origin: it should no doubt be considered to have grown up spontaneously in the corporate imagination. This is by no means true of another superstition we shall now study, but much more shortly, for it was in principle quite artificial, and hardly penetrated into the collective consciousness. I refer to the supposed respect shown to the royal blood by lions. This tradition was like the fables spread by the old bestiaries, yet it does not occur in these works. It begins to find expression in a fairly large number of French Anglo-Norman or English romances about the same time as the appearance of the royal cross theme; and often in the same poems as the cross. It is set forth to perfection by the author of one of the versions of *Beves of Hamtoun*, and I will quote his actual words:

> Mais coustume est, ce tesmoigne li brief,
> K'enfant de roy ne doit lyons mengier,
> Ainçois le doit garder et essauchier.[161]

This is certainly not a very ancient belief. It was unknown to the author of the *Chanson de Roland*, for he contrived a dream in which Charlemagne sees himself being attacked by a lion.[162] On the other hand, it had a good long life: its echoes can still be heard in English Elizabethan literature, in Sir Philip Sidney and even in Shakespeare, who makes very clear allusion to it through the mouth of Falstaff. In our climate, lions are not ordinarily a danger to kings or their subjects, and that for very good reasons. A superstitious theme bringing them into the picture might very likely have been in the first place no more than a piece of learned or literary imagination. In this case, however, we know that it was once used in diplomacy. When Friar Francis was holding forth to the Doge of Venice, we shall remember how he related that Edward III was willing to acknowledge Philip of Valois as king of France if he would expose his person to hungry lions and could escape unscathed from their claws. For, as he remarked, 'lions never harm a true king'.[163] In order to understand the political speeches of the Middle Ages, it is sometimes a help to read the romances on which they fed their minds. Besides, nothing could be more wrong-headed than to set literature and reality in permanent opposition to one another, for the success of fiction tinged with the miraculous in the Middle Ages can be explained by the superstitious outlook of the public to whom it was addressed. The professional story-tellers could certainly not have invented and propagated the lion motif unless their audience and readers had already been accustomed anyway to regard kings as miraculous beings.

5 Conclusions

Thus the conception of sacred royalty imbued with the miraculous runs all through the Middle Ages, as we saw at the beginning of this chapter,

1 A French king receiving Communion in both kinds and preparing to touch for scrofula. From a sixteenth-century painting in the Pinacoteca, Turin

2   A French king and St-Marcoul touching for scrofula. From a seventeenth-century altarpiece formerly in the church of St-Brice, Tournai

3   Henri IV of France touching for scrofula. An etching by Pierre Firens

without ever losing its vigour. Far from doing so, all this treasury of legends, healing rites, semi-learned and semi-popular beliefs constituting a large part of the moral strength of monarchy, was constantly on the increase. There is indeed nothing contradictory between these enrichments and the information given us by political history strictly speaking; they grew up side by side with the material progress of the Western dynasties. We ought not to be surprised at the appearance of the superstition concerning the royal mark towards the time of Philip Augustus, Henry II of England or Henry VI of Germany; nor at the blossoming of new monarchical legends under Charles V, for there is nothing here that goes against commonly held ideas. We can be quite sure through many other indications that the concept of royalty was most powerful at both these periods. But at first sight this would appear to offer a certain opposition to the general trend of events, in that under the early Capetians, for instance, the sacred character of royalty was currently attached to the person of the king at a time when the real power of royalty was very little, and the kings themselves were, in practice, often held in small esteem by their subjects. Does this mean that the phrases used by the authors of that period about the 'holiness' of monarchy were mere empty forms, devoid of any real feeling? Such a conclusion would betray a serious misunderstanding of the spirit of the age. Do not let us forget the brutal habits that are characteristic of turbulent societies; men of violence do not always manage to handle gently in practice even the things they hold in the deepest veneration. Soldiers in the Middle Ages sacked more than one church, yet we should be wrong in letting this persuade us that the Middle Ages were irreligious. But we can go still further. What ought to surprise the historian of the tenth and eleventh centuries is not, after all, the weakness of French royalty: the surprising thing is that this royalty, operating in a divided State where it no longer fulfilled any particular function, should have survived and retained enough prestige to take advantage later, from Louis VI onwards, of favourable circumstances and rapidly develop its latent energies, so that in less than a century it was able to assert itself as a great power, externally no less than internally. Does not at least part of the explanation of this long resistance and this sudden expansion lie in the intellectual conceptions and the sentiments we have been trying to analyse?

These ideas had their enemies in the shape of the partisans of Pope Gregory VII and their supporters; but in spite of these formidable adversaries, they triumphed. In the Middle Ages, men were never content with the picture of their kings as mere laymen and ordinary men. The religious and doctrinal movement of the eleventh century had been more or less successful wherever it had been supported by strong and ancient collective ideas, as in the battle for the celibacy of the clergy. The common people were always pleased to attribute a kind of magical virtue to chastity.

They would consider, for instance, that a man who had had intercourse with a woman the previous night could not be a valid witness at a trial by ordeal; and they were quite ready to maintain that for the full efficacy of the holy mysteries, a priest must abstain from all carnal impurity.[164] But because the notion of sacred royalty was so firmly entrenched in men's minds, the reformers failed in their efforts to uproot it. The long period of popularity enjoyed by the healing rites must be considered both as the effect and the proof of their failure.

IV

Some confused beliefs: St-Marcoul,
the kings of France and the seventh sons

1   *The legend and cult of St-Marcoul*

In France towards the close of the Middle Ages, the cult of a saint, St-Marcoul, became inextricably bound up with belief in the royal miracle. Let us attempt to unravel this confusion. But first of all, who was the person whose name became associated for good and all with the rite for scrofula?[1]

During the reigns of the early Carolingian emperors, there was in the diocese of Coutances, at a place called Nant, a monastery where they used to show the tomb of a pious abbot called Marcoul (Marculphus).[2] As often happens, the habit gradually grew up of calling the village clustered round the conventual buildings by the name of the monks' patron saint; and the name is probably embodied in the present day commune of St-Marcouf, not far from the sea, on the eastern coast of the Cotentin.[3] The primitive form has disappeared from the map.

On all sides in these early years of the eleventh century the religious orders in Frankish Gaul had found a new taste for letters, and were beginning to write—or re-write in better Latin—the biographies of their saints. The inmates of Nant were not behindhand in this respect, and one of them composed a Life of St-Marcoul.[4] Unfortunately this little work contains nothing but the most commonplace hagiographical fables— stories in which the devil, disguised as a fair shipwrecked maiden, pro- duces inaccurate quotations from Virgil. The only precise and perhaps credible information it contains concerns St-Marcoul's birthplace, Bayeux, and the period in which he lived, namely the time of Childebert I and Bishop St-Lô, that is to say, about the year 540.[5] A second Life, drawn up shortly after the first, only added some valueless amplifications. We must be content, in short, with a complete—or almost complete—absence of knowledge about the holy man of Nant. To judge by the Lives, the ninth century was not much better informed about him than we are.

Then came the Norman invasions. Like so many other monasteries in the Western provinces, Nant was burnt down in the course of a raid.[6] The monks had fled, taking their relics with them. No one took the trouble to tell us of the adventures of St-Marcoul on the roads of Gaul covered at that time by wandering bands of monks carrying similar treasures. We only know where the adventures finally ended. King Charles the Simple owned a property north of the Aisne, on the slopes that run down from the Craonne plateau to the river not far away, and stretching along the Roman road, called Corbeny; and here he offered asylum to the fugitives. A holy body was a precious possession, and Charles was intent upon keeping this one. Having obtained the permission of the prelates concerned, the Bishop of Coutances and the Archbishop of Rouen, he founded a monastery at Corbeny on 22 February 906, destined from then onwards to be the resting-place for these famous bones. They never returned to the Cotentin.[7]

The monks of Nant had lost their homeland, and before long they were to lose their independence too. Their new establishment was the property of the king who proceeded to marry a young girl called Frédérone and gave it to her as a dowry, together with all the surrounding estate. Some years later, when Frédérone in her turn felt that her time had come to die, she bequeathed the villa and the monastery to St-Rémi of Rheims. Truth to tell, the kings were loth to let one of their ancient family possessions be absorbed in the huge territories belonging to the Abbey of St-Rémi, especially because of its important and easily defensible military position. It provided an excellent observation-post over the whole valley, and contained some fortifications—a *castellum*—probably enclosing the whole of the monastic buildings, often mentioned in the history of the wars during this period. During his own lifetime, Charles the Simple retained possession of the little religious house where he had received the relics of 'the Confessor of Christ', in return for an annual rent. When he was dead, his son Louis the Foreigner managed to get it transferred to him on similar terms, and even added the village and land belonging to it. But in 954, on his deathbed, he restored the whole of it to St-Rémi, who was never again to lose possession of this important property. There was no longer an independent monastery at Corbeny, but only a priory, a *cellula* inhabited by a few monks under the superior authority of the Abbot of St-Rémi. And this was to be the situation right up to the time of the Revolution.[8]

At Corbeny, as at Nant, St-Marcoul had his worshippers who invoked his help for miracles and particularly for healings. But although he was considered to be a wonder-worker, like all the saints, it was a long time before he acquired any speciality. There was nothing special to mark him out particularly for the veneration of sufferers from scrofula. In the various Lives dating from the Carolingian period, there is no mention of scrofula among the cures attributed to him. From the twelfth century, we possess some particularly interesting information about the virtues commonly assigned to him. In 1101, the village of Corbeny suffered a series of appalling catastrophes, sent by Heaven, so we are told, 'as a punishment for the wickedness of the peasants': a murrain on the cattle, various depredations by soldiers, and finally a fire set alight by the troops of Thomas of Montaigu, 'a villainous and wicked tyrant, who had married his cousin'. The monks drew the greater part of their revenues from the dues levied upon their tenants, and these events therefore brought them severe financial difficulties. Their newly-appointed prior set about supplementing the ordinary resources of his house by alms. He had the idea of organizing a procession of the relics, in which the monks went through the roads of the Rémi district, the Laon region and Picardy, carrying their patron saint's reliquary on their shoulders; and everywhere they went there were miracles. We still possess a short account of this expedition.[9] Yet among all the illnesses relieved by the saint's body, there is no mention of scrofula. Rather more than a century later, there was consecrated in Coutances Cathedral a great pictorial stained glass window—which we can still admire today—in memory of the Abbot of Nant, whose cult was still alive in the diocese he had once served. It depicts only a single cure—a huntsman who, according to the Carolingian Lives, had been punished for his irreverence towards the saint by a serious hunting accident, and then had been restored to health by none other than the saint.[10] But there is still no mention of scrofula.

Nevertheless, Marcoul was destined to become the accredited doctor of this kind of affliction. The oldest testimony we have showing him in this role is unfortunately impossible to date with any precision. It is a sermon, certainly a good few years later than the relic-procession of 1101, but earlier that 1300 or thereabouts, since the first manuscript reference to it that we have clearly goes back to the end of the thirteenth century. It contains this sentence: 'This Saint has received such grace from Heaven for the healing of what is called the King's Evil that you can see crowds of sick people flocking to him [that is, to his body at Corbeny] as much from distant and barbarous parts as from the nations near at hand'.[11]

What were the reasons leading to the belief that St-Marcoul was a specialist in scrofula, about the twelfth and thirteenth centuries? As we have seen, there was nothing in the previous history of his legend to prepare men's minds for this idea. No doubt they were inclined in that direction by one of those apparently insignificant circumstances which often have the deciding voice in popular consciousness. In his *Apologie pour Hérodote* Henri Estienne wrote: 'Some saints have been assigned particular offices by virtue of their names, as for instance, among the medical saints, people have had the notion that such-and-such a saint would heal a particular disease because its name was similar to his'.[12] This remark was long ago applied to St-Marcoul. Scrofulous tumours seem to show a preference for the neck. Well, the name Marcoul—(Marculf) the final l being very lightly pronounced from early times[13]—contains the word *cou* (neck) and —what is generally forgotten—the word *mar*, an adverb often used in mediaeval language in the sense of bad or badly. Hence a sort of pun or play on words, which may have been exploited by some astute monks, and could well have been instrumental in attributing to the saint of Corbeny a special skill in healing an affliction of the neck. The credentials on St Clair, for example, as a supernatural oculist, are more obvious, but they are precisely of the same kind.

About the same time as Marcoul thus unexpectedly found himself endowed with a special power, he also became a popular saint. Up till then, before as well as after his exodus, he had hardly enjoyed more than a regional reputation, either in Neustria or in the province of Rheims. In the ninth century, there was another church besides the one at Nant—probably in Rouen—that held a part of the saint's remains. This is clearly brought out by an episode added to the traditional picture given in the older Life by the author of the second Carolingian Life, perhaps under the influence of recent events. St-Ouen, when Bishop of Rouen, as the hagiographer tells us, wanted to obtain possession of St-Marcoul's head, which had been taken out when the tomb had been opened up. But a letter, suddenly coming down from heaven, commanded him to give up his intention and be content with simply taking another fragment from the body. This little story clearly had no other object than to humble the pretensions of a rival house, and while not denying it a share in the relics, to refuse it any claim to the most precious relic of all.[14] The Neustrian versions of the great 'martyrology of St Jerome' mention St-Marcoul, but they are the only ones to do so.[15] Three French villages bear his name, all in Normandy and south of the Seine.[16]

Then came the departure for Corbeny. The fugitive saint had gained through this exile the advantage of being henceforth invoked by the pious in two different regions. He had never ceased to be remembered in his first homeland, and particularly at Coutances; and when its cathedral was rebuilt between 1208 and 1238, a chapel was dedicated to him, adorned by the fine stained glass window mentioned above. The diocesan breviaries also preserved his memory.[17] But above all he had his faithful followers at Corbeny and at Rheims, where the monastery of St-Rémi was situated, the mother house of the priory by the banks of the Aisne; and the liturgical books and legends of the archdiocese of Rheims contain a good number of references to him.[18] But for a long time his cult only covered a narrow radius. Outside Normandy, Corbeny and Rheims, he was more or less completely unknown before the fourteenth century, so it would seem, and even there—apart from Corbeny—his fame was certainly not of the first order. Neither at Rheims nor at Laon, the capital of the diocese to which Corbeny belonged, is there any effigy of him on the cathedral walls, although there were special places reserved for the regional saints.[19]

There is no mention of him in the *Chansons de geste*, which contain so many names of saints, often by way of assonance or to suit the rhyme.[20] In Vincent of Beauvais' *Speculum Historiale*, there are only a few words about St-Marcoul;[21] and he is not mentioned in the other big hagiographical compilations drawn up in France or outside in the thirteenth century or the first half of the fourteenth.[22] His name was not included in the calendar of St-Louis' psalter, and was certainly never invoked by this king.[23]

But towards the close of the Middle Ages, his name and stature increased. The most characteristic symptom of his new popularity was a distinctly impudent attempt on the part of the church of Our Lady at Mantes to claim the ownership of the saint's relics at the expense of Corbeny. At an unknown date, but certainly before the year 1383, there was discovered not far from Mantes and on the road to Rouen a grave containing three skeletons. Because of the care with which they had been buried, people thought these must be holy bodies, and their bones were taken to the neighbouring collegiate church of Notre-Dame. At first, they were at a loss what names to give them. The inventory of the furnishings of Notre-Dame drawn up in 1383 by Canon Jean Pillon shows them as still without precise identification; they were all placed in a great wooden chest—which does not suggest they were held in great respect. Rather less than a century later, on 19 December 1451, we see the Bishop of Chartres, Pierre Beschebien, presiding at their solemn translation in three reliquaries, more fitting for eminent servants of God. The fact is, as the written account of the ceremony bears witness, that in the interval between these dates identities had been assigned to the bodies. The authorities had thought they recognized in these remains—or deliberately contrived to do so—the remains of St-Marcoul himself and his two legendary companions attributed to him in the ancient Lives, called respectively Cariulphe and Domard. It was suggested that the monks from Nant, fleeing before the Normans and in danger of being overtaken by them, had only been able to preserve their precious burden by burying it in a ditch near the road. Much later on some shepherds were supposed to have had revealed to them—perhaps through their sheep—where the three bodies were buried.[24]

As was only to be expected, these inventions raised a storm of protest at Corbeny; and there followed a long polemical argument, which became particularly heated in the seventeenth century.[25] The monks of the ancient priory where Charles III had gathered together the bones of the Neustrian saint had rights firmly based upon history. They could quote authentic documents, first and foremost of which was their foundation-deed, and they were not slow to do so. But they also invoked certain signs of a more striking kind, as their fancy suggested. On Ascension Day, 21 May 1648, while St-Marcoul's reliquary was being carried in procession, a written account drawn up thirty three years later tells us that 'there suddenly appeared in the heavens three crowns, whose circular forms seemed to touch one another, and to be flecked with yellow and green and blue . . . These crowns . . . continued to hang in mid air above the reliquary'. During High Mass 'they were again seen with great distinctness. When the Mass was ended, they began to vanish one after the other.' The monks and devout followers—'more than 6,000 in number'—saw fit to take these meteoric appearances as 'public and incontrovertible testimony' vouchsafed by God himself in order to bring to nought the pretensions of the men of Mantes.[26] But it was all to no purpose: in spite of the most assured documentary evidence, and in spite of the miracles, the relics of St-Marcoul continued to be venerated at Mantes. Though they never attracted crowds of sufferers like those who came flocking to the banks of the Aisne, they still continued, so it was said, to heal some persons of the scrofula from time to time.[27]

Elsewhere, the saint's renown spread abroad more peacefully. Towards the end of the *ancien régime*, he was venerated in a fairly large number of churches, and still is today. They still often display some relics of his, and make them a centre of pilgrimage for the sick of the surrounding country. Many of the dates concerned with this pious victory defy all efforts to fix them precisely. Facts of this kind were rarely put in writing, which is a great pity, for they were for a long period one of the essential aspects of the common man's religious outlook. I have not been able to arrive at even a distant estimate of the date when Marcoul was invoked for the first time at Carentoir in the diocese of Vannes;[28] at Moutiers-en-Retz in the diocese of Nantes;[29] at St-Pierre de Saumur, and Russé near there;[30] at Charray en Dunois;[31] in the great abbey of St-Valery-sur-Somme;[32] at Montdidier, where he was chosen as the cloth merchant's patron saint;[33] at St-Pierre d'Abbeville;[34] at Rue and Cottenchy in the Amiens diocese;[35] at Ste-Elisabeth de Valenciennes; at Cysoing Abbey;[36] at St-Thomas Argonne;[37] at Balham in the Ardennes;[38] at Dinant;[39] at the Dominican Friars of Namur;[40] in various villages and small towns in the Walloon region, such as Somzée, Racour,[41] Silly, Monceau-Imbrechies, Mont-Dison;[42] at Erps, Zellick[43] and Wesembeck[44] in Brabant; at Wondelgem in Flanders;[45] and lastly in Cologne[46]—and no doubt in many other places which have eluded my research through lack of any appropriate records of the local saints. But whenever I have been able to pick up some definite or approximate indication of date, I have observed that it belongs to a relatively recent time.[47] At St-Riquier in Ponthieu, our saint was known from the fourteenth century onwards, for he is mentioned in a martyrology of this house drawn up about that time, and he was certainly venerated in a fairly active manner from the beginning of the sixteenth century at latest, as iconography bears witness.[48] In the church of St-Brice at Tournai, there was a statue and altar to him as early as the second half of the fifteenth century.[49] At Angers,[50] at Gissey in Burgundy,[51] there is evidence of his cult in the sixteenth century; and about the same time his effigy begins to figure on pious medallions, along with various local saints, in the Arras region.[52] In 1533 and 1566 the missals of the diocese of Troyes and the abbey of Cluny borrowed a prose passage in his honour from the liturgical books of St-Rémi of Rheims.[53] Likewise in the sixteenth century, a fragment of his skull stolen from Corbeny was taken to the church at Bueil in Touraine, where it subsequently began to attract the faithful.[54] In 1579, other portions of his relics, taken away by more lawful methods, gave rise to the great pilgrimage to Archelange in Franche Comté.[55] From the seventeenth century onwards, we sometimes find his name associated with the Virgin's on medallions in Notre-Dame de Liesse.[56] In 1632, thanks to the generosity of the Chapter at Angers, Coutances recovered some fragments of his body which had been seized and removed from the diocese in days gone by during the Norman invasions;[57] in 1672 Cologne sent some other fragments to Antwerp;[58] and thanks to a legacy by Anne of Austria, some others came into the hands of the Carmelites of the Place Maubert in Paris, about the year 1666.[59] Then more especially at the end of the sixteenth century and during the seventeenth, confraternities under his others came into the hands of the Carmelites of the Place Maubert in 1581,[60] at Notre-Dame, Soissons, in 1643,[61] at Grez-Doiceau, in the Duchy of Brabant, in 1663,[62] in the church of Notre-Dame du Sablon at Brussels, in 1667,[63] and even at Tournai, about 1670,[64] although the cult was already longstanding in that town. We only know of its existence among the Grey Friars at Falaise from a seventeenth century engraving.[65]

But pre-eminent above all these little local centres there was always the principal centre of St-Marcoul de Corbeny. Like Nant before, the village of Corbeny almost lost its name. From the fifteenth century onwards, the documents often call it Corbeny-St-Marcoul, or even simply St-Marcoul. It was hardly known for anything except its church. Here too a confraternity had come into existence, partly religious and partly economic; for the saint had been chosen—perhaps also by virtue of some assonance between the names—as the patron saint of the mercers in that district. Towards the beginning of the sixteenth century, we begin to see these tradesmen grouped all over France into a number of large associations under the careful scrutiny of the royal power, represented in this particular matter by the Great Chamberlain.[66] Each of these groups was presided over by a 'King of the Mercers', though he was officially known as 'Master Visitor', since the royal title would have sounded rather shocking if applied to a mere subject. One of these groups covering a large part of Champagne and Picardy was centred on the Corbeny Priory. It was known as the 'Congregation and Confraternity of St-Marcoul', and its 'king' as 'Brother Superior'. Its seal carried side by side the figures of St-Louis, the great protector of the monarchy, and St Marcoul, the great protector of the 'Congregation'. At that time, the 'mercers' were chiefly pedlars, going from one market-town to another; and one can hardly imagine any better propagandists for the cult of a particular saint.[67]

But the chief glory of Corbeny's wonder-working saint was, of course, the pilgrimage to his tomb. From the fifteenth century onwards, the monks used to sell pilgrims little medals or *bulettes* of gilded or ungilded silver, or —for the poorer sort—simple tokens in gilded silver, German silver, lead or pewter. They bore the pious abbot's effigy, and probably made his face and person familar throughout France to many who had never seen his tomb.[68] They also sold little pottery bottles containing water sanctified by the 'immersion' of one of the relics, and meant for washing the affected parts of the body. It was even sometimes drunk by the extra-zealous.[69] Later on, the monks also used to distribute little booklets.[70]

The regulations governing these pilgrimages as they existed at the beginning of the seventeenth century are known to us through a copy procured, about 1627 perhaps, by a man called Gifford, a delegate from the archbishop, and annotated in his own hand. His reflections are an extremely valuable testimony to the impression made upon an enlightened cleric of those days by the practice of popular devotion, where there was not always a very clear dividing line between religion and magic. As soon as patients arrived, they had their names inserted in the confraternity register and made a small contribution to the monks. They were then given a 'printed sheet' instructing them as to their duties. They were put under a number of restraints, dietary and otherwise. In particular, they were forbidden during their stay to touch any metal object; and this was so important that in former times, says Gifford, they had to wear gloves so as to prevent the said touching, in case any were absent-minded or careless. Of course, their primary duty was to follow the offices in the priory church. Strictly speaking, they were expected to make a novena; but those who were unable to spend nine full days at Corbeny were allowed to appoint a proxy from among the local inhabitants;[71] and this person had then to observe the same restraints as those that would have been incumbent upon the patient. In the detached view of Gifford, this custom was one of those 'not altogether free from superstition'; for in his opinion such arrangements could only be legitimate if their aim was to get patients to abstain from things that were 'naturally' harmful to them—that is, outside the sphere of the supernatural; in which case it was not at all clear how they could apply to people in perfectly good health.[72]

When the sick persons left Corbeny, they were still considered in principle as members of the confraternity, and the more conscientious would continue to pay their subscriptions from a distance.[73] The monks, for their part, did not lose sight of their visitors. They begged them, if after their 'voiage du grand St-Marcoul' they should eventually find that they had been healed of their disease, to obtain, as far as practicable, a certificate to this effect from their cure or the nearest judicial authority and send it to the monastery. There were whole files of these precious documents in the priory archives testifying to the saint's renown; and many of them have come down to us, the oldest from 17 August 1621,[74] the most recent from 17 September 1738.[75] Thay give us admirably precise information about the popularity of this sanctuary, showing that people came on pilgrimage to it not only from all parts of Picardy, Champagne and the Barrois district, but even from Hainault and the region of Liège,[76] from Alsace,[77] from ducal Lorraine,[78] from the Île de France,[79] from Normandy,[80] from Maine and Anjou,[81] from Brittany,[82] from the Nivernais, the Auxerre region and Burgundy,[83] from Berry,[84] the Auvergne,[85] the Lyons district,[86] and from Dauphiné.[87] The saint was called upon for the relief of divers diseases, but much the most frequent was scrofula.

When they returned to their native country, the Corbeny pilgrims would spread the cult of the saint at whose tomb they had gone to worship, often from great distances. At the head of the register of the confraternity at Grez-Doiceau in Brabant, opened in 1663, one can still read the regulations of the Corbeny brotherhood today.[88] There on the slopes of the Craonne plateau was the mother-house of the association; many of the local ones, at Grez-Doiceau or elsewhere, were no doubt only branches. The expansion of the cult of St-Marcoul, that we have just described, must have been largely the work of ex-patients who felt they owed a debt of gratitude to the wonder-worker whom they believed to have assuaged their sufferings.

What was the secret of the old abbot of Nant's success—or 'Nanteuil', as the place often came to be called from the sixteenth century onwards, by a strange and perhaps deliberate confusion of names? And why was his success so tremendous, but so long in arriving? Clearly, the chief factor in it was the speciality that it had become customary to attribute to him. As long as he was an ordinary healer, there seemed nothing particular to draw the faithful after him. But from the moment when he could be called upon to heal a specific disease, which was quite common, he found as it were a ready-made clientèle. His fortunes were helped, moreover, by the general evolution of religious life. He seems to have come into fashion during the last two centuries of the Middle Ages; and by the fifteenth century, his star was so much in the ascendant that an ambitious church thought it would be good business to stake a claim for his remains. During this period, Europe was laid waste by all sorts of plagues and calamities; and these—together perhaps with certain obscure movements of collective feeling, perceptible especially in their artistic expressions—gave a new direction to devotion. It became more tormented, more supplicating, so to speak; men's souls were more inclined to dwell anxiously upon the miseries of this world and to turn for relief from them to intercessors who nearly all of them had their particular specialized sphere.

Crowds flocked to the saint of scrofula, just as even larger ones did to the feet of St Christopher, St Roch, St Sebastian, or the Fourteen Helpers. His growing fame was only a particular example of the unanimous favour being shown to the doctor-saints at that same period.[89] In the same way the spreading of his renown in the following centuries coincides with the vigorous and successful efforts of many active Catholics in reaction against the Reformation. They strove to revive the cult of the saints among the masses by founding confraternities, procuring relics, and showing preference for those servants of God who seemed likely to attract suffering humanity in more lively fashion by virtue of their power over specific diseases. There are thus a good many reasons of a universal kind that explain St-Marcoul's new popularity. Yet it was also largely due, without the slightest doubt, to the close association which had gradually grown up in men's minds between his name and the royal dynasty. It is no mere chance that the mercers' seal bore the two conjoint images of St-Louis and St-Marcoul, for each in his own particular way was a saint of the House of France. Let us now see how this unexpected role came to the patron of Corbeny.

2 St-Marcoul and the wonder-working power of the French kings

Who was the first king to come and pay his devotions at St-Marcoul's tomb after his coronation? When this question was put to the monks in the seventeenth century, they would answer 'St-Louis'.[90] This idea, which was so flattering to them, had no doubt been suggested by the saintly king's effigy engraved upon the confraternity's seal. But it would seem that they were in fact mistaken, for St Louis was consecrated while still a child on 26 November 1226, in great haste and in conditions of insecurity extremely unfavourable to an innovation that would have delayed the young prince's return to his faithful Parisians. Besides, in Philip the Fair's reign the tradition of this solemn pilgrimage was certainly not yet firmly established. We know the itinerary followed by the royal retinue in 1286, after this sovereign's consecration: it cut south-westwards in a straight line, without making a detour towards the Aisne valley. Louis X, when he left Rheims in 1315, may have visited Corbeny; but if this is so, it must be admitted that Philip of Valois did not take this as a binding precedent, for in 1328 he followed more or less the same route as Philip the Fair. But from the time of John the Good, who stopped at Corbeny two days after his coronation, no king up to Louis XIV seems to have omitted this pious custom—except, of course, Henry IV, because the League were in possession of Rheims, and he was therefore forced to receive unction at Chartres. A whole ceremonial developed, which we find clearly described in an early seventeenth-century document. A procession would go to meet the illustrious visitor; the prior carried the saint's head and placed it in the 'sacred hands' of the king, who took possession of it, and brought it back to the church himself, or handed it over to his almoner. On reaching the church, he knelt in prayer before the saint's reliquary.[91] In the fifteenth century a special pavilion was erected among the conventual buildings called 'the royal pavilion', which served from then onwards as the royal quarters.[92]

Louis XIV modified the old custom. When he was consecrated in 1654, the town of Corbeny had been reduced to ruins by warfare. Moreover, the country round may also not have been very safe. Mazarin did not want to risk letting the young sovereign go outside Rheims. So St-Marcoul's reliquary was fetched from Corbeny to the Abbey of St-Rémi in Rheims itself, and the pilgrimage was thus able to take place without any inconvenience to the royal pilgrim. This seemed to be an agreeable procedure, and it was imitated, under various pretexts, by Louis XV and Louis XVI.[93] Henceforward, the kings no longer undertook the inconvenient journey to Corbeny; but somehow or other, they were still bound to pay their devotions to St-Marcoul. About the time of the early Valois, prayers before the relics of this saint had become an indispensable rite, which had almost necessarily to follow the solemnities of coronation; and such they remained up to the end of the monarchy. By Charles VII's time, it was commonly thought that this had always been so. 'Now it is true', says the *Chronique de la Pucelle*, 'that at all times the kings of France have been accustomed to go after their coronation to a priory . . . called Corbeny'.[94]

What inspiration first caused the king—let us say Louis X—to leave the usual road from Rheims and turn aside towards Corbeny? From that moment onwards, St-Marcoul, whose great popularity was already growing, was considered as a healer of scrofula. Was this the reason why the French prince, who himself specialized in the same illness, turned aside to seek the saint? By offering his devotions to a saint whom God seemed particularly to have entrusted with the cure of scrofula sufferers, did he hope that the saint's protection would bring him the power to work even finer cures than before? Such indeed we may imagine to have been his feelings. But of course no one has made it his business to leave us a precise record. On the other hand, we can clearly see that this was the notion quickly spread among men's minds by the pilgrimages, once they had become part of the customs and habits of the time.

Up till then, the wonder-working powers of the French kings had been considered a result of their sacred character, expressed in and sanctioned by unction. From this time onwards, people became accustomed to the idea that they were due to St-Marcoul's intercession, which had procured this signal grace from God. Such was the general belief in the time of Charles VIII and Louis XI. We have testimony to this in Jean Chartier, the author of the *Chronique de la Pucelle* and Lefèvre de Saint-Rémi, the author of the *Journal du Siège*, as well as in Martial d'Auvergne and Aeneas Piccolomini.[95]

In Francis I's day, the gift of miraculous power manifested by kings was almost universally attributed, as Fleuranges tells us, to this 'most meritorious' of saints.[96] And this was also the report gathered from court circles when the traveller Hubert Thomas of Liège passed that way.[97] But when he subsequently wrote up his memoirs, he became confused about French hagiography, and attributed to St-Fiacre what he had been told about St-Marcoul. This proves that the fame of the Corbeny saint in his new role had hardly had time to spread across the frontiers, though it was already firmly established in France.

If only the kings had confined themselves to attending a religious service and saying a few prayers before the relics of St-Marcoul! But quite early on there was added to these pious rites, the current coin of all pilgrimages, a practice better calculated to confirm the saint's reputation as the author of the royal miracle. When he had finished his devotions, the new sovereign would there and then in the priory lay his hands on some sick folk. The earliest testimony we have of this practice refers to Charles VIII in 1484. No doubt this was not at that time a very ancient custom, for the sufferers from scrofula had not yet adopted the habit of flocking to Corbeny when the king went there after consecration. There were only six who sought the presence of Charles VIII; but under Louis XII, fourteen years later, there were already eighty; and in Henry II's time, there were also a number of foreigners included in the company. In the seventeenth and eighteenth centuries, hundreds or even thousands thronged to Corbeny on such an occasion, or—since Louis XVI's time—to the grounds of St-Rémi in Rheims. But there is a further point to be made. At least since Louis XII's reign, and perhaps even earlier, this laying on of hands at the reliquary was the first to take place in each reign; before that day, no patient had access to the august healer. It is very tempting to explain this rule by supposing that before proceeding to heal, kings needed to wait until they had received from the saint the power to do so. This was at any rate the general opinion, and it may well have been shared by the kings themselves.[98]

The canons of Rheims viewed the new theory with great disfavour. It seemed to them to weaken the prestige of unction, which they considered the true source of the miraculous power to heal scrofula, and so—indirectly —to impugn the honour of their cathedral in which the successors of Clovis had come to receive consecration with the holy oil. They took advantage of the festivities marking Charles VIII's coronation in May 1484 to make a strong reaffirmation of the ancient doctrine. In his speech at the city gate to the youthful king, on 29 May, the dean reminded him that it would be to unction that he owed 'the divine and heavenly gift of healing and alleviating the pains of those poor sufferers from the diocese we are all familiar with'. But mere words were not enough: pictures were more effective for striking the imagination of the masses and the prince himself. All along the processional route to be followed by the sovereign and his train once they had crossed the ramparts they had put up, as was then the custom, 'stages' with a whole series of *tableaux vivants* recalling the most famous memories or the most splendid privileges of the monarchy. On one of these stages there was 'a young lad arrayed in an azure robe studded with golden fleurs-de-lis, wearing a golden crown upon his head'—in short, an actor representing a king of France, and a young king at that. Round about him were servents 'pouring out water for him to wash in', and sick persons whom he 'healed by touching them and signing them with the Cross'. This was in effect a representation of the royal touch, as Charles VIII was shortly to practise it. Underneath was an inscription carrying some lines composed, no doubt, by one of the gentlemen of the Chapter, probably the poet Guillaume Coquillart:

> En la vertu de la saincte Onction
> Qu'a Rheims reçoit le noble Roy de France
> Dieu par ses mains confere guerison
> D'escrouëllez, voicy la demonstrance.

This 'representation' and the four lines of verse which described it were evidently designed to highlight the 'power of the holy unction'. But 'as they passed before the aforesaid scene' the horsemen in the procession were in somewhat of a hurry, and merely gave it a cursory glance, without stopping to read the placard. They only noticed that it was a scene representing the healing of scrofula, and imagined 'it was a miracle wrought by St-Marcoul'; and this is what they said to the royal child, who no doubt believed them. The saint's reputation had so entered into the common consciousness that everything worked in his favour, even the insinuations of his opponents.[99]

If the canons of Rheims thought that their honour was involved in the renown of royal unction, all the more so did the various religious communities deriving prestige and profit from the cult of St-Marcoul. They were bound to give their utmost support to the theory basing the royal wonder-working powers upon this saint's intercession. First and foremost, of course, were his chief supporters, the monks of Corbeny. But there were others too. We know that at least since the fourteenth century the great abbey of St-Riquier in Ponthieu had paid him particular veneration. Soon after 1521, the community's treasurer, Philip Wallois, decided to decorate with frescoes the treasury chamber of which he had official control. One can still see today the full pictorial scene running round the panels of this fine room with its delicate rib vaulting, to a design probably sketched out by himself; and among these scenes he took good care to include St-Marcoul. In a boldly conceived picture, he is shown in the very act of imparting the marvellous gift. The Abbot of Nant is standing, holding his crozier; and at his feet kneels a French king in grand array, wearing a crown, a cloak with fleur-de-lis, and the collar of the order of St Michael. The saint is touching the prince's chin with his holy hand, with the gesture in which the king was usually represented on miniatures and engravings when touching for scrofula, since this illness normally attacked the glands in the neck. The artist could think of no more eloquent way of indicating to everyone the transference of healing power. Beneath the picture there is a Latin inscription making the meaning quite clear, which may be translated as follows:

O Marcoul, thy sufferers from scrofula receive from thee, great doctor, the gift of perfect health; and thanks to the gift thou bestowest upon him, the king of France, who is also a doctor, enjoys an equal power over the scrofula. May I then, through thee, who art resplendent with so many miracles, be granted grace to come safely at the last to the starry courts of heaven.[100]

Prayers had no doubt always accompanied the ceremony of the royal touch; but we know nothing of them before Henry II's reign, nor indeed subsequently. But for this prince there was composed a magnificent Book of Hours, a treasure of French art. On folio 108 of this manuscript, opposite a miniature of the king going from one sick person to another in a covered passage of classical architectural style, are the following words: '*Les oraisons qu'ont acoustumé dire les Roys de France quand ilz veulent toucher les malades des escrouelles*'. What does it contain? Simply a number of antiphons and responses in honour of St-Marcoul. These are indeed very commonplace compositions: their specific content consists purely and simply of material culled from the lives of the saint written in Carolingian times, and they contain no allusion to him as the initiator of the royal miracle.[101] Nevertheless if the king thought himself bound to pay his devotions to this same servant of God whom he had gone to venerate at Corbeny before attempting to heal for the first time—bound so to do every time he accomplished the customary miracle—this is clear evidence that he felt an obligation to express his gratitude to the saint for the marvellous power he was preparing to display to the eyes of all men. The liturgy for scrofula was a kind of acknowledgment of the glory of St-Marcoul, given by the kings, or by the clergy of their chapel.

The belief had thus become almost officially established by about the middle of the sixteenth century, and persisted through subsequent centuries. In 1690, the Abbot of St-Riquier, Charles d'Aligre, was intent upon reviving the splendour of his church, which had been ruined by warfare and the commendam system. He conceived the idea of commissioning from the best artists of the time a whole series of altar pictures, and he dedicated one of them to the glory of St-Marcoul, entrusting the work to an acknowledged painter of religious scenes, the worthy and prolific Jean Jouvenet. Under Louis XIV, a work referring to the royal miracle could not fail to put the king in the foreground, and in Jouvenet's canvas, carried out with his usual solid matter-of-factness, you see at first glance only a monarch, with the features of Louis XIV, touching the scrofulous. But then you pick out a little to his right, slightly in the background, as was fitting and proper, and even a little hidden by the royal doctor, an abbot bowing his head as though in prayer, with a halo round his head. This is St-Marcoul, present there at the rite his intercession has made possible. About the same time, at St-Wulfran of Abbeville, quite close to St-Riquier, an unknown painter, perhaps under the inspiration of Jean Jouvenet's model, also portrayed Louis XIV performing the healing act; and alongside the great king he placed St-Marcoul. In the church of St-Brice at Tournai there was another altar picture,* painted no doubt when the town belonged to France, between 1667 and 1713, by a talented artist thought to be Michel Bouillon, who had a school there between 1639 and 1677. Side by side in the picture are the Abbot of Nant, mitred like a bishop, and a French king with rather indeterminate features, draped in an ermine-lined cape decorated with fleur-de-lis. In his left hand the prince holds a sceptre, the churchman a crozier; their right hands are raised in almost the same gesture of blessing for the sick who crowd round their feet in dramatic postures. A similar motif occurs in works of lesser importance. In 1638 Don Oudard Bourgeois, prior of Corbeny, when publishing his *Apologie pour Saint Marcoul*, gave it a frontispiece depicting a king—this time duly provided with the little pointed beard characteristic of Louis XIII—stretching out his hand over a sick person; and as a third figure, there is the priory saint. Here again are two productions probably also dating from the seventeenth century, appealing to the popular piety of the time: an engraving by H. Hébert, and a medallion struck for the church of Ste-Croix at Arras. Both of them portray a king and St-Marcoul face to face, and there is only one important difference between them. On the engraving, as in the St-Riquier treasury fresco— and perhaps in imitation of it—the saint is touching the king's chin; but on the medallion, he is laying hands on him. Yet both gestures express the same idea—the idea of a supernatural transmission of power.

Finally, let us glance outside the boundaries of France. On 27 April 1683 a confraternity had been founded at Grez-Doiceau in Brabant, in honour of our saint. According to the Low Countries' custom, pilgrims were given pictures in the form of pennons known as *drapelets ;* and we still have a Grez-Doiceau *drapelet* dating apparently from the eighteenth century. At the feet of St-Marcoul, and kissing a round object—no doubt a reliquary—held out to him by the saint, is a French king, dressed as usual in a long cloak embroidered with fleur-de-lis. Beside him on a cushion are the sceptre and crown. Thus even on foreign soil people could hardly imagine the saint without the accompanying figure of the king. Everywhere iconography was spreading the idea that this ancient saint, of whom so little was known—hermit founder of an abbey, and the devil's antagonist in Merovingian times—had been instrumental in the origin, and was active in the continuance, of the royal healing power.[102]

* Until its destruction by fire in 1940.

What really was the saint's role? Perhaps ideas on this point have never been very clear, for the earliest notion, which had seen the miraculous virtue of kings as an expression of their sacred power, had never altogether disappeared. Moreover, over a long period there had scarcely been any reason to discuss the problem. But towards the close of the sixteenth century and at the beginning of the seventeenth, when the upholders of absolutism attempted, in reply to the 'opponents of monarchy', to exalt the prestige of royalty, they conceded—as we shall see—a fairly large place to the miraculous healing of scrofula. Their primary object was to bring out the divine character of the royal power, so they could not accept as the origin of the miraculous virtues of the royal touch anything else but that selfsame divine character, which they held to be ratified, and even reinforced, by the rites of consecration. For as we shall be seeing in due course, they did not share with regard to these religious solemnities the intransigence formerly shown by the author of the *Somnium Viridarii*. They tended either to keep silence about the influence commonly attributed to St-Marcoul, or even to deny it explicitly. This was for example the attitude of the jurist Forcatel, who is simply silent on the subject, and of the doctor du Laurens, and of the almoner Guillaume du Peyrat, who indulge in polemics against the saint's partisans.[103] Moreover, they argued, had not St Thomas Aquinas, as they interpreted him—confusing him in fact with his continuator Tolomeo of Lucca—had not he expressly attributed to holy unction the cures performed by the Capetians? Even the patron of Corbeny's defenders, like prior Oudard Bourgeois, no longer claimed more for him than a secondary role in the origins of the royal touch. 'I do not wish to infer', he writes in so many words, 'what has been maintained by some, that our kings owe their power to cure the scrofula to the intercession of St-Marcoul . . . The sacring of our kings is the prime source of this gift'. St-Marcoul's part, then, would have been confined to 'assuring' this grace (that is, obtaining a confirmation and continuance of it from God) in gratitude for the benefits received by him from Childebert (for it was believed that all the Merovingians from Clovis onwards had performed healings.) But this was an awkward effort to reconcile two sharply contradictory theories.[104]

Contradictions of this kind, however, were hardly any impediment to public opinion. The majority of the sick were pilgrims to Corbeny or seekers of the royal touch; and they continued vaguely in the notion that the Abbot of Nant played some sort of part in the royal miraculous power, without troubling their heads about the precise way in which his action operated. This belief is naively expressed in several of the healing certificates preserved in the Corbeny archives. They show that in the seventeenth century certain scrofula sufferers who had been touched by the king thought they could only obtain complete relief if they then went and made a novena at the tomb of St-Marcoul. Or they would express their thanksgivings in that direction; for even when they had been touched by the royal hand and found themselves free of their ills without the intervention of any other pious practices, they still thought the saint's intercession had somehow contributed to the miracle.[105] And the monks at the priory encouraged these ideas.

The regulations for the Corbeny pilgrimage drawn up about 1633, preserved in the Confraternity register at Grez-Doiceau in Brabant, read word for word as follows: 'In a case where he [the patient] is touched by the Most Christian King (the only one of all the princes on this earth who possesses this divine power to heal the scrofula through the merits of this blessed saint), [he] must, after being touched, come in person or send a deputy to have himself registered in the said confraternity, and must then make there, or cause to be made on his behalf, a novena, and then send to the aforesaid Corbeny a certificate of his healing, signed by the Curé or the Justice of his home.'[106] On the other hand the Rheims Chapter, as in the past, continued to view with disfavour this bid on the part of the saint for a share in the royal anointing. On 17 September 1657 a woman in Rheims, Nicolle Regnault, who had formerly suffered from scrofula and had now recovered her health, produced a double certificate of cure on the same piece of paper. One was signed by the Curé of St-Jacques of Rheims, M. Aubry, who was also a Canon of the metropolitain church. It testifies that Nicolle 'having been touched by the king at the time of his consecration was healed thereby'; there is no mention of St-Marcoul. The second was given by the treasurer of Corbeny. This monk testified that the sick woman 'has been perfectly healed by the intercession of the blessed St-Marcoul,' to whom she then made her novena by way of thanksgiving; and there is no mention in it of the king.[107] As for the higher ecclesiastical authorities, the prestige of unction had become one of the firmest links between the Church and royalty, and they set equal store by the cult of the popular saints. They were therefore in no hurry to decide the matter one way or the other. Their desire to have it both ways is perfectly expressed in the treatise *On the beatification and canonization of the servants of God*, the work of Cardinal Prospero Lambertini, later to become Pope Benedict XIV, that witty man to whom Voltaire dedicated his *Mahomet*. In Book IV of this famous work, which is still said to be authoritative for the Congregation of Rites, we read these words: 'the kings of France have received the privilege of healing scrofula . . . by virtue of a favour graciously imparted to them, either at the conversion of Clovis . . . [the unction theory] or when St-Marcoul begged this favour from God for all the kings of France'.[108] After all, as Marlot roundly observes, 'it is not impossible to possess one and the same thing under two different titles'.[109]

Truth to tell, St-Marcoul was an intruder into the theory of the royal miracle, and he never enjoyed complete success. But how is this intrusion to be explained? There is nothing whatsoever in his legend to justify it, in general or in particular; for when we read in the ancient lives that he received some presents from Childebert, there is no mention (in spite of what Oudard Bourgeois says) of his being in return '*magnifique à l'endroit de Sa Majesté*',[110] that is, obtaining for the king some marvellous gift, or at least a 'continuation' of such a gift. The idea of the saint's intercession arose towards the end of the Middle Ages from the spectacle of the early royal pilgrimages to his tomb, which were interpreted as acts of gratitude in return for benefits received; and this interpretation was subsequently saddled upon the kings themselves, for it was clearly to the advantage of the communities of confraternities interested in the cult of this saint that the idea should spread far and wide. Such at any rate were the incidental circumstances which enable us to give some account of why this curious conception, which has no parallel at all in England,[111] should have developed in France at the end of the Middle Ages. Yet it cannot be fully understood without considering it first and foremost as an example of the general tendency of the popular consciousness towards the confusion of beliefs; or if one may venture to borrow a term from classical philology, one might call it the 'contamination' of beliefs. There had been French kings since the eleventh century more or less who had healed scrofula; there was also in the same country a saint to whom a similar power was attributed one or two centuries later, and the illness had been called both the 'King's Evil' and 'St-Marcoul's disease';[112] surely there must be some connection between these two marvels? The popular mind sought for a link between them, and because it sought, it found one. We shall see that it was thus obeying a constant need of collective psychology if we now go on to study the history of another contamination of the same kind, in which the wonder-working kings and the saint of Corbeny were both simultaneously involved.

3   The seventh sons, the kings of France and St-Marcoul

From time immemorial, certain numbers have been considered to be endowed with a sacred or magical character, pre-eminently the figure 7.[113] It should therefore not seem surprising that in a good many different countries a particular supernatural power was attributed to the seventh son, or, more precisely, to the last representative of a continuous series of seven sons with no intervening daughters. Sometimes, but much more rarely, it was attributed to the seventh daughter at the end of an uninterrupted series of the same sex. This power sometimes takes on an unpleasant and on the whole rather annoying character for its recipient. In certain regions of Portugal, it seems, seventh sons are thought to change into asses every Saturday—I do not know whether voluntarily or not—and in this guise may be hunted by dogs until dawn.[114] But this power is nearly always thought of as beneficent; and in some places the seventh son is held to be a magician.[115] Above all, and almost everywhere, he is looked upon—and likewise a seventh daughter—as a born healer, a *panseux de secret*, as they say in Berry,[116] or, in Poitou, a *touchou*.[117] This kind of belief has been, and no doubt still is, very widespread in central and western Europe. It has been noted in Germany,[118] Biscay,[119] Catalonia,[120] and over almost the whole of France,[121] in the Low Countries,[122] in England,[123] Scotland[124] and Ireland,[125] and even outside Europe, so it is said, in Lebanon.[126]

Is this a very ancient belief? As far as I know, the first testimonies we have on this subject go back to the beginning of the sixteenth century. I have not come across anything earlier than Cornelius Agrippa's reference to it in his *De Occulta Philosophia*, first published in 1533.[127] Are we to believe that before thus emerging into the world of books this superstition —apparently unknown to the ancient world—had for a long time been in existence during the Middle Ages without leaving any written evidence? It may be so; and it is also possible that some mention of it will be discovered one day in mediaeval texts that have escaped my notice.[128] But I am inclined to believe that it only became really popular in modern times; for it would seem to have owed a good deal of its popularity to the little printed volumes hawked about on the chapmen's trays, which from about the sixteenth century onwards placed the old hermetical knowledge, and in particular the speculations about numbers, within the reach of simple people, whereas before this time they had not been at all familiar with such matters.[129] In 1637, a certain William Gilbert, of Prestleigh in Somerset, who had seven successive sons, employed the last of them, called Richard, to 'touch' the sick. At the same time, for reasons that will be later apparent, Charles I's government was taking quite stern measures against this kind of healer. The Bishop of Wells, to whose diocese Prestleigh belonged, was instructed to institute an enquiry into Gilbert's case; and he was thus able to learn— and we must be duly grateful for his report—how little Richard had began working his cures. A yeoman of the neighbourhood had a niece who suffered from scrofula; and he remembered having read in a book entitled *A thousand notable things of Sundry Sortes* that this illness could be cured by a seventh son. So he sent the little girl to the Gilberts, and she became the child-doctor's first patient.[130] Now we know the work in which the yeoman discovered this valuable information. It was composed by a certain Thomas Lupton, and published for the first time in 1579; it went through a good number of editions.[131] We may well believe that more than one father with seven sons borrowed from it, either directly, or, like William Gilbert, through a second party, the idea of utilizing the miraculous talent imparted to the last-born of this splendid series of sons. For that matter, Lupton himself cannot be considered in this particular case as the direct interpreter of a popular tradition; for he too owed something to books, and had the honesty to say so. Strangely enough, his chief source was a foreign work, *Memorabilium, utilium ac iucundorum Centuriae novem* by the French doctor and astrologer Antoine Mizauld; and it was from this that he drew the information destined to settle the vocation of the youthful healer of Prestleigh.[132] This book, too, was reprinted many times after its first appearance in 1567, particularly in Germany. Who will ever know how many of those *touchoux* in various countries owed to this book, at first or second hand, the inspiration that decided their careers? There may have been other similar books elsewhere with the same effect. For the results of printing throughout the world were not solely to further the progress of rational thought.

What diseases were these *septennaires*—to give them the name by which they were often called in ancient France—supposed to relieve? In the beginning, they probably dealt with all diseases indiscriminately. Moreover in Germany their powers would seem to have kept this general character. But elsewhere they tended to specialize, though without losing all influence over illnesses as a whole. In different countries they were given different skills: in Biscay and Catalonia, it was the bites of mad dogs; in France, Great Britain and Ireland, it was scrofula.[133] Our oldest documents, starting from Cornelius Agrippa, Antoine Mizauld and Thomas Lupton, already display them in the role of doctors for scrofula, in which they are still met with today in certain country districts on either side of the Channel. What was the source of this particular virtue? It is very striking that it should have been attributed to them precisely in the two countries where kings also exercised this power.[134] Not that belief in the cures performed by seventh sons originally had any connection with faith in the royal miracle, for it was born of quite different conceptions, and, we might almost say, quite a different sort of magic. But there is no doubt that in France and in the states under the English Crown men had become accustomed to look upon scrofula as a disease essentially connected with extraordinary methods. Jean Golein calls it 'a miraculous disease'; and an English seventeenth-century pamphlet 'a supernatural evil'.[135]

In France and the British countries of the sixteenth and seventeenth centuries there were many seventh-son practitioners. In England, several of them were serious competitors with the sovereign, for certain sick persons preferred to turn to them rather than to the king.[136] Charles I and his advisers were jealously on the defensive in this, as in all other points concerning the royal prerogatives; and they therefore persecuted these rivals with severity. In France they seem generally to have been left in peace, and were likewise extremely successful.[137] All circles of society were conversant with their exploits, though people of good sense like Madame de Sévigné or the Princess Palatine only talked of them with a touch of irony.[138] Several of these healers are known to us. There was a student at Montpellier who practised his art about 1555;[139] a hermit at Hyères in Provence, about whom one of his admirers, who has remained anonymous, wrote in 1643 a *Traité curieux de la guérison des écrouelles par l'attouchement des septennaires*, worthy to figure as one of the most singular monuments of human stupidity;[140] in 1632, the son of a tailor at Clermont-en-Beauvaisis; and at the same time a professed member of the Carmelite convent in the Place Maubert, Paris.[141] This last person practised his calling with the full approval of his superiors, a sign that the Church had not officially condemned this superstition. Moreover, we shall be seeing in a moment how the monks at Corbeny turned this business to good account. But of course the stricter and the more enlightened ecclesiastics were decidedly disapproving. We have a very curt letter from Bossuet to the Abbess of Faremoutiers, who was interested in a young man said to possess this gift: 'Permit me, Madam, to have the honour to inform you that I have only had dealings with these seventh sons in order to prevent them from deceiving the world by exercising their so-called prerogative, which is altogether without foundation'.[142] The same conclusion is reached by Jean Baptiste Thiers in 1679, in his *Traité des Superstitions*, and in 1704 by Jacques de Sainte-Beuve in his *Résolutions de plusieurs cas de conscience*.[143] As might be expected, these doctors' opinions were no bar to the survival of this belief. I have already pointed out that in some places it has survived up to the present day. Towards the middle of the nineteenth century, a peasant from the small village of Vovette in Beauce, the seventh of a succession of sons, carried on a very fruitful practice as such over a good many years.[144]

Thus France under the *ancien régime* possessed three different kinds of scrofula healers, all equally miraculous, and all thought to be equally endowed with power: a saint—St-Marcoul, the kings, and the seventh sons. The power attributed to them had a quite different psychological origin for each of these categories. For St-Marcoul, it was a general belief in the miraculous virtues and the intercession of the saints; for the kings (in principle, and with the necessary reservations respecting the late legend of Corbeny), it was the conception of sacred royalty; and finally for the seventh sons, what were really pagan speculations about the magic powers of numbers. But these diverse elements were brought together and amalgamated in the popular mind; and for the seventh sons, as well as for the kings, the tendency to 'contamination' was clearly at work.

It was a fairly widespread opinion among the common people that individuals endowed with particular magical powers carried a distinctive mark on their bodies at birth, indicating their talents and sometimes their illustrious origin. Such for instance was the wheel, 'entire or broken', testified to by several authors of the sixteenth and seventeenth centuries, seen on the 'family of St Catherine'. (The wheel had become the emblem of this saint, having originally been the instrument of her martyrdom.) Such again—according to the same writers—was the 'figure' shaped like a serpent shown by 'the relations of St Paul', 'imprinted upon their flesh', the relations who were thought in Italy to have inherited from the apostle to the gentiles the gift of healing poisonous snake-bites.[145] And the seventh sons were no exception. In Biscay and in Catalonia, people thought they saw a cross on their tongues or palates.[146] In France, the sign attributed to them by public credulity took another and more specific shape—that of a fleur-de-lis, which, people said, was imprinted from birth upon their skin; some even said on the thigh. This superstition appears in the seventeenth century.[147] At that period, were there still many people who thought that kings too were born with a mark of this kind? In his *Monarchie sainte, historique, chronologique et généalogique de France*, Father Dominique de Jésus attempted with absurd ingenuity to make as many family links as possible between the saints and the royal dynasty. When he reached St Leonard of Noblat, he gave the following proof of the relationship of this pious abbot to the House of France: 'One can see on his bare head a lily imprinted by nature, as I myself have seen and touched in the year sixteen hundred and twenty four'.[148] This, it would seem, is a distorted echo, as it were, of the old belief. I do not know of any other written evidence for the same period. No doubt it gradually died out about that time; and we should probably see in the miraculous mark attributed to the seventh sons one of its last manifestations. There can indeed be no doubt that this lily was commonly held to be the royal lily. The Jesuit René de Ceriziers in 1633 and the Rheims priest Regnault in 1722 both consider it to be a proof that the power of the 'seventh sons comes from the credit enjoyed in heaven by our kings'.[149] But this is already a half-rationalized interpretation: we shall remain closer to the popular truth if we simply say that the masses, with a minimal respect for logic, established a mysterious relationship between the magicians, who were born healers of scrofula, and the kings of France. And the outward expression of the former was a congenital sign on their bodies, reproducing the emblem characteristic of the Capetian coat-of-arms, and like the mark that the kings themselves had long been believed to carry, and perhaps were sometimes still believed to carry. Moreover, that was certainly not the only expression of this relationship. During the seventeenth century, before they began to practise their art, the seventh sons may well have sought the royal touch for themselves, so as to borrow through this contact, as it were, a little of its magnetism.[150] And even today in certain country parts their virtue is considered specially efficacious if their parents have taken the precaution to give them the name Louis. This tradition is clearly nothing but a memory of the times when the French kings bore this name from generation to generation.[151] We can see from this last example that this kind of superstition, originating in a monarchical outlook, sometimes even survived the monarchy itself. The same is true of the fleur-de-lis. As late as the middle of the nineteenth century, the healer at Vovette, who did so well out of the chance of his birth, used to display the heraldic imprint, which he claimed to have had ever since he was born, on the tip of one of his fingers. When occasion required, ingenuity was able to supplement nature. In the sixteenth and seventeenth centuries, it was strongly suspected that the 'relatives of St Catherine' and of St Paul used artificial means to produce marks like the wheel or the serpent, of which they were so proud.[152] In 1854, Dr Menault wrote an interesting article on the man from Vovette. Its tone is distinctly sceptical. He assures his readers that charlatans of this sort, if unfortunate enough to be born without the mark, would make one for themselves by means of cuts in the skin that left scars of the required shape.[153] Such was the final avatar of the 'sign' of the French kings.

The relationship with St-Marcoul was much closer still. Quite early on—but not before the beginning of the seventeenth century—the seventh sons placed themselves under the protection of the heavenly doctor of scrofula. Most of them would intercede with him on each occasion before touching the sick. But they went further still. At the beginning of their career, and even before they started to practise, they would nearly all go and carry out a novena at Corbeny. In observing these customs, they were once more imitating the French kings, or rather, obeying the same feeling that had sent the princes on their pilgrimage to the banks of the Aisne, and that was also expressed, as we have seen, in the liturgy of the royal miracle. In order to perform notable cures, they thought it as well to make sure at the outset of the intercession of the great protector of the scrofulous—'*tes* scrofuleux', to give the actual words of the inscription to St-Marcoul at St-Riquier, quoted above. They preferred to practise their art on the saint's days; and they sometimes even ventured to heal in the name of St-Marcoul. In short, they contracted what might be called, in all reverence, a kind of pious alliance with him.[154]

After all, at such a time and in such circles, nothing could have been more natural than such an association. A study of popular traditions offers us another example, similar in all points, but this time outside France. In Catalonia, the seventh sons were called *setes* or even *saludadors*, but they were not concerned with sufferers from scrofula: as we already know, their speciality was rabies. As healers of suspected bites, and as the possessors of secrets calculated to preserve both man and beast in advance against their bad effects, they were still exercising their art with enviable success during the last century, in Spanish Catalonia, and sometimes even in Roussillon. Now throughout the Iberian Peninsula, there is one heavenly intercessor above all others against rabies—a woman saint little known to historians, but possessing nonetheless a great many followers, namely St Quiteria.[155] Just as in France a common ability to relieve the same illness had established certain common bonds between the seventh sons and St-Marcoul, so in Catalonia a similar vocation gave rise to links between the *saludadors* and St Quiteria. The *saludadors* used to give their patients a cross to kiss that was said to belong to St Quiteria; and before blowing upon the sore and sucking it, which was their habitual remedy, they would address a short prayer to this saint. They would not begin their practice before they had paid a visit to a church where she was specially venerated—such as the abbey at Bezalu: there they would make their devotions, and after producing a certificate stating the details of their birth, they would be given by the monks a rosary with large beads, ending in this cross, which they were to get all their future patients to kiss.[156]

It is worth while reflecting upon this last feature, for it gives a clear picture of certain individual wills pursuing a well-defined line of policy. The idea of such collaboration between a saint and a magician must have grown up almost spontaneously in the minds of the people or the *saludadors* themselves; but the monks presiding over the cult of this saint must also have encouraged it. In the same way, the monks at Corbeny in France encouraged the seventh sons to link up with their patron saint, thus serving the interests of their house. These very popular healers might well have become formidable rivals to the pilgrimage. But the link established between them and St-Marcoul turned them, on the contrary, into his propaganda agents, especially when they followed the monk's invitation to make it compulsory for their patients to join the Corbeny confraternity. So there grew up between the seventh sons and the ancient community founded by Charles the Simple a real *entente*; and it so happens that we still possess two documents, both of the year 1632, which reveal some extremely interesting effects of this bond.

The prior at that time was the self-same Dom Oudard Bourgeois, whom we have already seen writing to defend his house's glory, which was disputed by the people of Mantes. He was an extremely busy and active man, and it was to him that the church was indebted for a new High Altar, in the style of the time.[157] In fact, he worked in all possible ways to establish the prosperity of the institution under his care. Whenever a seventh son made his appearance at Corbeny, armed with an extract from his parish register, stating, beyond all possibility of fraud, that he was indeed the seventh successive son, without any intervening females, he would first pay his devotions and then receive from Dom Oudard a certificate officially licensing him as a healer of scrofula. A copy would be filed in the priory archives. Two documents of this kind have come down to us, one relating to Elie Louvet, the son of a tailor at Clermont,[158] and the other to Antoine Baillet, a professed member of the Carmelites of the Place Maubert. Their naive composition is not lacking in zest. Here are the essential passages of the second one[159] (here given in translation, but see p. 375 for the original, with the fanciful spelling characteristic of the *grand siècle*):

We, Dom Oudard Bourgois, Prior of the Priory of St-Marcoul of Corbeny in Vermendois, of the diocese of Laon . . . having seen, read and attentively examined the record and witnesses of the birth of the Reverend Father Anthoine Baillet, priest and religious of the Order of Our Lady of Mount Carmel, and professed in the great convent of the Carmelite Fathers in the Place Maubert, Paris, namely

that he is the seventh male issue, without any female interposition, . . .
and seeing that the said Fr. Anthoine Baillet is the seventh male son,
and that the seventh can touch and lay hands upon those poor persons
afflicted with the scrofula, as is piously believed by the common
people, and by ourselves as well, as we all know by experience every
day . . . therefore since he has visited on two separate occasions
the royal church of St-Marcoul of Corbeny where the relics and
sacred bones of this great saint repose, this saint who is principally
called upon for the evil of scrofula; and on his second visit he has
made his novena along with the sick persons, and observed point by
point and to the best of his ability all that is required to be observed
in the said novena, and also caused himself to be inscribed as a
member of the royal confraternity, and before proceeding to touch, he
made proof to us—over and above the aforesaid documents and
attestations—of his obedience to his superiors, duly signed and
sealed, and dated the 15th of September 1632, and of the certificate
and approval of the doctors, bachelors and reverend fathers of his
monastery, to the effect that he always lived among them as a worthy
religious, in good odour and reputation . . . we therefore permit and
authorize him to lay hands charitably[160] upon those who suffer from
the scrofula on certain days in the year, to wit, the first day of May,
the feast day of St-Marcoul and the seventh day of July, which is
specially related to him, and the second of October, his translation,
and on Good Friday, and on the four Ember Day Fridays[161] (may
the whole be done to the glory of God) and when he has thus
touched the aforesaid sick persons, he shall send them back to us to
the said Corbeny, in order to register themselves as members in the
royal confraternity of St-Marcoul, set up in this place by our kings of
France, who are its first members,[162] and to make, or cause to be
made, a novena, to the glory of God and of this glorious saint.

In witness whereof we have signed these documents and affixed
the royal seal of the aforesaid Confraternity, given this twenty-
fourth of September, one thousand six hundred and thirty-two.

And so, provided with this testimony, Brother Antoine returned to his
convent. His talents seem to have been appreciated, for the sufferers from
scrofula were frequent visitors to the convent in Place Maubert, and after
Anne of Austria's death in 1666, the Carmelites were able to offer the further attraction of an authentic relic of St-Marcoul, left them by this
princess, on whose behalf it had formerly been taken from the reliquary at
Corbeny.[163] We still have the printed propaganda-sheet distributed among
the public by the Carmelites, no doubt about that date.[164] It contains the
strangest possible jumble of items. Side by side there are medical prescriptions, some of which seem to be connected with magical ideas,[165] antiphons

and prayers to St-Marcoul as well as to St-Cloud, another of the convent's patron saints; and after a deferential allusion to the royal miracle, there is the straight advice to the scrofula-sufferers to go and seek the laying on of hands from a 'seventh male child, well attested to be such without any interruption of the feminine sex'. Antoine Baillet is not mentioned by name, but there can be little doubt that this advice had him particularly in mind. At the head of the sheet is a little engraving of the saint.

The tradition firmly established by the protégés of Corbeny lasted on into the nineteenth century. The seventh son at Vovette used to practise in the presence of a little statue of St-Marcoul, after both he and his patient had first said a short prayer before it. This ceremony, and the accompanying treatment, which consisted of a simple laying on of hands with the sign of the cross, like the ancient royal gesture and probably in imitation of it, unless we are to believe in pure coincidence, were repeated each day for nine consecutive days. At the end of this period, the patient did not depart until he had received a prescription laying down certain dietary recommendations of a very strange kind, and a particularly strict observance of the feasts of St-Marcoul. He would also take away with him a little book containing the saint's office, and a devotional image, with a prayer of invocation to St-Marcoul inscribed beneath it. Moreover, by this time the intimate link between the seventh sons and the ancient wonder-worker of Nant and Corbeny had become evident enough to the general public to find strong expression in contemporary language. These scrofula healers would sometimes receive at baptism, from far-sighted parents or godparents, names that were appropriate to their future vocation, thought, no doubt, to call down beneficent influences upon them. Louis was very popular, as we have seen; and even more so, Marcoul.[166] This latter name gradually ceased to be a Christian name, and became a kind of generic name. By the nineteenth century, and probably much earlier still, in all the provinces of France, a man who had been fortunate enough to come into the world in succession to six other boys was commonly known as a *marcou*.[167]

This study of the cult of St-Marcoul and the belief in the powers of the seventh son has brought us down to the present day. We must now go back and trace the fortunes of the royal miracle from the Renaissance and the Reformation onwards. From that time, St-Marcoul was certainly held, though in a rather vague way, to be one of the originators of this royal power.

V

The royal miracle during the Wars of Religion and the absolute monarchy

1   *Wonder-working royalty before the crisis*

Around the year 1500, and well on into the sixteenth century, the royal miracle appears to have been growing in extent and fame on both sides of the Channel.[1]

Let us first consider the position in France. For this period, we have figures of exceptional precision drawn from certain account-books of the Royal Alms which had the great good fortune to escape destruction. The oldest of them goes back to the end of Charles VIII's reign and the most recent belongs to the reign of Charles IX, right in the middle of the Wars of Religion, and dates from 1569.[2] They contain very complete information about the financial transactions they cover. At the period we have now reached, the royal generosity was no longer a matter of a selection among the various sick persons touched, as it was under Philip the Fair. Now, all those who had been touched shared in the royal largesse, without any discrimination whatsoever.[3] Here are the yearly statistics of which we can be certain: Louis XII touched no more than 528 persons between 1 October 1507 and 30 September 1508;[4] but Francis I touched at least 1,326 in 1528; in 1529, more than 988; in 1530, at least 1,731.[5] Strangely enough, the record is held by Charles IX. In 1569, a year of civil war, but brightened by some royal victories—the year of Jarnac and Moncontour—this king distributed the usual sums through his almoner, the famous Jacques Amyot, to 2,092 scrofula sufferers, whose sores had been touched by his youthful hand.[6] These figures will stand comparison with those we have cited from other sources for a different period and country, the details given in the English account-books of Edward I and Edward III; for in the sixteenth century the Valois in France, like the Plantagenets in former times in England, witnessed the spectacle of crowds flocking to them in their thousands.

Where did these huge crowds come from? On this point, the sixteenth-

177

century documents are less explicit than the tables of Philip the Fair. The recipients of the royal touch listed in the former are usually nameless, or— if their names are sometimes known—their place of origin is hardly ever mentioned. Nevertheless there is a special category of foreigners, who were customarily given a special alms 'to assist them to return to their homeland', and this is often noted, at least under Henry II, though his accounts are too fragmentary to be included in the annual statistics given above, and also under Charles IX; and they seem to have been Spaniards.[7] We have other documentary evidence of their eagerness. It would seem then that the political antagonism between France and Spain during almost the whole of this century did not erode the faith of the peninsula's inhabitants who were scourged by the scrofula in the supernatural virtues of a prince who was their master's political enemy. Moreover, in spite of the rivalries of governments, there were still frequent comings and goings between the two countries; there were Spaniards in France, and more particularly a good many Frenchmen in Spain. And these migrations were bound to spread the fame of the French royal miracle beyond the Pyrenees. As soon as peace was re-established for the time being, those suffering from the scrofula—nobles and ordinary folk alike—would cross the mountains and hasten to visit their royal doctor. They seem to have formed into regular caravans, each one led by a 'captain'.[8] On arrival, they would receive large gifts—for persons of quality, up to as much as 225 or 275 *livres*; this generosity gives some idea of the importance attached by the French court to spreading the wonder-working prestige of the dynasty outside the king-dom.[9] Besides the Spaniards, there is mention of other foreigners, whose nationality is not specified, among the crowds that thronged round Henry II at Corbeny, on the way back from his consecration.[10]

Even beyond the frontiers of France, our kings sometimes performed acts of healing, notably in Italy, where their ambitions so often took them during this period. Charles VIII carrying out this miraculous rite at Naples, and Louis XII at Pavia and Genoa, were working in towns considered by them as an integral part of their states; but they were not afraid of some-times also practising their art on avowedly foreign soil, for example in the Papal States. In December 1515, Francis I, finding himself the guest of Leo X at Bologna, made a public announcement that he would lay hands on the sick, and in fact did so in the chapel of the Pope's Palace; among the persons touched was a Polish bishop. And even in Rome, on 20 January 1495, Charles VIII touched about 500 persons in the chapel of St Petronilla. If we are to believe his panegyrist, André de la Vigne, he threw the Italians into a state of 'extraordinary admiration'.[11] True, as we shall note in due course, the miraculous manifestations did not fail to evoke a certain scep-ticism among the free-thinkers in those parts; but the common people, and even the doctors, were less difficult to convince.[12] And what is more, when Francis I had been taken prisoner at Pavia and landed on Spanish soil at the end of June 1525, first at Barcelona and then at Valencia, the President of the Parliament of Paris, de Selve, writing a few days later, tells us that 'he saw so many sufferers from the scrofula . . . with great hopes of being cured, thronging round the king, greater than any crowds that ever pressed round him in France'.[13] Even in defeat, the august healer had as much success among the Spaniards as when they had come to implore his aid in all the pomp of the consecration ceremonial. The poet Lascaris sang of this episode in two Latin distichs that were famous in their day:

> Behold how the king cures the scrofulous with a
>   single gesture of his hand;
> Though captive, he has not lost the favours from
>   on High.
> By this sign, O most blessed of Kings,
> Methinks I see that thy persecutors are hated
>   by the gods.[14]

As befitted a better-policed State and a more sumptuous court, the scrofula ritual had gradually taken on a new and more regular solemnity and splendour in France. Louis XI, it will be recalled, used still to administer the royal touch every week; but after Charles VIII, who seems to have been criticized on this account by Commines, the ceremony hardly ever took place except at fairly infrequent intervals.[15] No doubt it still happened that when a king was on his travels, as when Francis I was passing through Champagne in January 1530, he would consent to receive a few sick persons at every stage of his journey;[16] or he would be touched by the plea of some poor old man he happened to meet all on his own 'out in the country'.[17] But usually the scrofula sufferers were put into groups as they arrived by the Royal Almoners, and were given a certain amount of assistance '*pour leur ayder a vivre*' until the day they would be received; and they then had to wait close at hand, until the chosen moment for the miracle. Otherwise, in order to get rid of this ever-moving procession that was probably not very pleasant for the court either to see or to rub shoulders with, it was sometimes preferred to give them a sum of money to induce them to 'retire' and not appear again until the appointed day.[18] In principle, of course, the days when the king was graciously pleased to perform his wonders were the chief religious festivals of the year, though their number was variable,[19] namely Candlemas, Palm Sunday, Easter or one of the days in Holy Week, Pentecost, Ascension Day, Corpus Christi, the Assumption, the Nativity of the Virgin and Christmas Day. Exceptionally, there would be some festival not in the liturgical calendar. On 8 July 1530, Francis I celebrated his '*espousailles*' to Eleanor of Austria at Roquefort, near Mont-de-Marsan, and showed himself to the new queen of France in all the splendour of the hereditary miracle.[20]

Thanks to this grouping system, the king would find real crowds, often several hundred strong, gathered together for the appointed moment, after the court physician had carried out his preliminary sorting.[21] In that way the ceremony assumed a particularly imposing character. Before proceeding to heal, the king would each time receive Holy Communion in both kinds, according to the privilege of his dynasty, which seemed, along with the gift of healing, to affirm the sacred character of the French monarchy. There is a little picture dating from the early sixteenth century which brings home to us the close connection in the loyalist outlook between these two glorious prerogatives. On the left, it shows the king, in a chapel that opens onto a courtyard, receiving the paten from a bishop, and holding the chalice in his hands; on the right, waiting in a little courtyard, and even kneeling on the chapel steps, are the sick.[22] The essential features of the rite have not changed since the Middle Ages: the contact with the bare hand passing lightly over the sores or tumour, followed by the sign of the cross. From the sixteenth century onwards, there was a fixed formula pronounced over each patient: 'The king touches thee, and God heals thee'; and this was to last, with a few variations, up to the final days of the monarchy.[23] More particularly, the solemn rite was now preceded by a very shortly liturgy, concerned entirely, as we have seen, at least since Henry II's time, with St-Marcoul, who had become the patron saint of the royal miracle.[24] In the same missal that has preserved it there is a fine miniature, vividly portraying for us the scene on one of these days for the royal touch. We see Henry II, followed by his almoner and a few nobles, making the round of the kneeling crowds, and going from one sick person to another. And we know that this was in fact what actually happened.[25] But this little painting must not be taken too literally. The royal dress—the crown, the great cloak adorned with fleur-de-lis and lined with ermine—is in this case purely conventional; the sovereign did not in fact put on his coronation vestments every time he laid hands on the sick. Moreover, the scene seems to be taking place in a church, and this was indeed often the case, though not invariably. The fanciful architecture in the Renaissance style imagined by the artist must be replaced in our minds by something less unreal and more varied in the way of setting; for instance, the Gothic pillars of Notre-Dame in Paris. There, on 8 September 1528, and watched by the good citizens—one of whom recorded his recollection of the scene in his journal—205 scrofula sufferers were assembled.[26] But the act did not always take place in a religious building or even in an enclosed space. There was the occasion on the Feast of the Assumption, 1527, when in the cloisters of the Bishop's Palace at Amiens Cardinal Wolsey watched Francis I touch about the same number of sick persons;[27] or again, in troublous times, it took place in a warlike setting, such as the camp near St-Jean d'Angély in the Landes, when on All Saints' Day, 1569, Charles IX momentarily exchanged the role of army leader for that of healer.[28]

4   Charles II of England touching for scrofula. An etching by Robert
White, the frontispiece to J. Browne, *Charisma Basilikon* (Part 3 of
Adenochoiradelogia), 1684

DE PAR LE ROY,

ET MONSIEVR LE MARQVIS DE SOVCHES,
Preuoſt de l'Hoſtel de ſa Maieſté, & Grande Preuoſté de France.

ON faict à ſçauoir à tous qu'il appartiendra, que Dimanche prochain iour de Paſques, Sa Maieſté touchera les Malades des Eſcroüelles, dans les Galleries du Louure, à dix heures du matin, à ce que nul n'en pretende cauſe d'ignorance, & que ceux qui ſont attaquez dudit mal ayent à s'y trouuer, ſi bon leur ſemble. Faict à Paris, le Roy y eſtant, le vingt-ſixieſme Mars mil ſix cens cinquante-ſept.   Signé, DE SOVCHES.

Leu & publié à ſon de Trompe & cry public par tous les Carrefours de cette Ville & Faux-
bourgs de Paris, par moy Charles Canto Crieur Iuré de ſa Maieſté, accompagné de Jean du
Bos, Jacques le Frain, & Eſtienne Chappé Jurez Trompettes dudit Seigneur, & affiché, le
vingt-ſixieſme Mars, mil ſix cens cinquante-ſept.   Signé, CANTO.

5   Notice announcing that Louis XIV will touch for scrofula on Easter Day 1657

In England, there is the same picture, at least in broad outline. As far as the touch for scrofula is concerned, we cannot be as precise about the main features, for statistics are lacking, and the occasional mention of sick persons 'healed' by the king scattered through Henry VII's or Henry VIII's account-books are probably no more than exceptional cases. The Almonry records, which are most likely to have contained a summary of the money distributed to the sick touched by the king as a whole, have disappeared for good and all.[29] There is no reason to doubt that the English kings of the sixteenth century enjoyed great popularity as doctors of the King's Evil, for numerous authors extol their powers in this direction; but we have no means of assessing this popularity in figures.

At any rate we have a very accurate knowledge of the ritual used in miraculous healing under Mary Tudor, and no doubt also under Henry VIII[30]—and perhaps even by Henry VII.[31] The English ceremony differed in a good many points from what was customary at the French court; and it will be worth while setting down the differences.

In the first place, the whole ceremony was accompanied throughout by a considerably more developed liturgy, the essentials of which were a *Confiteor* said by the king, an absolution given by the chaplain, and a reading of two passages from the Gospels—the verse from St Mark referring to the miracles performed by the Apostles—there is no missing the allusion—and the first words from the Gospel according to St John, which were frequently used in all forms of blessing or exorcism.[32] As we should expect, there is no reference to St-Marcoul or any other particular saint.

In contrast to French usage, the sovereign remained in one place—seated, no doubt—throughout the ceremony, and a Church official brought the sick to him one by one. Thus the prince would perhaps have preserved rather more dignity; though to judge by certain seventeenth-century engravings, there was a constant coming and going in the room where the ceremony took place. The same rules were still in force then, and the scene seems to have had the rather untoward picturesqueness of a procession in the 'Cour des Miracles'.[33] No doubt the principles of the arrangements went back to ancient times, for a thirteenth-century miniature already shows us Edward the Confessor in a sitting posture, and touching a woman who is being brought to him.[34]

The stir was all the greater in that each patient went before the king twice over. First they all passed before him in succession, and he laid his bare hands upon them; then, when this was finished, they came back again, still one at a time, and the king made the traditional sign of the cross over their sores. But not like his French rival, with his hand only, for he held in his fingers, while making the sacred sign, a piece of money—a gold coin. As soon as the gesture had been made, he would hang this coin (which had probably been previously pierced with a hole and provided with a ribbon) round each patient's neck. This is the part of the ceremony that contrasts most sharply with French custom. At the Valois court, too, the scrofula sufferers used to receive some money, generally two shillings each; but this alms—incidentally much more modest than its English counterpart—was given to them without any ceremony by a Church official discreetly following behind the king. In England, on the other hand, the royal gift had come to occupy a central position in the rite itself. This must be seen as a strange shift of belief, which should be dealt with once and for all at this point.

It will be remembered that during the Wars of the Roses, the English sovereigns had acquired the habit of attracting sufferers to themselves by the tempting offer of a handsome present in a form that soon became traditional—a gold coin, always of the same value, an 'angel'. Although these pieces continued—at least up to James I's time—to be current coin, they tended more and more to be not so much a means of exchange as genuine medals, specially to be used in the royal touch. And this tendency became so strong that it brought about an adaptation of the legend they bore to suit this particular ceremony. Under Mary Tudor, the old commonplace formula which had long run round their edge: 'O Christ, Redeemer, save us by thy cross', was replaced by one more appropriate to the royal miracle: 'This was the Lord's doing, and it is marvellous in our eyes'.[35] And as we shall see in a moment, when James I changed the rite, he also modified the appearance of the 'angel', and the legend inscribed on it. By the sixteenth century, people had ceased to regard this gold coin, so closely linked to the healing rite, as the simple charitable gift it had originally been: from then onwards, it was commonly looked upon as a talisman possessing its own intrinsic medicinal power.

On 4 April 1536 the Venetian Faitta arrived in England as a member of Cardinal Pole's suite. He tells us that he saw Mary Tudor touching the sick, and making each patient promise 'never to part from the piece of money [which she hung round his neck] except in case of extreme need'.[36] Whether the queen actually used these words or no, the very fact of their attribution to her proves that the 'angel' was no longer considered an ordinary coin. In Elizabeth's reign, belief in the medicinal virtues of this new amulet is clearly testified by the queen's chaplain, Tooker by name, the author of the first English book on the royal healing power. He rejects this belief as simply a popular superstition.[37] This attitude would subsequently be adopted by all the royal miracle's apologists. But in the seventeenth century they were having some difficulty in upholding it; for the more serious authors, such as the doctors Browne and Wiseman, no longer made anything but a formal protest against a popular idea which the love of the supernatural fastened at that time upon the common consciousness.[38]

There was a little story current in England about then, in which the characters changed, while the theme remained always the same.

A certain woman had been touched by the king, who had of course made a point of giving her the 'angel'. As long as she kept this pledge of health, she had appeared to be cured; but one day she lost it, or parted with it, whereupon she was immediately struck down by the old illness.[39] This opinion was shared by all classes of society. The Dutch doctor Diemerbroeck, who died in 1674, tells us that he once looked after an English officer in the service of the States General. This nobleman, who had formerly received a miraculous cure, wore on a ribbon round his neck the coin once given him as a young man by his prince. He refused to be parted from it, in the firm belief that his cure was intimately bound up with it.[40] Charitable people in the parishes would offer to renew the ribbons on which the 'angels' hung for poor persons suffering from scrofula.[41] Moreover, the Government would sometimes associate itself with this common prejudice. A proclamation of 13 May 1625 mentions certain persons who 'were formerly cured, but then disposed of the gold coins [from the king's gift] in unlawful ways, and consequently experienced a relapse'.[42] It is not difficult to imagine how these perverse individuals had disposed of the royal presents: they had obviously sold them. Indeed, we know that there was a considerable trade in these talismans.[43] Sick people who were unable, for one reason or another, to visit the court in person, or were perhaps frightened by the expense of the journey, used to buy these coins, with the idea of thus acquiring—no doubt at a reduced cost—some share in the miraculous benefits distributed by the sacred hand of the sovereign. Hence the indignation felt by the zealous supporters of royalty, who held that relief could only be obtained by direct contact with the august and royal hand. The seventh sons, who were faithful imitators of their sovereign, both in England and in France, also adopted the habit of hanging pieces of money round their patients' necks, though these were of silver, for their means did not allow them to imitate their royal competitor's munificence. This custom continued, at least in certain regions, up to the nineteenth century.[44] As we shall be seeing later on, it was in the form of a monetary amulet that this belief in the wonder-working gift of kings also survived in Great Britain well on into the nineteenth century.

Thus faith in the royal miracle was still vigorous enough in the mid-sixteenth century to give rise to a new superstition. How had the idea come into the minds of the English that the 'angels' were vehicles of healing power? They had first been used in the ceremony of the royal touch—always this same gold coin—as a result of rival dynastic ambitions, and then hallowed by tradition; and this had doubtless gradually inclined people to believe that something so essential to the rite must play some more important part than that of a mere coin given as alms. The kings themselves, at least from Henry VIII's time onwards, had adopted the habit of holding the coin in their hand while making the sign of the cross; and this action, whether intentional or not, had encouraged such a conclusion. Yet it would seem probable that general opinion only inclined so easily in that direction because another rite, finally linked on to the royal ceremonial towards the end of the Middle Ages, already provided an example of talismans consecrated by kings. I refer to the medicinal rings, which were held from this time onwards to receive from the contact with the hands of royalty a virtue that became part and parcel of their own substance. To the common mind, the old miracle of the royal touch began to take on in the end something of the character belonging to the newer miracle of Good Friday. It looks as though people ended by believing that the royal touch could also be endowed with a special efficacy by taking place on Good Friday.[45] The fact is that about the year 1500 the more recent of the two manifestations of royal supernatural privilege was at the height of its popularity—we might almost say, it was in full flower.

The success of the royal touch for scrofula can be gauged by the number of the sick who flocked to the ceremonies. For the healing rings, it can be judged by the public eagerness to get hold of these golden or silver rings which had been blessed after the adoration of the cross. To judge by the correspondence or accounts of the time, this eagerness seems to have been extremely lively in the days of the Tudors. Nothing could be more characteristic than the example of Lady Lisle. In 1528, Honor Grenville had married Viscount Lisle, the natural son of Edward IV. In 1533, she followed her husband to Calais, of which he was governor; and from there she carried on a very active correspondence with England. A chance confiscation, following upon a political lawsuit, has preserved for us the letters she received. Glancing through them, one is astonished at the place occupied by the cramp rings. Lady Lisle—who perhaps suffered from rheumatism—collected them with a sort of fervour; and she rated their virtue so highly that she even considered them a sovereign remedy against the pains of childbirth. Her children, her friends and her business acquaintances went out of their way to get her these rings, for it was clearly the surest way of giving her pleasure. No doubt, such a strong passion was not common: we may well believe that there was a touch of eccentricity about this great lady, and towards the end of her life, her mind did become totally deranged.[46] Yet to a lesser degree her faith seems to have been generally shared. Cramp rings often figure in contemporary wills among the precious things bequeathed to intimate friends.[47]

The reputation of the Good Friday ritual did not end at the English frontier. The medicinal rings were much appreciated in Scotland, and the English envoy used to give them to the Scottish notables with whom he wished to curry favour.[48] In 1543, a great Scottish nobleman, Lord Oliphaunt, who had been taken prisoner by the English and then released in return for a promise to serve Henry VIII's interests, was well loaded with cramp rings when he set out for his own country.[49] On the continent, too, royal propaganda helped to spread the fame of the miraculous rings: Henry

VIII would offer with his own hand to distinguished foreigners who visited him these metal rings consecrated by himself.[50] His own envoys would also distribute them in the countries to which they were accredited— in France,[51] at Charles V's court,[52] in Venice[53] and, before the schism, even in Rome.[54]

Truth to tell, the visitors received by the royal magician could hardly do otherwise than appear to receive these wonderful gifts with gratitude, whatever their secret feelings about them might be. On the other hand, by insistently claiming from the English government these talismans blessed by the king, its representatives in the various European courts were perhaps equally intent upon flattering their master's wonder-working pride as upon serving his interests by an astute distribution of this largesse. Imported into these countries by various means, these cramp rings had become an object of commerce, as they had also in England. And it was probably with a view to making money out of them that the Genoese Antonio Spinola, a secret agent in the service of the English court, when detained in Paris by his creditors in June 1515, applied to Wolsey for a dozen of them, saying that he had been pressed to supply them by 'some wealthy noblemen'.[55] However, although they were sold more or less everywhere, they did not always fetch a high price. In his memoirs, Benvenuto Cellini, as an example of inexpensive rings, instances 'those little rings for the cramp which come from England and are worth a *carlin*'—a small coin—'or thereabouts'.[56] After all, though, a *carlin* was still something. The testimony of diplomats may be suspected of insincerity; but we have other more reliable proofs that even outside England these *anelli del granchio* were more sought after than Benvenuto's phrase might suggest—though perhaps not held in as high esteem as Henry VIII had been persuaded to believe. And this was even true in circles that would naturally have been considered the least open to this kind of superstition. In Germany, Catherine of Schwarzburg, a friend of Luther, asked her correspondents to procure her some.[57] The English humanist Linacre, a doctor by profession, who was in friendly contact with the great Guillaume Budé, thought he would certainly give him pleasure by sending him some of the rings, accompanied by an elegant letter in Greek. In Budé's reply, written in the same learned tongue, we may perhaps detect a certain irony, but so gentle and well-veiled that the reader is left in two minds about it.[58] And even in France in Henry IV's reign, if we are to believe the word of the doctor du Laurens, a good many private individuals still kept specimens of these healing rings among their personal treasures, though the English kings had ceased fifty years before to have any more of them made.[59] In Renaissance Europe, faith in all aspects of the royal miracle was still very much alive and, as in the Middle Ages, hardly paid any heed to national rivalries.

Towards the second half of the sixteenth century, however, it was destined to feel a sharp reaction from the great upheaval that shook so many political and religious institutions throughout the Western world.

2 *The Renaissance and the Reformation*

In 1535, Michael Servetus produced in Lyons a translation, with additional notes, of Ptolemy's *Geographia*; and among the supplements were the following words:

> Two memorable things are related of the kings of France: first, that there is in the church at Rheims a vase of chrism which remains ever full, sent down from heaven for the coronation, and used for the anointing of all the kings; secondly, that the king, by the laying on of hands alone, cures the scrofula. I have seen with my own eyes this king touching several sufferers from this affection. If they were really restored to health—well, that is something I did not see.

Here there is a barely-concealed note of scepticism, though it is discreetly expressed . . . In 1541, again at Lyons, a second edition of this book appeared, in which the final phrase was suppressed, and replaced by: 'I have heard say that many sufferers were restored to health'.[60] That was in effect a retraction.

This little biographical episode is very instructive. It shows in the first place from what kind of intellectual milieu there was any likelihood of writers being forthcoming, over a good long period, who would be bold enough to cast doubts upon the royal miracle. They were hardly to be met with except among the impenitently heterodox, accustomed to reject many other beliefs that had hitherto been accepted as articles of faith. Men like Servetus, or later on like Vanini—who will cross our path in due course— were quite capable of ending up at the stake as the victims of one or other of the contemporary religious orthodoxies. But Servetus made a retraction: and we may well surmise that this was not a spontaneous repentance, but rather something imposed upon him from without. Over a long period of years, it was hardly possible in a book printed either in England or in France to launch an open attack on a superstition with which the prestige of the monarchy was bound up. At the very least, it would have been a useless act of temerity that no one would readily commit.

Naturally enough, foreign writers were under no such restrictions. In the sixteenth, and early years of the seventeenth century, there was a group of authors who might be called naturalists—if the term be taken to mean those who had received from their predecessors the picture of a universe full of marvels, but had set themselves to eliminate from it all supernatural influences. Their conception of nature was no doubt very different from our own; it seems to us nowadays full of ideas that conflict with experience or reason, and they were ready and eager—in spite of their free thinking—to appeal to astrology or magic. But in their view, this magic or astrology was an integral part of the order of things, and served to explain a whole variety of mysterious phenomena which contemporary science could not account for, but which they were yet unwilling to interpret, according to the doctrines professed before their time and round about them, as the arbitrary manifestations of superhuman wills.

How could anyone preoccupied with miracles at that time ignore that patent miracle of the royal healing, which was a familiar and almost daily occurrence? We might pick out among the principal representatives of this Italian School such notable men as Pomponazzi, Cardano, Giulio Cesare Vanini, and the humanist Calcagnini. They were all intent upon expressing at least a passing opinion on this topical subject. None of them doubted that cures did actually exist, but they were anxious to explain them by natural causes, that is, according to their ideas of nature. There will be an opportunity later on of examining their proposed solutions, when we reach the end of this study and have to come back to the problem they had the intelligence to pose. The important point to be noted here is their refusal to accept the traditional theory. In their eyes, the sacred character of kings was no longer an adequate explanation of their healing power.[61]

But the ideas of this handful of 'free-thinkers', who were moreover, as foreigners, not directly concerned with the two countries immediately involved in the royal gift, could hardly have much influence upon the common mind. The attitude of the religious reformers was destined to be far more decisive. They were far from denying the supernatural, nor did they dream—at least so long as they were not persecuted—of attacking the royal prestige or power. Without taking account of Luther, has it not been justly said of Calvin himself that in his *Institutes of the Christian Religion* 'the theme of the divine right of kings . . . is as solidly based upon "the very words of Holy Scripture" as it was to be in the works of Bossuet'?[62] The reformers were for the most part firmly conservative—in principle, at least—over political matters, and firmly opposed to any purely rational interpretation of the universe. Why should they have set themselves up in point-blank opposition to belief in the wonder-working virtue of kings? We shall in fact see that for a long time they were quite happy to accept it.

But the example of France is in this respect rather misleading. In the camp of the French reformers, there were no signs for a good many years of any protests against the touch for scrofula. Yet, as we have already seen, this silence was dictated more by elementary prudence than by any other reason. And it extended to everything relating to the royal miracle; it was probably only an oversight that made Henri Estienne omit the name St-Marcoul from the list of saints owing their healing role to a play upon words in his *Apologie pour Hérodote*. But now let us take a look at the Protestant countries themselves.

In Germany, as we already know, Luther, though dominated in so many points by ancient popular ideas, admitted quite candidly that a remedy given by the hand of a prince was made thereby all the more efficacious. Catherine of Schwarzburg, a heroine of the new faith, used to search out the English cramp rings.[63] In England, the two healing rites continued to be practised after the schism; and not only by Henry VIII, who could hardly be called a Protestant king, but even by Edward VI, in spite of his keenness to wipe out all traces of 'papist' superstitions. In this prince's reign, the Good Friday office shed its Roman forms; and at least from 1549 onwards, English people were forbidden to 'creep' towards the cross.[64] Yet this young theologian king never gave up the practice of consecrating the healing rings on the anniversary of the Passion; and even in the year of his death, when nearly on his deathbed, he still performed the ancestral gesture 'according to the old order and custom', as is recorded—perhaps with a touch of apology—in his account-books.[65]

In the long run, however, the Reformation was to deal a severe blow at the royal healing. The kings' wonder-working power derived from their sacred character; and this was created or confirmed by the ceremony of anointing, which counted as one of the solemn rites of the ancient religion. Protestantism looked with horror upon the miracles popularly attributed to the saints; and were not those attributed to kings remarkably like them? Moreover, St Edward in England and St-Marcoul in France were the accredited patrons of the touch for scrofula; and certain persons regarded this as a compromising connection. The innovators were far from excluding everything supernatural from their universe; but many of them were reluctant to allow these influences any such frequent intervention in daily life as previous generations had taken for granted. Here are the reasons given by James I of England in 1603—according to the account of a papal spy—for his reluctance to perform the royal touch: 'he said . . . he could not see how he could heal the sick without a miracle; but miracles had ceased—they no longer happened'.[66] In the atmosphere of miracles surrounding the western monarchies, almost everything was calculated to shock the adherents of a purified faith; and one can sense the effect likely to be produced by the legend of the Holy Phial on men thoroughly imbued with a kind of religious sobriety. It is hard to see how the Reformed sects, entering gradually into a clearer appreciation of their own ideas, and especially on the advanced wing of Calvinism, could have failed in the end to view the royal miracle as foreign to the truth of primitive Christianity. They came to see it as one of the ingredients in the system of practices and beliefs they rejected as the sacrilegious innovation of idolatrous ages; in a word, they considered it—as one of the English nonconformists was to say quite bluntly—a 'superstition' which must be rooted out from the faith. But it was not only, or even principally, by its strictly religious action that the Reformation imperilled the old respect for the medicinal powers of royalty. Its political consequences in this direction were also extremely serious. In the troubles it let loose in England and France, the privileges of royalty came under formidable attack, and amongst them the privilege of miraculous healing. Moreover, this crisis was by no means equally acute in the two kingdoms, whose history diverges along ways that are different in all respects during the sixteenth and seventeenth centuries. The crisis was much the more acute and decisive in England, so we will begin with that country.

The most recent of the acts manifesting the supernatural powers of the English monarchs was also the first to succumb to the new spirit. The consecration of healing rings did not survive the sixteenth century.

It was already threatened in the reign of Edward VI. One Ash Wednesday perhaps in the year 1547, an advanced preacher, Nicholas Ridley, speaking in the presence of the king and his court, held forth against a number of practices he considered idolatrous, and notably against the adoration of images and the use of the holy water in exorcism. Did he also venture in the same breath to come out openly against the 'medicinal' rings? He certainly seems to have given his hearers the impression that he was condemning them, implicitly at least. At this time the supporters of more moderate reform, the lawful heirs of Henry VIII's thought, were doing their best to gain the young king's allegiance; and they had every reason to carry the struggle into a field where the prestige of the monarch appeared to be at stake. One of this party, and a notable figure in it, Bishop Gardiner by name, wrote a letter of protest to Ridley,[67] in which he championed all that this zealous preacher had expressly or implicitly attacked, particularly the blessing of the cramp rings, which he said were 'a gift from God' and the 'hereditary prerogative of the kings of this land'. This controversy shows clearly enough what it was in this ancient magical custom, and more still in the touch for scrofula, that shocked the enemies of the Romanist religion. They could not fail to see in it, and rightly enough, a kind of exorcism, for the holy water with which the rings were sprinkled seemed to them a sure sign of superstition.[68] Edward VI subsequently persecuted Gardiner, but made Ridley Bishop of London. Yet as regards the royal miracle, it was, as we have seen, the wish of the former —'that he should not neglect the gift of healing'—that the king carried out to the end of his reign. In his case, his sense of royal humour prevailed over his evangelical doctrines.

Under Mary Tudor, of course, the Good Friday ceremony continued to be regularly carried out, with a pomp we have already referred to. But after Elizabeth's accession (1558), the court was once again Protestant, and the ceremony ceased to take place. It disappeared quite unobtrusively, probably at the beginning of the reign.[69] For some time, the cramp rings blessed by former sovereigns continued to be treasured and hoarded by the general public;[70] then people gradually ceased to value these unpretentious metal rings, which were not distinguishable by any external signs from those that were generally worn. Not a single genuine cramp ring has come down to us;[71] or if any have, we handle them without being aware of the fact. The secret of their virtues became a matter of indifference to unbelieving generations, and it has not been handed down to us. Elizabeth had effectively killed the ancient rite.

Elizabeth was a much less zealous reformer than her brother: why did she consider it her duty to break with a tradition he had always maintained, in spite of Ridley and his party? Perhaps the Catholic reaction that had been so violent under Mary had made men's minds more sensitive. The queen was clearly determined to preserve, in spite of all opposition, the royal touch for scrofula; and she perhaps thought it advisable to offer a sop to the opponents of the old beliefs by sacrificing the one of these two healing rites which did not bring the sovereign face to face with the suffering crowds, and so was of less value to the royal prestige.

Elizabeth indeed never broke off the 'healing' of scrofula.[72] She faithfully preserved the traditional ceremonial, merely cutting out from the liturgy a prayer that mentioned the Virgin and the saints, and probably translating into English the Latin ritual of the previous ages.[73] For her reign, we do not possess any documents giving the exact number of the sick who sought her help; but everything would seem to indicate that she exercised her miraculous power with full success.[74] Yet this was not without a fairly strong opposition from certain free thinkers like Reginald Scott. Under the direct inspiration of the Italian philosophers, he was one of the first English opponents of belief in sorcery; yet his discreet scepticism cannot have been very dangerous.[75] But there were two influential groups of men who refused to recognize that their sovereign possessed the gift of miraculous healing: the Catholics, because she was an excommunicated heretic; and the advanced Protestants, or Puritans, as they were beginning to be called, who had taken up a definite position for doctrinal reasons already indicated against a practice they roundly called superstitious. It became necessary to defend the ancient privilege of the English dynasty against the unbelievers. The official preachers set about the task from their pulpits on high,[76] and the writers of books joined in from this time onwards. The first book to be devoted to the royal touch dates from this reign, *Charisma sive donum Sanationis*, published in 1597 by 'the most humble chaplain of her Most Sacred Majesty', William Tooker. It was dedicated to the queen herself, and was naturally enough a dithyramb in praise of the royal miracle. Incidentally, it was a pretty inferior production, and one can hardly believe that it ever converted anyone.[77] Five years later, one of the queen's surgeons, William Clowes, jealous of the lead taken by the chaplain, wrote in English (at a time when the Church still remained faithful to Latin) a 'fruitful and well-founded' treatise on the healing of scrofula by the kings and queens of England.[78] The appearance of these pleas was a sign of the times. The ancient faith in the wonder-working virtue of kings was far from being dead in England; but it was no longer unanimously shared by all, and therefore needed apologists.

The accession of James I in 1603 came near to dealing it a mortal blow. In his political writing, this prince stands out as one of the most intransigent theoretical supporters of the divine right of kings;[79] and it seems strange that he should have hesitated to practise a rite that was such a perfect expression of the superhuman character of monarchical power. Yet this apparent paradox can be easily explained. James had been brought up in the rigorously Calvinistic environment of Scotland. In 1603, he was still thoroughly imbued with the lessons taught him by his earliest masters. True, from the beginning of his reign he defended episcopacy, because he considered the ecclesiastical hierarchy the surest support of royalty; but his religious sentiments continued to be those he had been taught; and this explains his reluctance to perform a so-called miracle, which he had been instructed to view as sheer superstition or imposture. At first he expressly asked to be excused from this ceremony.[80] But he subsequently resigned himself to it when his English advisers remonstrated with him, though not without some repugnance. A spy from the Roman Curia has left us a piquant account of the king's first ceremony of touching, which must have taken place in October 1603. The rite was preceded by a sermon from a Calvinist minister. Then the king himself, who despised neither theology nor the art of oratory, proceeded to take up the word. He explained the cruel dilemma confronting him: he was faced with either performing an act that might well be superstitious, or breaking an ancient custom, formerly instituted in order to benefit the subjects of his kingdom. He had therefore decided to make the experiment, but he wished to consider the rite he was about to perform as no more than a kind of prayer addressed to Heaven for the healing of the sick, a prayer in which he invited all those present to join him. At this point, he began to touch the scrofulous; 'and [our informer slyly adds] during the whole of this speech it was noticeable that the king several times looked towards the Scottish ministers by his side, as though expecting some sign of approval, since he had previously discussed the matter with them'.[81]

We do not know whether this reluctant wonder-worker there and then carried out some purification in the traditional ceremony. At all events, he did so soon afterwards. Like her Catholic predecessors, and like Henry VIII himself, Elizabeth had made the sign of the cross over the affected parts—to the great indignation, moreover, of some of her Protestant subjects.[82] James refused to imitate her in this matter. When the sick had been touched, and then passed before him a second time, he was content to hang —or have someone else hang—the gold coin round their necks, without making the symbolical sign that was an uncomfortable reminder of the old faith. At the same time, the cross disappeared from the 'angels', on which it had figured up till then, and the legend was shortened so as to cut out the word 'miracle' (*mirabile*).[83] Thanks to these modifications, and thanks, we may believe, to becoming accustomed to the ceremony in course of time and separated from the teachings of his youth, James I finally accepted the regular performance of this healing rite, though probably without repeating on each occasion the oratorical precautions accompanying his first attempt. Moreover, he does not seem always to have taken the matter very seriously. In 1618, when a Turkish ambassador, displaying a distinctly amusing religious eclecticism, asked the king to touch his son, who suffered from scrofula, we are told that the king laughed heartily, and did not refuse to comply.[84]

It was in the early years of this reign that Shakespeare staged his *Macbeth*. The play was intended to please the new king, for the Stuarts were thought to be descended from Banquo. In the prophetic vision of the fourth act, when there passes before the horror-struck Macbeth a vision of the line that is destined to spring from his victim, the last of the eight kings who go by to the sound of the hautboy is James himself, carrying the three-fold sceptre of his three kingdoms. It is striking that the poet should have thought good—as we have already noted—to introduce into this same tragedy a eulogy of the royal wonder-working power: 'A most miraculous work in this good king'.[85]

Was it just an allusion, or a piece of discreet advice? Or simply ignorance of the early hesitations shown by the last descendant of Banquo in carrying out this 'miraculous work'? We cannot say. At all events, on this point as on so many others, Shakespeare was a faithful interpreter of the popular mind. The mass of the nation could not as yet conceive of a king who was really without the grace of 'the healing benediction'. The opinion of those who staunchly supported the monarchy was strong enough even to triumph over the scruples of the monarch himself.

Charles I, like his father, administered the royal touch, but having been brought up an Anglican, he did not share his conscientious scruples. Under the first Stuarts, therefore, attitudes became definitively fixed. Belief in the royal miracle was part of that body of half-religious and half-political doctrines to which the partisans of the royal 'prerogative' and of the Established Church remained attached—that is, the great majority of the country. It was rejected by small groups animated by a burning religious zeal, who saw it both as the sorry heritage of ancient superstitions, and as one of the manifestations of the royal absolutism they had made up their minds to detest.

In France, as we have already seen, the Calvinists remained silent for a good long time on the subject of the healing power ascribed to kings—out of respect, perhaps, or out of prudence. True, their very silence was sometimes eloquent: what could be more significant, for example, than the attitude of Ambroise Paré? In the chapter 'Des Scrophules ou Escroulles' in his treatise on surgery, he avoids any allusion to the miraculous treatment of the King's Evil, quite contrary to the usual practice in the medical literature of his time.[86] Moreover, it would appear that at least after the beginning of the upheavals, the reforming party sometimes went further than a silent protest. Father Louis Richeome, of the Society of Jesus, in his *Trois Discours pour la religion catholique*, which came out in 1597, treats of the 'gift of healing the scrofula given to the Most Christian kings of France', and inveighs against 'the miscreance or impudence of certain French surgeons with evil hands and worse consciences, and certain fault-finders of Pliny, intoxicated with the potions of Luther, who have attempted to mitigate and calumniously demean this miracle'.[87] I have not been able to discover the meaning of these allusions, which are obviously aimed at specific people, but it is clear that they are directed against Protestant authors. Yet the Reformers' polemics as a whole never seem to have been very actively directed to that quarter. The writers of this camp were not very keen to attack royalty in one of its most popular privileges. In spite of so many disappointments, they mostly did not altogether despair of winning it round to their side, or at any rate obtaining its toleration. It was from a different direction that the most vigorous attack was launched against the wonder-working power, not of kings in general, but of one king in particular.

After Henry III had finally fallen out with the League, the League came to the conclusion that his godlessness had made him unworthy of exercising the supernatural power imparted to his race. It was said that one of his household who had been struck down by scrofula had several times been touched by the hand of the king, but without success. After the death on Henry III, Canon Meurier wrote a treatise on anointing, *De Sacris Unctionibus*, against Henry IV, in which he saw this medical failure as a divine warning given to the French people. If they accepted a king who had not been duly consecrated (Henry IV at this time was still a Protestant and Rheims in the hands of his enemies), the sufferers from scrofula would never again receive the benefit of miraculous healing.[88]

Then the man from Béarn became a Catholic; he was consecrated, not, it is true, at Rheims, nor with the chrism from the Holy Phial, but at least at Chartres, with an oil said to have been brought to St Martin in former times by an angel. He then proceeded to give the royal touch, and whatever might be the opinions of Meurier's supporters, the crowds flocked round him. The first ceremony took place, not immediately after the consecration, but in Paris on Easter Sunday, 10 April 1594, eighteen days after the entry of the royal forces. Paris had seen nothing of the kind since Henry III's flight in 1588; and the sick came forward in large numbers—between 600 and 700, according to Favyn, or 960 according to de Thou.[89] Subsequently, Henry IV went on dispensing the grace of healing to the scrofulous, who always flocked to him in hundreds or even thousands,[90] on the four great festivals— Easter, Pentecost, All Saints' and Christmas—and even more frequently, if occasion arose. Like all the French kings, he administered the touch standing, and found it a tiring business;[91] but he took good care not to avoid it. Desirous as he was of reconstructing the monarchy, he would surely not have neglected this part of the royal task. Purely administrative methods could not have been enough to give solid support to an authority that had been shaken by so many years of civil strife. It was also necessary to strengthen in his subjects' hearts the dynasty's prestige, and faith in the legitimacy of the reigning prince; and the hereditary miracle was certainly one of the best instruments for strengthening this prestige, just as it was the most striking proof of legitimacy. That is why Henry IV was not satisfied with effectively practising this marvellous rite; either he or his entourage put out a whole propaganda to commend the wonder-working gift.

The first method chosen was through books. In 1609, the king's personal physician, André du Laurens, published and dedicated to his master a treatise on 'The miraculous power to heal the scrofula, divinely and solely entrusted to the Most Christian kings of France'. It was a lengthy piece of pleading, whose theme is sufficiently indicated by these chapter titles: 'The miraculous power of healing the scrofula vouchsafed to the kings of France is supernatural, and does not come from the devil . . . . It is a grace given freely by God.'[92] The book seems to have been a great success: it was several times reprinted and translated.[93] As Gui Patin wrote in 1628 in a kind of Latin verse preface that headed one of these new editions: 'It would be hard to say whether it more brilliantly sets forth the royal splendour, or the author's learning'. But along with the public who read big books, it was necessary to attract the much larger public who looked at pictures. The engraver P. Firens—a Fleming who had his establishment in the Rue St-Jacques at the sign of the Taille Douce Press —offered for sale about the same time an engraving faithfully portraying the ceremony of the royal touch.[94] It shows the king passing along the rows of the kneeling sick, followed by his almoners, with his chief physician holding the head of each person as the king lays his hand upon the sores. The scene is set in the open air, in the midst of some rather heavy architecture, and a great display of military pomp. At the bottom of the engraving there is a lengthy legend in honour of kings in general, 'living portraits of Divinity', and in particular of the Most Christian King and his miracles. It ends as follows: 'Gentle readers, please excuse my boldness; my defence must be the support of a great king, and my safeguard the ardent desire I have to display to all men the wonders of the Most High'.[95] 'The support of a great king': I think we shall be quite justified in taking these words literally. Besides, we know from other sources that Firens often put his graver at the service of monarchist propaganda.[96] Thus the chief physician and the engraver, each in his own way, served the same policy, the theme of which was given to them from above.

And so in France and in England, after the struggles of the sixteenth century, the old belief in the supernatural gifts of royalty had once more triumphed—at least to outward appearance. It formed one of the articles in this monarchical faith which went on expanding in France during the absolutism of Louis XIV. In England, on the other hand, it gradually perished—though not without some ups and downs—under the impact of a new political and religious drama. We must say a word here about this faith in general; for unless we do this, there is a risk that the vitality of the wonder-working power of kings will appear quite inexplicable.

3   Sacred royalty and absolutism: the final legend in the French monarchical cycle[97]

To us nowadays, there is something surprising and even shocking about the habits of political thought and action displayed by the majority of Frenchmen in the time of Louis XIV, and likewise of a section of English opinion under the Stuarts. We find it hard to comprehend the idolatry of which royalty and kings were then the object; we can scarcely refrain from putting an adverse interpretation upon it, as though it were the result of some base servility. The difficulty we feel in penetrating the mentality of a period, however familiar to us in literature, on such an important point is perhaps due to our tendency to study its ideas of government solely through the great theorists who expounded them. Absolutism is a kind of religion; and to know a religion only through its theologians would be to condemn oneself to remaining ignorant of its vital springs. In this particular case, the method is all the more dangerous because these great doctrinaire writers often give only a kind of disguised version of the thought or sentiment of their time. Their classical education had instilled into them a taste for logical demonstration along with an insurmountable aversion to all political mysticism. They were therefore inclined to omit or conceal everything in the ideas of their world that could not be rationally expressed. This is true of Bossuet, who was impregnated with Aristotelianism, directly or through St Thomas Aquinas, almost as much as of Hobbes. There is a striking contrast between the *Politique tirée des propres paroles de l'Ecriture Sainte*, so basically reasonable, and the almost worshipping monarchism in which its author, like everyone around him, was involved. There was in fact a huge gulf between the abstract sovereign presented to us in this highly scientific treatise and the miraculous prince, anointed at Rheims with the heavenly oil, in whom Bossuet really believed with all his soul, both as priest and as faithful subject.[98]

So do not let us be led astray. In order to have true knowledge of even the most famous doctors of the monarchy, it is as well to be acquainted with the collective ideas handed down from the preceding ages, which were still vigorously alive at the time. For—to take up the comparison I was using just now—these men, like all theologians, were principally engaged in giving intellectual form to the very powerful sentiments that were widespread in their environment, and which they themselves more or less unconsciously shared. Hobbes subordinates the subject's beliefs to the prince's decisions. He writes—in terms worthy of the imperial polemical writers of the eleventh century—that 'although kings take not upon them the ministerial priesthood, yet they are not so merely laic, as not to have sacerdotal jurisdiction'.[99] For the full understanding of the deeply-rooted origin of these ideas, it is not enough merely to explain them by the social pessimism and political indifferentism professed by Hobbes; nor is it enough to remember that this great philosopher was a citizen of a country whose sovereign called himself 'supreme governor of the kingdom, as well in things spiritual as in things temporal'. What lies behind these ideas is in fact the whole conception of sacred kingship. When Balzac affirms that 'the person of Princes, whoever they may be, should be held by us as sacred and inviolable', or when he speaks of 'the impress of the divine finger' marked upon kings,[100] he is really expressing fundamentally the same sentiment, in a purified form, as that which had for so many generations impelled the sufferers from scrofula to seek healing from the kings of France.

It is probably a mistake for the historian to have constant recourse to these great front-line thinkers. He would probably do better to go to the second-rank authors, and consult those summaries of common law concerned with the monarchy, or eulogies of the monarchy—treatises on the majesty of kings, dissertations on their origin and authority, panegyrics on the fleur-de-lis—produced with such abundance in sixteenth- and seventeenth-century France. Not that the reader of such works should expect any great intellectual enjoyment, for as a rule they do not rise above a fairly low ideological level. Jean Ferrault, Claude d'Albon, Pierre Poisson de la Bodinière, H. du Boys, Louis Rolland, the Rev. Fathers Hippolyte Raulin or Balthasar de Riez, and other names that could easily be added—none of these has any claim to a place of honour in the history of social philosophy. Even the names of Charles Grassaille, André Duchesne and Jérôme Bignon, though perhaps rather worthier of esteem, none the less deserve the oblivion into which they have fallen.[101] But writings of this kind, by their very mediocrity and even sometimes coarseness, have the advantage of keeping very close to common ideas. And if they are sometimes to be suspected of having been composed by paid pamphleteers, more interested in earning their money than in following out an unprejudiced line of thought, so much the better, as far as we are concerned, for our primary aim is to grasp public opinion in its reality. Clearly, the arguments these professional propagandists choose to develop are the ones they expect to have most influence upon their readers.

The current ideas put out by these royal publicists of the seventeenth and eighteenth centuries often seem commonplace to anyone who has glanced at the literature of the preceding periods. They are only astonishing, however, if one fails to sense in them the long heritage from mediaeval times. It is no more advisable in the history of political doctrines than in any other sort of history to lay too much stress upon the traditional break generally introduced into European history about the year 1500, under the influence of the humanists. The sacred character of kings, so often affirmed by the writers of the Middle Ages, remains an obvious truth for modern times, and has constantly received fresh illustration.[102] The same is true of their quasi-sacerdotal character, though the writers are less unanimous on this point.

There had always been some hesitation about this matter, even among the most fervent royalists; and there would seem to have been more and more. Grassaille is full of the splendour of the French monarchy, and ready to accept all the legends that encircled it with a kind of marvellous halo; yet he repeatedly feels it incumbent upon him to state that the king, in spite of all his ecclesiastical privileges, is fundamentally a mere lay person.[103] Later on, at least in Catholic France, the Counter-Reformation, following upon the Council of Trent, and reinforcing the Church's discipline, made a clearer distinction than before between the regular priesthood and the status of the laity; with the result that a great many people became even more reluctant to accept the ill-defined position of a king, who was almost a priest but not quite. In spite of this, however, the ancient notion embodied in so many customs and rites retained a numerous following, even in the ranks of the clergy. We find the Bishop of Evreux, Robert Ceneau, writing in 1597:

> The majesty of the kings of France cannot be called altogether lay. And of this there are sundry evidences: first, holy unction, which takes its very origin from above; then the celestial privilege of the healing touch for scrofula, due to the intercession of St-Marcoul . . . and finally, the right of patronage, especially ecclesiastical patronage, containing—as we commonly see—the power to confer ecclesiastical benefices as of special right.[104]

André Duchesne, writing in 1609, holds that 'our great kings . . . have never been considered pure laymen, but have been held to be decked both with priesthood and with royalty, all in one'.[105] In 1611, a priest called Claude Villette published, under the title *Les Raisons de l'office et ceremonies qui se font en l'Eglise catholique*, a liturgical treatise whose success is testified by the number of editions it was to go through in subsequent years. It contains a long commentary on the consecration rites; and from several of these—unction upon the hands, the offerings made by the king, and above all Communion in both kinds—he concludes that the king is 'a mixed and ecclesiastical person'.[106] And in 1645, the almoner Guillaume du Peyrat came out even more clearly with the following justification for the eucharistic privilege accorded to the French monarchs: 'In my opinion, the reason for it is that although the kings of France are not priests like pagan kings . . . they nevertheless partake of the priestly character, and are not purely laymen'.[107] Then in a long and dull eulogy of the dynasty produced by Father Balthasar de Riez in 1672, the view is expressed that it is consecration which makes royal personages 'sacred and in some sort priestly'.[108]

The same attitude is observable among the English royalists. Witness these words put into the mouth of the captive Charles I by the author of the *Eikon Basilike*, on the subject of the refusal to allow him a chaplain: 'It may be, I am esteemed by my deniers sufficient of myself to discharge my duty to God as a priest: though not to men as a prince. Indeed, I think both offices, regal and sacerdotal, might well become the same person, as anciently they were under one name and the united rights of primogeniture.'[109]

Furthermore, the science of Christian antiquities had now come in to offer its support to this very old confusion between the two offices, and to put forward arguments unknown to the polemical writers of earlier ages. The Late Empire, after Constantine's conversion and even after Gratian, in the year 382, had renounced the traditional title of *pontifex maximus*, had not straightaway given up the idea of a sort of pontifical dignity attached to the Emperor. In the seventeenth century certain ancient documents expressing this conception and which had not been known to the Middle Ages, were brought to light. 'Long live the priest, the *basileus*!' the Fathers of Chalcedon had exclaimed in salutation to Marcianus. This salutation had no doubt been adopted as a fixed form by the Byzantine court ceremonial; and it was this that Daguesseau pronounced before the Parliament of Paris in 1699 in his *Réquisitoire pour l'enregistrement de la Bulle contre les Maximes des Saints*, applying it in praise of Louis XIV: 'Both king and priest, such are the terms used by the Council of Chalcedon'.[110] Most important of all, there was the life of Constantine by Eusebius, which had been often reprinted. In it there occurs the famous passage in which the Emperor calls himself τῶν ἐκτὸς ὑπὸ θεοῦ καθεσταμένος ἐπίσκοπος which was usually translated—no matter whether rightly or wrongly—'outwardly bishop'.[111] From the seventeenth century onwards, it became quite common to apply these words to the French king.[112] Thus the rebirth of scholarship assured the survival of these ancient remnants of paganism, now wearing a Christian mask.

Never has there been a time when the quasi-divine nature of the institution, and even the person, of royalty, was as directly or even bluntly emphasized as in the seventeenth century. 'Therefore (my Sonne),' said James I of England to his heir, the young prince, 'first of all things, learne to know and love that God whom-to ye have a double obligation; first, for that he made you a man; and next, for that he made you a little God to sit on his Throne and rule over other men.'[113] For the Frenchman Jean Savaron, the president and lieutenant general of the Seneschalsy of the Auvergne, monarchs are gods in bodily form;[114] for André Duchesne, they are gods come down to earth.[115] On 13 November 1625, the Bishop of Chartres, speaking for the Assembly of Clergy, expressed himself as follows:

> . . . let it then be known that, apart from the universal consensus of the peoples and nations, the Prophets announce, the Apostles confirm, and the Martyrs confess, that kings are ordained by God; and not only this, but that they are themselves gods, a thing that cannot have been invented by the servile flattery and complaisance of the Pagans; but this same truth is so clearly set forth in Holy Scripture that no man may deny it without blasphemy, or doubt it without sacrilege . . .[116]

Many other examples could be quoted, including the title of a royalist pamphlet in the time of the Fronde, entitled: *L'Image du Souverain ou l'Illustre Portrait des Divinités Mortelles.*[117] 'You are gods, although you die, and your authority never dies,' exclaimed Bossuet, when speaking on the Duties of kings at the Louvre on Palm Sunday 1662.[118] No one listening to him that day would have been astonished to hear such an expression on the lips of a preacher, although nowadays it sounds singularly bold, if not positively blasphemous. In those days it was perfectly commonplace.

It is not difficult to discover the source from which writers and orators derived it. First and foremost, from the Bible. The first two verses of Psalm 82 were generally considered to refer to kings: 'I have said, ye are gods, and ye are all children of the Most High, yet ye shall die like men'. In his commentary on the Psalms,[119] Calvin, like Bossuet in the above-mentioned sermon, applied this text to royalty. Nor is this all. Contemporary literature, steeped as it was in Holy Scripture, was equally steeped in the literature of antiquity. In vain did the Bishop of Chartres stigmatize 'the servile flattery and vile complaisance of the pagans'; he had to admit that they had been right in equating kings and gods. Even before his time, Claude d'Albon quoted the example of 'the ancient Philosophers' in support of his contention that 'the Prince is more than a man . . . nay, he is a god', or at least 'a demi-god'.[120] Here too, learned memories of antiquity constrained these fervent Christians to use language heavily loaded with pagan thought. We may conveniently remind ourselves of what that great twelfth-century humanist John of Salisbury, who was at the same time one of the most vigorous champions of the supremacy of the spiritual, said about the Romans: 'This nation invented the words we use in order to lie to our masters'.[121] Even in the Middle Ages, these influences were already sometimes making themselves felt. Towards the end of the twelfth century, Godfrey of Viterbo, speaking to the Emperor Henry VI, exclaimed: 'Thou art god, born of a race of gods'. Godfrey was a pedant, a worthy emulator of his compatriot and contemporary Peter of Eboli, who was accustomed to call this same sovereign 'Jupiter the Thunderer' and his wife 'Juno'.[122] About a century later, Egidio Colonna was calling kings 'demi-gods';[123] he too was familiar with the authors of antiquity, and was thereby induced to use a term at variance with his political system as a whole, which was usually not very favourable to the temporal power. In general, however, such deviations are rare in the Middle Ages. It must be recognized that such abuses of the divine name hardly became general before the seventeenth century. We must not, of course, exaggerate the importance of verbal excesses of this kind: the element of purely literary reminiscence in them should warn us not to take them too seriously. Yet their significance should not be minimized, for words are never entirely separable from the things they represent. It is very striking to find this constant use, in an age of faith, of expressions which previous ages would almost unanimously have rejected as idolatrous. What would Gregory VII have thought of the language used by the Bishop of Chartres?[124]

Towards the end of the sixteenth and at the beginning of the following century, the religious struggles had momentarily seemed to revive the ancient polemics concerning the *regnum* and the *sacerdotium*. The controversy between Cardinal Bellarmine and James I of England is as it were a last echo of Gregorian times;[125] and the same is true of the long discussion among theologians on the subject of tyrannicide. But ecclesiastical opinion as a whole, especially in France, had become more and more favourable to the concept of sacred royalty. The Church was now inclined to see the sacred character claimed by kings more as a homage to religion than as an encroachment on the privileges of the clergy. In particular, no Catholic dreamt any longer of ostracizing the royal miracle for theological reasons. In 1572, a Spanish priest, the Blessed Luis of Granada, a jealous champion of orthodoxy, quoted quite naturally in his *Introduccion al simbolo de la Fe* —a work many times republished and translated—as an example of contemporary miracles 'the virtue possessed by the kings of France to heal the contagious and incurable disease of scrofula' (just as Bradwardine had done in days gone by), and devoted considerable space to developing the theme.[126] Moreover, as early as 1547, at a time when his difficulties with Charles V inclined him to treat the Valois with some benevolence, Pope Paul III had expressly recognized the authenticity of this 'virtue'. In the Bull founding Rheims University, dated 5 January of that year, he sang the praises of 'the city of Rheims where the Most Christian kings receive from the archbishop's hands, as a bounty sent down from on high, the gift of Holy Unction, and the power to heal the sick.'[127]

Yet the miraculous gift did not always receive the same treatment by writers in every period. In the sixteenth century, all—or nearly all—the apologists of royalty, from Vincent Cigauld under Louis XII or Grassaille under Francis I to Forcatel under Henry III, give it an honourable place in their works.[128] In the seventeenth century, on the other hand, it serves as a touchstone to distinguish between the two categories into which the political literature of absolutism was quite sharply divided at that time: what may be called philosophical literature, and popular literature. Writers of the second class, such as Arroy, Hippolyte Raulin, Maimbourg, make extensive use of it as an argument eminently likely to go home to their readers. Writers in the first class, however, avoid any mention of it. For example, neither Balzac in his *Prince* or his *Aristippe*, nor Bossuet in any of his major works, makes the slightest allusion to the royal healings. This silence can certainly not be ascribed to scepticism on their part, but must be viewed as no more than one among many other signs of the repugnance felt by these thinkers for anything not constructed on strictly rational lines. But it was none the less an ominous sign for the future of the royal hand. This great miracle was no doubt still believed in by almost all circles, and Bossuet mentions it as something he takes for granted in an informal letter;[129] but the learned felt a kind of bashfulness in speaking of it, as though it were a rather too popular belief; and later on, they became ashamed to believe in it at all.

As we saw above, it was unction, and especially the miraculous oil from the Holy Phial, that Paul III considered the source of the healing gift; and here he was in line with ancient tradition. In this way a power that had always been somewhat suspect in principle became linked to an entirely Christian rite. There were now hardly any opponents of this view except among the most zealous supporters of St-Marcoul, and even these, as we know, soon gave in. Among the most fervent royalists, no one any longer dreamt of denying the role attributed to unction in this context. No doubt, it was still perfectly understood among all the theorists on this side that consecration, as du Haillan expressed it, was no more than 'a thoroughly reverent ceremony', not 'in any way concerning the essence of sovereignty'. In default of it, a king did not fail 'd'estre roi'; and the events marking the beginning of Henry IV's reign gave the political writers one more chance of reiterating this doctrine, which had by now become an official dogma.[130] But the theorists would not admit that the dignity of kingship was dependent upon an ecclesiastical solemnity. Yet they would seem to have been less touchy on the question of the healing power. Henry IV was king a good while before he was consecrated; but he did not do any laying on of hands before this event. He never visited Corbeny, access to it being blocked at the time of his coronation; so that at least in his case, it was consecration with the holy oil, and not the intercession of St-Marcoul, that was waited for as a necessary prelude to healing.[131] As regards the origin of the royal miracle, as on so many other points, the seventeenth century saw a kind of reconciliation between the defenders of the Church's rights and the most zealous champions of royalty.

The old legends about the Holy Phial, the fleur-de-lis or the oriflamme continued to circulate in France. Towards the end of the sixteenth century, a new story came in to join the traditional cycle. This was the legend of the first healing of scrofula by Clovis, which is of particular interest to us here.

According to the most generally held opinion, consecration conferred upon kings the right to heal. Now Clovis was said to have been the first French prince to receive unction, and unction direct from heaven; it was natural enough to think that this monarch, with the favour shown him from on high, had likewise been the first to relieve the pains of scrofula. Truth to tell, there is only one surprising thing—namely that this myth should have come so late upon the scene.[132] To create this myth, it needed the fluency of a certain southern publicist, Étienne Forcatel of Béziers. In the history of jurisprudence he has acquired a somewhat doubtful celebrity for having been preferred by the professors of Toulouse to the great Cujas, when the latter—whose novel methods frightened the traditionalism of the university faculties—was canvassing for a university Chair in the Faculty of Law. 'An incompetent man, quite incapable of teaching' (*homine insulso et ad docendum minus idoneo*) says Cujas' biographer, Papire Masson.[133] At any rate, he was an entirely unoriginal thinker, and a writer surprisingly lacking in order and clarity, as can be seen from his *Traité de l'empire et la philosophie des Français*, which first appeared in 1579. In spite of its second-rate quality, this book went through several editions.[134] But there is more to it than this; for it would seem that it is to this book that the honour belongs of having launched upon the world the anecdote about Clovis as a miraculous healer, an anecdote that was destined to enjoy so much fame. I have not been able—nor were the seventeenth century writers who quote it—to find this anecdote in any earlier writer; and we must admit that it issued in full array from Forcatel's inventive brain. Here it is, in summary form.[135] Clovis had a squire to whom he was much attached called Lanicet (by which we see that our author was very imperfectly acquainted with Merovingian proper names) and this man was struck down by scrofula. He tried various remedies but in vain; and notably—twice over—the remedy prescribed by Celsus, namely to eat a snake. Then Clovis had a dream, in which he saw himself healing Lanicet simply by touching him; and at the same time his room seemed to be filled with a flaming light. As soon as he woke up, he gave thanks to God, and touched his squire, whose disease of course departed from him.[136] This was the origin of the miraculous gift, which was then passed down from Clovis to his sons, and so to all his successors. The enormous success of this very second-rate fable shows that it corresponded to a kind of logical need in men's imaginations. It was reproduced by Canon Meurier as early as 1597;[137] and it very rapidly became a commonplace, or rather an article of faith, for the apologists of royalty;[138] though the good historians like du Peyrat or Scipion Dupleix no doubt rejected it; but who listen would to them?[139] In spite of du Peyrat's protests, du Laurens includes it in his famous treatise on the healing of scrofula; and this work soon became authoritative.[140] Then it crossed the frontier, and turned up as early as 1628 in the works of a Spanish historian.[141] It soon formed an integral part of the legendary and sentimental patrimony of France. The author of the little work entitled *Codicilles de Louis XIII roi de France et de Navarre à son très cher fils aîné* . . ., which appeared during Louis XIV's minority, worked out a curious programme of patriotic feasts, among which he suggested one on 'the second Sunday after Easter' for 'thanking God for the gift He made to the said S.Clovis (*sic*) and all the kings of France for the gift of the Holy Phial and the healing of the scrofula'.[142] A little later on, Desmarets de St-Sorlin, when composing his great national and religious epic *Clovis ou la France chrestienne*, was careful not to omit such a splendid episode; and if he made a few adjustments in order to give weight to the dramatic elements in the story, it still remains the same tale first elaborated by Étienne Forcatel.[143] This jurist from Toulouse, apparently unrestrained by any scruples of scholarship or simple honesty, had been brazen enough to supply the public with the legend it needed to complete the cycle of miraculous royalty. There would be cause for astonishment at the success of this kind of fraud if the same cycle did not already contain so many examples of the ease with which an individual invention can spread when it is carried along on a current of collective credulity.[144]

But what proves the power of miraculous royalty better than anything written by the publicists, and better than all the legends, is the popularity of the royal miracle in seventeenth-century France, and the part that it played at this same time in the civil strife in England.

4 *The touch for scrofula in the period of French absolutism and the early struggles of the English civil war*

In the French monarchy of the seventeenth century, the touch for scrofula definitely took its place among the solemn ceremonies with which the sovereign's splendour was surrounded.[145] Louis XIII and Louis XIV practised it regularly on the great festivals—Easter, Pentecost, Christmas or New Year's Day—and sometimes on Candlemas, Trinity Sunday, the Assumption, and All Saints' Day.[146] When the ceremony took place in Paris, the Grand Provost would announce it some days in advance, with the sound of the trumpet and by public notice. We still possess some of these placards from Louis XIV's time;[147] (one of them is reproduced as Plate 5 in the form in which they must often have been read by passers-by in those days, displayed on the walls of their town, in the open air). The ceremony used to take place in different places, as the particular occasion required. In Paris, it was usually in the Great Gallery of the Louvre, or more rarely in a ground floor room of the same palace; elsewhere, it would be in one of the rooms or courtyards of a *château*, or in parks, cloisters or churches. As it was attended by large crowds, the ceremony was very tiring, especially in hot weather and for a youthful king like Louis XIII at the beginning of his reign.[148] But unless the sovereign was seriously indisposed, he could not get out of this duty, which was an essential part of his office; he had to sacrifice himself for the health of his subjects. Only when there was an epidemic were the sick excluded, for fear of spreading the infection and exposing the king to it.[149] But the sick would come all the same: 'they won't leave me alone; they say that kings never die of the plague . . . they think I'm only a king on a pack of cards', said the young Louis XIII, who used to be enraged by this 'persecution'.[150] The fact is that the wonder-working gift had lost nothing of its ancient popularity. We still possess some figures for Louis XIII's reign, and—usually less accurately —for Louis XIV. They are much like the figures of former days: several hundreds, and sometimes more than a thousand at each session. In 1611 for the whole year it was at least 2,210, in 1620, 3,125; on Easter Day 1613, 1,070 at a single session;[151] on 22 May 1701, Trinity Sunday, 2,400.[152] When the usual regular sequence had been interrupted for one reason or another, there was a really frightening crowd for its first resumption. At Easter 1698, Louis XIV had an attack of gout, and was unable to touch; and when Pentecost came round, he was faced with nearly 3,000 sufferers from scrofula.[153] In 1715, on Saturday 8 June, the eve of Pentecost, 'in very hot weather', the king—who was already very near death— performed the healing act for the last time; he touched some 1,700 persons.[154]

As in the past, a cosmopolitan crowd milled around the approaches to the royal palaces on the appointed days. The great reputation of the French miracle was no more confined to the national boundaries than it had been in days gone by. Truth to tell, we can adopt the words of Father Maimbourg, when he wrote that this marvellous king's 'empire' was bounded neither by the natural frontiers 'nor by the chain of the Pyrenees or the Alps, nor by the Rhine, nor by the Ocean'; for 'nature herself was subject to him'.[155] An eye-witness, Josué Barbier by name, who happened to be at the court at St-Germain-en-Laye in June 1618, has left us a picturesque account of all this motley throng—'as many Spaniards, Portuguese, Italians, Germans, Swiss and Flemings as Frenchmen'—whom he saw that Pentecost strung out all along the main road and in the shade of the park, waiting for the youthful king.[156] Churchmen were as ready to present themselves as others: we know of at least three Portuguese Jesuits who journeyed to France at this time in order to receive the royal touch.[157] The arts sometimes placed themselves at the service of this universal fame. When the citizens of Bologna visited their municipal building, they had only to lift up their eyes to see an immediate reminder of the astonishing power 'over nature' possessed by the king of France. Between 1658 and 1662, Cardinal Girolamo Farnese, who was governing this city as legate, had adorned a gallery in the old *palazzo* with frescoes in the pompous and theatrical style of the Bologna school. There were eight large compositions, each of them representing a historical scene, real or legendary, in the life of the ancient city, which belonged to a princely house then fairly closely linked to France by political bonds. The cardinal opportunely remembered that in 1515 Francis I had shown himself to the inhabitants of Bologna in the role of miraculous healer. On the right-hand wall you can still see the king, as portrayed by Carlo Cignani and Emilio Taruffi, passing his hand over the neck of a kneeling woman, while all round him there are pages, men at arms and patients standing or squatting in groups, the whole being nicely balanced according to the rules of classical art.[158]

Among the foreigners who thus sought the healing hand of the French king, the most numerous were always the Spaniards. As though in reward for their zeal, they were always placed in the forefront when the sick were arranged in order before the ceremony began.[159] Moreover, as they were, generally speaking, not regarded with much favour as a nation by the French, there was a tendency to make fun of their eagerness to come forward. It used to be said in Louis XIII's time by the politicians and the Protestants that everyone knew why in the days of the League Bellarmine, Commolet and the other leading lights in the Society of Jesus were so keen to hand over the kingdom of France to the House of Spain: it was out of charity, in order to make it easier for this scrofulous people to have access to their accredited physician.[160] Or they would tell the amusing little story with which Father Maimbourg delighted the pupils at the Collège de Rouen on a prize-giving day. A Spanish grandee who suffered from scrofula knew that he would only regain his health if he was touched by the French king; but his pride prevented him from acknowledging the disease, and more particularly his faith in the virtues of an enemy prince. He therefore went as it were on a visit to Fontainebleau, where Henry IV was then in residence, hiding all signs of the disease disfiguring his neck beneath his cuirass and the folds of his broad ruff, after the fashion of his country. The king embraced him in order to bid him welcome, and he was healed.[161] But these astute politicians were not merely joking: they were using the well-known feelings of the Spanish sufferers as a useful means of propaganda. In Richelieu's time, a publicist of the French party in Catalonia appealed to the royal miracle as an argument calculated to convert his compatriots to the Bourbon cause.[162]

This fame spreading far and wide through Europe was a thorn in the flesh of the rival dynasties. There could be no finer homage to it than their anxieties, manifest in the bitter attacks launched by writers in the pay of the House of Austria. All these pamphleteers—and they were particularly numerous during the first half of the century—were extremely preoccupied with the miraculous privilege claimed by the French kings; and they often claimed for their own masters—a Hapsburg in Vienna or in Madrid—a similar privilege, based (as we have seen) on nothing but the memory of ancient and long-discredited attempts at healing, or more simply still on their own imaginative inspirations. In any case, they were bent upon playing down the value of this very popular gift.

Here is a rather interesting example of this state of mind. There appeared in 1635, under the title of *Mars Gallicus*, a small book displaying a Spanish bias, which enjoyed a certain celebrity. It was written under the pseudonym of Alexander Patricius Armacanus, and did not deny the French miracle, for it would have been highly audacious to do so! But it set out to show that the miraculous gift is received from God as something freely given, and proves neither holiness nor any kind of superiority in the person upon whom God has chosen to bestow it. Balaam's ass prophesied: does that prove that it possessed the prerogative of supreme power over all the race of asses?[163] This was a basically orthodox theory; but it has been seldom developed to this vigorous extreme. The fact is that this pseudonym was a mask for a weighty theologian, Jansenius, Bishop of Ypres. This was a case where political passion found its support in certain theories about divine grace and freewill, which were destined to create something of a stir throughout the world. But in spite of all the assertions of the writers of books the Spaniards continued to flock to the king of France.

As for distinguished visitors touring Paris—even Lutherans—they were invariably taken to witness the royal touch. It was one of the sights of the city, something to be seen in an interval between a sung Mass and a solemn session of the Académie des Inscriptions.[164]

Thus the history of the royal miracle in seventeenth-century France is a thoroughly peaceful one. No doubt there were unbelievers: the majority of Protestants would seem to have been decidedly in this class. A writer who had formerly belonged to them, the former pastor Josué Barbier, who was converted to Catholicism towards the beginning of Louis XIII's reign, and appears to have been extremely anxious to get the maximum personal advantage from this change of religion, thought he could best pay court by devoting to the royal miracle a dithyrambic work entitled: *Les miraculeux effects de la sacrée main des Roys de France tres chrestiens : pour la guarison des Malades et conversion des Heretiques*. In it, he directly accuses his ex-co-religionists of not believing in these 'miraculous effects' and either attributing the so-called cures to 'diabolical illusions' or quite simply denying their reality.[165] Not that public opinion among the Reformed Churches was generally hostile to the monarchy, either before or after the revocation of the Edict of Nantes. There is an absolutist literature coming from Protestant sources, such works as the *Discours sur la Souveraineté des Roys*, published in 1650 by Pastor Moyse Amyraut and directed against the English revolutionaries, or the *Traité du pouvoir absolu des Souverains*, published in 1685 by Pastor Elie Merlat. Both of these would seem to be the sincere opinions of profoundly loyal subjects. But the monarchy thus presented to their readers is a monarchy shorn of legend and miracle, hardly resting upon any other sentimental support than respect for the Bible, interpreted in a sense favourable to the divine right of kings. One may well doubt whether the loyalty of the masses could in the long run be sustained in all its blind fervour without the basis of the mystical and the miraculous that Calvinism was now taking away from them. Moyse Amyraut took as the theme for his discourse the biblical text: 'Touch not mine anointed'. These words were full of rich significance for believers watching their master being anointed on his consecration-day with the heavenly balm once brought down from heaven by the dove; but they were bound to sound hollow to men who were far from recognizing anything supernatural about the oil of Rheims, and as a matter of faith refused to admit that unction itself possessed any inherent efficacy. They only attributed to it—as Amyraut himself teaches—a purely and strictly symbolical value.[166] In this sense, Josué Barbier was not perhaps altogether wrong in pointing out a sort of incompatibility between the reformed religion and the monarchical sentiments, at least as ordinarily understood by the fervent French monarchists of the seventeenth century.

Even at court, not everyone took the miracle very seriously. Louis XIV's own sister-in-law, the Duchess of Orléans, who had been brought up a Protestant, ventured to express her private opinion in a letter written, it must be mentioned, after the Great King's death. 'People here also believe that a seventh son can cure the scrofula by a touch of his hand. For my part, I think his touch has just as much power as the French king's' [by which we should obviously understand 'as *little* power'].[167] Later on, we shall see Saint-Simon's opinion—though it, too, was given in another reign and perhaps under the unconscious influence of a new movement of thought.[168] Among the royal entourage, and especially among the free-thinkers, there were probably other people of very slender faith who kept their mouths shut. But there is no doubt at all that the masses believed wholeheartedly. The eagerness of the sick to come forward is sufficient proof of the popular fervour. But the history of the miracle in England at this same period did not run such a smooth course.

At first sight, there would not seem to have been any point in the events of Charles I's reign that differed from the situation in France. The royal touch generally took place more frequently than at the court of the Bourbons. It was apt to be interrupted by epidemics, or by seasons of excessive heat. The appointed days were announced in advance by royal proclamations throughout the country.[169] The solemn ceremony followed the liturgical forms adapted by Elizabeth and James I to the use of the Anglican Church. There was great enthusiasm, and although we have no accurate figures for this reign, all the evidence indicates that the faith and zeal of the sick were in no way diminished. It was even necessary to take precautions against excessive crowds, who might have imposed too great a strain upon the king, and doubtless also on his treasury. After having been touched once, some people used to try and slip in again. Either they had not found adequate relief on the first occasion, and hoped to improve the results by a second touch; or they were simply tempted by the very generous amount of the alms, especially as the traditional 'angel' was easily negotiable as a talisman. In order to prevent this abuse, it was laid down that no one might present himself more than once. In order to ensure that this provision was carried out, every sufferer from scrofula wishing to take part in the ceremony had to provide himself in advance with a certificate from the pastor and the various parish authorities stating that he had never before received the royal touch.[170]

In this reign, the miraculous rite became an integral part of the country's regular life. In 1633, a significant innovation was introduced, by which the service of 'healing' was incorporated into the *Book of Common Prayer*, which the Church put into the hands of everyone.[171] In short, the picture we get is that of a well-supported miracle, which had become one of the institutions of a well-ordered monarchical State.[172]

Moreover, it was an uncompromisingly absolutist State. In France, the monarchy under Louis XIII and Louis XIV showed itself tolerant towards the 'seventh sons', who were nevertheless fairly hot competitors with the kings as healers. It is true that under Louis XIII the Archbishop of Bordeaux, Henri de Sourdis, had forbidden certain persons to continue their practice—probably 'seventh sons', who claimed to heal scrofula in his archiepiscopal city. His veto was based upon the principle that 'the privilege of touching such sick persons is reserved to the sacred person of our most Christian King'.[173] But this would appear to be an absolutely isolated instance. In England, on the other hand, Charles I or his ministers declared relentless war against the competitors with the royal prerogative. To touch the scrofulous, for anyone who was not a king, was declared to be a crime of lèse-majesté which could, if necessary, be brought before the famous Court of the Star Chamber.[174] This showed a somewhat touchy susceptibility, indicative perhaps of an absolute power less firmly based than that of the Bourbons.

Indeed, it is not difficult to see why the Stuarts should have preferred to keep a monopoly of this miracle. Sick people who had been healed, and who thought they owed their healing to the royal hand, were likely to be assured supporters of the monarchy. One of these chances that happen only too rarely has preserved a document giving a vivid picture of the mental state that could be produced by a fortunate royal touch. A certain nobleman, Lord Poulett, had a daughter who, poor child, was entirely disfigured by scrofula. He sent her to court, where she received the royal touch in 1631, and at once improved in health. A Secretary of State, Lord Dorchester, had obligingly undertaken to present her to the king, and after the event her father wrote to thank him. We still possess this letter, which is couched in really moving terms.[175] The feelings expressed on that occasion by this noble lord must no doubt have been shared by more than one father or mother of humbler station, whose voice has not reached us down the years. What does it matter to us today that such joys should have been based upon what was no doubt an illusion? It is impossible to have a sound appreciation of the strength of loyalty towards the monarchy if one allows prejudice to rule out from historical evidence the effusions of these grateful hearts. Although Lord Poulett came of a Puritan line he later on joined the king's side against Parliament. To be sure, the memory of the royal miracle cannot have been the sole, nor even the principal, reason for his attitude; but it is surely hard to believe that on the day when he made his decision, he did not go back in mind to the sick little child who had been healed when there seemed to be no hope.

Then came the Civil War. Belief in the wonder-working power now became one of the dogmas of the royalist faith rejected by the supporters of the Long Parliament, but still alive in the hearts of the common people. In 1642, Charles I had left London, where the middle classes and the artisans were making common cause with the parliamentary party; and he soon set up his headquarters in Oxford. The following year there was printed and circulated in London, a 'humble petition to His Excellent Majesty the King, presented by several hundreds of his poor subjects afflicted with this painful infirmity known as the King's Evil'. The sufferers said, in fine, that they were afflicted with a 'supernatural' disease, only to be cured by those 'supernaturall meanes of cure which is inherent in your sacred Majesty'. They said they could not have access to him at Oxford, where he was 'invironed with so many legions of souldiers'; and they therefore begged His Majesty to return to Whitehall. The so-called petitioners affirm that they have no wish to interfere in politics, 'having enough to reflect and consider our owne miseries'. This protest cannot be taken at its face value. It is clearly no more than a royalist pamphlet. Its authors lift the mask when they declare at the close that they hope the king's return will bring with it not only the healing of the sick, but also the healing of 'the State, which hath languished of a tedious sicknesse since your Highnesse departure from thence, and can no more be cured of its infirmitie then wee, till your gracious returne hither'.[176] Besides, it was not Charles I who was unwilling to return to London; it was the Londoners who refused to allow him to, at least as an absolute sovereign; they were the people who had to be appealed to. An ingenious publicist had the idea of stirring up public opinion in the capital by this supposed plea from the scrofulous. No doubt he had his reasons for striking this note. The sights that must have been seen during the king's captivity were such as to suggest beyond doubt that the sufferers from scrofula did miss the presence of their physician-in-ordinary. In February 1647, Charles, recently handed over by the Scots, was brought south by the Parliamentary commissaries; and during the whole of the journey sick people flocked to him, bringing with them the coin—gold, if possible, or failing that, silver—which the prince was no longer rich enough to bestow from his own privy purse, but which was commonly believed to be necessary for him to hang round their neck if the rite was to be fully efficacious. The commissaries did their best to keep the crowds away, with the somewhat hypocritical excuse that there was a danger of infection, since 'many of them are in truth infected with other dangerous diseases, and are therefore altogether unfit to come into the Presence of His Majesty'.[177] When the king, still a prisoner, was installed at Holmby House, there was a repetition of the same scenes. The House of Commons then decided to act in the matter, and appointed a committee to draw up 'a Declaration to be set forth to the People, concerning the Superstition of being Touched for the Healing of the King's Evil'.[178] The text of this proclamation appears to have been lost, which is a great pity, for we should like to know the reasons put forward in it, which would doubtless throw an interesting light upon the feelings of one party about the sacred nature of royalty. Moreover, we have good reason to doubt whether it had much effect on the masses. The so-called petitioners of 1643 were not altogether wrong in affirming that the touch was the only prerogative the person of royalty could never be deprived of.[179] When Charles had been beheaded, special powers of healing were attributed to his relics, especially to handkerchiefs dipped in his blood—the selfsame power that had resided in his hands when he was alive.[180] A royal martyr, even in a Protestant country, was always liable to become a kind of saint.

Later on, the royalists claimed that Cromwell had tried to exercise the miraculous gift, thus usurping for his own advantage even the supernatural privileges of royalty,[181] but that was certainly no more than a wanton calumny. Under the Republic and the Protectorate, there was no more touching by anyone in Great Britain. Yet the old faith was not dead. Charles II in exile performed the hereditary miracle; seeing that his treasury was in a sorry state, he could only distribute silver coins instead of gold, but people still came to him. An ingenious merchant ran organized tours by sea for the English or Scottish scrofula sufferers to the Low Country towns where the prince had his meagre court.[182] What is more, the relics of the living pretender were credited with the same power as those of the dead king. A handkerchief used by him to staunch a nose-bleed during his flight to Scotland after the battle of Worcester was said to be able to heal the scrofula.[183] It is as well to bear these facts in mind when we attempt to explain the Restoration of 1660. Not that one should imagine, of course, that the king was called to the throne for the specific purpose of relieving the scrofulous; but the persistent belief in the wonder-working gift is one of the symptoms of a state of mind the historians of these events cannot afford to ignore.

Again, those who brought about the Restoration, desirous of reviving the monarchical religion in men's hearts, did not forget the prestige enjoyed by the royal miracle. As early as May 1660, when Charles II had just been recognized by Parliament, but was still on foreign soil, at Breda, he carried out a particularly solemn healing ceremony.[184] As soon as he returned to England, he proceeded to touch on several occasions, in the Banqueting Hall of the Palace of Whitehall, and there were crowds of sufferers thronging round him.[185] The defenders of royalty fostered the popular enthusiasm both by word of mouth and by pen. Preaching at Westminster on 2 December 1660, Sancroft exhorted the faithful to hope for relief from the sufferings being undergone by the Church and the people through 'those very hands upon which God hath entailed a Miraculous Gift of Healing'.[186] This was a significant allegorical allusion, which recurs in 1661 as the theme of a very wordy and rather mad pamphlet of John Bird, called *Ostenta Carolina*.[187] In 1665, there appeared a small anonymous work devoted directly and without any metaphor to the royal touch itself, entitled Χειρεξοχη or *The Excellency of Handy-work of the Royal Hand*.[188] Finally, in 1684, came the turn of one of the king's physicians, John Browne, whose *Adenochoiradelogia* is the exact English counterpart, though more than seventy years removed in time, of the treatise by du Laurens. It was a lengthy demonstration, strongly reinforced by argument and anecdote, in favour of the prince's healing power.[189]

It is no part of the historian's duty to sound the secrets of the heart. We shall never know what Charles II really thought deep down inside of the singular talent so liberally attributed to him by his subjects. Do not let us be in any hurry, however, to proclaim it all scepticism and imposture; for that would be to set too slight a value upon the power of dynastic pride. Moreover, a certain degree of moral laxity does not necessarily exclude credulity. At all events, whatever the king's intimate feelings may have been, the performance of this miraculous healing was perhaps the one of his royal duties that he carried out with the greatest conscientiousness. He touched much more frequently than his French neighbour, regularly on Fridays in the ordinary way, except in times of great heat. The ceremonial remained the same as in his father's and grandfather's time; except that after 1665 the coin formerly given to the sick was replaced by a token specially struck for the occasion, and valueless as currency.[190] Even nowadays collections of English coins quite often contain examples of these fine gold tokens, bearing—like the 'angels'—the impress of St Michael slaying the dragon, and the legend *Soli Deo Gloria;* on the reverse is a three-masted ship with its sails swelling in the wind. Those who had come for healing would most carefully preserve these medals, treating them like amulets; and a good number have come down to us because a much larger number still were originally distributed.

The figures give us some idea of Charles II's popularity as a healer. Here are some of them: from May 1660—the beginning of the rite—to September 1664, rather more than four years, about 23,000 persons were touched; from 7 April 1669 to 14 May 1671—scarcely more than two years—at least 6,666, and perhaps even more; from 12 February 1684 to 1 February 1685—about a year, and at the extreme end of Charles's reign (for he died on the following 6 February)—6,610. Browne was certainly exaggerating when he affirmed in 1684 that 'near half the Nation hath been Toucht and Healed by His Sacred Majesty since His Happy Restauration'.[191] But we can quite confidently estimate that the number of sick persons Charles must have seen pass before him was something like 100,000 during his twenty-five years' reign.[192] It was a mixed crowd, in which (according to Browne) there were a number of foreigners—Germans, Dutch, and even Frenchmen—and at any rate some colonists from America—Virginia and New Hampshire—who had come to seek healing in Whitehall. We know this for certain, because there is documentary proof.[193] There is no doubt, however, that the majority were English or Scottish. In short, no wonder-working king ever enjoyed greater success. The long interruption during the Long Parliament and the Cromwellian period had only resulted in a revival of popular faith in the miracle. The sick, who had long been deprived of the supernatural remedy for their disease, thronged around their august healer from the moment of his return with a kind of fury. But this eagerness was no transient blaze, for—as we have seen—it continued throughout the reign. The notion of miraculous royalty, though so disdainfully regarded as a superstitious practice by the House of Commons in 1647, was very far from being on its deathbed.

Yet it had its adversaries, and they had by no means laid down their weapons. Browne's polemics in his *Adenochoiradelogia* against the noncon-formists, and the edifying little stories in which he delighted of nonconformists converted to respect for royalty by the results of miraculous healing, are eloquent proof that not everybody shared the popular belief. In 1684, a Presbyterian minister was prosecuted for having spoken slightingly of the royal touch.[194] Nevertheless, even this party could not afford to neglect the weapon of miracle. In 1680 Monmouth, a natural son of Charles II, and considered by the Whigs as the heir designate, instead of his uncle the Duke of York, who was thought to be barred from the throne by his Catholic faith, made a triumphal procession through the western counties. It would seem that on this occasion, although he was only, even in his supporters' eyes, the future king, he touched at least once for the scrofula.[195]

And when in 1685, still in the name of Protestantism, he took up arms to challenge the right of his uncle to the crown—who had by then become James II—he carried out all the usual royal acts—among others, the rite of healing. In the posthumous Bill of Indictment drawn up against him by James II's magistrates, this figures as one of the charges.[196] There could still, it seems, be no real king without the presence of miracle.

Nevertheless in England, this ancient rite, though sending out a last blaze of glory, was near its final demise and, even in France, it was at least beginning its decadence.

VI

The decline and death of the royal touch

The disappearance of faith in the royal miracle

The final disappearance of the royal touch had as its immediate cause—first in England, and then in France—political revolutions; but these contingencies were only effective because of the deep-down shattering of faith in the supernatural character of royalty that had taken place almost imperceptibly in the hearts and souls of the two nations. We cannot pretend here to give a true account of this obscure travail of soul; we can do no more than indicate some of the causes that contributed to the destruction of the old belief.

Royal healings were only one example among many others of the marvellous cures which, over a long period, had hardly called forth any sceptical disbelief. A few facts will cast light on this state of mind. In France, from Henry II at least to the time of Henry IV, there was the long-standing reputation of the Bailleul family, a veritable dynasty of bone-setters, who handed down from father to son 'the secret power to reset bones displaced by a violent shock, or broken by some blow received, to remedy the contusions occurring to nerves and limbs, to put them back into place if they had been dislocated, and to restore them their former wholeness and strength'. After having exercised this hereditary talent more or less in obscurity in their native province, the Pays de Caux, the Bailleuls appear at the court of Henry II; and there, as well as holding the highest offices, Jean, abbot of Joyenval and Royal Almoner, Nicolas—the first of that name—Groom in Ordinary to the Royal Stable and Gentleman of the Chamber, perhaps also Nicolas the second, destined to be Parliamentary Magistrate and head of the Exchequer under Louis XIII, continued to heal all sorts of sprains and fractures. They would seem, no doubt, to have owed their success to nothing more than a skilful technique handed down from father to son, with nothing supernatural about it; but quite clearly, this was not how their neighbours and contemporaries viewed the matter. It was not for nothing that the poet Scévole de Ste-Marthe wrote a eulogy of them in Latin verse, in his book on 'illustrious Gauls', comparing the 'graces' granted to this family by God with 'the extraordinary and altogether celestial favour' that allows the Most Christian Kings 'simply by a touch of their hands' to 'heal the painful and incurable evil of scrofula'.[1] For most contemporaries, the two healing powers had the selfsame superhuman origin, and the faith they had in both of them was the outcome of one and the same attitude of mind.

Moreover, all sorts of diseases had their own particular hereditary doctors of various kinds. We have already several times come across the 'relatives' of St Paul in Italy, the 'relatives' of St Catherine in Spain, of St Roch, St Martin, and St Hubert in France. These last-mentioned healers in particular enjoyed an extremely brilliant career in the seventeenth century. We know of several, nobleman, or people claiming to be such, among them; for what could give a better title to nobility than this illustrious ancestry? Or again, there were nuns, who did honour to their respective convents. The most famous was a certain Georges Hubert, expressly recognized by Royal Letters Patent, dated 31 December 1649, as 'of the line and generation of the glorious Saint Hubert d'Ardenne', and able, by virtue of this connection, 'to heal all persons bitten by wolves and mad dogs and other beasts suffering from rabies, solely by touching on the head, without the use of any other remedies or medicaments'. The 'chevalier de Saint Hubert'—for that is the name he went by—exercised his art over many years with much fame and profit. In 1701, quotations were still being made from a printed prospectus 'in which he recorded his address for the benefit of those who might want to come and be touched'. He reckoned among his clientèle (all the more numerous in that his touch was also thought to have a preventive effect) two kings of France—Louis XII and Louis XIV—Gaston d'Orléans, the Prince de Conti, and a Prince of Condé who was no doubt the victor at the battle of Rocroy. All these great lords were ardent huntsmen, for whom dog-bites were a very real hazard. By special permission of the Archbishop, Jean François de Gondi, renewed by his successors, he used to touch when in Paris at a chapel in the parish of St-Eustache. He was given permission by more than thirty bishops or archbishops to practise in their respective dioceses. On 8 July 1665 the Estates of the province of Brittany voted him a bounty of 400 livres. Here, too, public opinion did not fail to establish a connection between the marvellous talent of this born wonder-worker and the miraculous virtues officially attributed to royalty. When any odious sceptics ventured to question the cures performed by the *chevalier* or his colleagues, we are told by the abbé Le Brun (who was himself an unbeliever) that the faithful replied by quoting the example of the Prince himself. Since everyone admitted the efficacy of the royal touch, why should it be thought so extraordinary, they said, 'that persons of a certain line should heal certain diseases'?[2]

Moreover, the Bourbons were not the only ones, even in their own kingdom, to heal the scrofula by right of birth. Not to mention the seventh sons, who have been sufficiently dealt with above, seventeenth-century France contained at least one family in which there was handed down through the blood a gift very much like the one that graced the royal dynasty. The eldest sons of the house of Aumont—a noble Burgundian house with possessions also in Berry—were thought to be capable of restoring health to the scrofulous by giving them holy bread. A 'fabricated' tradition, André Favyn calls it in his *Histoire de Navarre*; it was distasteful to the usual apologists of the monarchy, who considered it more secure to reserve jealously to the royal line the privilege of relieving the 'King's Evil'. But this tradition is mentioned by too many serious authors for us to avoid the conclusion that it enjoyed a certain measure of popularity, if only on a regional scale.[3]

In England, under Charles II, an Irish nobleman, Valentine Greatrakes by name, discovered one fine day by divine revelation that he possessed a talent for healing scrofula. He was visited by crowds of sufferers from all over the world. The Worcester municipality—about the same time when the Breton Estates were voting the 'chevalier de Saint Hubert' a bounty—granted the Irish toucher (or stroker, as he was called), a sumptuous banquet. Greatrakes' success was complete: he even waged written warfare, and learned pamphlets were exchanged by his partisans and his opponents. His supporters were by no means only people of no standing. Robert Boyle, a member of the Royal Society, and one of the founders of modern chemistry, proclaimed his faith in this healer and likewise, incidentally, in the royal miracle.[4]

Moreover, the attitude of those who believed in the power of the touch is clearly reflected in the works themselves that deal with the wonder-working virtue of kings. For instance, Browne, although a doctor and a contemporary of Newton, would seem to be still steeped in notions of primitive magic. Witness his extraordinary story of the innkeeper from Winchester who, as a sufferer from scrofula, had bought from the apothecary an earthenware flask of medicinal water. At first the remedy did not seem to do any good; but when he had received a blessing from Charles I—though at some distance, because the Parliamentary forces prevented him from coming close—he resumed his medicinal water and was cured. As his sores dried up and the tumours died down, mysterious scabs began to show themselves on the sides of the flask, and cracked the glaze. One day someone had the unlucky idea of scraping them, whereupon the disease reappeared. The cleansing was stopped, and the healing then became complete. In other words—though Browne does not explicitly say so—the scrofula had passed from the man into the earthenware vessel . . .[5] Truth to tell, the notion of the royal miracle would seem to have been related to a whole magical outlook upon the universe.

Now, there can be no doubt that this conception gradually lost ground during the Renaissance, and especially during the eighteenth century. It is not our business here to enquire into the reasons. It will be enough to remind ourselves of the obvious truth that the decadence of the royal miracle is intimately bound up with the mental efforts of the time—at least among the élite—to eliminate the supernatural and the arbitrary from the world order, and at the same time to work out a purely rational conception of political institutions.

For these efforts reflected a second aspect of the same intellectual evolution, which was as fatal as the first to the old belief whose fortunes we are following. The 'philosophers' were accustoming public opinion to consider sovereigns as no more than the hereditary representatives of the State; and at the same time they were discouraging belief in any attempts to discover the marvellous or miraculous in royalty. One may well expect miracles of a chief by divine right, whose very power is rooted in a kind of sublime mystery; they will clearly not be expected of an official, however exalted in rank, however indispensable the part he plays in public affairs may seem.

More specific causes combined to hasten the ruin of the faith long held by the two kingdoms respecting the virtues of the royal touch. It was affected by repercussions from the civil and religious wars. In England, as we have seen, the more extreme Protestants were hostile to it from the beginning, both for doctrinal reasons and out of hatred for the absolute monarchy under whom they were suffering persecution. Above all, the miraculous claims put forward simultaneously in both countries, by a Catholic and by a Protestant dynasty, did not fail to spread dissension among the adherents of both confessions. Up to the Reformation, the subjects of the French king had quite happily accepted the ambitions of the English king, and vice versa; but when the religious rupture had taken place, this equanimity was no longer acceptable. Truth to tell, English writers did not generally make much difficulty about admitting the cures performed by the kings of France; they were content—flying in the face of historical fact—to claim for their own country the privilege of having been the first to possess physician-kings.[6] The Catholics usually took a more intransigent line. As long as the English princes maintained the sign of the cross, their 'papist' subjects were reluctant, in spite of everything—even if only out of national pride—to contest the miraculous royal prerogative in which so many generations of Englishmen had believed. They fell back as a last resort upon attributing the effective power of healing to the sign of the cross itself, even when it was made by heretical hands.[7] James I deprived them of this last loop-hole.

In France, and on the continent in general, Catholic writers were not restrained by any patriotic scruples, and so nearly all went to the extreme point of denying the miracle in England.[8] As early as 1593, we find the

Spanish Jesuit Martin del Rio taking up this position in his *Disquisitionum Magicarum, libri VI*, which went through many editions, and was considered authoritative over a long period.[9] The same attitude was adopted a few years later by the Frenchmen du Laurens and du Peyrat,[10] who held the English royal touch to be powerless: the privilege claimed by the English kings was a mere illusion or imposture. This view involved recognizing the possibility of an enormous collective error—a dangerous suggestion for, after all, the reality of the miraculous gift attributed to the Bourbons was founded upon the selfsame kind of proof as that invoked on behalf of the Tudors or Stuarts by publicists across the Channel. If the English were mistaken about the virtue of the royal hand, might not the same be true of the French? Martin del Rio in particular displayed a formidable and critical vigour in this controversy. Not being French, he probably felt he could speak more freely. Not that he denied the reality of the prodigies performed by the Catholic dynasty then reigning in France. In this respect, religious zeal was predominant over national pride, and he was prepared to acknowledge them explicitly as authentic. But he was clearly not as careful to put forward nothing that could even remotely risk undermining the prestige of our physician-kings as he would have been as a French subject. In his efforts to explain the wonder-working renown of Elizabeth without recourse to the miraculous, he hesitates between three solutions: the use of secret plasters—in other words, gross fraud; diabolical influence; and finally 'pretence'—the queen only heals people who are not really ill at all. For, as del Rio observes, it is an established fact that she does not heal all who come before her.[11] This last remark in particular, and the hypothesis underlying it, were full of ominous suggestion. Among the numerous readers of *Disquisitionum Magicarum*, surely someone must have thought of applying its reasoning to the French kings themselves. In 1755, Louis Chevalier of Jaucourt wrote an article entitled 'Scrofula' in the *Encyclopédie*. He certainly did not believe—even as far as his own country was concerned—in the wonder-working power of kings. The *philosophes* of this time had fundamentally shaken the old faith; but the writer does not dare to launch a frontal attack on the privilege claimed by the ancient dynasty of France; he is content to make brief mention of it, and reserves all his critical irony for the claims of the English sovereigns. This is obviously simply a device for avoiding a clash with authority and for getting out of an awkward situation; the reader would realize that the blows were in fact aimed equally at both the monarchies. But this lexicographical duplicity represents what must have been a sincere intellectual attitude in the minds of many. People began by doubting the foreign miracle, which religious orthodoxy forbade them to believe in; and their doubts gradually spread to the miraculous at home.

2 *The end of the English rite*

It was in England that political events first put an end to the ancient custom of the royal touch.

James II was naturally not the kind of man to allow the most wonderful of all the monarch's privileges to fall into disuse. He would sooner have added something on this count to what he had inherited from his predecessors. There cannot be much doubt that among his entourage there were some who even toyed with the idea of reviving the old rite of the medicinal rings. But it remained no more than a wish, and was not translated into action.[12] On the other hand James II frequently administered the royal touch and—like his brother—was visited by large crowds of sufferers. There were 4,422 of them between March 1685—apparently the first month when he began the practice—and December of the same year.[13] On 28 and 30 August 1687, scarcely more than a year before his fall, in the choir of Chester Cathedral, he touched 350 and 450 persons respectively.[14] At the beginning of his reign he had accepted the help of Anglican priests in the ceremony; but from 1686 onwards he became more and more reluctant to call on their services and preferred to turn to the Catholic clergy. At the same time, it would seem, he replaced the ritual in use since James I's reign by the ancient liturgy attributed to Henry VII, and resumed the Latin prayers, the invocation of the Virgin and the saints, and the sign of the cross.[15] This return to the past only served to discredit the royal miracle among a section of the Protestants, for it seemed to be involving it in all the trappings of a detested creed.[16]

William of Orange, who was brought to the throne by the revolution of 1688, had, like James I, been educated in the Calvinistic faith; and, like him, he saw nothing but superstition in the healing rite. Taking up a more decided position than his predecessor, he refused to touch, and held by this refusal for good and all.[17] Was this merely a difference of individual temperament, a difference between a weak-willed and a more resolute man? There was something in this, no doubt; but it was also a difference between two states of the popular way of thinking. Whereas public opinion had not been willing to renounce this practice under James I, it would seem to have done so less than a century later without being too scandalized. In certain orthodox circles, they consoled themselves by relating that a sick person on whom the king—in spite of proclaiming his disbelief—had gone so far as to lay a passing hand, had made a complete recovery.[18] The Tories, however, did not consider things satisfactory. In 1702, Queen Anne came to power; and after only a year they persuaded her to renew the miraculous tradition. She proceeded, like her ancestors, to touch the sick, but with a simplified rite, and there seem to have been plenty of scrofula sufferers to seek her help.[19] In this reign, we can still find an author, Jeremy Collier, writing as follows in his celebrated *Ecclesiastical history of Great Britain*: 'To dispute the matter of fact is to go to the excesses of scepticism, to deny our senses, and to be incredulous even to ridiculousness'.[20] A good Tory felt bound to profess belief in the efficacy of the royal hand, and Swift did not fail to do so.[21] A patriotic card-game engraved at this time showed on the nine of hearts a vignette of 'Her Majesty the Queen touching for scrofula'.[22] 'Her Majesty' would seem to have performed the healing gesture for the last time on 27 April 1714, rather more than three months before her death.[23] This is a memorable date, for it marks the end of an ancient rite. From that day onwards, no English king or queen, on English soil, ever hung the coin round the neck of those who were suffering from disease.

Indeed, the princes of the House of Hanover, who were called to the throne of Great Britain in 1714, never attempted to resume the miraculous healing of scrofula. For a good many years subsequently, until right on in George II's reign, the official prayer-book continued to include the liturgical service for the 'healing' of the sick by the king;[24] but from 1714 it became no more than an empty survival: the ancient prayers were no longer used. What was the reason for this omission on the part of the new dynasty? Was it simply due to the horror felt by the Whigs, who were the dynasty's chief supporters and counsellors, for everything reminiscent of the ancient monarchy and its divine right? Was it a desire to avoid shocking a certain kind of Protestant feeling? No doubt there was something of both these in it; but it would seem that although these considerations certainly played their part in the Hanoverians' decision, they do not completely explain it.

Only a few years earlier, Monmouth, who also relied on the most vigorous Protestantism for support, had touched the sick; and his friends do not appear to have been scandalized by the fact. George I was called to the throne by very much the same party: why should not he too have essayed to heal? He might perhaps have made the attempt if there had not been a great difference between Monmouth and himself from the point of view of strict monarchical right. Monmouth, although the son of Charles II and Lucy Walter, posed as having been born in wedlock, and as therefore of the royal blood. No such claim could be seriously advanced by the Elector of Hanover, the great-grandson of James I, who had become king of England through the requirements of the Protestant Succession. The story was told in Jacobite circles that a certain nobleman who came to George, begging him to touch his son, was gruffly advised to go and seek out the Stuart Pretender, who was in exile overseas. This advice was followed—so the story ran—and the nobleman, whose son was healed, became a faithful adherent of the old dynasty.[25] It may well be that this story was entirely invented by the party spirit; but it possesses a certain degree of psychological probability, which assured its success. No doubt it expressed fairly accurately the state of mind of these Germans transported to English soil. They were not the legitimate heirs of the sacred line, and they did not consider themselves suitable successors to the hereditary miracle.

When in exile, neither James II nor his son after him ceased to practise the healing act. They continued to touch in France, at Avignon, and in Italy.[26] People still came to them from England at the same time as those from countries near to where they were residing. The Jacobite party carefully fostered the old belief. In 1721, a polemical writer belonging to this group brought out a would-be letter from 'a nobleman of Rome, giving an account of certain amazing cures recently performed in the vicinity of this City'. In a rather more veiled form, this is still the same theme we have seen developed a little less than a century earlier in the scrofula-sufferers' pseudo-petition demanding the return of Charles I to London. 'For shame, *Britons*, awake, and let not an universal Lethargy seize you; but consider that you ought to be accounted unworthy the knowledge and Benefits you may receive by this extraordinary Power, if it be despised or neglected'.[27] This little work must certainly have enjoyed some success, seeing that the opposite camp thought it necessary to issue a reply. A doctor—William Beckett by name—assumed the task. His *Free and Impartial Enquiry into the Antiquity and Efficacy of touching for the Cure of the King's Evil* is the work of a rational and reasonable mind, and moderate in tone; in short, one of the most sensible productions ever devoted to the ancient monarchical 'superstition'. Not everybody kept to this dignified tone, for anti-Jacobite polemics did not always eschew heavy irony and Rabelaisian allusions (since we are not yet in the Victorian era!). Witness the violent little anonymous article which appeared in a Whig journal in 1737, called *Common Sense*.[28] The controversy was revived with renewed vigour in 1747. In that year, the historian Carte slipped into a note at the bottom of a page in his *General History of England* an anecdote relating to an inhabitant of Wells in Somerset. This man, suffering from scrofula, had been cured at Avignon in the year 1716 by 'the eldest lineal descendant of a race of kings, who had indeed, for a long succession of ages, cured that distemper by the royal touch'.[29] The note did not pass unobserved: the City of London withdrew from Carte the subscription with which they had honoured his work; and the Whig newspapers were filled with letters of protest for several months.[30]

Truth to tell, the Stuarts' opponents had good reason at that particular time for showing themselves rather sensitive. Less than two years before, Charles Edward had made a triumphal entry into Edinburgh, and had occupied the ancient castle of Holyrood. He did not give himself out to be king, but simply the representative and heir of the true king, whom the Jacobites considered to be his father, 'James III'. It is interesting that he should nevertheless have practised at least once the healing rite, and in this very palace of Holyrood.[31] Already, as we have seen, Monmouth, although only a pretender to the inheritance and not to the actual crown, had dared to practise the royal rite in 1680.[32] These improper proceedings which previous ages, with a better knowledge of monarchical religious dogma, would doubtless not have tolerated, prove in their own way how decadent the ancient faith had become.

When Charles Edward returned to Italy and became the legitimate king by the death of his father, he continued to perform the miraculous act.[33] There have come down to us from his time, as well as from James II and 'James III', medals struck on foreign soil for hanging round the necks of the sick who had been touched. These touch-pieces of the exiled Stuarts are usually in silver, and only very rarely in gold, for the hard times scarcely allowed the use of the traditional precious metal. After Charles Edward's death, his brother Henry, Cardinal of York, who had now become the Pretender, also practised the healing rite. His usual medalist, Gioacchimo Hamerani, also produced the customary medal for him. It bears the usual figure of St Michael slaying the dragon, and on the reverse the Latin legend: 'Henry IX, king of Great Britain, France and Ireland, cardinal, bishop of Tusculum'.[34] 'Henry IX' died in 1807, the last of the Stuart line. And with his death, the touch for scrofula came to an end. The royal miracle and the royal race died at one and the same time.

In 1755, Hume wrote in his *History of England*: 'the practice [of the royal touch] was first dropped by the present royal family, [the house of Hanover] who observed that it could no longer give amazement to the populace, and was attended with ridicule in the eyes of all men of understanding'.[35] On this second point, we shall have no difficulty in agreeing with Hume; but on the first, he was certainly wrong. He was carried away by the optimism that was a common feature of all the rationalists of his day, and was, like so many of his contemporaries, too ready to believe in the triumph of 'advancing knowledge'. The popular mind was not destined to desert the old belief for many a long day yet: the refusal of the Hanoverians to subscribe to it had not robbed it of all sustenance. Certainly, it was now given to only very few sick persons to obtain direct contact with a royal hand. In Hume's time, the exiled Stuarts were still wonder-working figures; but the number of English people who came to seek healing at their hands in their distant abodes would never appear to have been very considerable. The faithful supporters of the miracle had to be content for for the most part with substitutes. The medals, originally struck for the distribution on the days of the royal touch, and being of a durable material, were preserved by the common people as amulets. In 1736 the churchwardens of Minchinhampton parish, in Gloucestershire, still offered to renew the ribbons for those scrofula sufferers who had formerly been touched by the king and wore the gold coins round their necks.[36] Similarly, and over a longer period, a like virtue was ascribed to certain coins originally struck purely as money, but endowed with a special kind of dignity by the fact that they bore the effigy of Charles I, king and martyr. Crowns and half-crowns of this prince were held to be sovereign remedies against scrofula, and were handed down from one generation to another in the Shetland Islands up to the year 1838, and perhaps even later.[37] The same kind of power was ascribed to certain personal relics, such as a handkerchief stained with the Cardinal of York's blood, which was considered capable of curing the 'King's Evil' in Ireland as late as 1901.[38] Moreover, as far as relics are concerned, in the Scottish county of Ross even during the reign of Queen Victoria, the ordinary gold coins were held to be universal panaceas simply because they bore 'the image of the Queen'.[39] Of course people were well aware that all these talismans, however much appreciated they might be, were after all only indirect means of entering into *rapport* with the royal person; and something more direct would have been more valuable still. Here is something Miss Sheila Macdonald tells us in a note on survivals from former times in the county of Ross:

> An old shepherd of ours who suffered from scrofula or king's evil, often bewailed his inability to get within touching distance of Her late Gracious Majesty [Queen Victoria]. He was convinced that by so doing his infirmity would at once have been cured. 'Ach! no,' he would say mournfully; 'I must just be content to try and get to Lochaber instead some day and get the *leighiche* [healer] there to cure me.' . . .[40] [The healer was a seventh son.]

Indeed, if circumstances had not imposed upon the English a dynasty who could hardly claim to base their legitimate authority upon sacred blood, but only upon the national choice, we may well wonder how long the popular mind would have gone on demanding that kings should practise the royal miracle. Great Britain owed the consolidation of her parliamentary regime to the accession of a foreign prince in 1714 who could not fall back upon divine right, or upon personal popularity. It was the same circumstance, no doubt, that also led to the suppression of the ancient rite, which was such a perfect expression of sacred royalty in olden days, and so eliminated the supernatural element from politics earlier in England than in France.

3 The end of the French rite

The healing rite went on being solemnly performed in France by her kings during the eighteenth century. We only have a single figure for Louis XV— and that only approximate—for the number of sick touched; this was on 29 October 1722, the day after his consecration, when more than two thousand scrofula sufferers appeared before him in the St-Rémi park at Rheims.[41]

It is clear that there was no falling off in the old popularity of the rite.

Nevertheless this reign, remarkable all through for the decadence of the monarchy's prestige, delivered a severe blow to the ancient ceremony of the royal touch. Three times at least, it failed to take place through the fault of the king. By ancient custom, the king could not proceed to heal until he had first received Communion. Now in 1739, Louis XV, who had just become involved in an intrigue with Mme de Mailly, was refused access to the Holy Table by his confessor, and so did not make his Easter Communion. Likewise at Easter 1740 and Christmas 1744 he had to abstain from Communion; and on these three occasions he did not give the royal touch. There was great scandal about it in Paris, at any rate in 1739.[42] These interruptions in the miracle, occasioned by the king's misconduct, seemed likely to break the habits of the crowds who normally flocked to him. As for cultivated circles, there was less and less attempt to veil their scepticism. As early as 1721, the *Lettres Persanes* were already treating 'the royal magician' with a certain frivolity.[43] Saint-Simon, writing his memoirs between 1739 and 1751, makes fun of the poor Princesse de Soubise, Louis XIV's mistress, who was said to have died of scrofula. There is a fierce flavour about this anecdote, but it is probably inaccurate, for it is quite likely that Mme de Soubise was never the king's mistress, and it appears certain that she did not suffer from scrofula. Saint-Simon probably picked up this slanderous tale from the court gossip heard in his younger days; but the twist he gives it certainly seems to prove that almost in spite of himself he had been influenced by the new spirit. He even goes so far as to speak of 'the miracle that people *claim* to be associated with the touch of our kings'.[44] Not only in his *Correspondance*, but even more openly in his *Questions sur l'Encyclopédie*, Voltaire cannot resist making fun of the dynasty's miraculous virtues, and delights in picking out certain resounding failures. According to him, Louis XI proved incapable of healing St Francis of Paula and Louis XIV one of his mistresses—Mme de Soubise, no doubt—although she was 'well and truly touched'. In his *Essai sur les Moeurs* he puts before the French kings as a model the example of William of Orange, who renounced this 'prerogative', and dares to add: 'The time will come when reason, which is already beginning to make some headway in France, will abolish this custom'.[45] The disrepute into which this age-old rite had fallen has one very serious disadvantage as far as we are concerned: it makes the writing of its history particularly difficult. For the journals of the later eighteenth century, even those which give the fullest court news, seem to have considered it beneath them to report such a vulgar ceremony.

Yet Louis XVI, faithful to ancient usage, was confronted on the day after his consecration with a crowd of 2,400 sufferers from scrofula.[46] Did he, like his predecessors, continue to touch on the great feasts? It seems extremely likely that he did so, but I have not been able to discover any documentary proof. In any case, the miracle certainly no longer took place in the same peaceful atmosphere as in the past. It would seem that under Louis XV, and from the consecration ceremony onwards, the king—doubtless with the best intentions, and sincerely believing that he was following ancient custom—had slightly changed the traditional form of words accompanying the royal touch on each occasion. In the second clause, the words '*Dieu te guérit*' (God heals thee) had been altered to '*Dieu te guérisse*' (May God heal thee).[47] It is true that since the seventeenth century, some writers who depict the ceremony give this turn of phrase; but they are of no value as witnesses, for they were travellers who wrote up their recollections or diaries after the event, and had no authority or official standing. All good authors, and the ceremonial itself, as drawn up in this century, use the indicative tense. Du Peyrat explicitly rejects the subjunctive as unseemly. It was left to our last wonder-working monarchs to show an unconscious inclination towards the mood of doubt—an almost imperceptible nuance, yet one we may rightly consider symptomatic.

More instructive still is the episode of the healing certificates, which offers a vivid contrast between the beginning and the end of the eighteenth century. Not long after Louis XV's coronation, the Marquis of Argenson, then intendant of Hainault, discovered within his jurisdiction an ex-patient who had been touched by the king on his journey to Rheims, and three months later had found himself cured. The Marquis at once drew up a case-history, after many enquiries and authentic attestations of the facts, and sent it with all speed to Paris, thinking it to be flattering to the king's pride, and a means of paying his court. But he received a disappointing response. The Secretary of State, La Vrillière, 'replied curtly that things were just as they should be: no one had any doubts about the gift of performing these marvels possessed by our kings'.[48] The desire to prove a dogma might well seem to true believers to cast a suspicion of doubt upon its truth. But fifty-two years later, things were very different. A certain Rémy Rivière of the parish of Matougues had been touched by Louis XVI at Rheims, and was cured. The intendant of Châlons, Rouillé d'Orfeuil, learnt of the fact and hastened to send to Versailles on 17 November 1775 a certificate 'signed by the surgeon of the place, as well as by the curé and the chief inhabitants'. The Secretary of State, Bertin by name, who had charge of the correspondence with Champagne, replied on 7 December in the following terms:

Sir, I have received the letter you wrote to me concerning the healing of the said Rémy Rivière and I have placed it before His Majesty; if hereafter you should learn of any like healings, you will please be so good as to communicate them to me.[49]

We also possess four other certificates issued in the same area of jurisdiction and in that of Soissons, in November and December 1775, for four children touched by Louis XVI after his consecration, and said to have been restored to health. We do not know on reliable authority if these cases were communicated to the minister and to the king; but it would seem likely that Bertin's letter—if known to the other intendants—would have decided them not to put them away in the files.[50] People could no longer afford to despise experimental evidence of the miracle.

To be sure, the moment did come—probably in 1789—when Louis XVI had to give up exercising the miraculous gift, along with everything else reminiscent of divine right. When did the last act of touching take place in this reign? Unfortunately, I have not been able to discover. All I can do is to confront researchers with this interesting little problem. If we could solve it, we should have a pretty accurate idea of the date when the ancient sacred royalty ceased to seem tolerable to public opinion.[51] Among the relics of the 'Martyr King', none apparently was ever considered, like those of Charles I of England, to possess the power of curing the King's Evil. The royal miracle would seem to have died, along with belief in monarchy.

Yet there was to be one further attempt to revive it. In 1825, Charles X was anointed. In one final burst of splendour, holy and quasi-priestly royalty displayed its somewhat antiquated pomp and circumstance. 'So he is both priest and king!' exclaimed Victor Hugo, in his 'Ode on the Consecration', where he depicts the unction of this new king, the Lord's Anointed.[52] Was the tradition of the royal touch destined also to be resumed? Those around the king were divided on this point. Baron de Dalmas, who was then Minister for Foreign Affairs, and filled with ardent personal faith in the virtues of the royal hand, has left us in his *Mémoires* an echo of these disagreements. He says:

> Several men of letters who had been set to study this question, had seriously affirmed this touch for scrofula to be no more than an old popular superstition, which it would be most inadvisable to revive. We were Christians, and yet this idea was adopted, and it was decided—in spite of the clergy—that the king should not resume the practice. But that was not the way it appeared to the common people . . .[53]

These 'men of letters' no doubt recognized their right to pick and choose from the heritage of the past. They loved the Middle Ages, but only as accommodated to the taste of the day, that is, somewhat romanticized; they wanted to revive such of the customs as seemed poetical, but rejected all that seemed to them to smack too strongly of 'Gothic' barbarism. A Catholic historian, who thought it impossible to be a half-and-half traditionalist, has poked fun at this squeamishness: 'Chivalry was delightful; the Holy Phial was rather too daring; and as for scrofula, it was positively unmentionable'.[54]And then, as the *Ami de la Religion* wrote in retrospect, there was a fear of 'providing a pretext for the derisions of disbelief'.[55] All the same, there was a small active group headed by a priest with extreme views, abbé Desgenettes, curé of the *Missions Etrangères*, and the Archbishop of Rheims himself, Mgr Latil, who were determined to renew the links with the past, on this point as on all others. These strong-minded men seem to have made up their minds to force the hand of the wavering monarch. They scorned the wishes of the inhabitants of Corbeny, who had asked Charles X to renew the ancient pilgrimage upon their territory, and gathered together in Rheims itself, at the Hospice of St-Marcoul —a hospital founded in the seventeenth century—all the available sufferers from scrofula.[56] Moreover, it is possible—as Baron Dalmas suggests—that a part, if not the whole, of popular opinion was easily persuaded to lend them some support; for the memory of the old marvels and the enthusiasm they had formerly aroused were doubtless not altogether extinct in the minds of the humble. Up to the very last moment, Charles X seems to have hesitated to give way to this pressure. One day, he gave orders to dismiss the poor people who had assembled in expectation of the healing rite; but then he changed his mind, and on 31 May 1825 he went to the hospice. The order to disperse had thinned the ranks of the sick, and there were no more than about 120 to 130 of them left. The king, 'the first physician of the kingdom', as a contemporary publicist expresses it, touched the sick without much display and pronounced what had now become the traditional formula: 'The King touches thee, *may God heal thee*', and said a few comforting words to them.[57] Later on, as under Louis XVI, the nuns of St-Marcoul drew up some certificates of healing, to which we shall come back in due course.[58] To sum up, it may be said that this resurrection of an archaic rite ridiculed by the philosophy of the preceding century would seem to have been considered rather out of place by all parties, with the exception of certain exalted extremists. On the eve of the consecration, that is, before Charles X had announced his decision, Chateaubriand (if we may trust his *Mémoires d'Outre-Tombe*) wrote the following words in his journal: 'There are no longer any hands virtuous enough to heal the scrofula'.[59] After the ceremony was over, neither the *Quotidienne* nor the *Drapeau Blanc* showed much more enthusiasm than the *Constitutionnel*.

If the King [says the *Quotidienne*] in the accomplishment of the duty imposed upon him by an ancient custom, approached those unfortunate people in order to heal them, he must, as a right-thinking person, have been sensible that even if he could not remedy the sores of the body, he could at least lessen the sorrows of the soul.[60]

The Left were disposed to make fun of the wonder-worker:

'Oiseaux, ce roi miraculeux
Va guérir tous les scrofuleux',

sang Béranger in some rather uninspired lines in the *Sacre de Charles le Simple*.[61]

It was only natural that Charles X should be unfaithful to his ancestors' example in this matter, and never touch on the great festivals. After this date, 31 May 1825, no king in Europe ever laid his hands upon the sores of those who were afflicted with scrofula.

Nothing makes us feel the final decline of the ancient monarchical religion more acutely than this last tentative effort, with its timid approach and its lukewarm reception, to restore to royalty the former lustre of the miraculous healing. The touch for scrofula came to an end later in France than in England. But there was this difference between the two countries, that in France, when it ceased to be practised, the faith which had so long sustained the rite had well-nigh been extinguished, and was about to perish completely. No doubt, a few outmoded believers would still sometimes make their voices heard. In 1865, a priest from Rheims, abbé Cerf, the author of an estimable memoir on the history of the royal touch, was to write: 'When I began this work, I only believed half-heartedly in the prerogative of the French kings to heal scrofula. Before I had finished my research, I had become a firm believer in the incontrovertible truth of this prerogative.'[62] That was one of the last testimonies to a conviction that had incidentally become purely Platonic, since it no longer ran the risk at that actual time of being tested by facts. In the United Kindgom, certain popular survivals of the ancient belief could even be discovered in the nineteenth century; but I can find nothing comparable in France except the royal mark—the fleur-de-lis—which, as we have seen, the seventh sons had inherited from the kings. Yet hardly anyone among the clients of the Vovette healer or any other of the numerous healers thought of the link formerly and vaguely established by the popular consciousness between the powers of the 'seventh' and the hand of royalty. Among our contemporaries, many no longer believe in the miraculous in any shape or form; as far as they are concerned, the question has long ago been settled. There are others who have not altogether rejected the miraculous; but they no longer believe that political power or even royal lineage can confer supernatural grace. In this sense, Gregory VII has indeed won the day.

BOOK 3

A CRITICAL INTERPRETATION
OF THE ROYAL MIRACLE

I

A critical interpretation of the
royal miracle

1 *The first attempts at a rationalist interpretation*

We have so far been following the age-long vicissitudes of the royal miracle as far as the documentary evidence permits. In the course of our research, we have done our utmost to throw light upon the collective ideas and the individual ambitions which blended in a kind of psychological complex and led the kings of France and England to claim this wonder-working power, and their subjects to recognize it. We have thus to a certain extent explained the miracle, as far as its origins and its long years of success are concerned. Yet the explanation remains incomplete, and one point in the history of the marvellous gift is still obscure. After all, the crowds who formerly believed in the reality of the cures effected through the royal touch or the medicinal rings, saw them as a fact of experience, 'a truth as clear as the sun', as Browne exclaims.[1] If the faith of these countless believers was mere illusion, how did it manage to survive when confronted by practical experience? In other words, did the kings actually heal? If they did, what was the procedure? If on the other hand this question must be answered in the negative, how did people manage for so many years to persuade themselves that kings really did heal? Of course, the question would not even arise if we were to admit the possibility of appealing to supernatural causes; but—as we have already said—hardly anyone nowadays would dream of invoking them in the matter under discussion. Now, it is obviously not good enough simply to reject the ancient interpretation out of hand because it is repugnant to reason; we must try to discover and substitute a new interpretation acceptable to reason. This is a delicate task; yet to evade it would be a kind of intellectual cowardice. Moreover, the problem has an importance going far beyond the history of monarchical ideas. We are confronted here with a sort of crucial experience invoking the whole psychology of the miraculous.

231

The royal healings do indeed constitute one of the so-called super-natural phenomena that are the best-known, and easiest to study, and one might almost say one of the best-attested in the whole of history. Renan was fond of observing that a miracle had never taken place in the presence of the *Académie des Sciences*; this one at least was witnessed by numerous doctors who were not without at least a smattering of scientific method. As for the crowds, they believed in miracles with whole-hearted passion. Thus we possess a large number of testimonies to them from very varied sources. After all, what other manifestation of this kind has ever continued as regularly and uninterruptedly over nearly eight centuries of history? Even in 1610, we find the historiographer Pierre Mathieu, a good Catholic and a zealous monarchist, expressing his opinion that this was 'the only miracle to take place continually in the Christian religion and in the House of France'.[2] Now it so happens, by an extremely fortunate chance, that this miracle, although extremely well-known and of admirably long continuance, is one of those no longer believed in by anyone today; so that historical study of it by critical methods runs no risk of shocking pious souls. And this is a rare privilege, to be used to the full. Others may then feel free to apply to other facts of the same kind the conclusions derived from our study of this particular phenomenon.

Nor is it only nowadays that minds whose general outlook inclines them to deny the supernatural are impelled to find a rational explanation for cures long attributed by the popular mind to the hand of kings. If the modern historian feels this need today, how much more forcibly must it have been felt by the thinkers of the past, to whom the royal miracle was more or less an everyday experience.

True, the case of the cramp rings has never been very much discussed. To a large extent, this would seem to have been because they ceased to be made too long ago for them to be for any length of time a subject of study by the free thought of modern days. Nevertheless the Frenchman de l'Ancre, writing in 1622 a little treatise against 'sorceries', mentioned them in passing; no doubt people round about him had not yet completely lost the habit—attested thirteen years earlier by du Laurens—of treasuring them up as talismans. The author does not deny their virtue; but he refuses to see anything miraculous in them. Not that incredulity in general was his philosophical attitude; but national pride forbade him to admit the authenticity of an English miracle. For him, these 'rings of healing' owed their effectiveness to some secret and more or less magical remedy—'elk's-foot' or 'peony-root'—surreptitiously introduced into the metal by the English kings.[3] In short, the so-called consecration was only a fraud. When dealing with the scrofula miracle, we shall come across more than one explanation of this sort. For unlike the explanation given for medicinal rings, the interpretation of the royal touch has frequently been a theme for discussion.

As we have seen, this question was first taken up by the early Italian 'free thinkers'. It was next raised by some Protestant theologians in Germany—Peucer at the end of the sixteenth century, Morhof and Zentgraff in the following century—in a broadly similar frame of mind. Although they did not, like their predecessors, deny the whole realm of the supernatural, they were no more ready than these to attribute miraculous grace to the Catholic king of France, or even to the Anglican dynasty. In the seventeenth century, the enigma of the royal healings would seem to have become current material for the public dissertations which periodically enlivened the somewhat dreary life of the German universities. At all events, the studies by Morhof, Zentgraff and no doubt also Trinkhusius, unfortunately known to me only by its title, owed their origin to theses upheld in this fashion before academic assemblies at Rostock, Wittenberg and Jena.[4]

Up till now, it will be observed, discussion took place in the countries outside the two kingdoms directly concerned with the royal miracle. In France and England, the sceptics were reduced to a policy of silence. It was no longer so in eighteenth-century England, where the kings had given up any claim to heal. I have already mentioned the polemics which brought the Whigs and the Jacobites into conflict on this particular point. The debate became of more than merely political interest. Hume's celebrated *Essay on Miracles*, published in 1749, restored to it a certain philosophical and theological dignity. Not that these strong and full-bodied pages contain any reference to the claims of the royal hand, for Hume is speaking as a pure theorist, and hardly pauses to carry out a critical examination of the facts. His opinion on this particular point must be sought in his *History of England*. This, as we have seen and as we should expect, was resolutely sceptical, and breathed that slight air of disdain that the word 'superstition' so readily invoked in the men of the eighteenth century. But his *Essay*, by directing attention to a whole order of problems, gave miracles in general a sort of intellectual topicality, in which the ancient monarchical rite to some extent shared.

In 1754 an Anglican minister, John Douglas, brought out under the title *Criterion* a refutation of Hume's *Essay* in which he resolutely took up a historical position. Whatever may be thought of its conclusions, this little treatise, which is full of acute and judicious observations, deserves to occupy an honourable place in the history of critical methods. It does not put forward an indiscriminate defence of all phenomena currently thought to be supernatural. As he expressly states in his subtitle, Douglas sets out to refute 'the pretensions' of those who would

compare the miraculous Powers related in the New Testament with those said to have continued almost down to modern times; and to show the great and fundamental difference between these two kinds of miracle from the evidential point of view; whence it will be seen that the former must be considered true, and the latter false.

In short, he was concerned to rescue the Gospel miracles by repudiating all connection between them and other more recent manifestations, which enlightened contemporary opinion had firmly refused to believe. Among these false prodigies of the present time, he includes—along with the healings said to take place at the tomb of the deacon, François de Paris— 'the cures of scrofula by royal touch'. These were, in the eyes of a man of the eighteenth century, the two most familiar examples of an action popularly regarded as miraculous.[5]

Now all these writers, from the oldest naturalistic thinkers of Italy, from Calcagnini or Pomponazzi to Zentgraff and Douglas, take up a common attitude to the wonder-working power of kings. They all agree— though for different reasons—in refusing to credit it with a supernatural origin; but they do not deny its existence: they do not in the least dispute the fact that kings do perform healings. This was a rather embarrassing position for them, for it forced them to seek natural, or so-called natural, explanations for these cures they admitted to be real, those 'extraordinary mockeries of events',[6] as Peucer calls them; and these explanations are not at all easy to find.

Why did they adopt this position? Would it not have been more convenient to come to the simple conclusion that the healing gift did not exist at all? Their critical powers were no doubt not yet sharp enough to be capable of taking up such a bold position. Public opinion was unanimous in affirming that great numbers of sufferers from scrofula had been healed by the kings. The rejection of a fact proclaimed by a multitude of witnesses—or so-called witnesses—would have required a boldness that could only be supplied and justified by an expert knowledge of the results obtained by a study of human testimony. Well, even nowadays, the psychology of testimony is still in its infancy. In the days of Pomponazzi or even Douglas, it had hardly come into existence. In spite of appearances, the simplest—and perhaps also the most sensible—intellectual method at that time was to accept the fact as proven by common experience, even if it had to be explained by causes different from those supplied by the popular imagination. We can no longer realize nowadays the difficulties encountered in former times by certain minds—even when relatively emancipated—if confronted by affirmations supported by universal consent. They must have found it impossible to deny them as deliberate falsehoods. Wyclif, at any rate, when confronted with the marvels accomplished by so-called saints, compromised in his eyes by their participation in the wealth of the Church, retorted by ascribing their origin to the demons, who were well known to be capable of imitating divine grace.[7] In the same way the Jesuit del Rio insinuated that the devil might well have a hand in the cures performed by Queen Elizabeth, if indeed there was any substance of reality about them.[8] And the French Protestants, as Josué Barbier tells us, sometimes preferred to consider their king in league with the evil one rather than credit him with the gift of working miracles.[9] But that was an argument the Reformation theologians themselves did not care to abuse; and one that was entirely ruled out for naturalistic philosophers.[10]

The first explanations of the royal touch given by the thinkers of the Italian Renaissance appear very strange to us, if not frankly quite absurd. To start with, we have some difficulty in believing that they did indeed represent an advance upon the explanation in terms of miracle. The fact is that almost the whole world of physical and natural science lies in between those thinkers and ourselves. But we must be just to these fore-runners.[11] It was a step forward, as we have already noted, to bring within the discipline of natural law—even if inaccurately conceived—a phenomenon up till then considered as outside the normal world order. The clumsiness of these tentative efforts was like the awkward first steps of childhood. Moreover, the very diversity of the proposed interpretations betrays the hesitations in their authors' minds.

The Florentine astronomer Giuntini, who was Almoner to the Duke of Anjou, the fourth son of Catherine de' Medici, was said to have sought the cause of the royal healings in some mysterious influence from the stars.[12] Weird as this notion may seem to us, it was in keeping with contemporary taste, though it appears not to have enjoyed much success. Cardan believed in some kind of imposture: he thought that the French kings fed upon aromatic herbs containing medicinal virtues that were imparted to their persons.[13] Calcagnini thought in terms of a different kind of fraud: he tells how Francis I was said to have been discovered at Bologna moistening his thumb with saliva, showing that the Capetians' healing power resided in their saliva, no doubt as a physiological quality belonging to their line.[14] This gives us a glimpse of an idea occurring almost in-evitably to the men of that age, the notion that healing power was handed down in the blood, for in the Europe of that time there were so many charlatans who claimed by family vocation to be able to relieve such and such specific diseases! We saw above how the Italian canonist Felino Sandei—who died in 1503—refused to recognize the privilege of wonder-working attached to the French monarchs as miraculous—profoundly shocking one of the oldest apologists for the Valois, Jacques Bonaud de Sauset. He merely ascribed it to 'the force of blood relationships'.[15] The most famous representative of the philosophical school of Padua, Pietro Pomponazzi, took up the same hypothesis, and categorically freed it from any appeal to the miraculous. 'Just as such-and-such a herb or stone or animal . . . possesses the power to heal a specific disease . . . so like-wise can a man possess a power of this kind as a personal attribute'. Where the kings of France are concerned, he holds this attribute to be the prerogative not of an isolated individual, but of a whole line. Then he proceeds, with small reverence, to compare these great princes to the 'relatives of St Paul', Italian sorcerers who, as we know, gave themselves out to be able to cure poisonous bites. He does not call in question the genuine talent of either; but in his system of thought, such hereditary predispositions are entirely natural, as much as the pharmaceutical properties of particular kinds of mineral or vegetable.[16] The same line is taken, in a general way, by Giulio Cesare Vanini.[17] But with him, mixed in with the theory of heredity that he holds in common with Pomponazzi, we begin to see the emergence of a different kind of explanation, which will be met with again in Beckett and Douglas.[18] According to these authors, the cures were the effect of 'imagination', though they did not mean by this that they were imaginary, that is to say, unreal. They thought that the sick people were stirred in spirit by the solemn occasion and the pomp of the royal ceremonial, and above all by the hope of recovery, and thus underwent a kind of nervous shock capable in itself of bringing about a cure. In short, the royal touch was a sort of psychotherapy, and the kings were unconscious Charcots.[19]*

Nowadays, no one any longer believes in the physiological influence of the stars, in the medicinal power of saliva, in the force that could be communicated by a diet reinforced with aromatic herbs, or in an innate curative virtue handed down in families. But the psychological explanation of the royal miracle would still seem to have some supporters. Not, it is true, in the same simplified forms as in days gone by: no one would say, like Beckett, that the imagination could set the blood in motion and so force a way through the obstructed channels of the glands. It would rather take on more subtle and more specious neurological forms; and it would therefore seem as well to add a few words on this subject.

At this point we should do well, no doubt, to consider the healing rings by themselves. As far as it applies to this manifestation of the wonder-working gift, the hypothesis adopted by Vanini and Douglas is not altogether devoid of probability. We may well retain it as a possible explanation, if not of all cases, at least of a certain number. Let us remind ourselves what affections these gold or silver rings consecrated on Good Friday were supposed to cure: epilepsy and 'cramp', that is to say, all kinds of spasm or muscular pain. Now neither epilepsy nor rheumatism or gout—to take two of the rather vague categories of muscular 'pains'—are amenable to psychiatric treatment. But it is necessary to bear in mind what the medicine of earlier times was like, even in its learned forms; not to mention the permanent characteristics of popular medicine. In neither of them could much precision be expected in the matter of clinical definitions; nor could

* Jean-Martin Charcot (1825-93) the celebrated neurologist, whose studies and experiments in hypnotism and hysteria at the Salpétrière in Paris attracted world-wide attention.

one look for very reliable diagnosis. In the days when the English kings were blessing the cramp rings, it was certainly easy to lump together under the name of epilepsy, or one of its numerous synonyms, such as the *mal St Jean*, or the *morbus comitialis*, along with genuine epileptic troubles, many other kinds of nervous disorder, like convulsions, tremors, contractions, which were purely emotional in origin, or which modern neurology would assign to the group of phenomena arising from suggestion or autosuggestion, and which are curable by persuasion (pithiatic). All these are accidental conditions perfectly capable of being removed by a psychic shock or by the suggestive effect of a talisman.[20] Likewise among the 'pains', there were probably some of a neuropathic kind, on which 'imagination'—in the meaning given to this word by the old authors—could well have had some effect. Some of those who wore the rings, it would seem, owed relief from their ailments—or some degree of improvement—quite simply to the sturdy faith they had in the royal amulet. But let us come back now to the oldest, most striking and best known form of miracle—the touch for scrofula.

In the seventeenth century, the supporters of the supernatural character of royalty frequently protested against the idea that these cures, which they attributed to the royal hand, could possibly be the effect of imagination. The usual argument they advanced was that quite young children were often cured, although they were obviously not amenable to suggestion, since they were incapable of understanding. This observation is certainly valuable; for why should one deny that young children were healed, yet admit the healing of adults, though there is the same evidence for both?[21] But the chief reason against accepting the psychic interpretation of the royal miracle is of a different order. Some fifty years ago, it would perhaps have found few opponents among neurologists and psychiatrists. For after the work of Charcot and his school, there was a ready disposition to allow that certain nervous troubles called 'hysterical' could produce sores or swellings. It was only natural, of course, that lesions supposed to have been caused in this way could yield to the influence of another shock of the same kind. Once this theory is accepted, nothing could be simpler than to assume that at least a certain number of the tumours or sores thought to be scrofulous which came under the royal touch were in fact 'hysterical' in character. But these conceptions are almost unanimously rejected today (1923). More accurate studies have shown that the organic phenomena formerly attributed to the action of hysteria should, in all cases admitting of precise observation, be attributed either to simulation, or to affections of an entirely non-nervous character.[22] In conclusion, we must ask ourselves whether suggestion can bring about the healing of scrofula proper, that is to say, tubercular adenitis, or adenitis in general. Since I rightly distrusted my own incompetence in this matter, I referred this question to several doctors or physiologists. Their answers varied in form, in accordance with their varieties of individual temperament; but fundamentally they were in agreement, and could be summed up very accurately in the words of one of them: to uphold such a thesis would be to support 'a physiological heresy'.

2 How people believed in the royal miracle

In short, the Renaissance thinkers and their immediate successors never succeeded in finding a satisfactory explanation of the royal miracle. Where they went wrong was in the way they posed the problem. They possessed too slight a knowledge of the history of human societies to allow for the strength of collective illusions, the astonishing power of which we acknowledge today. It is the same old story as Fontenelle so charmingly related. A solid gold tooth was said to have appeared in the mouth of a young boy in Silesia. Scholars discovered a hundred and one reasons to explain this phenomenon. In the end, someone thought of actually looking at the miraculous jaw; and what they observed was a piece of gold leaf cunningly applied to a very ordinary tooth. Let us beware of imitating these misguided scholars: before asking how the kings healed, let us not forget to ask whether they did in fact really heal. We have only to glance over the clinical dossier of the miraculous dynasties to be left in no doubt upon this point. The 'physician-princes' were not impostors; but they no more ever restored a person to health than the Silesian boy ever had a golden tooth. The real problem, then, will be to understand how people believed in their wonder-working power when they did not in fact heal. Here, too, the clinical documents will help us.[23]

In the first place, it is as clear as daylight that the effectiveness of the royal hand was liable to suffer eclipse. We know from fairly numerous instances that many patients came repeatedly for the laying on of hands—a plain proof that the first attempt had not been fully successful. Under the later Stuarts, a certain churchman came twice before Charles II and three times to James II.[24] Browne freely recognizes this: 'others again having been healed upon His second Touch, which could not receive the same benefit the first time'.[25] A superstitition grew up in England that the royal touch was only really effective if repeated; and this could only have come about through the first touch being often ineffective.[26] In the same way in nineteenth-century Beauce, the patients of the Vovette *marcou* would make repeated visits to this rustic doctor if they failed to obtain relief the first time.[27] Thus neither kings nor seventh sons were successful on every occasion.

But there is a further point. In the heyday of faith in the monarchy, believers in France or England would never of course have admitted at any price that their kings had never healed anyone at all; but most of them readily admitted that the kings did not heal everyone, even with repeated attempts. Douglas calls attention to this precise point: 'It never was claimed that the Royal Touch was beneficial in every Instance when tried'.[28] As early as 1593, the Jesuit del Rio made the most of Tooker's admissions on this point as a weapon against the English miracle,[29] for he was intent upon bringing down the pretensions of a heretical princess. Only eyes that had been opened by religious passion could light-heartedly proceed to draw such a serious conclusion. Ordinarily, as we see from Tooker himself and then from Browne, the tone was more accommodating.

Let us listen to what Josué Barbier has to say in answer to the doubts of his former Protestant co-religionists:

> You say, in order to darken still further this miraculous virtue, that there are only a very few from among the scrofulous receiving the royal touch who are healed. . . . But even if it be granted that the number of those cured is smaller than the number remaining sick, it does not follow that the healing of the former is not miraculous and admirable, any more than for the healing of the one who first entered the Pool of Bethesda, after an angel had troubled the waters, descending once a year for this very purpose. And although the Apostles did not heal all the sick, yet they did not cease to work miracles for those who were healed.

Then there follow other examples taken from the Holy Scriptures: 'Naaman the Syrian' was the only one 'cleansed by Elisha', although—as Jesus Himself says—'there were many lepers in Israel'; Lazarus alone was raised from the dead by Christ; the woman with an issue of blood was the only one healed because she had touched the hem of the Saviour's garment, when 'many others touched it, but received no benefit'![30]

In a similar vein, the Englishman George Bull, a theologian of considerable knowledge and perfect loyalty to the throne, wrote as follows: 'And yet they say some of those diseased persons return from that sovereign remedy *re infecta*, without any cure done upon them . . . God hath not given this gift of healing so absolutely to our royal line, but he still keeps the reins of it in his own hand, to let them loose, or restrain them, as he pleaseth'. After all, the Apostles themselves had received from Christ the gift of relieving sickness so 'as not to be at their own absolute disposal, but to be dispensed by them, as the Giver should think fit'.[31] Nowadays, we tend to think of miracles in uncompromising terms. It seems to us that as soon as an individual enjoys supernatural powers, he must necessarily be able to exercise them all the time. But the ages of faith, for whom manifestations of this order were part of the familiar framework of existence, thought of them more simply. They did not demand that wonder-workers, whether saints or kings, dead or living, should always display an unvarying efficiency.

Moreover, if the sick person who had failed to obtain a miraculous cure was ill-bred enough to complain, the champions of royalty had no difficulty in giving him an answer. They would say, for instance, like Browne in England[32] or Canon Regnault in France, that he had been lacking in faith, a faith, as Regnault writes, which has 'always been a disposition necessary for miraculous cures'.[33] Or they would conclude that the diagnosis had been at fault. In the reign of Charles VIII, a poor fellow called Jean l'Escart received the royal touch at Toulouse, but was not cured. Later on, St Francis of Paula freed him from his trouble by advising him to practise certain pious exercises and to take an infusion of herbs. During the proceedings for the saint's canonization, Jean made a deposition, in which he seems to have admitted of his own accord that if he had importuned his prince without success, it was because he did not suffer from the proper disease.[34] After all, it was only the King's Evil that could be relieved by the king.

So the 'sacred hand' of the 'physician-princes' was not always successful. It is a pity that we cannot as a rule ascertain the ratio of failures to successes. The certificates given after Louis XVI's consecration were completely random, and without any kind of overall plan. After Charles X's consecration, an attempt was made at something better co-ordinated. The Sisters of the Hospice St-Marcoul, in a well-intentioned but perhaps imprudent attempt, had the idea of following up the patients and collecting some information about the further results. About 120 to 130 persons had been touched. In all, they were able to collect eight cases of cures, and even three of these were only known by somewhat dubious testimony. The figure is so low that one can hardly believe it represents the usual proportion. The Sisters had made the mistake, no doubt, of being in too much of a hurry. The first five cases—the only certain onces—were noted in the first three and a half months after the ceremony; after this time had elapsed, the enquiry does not seem to have been taken any further. But it should really have been pursued perseveringly. If there had been further observation of those who were touched on 31 May 1825, it is probable that new cases of healing would have been recorded.[35] During the ages of real faith, it was a very wise rule to exercise patience in this matter.

Indeed, we should be wrong in supposing that there had ever been any demand for the royal touch to be immediately successful. There was no expectation that the sores would suddenly dry up or the tumours suddenly go down at a touch of the royal hand; though the hagiographers, it is true, did attribute an instantaneous triumph of this kind to Edward the Confessor. Nearer our own time, a similar effect was attributed to Charles I. A young girl had lost the sight of her left eye as a result of scrofula; but when she had received the royal touch, she recovered the use of it on the spot, though the sight was still rather imperfect.[36] In everyday life, people did not expect this degree of rapidity. They were satisfied if the relief took place some time—even quite a long time—after the performance of the rite. That is why the English historian Fuller, who was no more than a very lukewarm supporter of wonder-working royalty, only regarded the healing power of sovereigns as a 'partial' miracle; 'for a complete miracle is done *presently* and *perfectly*, whereas this *cure* is generally advanced by Degree and some Dayes interposed'.[37] Yet Fuller was at least half way towards being a sceptic. The true believers were much less particular. The Corbeny pilgrims did not withhold their gratitude from St-Marcoul even when they had only been healed a certain time after their 'journey'. The scrofula-sufferers who had received the royal touch considered they had been miraculously healed if the cure took place at any time, no matter when. In Louis XV's reign, d'Argenson thought he was paying due homage to the crown when he informed the appropriate authorities of a result that only took place after three months. William Clowes, Queen Elizabeth's physician, reported with admiration the story of a patient who was delivered from his ills five months after being touched by the Queen.[38] We have already noted the moving letter written in all the joy of a father's heart by the Englishman, Lord Poulett, whose daughter had been touched and, as he believed, healed by Charles I; her health, he says, 'improves from day to day'—implying that his precious child's health was not yet fully re-established. We may if we like assume that the child ended by recovering completely. But even if we take the most favourable interpretation—in this as in so many other cases—the influence of the august laying on of hands was only felt, as Fuller says, 'by Degree and some Dayes interposed'. This super-natural action, when it took place, was generally only a delayed action.

No doubt, the effect produced sometimes remained only partial. Con-temporaries appear to have accepted these half-successes with equanimity, though they were really no more than superficial. On 25 March 1669, two doctors from Auray in Brittany signed a certificate of healing without a second thought for a man who had had several scrofulous ulcers, and had then been touched by the king; after which, as an extra precaution, he had gone on a pilgrimage to St-Marcoul at Corbeny. The result was that all the ulcers had disappeared—except for one.[39] Modern science would say in such a case that certain manifestations of the disease had disappeared, but not the disease itself; it was still there, and ready to break out at other points. Then there were sometimes relapses, which do not seem to have occasioned much surprise or scandal. In 1654 a woman called Jeanne Bugain was touched by Louis XIV the day after his consecration. She 'experienced some relief', but the illness then came on again, and was only definitely cured after a pilgrimage to Corbeny. These facts were vouched for in a certificate drawn up by the village curé.[40] The country priest responsible for it certainly did not imagine that anyone could draw conclusions from it that were disrespectful to the monarch, for a solid faith is not easily shaken.

I have already mentioned above Christopher Lovel, of Wells in Somerset, who went to Avignon to seek out the Stuart Pretender in 1716 and was said to have been healed by him. This splendid triumph evoked great enthusiasm in Jacobite circles and was the prime cause of the historian Carte's misadventures. But it appears to be a fact that the unfortunate Lovel fell ill again, set off full of faith on a second journey to his prince, and died on the way there.[41]

Finally, we must take note of relapses of a different kind, which the medicine of the day was more or less incapable of diagnosing. We know at the present time that the disease our forefathers called scrofula was more often than not a form of tubercular adenitis, that is, one of the possible local symptoms of a bacillus disease capable of attacking many organs of the body. It sometimes happened that with a remission of the adenitis the tuberculosis took on another and often much more serious form. We read in the *Synopsis Annalium Societatis Jesu in Lusitania*, published by Father Antonio Franc in 1726, that on 17 January 1657 there died at Coimbra 'the scholastic, Michel Martin. He had been sent to France for the healing of his scrofula by laying on of hands from the Most Christian King, and came back cured to Portugal; but he then succumbed to another disease, and fell victim to a slow consumption'.[42]

We may sum up our review as follows. Only a certain number of the sick recovered their health—sometimes incompletely, or only temporarily; and the majority of the cures only took place a considerable time after the healing rite. Now it will be as well to remind ourselves what this disease was over which the French and English kings were supposed to have miraculous power. The doctors of the day did not possess either an accurate terminology or very certain methods of diagnosis. A perusal of the old treatises, like the one by Richard Wiseman, clearly shows that the name scrofula was often used to cover a large number of lesions of various kinds, some of which were benignant; and these last would sometimes disappear by themselves, sometimes after quite a short time.[43] But let us leave on one side these spurious cases of scrofula, and concentrate on the genuine article, tubercular in origin, which always constituted the large majority of the cases dealt with by the royal touch. Scrofula is not a disease that is easily cured: it often recurs over a long period, sometimes almost indefinitely; but it is pre-eminently a disease that easily gives the illusion of being cured; for its symptoms—tumours, fistulas, suppurations and the like—fairly often disappear of themselves, only to come back again later on at the same spot or elsewhere. Given a temporary remission of this kind, or even a real cure (not of course impossible, but not so common), some time after the royal touch, there was justification for belief in the wonder-working power. This, as we have already seen, was all the faithful subjects of the French or English kings asked for. No doubt there would not have been this readiness to proclaim a miracle unless there had been the predisposition to expect no less from the hand of royalty. But we need hardly remind ourselves that everything favoured such an expectation.

The idea of sacred royalty was a legacy from almost primitive ages; it was strengthened by the rite of unction and by the whole expansion of the monarchical legend, and it was also cleverly exploited by certain astute politicians, all the more subtle at making use of the legend because they themselves often believed in it. No wonder, then, that people were prejudiced in favour of it, and that it haunted the popular mind. Now, there were no saints that did not have their miraculous exploits; no sacred things or persons without their supernatural powers. Moreover, in the world of marvel inhabited by our ancestors, there was hardly any phenomenon they were not prepared to explain by causes outside the normal order of the universe. One day, certain kings in Capetian France and Norman England —or perhaps certain counsellors on their behalf—conceived the idea of trying their hand as wonder-workers, in order to strengthen their rather fragile prestige. Persuaded as they were themselves of the sanctity conferred on them by their function and their royal lineage, they probably thought it a simple thing to claim this kind of power. It was noticed that a much-feared disease would sometimes yield—or appear to yield—after they had laid hands, which were almost unanimously considered as sacred, upon it. They could scarcely avoid seeing it in terms of cause and effect and concluding that the looked-for miracle had indeed occurred. What created faith in the miracle was the idea that there was bound to be a miracle. And this was what kept the belief alive, as well as the accumulating witness of the generations down the ages, all those whose testimony, apparently based upon experience, seemed impossible to doubt. As for the probably fairly numerous cases where the disease resisted the touch of the august hands, they were soon forgotten. Such is the happy optimism of believing souls.

Thus it is difficult to see faith in the royal miracle as anything but the result of a collective error—a more harmless one, incidentally, than most of those which bestrew the human past. Even by William of Orange's time, the English doctor Carr observed that whatever opinion might be held about the efficacy of the royal touch, it possessed at least one advantage: it was not in any way harmful.[44] And in that it was greatly superior to a good many of the remedies for scrofula contained in the pharmacopoeia of olden times. The possibility of recourse to this miraculous treatment universally held to be effective must sometimes have prevented patients from using more dangerous remedies. From this purely negative point of view we are no doubt quite right in imagining that more than one poor sufferer may have owed a debt to his prince for the relief of his ills.

Appendix I

The royal miracle in the
French and English royal accounts

The healing rites involved the kings in certain expenses. That is why there is a
need to consult the English and French account-books on this subject. But documents of this kind are extremely difficult to interpret. It is no good simply
sampling them at random: to obtain fruitful results, one must explore them
methodically. More particularly when they are examined in detail, it becomes
clear that although they are very rich in information for certain periods, at other
times they yield none—or almost none. This apparent capriciousness needs to be
explained, and I shall attempt to do so in the following critical study.

We will begin with France.

1   *The touch for scrofula in the French account-books*

To start with, we shall do well to remember one general fact that historians often
have reason to deplore, namely how very few of the French monarchy's financial
archives still survive. There are many causes for this scarcity, some of which are
debatable; but the chief reason is well known. On the night of the 26/27 October
1737, there was a fire in the building within the Palais on the Île de la Cité,
which housed most of the documents of the Chambre des Comptes; and almost
everything that still remained of the old administrative accounts perished in the
disaster.[1] All we have to work on is a few scattered remains that chanced to escape
destruction.

The earliest accounts containing some information on the scrofula rite come
from the reign of Philip the Fair. In those days, not all the sick who were touched
used to receive alms; it was only foreigners, or Frenchmen who came from places
far away from the royal residence.[2] They were given the money either by the
almoner himself, or by some subordinate valet or porter; and the money came
from the Royal Household Chest. Now we happen still to possess a certain
number of the wax tablets from the time of St-Louis, Philip III and Philip IV
on which the officials who managed these funds used to write down their operations in detail.[3] The oldest of these contain no mention of any gifts to the scrofulous. This is probably not because the scrofulous were excluded on principle

from the royal bounty. Our tablets simply indicate on several occasions that certain sums were distributed as alms, without any more detail than now and again a man's name; and some of these amounts may well have been paid out to persons who had come for the royal touch. The absence of any indication simply means that the precise destination of this kind of expense was of no interest to the cashier. It mattered little whether it had gone to a scrofula sufferer, or to some other poor man: it was alms—and that was all he needed to know.

But fortunately for the historian there came a moment when an accountant with a more enquiring mind took over the funds. Between 31 January 1304 and 18 January 1307, the Royal Household Chest passed from Jean de St-Just into the control of Renaud de Roye. We possess some of the tablets from the time of the latter in two groups, stretching respectively from 18 January to 28 June 1307 and from 1 July 1308 to 30 December of the same year.[4] They contain a note of a fairly large number of payments to individuals 'suffering from the King's Evil', entered with remarkable care, since on each occasion the name and place of origin of each recipient are meticulously recorded.[5] It is to this wonderfully accurate official that we owe some of the most precise data we possess concerning the royal miracle.

Now let us jump ahead nearly a couple of centuries. From Philip the Fair to Charles VIII, there are no accounts referring to the healing power. It is probable that at a fairly early date, the administration of funds for providing gifts to scrofula sufferers, and for more general alms, ceased to belong to the Royal Household accounts; for the latter, even by Charles VI's time, already contain no mention of this kind.[6] From that time onwards, the almoner had his own special account, managed by himself or an expert under his orders. No doubt he also had his own books; but most of them have perished. The only ones, it seems, to have survived before Charles VIII, the registers classified under KK 9 and KK 66 in the National Archives, dating from the reigns of John II, Charles V and Charles VI, and partly from Louis XI, concern offerings made to religious establishments or on the occasion of religious solemnities—the first batch entirely, and the second as regards the major part of them. They are not of interest to us here.[7] Not till the year 1485 do we meet with proper account-books. Here is a list of them, though I must warn the reader that I have only been able to search the Archives Nationales and the Bibliothèque Nationale, and so cannot claim to have covered all possible sources. The catalogue details given without further additions all refer to the Archives Nationales.

1 The fragment of a register: expenses—a part of September 1485; K 111, fol. 49–53.[8]
2 Fragment of a register: expenses—a part of March and April 1487; KK 111, fol. 41–8.
3 Register for 1 Oct. 1497–30 Sept. 1498; KK 77.
4 Account of expenses apparently not forming part of a register, Oct. 1502; Bibl. Nat. fr. 26108, fol. 391–2.
5 Register for 1 Oct. 1506–30 Sept. 1507; K 88.
6 Register going from 19 May 1528 to 31 Dec. 1530; the greater part of it has been preserved in the Arch. Nat. KK 101; but the volume has numerous gaps, all of them to do with the expenses. The fol. 15–22 (May, June and part of

July 1528) today constitute folios 62–9 of Bibl. Nat. fr. 6762; fol. 47–62 (part of Dec. 1528, January, February, part of March 1529) constitute sheets 70–85 of the same MS. Fol. 71–94 (part of April, May and part of June 1529), 171–86 (part of August and September 1529), 227–58 (November and part of December 1529), 275–96 (part of January and February 1530), 331–54 (part of April and May 1530), 403–34 (part of August, September and part of October 1530) all appear to be definitely lost.

7 Fragment of a register: expenses for part of July 1547 (the year is not given, but is deducible from the fact that a certain number of the articles are concerned with the consecration journey): KK 111, fol. 33–40.

8 Fragment of a register: expenses for part of April, May, June, July, and part of August 1548: KK 111, fol. 17–32.

9 Fragment of the register of the financial year stretching from 1 January to 31 December 1549: total receipts, expenses for January and a part of February: KK 111, fol. 1–16.

10 A register: 1 January–31 December 1569: KK 137 (in a bad state).

In all these registers, fragments of registers, or accounts—with the exception of no. 2—one comes across references to the touch, but mostly in simple numerical form. The names of the sick are only occasionally mentioned.

From 31 December 1539 onwards up to the end of the French monarchy I have not found any further alms registers.[9]

2 The English accounts

The old English Royal Houses have left us a fine array of financial archives, beside which the Paris remnants cut a very poor figure. They did not suffer any disaster comparable to the fire of the Palais. Confronted by such riches, a Frenchman feels both full of admiration and somewhat frightened: how is he to find his way among so many treasures? The administrative history of England is very imperfectly known—not that it would be impossible to write it, but rather because it has not attracted anyone for a long time. The brilliant episodes of parliamentary life attracted everyone's attention, and scholars were not keen to lower their gaze to the obscure labours of clerks in offices. Lately, however, a new generation of workers have valiantly set about the task;[10] and some day we shall owe to their efforts the power to plumb the secrets of many constitutional and social transformations that are little more than guess-work at present. But their task is far from complete. In particular, the study of financial documents— the whole business of classification, comparison and discussion, which appears so thankless, yet yields such important results—is still in its very early stages. Nevertheless, I felt compelled to make use of these difficult documents here, for they contain a mass of data essential to any knowledge of the healing rites. Above all, I have had to concentrate on a special class of them—the accounts of the Royal Household. As I used them, I could not abstain from making a critical analysis, for no work previous to mine gave me enough information.[11] I have done my best; but I fully recognize the risk of making mistakes in research work of this sort under the conditions in which I undertook it. In order to reconstitute with some certainty the methods followed by an administrator in setting out his accounts, it would be necessary to break down all the available material between two carefully chosen points of time. In other words, one would have to limit one-self to a relatively short period, and study it thoroughly. I, on the contrary, was forced to take in an extremely long period; and I have only been able to make soundings here and there, fairly numerous, indeed, but necessarily incomplete. In what follows, the reader will find some positive facts, which will in any case prove useful; but their interpretation must remain a matter of conjecture. I have given in the notes the exact nomenclature of the documents examined by me. This will give some idea of the foundation for my hypotheses.[12]

Up to the beginning of Edward I's reign, there are only a few accounts that have come down to us; and they tell us nothing about the subject of our present interest.[13] From Edward I onwards, however, the organization becomes better, more accurate and more fully documented, with everything carefully preserved. That is when the series of the admirable Exchequer Accounts of the Public Record Office in London really begins; and it is to some extent duplicated by the collections in the British Museum, where a good number of odd documents re-moved at various periods from the official place of deposit have found a resting-place. We must study separately the information available in the financial archives of the old English kings in so far as it concerns the touch for scrofula and the healing rings respectively.

I THE TOUCH FOR SCROFULA IN THE ENGLISH ACCOUNTS

The sick who had been 'signed 'or 'blessed' by the king used each to receive a small sum of money. In Edward I's time the distribution of the gifts was carried out by the almoner, and there are three kinds of document that allow us to trace the payments made on those occasions.

They are as follows:

1 The almoner's 'rolls': these are simple memoranda noting for a given period —usually a year—the sums disbursed by this personage. The expenses are shown day by day or week by week—occasionally, by the fortnight.[14]

2 A summary account for each financial year, that is, for *each year of the reign*, by the Keeper of the Wardrobe (*custos garderobe*).[15] This was the title given to the official who managed the finances of the Royal Household. This word 'Ward-robe' is somewhat misleading, since it apparently covered sometimes simply one of the Household offices, the section whose business it was to look after the clothes, jewels and similar objects, but at other times (usually with the added epithet 'Great'—*Magna Gardaroba*) the Royal Household as a whole (elsewhere called *Hospicium*). The relationship between the Wardrobe properly speaking and the Great Wardrobe are indeed obscure; and I make no claim here to decide the question, or even to put it in precise terms, for it is a most intricate problem. But I thought it as well to indicate an ambiguity in the terms used which sometimes makes research into the royal accounts far from easy.[16]

3 The accounts—also annual—of the Comptroller of the Wardrobe (*contrarotu-lator Garderobe*).[17] This document called the *contrarotulamentum* was apparently intended to make it possible to check the management. One can conjecture that

the roll and the counter-roll, both on the same pattern, but—in principle at least—independent of one another, were meant to be compared in due course by the inspectors of the accounts. I had occasion to compare the accounts for the twenty-eighth year of Edward I's reign as regards the amounts recorded for the royal touch, on the one hand by the Keeper of the books, on the other by the Comptroller; and I found that they tallied. But this was only possible on that one occasion; for generally one or the other of the two documents had been lost. Yet this is of small importance, for they were no doubt almost always approximately in agreement. Thanks to the principle of double accounting, probably invented by suspicious officials, we are able today to use the Comptroller's account to replace the Clerk of the Wardrobe's, where this has disappeared, and vice versa.

But in the eyes of the historian concerned with the royal miracle, all these accounts have one grave defect: they only give figures, and never names. They tell us that in such-and-such a week Edward I touched so many sick, and even this is worth a good deal; but we should like to have more. All these poor people who came to the king asking to be healed, where did they come from? The Royal Household Accounts of Philip the Fair gave this information, but the Royal Household accounts of Edward I are always silent on the point. Such as they are, however, they are very valuable. For the following reigns we have much less information; and the fault lies in a series of changes in administrative practice, which we shall now explain.

In Edward II's time, the role of almoner suddenly vanishes for good and all.[18] What was the reason for this? We can only hazard a conjecture. It is most unlikely that the almoners ceased to enter their expenses; but no doubt they gradually fell into the habit of keeping their accounts in their own possession. For we know that there was over a long period a completely distinct Almonry fund. But in the course of time the ancient section of this fund completely disappeared, partly in a fire, partly as a result of disorder or dilapidations.[19] It may be mentioned straight away that the same thing has happened with another set of records from which we might have hoped to gather useful information, those of the Chapel Royal.[20]

There remain the summary figures recorded for each occasion of the royal touch,[21] either by the Keeper of the Wardrobe or by the Comptroller. Unfortunately they ceased to be kept with the same minute accuracy from about the middle of Edward II's reign, as far as concerns the material we are interested in.[22] It became a habit no longer to put down in chronological detail the sums given to the scrofula sufferers touched by the king. From that time onwards, they were content with a summary mention, specifying that so many pounds, *sous* or *deniers* had been paid out by the almoner to so many sick persons 'blessed', in the course of the particular exercise; or, exceptionally, for a certain period demarcated within this exercise; and working out at so much per sick person. No further details are given.[23] This was the practice, it would seem, regularly followed during the second half of Edward II's reign and the reign of Edward III in its entirety.[24]

From Richard II's reign, the summaries relating to each finished exercise cease entirely to give us any information about the royal touch for scrofula.[25] Could it be that the English sovereigns then abruptly gave up the use of their wonder-working power? That cannot be so, for we know that they went on posing as miraculous doctors, as they had done in the past. This sudden silence is probably to be explained by a modest bureaucratic reform. In the accounts or counter-rolls of the Wardrobe, the section relating to expenses must have been divided into two parts, one for current expenditure—in chronological order— and the other comprising a series of chapters giving the details office by office— the *particule*—of the expenses not falling within the preceding framework. This arrangement, which was clear enough, was no novelty; but from this moment it became the regular practice. In the oldest accounts of this type from the preceding reigns, the gifts made by the king to the sick he had 'blessed' were always entered together—*en bloc*, as we have seen—in the second part, in the section (*titulus*) covering the Royal Alms. They were therefore clearly considered as extraordinary expenses. But under Richard II, the item referring to the royal touch disappeared for ever from the Alms section or *titulus*. The explanation would seem to be that henceforward it was decided to class these payments as normal expenditure, and they therefore had to be transferred to the first part, arranged in the form of a day-by-day account. Unfortunately, this day-book was drawn up in a rather vague fashion. It was considered sufficient to show what each office had disbursed each day or each week, without specifying the exact object of each disbursement—so much for the cellar, so much for the kitchen, etc., so much for the Royal Alms.[26] The almoner had paid out a certain sum; but the details as to whom and for what were not of interest. And so under this system the expenses incurred for the royal touch became concealed in the mass of the other royal bounties. For nearly a century, one could look in vain for any trace of the royal miracle in these accounts.

But under Henry VII and Henry VIII it reappears. Not that the annual registers of the Clerk of the Wardrobe or the Comptroller give us more informa-tion than in the past.[27] But for this reign we possess certain day-books from the court, which indicate on several occasions sums paid out to 'sick persons healed' by the king.[28] These payments do not appear to have been made by the almoner; for one of them, in Henry VIII's reign, we know the name of the official who advanced the money and was then reimbursed: it was the First Gentleman of the Privy Chamber.[29] Moreover, the references to the royal touch are fairly infre-quent in these registers. One wonders whether they really cover all the cases in which an expense of this kind was involved. I can well believe that a certain number—perhaps the majority—of the sums paid out to the sick still passed through the hands of the almoner, who no doubt entered them as part of his general disbursements, which are no longer known to us in detail.

As we come on to the seventeenth century, we find that the accounts of the Royal Household will no longer serve our purpose:[30] we shall get our information from financial documents of another kind. About the fifteenth century, the English kings had formed the habit of giving the sick they touched neither a variable sum of money, nor even a fixed sum in coins of any kind, but always the same gold piece, an 'angel'.[31] Gradually, the 'angel' ceased to be an ordinary coin, and was hardly minted any more except for the healing rite. In Charles II's reign, it was replaced by a medal no longer possessing any monetary character, called the 'touch-piece'. In the seventeenth century, 'angels' and 'touch-pieces' were struck at the Tower of London Mint. We possess a certain number of directives on this subject addressed by various government authorities to the keepers of this establishment; we also have some accounts, giving us some idea of the amount produced.[32] These statistical data are interesting; for at least from the time when the 'angel' ceased to be used for anything else but the royal touch, the figures for the coins or medals coming from the mint give us some idea of the number of sick touched by the king. This method, however, will not provide us with any very accurate details; it can only give us a rough idea of quantity, because we do not know for certain over what period of time the coins or medals struck at a particular moment were subsequently distributed. Or rather, we do not know this as a rule; but for Charles II's reign and the beginning of James II's we are better informed.

The accounting system for producing the royal touch medals in these two reigns was as follows.[33] The official in charge of the court finances, the Keeper of the Privy Purse, used to deal directly with the mint, buying the medals from them in fairly large quantities, and then passing them on gradually as they were needed. The sum needed for each purchase was advanced to him by the Treasury; but he subsequently had to justify to the central financial administration the use he had made of it. It was not of course sufficient to produce a receipt for the total amount of coin; he had to render account of the way it had been distributed. Before issuing him with a fresh sum for a new minting, the Treasury would want to be sure that he had completely used up the first, and spent it for the proper purposes. So the official would issue a certificate over a given period, giving day by day the number of sick persons touched, which would in principle be equal to the number of medals distributed. These papers were then signed by the two officiating doctors, countersigned by the ecclesiastical official, the Clerk of the Closet, whose business it was at this time to manage the ceremony, and finally produced at the appointed time to the authorities who checked the accounts. They were excellent supporting testimony, and they provide us today with admirably precise information for our documentary history. Unfortunately, they have not been at all well preserved. They were only of temporary interest, and no doubt no one bothered to clutter up the files with them. Five of them—we cannot say how or when—fell into the hands of a collector, and eventually ended up in the Surgeon-General's library in Washington.[34] But not all the certificates of this kind have left the Public Record Office. I had the good fortune to light upon a bundle that had gone astray among the 'miscellaneous books' in the Exchequer files, which contained fifteen of them.[35] More thorough search would no doubt unearth some more of them. But for the present the one drawn up in 1685, when N. Duresme was Clerk of the Closet, must be considered the latest financial document concerned with the royal miracle.[36]

II THE MEDICINAL RINGS IN THE ENGLISH ACCOUNTS

On the subject of the medicinal rings, the accounts give us much more exact and continuous information than about the touch for scrofula. The Good Friday rite —sufficiently described above—required each year a payment in coins, which of course had to be recorded. This expense was naturally incurred only once in the year, which no doubt explains the fact that it was always entered not in the first part of the annual accounts (which, it will be recalled, were in chronological form), but in the second, under the heading of exceptional disbursements by the Almonry. From Edward III to Edward VI, this was the regular practice.[37] This business was very simple in its main lines, and only involves one delicate point that deserves a little further attention.

During the reigns of Edward III, Richard II, Henry IV and under Henry V at least in 1413, the items in the alms section dealing with the cramp rings are always entered in the same form, and this fits in perfectly with what we know of the essence of the rite. Two successive payments of equal value are shown, the first relating to the coins placed by the king upon the altar, and then taken away to be melted down and transformed into rings; the second to the final offering, which was considered to be the 'redemption' of the first one.[38] From the year 1442 onwards (the first mention I have discovered for Henry VI's reign) the method of entry changes. There is now one single entry, and the wording is not very clear: 'Offerings of my lord the king, made at the adoration of the cross on the day of Good Friday, in gold or in silver, for the making of medicinal rings, 25 shillings';[39] or from Henry VIII's time: 'For the offerings of my lord the king made at the adoration of the cross on the day of Good Friday, and for the redemption of the medicinal rings to be made of them, gold and silver, 25 shillings'.[40] If this style is obscure, it is because the accountants continued to use old-fashioned expressions suggesting that the old practices of redemption and manufacture of the rings from the coins offered on the altar were still in existence. What actually took place can be deduced with certainty from the reduction of the primitive double payment, which—at least since 1369—was invariably twice twenty-five shillings[41] to a single payment equal to half the total originally disbursed. The kings had not become any less generous: they still always made the same gift to their chapel, for in fact it was only the second offering that used to be retained by it—namely twenty-five shillings. The first offering used formerly to be reclaimed for making the rings, and this is what had disappeared. Why was this? We shall find the explanation in some documents not belonging to the accounting departments, namely *A Defence of the rights of the House of Lancaster*[42] written by Fortescue and a ritual from Henry VIII's time. The rings were from this time onwards brought in ready made on the morning of Good Friday. The metal for them was taken from the Royal Treasure a good while beforehand. The expenditure corresponding to this provision of precious metal no longer had any reason to figure in the alms section of the accounts; it must now be sought in the special accounts relating to the royal jewels; and that is where, at least from Edward IV's time, we do sometimes actually come across it.[43]

To sum up, we may say that the financial archives of the old English monarchy only offer us fragmentary, and too often vague, information about the healing rites, and more particularly about the touch for scrofula. The French archives, though much poorer in material, are in certain respects more fruitful. This is the sort of surprise quite normal to this kind of source-material, which is as full of disappointments as of unexpected discoveries.

In a series of pieces of a well-defined type, the slightest change in the arrangement of the entries coming in at a particular moment, though at first sight insignificant, may often be enough to conceal from the eyes of the historian a whole category of information of the utmost importance. We are at the mercy of the whims of a minor civil servant, who may decide to change the routine of his predecessors. That is why it is seldom wise to base an argument on the apparent silence of an account.

Appendix II

Notes on the iconography

I have collected below a few summary indications concerning the pictorial or plastic representations of the royal miracle that I have been able to gather. A scholar as well informed as Salomon Reinach declared in 1908 in reference to no. 3 in my list that he had never come across any other picture on that subject (*Rev. archéologique*, 4th series, XII (1908), p. 124, n. 1). The reader will see that I have been fortunate enough to effect a notable increase in the size of the iconographical dossier relating to the royal touch and the healing rites in general. Such as it is, however, it is not very rich; though no doubt searchers more fortunate than myself may one day be able to extend it, at least as regards the last two or three centuries of the wonder-working monarchies. For the Middle Ages, I do not think there is much more to be found. Moreover, when I applied to le comte Durrieu and Henry Martin, they were kind enough to reply that they did not know of any miniatures relating to the touch for scrofula other than the ones listed here. For the modern period, Jules Robiquet, the curator of the Musée Carnavalet, and Charles Mortet, head of the Bibliothèque Ste-Geneviève, assured me that the collections in their care did not contain any representation of the touch for scrofula.

As a method of classification, I have adopted the chronological order within each subdivision. The numbers marked with an asterisk are the works known to me only through earlier authors, either because they have disappeared, or because I have been unable to find them.

For each work, I have indicated the reproductions that have been made of it, then the studies produced on it; when it seemed apposite, I have added a short critical discussion. A thorough-going description—which, to be really useful, would always need to be fairly long—would often have duplicated what had already been said in the text. I have only given one in two cases: first, when it was necessary for the discussion; and secondly, when the work had not been published or reproduced in any printed work, including this present book. As for reproductions in the text, I was obliged to set certain limits—for reasons that will be easily understood. I have been guided in my choice by the following considerations: I have put before the reader two engravings, one of them representing the French rite, the other the English, in the royal touch (nos. 8 and 13);

an altar picture which throws light upon the association between the healing king and St-Marcoul, peculiar to France (no. 16); and finally, that delightful picture of the sixteenth century in which an unknown artist has ingeniously brought together the two most striking aspects of sacred royalty, its quasi-assimilation, through the Communion rite, with the priestly dignity, and its wonder-working power (no. 3). I should have liked to add to these characteristic documents the St-Riquier fresco (no. 20), which so happily symbolizes the role assigned to St-Marcoul of intercessor for the royal miracle; but I was not able to photograph it myself when I went to study it on the spot, and I did not subsequently succeed in obtaining any photograph or other copy of it.

I should like to thank all those persons who were kind enough to help me in a variety of ways to bring these widely dispersed documents together: le comte Durrieu; Henry Martin; Salomon Reinach; Jules Robiquet; Charles Mortet; Henri Girard; the archpriest of St-Wulfran's, Abbeville; François Paillart, the well-known printer; Paul Gout, chief architect of the Monuments Historiques; Mr Hocquet, the city archivist at Tournai; Guglielmo Pacchioni of the Reale Pinacoteca in Turin; Professors Martinotti and Ducati of Bologna; and Miss Helen Farquhar.

I   *The touch for scrofula*

1   *Edward the Confessor touching the scrofulous woman.* A 13th century miniature in Cambridge University Library MS. Ee III 59, containing the poem entitled *La Estoire de Seint Aedward le Rei*, p. 38.

Reproductions: Crawfurd, *King's Evil*, opp. p. 18; C. Barfoed, *Haands-Paalaeggelse*, p. 52 (from Crawfurd). *Studies*: H. R. Luard, *Lives of Edward the Confessor* (Rolls Series), London, 1858, p. 12, no. XXXVII; cf. above pp. 24 and 181.

2   *Un roi de France touche les écrouelles.* The second upper medallion of the stained glass picture of the consecration, in the chapel of St-Michel du Circuit, the Abbey Church of Mont St-Michel, executed in 1488 on the orders of Abbot André Laure.

This window, which has been destroyed, is only known through past descriptions of it, notably by Abbé Pigeon, *Nouveau Guide historique et descriptif du Mont Saint-Michel*, Avranches, 1864, reproduced by Paul Gout, *Le Mont Saint-Michel*, II, pp. 556-7. I have quoted a part of this description above (p. 83); here it is in full:

The second medallion represents the king, who having taken Communion
in both kinds, has gone to a park where a considerable number of
sick folk are assembled. He touches them one after the other with
his right hand, from forehead to chin and from one cheek to the other,
as he repeats these hallowed words: 'May God heal thee, the king touches
thee'.
In a corner of the picture there is a cage from which several birds are
escaping, a symbol of the freedom just given by the new king to those who
have been captive, and the freedom he will give to his subjects . . .

The form of words *Dieu te guérisse, le roi te touche'*, was certainly not part of the original window; as far as I can see, Abbé Pigeon only mentions it in order to prove his own learning. But it must be admitted that on this point his text is far from clear.

Studies: see above p. 83.

3 *A French king receives Communion in both kinds and prepares himself for touching the scrofula.* A 16th century picture; in the 18th century it was at Genoa, in the Palais Durazzo, via Balbi (cf. Ratti, *Guido di Genova*, 1780, I, p. 209); acquired by the King of Sardinia in 1824; now in the Reale Galleria at Turin, no. 194.

Reproductions: Reale Galleria illustrata, IV, p. 153; Paul Richer, *L'art et la médecine*, n. d., p. 296; Eugen Hollaender, *Die Medizin in der klassischen Malerei*, Stuttgart, 1903, p. 265; S. Reinach, *Répertoire de peintures du moyen-âge et de la Renaissance*, 4, 1918, p. 663; Martinotti, 'Re Taumaturghi' p. 133; here Plate 1.

Studies: Hollaender, loc. cit., S. Reinach, *Revue archéologique*, 4th series, 12, 1908, p. 114, n. 1; cf. above p. 180. I owe to a letter from Guglielmo Pacchioni, curator of the Reale Galleria, a large amount of valuable information made use of above and in the discussion that follows below.

What exactly is the subject of this picture? In order to answer this question, it will be as well first of all to give a short description of the work.

On the left, and in a chapel open on the right-hand side, is a French king, bearded, wearing a cloak decorated with fleur-de-lis, a crown on his head, his sceptre and a baton, the symbol of royal justice, at his side. He is kneeling before a kind of marble table, which must be an altar. He seems to be holding in both hands a chalice covered with a lid. Opposite to him is a kneeling bishop, also holding in both hands an object I think I recognize quite certainly as a paten, which is empty. Round the altar there are another bishop and a monk, kneeling, and another monk and three laymen standing (one a page holding the train of the first bishop, and a person holding an object which is perhaps a helmet surmounted by a crown). On the right, in a courtyard onto which the chapel opens, bordered by a battlemented wall pierced by a monumental door, there are two sick persons with crutches, one kneeling and the other standing, a woman holding a little child in her arms, two other people, one with joined hands, and near the door, some guards. Beyond the wall is a landscape with a town, towards which a mounted procession is making its way.

Everyone, it seems, is agreed in recognizing in the right-hand figures (except for the guards) sufferers from scrofula waiting for the royal touch. As regards the scene on the left, Hollaender and Reinach interpret it as representing the king's unction. I think it should rather be taken as the king receiving Communion in both kinds, according to the privilege of his dynasty. The presence of the paten puts the matter almost beyond doubt. The king has just received the Host, and is about to receive the wine from the chalice. He will then go on to touch the sick. Is this Communion at the consecration service? At first sight, the king's costume might incline one to think so; but it is well known that in the art of the period this costume was only a conventional device for indicating the figure to be that of a king, and a king of France. In all probability, the artist's intention was simply to set the two scenes side by side to bring out the two outstanding prerogatives of the French monarchy—Communion on a level with priests, and the healing miracle. It would seem that the author of the Mont St-Michel stained glass window had already been inspired by a similar idea; but there, as the subject of the entire window was the royal consecration, the Communion depicted was doubtless the one taking place during this ceremony.

There remains the question of probable authorship. The picture, which is unsigned, has been successively attributed to Albrecht Dürer (Ratti, loc. cit.), to the Cologne School, to Lucas van Leyden and to Bernard van Orley; this last opinion has acquired a semi-official value owing to its adoption by Burckhardt, *Cicerone* (Fr. trans. II, p. 637), and by the Galleria catalogue, the work of Baudi de Vesme. Yet it presents a certain difficulty: how would van Orley, the accredited painter of Margaret of Austria and Mary of Hungary, have been induced to devote one of his works to the glory of the French miracle? (For his career cf. A. Wauters *Bernard Van Orley*, 1893.) Our picture is probably from the hand of some artist from the Low Countries subjected to an Italian influence. It would seem that this rather vague attribution is as far as we can go.

4 *A French king touching a scrofulous man*. A woodcut in Degrassalius (Grassaille), *Regalium Franciae iura*, 1538, p. 62.

5 *Henry II touching for scrofula*. A miniature in Henry II's Book of Hours, Bibl. Nat. lat. 1429, fol. 106v.

Reproductions: du Bastard, *Peintures et ornements des manuscrits*, VIII (in colour); *Livre d'heures de Henri II, reproduction des 17 miniatures du ms. latin 1429 de la Bibliothèque Nationale* (1906), pl. XVII; Landouzy, *Le Toucher*, unnumbered; Crawfurd, *King's Evil*, opp. p. 58 (back to front); Farquhar, 'Royal Charities', I, opp. p. 43.

Studies: on the MS. as a whole, cf. among others L. Delisle, *Annuaire-Bulletin de la Soc. de l'Histoire de France*, 1900, and *Exposition des primitifs français . . . Catalogue . . .*, 1904, *Manuscrits à peintures*, no. 205 on the above miniature, p. 316.

6 *Mary Tudor touching a young scrofula patient*. A miniature in the Queen's missal, Westminster Cathedral Library.

Reproductions: Crawfurd, *King's Evil*, opp. p. 68.

Studies: for the missal, see a communication by Sir Henry Ellis, *Proceedings of the Society of Antiquaries*, 1st series, 2, 1853, pp. 292–4, and Sparrow Simpson, 'On the forms of prayer', pp. 285–7.

7* *Queen Elizabeth touching for scrofula*. An engraving by the Flemish engraver Joos de Hondt, probably carried out during his stay in England (1583–94).

I only know of this work from the mention made of it by Tooker in his *Charisma, Epistola Dedicatoria*, p. 10: '. . . cum nuper in *Tabulis Geographicis et Hydrographicis* depictam vidimus, et exaratam salutiferae hujusce sanationis historiam, et quasi consecratam memoriam oculis contemplati sumus', with the marginal note: 'Iodocus Flandr. in descript. sive tab. orbis terr'; cf. Del Rio, *Disquisitionum*, 1606 ed., p. 61, for an enumeration of the proofs given by Tooker in support of the power supposed to have been exercised by Elizabeth: 'Probat etiam quia quidam Judocus Hundius eam curationem pictam in lucem dedit'. I have not found anything resembling this in the various atlases of J. de Hondt's work I have been able to consult: *Theatrum imperii Magnae Britanniae . . . opus nuper a Iohanne* Spedo . . . nunc vero *a Philemone* Hollando . . . *donatum*, Amsterdam, 1616, 'ex Officina Judoci Hondii'; *Thrésor des Chartes*, The Hague, n.d.; Pierre Bertius, *La Géographie raccourcie . . . avec de belles cartes . . .* par Judocus Hondius, Amsterdam, 1618; and his various editions of Mercator's work.

For J. de Hondt's stay in England, see *Bryan's Dictionary of Painters and Engravers*, ed. by G. C. Williamson, and the *Dictionary of National Biography*, under his name.

8   'Représentation au Naturel . . . the Most Christian King Henry IIII, king of France and Navarre, touching for scrofula.' An etching by P. Firens, n.d. I know of the following copies: (1) Bibl. Nat. Estampes, coll. Hennin, XIV, fol. 5; (2) Bibl. Nat. Imprimés, coll. Cangé, L b³⁵ 23b, fol. 19 (proof before lettering); (3) ibid., fol. 21; (4) mounted on a guard, at the head of *Discours des Escrouelles*, in a copy of the *Oeuvres de Mᵉ André du Launres*, Paris, 1613, Bibl. Nat. Imprimés, T²⁵ 40b (proof before lettering); (5) mounted on a guard at the head of a copy of Andreas Laurentius, *De Mirabili strumas sanandi vi . . .*, Paris, 1609, B.M. 1187 a 2 (proof before lettering); (6) ibid., at the head of another copy of the same work, in the same library (proof before lettering).

Reproductions: Abel Hugo, *France historique et monumentale*, 5, 1843, pl. I (very second-rate); *Nouvelle iconographie de la Salpêtrière*, 4, 1891, p. XV; A. Franklin, *La Vie privée d'autrefois, Les Médecins*, opp. p. 15 (detail); Landouzy, *Le Toucher*, p. 2; Crawfurd, *King's Evil*, opp. p. 78; Martinotti, 'Re Taumaturghi', p. 136; Roshem, *Les Escroulles*, p. ix (very much reduced); here Plate 3.

Studies: above, p. 194. The fact that this engraving figures at the front of a certain number of copies of du Laurens' treatise on the healing of scrofula, or the translation of it, has fairly often led to the belief that it was engraved as a frontispiece to this work, and in particular for the *editio princeps* of 1609 (on account of the two copies in the B.M.); but it is clear enough that in these two copies—as in the translation of 1613 in the Bibl. Nat—the engraving has been mounted on a guard at a later stage. Moreover as it measures (without the lettering) approximately 15½ in by 11¾ in, it is much too large to have been meant for a 'frontispiece' for a small octavo volume like the edition of 1609; and—a conclusive point—there are numerous copies of this edition which do not contain it at all.

9   *A king touching a scrofulous woman.* An etching, opp. p. 1 in S. Faroul's *De la Dignité des roys de France*, 1633.
Reproduction: Landouzy, *Le Toucher*, p. 20.

10   *A king with the features of Louis XIII touches for scrofula, in the presence of St-Marcoul.* An etching, on the title-page of Oudard Bourgeois' *Apologie*, 1638.
Reproduction: Landouzy, *Le Toucher*, p. 18.
Study: above p. 164.

11   *Francis I touching for scrofula at Bologna on 15 December 1515.* A fresco carried out by Carlo Cignani and Emilio Taruffi by order of Cardinal Girolamo Farnese, legate at Bologna from 1658 to 1662; Bologna, Palazzo Comunale, Sala Farnese. In an insert are the words: 'Franciscus primus Galliarum rex Bononiae quam plurimos scrofulis laborantes sanat'.

Reproductions: G. Martinotti, 'Re taumaturghi' in *L'illustrazione medica italiana*, 4, 1922, p. 134.

Studies: G. Martinotti, loc. cit., cf. above, p. 205 (where I have used information obligingly sent me by Prof. Ducati, some of it taken from Salvatore Muzzi, *Annali della città di Bologna dalla sua origine al 1796*, 8, Bologna, 1846, pp. 12ff.)

12   *Charles II touching for scrofula*. An etching by F. H. van Houe, the frontispiece for a printed sheet or 'broadside' (printed on one side only), giving the ritual of the royal touch: London, Dorman Newman, 1679.

Reproductions: Landouzy, *Le Toucher*, p. 25; Crawfurd, *King's Evil* (unnumbered); Eugen Hollaender, *Wunder, Wundergeburt und Wundergestalt in Einblattdrucken des fünfzehnten bis achtzehnten Jahrhunderts*, Stuttgart, 1921, p. 265.

Noted: above, Book 2, Ch. V, n. 33.

13   *Charles II touching for scrofula*. An etching by R(obert) White, frontispiece to J. Browne, *Charisma Basilikon*, forming part 3 of his *Adenochoiradelogia*, London, 1684.

Reproductions: Landouzy, *Le Toucher*, p. 27; *Home Counties Magazine*, XIV (1912), p. 118; Crawfurd, *King's Evil*, opp. p. 114; Farquhar, 'Royal Charities', II, unnumbered; here Plate 4.

Study: above, Book 2, Ch. V, n. 33.

14   *Louis XIV touching for scrofula in the presence of St-Marcoul*. A picture by Jean Jouvenet, in the former abbey church of St-Riquier (Somme), the St-Marcoul chapel: Signed 'Jouvenet, p (inxit) 1690'.

Reproductions: *La Picardie historique et monumentale* (Soc. des antiquaires de Picardie; fondation E. Soyez), IV, 1907–11, monograph on *St-Riquier*, by Georges Durand, pl. LV.

Studies: G. Durand, loc. cit., pp. 337, 338; cf. p. 230; above p. 165. On the author, the essential work is still F. M. Leroy, *Histoire de Jouvenet*, 1860; cf. Pierre-Marcel Lévi, 'La Peinture française de la mort de Lebrun à la mort de Watteau', n.d. (thesis, Paris).

15   *Louis XIV touching for scrofula, in the presence of St-Marcoul*. An unsigned picture of the 17th century, in the choir of St Wulfran's church at Abbeville.

Noted: *La Picardie historique et monumentale*, 3, p. 39; cf. above, p. 165. The archpriest was kind enough, through F. Paillard, to provide me with some most useful information.

The picture is in a rather poor state of preservation. Louis XIV—whose features are distinctly vague in delineation—is wearing an ermine-caped cloak with a jewelled collar and is turning to the right and leaning down to touch a kneeling sufferer on the forehead. On his right is St-Marcoul holding a crozier. Beside the sick man who is being touched there is another person, also kneeling. In the background and on the right, under an open arcade, there are various persons (patients and guards) rather indistinctly portrayed.

16   *A French king and St-Marcoul healing the scrofulous*. An altarpiece from the second half of the 17th century, church of St-Brice, Tournai.

Reproduction: here Plate 2.

Study: above, p. 165; I owe some extremely valuable information to Mr Hocquet, the archivist. This picture is commonly attributed by local tradition to Michel Bouillon, who ran a school at Tournai from 1630 to 1677. The St-Brice archives do not contain any mention of this.

17* *Queen Anne touching a little boy*. A vignette on a nine of hearts in a card-game with patriotic pictures, described by its owner, G.W.L., in the *Gentleman's Magazine*, 1, 1814, p. 129 (*Gentleman's Magazine Library*, 9, p. 160). The nine of hearts is described as follows: 'Her Majesty touching for the evil. Her right hand is placed on the head of a little boy, who is kneeling before her.'

Noted: above p. 220.

DOUBTFUL:

18 *Bas-relief supposed to represent a king touching for scrofula*. The fragment of a bas-relief discovered at La Condamine (Principality of Monaco): in the Monaco museum (impression in the St-Germain-en-Laye museum).

Reproductions: *Rev. archéologique*, 4th series, 12, 1908, p. 121; E. Espérandieu, *Recueil des bas-reliefs de la Gaule* (unpublished documents), II, no. 1684.

Study: S. Reinach, 'Sculptures inédites ou peu connues', *Rev. archéologique*, loc. cit., pp. 118 ff. E. Espérandieu, loc. cit.

The bas-relief would seem to belong to the Middle Ages (13th century?); but it is not easily interpreted. The suggestion that it represents a king (since the central figure is wearing a crown) touching for scrofula was only put forward by Reinach—and followed by Espérandieu—as a conjecture. Apart from the fact that the 'king' is not really 'touching' the men close to him, representations of scenes connected with the royal touch do not seem to have been at all customary in mediaeval iconography.

II *The consecration of the medicinal rings*

19 *Mary Tudor at prayer preparatory to consecrating the rings*
Reproduction: Crawfurd, 'Cramp-rings', opp. p. 178.
Study: above, pp. 104 and 105; for the missal, cf. no. 6.

III *St-Marcoul and the French kings*[1]

20 *St-Marcoul granting a French king the power to heal scrofula*. A fresco probably executed soon after 1521, commissioned by Dom Philip Wallois, treasurer of the Abbey of St-Riquier; in the treasury of the church of St-Riquier (Somme), west wall.

Reproduction: *La Picardie historique et monumentale*, 4, Saint-Riquier, pl. XXXII (including the whole decorative pattern of this panel).
Study: G. Durand, *La Picardie*, loc. cit., p. 305; above, p. 163.

21* *St-Marcoul granting a French king the power to heal scrofula.* An engraving by H. Hébert; only known from the description by L. J. Guénebault, *Diction-naire iconographique des figures, légendes et actes des saints*, in Migne, *Encyclopédie théologique*, 1st series, 45, col. 388. The saint is here represented touching the lower jaw of a king kneeling near him. Guénebault had seen this engraving at the Bibliothèque Mazarine, 'portefeuille no. 4778 (38), fol. 58, no. 8'. On 15 Nov. 1860 this portfolio, with a whole collection of engravings, was added to the Cabinet des Estampes in the Bibl. Nat. As no detailed list of the items thus added was then drawn up, I found it impossible to discover Hébert's engraving in the Cabinet des Estampes; it does not form part of the *Collection des Saints*.

Study: above, p. 164.

22 *St-Marcoul stretching out his right hand over the head of a kneeling king.* A devotional medal, no doubt belonging to the end of the 17th century or the beginning of the 18th, coming from Arras. It bears the legend: S. Marco. On the reverse, S. Liévin, who was honoured along with St-Marcoul in the church of Ste-Croix, Arras. In the collection Dancoisne.

Reproduction: J. Dancoisne, 'Les Médailles religieuses du Pas-de-Calais'; *Mémoires Académie Arras*, 2nd series, 11, 1879, pl. XVIII no. 130.

Studies: ibid., p. 123 and above, p. 165.

23 *A French king worshipping St-Marcoul.* An etching on a 'banner' from the Grez-Doiceau (Brabant) pilgrimage, n.d. (18th century); in the Van Heurck Collection, Antwerp.

Reproductions: Schépers, 'Le Pèlerinage de Saint Marcoul a Grez-Doiceau', *Wallonia*, 1899, p. 180, perhaps from a different copy from the one in the Van Heurck Collection; E. H. Van Heurck, *Les Drapelets de pèlerinage en Belgique et dans les pays voisins*, 1922, p. 157.

Studies: Van Heurck, loc. cit.; above p. 165.

The same motif is again reproduced in two other forms in the church at Grez-Doiceau: 'Another statuette shows St-Marcoul holding out a round object to be kissed by a king kneeling down in front of him; a very badly drawn picture represents the same subject in the foreground, and in the distance pilgrims approaching the church at Grez-Doiceau' (Van Heurck, p. 158); I do not know the date of these two works of art, which is not given by M. Van Heurck—very possibly (as one can well understand) because he could not arrive at any exact figure. Cf. Schépers, loc. cit., p. 181.

24 *Louis XVI making his devotions before the St-Marcoul reliquary after his consecration.* An altarpiece from the end of the 18th century, unsigned, in the church of St-Jacques (second side-chapel on the left-hand side) at Compiègne.

In the centre of the picture the king, wearing a blue cloak decorated with fleur-de-lis and an ermine collar, is kneeling with clasped hands at the foot of an altar towards the right of the picture; and on the altar is the reliquary, surmounted by a statuette of the saint.

To the right of the altar is a cardinal, and to the left a priest in liturgical dress, holding a book. Behind the king are two lords wearing a decoration, two ecclesiastics and two guards. In the background, behind a balustrade, there is a crowd of common people (sick persons?). The scene takes place in a Gothic church. At the bottom left corner, in a square frame, is the inscription: 'Louis XVI after his consecration—gives thanks to God before the—reliquary of Saint-Marcoul before—touching the sick—11 June 1773'.

The workmanship is very second-rate.

Appendix III

The beginnings of royal unction
and consecration

I have brought together below some material in support of the statements made earlier in this book, in cases where the exigencies of typography compelled me to present my material without the apparatus of proof (Bk. 1, Ch. II, pp. 37 ff). I only have in mind, of course, the countries of Western Europe where royal unction first made its appearance—Spain, the Kingdom of the Franks, England, and perhaps some Celtic countries. I shall also have a word to say about Byzantium. I am not concerned to follow out the rather late spread of the rite to other European States. To take Navarre and Scotland by way of example, it may be noted that unction was authorized in them by Papal Bull respectively in 1257 and 1329: Baronius-Raynaldus, ed. Theiner, XXII, p. 14, no. 57, and XXIV, p. 422, no. 79. In Scotland, the privilege had been solicited long before it was granted. The canonist Henry of Susa, generally known by the surname Hostiensis, wrote in his *Summa Aurea*, composed between 1250 and 1261, lib. I, c. XV, fol. Lyon, 1588, fol. 41 v.: 'Si quis de novo ungi velit, consuetudo obtinuit quod a papa petatur, sicut fecit Rex Aragonum[1] et *quotidie instat Rex Scotiae*'; cf. above Book 2, Ch. III, n. 17.

Wherever the facts do not lend themselves to discussion, I shall confine myself to very brief references.

1 *The Visigothic kingdom of Spain*

The history of royal unction among the Spanish Visigoths has been set out by Dom Marius Férotin, in his *Liber ordinum en usage dans l'église wisigothique et mozarabe d'Espagne (Monumenta ecclesiae liturgica V)*, 1904, Appendix II, col. 498–505. I have borrowed largely from this excellent work.

The first Visigoth king of whose unction we have reliable evidence is Wamba, in Sept. 672 (Julian of Toledo, *Liber de historia Galliae*, c. 3 and 4; Migne, *Patrologia Latina*, vol. 196, col. 765–6). But the contemporary writer who relates this ceremony obviously considered it traditional. After Wamba, there are frequent examples of the continuity of the rite.

To put the matter shortly, it may be stated that the rite was certainly earlier than Wamba's time. But can we arrive at any precise date? Dom Férotin does not think that the documentary evidence makes this possible. It would be tempting to attribute the initiative for such a reform to the first Catholic king to reign over the Visigoths, Reccareddi (586–601). Schücking, *Regierungsantritt*, p. 74, has drawn attention to a passage in Isidore of Seville's *History of the Goths*, where the following words occur concerning this prince's accession: 'regno est coronatus' (*Monum. German. AA.*, XI, p. 288). But it is difficult to give these words any exact meaning. What are we to understand by the words 'regno coronatus'? Do they mean a coronation in the proper sense of the term, that is, a solemn handing over of the crown in the setting of a church ceremony of the pattern of Byzantium, whose practices were indeed imitated by Visigoth royalty in more than one point? We might well think so, if the detailed description of the accession solemnities given by Julian of Toledo in Wamba's case did not compel us to admit that the Visigoths were acquainted with royal unction, but not with coronation. Is Schücking then right in his suggestion that what Isidore of Seville claims to be recalling is the ceremony of unction itself? But if we adopt this suggestion, it must mean that the phrase in question could only have been used in a metaphorical sense. Once this possibility is accepted, we must clearly be prepared to go the whole way. Isidore considers the crown as the royal emblem *par excellence*, and that is just what it was from that time onwards in Byzantium, and just what the Bible proclaimed it to be (cf. below p. 269) and it is possible that the Visigoth kings, although they did not receive a crown at their accession in the course of a religious ceremony, did sometimes wear it as an emblem of their royal dignity.[2] May not Isidore simply have used the expression *coronatus* pictorially— as a kind of literary ornament, if one may so call it—as we today speak of a king 'ascending the throne' without alluding to any precise rite? In short, although we can consider it certain that royal unction was introduced into Spain before 672, our documents do not allow us to fix precisely the date of its introduction.

As for the Council of Toledo in 638, erroneously quoted by Eichmann, *Festschrift G. von Hertling dargebr.*, p. 263, its decisions do not contain the slightest reference to unction, nor to any kind of royal consecration; cf. Mansi, *Concilia*, 1764 ed., X, col. 659 ff. On the other hand, there is a very clear allusion to royal unction in c.1 of the Council held in this same time in 681: ibid., XI, col. 1028.

When the Moslem invasion had ruined the old Visigoth royalty, the new Christian dynasty in Oviedo appears—at any rate from 886 onwards—to have renewed the tradition of unction (Férotin, col. 505; cf. Barrau-Dihigo, 'Recherches sur l'histoire politique du royaume asturien' (thesis), Paris, 1921, p. 222, n. 2). Was this the survival of an autochthonous rite? Or, on the other hand, are we to suppose that this had been forgotten, and that what we have here is an imitation of the new Frankish usages? Our documents do not allow us to decide between these two possibilities.

2   The kingdom of the Franks

For the numerous pieces of evidence relating to Pepin's unction in 751, the reader should refer to Böhmer-Mühlbacher, *Die Regesten des Kaiserreichs*, 2nd ed., p. 32. As regards that date, see M. Tangl, 'Die Epoche Pippins' in *Neues Archiv*, XXXIX (1914), pp. 259–77.

We know that Pepin had himself anointed a second time, by the Pope, on 28 July 754; Böhmer-Mühlbacher, p. 38; for the date, Erich Caspar, *Pippin und die römische Kirche*, Berlin, 1914, p. 13, n. 2.

Was Pepin really the first Frankish king to receive unction? Up till now, this had been almost unanimously believed. Recently, Dom Germain Morin, in an article entitled 'Un Recueil gallican inédit de bénédictions épiscopales' in *Revue bénédictine*, XXIX (1912), has expressed a doubt on this point. Dom Morin has discovered in a Munich MS. of the ninth century an unction ritual which he considers—on good grounds, I think—as the oldest known in a Frankish country (p. 188; cf. above, Book I, Ch. I, n. 45); but as this MS. is—I repeat—of the ninth century, I cannot understand how it can be used as an argument for doubting the 'commonly received opinion' that 'the anointing of kings with holy oil . . . was unknown in Gaul' at the Merovingian period (p. 188 n. 3). Unless new discoveries come to light, 'the commonly received opinion' does not seem to be in danger of being abandoned.

3 *Imperial unction*

The history of imperial anointing—in the Western Empire as renewed by Charlemagne—has been completely unravelled by René Poupardin, 'L'onction royale' in *Le Moyen-Age*, 1905, pp. 113–26. I can only add one not very important detail to this remarkable memoir.

Charlemagne had been anointed king—perhaps even twice (Böhmer-Mühlbacher, pp. 38, 57); the majority of the documents agree that he was not re-anointed as Emperor (ibid., p. 165); Pope Leo II thought it enough to crown him. All the same, various authors at different periods have re-echoed a tradition to the contrary, according to which the Frankish prince was said to have received unction on this occasion, as well as the crown. Truth to tell, all the evidence really goes back to one source, the Byzantine chronicler Theophanes (*Chronographia*, ed. C. de Boor, I (1883), p. 473). There can indeed be no doubt at all that Theophanes was the source from whom not only the Byzantine Constantine Manasses derived his evidence in the twelfth century (*Histor. de France*, V, p. 398), but also the author of the famous letter of the Emperor Louis II to Basil of Macedon, written in 871 or 879 (*Chronicon Salernitanum*, Pertz, *SS.*, III, p. 523). Poupardin, who is usually so accurate, does not seem to have noticed the relationship of dependence linking this last document to Theophanes. Yet the connection is obvious. There can in fact be no doubt that the letter was really drawn up by Anastasius, called 'the librarian'. Now Anastasius could hardly have been ignorant of the work of Theophanes, since he had translated it into Latin in his *Chronographia tripartita*; this work moreover contains the passage relating to Charlemagne's unction, reproduced in very correct form (Theophanes, ed. de Boor, II, p. 315).[3] It was from the *Chronographia tripartita* that this detail was taken over into the *Chronicon Casinense* (Muratori, *Scriptores*, II, p. 364 E), an inferior compilation, issued under the name of Anastasius, but really from the hand of Peter the Deacon (first half of the twelfth century). It only remains to examine how much faith we should have in the evidence derived—solely—from Theophanes.

He wrote at the beginning of the ninth century, and consequently near to the events in time, but far removed from them in point of distance. What he says cannot be sustained in face of the accurate information coming from Frankish and Roman sources. In all probability, there was a confusion in his mind or in his informers' between the imperial consecration given to Charlemagne by the coronation (and the ritual acclamation), and the unction received likewise from the Pope on the same day by the new emperor's eldest son, also called Charles after his father (Böhmer-Mühlbacher, p. 165). It would seem, moreover, that in Byzantium the rite of unction with holy oil was ridiculed, being unfamiliar to the Eastern liturgies. Theophanes relates that the Pope anointed Charlemagne from head to foot: χρίσας ἐλαίῳ ἀπὸ κεφαλῆς ἕως ποδῶν—an assertion then repeated by all the documents derived from him, except for the letter from Louis II. This, being written in order to justify the imperial title adopted by the Frankish kings, could obviously not include a detail calculated to throw ridicule upon the greatest of these princes (cf. above, p. 35).

The first sovereign to be anointed as Emperor was Louis the Pious, who received from Pope Stephen IV at Rheims in 816 in one single ceremony both consecration with holy oil and the crown (Böhmer-Mühlbacher, p. 265). From this time onwards, the rite of unction would appear to have become an integral part of the imperial consecration ceremonial.

4 *England*

The Anglo-Saxon royal anointing has sometimes been thought to be older than the Frankish rite, and the latter has even been regarded as an importation from the neighbouring island. This theory is still held by H. Brunner, *Deutsche Rechtsgeschichte*, II, p. 19. An argument was based upon the consecration ritual contained in the so-called Egbert Pontifical (ed. in *Publications of the Surtees Society*, XXVII, 1853; cf. Dom Cabrol, *L'Angleterre chrétienne avant les Normands*, 2nd ed., 1909, and the article 'Egbert' by the same author in the *Dictionnaire d'archéologie chrétienne*). This document would not seem, however, to justify such a conclusion. It is of uncertain date: the manuscript in which it has come down to us (Bibl. Nat. lat. 18575) is not earlier than the tenth century. Truth to tell, the text bears witness to a liturgical stage older than the manuscript but its attribution to Egbert Archbishop of York (?732–66) has no serious evidence to support it, being based solely on the presence at the head of the manuscript of a fragment of the penitential (certainly authentic) composed by Egbert. It goes without saying that two works by different authors may well have been copied one after the other. As for the statement in fol. 3 of the manuscript (ed., pp. xi–xii), expressly attributing the Pontifical to Egbert, it comes from the hand of Nicolas Clement, author of the *Catalogue* of 1682, and has therefore no evidential value. Moreover, the Service of the *Coronatio regis* certainly seems not to have belonged to the original collection (cf. Dom Cabrol in the *Dictionnaire*, col. 2213). And finally, even if Egbert were to be deemed the author of the Pontifical, and more especially the *Coronatio*, we must not forget that this prelate died fifteen years after the first Frankish anointing.

In actual fact, the first English prince of whom it may be affirmed that he was anointed is Egbert (there is of course no significance in the name being identical with that of the Archbishop of York), son of King Offa of Mercia, who was associated with his father during his lifetime. The ceremony took place at the Council of Chelsea (*Cealchythe*) in 787, in the presence of papal legates: cf. *Two of the Saxon chronicles parallel*, ed. C. Plummer, Oxford, I (1892), pp. 53–4 and the corresponding notes in vol. II; A. W. Haddan and W. Stubbs, *Councils and ecclesiastical documents relating to Great Britain and Ireland*, III, Oxford, 1878, pp. 444 ff. To be sure, our documents do not use the actual word *unction*: the chronicles state that Egbert was *consecrated* king (*to cyninge gehalgod*). But this is the very term commonly used for the ordination of bishops, which in the Anglo-Saxon ritual implied the use of holy oil. Furthermore, the decisions of the council, as reported to Pope Adrian II by the legates (Haddan and Stubbs p. 447 and *Monum. Germaniae*, *Ep.*, IV, p. 19, no. 3), are evidence of a very clear tendency to subject the royal 'election' to the same conditions of validity as entry into the priesthood. The passage runs as follows: 'There shall not be elected as king anyone born of adultery or incest; even as today, by the same token, the canons forbid that any child of adultery may attain to the priesthood; and likewise he who has not been conceived in lawful wedlock may not be the Lord's Anointed, king of the whole realm and heir of the fatherland'.[4] This comparison between these two dignities, which was quite certainly made in the sphere of discipline, probably spread at the same time into the field of ceremonial. Finally, let us note the term 'Anointed of the Lord', which will recur once again further on (and cf. above, p. 38). In other cases, it may have been used in a purely metaphorical sense: this would seem to have been so, for instance, in a number of Byzantine texts (cf. above, no. 3, p. 265); but here, when the expression is put side by side with the *gehalgod* of the chronicle, the obvious suggestion is to give it a more definite interpretation and see it as a direct allusion to the specific rite of unction.

Now in this affair of the Council of Chelsea all the indications point to the possibility of Frankish influence. The relations of Offa with his powerful neighbour on the continent are well known. But over and above this, the pontifical legates who presided over the council had been accompanied, during their English mission of 786–7, by a Frankish abbot called Wigbod, expressly delegated by the 'Most Excellent King Charles' (Haddan and Stubbs, pp. 447–8; *Monum. Germ.*, p. 20). Finally another institution, tithe—which, like unction, was both biblical and Frankish—was sanctioned by the decisions of the council (c. XVII). In the face of these facts it can scarcely be doubted that the mode of consecration applied to Egbert was directly inspired by the Carolingian example, which we know to have preceded it by about thirty-six years.

This will be a convenient place to call attention to a rather curious analogy. At about the same time as the rite of unction appeared in the Frankish State, the Royal Chancery—perhaps already in Pepin's time, but certainly under his sons Charles and Carloman—had the idea of expressing in its own way the religious character assumed by the monarchy by introducing into its title the famous words *gratia Dei*. Certain scholars saw this formula as a borrowing by the

Carolingian princes or their clerics from the habits of the Anglo-Saxons. But it would seem that they were wrong; for recent research has shown that the two words in question only occur in the Anglo-Saxon decrees—and particularly those of Offa of Mercia—several years later than the date of their adoption by the official scribes. Here again, the initiative came from the continent (Karl Schmitz, *Ursprung und Geschichte der Devotionsformeln*, Stuttgart, 1916, pp. 174–7). In things great and small the Visigoth royalty's collapse deprived it of widespread influence; and it was to the Carolingians that the honour fell of providing Western Europe with the model for a royal line that had become sacred in a Christian sense.

There can be no doubt that from Egbert's anointing in 787 the rite he had inaugurated spread and became consolidated throughout the whole Anglo-Saxon realm. The so-called Egbert Pontifical is the oldest known document to give us the liturgy of the English consecration; cf. also the other texts quoted below, p. 269 and W. Stubbs, *Constitutional History of England* (French trans. by Petit-Dutaillis, I, pp. 186 ff.). All the same it should be noted that Edgar, King of Northumbria and Mercia from 957 onwards, and of the whole of England from 959, was not anointed—and crowned—till 973; we have no idea of the reasons for this astonishing delay, though the reasons invented later by ecclesiastical legend are valueless: cf. *Two of the Saxon Chronicles Parallel*, ed. Plummer, II, p. 160–1. Yet the fact of this delay proves that at this period it was possible to be king by hereditary right or election without having received unction; cf. below, p. 270, for the delay in his consecration brought about likewise by Charles the Bald, and for the refusal by Henry I.

For the anointing of an heir while his father was still alive—as in the clear case of Offa and Egbert at the very start of the rite—see another case noted in my edition of Osbert of Clare, *Analecta Bollandiana*, 1923, p. 71 n. 1.

5   The Celtic countries

I pointed out above (p. 37) how the current of ideas favourable to imitating the Old Testament developed by Irish influence in Gaul made it easier for the Frank-ish State to introduce royal unction. People have sometimes wondered if the Celtic countries—Ireland in particular—may not have provided either Frankish Gaul or Anglo-Saxon England with a more concrete example. It has been sug-gested that the very rite of royal unction may have been practised from very early times by the churches in these regions. Unfortunately, it is impossible to come to a firm conclusion on this point, for the documents bearing upon it are not decisive.

Gildas, writing in the sixth century his *De Excidio et Conquestu Britanniae*, uses in c.21 (*Mon. Germ., AA.*, XIII, p.37), in connection with the disasters in Great Britain subsequent to the departure of the Roman legions, the expression *ungebantur reges non per deum*. Is this an allusion to a specific rite or a purely verbal reminiscence of a biblical phrase? We cannot be certain, for Gildas is a very imprecise historian. We owe to Adaman, Abbot of Iona (d. 704) a life of St Columba, in which (III, c. V, ed. J. T. Fowler, Oxford, 1894,[5] p. 134) the saint 'ordains' a king as a result of a dream; but the rite described only involves a lay-ing on of hands and a blessing; there is no mention of anointing.

Finally, there is a canonical Irish collection, the *Hibernensis* (ed. H. Wasserschleben, *Die irische Kanonensammlung*, 2nd ed. Leipzig, 1895; for the bibliography, see Sägmüller, *Lehrbuch des katholischen Kirchenrechts*, 3rd ed., I, p. 152); in XXV, c.1, *De ordinationi regis*, certain biblical texts are quoted in reference to unction. The *Hibernensis* probably dates from the eighth century, and its influence on the Frankish Church was considerable. Unfortunately, we do not possess any satisfactory edition of it, distinguishing from the original text the additions made by a later age (cf. on the Wasserschleben edition, S. Hellmann in his edition of Sedulius Scottus, *Liber de rectoribus*, p. 141, and P. Fournier, *Revue celtique*, 1909, p. 225, n. 3). Besides, even if we take the passage referring to 'ordination' to be primitive, we should still hesitate to draw a definite conclusion from it about the rites actually practised in the circles where the *Hibernensis* saw the light of day. We should not be warranted in deducing from a biblical quotation the existence of an institution which might be justified by the quotation. It may be noted that when the Breton chieftain Nominoe caused himself to be proclaimed king under Charles the Bald, he at once had himself anointed; cf. J. Flach, *Les Origines de l'ancienne France*, IV, p. 189, n. 3. But here, it is clearly only a matter of imitating Frankish usage, though the imitation is interesting, for it proves that as early as this period no man was considered truly king in Gaul unless he had received anointing.

To sum up, we may say that unless some unforeseen documentary discoveries are made, the problem seems likely to resist all attempts at solution, negative or positive. If the Celtic Christian kingdoms were really acquainted with the anointing of kings before Frankish Gaul, England, or even Spain, they were very successful in keeping the matter to themselves.

6 *The coronation; the establishment of a single ceremony for handing over the crown and for unction*

I have already indicated above (p. 38) how the rite of coronation proper in the West was brought in from Byzantium. Charlemagne received the crown from the Pope in imitation of the Eastern emperors who used to receive it from the patriarchs of Constantinople. Louis the Pious was the first to be anointed and crowned in the course of one and the same solemn ceremony (Böhmer-Mühlbacher, pp. 165, 265). For the diadem and the crown in Byzantium, see Jean Ebersolt, *Mélanges d'histoire et d'archéologie byzantines*, pp. 19 ff. and esp. p. 67. For Roman usage, consult the articles 'Corona' and 'Diadema' in the dictionaries by Daremberg and Saglio and Pauly-Wissowa; cf. also the article on 'Crown' in J. Hastings, *Encyclopaedia of Religion and Ethics*.

As a matter of fact, the crown and the diadem as emblems of royalty had perhaps not been altogether unknown among barbarian kings. For the Visigoths, cf. above, p. 263. Among the Frankish kings, Clovis (according to Gregory of Tours—*Hist. France*, II, 38; cf. above, p. 34), showed himself to his subjects in the town of Tours adorned with a diadem. Did his successors sometimes deck themselves in the same insignia? They are often shown wearing it on their coins; but it is difficult to see these second-rate effigies as anything but clumsy imitations of the imperial money. The other documents, whether historical or archaeological, are hard to interpret, cf. W. Schücking, *Der Regierungsantritt*, p. 131. One fact alone is certain: even if it were to be admitted that the Frankish kings before Charlemagne did sometimes wear the diadem, they never received it, or any other insignia, in the course of a religious ceremony marking their accession.

On the other hand, it is as well to take note that the use of the crown, and likewise unction, as emblems of supreme political power was facilitated by biblical precedents. Not that the Bible provided a precise model for the solemnity of coronation, as it did for the use of holy oil; but the Old Testament several times mentions the crown as a symbol or emblem of royalty (for particular passages, see Vigouroux, *Dictionnaire de la Bible*, under the word 'Couronne'. And finally, as soon as coronation properly speaking had been introduced into the West, the idea was conceived of giving the royal crown a mystical meaning by comparing it with that 'glorious crown' which the Sacred Books promise to the elect, either directly or metaphorically, in a number of passages; cf. the prayer (first attested for the consecration of Charles the Bald) which was quoted above, Book 1, Ch. II, n. 45.

The coronation of Louis the Pious had only been an *imperial* coronation. But the crown very quickly took its place alongside unction in the rites of *royal* accession. As early as 838, and without any religious ceremony, Louis the Pious had handed a 'royal crown' to his son Charles—the future Charles the Bald (B. Simson, *Jahrbücher des fränkischen Reichs unter Ludwig dem Frommen*, II, p. 180). When Charles decided in 848 to seek consecration from the Archbishop of Sens, he did not receive anointing only: the prelate handed him a crown and—what was a new gesture—a sceptre (references below, p. 270). And so consecration, constituted by the union of coronation, or—more generally—the handing over of the insignia of royalty with the act of anointing, had really come into being.

Much the same took place in England—I need not investigate the other European countries (though for Germany, see below, no. 7). This same joining together of the two essential actions took place fairly quickly. The most ancient Anglo-Saxon *ordo*, that of the pseudo-Egbert (above, p. 267), which must date from about the ninth century, already shows us bishops handing the king a *galeum*, which must be a crown (p. 103 of the Surtees Society ed.). The so-called Ethelred *ordo* (J. W. Legg, *Three Coronation Orders*, Henry Bradshaw Soc., XIX, p. 57) and the Robert de Jumièges' *Benedictional* (ed. Wilson, Henry Bradshaw Soc., XXIV, p. 144) expressly mention the crown; similarly in the description of the consecration of Edgar in 973; *Vita S. Oswaldi* in J. Raine, *The historians of the church of York* (Rolls Series), I, p. 437–8. These four documents likewise bear witness to the use of the sceptre. Thus the Frankish and Anglo-Saxon rites seem to have developed in parallel, and we may very well believe that there was mutual influence between them.

7   *The persistence of the rite of unction; its interruption in Germany*

It would seem to have been part of the nature of a rite like royal unction that once it had been introduced into the monarchical practice of a given country, it tended to perpetuate itself almost indefinitely. Indeed, it would appear to have had a fine continuity in Visigoth Spain (above, p. 262), and Anglo-Saxon and Norman England (above, p. 265). The same is true of the states that evolved from the

Carolingian Empire, of Western France—or just plain France. On 6 June 848, at Orléans, Charles the Bald received from Ganelon, Archbishop of Sens, unction, the 'diadem', and the sceptre (Levillain, *Le Sacre de Charles le Chauve à Orléans*, Bibl. de l'École des Chartes, 1903, p. 31, and F. Lot and Louis Halphen, *Le Règne de Charles le Chauve*, 1909, pp. 192ff.). This consecration came very late in the day, for he had long been king, without having been anointed. As we have seen (p. 269), he had already received a royal crown from his father Louis the Pious in 838—and without any ecclesiastical ceremony;[6] but he thought that the handing over of the crown and the sceptre by a prelate, in the course of a solemn ceremony, was indispensable to his prestige. His successors were equally persuaded that they could not do without this ritual. Unction together with coronation seems likewise to have been practised in Italy (cf. Ernst Mayer, *Italienische Verfassungsgeschichte*, II, pp. 166ff.), in Lorraine (Robert Parisot, *Le Royaume de Lorraine sous les Carolingiens*, 1899, p. 678), and even in the little kingdoms of Provence and Burgundy (René Poupardin, *Le Royaume de Provence*, 1901, pp. 112, n. 8, and 457, n. 4; *Le Royaume de Bourgogne*, 1907, p. 66, n. 2). But in Eastern France, or—to use the convenient though anachronistic term, Germany—the history of royal consecration is not equally simple.

As regards Louis the German, his sons and Arnulf, there is no documentary mention of religious consecration (cf. G. Waitz, *Verfassungsgeschichte*, 4th ed., VI, p. 208 and n. 4; U. Stutz, *Der Erzbischof von Mainz und die deutsche Königswahl*, Weimar, 1910, p. 5, n. 3). Is this silence merely a matter of chance? One does not deny the possibility, seeing that our sources are far from perfect; all the same, there is something surprising about the unanimous silence of these texts, and at the very least it would prove the indifference of the annalists towards this kind of ceremony. It would therefore seem certain that ecclesiastical accession-rites were of less importance at this time in Germania than in Gaul; and it is distinctly questionable whether the kings up to and including Arnulf ever had recourse to them at all.

For Louis the Child, the evidence is ambiguous (cf. Stutz, loc. cit. and Böhmer-Mühlbacher, p. 796).

On the other hand Conrad I certainly had himself anointed and crowned (Böhmer-Mühlbacher, p. 823).

Finally, let us come on to Henry I. With regard to him, the evidence is explicit. He declined the offer of unction and coronation made him by the Archbishop of Mainz (for the documents, and a certain number of modern historians' opinions, see G. Waitz, *Jahrbücher des deutschen Reichs unter König Heinrich I*, 3rd ed., *Excursus* 10; cf. Böhmer-Ottenthal, *Die Regesten des Kaiserreichs unter den Herrschern aus dem Sächsischen Hause*, p. 4). There is a curious passage, reflecting the scandal caused by this decision in certain ecclesiastical circles, in the *Vita Udalrici* (Pertz, *SS.*, IV, p. 38), where the Apostle St Peter appears to St Ulrich, Bishop of Augsburg, carrying two swords, one with and the other without a hilt. He addresses the prelate as follows: 'Dic regi Heinrico, ille ensis qui est sine capulo significat regem qui sine benedictione pontificali regnum tenebit; capitulatus autem, qui benedictione divina tenebit gubernacula'. Why did Henry I obstinately insist on reigning like this 'without the pontiffs' blessing'? I have already indicated above (p. 39) that on this point I agreed with the opinion held by the majority of historians. It seems clear to me that there can have been only one motive behind such a refusal—the fear of seeming to hold his royal dignity solely from the hands of the clergy. It is worth noting in this connection that episcopal influence would seem by all accounts to have been rather weak at the court of Henry I (A. Hauck, *Kirchengeschichte Deutschlands*, 3rd ed., III, p. 17, n. 3). Nevertheless, such a lively sense of the possible dangers to royalty from ecclesiastical dominance seemed rather surprising in a sovereign of the tenth century, well before the time of the Gregorian reforms. Hence the bold solution proposed by M. J. Krüger, 'Grundsätze und Anschauungen bei den Erhebungen der deutschen Könige in der Zeit von 911–1056', *Untersuchungen zur deutschen Staats- und Rechtsgesch.*; Part 110, pp. 42ff. This scholar rejects as pure 'fantasy' the evidence of the chronicler Widukind, which is the principal source of our information about Henry I's behaviour. But in that case, what are we to make of the *Vita Udalrici*, which is only very slightly later than Widukind, and which there is no reason at all to believe dependent upon him? After all, isn't it really rather too simple to treat documents as mendacious as soon as they do not fit in with our own theories? Surely, Krüger's surprise at Henry I's anxieties is unnecessarily great: I had occasion above (pp. 39 and 125) to recall the fact that Church writers had not waited for Gregory VII to interpret royal unction in a sense that was most favourable to their own pretensions.

As soon as he came to the throne in 936, Otto I had himself anointed and crowned (Böhmer-Ottenthal, p. 34, and Köpke-Dummler, *Otto der Grosse* (*Jahrbücher der deutschen Geschichte*), I, pp. 27ff.). This example was followed by all his successors.

8 *The Byzantine empire*

I shall make no attempt here to examine the history of Byzantine consecration as a whole. I shall only concentrate upon one element in this ceremony—the element of unction. It is indeed important for anyone studying the history of consecration in the western monarchies to determine the time when imperial unction was introduced in Byzantine; and this for two reasons. If we were to recognize that this usage was first established in the East, we should be bound to ask whether the first of the Lord's Anointed in Spain or in Frankish Gaul did not simply imitate an example that had come to them from the East. Moreover, we should be forced more or less into modifying our conclusions from the comparative history of the accession ritual in the different European states, according as this biblical rite was proved to have appeared at any earlier or later date in a country where the cult of monarchical traditions was so firmly established.

But first of all, we may affirm that this much is quite certain. If one disregards the consecration of Baldwin of Flanders in 1204, which—having been celebrated according to the Latin rite—is clearly not relevant, the first certain document explicitly mentioning an imperial unction is the description of the coronation of Michael IX Paleologus by George Pachymeres. Michael IX was crowned on 20 May 1295, and George Pachymeres was writing about 1310: *De Andronico Paleologo*, Migne, *Patrologia Graeca*, vol. 144, col. 216. Nicephorus Gregoras represents Theodorus Lascarus as having received unction in 1254 (*Byzantinae Historiae*, lib. III, Cap. II; *P.G.*, vol. 148, col. 181); but Nicephorus was writing about 1359, and his account may have been influenced by the practice of his own time and proves nothing certain about an event of more than a century earlier. The Emperor John VI Cantacuzenus in his *Four books of history*, describing the coronation of Andronicus III Paleologus, which took place in 1325, likewise includes a ceremony of unction; he was writing between 1355 and 1383 (*Histor.*, lib. I, cap. XLI, *P.G.*, p. 153, col. 276ff.).

Thus by the beginning of the fourteenth century the Emperors were indubitably receiving the impress of the holy oil, and the rite was destined to last till the end of the Empire. But when did it actually begin? This is where controversy really has free course.

There are a good many documents, well before the fourteenth century, which use the words *unction* and *anoint* (χρίσμα and χρίειν) to designate the creation of an Emperor, or give the Emperor himself the title of the *Lord's Anointed* (χριστὸς Κυρίου). The whole problem is to know if they are to be taken in a literal or in a purely metaphorical sense, since these pictures are borrowed from the vocabulary of the Bible. The first solution—the literal sense—has been adopted by W. Sickel, 'Das byzantinische Krönungsrecht bis zum 10. Jahrhundert' in *Byzantinische Zeitschrift*, VII (1898), p. 524 and especially pp. 547 ff., n. 80–3. Incidentally, it is important to note straight away that the oldest evidence invoked by Sickel only goes back to the second half of the ninth century. It is a letter from the famous patriarch Photius to the Emperor Basil I, in which the prelate reminds the Emperor of his consecration as 'unction and the laying on of royal hands': χρίσμα καὶ χειροθεσίαν βασιλείας (Ep. I, 10; *P.G.*, vol. 102, col. 765). Basil's accession can be dated in 867—more than a century after Pepin had been anointed —the first of the Frankish kings to receive unction; and more than two centuries after the first Visigoth unctions. Interpret it as you may, it is thus impossible to take the document produced by Sickel as proof of borrowing on this score from the oriental uses by the Western monarchies.

In the opposite camp to Sickel are the scholars who see in the expressions used in Photius' letter or similar documents nothing more than simple metaphors: J. J. Reiske, in his edition of *De Cerimoniis* by Constantine Porphyrogenitus (*Corpus S.S., historiae Byzantinae*) II, p. 351; and especially Brightman, 'Byzantine imperial coronations' in *Journal of Theological Studies*, II (1901), p. 383, and Jean Ebersolt, *Mélanges d'histoire et d'archéologie byzantines* (extracted from the *Rev. d'hist. des religions*, LXXVI (1917), pp. 22–3, 27).[7] Their reasoning seems to me to be thoroughly sound. Even in the text of Photius the word χειροθεσία can obviously not be considered as anything but pictorial, for no laying on of hands ever figured in the imperial consecration ritual. Why, when the two words χρίσμα and χειροθεσία are closely joined to one another in the same clause, should one attribute to the first a concrete sense, while only being willing to give the second a purely symbolical value? But there are further considerations. The celebrated book *De Cerimoniis*, composed by the Emperor Constantine Porphyrogenitus (949–59), contains a detailed description of consecration, but it contains no reference to unction. In the same way a Euchology from the early twelfth century contains the consecration liturgy; but still there is no mention of unction (Brightman, p. 378). This double silence would be inexplicable if it were not for the quite simple explanation that the rite in question was not yet being practised, either in the tenth or even in the early twelfth century.[8]

But it certainly seems to have been practised by the end of the twelfth century, that is to say—whatever Ebersolt (loc. cit., p. 27) may maintain—before the Latin conquest of 1204. It is hard to avoid seeing an allusion to a concrete act in the words used by Nicetas Acominatus, writing about 1210, to describe the consecration of Alexius III Angelus in 1195 (*De Alexio Isaacii Angeli fratre*, lib. I; *P.G.*, vol. 139, col. 829: 'ὅπως κατὰ τὸ ἔθιμον ἐς βασιλέα χρισθῇ καὶ περιβαλεῖται τὰ τοῦ κράτους σύμβολα'—'so that, according to custom, he might be made *basileus* by anointing and might receive the symbols of supreme power'. Unction and the handing over of the insignia: are not these the two fundamental features in a ceremony essentially similar to the Western consecrations? In particular, there is one document which Brightman does not appear to me to have interpreted in strict enough terms. It proves incontrovertibly, as I read it, that by about the year 1200 imperial unction had begun to be part of the customs of Byzantium. The text in question is a commentary on the twelfth canon of the Council of Ancyra, composed about that date by Theodoros Balsamon (*P.G.*, vol. 137, col. 1156). Balsamon relates that in 969, the Emperor John Tzimisces, having assassinated his predecessor Nicephorus Phocas, was at first forbidden by the patriarch Polyeuctes to enter 'the great church'; but he was then admitted as the result of a synodical decree analysed by our author as follows:

'Εἶπε γὰρ μετὰ τῆς ἁγίας συνόδον, ἐν τῇ γενομένῃ τηνικαῦτα συνοδικῇ πράξει, τῇ ἐν τῷ χαρτοφυλακείῳ ἀποκειμένῃ, ὡς, ἐπεὶ τὸ χρίσμα τοῦ ἁγίου βαπτίσματος τὰ πρὸ τούτου ἁμαρτήματα ἀπαλείφε οἷα καὶ ὅσα ἂν ὦσι, πάντως καὶ τὸ χρίσμα τῆς βασιλείας τὸν πρὸ ταύτης γεγονότα φόνον παρὰ του Τζιμισκῇ ἐξήλειψεν'
(For translation, see above, page 115).

It is difficult to know whether Balsamon has given a very accurate reproduction of the wording of the synodical decision; but this is of no great importance. Even if it were admitted that the word χρίσμα formed part of the text 'preserved in the archives', there is nothing to prevent us from giving it the metaphorical sense it normally carried in the tenth century. But let us go on with Balsamon's commentary. He observes that many have drawn the conclusion from this decree that in the same way a bishop's sins are wiped out by the anointing they receive at their consecration, διὰ τοῦ χρίσματος τῆς ἀρχιερωσύνης. What is the value here of this word χρίσμα? Obviously, it is purely symbolical, for in the Eastern rite, bishops were never anointed. Indeed, Balsamon gives a very clear explanation of his metaphor: 'In place of the oil with which, according to the Old Law, kings and high priests were anointed, [those who uphold this opinion] say that for bishops today it is enough that the Gospel should be placed [on their consecration day] like a yoke upon their neck, together with the impress made by the laying on of hands with the invocation of the Holy Spirit . . .'[9] 'It is enough for bishops today . . .': there is no mention of kings in the second clause. Why is this? It is unlikely that this silence is simply a question of forgetfulness. If our glossator has not indicated what was the contemporary liturgical equivalent of the royal unction prescribed by the Bible, it is in all probability because there was no question of an equivalent. The bishops of his day—whom he equates with the high priests under the Old Law (the Greek word ἀρχιερεύς is the same)—did not, unlike their Hebrew predecessors, receive consecration with holy oil; on the other hand the Emperors, apparently, were anointed, after the pattern of David and Solomon.

The question remains why unction took so long to penetrate into Byzantium. Mgr Duchesne (*Liber Pontificalis*, II, p. 38, n. 35) has very rightly observed that the ritual of consecration in the East, in rejecting for a long time the use of oil, was only falling in with a general habit of the Eastern Church, where unction has no place in the ceremonial for the ordination of priests or bishops. I think one should add, as I have already suggested, that the Byzantine monarchy, held to be sacred ever since its Roman origins, and resting upon the surviving traces of the imperial cultus, did not feel the need to sanctify itself by a rite imitated from the Bible as early as the barbarian royal lines of the West. Later on, the influence of the Western example made itself felt. In all probability, Byzantium borrowed rather late in the day from the States that had issued from the Frankish Empire the rite of royal unction; quite certainly, it was not borrowed from Byzantium by the Visigoth kings or by Pepin.

Appendix IV

Extracts from Jean Golein's Treatise on Consecration with a short analysis

(*translated by Anthony Goodman*)

The little treatise on the consecration of the French kings inserted by the Carmelite Jean Golein in his translation of the *Rationale Divinorum Officiorum* by Guillaume Durand, carried out by him for King Charles V in 1372, is important testimony to the ideas current in the 'wise and merciful' king's entourage (as we gather from the preface—Bibl. Nat., fr. 437, fol. 2 v., col. 1). At least in one part of it—the part concerned with the touch for scrofula—it professes to represent the very thoughts of the sovereign. I shall perhaps be reproached for not having published it in its entirety. But I could not indefinitely overload the already very lengthy Appendices. And then it must be admitted that Jean Golein's long disquisition on the *ordenance* of the consecration does not tell us anything about the ceremony that we do not know, it seems, from other documents, notably from the *ordo* published by the Henry Bradshaw Society.[1] As for the symbolical commentary—both subtle and long-winded—accompanying the description of each of the ritual details, it does not add much that is new to the knowledge we already have of the mental and spiritual tendencies of the intellectual circles in which Charles V was at home. After serious thought, I have therefore confined myself to a reproduction of extracts, linked together by a brief analysis. It will be observed that, as well as valuable information about the royal miracle, about the cycle of legend surrounding the French dynasty and about the theory of succession in the masculine line as then formulated at the Valois court, our treatise contains a mention of a strange tradition relating to Turpin, some iconographical information about the French king's 'ymages', a hint of the true significance of a statue in the Cathedral of Sens not hitherto properly understood, and an amusing etymology of the word *chapelain* (cf. below, pp. 278–9). And finally, by criticizing in regard to the healing of scrofula the expressions used by Raoul de Presles in the preface to his translation of the *City of God*, Jean Golein allows us to correct the date—about 1376—proposed for this book by Léopold Delisle in his *Recherches sur la librairie de Charles V*. It can now be taken as certain that this famous work was finished before 1372.

The translation of the *Rationale* was printed in 1503, by Vérard;[2] and in this form it would appear to have enjoyed a certain success. Charles Villette, who in 1611 published a liturgical treatise that was to go into a number of editions, had read it, and had drawn some inspiration from its treatment of consecration.[3] But Vérard's version is full of mistakes. As for manuscripts, there are several in existence, notably Bibl. Nat., fr. 176 (14th century), Arsenal 2001 and 2002 (15th); but only one is needed to establish the correct text, the one that is numbered 437 in the Fonds Français of the Bibliothèque Nationale. It was made specially for Charles V, and still carries on its last page the king's ex-libris autograph, dated 1374. The passage on the consecration occupies folios 43 v.–55 v.[4] I have faithfully followed it, and merely corrected one or two obvious mistakes, which I have indicated as they occur.

This manuscript presents one strange peculiarity. In the passage on the consecration—and in this passage only—there are in the margin a number of notes, in a good fair hand, contemporary with the manuscript, but not that of the copyist. They are not corrections by the author, since at one point the glossator contradicts the text itself (below, p. 278; cf. above, p. 135); they are emendations by an attentive reader. Could this have been the king himself? It would be tempting to suppose so; but there is nothing that would turn this hypothesis into a certainty. The writing, which is rather impersonal, does not appear to be Charles V's; it might be that of a secretary to whom the king had dictated his observations. But such a thing could hardly be proved. Some of these marginal glosses will be found below, placed in oblique parentheses < >.

Of the coronation of the king of France and of the queen[5]

PREFACE; NOBLE NATURE OF THE CORONATION; REGULATION BY CHARLEMAGNE OF THE SUCCESSION TO THE FRENCH THRONE; PARTICULARS OF THE CORONATION OF CHARLES V [fol. 43 v.–44]:
'But, because we have discussed only briefly the consecration of princes which by no means ought to be so neglected on account of the reverence due to my very redoubted and sovereign lord, who was consecrated king of France on Holy Trinity day by the archbishop of Rheims, Monseigneur Jean de Craon, in the year 1364.[6]

For, whereas the emperors of Rome and Constantinople are anointed, and also some other kings, such as the kings of Jerusalem, Spain, England and Hungary, and some others are not anointed, Charles VI[7] was crowned and consecrated at Rheims, in the manner of his predecessors, not indeed with oil or balm preserved by the hand of any bishop or apothecary, but with the holy celestial liquid which is in the Sainte Ampoule, kept and preserved at St-Rémi of Rheims, as that which was brought from heaven by angelic hands to anoint the noble and worthy kings of France more nobly and efficaciously than any other kings of the old law and the new. And for this reason he is called the most noble, the very Christian defender of the faith and of the Church, and does not recognize any temporal sovereign as his superior.

The emperor Charlemagne, by the counsel of the Church and of the Christian kings who had come to the aid of the Catholic faith and to the defence of Rome, after the marvellous victory which they had gained over the Saracens, caused this dignity to be ordained by the general council held there, consisting of prelates of the Church, as well as noble secular kings and the senators of Rome, of which he was patrician and emperor, and with the pope they decreed that the papal election should be confided to the cardinals, the election of the Emperor to the nobles of Germany and that the kingdom of France should appertain to the Kings of France descending as heirs male from the holy and consecrated line, so that this blessing would be transmitted continuously from one to another.

And on account of this the queen also has a coronation. And there was crowned, together with my said sovereign lord, Madame Jeanne de Bourbon, daughter of the noble prince the duke of Bourbon, who was descended of the same holy line; and was his cousin; but by the dispensation of the Church, he ventured to marry her. By reason of the holy consecration, from God without other means of blessed generation, I conclude that it is a higher dignity to be king of France than emperor or any other royalty: which chronicles and *gestes* amply show.'

(There follows the history of some Roman emperors who were 'elected from poor estate'.)

[fol. 44] 'And this reason led the emperor Charlemagne and the Church to ordain that the nobles elect the emperor of Rome, who should be crowned and anointed by the pope; but the Sainte Ampoule which God provided with his blessing contains a mixture of oil and balm entirely different in kind; for the vessel, that is to say the phial, is of a substance the like of which no one has ever seen or can counterfeit and the liquid within is more sweetly scented than anything else known. With this oil was anointed the wise, merciful and good king Charles VI, thus appointed, as was said before, on the feast of Trinity, by an election of holy devotion. Also, just as it pleased God the Father to say to his son as he received the unction of baptism: *Hic est filius meus dilectus in quo michi complacui*,[8] and the Holy Spirit descended in the form of a dove which anointed him *oleo leticie pre participibus suis*,[9] and the son in human form received this holy consecration, so the said lord in the true faith of the Holy Trinity received the sacred coronation with pure devotion, and with such favour that his enemies the English and others lacked the power and ability to attack him and his realm; but on his return he met several important prisoners taken at the battle of Cocherel, who had planned to attack him before the said coronation;[10] but the outcome was quite different from what they intended. So our good King gave thanks for it to the blessed Trinity and made fine offerings on his return to Paris to the poor mendicants and to other poor people, as one who feels the merciful grace of the unction, which had been carried out in accordance with the rite contained in the pontifical of the archbishop of Rheims, the significance of which will be explained hereafter.'

After this follows the significance of the coronation of the Kings of France.

(Description of the coronation, with explanations of its symbolical meaning —the 'mystical significance' of different rites. The following details are to be noted):

THE HEALING OF SCROFULA[fol. 46 and v.]: once the ceremony has finished, the Sainte Ampoule will be returned 'to the church of St-Denis or to the chapel of St-Nicolas'.[11]

'St-Denis testifies to the faith which he brought into France, that one should bring back the phial pledged to in good faith. The placing of the phial in the chapel of St-Nicolas is testimony to the oil which always issues miraculously[12] from his holy limbs, just as this oil, [which] is also in this phial through a divine miracle and holy decree, is likewise holy. For, when the king has been anointed and consecrated with it, just as those anointed with the oil which flows from the limbs of St-Nicholas are soon healed, so those who are infected with the disease of scrofula, if they are touched by the king's hand anointed from this phial, are soon cured and restored to health, And if anyone meddled in it who was not the rightful king and duly anointed, without delay he would contract St Remigius' disease, as has previously appeared.'[13]

THE STATUE OF CONSTANTINE AT SENS (Commentary on the coronation oath, by which the king promises to protect the Church): [fol. 47] 'and this symbolizes the oaths which the kings of Israel made to the priests, and which Alexander made in the history alluded to before;[14] and such as Constantine made at the church of Sens, as it appears at the west door of the church of Sens, where it is written in letters of gold above his statue where he swore thus: *Regnantis veri cupiens verus cultor haberi—Juro rem cleri libertatesque tueri*'.[15]

COMPARISON BETWEEN ROYAL ROBES AND LITURGICAL VESTMENTS [fol. 47]: 'the cloth . . . fashioned in the style of a tunicle for a subdeacon <and also, of a dalmatic>. And with this a surcoat worn over it <sackcloth in the style of a chasuble on one side and of a cloak on the other, all of it cut in a diamond pattern>.'

ORIGIN OF THE FLEURS-DE-LIS (After the listing and explanation of the royal robes, all marked with the fleurs-de-lis) [fol. 48]: 'And for this reason the abbot of St-Denis supplies all these ornaments: because Monseigneur St Denis gave the arms of the fleurs-de-lis to the kings of France <no, because God sent them miraculously at Montjoie[16]>.'

THE CORONATION 'CLEANSES' THE KING OF HIS SINS [fol. 48]: 'And when the king disrobes, this is testimony that he is relinquishing his former worldly state to take up that of the royal religion; and if he holds it in such reverence as he should, I believe that he is as fully cleansed of his sins as one just professed in a religious vocation; concerning which St Bernard says towards the end of his book *de precepto et dispensacione*: that just as sins are pardoned at baptism, so they are on reception into the religious life; the original passage from St Bernard commences: *Audire vult* etc.[17] Therefore, if in return for the intention to live penitently and serve God steadfastly sins are pardoned, how much more so to him who takes on an estate where he has so many diverse anxieties and afflictions.'

ETYMOLOGY OF THE WORD CHAPLAIN [fol. 48 v.]: 'for this victorious faith the noble kings of France, by ancient precept and custom, carry into battle the cap of Monseigneur St Martin, which is woollen, and kept by priests inside a reliquary with great devotion; wherefore one does not style them priests but chaplains in reverence to the said cap which is of wool; and this word is composed of cap (*chappe*) and wool (*laine*); for this reason they are said to be chaplains (*chappelains*).'

THE GLOVES, ROYAL INSIGNIA; RESPECT DUE TO THE HOLY CHRISM [fol. 49 v.] (after the conferment of insignia): 'Afterwards the gloves are put together and blessed; and then the archbishop puts them on his hands anointed by the holy chrism to protect them from any other contact. Some say that one should dry the parts anointed with cotton, and then put the gloves on the hands. And because the King of France is anointed on the hands in a more exalted way than other kings, one puts the gloves on his hands in painting their portraits.[18] Monseigneur St Louis understood this: when he was imprisoned by the Saracens of Outremer and was asked to decide when he wanted to wash his hands, before dining or afterwards, he preferred to do so afterwards so that he might wash only once, and after he had washed, he placed gloves on his hands in acknowledgment of the holy chrism or holy unction to which he owed reverence. For a similar reason, after the anointing of the head, the archbishop puts a cap on his head and he should always wear it, as a token that he has received the holy unction on the head, and of worthier holiness. And so that he has it always in mind, he should wear a cap all his life and should never have his head cropped with a razor: he is dedicated to God as a pure Nazarite.' (Likewise the shirt used on the coronation day is to be 'burnt'.)

(From fol. 50, col. 2 onwards description of the queen's coronation. Then)

COMMUNION OF THE TWO SOVEREIGNS [fol. 51]: 'The king and queen should descend from their dais and come humbly to the altar and take from the hand of the archbishop the Body and Blood of Our Lord; and in this the royal and priestly dignity is demonstrated: for one gives the Blood separately to no one, unless he is a priest.'

Finally BLESSING OF THE ROYAL BANNER [fol. 51 v.]: 'After this follows the blessing of the royal banner: *Inclina, Domine, aurem tuam ad preces.* . . . This benediction should be made over the royal banner at Rheims,[19] and afterwards over the oriflamme in the church of Monseigneur St Denis of France when the king intends to go to war.'

(There follows a history of the origins of the oriflamme. Manuel, emperor of Constantinople, during a Saracen invasion, had a dream in which he saw a fully armed knight on horseback at the foot of his bed, holding a lance 'shining all over as if it was gilt' from which issued a 'tongue of fire'. When he awoke an angel appeared to him and revealed that this knight would be the one to deliver his empire from the Saracens. Manuel then remembered Charlemagne's features, recognized him as the person in his dream and wrote to him appealing for help. Description of the raising of the oriflamme by Charlemagne at St-Denis.)

LEGEND ABOUT TURPIN [fol. 52 v.]: 'Some histories suppose that the first who carried the said banner against the infidels in the company of Charlemagne was Turpin, who had been for nine years a monk of Jumièges in the abbey where the sick are lodged, and who was later made archbishop of Rheims and performed valorous deeds for the faith against the enemies of Jesus Christ, as appears in several histories; and his body lies at Leschans beyond Arle le Blanc in Provence, and though it is in the wind and rain in the fields in a stone tomb which one opens, his skin is natural and his body preserved: this I have seen clearly.'[20]

CELESTIAL ORIGIN OF THE TWO ROYAL BANNERS [fol. 52 v.]: 'These two banners of France were given, the one with three fleurs-de-lis by a saintly hermit of Joyenval, and the other by the revelation of angels in a marvellous vision and clear apparition, and confirmed and proved by noble victory.'

(The elucidation of the two banners is dealt with at length.)

KINGS DO NOT TAKE THE REAL ORIFLAMME TO WAR [fol. 53]: 'When the kings of France go into battle, they take a copy of the one which Charlemagne brought back from Constantinople, and cause the new one to be blessed and leave behind the banner of Charlemagne, and carry the new one, and after victory they return it to Monseigneur St Denis.'

STORY OF THE ORIGINS OF THE ROMAN EAGLE (falsely attributed to Pliny) [fol. 53]: whilst the emperor Augustus 'was sitting in a garden, an eagle flying overhead dropped from its talons a white hen holding in its beak a sprig of laurel loaded with berries'; this incident was the origin of the laurel wreath with which 'were crowned victors who had had a triumph in battle, especially emperors' and of the eagle on the armorial bearings of emperors and the 'imperial standard';[21] in the author's time this eagle was to be seen on the red banner of the 'community of Rome'; there has been added to it, slantwise on the banner (from one 'corner' to the 'corner' opposite) four letters: 'SPQR' which some interpret as meaning 'the emblem of the Roman people' (*le signe du peuple romain*), others as 'Senatus Populusque Romanus.'

FRANCE AND THE EMPIRE [fol. 53 and v.]: 'So some wish to say that this standard bestowed on Charlemagne through the vision of the emperor of Constantinople foretold that he should be emperor of the Roman people, as he later was, and called patrician and emperor; and wished to leave this imperial emblem in France as a token of perpetual Empire through succession of heir male, and not at all by election as in the empire of Rome and Germany. Therefore it is a more fitting thing that the emperor of France anointed with such precious ointment brought down from Heaven should be more eminent and beget children who have the succession as their paternal inheritance, ordained by God.'

(Once having explained the celestial origin of the two standards and of the oil which was used to anoint kings, it is a question of deducing the necessary conclusions from these premises.)

CONCLUSIONS: THE CURE FOR SCROFULA; SUCCESSION BY HEIR MALE; ATTITUDE OF CHARLES V TOWARDS THE HEALING POWER [fol. 53 v.–54]: 'From which two conclusions are manifest: one is that the royal estate of France is of great dignity, because the king is anointed with the holy unction brought down from Heaven, through which properly received he cures the extraordinary disease called scrofula: not that it should be understood that the person is because of this called holy nor that he is working miracles, but because of the exalted royal estate he has this prerogative above all other kings whoever they may be.

And we should understand that although the priest, after his ordination, can consecrate as a minister the Body of Jesus Christ by reciting the words of consecration, such a priest is not therefore alleged holy or working miracles —for a priest who might be in a state of sin could consecrate on account of the authority and character conferred in the consecration—similarly I am not saying by any means that the king has such a character because of the unction, though he has such eminence because of the consecration and of the sacred lineage that it pleases our Lord to give him power against this unsightly disease, scrofula. And, just as the apostle says (I Timothy 5: 17): *Qui bene presunt presbiteri dupplici honore digni habentur*;[22] "Let the priests that rule well or have good rule be esteemed worthy of double honour", once for the authority of the priesthood which is a spiritual dignity and again for the goodness which should be in them, and this is personal, the royal authority on which is grounded the power to heal scrofula is received more from the spiritual authority in the sacred anointing which is not personal, but personal goodness is well fitted to be esteemed with priestly goodness. So one should not say that on this account the king is holy nor that he performs miracles, any more than the priest; for a usurer or notorious sinner who might be a priest could consecrate on account of the priestly dignity, and yet no one says that he performs miracles as if holy. So the royal nobility and dignity is to be understood in this sense; and I know well that in his great wisdom the sovereign lord who made me translate this treatise on the coronation, that is to say the wise and merciful King Charles the Fifth, does not by any means wish holiness or the ability to work miracles attributed to him, for he prefers that he should have merit for these things in the eyes of God rather than worldly adulation; though he does not by any means wish, nor ought to do so, that the royal estate be less esteemed than is reasonable, in accordance with the words of the apostle (Romans XI:13): *Quamdiu quidem ego sum gencium apostolus ministerium meum ego honorificabo* etc.;[23] "As long indeed as I am an apostle of God," says St Paul, "I will honour my ministry and office;" at all times he calls himself a miserable sinner and never a saint, but he attributes the miracles performed by the saints to God and to his glory.'

(Similarly Christ (Luke 7:28) said of John the Baptist that there had been none greater than he born of woman, but that the least of the kingdom of Heaven was greater still): 'So I certainly do not contend that it would be with the King's consent that it was said to him "you perform miracles in your lifetime", for that would ascribe to him vainglory to which he pays no heed, but ascribes all to God through whom he reigns and will reign to the honour of God and to the humbling of his enemies. This is evidently the first conclusion.'

(The second line of argument is that the queen is never anointed and that at the end of the coronation neither the banner of fleurs-de-lis nor the oriflamme is blessed. Here it is): [fol. 54 and v.] 'No woman ever approaches so near the priestly order as to receive the royal unction, nor has a woman been entrusted with the healing of the said disease. Wherefore it appears that women cannot and certainly should not inherit in France, but it would be wrong for the realm. For by the way of hereditary succession the first king anointed laid down that unction from the Sainte Ampoule never appertains to a woman. *Ergo* no woman has the royal succession, and not by election, for Charlemagne, to whom the oriflamme was committed and the disposition of the election of the pope, the emperor and the king of France, decreed with the Church, in the company of the pope, the holy college of cardinals and of prelates, kings, dukes and other Christian princes, with the assent of all, that the kingdom of France was held by succession of the heir male nearest in line of descent; for every reasonable man can readily conclude that neither the dignity of such unction nor of the arms rightfully belongs to a woman; for this seems more of a divine ordinance than a human one and a reflection of the blessed Trinity; for by the emblem of the fleurs-de-lis which is the sovereign royal emblem can be understood the Father who has a certain sovereignty; for whereas the other persons are equal to the Father as regards divinity, so have they, according as the son took on human form, a certain inferiority, concerning which it is written in the creed that *Filius est equalis Patri secundum divinitatem, minor Patre secundum humanitatem;*[24] therefore one can compare the three fleurs-de-lis to the sovereign lordship; whereas all of them abide together, they divide mysteriously in the unction which signifies the Holy

Spirit; also in the form of a dove it wills to bear the said phial, and thus it appeared at the baptism of Jesus, concerning which the Church chants: *In specie columbe Spiritus Sanctus visus est*; the red oriflamme symbolizes the son in human form raised on the cross drenched by his precious Blood, and stained red. Whence it is clear that this dignity appertains more to a man than to a woman and that Edward king of England who has for long held to this error, saying that because of his mother he has some right to the kingdom of France, has not been at all well informed about his case; or, if he was, covetousness has deceived him, and his sin is bringing and will bring him by the judgment of God to nought. This judgment is being discharged on him by my said sovereign lord King Charles the Fifth, who does not attribute to himself the miracles which God performs in his realm, but to the goodness and grace of God who of his mercy grants him the knowledge and understanding to say what David says devoutly in the psalter: *Tu es Deus solus qui facis mirabilia magna et qui facis mirabilia magna solus.*[25] And if some who have not used the terms of theology attribute to a creature what should be attributed to the Creator, this is not in the least surprising, for one often says: "such a saint performs miracles and such a one cures such a disease". But it is by the power of God which is in them and not in the least of their own merits, according to what St Bernard says in his fourth book to Pope Eugenius: *virtus vero in sanctis manens ipsa facit opera.*[26]

But I have not set this matter in order for the purpose of gainsaying my master Master Raoul de Presles, who says in his prologue to the book of *The City of God* that my said lord performs miracles in his lifetime and that this power is conferred on him who heals the scrofula.[27] But I have done it so that those who follow on in times to come, less subtle and experienced in learning than my aforesaid Lord, do not take occasion for vainglory nor hold themselves saints and miracle-workers. And on account of this and not without reason there was imprinted on the edges of coins: *Christus vincit, Christus regnat, Christus imperat.*[28] And God has given such grace to my said lord that he has put his subtle intelligence to study, so that he understands the terms of theology to his own salvation and to the honour of God, and the terms of other sciences, such that he applies to the government of his realm, as it clearly appears. For this purpose, to instruct nobles, Gervase wrote the book *de ociis imperialibus.*'[29]

Appendix V

The pilgrimage of the French kings to Corbeny after their consecration and the transfer of St-Marcoul's reliquary to Rheims

I have brought together here some references relating to the devotions paid by the French kings to St-Marcoul after their consecration, since I did not wish to encumber the notes in this book with them.

For the consecration of St-Louis, see Lenain de Tillemont, *Vie de Saint Louis* (Soc. de l'Hist. de France), I, pp. 429 ff.; for the faithfulness of Parisians during the minority, Joinville, chapter XVI. We know for certain that Louis visited Corbeny on several occasions, which is not surprising, seeing that this little market town is situated on an ancient Roman road that must have carried a good deal of traffic. One would imagine that he must have said his prayers at the saint's shrine on each occasion; but the earliest of these visits for which there is documentary evidence was on 28 May 1248 (*Histor. de France*, XXI, 275 J; for the other visits, see ibid., 399 C, 400 B, 402 A and G; Lenain de Tillemont, IV, p. 70 and VI, p. 276 (where *Nov.* should be corrected to *Dec.*), IV, pp. 126, 388; V, p. 22). Now by the year 1248 this pious king had certainly been long in the habit of touching for scrofula, in conformity with the tradition of his ancestors. Cerf, *Du Toucher*, p. 236, and Ledouble, *Notice sur Corbeny*, p. 193, who have recognized the impossibility of a pilgrimage immediately after the consecration, affirm that Louis went to Corbeny in 1229 (Cerf is more precise—1 Dec. 1229). But I can find no trace of this either in Lenain de Tillemont, or in the *Mansiones et Itinera* drawn up by the editors of *Histor. de France*, vol. XXI. Even if this fact were to be taken as certain, Louis could not be considered as the initiator of the custom of journeying to Corbeny, for the characteristic feature of this custom was precisely the obligation for the king to pay his devotions to St-Marcoul immediately after his consecration.

Philip the Fair's itinerary after his consecration is known to us from the record on tablets kept by the Keeper of the purse of the Royal Household; *Histor. de France*, XXII, pp. 492, 493.

Louis X: the Chancery Register, Arch. Nat. J.J. 52, fol. 118 v., no. 229, contains a deed by this prince, enacted in the month of August 1315 (the month of the consecration), at a place called *Corberiacum;* the authors of the *Itinéraire*, published in vol. XXI of the *Historiens de France*, p. 465, propose the correction *Corbeniacum* (Corbeny), which is quite probable. There should be another copy of this deed—confirming the foundation of a hospital at St-Just *in Angelo*, by Jean de Clermont, Lord of Charolais, and Jeanne, Countess of Soissons, his wife —in the register formerly numbered 51 in the Treasury at Chartres and kept at the present time in Petrograd, since this register is a duplicate of no. 52 (see lastly H. François-Delaborde, *Catalogue des actes de Philippe-Auguste*, p. lxv); I have not of course been able to see it.

Philip VI certainly did not come to Corbeny after his consecration: Jules Viard, *Itinéraire de Philippe VI de Valois* (Bibliothèque de l'Ec. des Chartres, 1915), p. 89, with the *Additions*, ibid., 1913, p. 168.

John the Good: M. E. Petit, 'Séjours de Jean II', *Bullet. historique et philologique*, 1896, p. 587, has worked out an itinerary for John the Good giving *Cormisiacum* for 30 Sept. 1350 (the king having been consecrated on the 26th). This should be corrected to *Corbeniacum*. There is in fact in the St-Rémi archives at Rheims, file 190 no. 2, an authentic extract, made at the order of the 'lords' (of the Chamber of Accounts) on 28 Nov. 1355, from the Christmas 1350 Royal Household accounts, which runs as follows: 'de gisto habitatorum villarum de Corbeniaco et de Craonne XXVᵃ octobris CCI pro uno gisto quod rex cepit de iure suo apud Corbeniacum supradictum adreditum sacri, die xxxᵃ septembris precedentis, computatum per Renerum Coranci ijᵉ xxiij l, x s, vd. p.'

The journeying of Charles V to Corbeny is not attested by definite documentary evidence, but may be adduced with some probability from his itinerary as a whole. This is the conclusion of M. Delachenal, *Histoire de Charles V*, II, 1916, p. 97.

For Charles VI, we have reliable evidence: E. Petit, 'Séjours de Charles VI', *Bullet. historique et philologique*, 1893, p. 409; cf. Douët d'Arcq, *Comptes de l'Hôtel des rois de France aux XIVᵉ et XVᵉ Siècles* (Soc. de l'Hist. de France), pp. 6, 64. Similarly for Charles VII, for whom there are several pieces of evidence: cf. above, Book 2, Ch. IV, n. 90; Vallet de Viriville, *Histoire de Charles VII*, II, 1863, p. 102, and de Beaucourt, *Histoire de Charles VII*, II, 1882, p. 234. The same is true for Louis XI, *Lettres*, ed. Dupont (Soc. de l'Hist. de France), XI, p. 4.

From Charles VIII to Francis II, there is definite evidence that each of them visited Corbeny, and the various testimonies support one another. I shall only refer the reader to Godefroy, *Ceremonial*, I, pp. 208, 234, 265, 293, 311; for Louis XII, cf. above, Book 2, Ch. IV, n. 98; for Henry II, Book 2, Ch. V, n. 10.

For Charles IX and Henry III, I have not come across any evidence; but there is no reason to suppose that these princes broke the old tradition.

All the authorities agree that Henry IV—who was consecrated at Chartres— did not make the pilgrimage to Corbeny. Oudard Bourgeois, *Apologie*, p. 64, affirms that he kept his novena to the saint in the château of St-Cloud, before entering Paris; but I do not know of any other documentary support for this information; and Oudard Bourgeois' constant concern to sing the praises of his saint makes him a rather dubious witness.

For Louis XIII, Godefroy, *Ceremonial*, I, p. 417; there is a legally attested certificate that the king began his novena (29 Oct. 1619) in the archives at St-Rémi, file 190, no. 5.

The transference of St-Marcoul's reliquary to Rheims at the time of Louis XIV's consecration: a public announcement on 17 June 1654, file 190, no. 14 (the king was prevented from going to Corbeny 'on account of urgent affairs and of the ruin and desolation of that town'); a letter of safe conduct, dated 3 July 1654 (in a grant of 10 July in the same year), ibid., no. 15 ('to the which place we should have made our visit and paid our devotions if we had not been prevented by the present warfare'). For the ravages caused by the soldiers at Corbeny in 1642 and 1653, see the same file, nos. 9 and 13.

The same transference under Louis XV: H. Dieudonné, 'La chasse de Saint Marcoul au sacre de Louis XV', *Revue de Champagne*, 1911, p. 84; cf. above, Book 2, Ch. VI, n. 41.

Under Louis XVI, Leber, *Des cérémonies du sacre*, 1825, p. 447; cf. above, Book 2, Ch. IV, n. 166.

Du Tillet, in his *Mémoires et recherches*, Paris, 1578, pp. 147 ff, and following his lead, but inaccurately, Godefroy, *Ceremonial*, I, p. 1, published the translation of an *ordo* of consecration said to have been used by Philip Augustus in 1710. M. H. Schreuer, in succession to other historians, including A. Luchaire, has denied this attribution; M. Buchner has upheld it against him (for a bibliography of this controversy, see *Revue historique*, CVIII, p. 136). The *ordo* mentions the pilgrimage to Corbeny (Du Tillet, p. 156; Godefroy, p. 11). We should therefore have to involve ourselves in this discussion if it were not obvious from Du Tillet's edition—truncated by Godefroy—that the phrase relating to the pilgrimage is an interpolation due to Du Tillet himself. He thought good to add to the text he had before him a development of the royal touch in which he refers to Philip the Fair. For the year 1179, this is a somewhat startling anachronism. Moreover, this is not the only example of this kind of gloss inserted even in the text of the *ordo* by this good clerk; on p. 155 there is a remark relating to the Duc de Berry, son of John II. Schreuer's negative inferences seem to me to be conclusive. But in order to be able to offer a positive opinion on the date of the *ordo*, falsely attributed to Philip Augustus, we should have to possess something more reliable than a doctored translation.

Appendix VI

Additions and corrections

I *The primitive republicanism of the Germanic peoples*

Pp. 31 ff.—In all the development of my theme, I shall perhaps be reproached for having treated with a rather too disdainful silence a theory that was once upon a time famous, that of the primitive republicanism of the Germanic tribes. To be sure, it is generally well known that a whole school of historians, Germans for the most part, have seen Germanic royalty as a somewhat late-developing institution, born, at any rate among the West Germans, from the great upheavals following the invasions. But does this theory really deserve a detailed discussion? In so far as it relies on documentary support, and is not simply a reflection of the seductive mirages of the Enlightenment or of Romanticism, it rests in the last resort upon a double misunderstanding. In the first place, the terminology of the Latin authors is interpreted quite uncritically. When describing Germanic society, they like to reserve the word *rex* for the chiefs of extensive groups; in their view, the heads of little tribal groups were only *principes*. By transposing their language into French or German without any preliminary exploration, we should simply end by producing nonsense. In terms of current sociological vocabulary, *principes* and *reges* are clearly kings, that is to say, monarchs possessing hereditary prestige. I use the word hereditary intentionally; for it is with regard to this word that the supporters of this retrospective republicanism fall into their second confusion. From the fact that election certainly played some part in the choice of the *principes* and even the *reges*, they are inclined to see both classes—and more particularly the former—as purely elective magistrates, and—if I may venture to say so—presidents of small-scale republics. But to do this is to forget that alongside a legitimate personal line there may exist a family legitimacy; heredity exists as soon as the people's choice is only made within a particular family—always the same one—endowed with a virtue handed down through the blood. And such would seem to have been the normal rule among the ancient Germanic tribes. I should like simply to refer the reader on this matter to the fine chapter by Heinrich Brunner, 'Königtum und Fürstentum', in Vol. I of his *Deutsche Rechtsgeschichte* (2nd ed. 1906, pp. 164–75; cf. also *Grundzüge der deutschen Rechtsgeschichte*, 7th ed., 1921, pp. 14–15); and as an excuse for having treated such a serious problem so briefly, I would finally refer the reader to the opinion quite recently expressed by an historian whom I shall not be suspected of favouring unduly—Alphonse Dopsch: 'Today there can hardly remain any doubt that kingship among the Germanic tribes existed from the very beginning' (*Wirtschaftliche und soziale Grundlagen der europäischen Kulturentwicklung*, vol. II, 1920, p. 23).

II *The Frankish kings as priests*

To the text of Venantius Fortunatus quoted above, p. 36, we must no doubt add the letter addressed by the Bishops gathered together at the Council of Orléans in 511 to Clovis, communicating to him their decisions: 'Quia tanta ad religionis catholicae cultum gloriosae fidei cura vos excitat, ut *sacerdotalis mentis affectum* sacerdotes de rebus necessariis tracturos in usum collegi iusseritis . . .' (*Concilia aevi merovingici*; Monum. Germ., Concilia, I, p. 2). Unfortunately, the text is not very clear. All the MSS. give *affectum*, which has astonished the editor; we should probably take it for a copying mistake instead of the proper *affectu*. If we allow this interpretation, there is no further ambiguity; the fathers in council clearly mean to call the spirit of Clovis *Sacerdotal*. Here, the similarity of the style with that of the Eastern Councils (cf. above, Book 2, Ch. III, n. 4) is very striking; moreover, it is remarkably interesting for the historian to note how the Gallic episcopate transferred a really imperial terminology in favour of the conquering Franks.

III *The iconography of the fleur-de-lis legend*

P. 136 and Book 2, Ch. III, n. 103: (1) Tapestries of Charles the Bold's marriage: substitute for the reference given to Jean de Haynin's *Mémoires* the following: *Mémoires de Jean, sire de Haynin et de Louvignies*, ed. D. D. Brouwers (Soc. des bibliophiles liégeois), Liège, 1906, II, p. 25.
(2) Works not indicated above:

The popularity of the legend in fifteenth-century Germany comes out in the two following works: *Triomphe de l'Empereur Maximilian*, engraved by H. Burgmair, ed. of 1796, pl. 105; Clovis is represented with a coat-of-arms, parted per pale, on the right three toads, on the left three fleurs-de-lis—a statue of Clovis in the Hofkirche at Innsbruck (a sculptured group on the tomb of Maximilian). The Frankish king is represented with the same escutcheon parted per pale, but the opposite way round, with the lis on the right (cf. K. Zimmeter, *Führer durch die Hofkirche*, pl. opp. p. 6); the statue was carried out from designs by Christopher Amberger.

IV *The consecration of the Norman Dukes*

Book 2, Ch. III, n. 16—The indications given above on the manuscripts from which the ritual of this ceremony has come down to us are altogether incorrect, and should be corrected as I shall shortly show. I owe the recognition and the possibility of correcting my mistakes to the kindness of M. Labrosse, the Director of the Bibliothèques et Archives Historiques of Rouen.

Chéruel and Delachenal only knew the ritual for the Norman Dukes through seventeenth-century copies, and each of them, it would seem, from a different copy. The former seems to have consulted the copy in the MS. kept in the Archives Municipales at Rouen under the reference no. A/38, the latter the copy in MS. S.I. of the same collection. Nevertheless a much older transcription of this text is extant, which can be read in fol. 181 of the celebrated *Bénédictionnaire* of Robert de Jumièges, kept in the Bibliothèque de Rouen under the reference Y 7, and published in 1903 by H. A. Wilson (*The Benedictional of Archbishop Robert*; Henry Bradshaw Soc., 24). The benedictional itself was drawn up in England, probably at Winchester, towards the end of the tenth century, and brought to Jumièges in Normandy in 1052 by Robert, Archbishop of Canterbury, who had been sent into exile as a result of the triumph of his enemy, Count Godwin. But fol. 181–3 are in a different handwriting from the MS. as a whole, and noticeably more recent. We should undoubtedly follow Omont (*Catalogue général des MSS. des Départments; Rouen*, no. 369) in dating them in the twelfth century. Wilson thinks they belong to the end of the thirteenth (op. cit., p. 157, n. 4); but Labrosse, after personally examining the MS., has been kind enough to assure me that this date is certainly much too late. The text given by the Wilson edition tallies in all respects with Martene's, but the latter does not indicate its source.

Moreover, Wilson (p. 196) has shown quite clearly that the redactor of the *Officium ad ducem constituendum* simply drew the material for his liturgy from the Anglo-Saxon *Consecratio regis* contained in the ancient portion of the benedictional (pp. 140 ff. of the edition). In effect, he composed the ritual for the ducal consecration out of extracts from the royal consecration ritual: (1) the king's oath; (2) liturgical formulae relating to the handing over of the ring and the sword; (3) the blessing, which closes the ducal ritual, but in the royal ritual it comes before the enthronement. It is instructive to note how in this way the ceremonial for the accession of a great feudal figure has been modelled upon that of the royal accession. But this copy is indeed no more than an abridged version; unction in particular remains a purely monarchical act.

V   *The posthumous miracle of King James II*

Book 2, Ch. VI, n. 26—In the *Bulletin de la soc. académique de Laon*, 15, 1805, pp. 14–22, Matton published the written report, dated 28 Sept. 1703, of a miraculous healing brought about by the intercession of James II. A young girl in hospital at the Hôtel-Dieu at Fère-en-Tardenois, where she was thought to be suffering from the 'falling sickness', was said to have been cured after performing a novena to the pious king. Moreover, it is very clearly evident from the written report that cases of nervous shock following an accident had been included under the term 'falling sickness'; and these effects could last for as much as nine years.

VI   *Gratia Gratis Data*

Many documents quoted above (in particular Félix Fabri, p. 150, Benedict XIV,

p. 291, n. 2, Du Laurens, p. 343), describe the healing granted by God to various princes as *gratia gratis data* or *donum gratis datum*. In reproducing, and sometimes translating, these documents, I omitted to point out that they are only intelligible in the light of a theological theory formerly familiar to all educated minds, but today perhaps less universally known—the distinction between *gratia gratis data* and *gratia gratum faciens*. The first of these two graces was not considered to change the recipient at all in his inmost being; it simply made him able to co-operate by certain actions in the salvation of others. But the second was of a much higher order, for it made the recipient acceptable in the sight of God; it 'united him to God', as St Thomas Aquinas puts it (*Summa theol.*, Ia, IIae, qu. CXI, a. 1). The gift of performing miracles is a classic example of *gratia gratis data;* the royal healings were only a particular form of miracle; hence the expressions quoted above.

VII   *The seventh sons or daughters; the fleur-de-lis of St-Marcoul*

Book II, Ch. IV, §3—I would add to what was said in the text about the powers of the seventh sons the following information, which is grouped under countries:

Hungary: 'According to an ancient belief which is widespread at Folso-Boldogfalva (in the department of Udvarhely) the seventh son of a mother, if he is pious, and does not swear, and if he has the thumb-nail of his right hand smeared at the age of seven with poppy-oil, possesses the gift of discovering hidden treasure by looking through the thumb-nail, which has become transparent' (*Revue des traditions populaires*, 13, 1898, pp. 120–1). (Note the obsession with the number seven: seventh son, seven years old.)

France, Brittany: 'Correspondence between the *intendant* and MM. de Breuteuil and Malesherbes in execution of the king's commands directing them to keep watch upon a certain Sieur Fouquet, of the parish of Lecousse, near Fougères, who claims to be able to cure the scrofula miraculously because he was born the seventh boy in his family and carries on his chin a kind of fleur-de-lis.' Summary of reports in the Departmental Archives, Ille-et-Vilaine, C 206; cf. *Rev. des trad. popul.*, 21, 1906, p. 405.

The Dol district: The seventh sons, or seventh daughters, carry the fleur-de-lis on some part of their body, and touch for scrofula at the Ember Seasons. 'If the scrofula is destined to be fatal, death will take place within a week of the touching' (*Rev. des trad. popul.* 8, 1893, p. 374).

The Nantes district and Vendée: The seventh son carries a fleur-de-lis under his tongue or on his arm and can heal all kinds of disease (*Rev. des trad. popul.*, 15, 1900, p. 591).

Lower Normandy: The seventh sons or seventh daughters touch 'du carreau', i.e. tuberculosis of the mesenteric ganglia. (*Rev. des trad. popul.*, 24, 1909, p. 65).

Loir-et-Cher: 'The youngest of seven boys in a family which consists only of boys has the gift of healing cold humours (the scrofula). He is called a *Marcou.*' (*Rev. des trad. popul.*, 15, 1900, p. 123.) Cf. ibid., p. 381, where we see that a *Marcou* can also heal certain other diseases.

Berry: I have been informed that even nowadays in a certain Berry village a seventh son was quite recently practising—and perhaps still is—his marvellous powers. He would touch, it seems, for all kinds of illness, but only in the night of Maundy Thursday to Good Friday. (We recognize here the specially favourable character for healing belonging, as we have already noted, to Fridays, and particularly Good Friday.) He enjoyed a big circle of patients who flocked to him, and not only from among the poor. On one of those nights, I am told, 'you could see a large number of carriages at his door, and even one car'.

Finally, I must note that F. Duine (*Rev. des trad. popul.*, 14, 1899, p. 448), gives the following reference to the seventh sons (which I have not been able to follow up): L. Morel, in his edition of *Macbeth* (English text, Paris, Hachette, 1888, p. 226).

VIII *Miscellaneous additions and corrections*

P. 75—The etymology of the name David given by Brother William de Sauqueville is obviously taken from St Jerome, *De nominibus hebraicis*; Migne, *P. L.*, vol. 23, col. 857.

Book 2, Ch. I, n. 87—Bibliography of Tolomeo of Lucca. It seems to be a question of Tolomeo's political writings in J. Bauermann, *Studien zur politischen Publizistik in der Zeit Heinrichs VII und Ludwigs des Bayern*, Breslau (Auszug einer Breslauer Diss.); but I only know the very short review of this work by Buchner, *Histor. Jahrbuch*, 41, 1921, pp. 336, 337.

P. 88—In the translation of the text of Alvarez Pelayo, line 5, substitute for the words 'king Sancho' the words 'the illustrious king don Sancho'.

P. 156—Cult of St-Marcoul. Add Blois, Church of St Nicholas (*Rev. des trad. pop.*, 15, 1900, p. 123).

Book 2, Ch. III, n. 42—For the history of Communion in both kinds one can now consult the summary put by G. Constant at the head of his work entitled *Concession à l'Allemagne de la communion sous les deux espèces* (Biblioth. des Écoles de Rome et d'Athènes, part 128), 1923, pp. 1 ff; very brief indications about imperial and royal communion p. 7, n. 1 and 6; Constant appears to believe—in which he is certainly wrong—that the French kings, from the time of Clement VI's Bull onwards, only partook of the chalice on their consecration day. For the concession of communion *sub utraque specie* to Maximilian II, ibid., p. 153.

Book 2, Ch. III, n. 83—For Hincmar's falsifications, references should also have been made to E. Lesne, 'La Lettre interpolée d'Hadrien Ier à Tilpin et à l'église de Reims au IXᵉ siècle', *Le Moyen-Age*, 1913, pp. 325, 389.

P. 159 and Book 2, Ch. IV, n. 77—By mistake I gave Saales, Bourg and Bruche as situated in Alsace. These localities, having been annexed by Germany in 1871, are today part of the Bas-Rhin *département;* but they are really *lorraine*, and under the *ancien régime* they were part of the ducal Lorraine.

P. 202, line 38—I have failed to find the passage in Celsus alluded to by Forcatel. The references of this inventive lawyer should probably not be taken as an article of faith.

Book 2, Ch. V, n. 145—Some figures of sick persons who were touched by Louis XIII are given as reported by the *Gazette de France* in the *Revue des traditions populaires*, 17, 1902, p. 417.

ADDITIONS AND CORRECTIONS

P. 208—For the attitude of the French kings to the seventh sons, compare with the measures taken by the Archbishop of Bordeaux the correspondence of the eighteenth century noted above on p. 289; but I discovered this information too late for me to be able to procure a copy of it in time.

P. 239—When speaking of George Bull, and quoting one of his sermons, I should certainly have indicated the exact period when this theologian lived. He formerly enjoyed a European reputation, but his name is entirely forgotten today. The edition I used, referred to in the note, turns out to be the one of 1816, which might be misleading. G. Bull was born in 1654, and died in 1710; but his sermons were only published after his death.

P. 258—*Charles II touching for scrofula.* The reader will find in the *Revue Historique*, 119, 1915, p. 431, a review of the edition of Macaulay's *History of England* kindly procured for me by C. H. Firth (vols. IV, V and VI), which contains a plate showing 'Charles II touching for scrofula'. I have not been able to see the work myself; most probably, it is a reproduction of one of the works classified above under nos. 12 and 13. Incidentally, to the reproductions of no. 13 indicated above we should add the one given by C. Barford in his *Haands-Paalaeggelse*, opp. p. 72.

P. 268—*Diadem and Crown*—According to J. Maurice (*Bulletin de la soc. nationale des Antiquaires*, 1921, p. 233), the flexible band of gold ornamented with uncut precious stones and pendant crystals as opposed to the diadem 'of the Eastern kings' and of Diocletian, was introduced into the Roman Empire by Constantine the Great, in imitation of the kings of Israel; it then became the insignia of the Emperors, as opposed to the diadem, which remained the insignia of the Caesars. The French kings' crown was derived from this form.

P. 275—For Jean Golein, the reader should also have been referred to the bibliography given by A. Molinier, *Les Sources de l'histoire de France*, IV, no. 3344. Note that the reference to A. Thomas, *Mél. [d'archéologie et d'histoire] de l'école de Rome . . .*, II, 455, should be omitted.

Notes

1 I likewise owe a very special debt of gratitude to my colleagues P. Alfaric and E. Hoepffner, who—along with L. Febvre—have been kind enough to help me with correcting the proofs.

INTRODUCTION

1 A little difficulty arises regarding this person. The Venetian document quoted below in n. 2 calls him Richard: 'fratri Ricardo Dei gratia Bisaciensis episcopus, incliti principis domini regis Roberti capellano et familiari domestico'. But in 1340 the Bishop of Bisaccia, who was a Dominican and in consequence a 'Friar', was called Francis; cf. Eubel, *Hierarchia catholica*, 2nd ed., 1913, and Ughelli, *Italia sacra*, vol. VI, Venice, 1720, col. 841. It can hardly be doubted that Francis was the person who held forth in front of the Doge; the Venetian scribe must somewhere or other have made a mistake in reading or copying (perhaps an incorrect initial?). I have thought it right to correct this.

2 Venice, Archivio di Stato, *Commemoriali*, vol. III, p. 171; analysed in *Cal. State Papers, Venice*, I, no. 25. I am indebted for a copy of this most interesting piece to the extreme kindness of M. Cantarelli, professor at the University of Rome. There is no mention of the Bishop of Bisaccia's embassy in E. Deprez, *Les Préliminaires de la Guerre de Cent Ans*, Bibl. Athènes et Rome, 1902. The analysis of the *Calendar* is not free of mistakes: it translates *comitatum de Pontyus in Picardiam* (le Ponthieu) as 'the counties . . . of Pontoise'.

3 '. . . ne tanta strages Christianorum, que ex dicto belo orta et oritur et oriri in posterum creditur, ipsi serenissimo principi Eudoardo imputaretur aliquatenus, in principio dicte guerre suas literas supradicto destinavit Philipo, continentes quod ad evitandum mala super inocentes ventura eligeret alterum trium: silicet quod de pari ipsi duo soli duelum intrarent,

vel eligeret sibi sex vel octo aut quot velet, et ipse totidem, et si[c] questio terminaretur inter paucos, Altissimo de celo justitiam querenti victoriam tribuente; aut si verus rex Francie esse[t], ut asserit, faceret probam offerendo se leonibus famelicis qui verum regem nullactenus lesunt; aut miraculum de curandis infirmis, sicut solent facere ceteri reges veri, faceret [MS: facerent]; alias indignum se regni Francie reputaret. Que omnia supradicta, ac plures et diversos [MS: diversi] pacis tractatus contempsit, se in superbiam elevando.'

4 For the belief relating to lions, see p. 148. For the four Venetians' journey, see p. 63.

5 Cf. d'Albon, *De la Maiesté royalle, institution et preeminence et des faveurs Divines particulieres envers icelle*, Lyons, 1575, p. 29v.

6 I am moreover well aware that in the course of my enquiry I have not always succeeded in holding the balance between the two countries whose parallel destinies I wished to follow. Sometimes England may seem to have been somewhat neglected. I have, I think, been able to study the healing rites in England just as thoroughly (except for a few details) as in France; but not the history of sacred royalty in general. The present state of Europe (1923) is unfavourable to travel and to the purchase of foreign books by public or private libraries; and it makes research in comparative history more difficult that ever. The remedy would no doubt be a good system of international loans, for both printed books and manuscripts; but it is well known that Great Britain, in particular, has not yet embarked on such a course. As I have already indicated, my work was only made possible by the generous gift on the part of M. de Rothschild, to whom the Institut de France owes its London house. Unfortunately, I was only able to fit in a single visit to England, at—or very near—the beginning of my labours, that is, at a time when the problems never show up in all the breadth and complexity they are destined to reveal later on. Hence certain gaps which I have not always managed to fill in, in spite of the kindness of my London friends.

7 On 17 May 1691; the speech was printed: *Speculum boni principis in Henrico Magno Franciae et Navarrae rege exhibitum exercitatione politica Deo annuente, in inclyta Argentoratensium Academia . . . Argentorati, Literis Joh. Friderici Spoor* (small quarto brochure, 54pp.). This little work must be very rare: I know of no other copies but those in the Bibl. Nat. and the Bibl. Wilhelmitana at Strasbourg. On p. 12 there is a eulogy of the Edict of Nantes, which—in spite of its brevity—might well have been significant in its day. Apart from the articles in the *Allgemeine deutsche Biographie* and *La France protestante*, the reader can consult for Zentgraff's career O. Berger-Levrault, *Annales des professeurs des Académies et Universités alsaciennes*, Nancy, 1892, p. 262.

BOOK I   CHAPTER I   *The beginnings of the touch for scrofula*

1 The confusion with affections of the face is still nowadays one of those against which there are warnings for practitioners in modern medical treatises; cf. de Gennes in Brouardel, Gilbert and Girode, *Traité de*

Médecine et de Thérapeutique, III, pp. 506 ff. For confusion with eye diseases, cf. e.g. Browne, *Adenochoiradelogia*, pp. 140 ff., 149, 168. Cf. Crawfurd, *King's Evil*, p. 99.

2 For Italy (the Lucca region), see Arnold of Villanova's evidence quoted by H. Finke, 'Aus den Tagen Bonifaz VIII' (*Vorreformationsgeschichtliche Forschungen 2*), Münster, 1902, p. 105, n. 2. For Spain, below, Book 2, Ch. V, n. 7.

3 What follows is taken from *De Pignoribus Sanctorum* by Guibert de Nogent, the most accessible edition of which is Migne, *Patrologia Latina*, vol. 156.

4 *P.L.*, vol. 156, col. 651ff.

5 Col. 664 at the beginning of Book III §IV: 'in eorum libello qui super dente hoc et sanctorum loci miraculis actitat'.

6 Col. 607 'nobis contigui'; col. 651 'finitimi nostri'.

7 Col. 652 'Attendite, falsarii . . .'.

8 Bibl. Nat. MS. Lat. 2900 which comes from this very monastery at Nogent.

9 See in particular the very interesting memoir by M. Abel Lefranc, 'Le Traité des reliques de Guibert de Nogent et les commencements de la critique historique au moyen âge', in *Études d'histoire du moyen âge dédiées à Gabriel Monod*, 1896, p. 285. M. Lefranc seems to me slightly to exaggerate Guibert's critical sense, though there is certainly no denying it. Cf. Bernard Monod, *Le Moine Guibert et son temps*, 1905.

10 Col. 615 and 616. Incidentally, the passage relating to the scrofula is rather strangely intercalated in the middle of the argument, between the examples from antiquity and the reminder of the prophecies of Balaam and Caiaphas. The treatise as a whole is very badly composed. The greater part of the examples quoted by Guibert de Nogent were the classical ones of that time; see e.g. the moral drawn by Peter Damian from the prophecy of Caiaphas— taken as the type of the Simonist—in *Liber gratissimus*, chapter X, *Monumenta Germaniae, Libelli de lite*, I, p. 31.

11 I quote from the manuscript, fol. 14: 'Quid quod dominum nostrum Ludovicum regem consuetudinario uti videmus prodigio? Hos plane, qui scrophas circa jugulum, aut uspiam in corpore patiuntur, ad tactum eius, superadito crucis signo, vidi catervatim, me ei coherente et etiam prohibente, concurrere. Quos tamen ille ingenita liberalitate, serena ad se manus obuncans, humillime consignabat. Cuius gloriam miraculi cum Philippus pater ejus alacriter exerceret, nescio quibus incidentibus culpis amisit'. The text of *P.L.*, vol. 156, col. 616, spelling apart, is correct.

12 Cf. G. Bourgin, the introduction to his edition of Guibert de Nogent, *Histoire de sa vie* (Collect. de textes pour l'étude et l'ens. de l'histoire), p. xiii. Bourgin seems not to have noticed a passage in the *De Pignoribus* relating to the healing of scrofula, or he would not have represented the meetings between Guibert and the king as merely 'probable'.

13 Ordericus Vitalis, Book VIII, chapter xx, ed. Le Prévost, III, p. 390.

14 It will be found collected together above, see p. 74.

15 Du Peyrat, *Histoire ecclésiastique de la cour*, p. 817. It will be noticed that in our time Sir James Frazer has taken up again the old theory of du Laurens and Pierre Mathieu (*Golden Bough*, 1, p. 370), without realizing the historical difficulties it raises.

16 *Historia Francorum*, 9, c. 21: 'Nam caelebre tunc a fidelibus ferebatur, quod mulier quaedam, cuius filius quartano tibo gravabatur et in strato anxius decubabat, accessit inter turbas populi usque ad tergum regis, abruptisque clam regalis indumenti fimbriis, in aqua posuit filioque bibendum dedit; statimque, restincta febre, sanatus est. Quod non habetur a me dubium, cum ego ipse saepius larvas inergia famulante nomen eius invocantes audierim ac criminum propriorum gesta, virtute ipsius discernente, fateri'.

17 *Bibliotheca Hagiographica Latina*, 1, p. 555.

18 *Histoire ecclésiastique de la Cour*, p. 806.

19 *Histor. de France*, 10, p. 115A and Migne, *P.L.*, vol. 141, col. 931: 'Tantam quippe gratiam in medendis corporibus perfecto viro contulit divina virtus ut, sua piissima manu infirmis locum tangens vulneris et illis imprimens signum sanctae crucis, omnem auferret ab eis dolorem infirmitatis.' I would particularly mention that the interpretation of this passage, developed later on, had already been indicated in its broad lines by Dr Crawfurd in his *King's Evil*, pp. 12, 13.

20 'Du toucher des écrouelles', p. 175, n. 1.

21 On this point, and on everything to do with the critical explanation of the royal miracle, see above Book III.

22 *Journal des Savants*, 1881, p. 744.

23 Migne, *P.L.*, vol. 207, letter XIV, col. 42; letter CL, col. 439.

24 For example, A. Luchaire in his attractive article on Peter of Blois in *Mém. Acad. Sc. Morales*, 171, 1909, p. 375. In order to have a right judgment of Peter of Blois' correspondence and the sincerity of his letters it is as well to remember that he composed a manual on the art of letter-writing, *Libellus de arte dictandi rhetorice*; cf. C.-V. Langlois, *Notices et extraits*, 34, 2, p. 23. For Peter's career, see finally J. Armitage Robinson, 'Peter of Blois' in his *Somerset Historical Essays* (published for the British Academy), London, 1921.

25 *P.L.*, vol. 207, col. 440 D: 'Fateor quidem, quod sanctum est domino regi assistere; sanctus enim et christus Domini est, nec in vacuum accepit unctionis regiae sacramentum, cujus efficacia, si nescitur, aut in dubium venit, fidem ejus plenissimam faciet defectus inguinariae pestis, et curatio scrophularum'. The text of the new acq. MS. lat. 785 in the Bibl. Nat., fol. 59, is in conformity with that of the editions, except for the insignificant inversion 'unctionis regie accepit sacramentum'.

26 *King's Evil*, pp. 25, 26. I owe a great deal to this excellent commentary.

27 These documents are discussed on pp. 67 ff., 76 ff.

28 *Charisma*, p. 84. Tooker also puts forward—though with rather less assurance—Joseph of Arimathea as the institutor of the English rite. Lucius (whose reputation was largely spread in England through Bede's *Historia Ecclesiastica*, I, 4) owes his origin, as we know, to a mention in the *Liber Pontificalis* of a letter said to have been addressed to Pope Eleutherius by 'Lucius, the Breton king.' Harnack proves that the redactor of the life of Eleutherius had erroneously converted a king of Edessa into a Breton prince: *Sitzungsberichte der kg. preussischen Akademie*, 1904, i, pp. 909–16.

29 Cf. J. F. Payne, *English Medicine in Anglo-Saxon Times*, (Fitzpatrick Lectures), Oxford, 1904, p. 158.

30 Cf. Holinshed, *Chronicles of England, Scotland and Ireland*, i, Book VIII, chap. 7, 1807, ed. I, London, p. 754.

31 For everything concerning the Lives of Edward the Confessor, I shall refer the reader once and for all to the introduction to my edition of Osbert de Clare, *Analecta Bollandiana*, 41, 1923, pp. 5 ff.

32 *Vita Aeduuardi regis qui apud Westmonasterium requiescit* in *Lives of Edward the Confessor*, ed. Luard (Rolls Series), p. 428; William of Malmesbury, *Historia Regum*, ii, I, 222, ed. Stubbs (Rolls Series), i, p. 272; Osbert of Clare, chap. XIII; Ailred, ed. R. Twysden, *Historiae anglicanae scriptores*, x, London, 1652, col. 390, and Migne, *P.L.*, vol. 195, col. 761.

33 Loc. cit., p. 273: 'unde nostro tempore quidam falsam insumunt operam, qui asseverant istius morbi curationem non ex sanctitate, sed ex regalis prosapiae hereditate fluxisse'.

34 'Super aliis regibus qualiter se gerant in hac re, supersedeo; regem tamen Anglicum neutiquam in talibus audere scio'. Such at any rate was the original text of the manuscript, and the one adopted by the editors; cf. Migne, *P.L.*, vol. 156, col. 616. What would seem to be a twelfth-century hand has sought to emend *scio* into *comperio* by adding the abbreviation of *com* before the *sc* and changing *sc* into *per*.

35 E.g. Mabillon, *AA.SS.ord. S. Bened.*, iv, 2, p. 523; this is still the modern interpretation, adopted by Delaborde.

36 *King's Evil*, p. 18. Crawfurd, who does not think that Henry I touched for scrofula, sees in Guibert's phrase an allusion to the miracles of St Edward.

37 P. 429: 'Quod, licet nobis novum videatur, hoc eum in adolescentia, cum esset in Neustria quae nunc Normannia nuncupatur, saepius egisse Franci testantur'.

38 For what follows, see my introduction to the *Life* by Osbert of Clare, in particular, pp. 20, 35.

39 The allusion to the Norman miracles does not occur in Ailred. By his time— the reign of Henry II—belief in the wonder-working power of kings was firmly established; there was no longer any point in insisting on the large number of scrofulous healed by Edward the Confessor. Besides, this appeal to rather unknown events, said to have taken place abroad, would have seemed somewhat odd. That is no doubt why Ailred, who was officially entrusted with the revision of Osbert's text, suppressed the sentence in question.

40 The Ashmolean Museum in Oxford possesses a medal of Scandinavian or Anglo-Saxon origin found in the seventeenth century, near the city of Oxford itself. It has a hole through its upper part, and carries an inscription that is hard to decipher. When it was first discovered, the inscription was thought to be *E.C.*, which certain scholars, by a strange aberration, interpreted as *Edward the Confessor*—as though Edward would have used this hagiological appellation during his lifetime! Now, the coins distributed by the kings of England in modern times to the scrofulous touched by them— the *touch-pieces*—were also pierced, so as to be hung round the patient's neck; so these over-ingenious scholars thought that what had been discovered was a touch-piece of St Edward. Their opinion scarcely needs refuting. Cf. Farquhar, 'Royal Charities', i, pp. 47 ff.

41 Between the reigns of Henry I and Henry II comes Stephen of Blois. He was only the nephew of the former, only on the maternal side at that, and reigned in spite of the last wishes expressed by his uncle. Did he nevertheless claim the healing power initiated by his uncle? Or did Henry II, on coming to the throne, have to revive a tradition that had momentarily been interrupted? In the absence of documentary evidence, this little problem remains insoluble.

BOOK I   CHAPTER 11   *The origins of the royal healing power*

1 *Cultes, mythes et religions*, 2, p. 21.

2 *Lettres Persanes*, 24.

3 *Golden Bough*, I, p. 371 (italics mine). Cf. ibid., III, p. 134.

4 I owe a great deal in the argument that follows to the fine book of Kern, *Gottesgnadentum*. There is a very full bibliography in this book, though there is unfortunately no classification. It will make it possible for me to make a large reduction in the bibliographical references, particularly with reference to consecration. Perhaps it will help researchers if I tell them there is nothing useful to be found in the article by Jos von Held, 'Königtum und Göttlichkeit: Am Ur-quell', *Monatschrift für Volkskunde*, 3, 1892. Since Kern's volume, a useful work has appeared on the subject of consecration by Reginald Maxwell Woolley, *Coronation Rites*, Cambridge (The Cambridge Handbooks of Liturgical Study), 1915, and a thesis in the Law faculty, Toulouse, by Georges Péré, *Le Sacre et couronnement des rois de France dans leurs rapports avec les lois fondamentales*, 1921, in which there is to be found certain judicial information, unfortunately marred by an astonishing ignorance of the literature of the subject; cf. also Ulrich Stutz, 'Reims und Mainz in der Königswahl des X. und zu Beginn des XI. Jahrhunderts', *Sitzungsber. der preussischen Akademie*, 1921, p. 414.

5 The sacred character of the ancient Germanic royalty has been brought out on many occasions. It is specially worth while consulting H. M. Chadwick, 'The Ancient Teutonic Priesthood', *Folklore*, 1900; cf.—by the same author —*The Origin of the English Nation*, Cambridge, 1907, p. 320. There are suggestive hints in J. Flach, *Les origines de l'ancienne France*, 3, pp. 236, 237, and Paul Vinogradoff, *Outlines of Historical Jurisprudence*, I, Oxford, 1920, p. 352. I have made use below of some information borrowed from the Scandinavian group. I am well aware that among these peoples the sacred character of royalty became much accentuated through the absence of a specialized priesthood, which appears on the other hand to have existed in many other Germanic tribes. The Northern kings always remained priests; but for the most part, the kings of Germania properly speaking did not possess—or no longer possessed—this kind of function round about the period of the great invasions. But we are not interested here in these differences, however important they may be, for in the South no less than in the North, the fundamental idea was the same; and this is all we need to know.

6 *Germania VII :* 'Reges ex nobilitate, duces ex virtute sumunt'. This sentence

from Tacitus has often, and rightly, been compared with a remark by Gregory of Tours, *Historia Francorum*, II, 9, on the subject of Frankish origins: 'ibique iuxta pagos vel civitates reges crinitos super se creavisse de prima, et, ut ita dicam, de nobiliori familia'.

7 *Getica*, chapter XIII, ed. Mommsen (*Momunenta Germaniae A.A.*, v), p. 76, on the subject of the royal family of the Amales: 'iam proceres suos, quorum quasi fortuna vincebant, non puros homines, sed semideos id est Ansis uocauerunt'. For the meaning of the word Ase, cf. Maurice Cahen, *Le Mot 'Dieu' en vieux-scandinave* (Collect. linguistique Soc. linguistique de Paris, 10, and thesis, Fac. Lettres, Paris), 1921, p. 10, n. 1. E. Mogk, in his article 'Asen' in Hoops, *Reallexikon der germ. Altertumskunde*, seems to think that the word was only applied to kings who had died and been posthumously deified; but I can see nothing of the kind in Jordanes. In an interesting passage of Justin, *Histor. Philippic.* vii, 2, we see the Macedonians being accompanied into battle by their infant king, 'tanquam deo victi antea fuissent, quod bellantibus sibi regis sui auspicia defuissent'. This suggests a belief similar to that testified among the Goths by the text of Jordanes.

8 Cf. among others Kemble, *The Saxons in England*, 1876 ed., London, i, p. 336; W. Golther, *Handbuch der deutschen Mythologie*, 1895, p. 299; J. Grimm *Deutsche Mythologie*, 4th ed., Berlin, 1878, iii, p. 377. The most recent study of genealogies is the essay by E. Hackenberg, *Die Stammtafeln der anglo-sächsischen Königreiche*, Berlin, 1918. I have not been able to consult it; but its chief conclusions are summed up by Alois Brandl, *Archiv für das Studium der neueren Sprachen*, 137, 1918, pp. 6ff. (esp. p. 18). There is perhaps an allusion to the would-be divine origin of the Merovingians in a phrase of the famous letter written by Avitus, Bishop of Vienne, to Clovis at the time of his baptism. Cf. Junghans, *Histoire de Childerich et de Chlodovech*, trans. Monod (*Bibl. Hautes Études*, part 37), p. 63, n. 4.

9 Cassiodorus, *Variae*, viii, 2: 'quoniam quaevis claritas generis Hamalis cedit, et sicut ex vobis qui nascitur, origo senatoria nuncupatur, ita qui ex hac familia progreditur, regno dignissimus approbatur'. ix, i: 'Hamali sanguinis purpuream dignitatem'.

10 This is what the German historians express by the contrast between *Geblütsrecht* and *Erbrecht*.

11 Procopius, *De Bello Gothico*, ii, 15. Cf. Kern, *Gottesgnadentum*, p. 22. In Procopius' view, the Heruli settled in 'Thule' were a group who had come rather late in the day from the Black Sea region, where the Herulian people had lived 'since time immemorial' (ii, 14). This is an obvious mistake, which has been unanimously rejected.

12 *Heimskringla*, ed. Finnur Jonsson, i, *Halfdana Saga Svarta*, K. 9. For the translation of this text and the others subsequently quoted from the same source, I owe a great deal to the kind help of my colleague Maurice Cahen.

13 This is what we gather from a passage from the Danish historian Saxo Grammaticus (Book xiv, ed. Holder-Egger, Strasburg, 1886, p. 537). According to this passage, when Waldemar I of Denmark travelled across Germany in 1164 on his way to the Diet at Dole, the mothers were said to have brought their children to be touched by him, and the peasants their corn, hoping in both cases to promote their favourable growth. Thus even in

foreign parts there would appear to have been a belief in Waldemar's marvellous powers. This is an obvious exaggeration, clearly attributable to
nothing else but Saxo Grammaticus' chauvinism. Nevertheless, this is an
instructive little story, for it tells us not so much about the Germans' mental
attitude, as about the Danes'. In order to vaunt the powers of his country's
king Saxo Grammaticus contrives to picture even the neighbouring peoples
as having recourse to the prince's sacred hand. Such a gesture on the part of
his own compatriots would probably have appeared too commonplace even
to mention. He certainly did not invent the belief he sets before us: where
did he get the idea from? One can only suppose that he has changed the
country in order to add to the effect of his story. Perhaps he himself shared
this faith: he evidently speaks of it with sympathy, though—no doubt out
of respect for the Church's teaching—he thought himself bound to add that
it was of a superstitious kind: 'Nec minus supersticiosi agrestes . . .'

14 Ammianus Marcellinus, XXVIII, 14: 'Apud hos generali nomine rex appel-
atur Hendinos, et ritu ueteri potestate deposita remouetur, si sub eo fortuna
titubauerit belli, vel segetum copia negauerit terra, ut solent Aegyptii casus
eiusmodi suis adsignare rectoribus'. For Sweden, see *Heimskringla*, I,
Ynglinga, K. 15 and 43. In the second of these passages, note the appearance
of the idea that bad harvests were due, not to a deficiency in the king of
this mysterious power, that *quasi-fortuna* spoken of by Jordanes, but to the
commission by him of some precise fault (such as neglect of the due accomplishment of the sacrifices). This is a first step towards a rationalistic
interpretation which begins to shake the old belief. On the same kind of
superstitions among primitive peoples, there is an abundant literature; see
as the latest authority L. Lévy-Bruhl, *La Mentalité primitive*, 1922, pp. 366 ff.

15 *Heimskringla*, II, *Olafs Saga Helga Konungs*, II, K. 155 and 189. Olaf died
in 1030. W. Ebstein, 'Zur Geschichte der Krankenbehandlung', *Janus*, 1910,
p. 224, has construed these texts (in the second of which we see Olaf healing
a little boy with a tumour on the *neck*) so as to attribute a Scandinavian
origin to the touch for scrofula, suggesting that the practice passed from
the northern countries to England (under Edward) and from there to France.
This theory certainly does not need to be refuted at length. It will be enough
just to recall the dates: Olaf's healing power is only attested by a thirteenth-
century document, and there is nothing to indicate that the Norwegian kings
exercised a dynastic gift. Edward the Confessor's miracles are only known to
us from an early twelfth-century document, which is in all respects highly
dubious. In France, the healing rite was certainly in existence in the second
half of the eleventh century (Philip I); and it is highly probable that the
wonder-working virtue of the French kings goes back to the end of the tenth
century, that is, to a time not only earlier than the *Saga* containing the account
of St Olaf's healings, but even than the reigns of this monarch and of St
Edward.

16 We may add certain noble families of Arabia, whose healing power seems
to have been specialized for the treatment of rabies, and would appear to go
back to the pre-Islamic period; cf. below, Bk. 1, Ch. II, n. 64. For classical
antiquity, documentary evidence is obscure. A passage in Plutarch's *Pyrrhus*,
chapter III, tells us that people used to attribute the gift of healing to

Pyrrhus; in his case, the seat of this marvellous power was his big toe; but there is nothing to indicate that he shared this power with the other kings of Epirus. Perhaps this is a case similar to that of the Merovingian Guntram: the application to a particularly famous individual—but not to a whole line —of the general belief in the magical character of royalty. Incidentally, two illnesses—leprosy and jaundice—appear in the ancient documents as *morbus regius* (see in particular Law Hussey, 'On the cure of scrofulous diseases', p. 188), without its being possible in any way to determine whether this name originally had any connection with a royal 'miracle'.

17 I am confining myself here to survivals which are certain, though others have also been suggested. According to some historians (e.g. Grimm, *Deutsche Rechtsaltertümer*, 4th ed., I, pp. 314 ff., and Chadwick, loc. cit.), the wagons drawn by oxen, which Einhard shows us to have been used by the last Merovingians, were sacred wagons, similar to those reported by Tacitus (*Germania*, 40) to have been used in the processions of the goddess Nertus. This is perhaps an attractive hypothesis but, after all, it is no more than a hypothesis. A legend first attested by the pseudo-Fredegarius (III, 9) makes Merowig the son of a sea monster. Is this a remnant of some old pagan sea-myth? Or is it a purely etymological legend, basically a play on words upon the name Merowig, which first arose in Gaul? No one will ever know. We must exercise caution. I may perhaps be allowed to reproduce at this point an amusing example of the excesses that too ardent folklorists are apt to fall into. In Grimm, loc. cit., I, p. 339, we read this sentence, supported by a reference to a Provençal poem *Fierabras*: 'Der König, der ein pferd tödtet, hat kein recht im reich'. Might this be a 'taboo'? If we go back to the documents, Fierabras is a pagan king, but a valiant knight. He engages in combat with Olivier. By accident, he kills his opponent's horse—a serious infringement of the rules of jousting courtesy; for nothing was considered more disreputable than to triumph over an adversary by depriving him of his mount. Hence Olivier's reproaches: a king who does such a deed no longer deserves to reign: 'rey que caval auci non a dreg en regnat' runs the Provençal text quoted by Grimm (I. Bekker, *Der Roman von Fierabras*, Berlin, 1829, v. 1388); 'Rois ki ceval ocist n's droit en ireté' runs the French poem (ed. Guessard in *Les anciens poètes de la France*, 1850, v. 1119). Fierabras then dismounts from his horse; the two heroes will now be on equal terms, and the combat can continue in due and proper form. The line I have just quoted, if isolated from the context, seems to supply the strangest information about royal magic, and this is certainly how it was understood by Grimm. But one has only to read the complete scene to see that it offers nothing more than some rather commonplace information about the code of combat in chivalry.

18 The oldest evidence is no doubt contained in Claudius IV, *Consul. Honor.*, 446; *Laud. Stilic.*, I, 203; Avitus, letter to Clovis on the subject of his baptism, ed. U. Chevalier, *Oeuvres de St. Avit*, Lyons, 1890, Letter XXXVIII, p. 192; Priscus, Ἱστορία Γοθική, chapter 16. On the battlefield of Vézeronce, Clodomir's dead body was recognized by his long hair, 'the honour of the royal line': see the very strange passage in Agathias, *Histor.*, I, chapter 3. The custom by which adult Franks were compelled to wear the

hair short is attested by Gregory of Tours, *Histor.*, III, 18. I will not enquire here whether long hair was likewise a mark of royalty among other Germanic nations. At least it is certain that among some of them, this privilege was common to all freemen. For the Suevi in the time of Tacitus, *Germ.*, XXXVIII; for the Goths, F. Dahn, *Die Könige der Germanen*, III, p. 26. For the magic value of long hair, cf. J. Frazer, *Folk-lore in the Old Testament*, 2, London, 1919, pp. 480 ff.

19 The same fact has been noted for Byzantium by Bréhier (in the work mentione below, n. 21), on p. 72: 'Another significant fact [for the survival of the imperial culture] is the frequency of imperial canonizations'.

20 The reader will find the documents relating to the accession of barbarian dynasties conveniently brought together and intelligently commented upon in W. Schuecking, *Der Regierungsantritt*, Leipzig, 1889. Briefly, it would seem that among the Merovingians the new king's accession to power was accompanied by various, and variable, practices, which never seem to have been collected and fixed in a co-ordinated ritual—carrying aloft on the buckler, investiture with the lance, a solemn progress through the kingdom . . . All these practices had one factor in common: they were strictly lay (in as much as they were considered to be emptied of their ancient religious character, which was pagan); the Church played no part in them. For a recent opinion to the contrary, cf. Germain Morin, above, Appendix III, p. 264.

21 See Louis Bréhier and Pierre Batiffol, *Les Survivances du culte impérial romain*, 1920, particularly pp. 35, 43, 59; cf. the review by J. Ebersolt, *Moyen Âge*, 1920, p. 286.

22 For Vespasian, see Tacitus, *Hist.*, IV, 81; Suetonius, *Vesp.*, 7; Dio Cassius, LXVI, 8. For Hadrian, *Vita Hadriani*, c. 25. Cf. Otto Weinreich, *Antike Heilungswunder (Religionsgeschichtliche Versuche*, 8, 1), Giessen, 1909, pp. 66, 68, 75; H. Dieterich, *Archiv. fur Religionswissenschaft*, 8, 1905, p. 500, n. 1. For Vespasian and messianism, see the fine account in Renan, *L'Antéchrist*, chap IX.

23 M. Batiffol (loc. cit., p. 17, n. 2), notes that in the Ostrogoth kingdom of Italy there are vestiges of the imperial cult; in the reign of Theodoric, the imperial purple was worshipped: Cassiodorus, *Variae*, XI, 20, 31. But from the point of view of political law, Theodoric's kingdom was in an uncertain position. Theoretically at least, it still formed part of the Empire; and it was in their capacity of imperial magistrates that the *primiscrinii* and the *primicerii* mentioned by Cassiodorus carried out the traditional rites.

24 Without wishing to enter into a discussion on this subject that would be completely beside the point here, I need only observe that an Italian inscription gives Theodoric—who was certainly a *magister militum*, that is to say, an imperial official—the title of 'semper augustus': *Corpus Inscriptionum Latinarum*, X, 6851. Common custom did not therefore preclude such linguistic confusions in Romanized countries under barbarian rule. Of course, several points still remain obscure, especially as regard the precise title given to Clovis by the Emperor Anastasius in the text of Gregory of Tours.

25 On the politico-religious theories of the Carolingian epoch, there is a useful collection of references with some intelligent hints in H. Lilienfein, 'Die Anschauungen von Staat und Kirche im Reiche der Karolinger', *Heidelb.*

Abh. zur mittleren und neueren Gesch., 1, Heidelberg, 1902; unfortunately the author tends to explain everything by the antithesis between 'Romanism' and 'Germanism'. When will scholars make up their minds to drop this puerile dichotomy? I did not get much help from W. Ohr, *Der karolingische Gottesstaat in Theorie und in Praxis*, Leipzig, 1902.

26 I, I, 3, Migne, *P.L.*, vol. 98, col. 1014, 1015. Much later on, Frederick Barbarossa, who should nevertheless have had a good deal to reproach himself with on this subject, was not afraid likewise to criticize the use of the word 'saint' as applied to the Byzantine Emperor: see Tageno de Passau in *Monumenta Germaniae, SS.* XVII, p. 510, lines 51ff.

27 E. Eichmann, in his *Festschrift G. von Hertling dargebracht*, p. 268, n. 3, quotes some examples, to which many others could be added. It will be enough to refer the reader to the index of the *Capitularia regum Francorum* and of the *Concilia* in the editions of the *Monumenta Germaniae*. Cf. also Sedulius Scottus, *Liber de rectoribus christianis*, chap. 9, ed. S. Hellmann (*Quellen und Unters. zur latein. Philologie des Mittelalters*, I, 1), p. 47; Paschasius Radbertus, *Epitaphium Arsenii*, Book II, chapters 9 and 16, ed. Duemmler (Kgl. Preussische Akademie, Phil.-hist. Klasse, Abhandl., 1900, II), pp. 71, 85.

28 *De ordine palatii*, chap. XXXIV, ed. Prou (Bibl. Ec. Hautes Études, part 58), p. 90: 'in sacris ejus obtutibus'. This treatise by Hincmar is known to be no more than the redaction of an earlier work composed by Adalard de Corbie which has not survived. The expression I have just quoted would fit in better with Adalard's ideas than with Hincmar's. Perhaps the latter had derived it from this source.

29 It is found in use in Germany in the days of the Saxon emperors: Waitz, *Verfassungsgeschichte*, 2nd ed., VI, p. 155, n. 5; and it naturally took on a new popularity under the Hohenstaufens: cf. Max Pomtow, *Ueber den Einfluss der altrömischen Vorstellungen vom Staat auf die Politik Kaiser Friedrichs I*, Halle, 1885, particularly pp. 39, 61. See also above, p. 200.

30 Above, p. 265; for the controversy relating to the introduction of anointing in Byzantium, above p. 271.

31 Genesis 14: 18; cf. Psalm CIX, 4; the symbolical role played by Melchisedech is already abundantly displayed in the Epistle to the Hebrews.

32 *Mémoires de l'Acad. des Inscriptions*, XXXII, I, p. 361.

33 II, 10: 'Melchisedek noster, merito rex atque sacerdos, complevit laicus religionis opus'. There is an article by F. Kern on the iconographical role played by Melchisedech in the Early Middle Ages in 'Der Rex und Sacerdos, in biblischer Darstellung', *Forschungen und Versuche zur Geschichte des Mittelalters und der Neuzeit, Festschrift Dietrich Schäfel . . . dargebracht*, Jena, 1915. The word *sacerdos* applied to a lay sovereign recalls certain formulae of official adulation, traces of which are found in fifth century Byzantium, and to which the pontifical Chancery itself used sometimes at that period to condescend in addressing the Emperor; cf. below Book 2, Ch. III, n. 3 and especially p. 198. But between Fortunatus' poetry and the language freely used more than a century earlier to Theodosius II, Marcion or Leo I, the only link is no doubt the common habits of mind implanted in men by centuries of imperial religion.

34 The text of the letter from Addu-Nirari, J. A. Knudtzon, *Die El-Amarna Tafeln*, Leipzig, 1915, I, no. 51, cf. II, pp. 1073, 1103. For unction in the Hebraic cultus, see among others T. J. Cheyne and J. Sutherland Black, in *Encyclopaedia Biblica*, under the word 'Anointing'. The Addu-Nirari letter naturally raises the question whether royal anointing was practised in ancient Egypt. On this subject, my colleague M. Montet has been kind enough to write to me as follows: 'In all the ceremonies of Egypt, they began by washing the hero of the feast, whether it was a god, a king, or dead body; then he was anointed with a perfumed oil . . . After that, the ceremony proper began. At the end of a coronation, there was much the same procedure: first the purifications and the anointings, then the handing over of his insignia to the heir to the throne. It was not then by unction that the heir and candidate for royalty was transformed into a Pharoah, Lord of the Two Lands.' The Tell-el-Amarna tablet certainly seems to allude to a rite in which unction played a more important part, no doubt a Syrian rite, with which the consecrating Pharoh had perhaps complied.

35 L. Duchesne, *Origines du culte chrétien*, 5th ed., 1920; cf. *Liber Pontificalis*, II, 1892, p. 38, n. 35. For the character of unction given to catechumens in the Gallican Rite—the unction that Clovis received at Rheims—a controversy has arisen between liturgiologists—or rather, theologians—which does not concern us here: see the articles by Dom de Puniet and R. P. Galtier, *Revue des questions historiques*, vol. 72 (1903), and *Revue d'histoire ecclésiastique*, 13, 1912.

36 For everything concerning the beginnings of royal unction, see the references and discussion in Appendix III, p. 262.

27 Cf. P. Fournier, 'Le Liber ex lege Moysi et les tendances bibliques du droit canonique irlandais', *Revue celtique*, 30, 1909, pp. 231 ff. It may be pointed out that the comparison of the king with David and Solomon is a commonplace in all the consecration rituals. The Popes, too, used it freely in their correspondence with the Frankish sovereigns: see some collected examples, *Epistolae aevi carolini* (*Monumenta Germaniae*), III, p. 505, n. 2; cf. also E. Eichmann in *Festschrift G. von Hertling dargebracht*; p. 268, n. 10. Did not Charlemagne call himself—in his familiar circle—by the name David? A comparison needs to be made between the history of royal unction and the history of tithe, which was also borrowed from the Mosaic Law. For a long time it had been simply a religious obligation, enforceable only by ecclesiastical penalties; it was Pepin who gave it the force of law.

38 *Monumenta Germaniae, Diplomata Karolina*, I, no. 16, p. 22, 'divina nobis providentia in solium regni unxisse manifestum est'.

39 See above, Appendix III, p. 268.

40 See above, p. 266.

41 It can be remarked that in spite of the dynastic troubles of the ninth and tenth centuries, the only king of France who died a violent death—and that was on the battlefield—was a notorious usurper, Robert I. Among the Anglo-Saxons, Edward II was assassinated in 978 or 979; but he was made a saint—St Edward the Martyr.

42 *Quaterniones*, Migne, *P.L.*, vol. 125, col. 1040: 'Quia enim—post illam unctionem qua cum caeteris fidelibus meruistis hoc consequi quod beatus

apostolus Petrus dicit: "Vos genus electum, regale sacerdotium", episcopali et spirituali unctione ac benedictione regiam dignitatem potius quam terrena potestate consecuti estis'. The Council of St-Macre, Mansi, XVII, 538: 'Et tanto est dignitas pontificum major quam regum, quia reges in culmen regium sacrantur a pontificibus, pontifices autem a regibus consecrari non possunt'. Cf. in the same sense a Bull of John VIII, addressed in 879 to the Archbishop of Milan, *Monumenta Germaniae, Epist.*, VII, i, no. 163, line 32. The importance attributed by Hincmar to anointing comes out particularly in the *Libellus proclamationis adversus Wenilonem*, drawn up in the name of Charles the Bald, but whose real author was undoubtedly the Archbishop of Rheims: *Capitularia*, ed. Boretius, II, p. 450, c.3.

43 Moreover, it is as well not to forget that in Eastern France, or Germany, tradition during this time appears to have insisted less forcibly on anointing than in France proper. Nevertheless, Conrad, Henry I's immediate predecessor, had certainly been anointed, and his descendants and successors in their turn were to be so likewise. For Henry I's refusal, see the references and discussion in Appendix III, p. 270.

44 Cf. Lilienfein, *Die Anschauungen vom Staat und Kirche*, pp. 96, 109, 146. The same idea had already been forcibly expressed—on the subject of the Byzantine emperor's pretensions—by Pope Gelasius I in a passage of *De anathematis vinculo* often quoted in the course of the great polemical battles of the eleventh and twelfth centuries: Migne, *P.L.*, vol. 59, col. 108–9. Cf. also, contemporary with Hincmar himself, Nicolas I; Mansi, *Concilia*, XV, p. 214.

45 We are still without a really critical survey of the *ordines* of consecration for all the countries. I have therefore had to confine myself here to some rapid and certainly very incomplete comments, but enough, after all, for the object I have in view. The ancient Gallican ritual published by Dom Germain Morin, *Revue bénédictine*, 29, 1912, p. 188, gives the benediction: 'Unguantur manus istae de oleo sanctificato unde uncti fuerant reges et profetae'. The prayer 'Coronet te Dominus corona gloriae . . . et ungat te in regis regimine oleo gratiae Spiritus sancti sui, unde unxit sacerdotes, reges, prophetas et martyres', was used for Charles the Bald (*Capitularia regum Francorum*, ed. Boretius, II, p. 457) and Louis the Stammerer (ibid., p. 461); it recurs in a Rheims Pontifical: G. Waitz, 'Die Formeln der deutschen Königs- und der Römischen Kaiser-Krönung' (*Abh. der Gesellsch. der Wissensch. Gottingen*) 18, 1873, p. 80. It perhaps originated in a *Benedictio olei* (deliberately, of course, without reference to royal unction) given in the *Gelasian Sacramentary*, ed. H. A. Wilson, Oxford, 1894, p. 70. The Anglo-Saxon prayer 'Deus . . . qui . . . iterumque Aaron famulum tuum per unctionem olei sacerdotem sanxisti, et postea per hujus unguenti infusionem ad regendum populum Israheleticum sacerdotes ac reges et prophetas perfecisti . . .: ita quaesumus, Omnipotens Pater, ut per hujus creaturae pinguedinem hunc servum tuum sanctificare tua benedictione digneris, eumque . . . et exempla Aaron in Dei servitio diligenter imitari . . . facias', in the Egbert *Pontifical*, ed. by the Surtees Society, 27, 1853, p. 101; Robert de Jumièges' *Bénédictional*, ed. H. A. Wilson, Henry Bradshaw Society, 24, 1903, p. 143; the Leofric *Missal*, ed. F. E. Warren, Oxford, 1883, p. 230; with a few differences, also

in the so-called Ethelred *ordo*, ed. J. Wickham Legg, *Three Coronation Orders*, Henry Bradshaw Soc., 19, 1900, p. 56; these last two collections preface this prayer by another, which is very closely reminiscent of the Carolingian prayer used for Charles the Bald and Louis the Stammerer; perhaps there was a choice between the two. The poet of the *Gesta Berengarii*, in a paraphrase of the consecration liturgy, mentions that the holy oil was used among the Hebrews to anoint their kings and *prophets* (IV, v. 180: *Monumenta Germaniae, Poetae Latini*, IV, i, p. 401).

46 *Gesta Berengarii*, IV, v. 133–4 (*Monumenta Germaniae, Poetae Latini*), IV, i, p. 399.

47 The libellus had been drawn up by Paulinus of Aqu ileia. *Monumenta Germaniae, Concilia*, II, i, p. 141: 'Indulgeat miseratus captivis, subveniat oppressis, dissolvat fasciculos deprimentes, sit consolatio viduarum, miserorum refrigerium, sit dominus et pater, sit rex et sacerdos, sit omnium Christianorum moderantissimus gubernator . . .' It may be noted that through a kind of contradiction quite frequent in such cases the bishops had, in the previous sentence, opposed the battle waged by the king with the *visible* enemies of the Church to the bishops' struggle against her *invisible* enemies—which amounts to a clear opposition between the temporal and the spiritual. See above, p. 111.

48 Jaffé-Wattenbach, 2381; the original text is I Peter 2: 9. The quotation recurs in Hincmar, *Quaterniones* (the passage reproduced above, n. 45), but applied to all the faithful with whom the kings share their first unction (baptismal unction); thus it cannot be doubted that Hincmar was very consciously taking the biblical words back to their primitive meaning for the special instruction of Charles the Bald.

49 *Histor. de France*, 10, letter XL, p. 464 E; LXII, p. 474 B. Fulbert (L. LV, p. 470E and LVIII, p. 472 C) likewise calls royal letters 'sacra'—according to an old Roman imperial custom, revived during Carolingian times (e.g. Lupus of Ferrières, *Monumenta Germaniae, Epist.*, VI, I, no. 18, p. 25). Later on, Odo of Deuil (*De Ludovici Francorum Regis profectione in Orientem*, Migne, *P.L.*, vol. 185, I, 13 and II, 19), seems to reserve this word for *imperial* letters (with reference to the Byzantine Emperor).

50 *In gloria martyrum*, chap. 27; *De virtutibus S. Martini*, I. chap. 11.

51 Jacques de Vitry, *Exempla ex sermonibus vulgaribus* ed. Crane (Folklore Society), London, 1890, p. 112, no. 268.

52 Jaffé-Wattenbach, no. 5164; Jaffé, *Monumenta Gregoriana* (*Bibliotheca rerum germanicarum*, II), p. 413: 'Illud interea non praetereundum sed magnopere apostolica interdictione prohibendum videtur, quod de gente vestra nobis innotuit: scilicet vos intemperiem temporum, corruptiones aeris, quascunque molestias corporum ad sacerdotum culpas transferre . . . Praeterea in mulieres, ob eandem causam simili immanitate barbari ritus damnatas, quicquam impietatis faciendi vobis fas esse, nolite putare'.

53 Jacques de Vitry, loc. cit.

54 For the medical superstitions relating to sacred things, there is a very useful collection of facts in the two works by S. Franz, *Die Messe im deutschen Mittelalter*, Freiburg, 1902, pp. 87, 107, *Die kirchlichen Benediktionen im Mittelalter*, Freiburg, 1909, especially II, pp. 329, 503. Cf. also A. Wuttke,

Der deutsche Volksaberglaube, 2nd ed., Berlin, 1869, pp. 131 ff; and for the Eucharist, Dom Chardon, *Histoire des sacrements*, book I, section III, chap. XV in Migne, *Theologiae cursus completus*, XX, col. 337 ff. The Eucharist and holy water have both been thought of as being useful for malevolent magical purposes; and in this guise they played a considerable role in the real or supposed practices of mediaeval sorcery. See numerous references in J. Hansen, *Zauberwahn, Inquisition und Hexenprozess im Mittelalter* (*Histor. Bibliothek*, 12), 1900, pp. 242, 243, 245, 294, 299, 332, 387, 429, 433, 450.

55 P. Sébillot, *Le paganisme contemporain*, 1908, pp. 140, 143; A. Wuttke, loc. cit. p. 135. For the wine used in the Mass, Elard Hugo Meyer, *Deutsche Volkskunde*, 1898, p. 265.

56 *In gloria martyrum*, chap. 84. The persons concerned were a Breton 'count' and a Lombard 'duke', both of whom, quite independently of each other, were supposed to have had this strange fancy.

57 Apart from the works quoted above, n. 54, see Vacant and Mangenot, *Dictionnaire de théologie catholique* under the word 'chrême', Dom Chardon, loc. cit., book I, section II, chap. II, col. 174, and for the use of holy oil in malpractices, Hansen, *Zauberwahn*, pp. 128, n. 3, 245, 271, 294, 332, 387. It may also be recalled that Louis XI, when on his deathbed, sent from Plessis-les-Tours for the Holy Phial from Rheims and the miraculous balm the Virgin was supposed to have given St Martin, and caused himself to be anointed with these two chrisms, hoping that they would restore him to health: Prosper Tarbé, *Louis XI et la sainte ampoule*, Rheims, 1842 (Soc. des bibliophiles de Reims) and M. Pasquier, *Bullet. histor. et philolog.*, 1903, pp. 455-8. The connection between the healing power claimed by the kings and the power commonly attributed to the Holy Chrism has already been pointed out by Leber, *Des Cérémonies du sacre*, pp. 455 ff. But unction was not, of course, the only source of this power, or of the notion commonly held of it, since not all anointed kings exercised this power; a particular hereditary virtue was thought to be needed as well. Cf. above, p. 130.

58 *Lettres*, ed. J. Havet (Collection pour l'étude . . . de l'histoire), no. 164, p. 146. For the opposition to the early Capetians, see especially Paul Viollet, *La Question de la légitimité à l'avènement d'Hugues Capet*, Mém. Académ. Inscriptions, 34, I, 1892. I need hardly remind the reader that for the events of 987 and the early days of the Capetian dynasty, reference must always be made to the classics by M. F. Lot, *Les Derniers Carolingiens*, 1891, and *Études sur le règne de Hugues Capet*, 1903.

59 IV, 11; 'Sed si de hoc agitur, nec regnum iure hereditario adquiritur, nec in regnum promovendus est, nisi quem non solum corporis nobilitas, sed et animi sapientia illustrat, fides munit, magnanimitas firmat.'

60 *Canones*, IV (*Histor. de France*, X, p. 628): 'Tres namque electiones generales novimus, quarum una est Regis vel Imperatoris, altera Pontificis, tertia Abbatis'.

61 After the Hundred Years' War, when the English kings still claimed as part of their official style and title the title king of France, it was readily believed in Europe that it was because of this claim that they put themselves forward as healers of the scrofula. See—among other reformers—the letter relating to James I from the Venetian envoy Scarramelli and the account of John

Ernest of Saxe Weimar's journey quoted below, Book 2, Ch. V, n. 80. The facts related above make it unnecessary to discuss this theory.

62 See especially the 4th treatise, *De consecratione pontificum et regum*, in which there is a running commentary on the consecration: *Libelli de lite* (*Monumenta Germaniae*), III, pp. 662ff. On the 'Anonymous' of York, cf. H. Boehmer, *Kirche und Staat in England und in der Normandie im XI. und XII. Jahrhundert*, Leipzig, 1899, pp. 177 ff. (previously unpublished extracts, pp. 433 ff.).

63 Cf. H. Boehmer, loc. cit., pp. 287 ff.; and my Introduction to Osbert of Clare, *Analecta Bollandiana*, 1923, p. 51.

64 J. Wellhausen, *Reste arabischen Heidentums* (*Skizzen und Vorarbeiten*, H. 3, Berlin, 1887), p. 142. Cf. G. W. Freytag, *Arabum proverbia*, I, Bonn, 1838, p. 488; E. W. Lane, *An Arabic-English Lexicon* I, 7, Leipzig, 1884, p. 2626, 2nd col. The superstition must be pre-Islamic in origin. The same power—attributed to the blood of the Banou-Sinan—is mentioned in an ancient poem included in the *Hamasa*, translated by G. W. Freytag, II, 2, Bonn, 1847, p. 583.

65 As was frequently noted by writers of the *ancien régime*; they saw this observation as an excellent argument against the naturalist thesis according to which the healing power was a family attribute of the royal line, more or less physiological in character (cf. below, p. 235): e.g. du Laurens, *De Mirabili*, p. 33. I am of course well aware that in the time of Robert II or Henry I of England the principle of primogeniture was as yet far from being universally established; but it already received solid support, and in France it had been applied, in spite of the Carolingian traditions, from the time of Lothair's accession in 954. As far as I know, no serious study has ever been made of the introduction of this novel idea into monarchical law; but this is not the place to undertake it. It must suffice to note that the very weight of monarchical conceptions led certain minds to consider as worthy of the throne, not the eldest son, but the son—whatever might be his place in the family—who had been born after his father's proclamation as king, or his consecration as such. In the eyes of these jurists, in order to be really a royal child it was necessary to be born not merely of a prince, but of a king. This conception never acquired the force of law; but it served as a pretext for the revolt of Henry of Saxony against his brother Otto I (cf. Boehmer-Ottenthal, *Regesten des Kaiserreichs unter den Herrschern aus dem sächsischen Hause*, pp. 31, 33), and there are echoes of it in various documents: e.g. Eadmer, *Vita S. Dunstani* (*Memorials of St Dunstan*, ed. Stubbs, Rolls Series, p. 214, c. 35); Matthew Paris, *Historia Anglorum*, ed. Madden, Rolls Series, I, p. 353, and *Chronica majora*, ed. Luard, Rolls Series, IV, p. 546.

BOOK 2   CHAPTER I   *Touching for scrofula*

1 Here is an example of the therapeutic use of the sign of the cross: in *Garin le Lorrain* (*Li Romans de Garin le loherain*, ed., P. Paris: *Les Romans des douze pairs*, I, p. 273), we see the doctors, after placing a plaster on the Duke of Bégon's wound, make over it the sign of the cross. The sign of the cross was so much a matter of course as a rite of benediction and exorcism in all

the ordinary actions of daily life that in St Columba's *Regula Coenobialis* there is a prescribed punishment of six strokes for any monk who shall omit to make this sign over his spoon, before drinking from it, or to get a senior monk to make it over the lamp he has just lit: *Zeitschrift für Kirchengeschichte*, 17, 1897, p. 220.

2 One example among many others: Public Record Office, *Chancery Miscellanea*, IV, i, fol. 17 v., 27 May 1378 'xvij egrotis signatis per regem xvij d'.

3 For the interpretation of an obscure text by Étienne de Conty, see below, n. 5.

4 Cf. the anonymous *Life*, ed. Luard, *Lives of Edward the Confessor*, p. 429, and especially Osbert of Clare, chapters XIV, XV, XVI, XVII (where the reader will find references to the corresponding passages in the other biographies); see also A. Franz, *Die kirchlichen Benediktionen*, I, pp. 79 ff., and esp. p. 84.

5 Bibl. Nat. lat. 11730, fol. 31 v.: 'Item post dictam sanctam unctionem et coronacionem regum Francie omnes predicti reges singulares quilibet ipsorum fecit pluries miracula in vita sua, videlicet sanando omnino de venenosa, turpi et inmunda scabie, que Gallice vocatur *escroelles*. Item modus sanandi est iste: postquam rex audivit missam, affertur ante eum vas plenum aque, statim tunc facit oracionem suam ante altare et postea manu dextra tangit infirmitatem, et lavat in dicta aqua. Infirmi vero accipientes de dicta aqua et potantes per novem dies jejuni cum devocione sine alia medicina omnino sanantur. Et est rei veritas, quod quasi innumerabiles sic de dicta infirmitate fuerunt sanati per plures reges Francie'. This passage has already been reproduced by d'Achery in his notes on the *De vita sua* by Guibert de Nogent and, following his lead, by Migne, *P.L.*, vol. 156, col. 1022-3. For the author, see a notice by L. Delisle, *Le Cabinet des manuscrits de la Bibl. Nationale*, II, p. 127, (published earlier, Bibl. Éc. Chartes, 1860, p. 421). The little treatise on French royalty is placed at the head of a continuation of the Martinian Chronicle, likewise from the hand of Étienne de Conty (a fragment of this continuation is published by J. H. Albanès and U. Chevalier, *Actes anciens et documents concernant le bienheureux Urbain V*, p. 73), where the last event related is the battle of Nicopoli (25 September 1396). The text quoted at the head of this note is not without its obscurities: according as one gives the word *lavat* an active or a neutral sense—both of which are perfectly in keeping with classical usage—the meaning will be either that the king washes the sores, or that he washes himself after touching them. I prefer the second, for the first, in spite of its general acceptance, runs clean contrary to all we know from elsewhere about the French rite.

6 *Histor. de France*, 20, p. 20, chapter XXXV (the text quoted below Book 2, Ch. III, n. 10).

7 Ives de Saint-Denis, *Histor. de France*, 21, p. 207, C and D: 'primogenitum iterum ad se vocatum secretius, praesente scilicet solo confessore, instruxit de modo tangendi infirmos, dicens ei sancta et devota verba quae in tangendo infirmos dicere fuerat assuetus. Similiter docuit eum quod cum magna reverentia, sanctitate et puritate deberet illum contactum infirmorum et mundis a peccato manibus exercere'. The interview of 26 November 1314 between Philip the Fair on his deathbed and the heir to the throne is also vouched for by the envoy from the king of Majorca (who was unaware of what was said), Bibl. Éc. Chartes, 58, 1897, p. 12.

8 Above, p. 164.

9 Below, n. 20.

10 For the accounts, among many other examples see: Public Record Office, *Chancery Miscellanea*, IV, i, fol. 20, 3 June 1278: 'tribus egrotis benedictis de manu Regis'; Exchequer Accounts, 352, 18, 8 April 1289: 'Domino Henrico elemosinario . . . die Parasceue, apud Condom . . . pro infirmis quos Rex benedixit ibidem: xxj d. st.' Bradwardine: text quoted below, n. 20. John of Gaddesden: *Praxis medica seu Rosa anglica dicta*, no place or date (1492), fol. 54 v. (cf. above p. 69).

11 For St-Louis, his life by Guillaume de Saint-Pathus, ed. Delaborde (Collection de textes pour servir à l'étude . . . de l'histoire), p. 99. For Philip the Fair, and the English sovereigns, see the accounts enumerated below. Appendix I, p. 244. For Louis XI, Commines, VI, c. VI, ed. Maindrot (Collection de textes pour servir à l'étude . . . de l'histoire), II, p. 41.

12 The preceding account follows the information given in the letter of remission dated from Romorantin, 23 October 1454, and granted to Henri Payot, 'pouvre simple homme, mareschal, demourant a Persay le Petit ou bailliage de Sens et diocese de Langres': Arch. Nat., JJ. 187, fol. 113 verso (pointed out by Charpentier, supplement to the article 'scroellae' in du Cange, *Glossarium*).

13 What follows is in accordance with the royal accounts, studied below in Appendix I.

14 No doubt, in accordance with the Royal Household practice, though not expressly indicated in the accounts, this was in money of Paris.

15 The poorest could moreover receive supplementary assistance in food: Exchequer Accounts, 350, 23, week beginning Sunday 12 July 1277: 'Sexaginta et undecim egrotis benedictis de manu regis per illam ebdomadam de dono regis per elemosinarium suum v. s. xj d. In pascendis quinque pauperibus dictorum egrotorum per elemosinarium regis vij d. ob.'

16 For all technical details about the accounts, whether French or English, see Appendix I. It contains in particular the list of the English Royal Household accounts I have consulted, year by year, which enables me to simplify the references given below. For interpreting the information given by Edward I's accounts, I have used Henry Gough, *Itinerary of King Edward I*, 2 vols, Paisley, 1900; cf. also an itinerary of the same prince by T. Craib, a typed copy of which exists in the Public Record Office in London. To be supplemented for Edward I's visits to Aquitaine by C. Bémont, *Rôles gascons* (*Documents inédits*), III, pp. ix ff. For Edward II, I have used C. H. Hartshorne, 'An itinerary of Edward II', British Archaeological Association, *Collectanea Archaeologica*, I (1861), pp. 113–14. I am well aware that these various itineraries, drawn up from Chancery documents, would need to be checked and perhaps corrected in detail with the help of the Royal Household Accounts themselves but I have not had time to do this. Moreover, only the broad lines were important for the purpose I had in view.

17 The twenty-eighth year of the reign extends from 20 November 1299 to 19 November 1300; the thirty-second year from 20 November 1303 to 19 November 1304; the eighteenth from 20 November 1289 to 19 November 1290; the twenty-fifth from 20 November 1296 to 19 November 1297; the

fifth from 20 November 1276 to 19 November 1277; the seventeenth from 20 November 1288 to 19 November 1289; the twelfth from 20 November 1283 to 19 November 1284. I have obtained the totals above by adding the figures given in the greatest detail by the various accounts mentioned in Book 2, Ch. V, notes 14 to 16. From the reign of Edward I, we possess in the Public Record Office (under *Chancery Miscellanea*, IV, i) a sort of cash-book from the Royal Household, extending from 31 January 1278 to 19 November of the same year. I have not been able to use it for statistics of the royal touch because alongside perfectly clear entries such as 'pro xxx egrotis egritudinis Regis' (fol. 9 v.), 'proc $\frac{xxx}{iii}$ xij egrotis de morbo regio curatis' (fol. 11 v.), it contains others simply in the form of 'pro egrotis', so that one cannot make out whether it is only a question of alms given to sick persons in general, or to scrofula sufferers touched by the king. In the same way, it was not possible to make use of the entries 'pro infirmis' in the alms-roll of year 21, Exchequer Accounts, 353, 16.

18 The first figure by B.M., Add. MS. 9951, fol. 3 v.; the second by Add. MS. 17632, fol. 5; the third is the result of adding the detailed items in the account analysed in *Archaeologia*, 26, pp. 319-20 (cf. below, n. 25).

19 The first figure from Exchequer Accounts, 388,5 (the last membrane of a roll); the second, Record Office, *Treasury of Receipt, Miscell. Books*, 203, fol. 177; the third, B.M. Cotton Nero C VIII, fol. 208 (an indication relating to the pittance received by the poor, fol. 207 v, allows us to determine, as far as this last account is concerned, the period to which the figure of sick persons touched applies). It will be noted that there is overlapping between the figures of Cotton Nero C VIII and those of Exchequer Accounts, 388, 5; cf. below n. 23.

20 Thomae Bradwardini, *De causa Dei contra Pelagium et de virtute causarum ad suos Mertonenses libri tres*, London, 1618, I, c.I, corol. pars 32, p. 39. 'Quicumque etiam negas miracula Christiana, veni et vide ad oculum, adhuc istis temporibus in locis Sanctorum per vices miraculosa gloriosa. Veni in Angliam ad Regem Anglorum praesentem, duc tecum Christianum quemcunque habentem morbum Regium, quantumcunque inveteratum, profundatum et turpem, et oratione fusa, manu impsita, ac benedictione, sub signo crucis data, ipsum curabit in nomine Jesu Christi. Hoc enim facit continue, et fecit saepissime viris et mulieribus immundissimis, et catervatim ad eum ruentibus, in Anglia, in Alemannia, et in Francia circumquaque: sicut facta quotidiana, sicut qui curati sunt, sicut qui interfuerunt et viderunt, sicut populi nationum et fama quam celebris certissime contestantur. Quod et omnes Reges Christiani Anglorum solent divinitus facere, et Francorum, sicut Libri Antiquitatum et fama Regnorum concors testantur: Unde et morbus Regius nomen sumpsit'. This work, which occupies a certain place in the history of mediaeval philosophy, dates from 1344. Cf. F. Ueberweg, *Grundriss der Geschichte der Philosophie*, II, *Die mittlere . . . Zeit*, 10th ed., 1915, p. 586.

21 This figure cannot in fact be fixed with complete accuracy. According to the alms-roll Exchequer Accounts, 351, 15, eight sick persons were touched during the week beginning 12 March (the feast of St Gregory the Pope).

Should these be ascribed to the period before 15 March—that is, to say, in England—or to the subsequent period—that is, in Wales? I have adopted the first solution, which seems to be the more probable. By choosing the second, moreover, we should only produce a very slight effect on our results.

22 The week beginning 17 September (the Sunday before St Matthew's Day).

23 108 from 25 January 1336 to 30 August 1337; 136 from 10 July 1337 to 10 July 1338; total 244; but the figures overlap. It may be pointed out that the Counterroll of the Wardrobe for the years 8 to 11 of Edward III, B.M. Cotton Nero C VIII, which (fol. 200 v.-8) contains a *Titulus de elemosina* stretching from 31 July of year 8 (1334) to 30 August 1337, does not give any indication of sick persons touched for the period 31 July year 8 to 24 January year 10, that is, from 31 July 1334 to 24 January 1336. During almost the whole of this period Edward was in Scotland or in the northern counties, and occupied by his Scottish adventure.

24 T. F. Tout, *The place of the reign of Edward II in English history* (Manchester Historical Series, 21), 1914, p. 9, writes as follows: 'Chronicles do not often all agree, but their agreement is absolutely wonderful in dealing with the character of Edward of Carnarvon'.

25 It should be added, in order to be entirely accurate, that from 20 June 1320 to 21 July of the same year Edward II went on a short journey to Picardy (cf. *Collectanea Archaeologica*, 1, 1861, pp. 135 ff.). So for the period from 20 March to 7 July 1320, during which he touched 93 sick persons, we must deduct 18 days for absence, and from the fourteenth year of the reign (beginning 8 July 1320) we must cut off 14 days. But these deductions are too slight to have a perceptible effect on totals running over four months in one case, and a whole year in the other. I only know the account for the tenth year of the reign (8 July 1316 – 7 July 1317) by the analysis given in the *Archaeologica*, 26, pp. 318 ff. If this analysis is complete, it only includes mention of the royal touch for the period from 27 July to 30 November 1316, but the absence of this kind of mention for the rest of the year seems to me difficult to explain. This account is preserved in the library of the London Society of Antiquaries. I can only hope that this present work may encourage some English scholar to seek a solution to the little problem I have just raised.

26 Cf. J. C. Davies, *The baronial opposition to Edward II*, Cambridge, 1918, p. 109.

27 Alms-Roll, Exchequer Accounts 352, 18. Between 29 June and 1 July, Edward went to Poitou. He landed at Dover on 12 August, and during the interval he stayed or travelled in the kingdom of France, outside his own fief of Aquitaine, and so naturally did not 'touch' anyone. It is true that from 29 July to 4 August at least he stayed in the little county of Pontheiu, at the mouth of the Somme, which belonged to him; but he does not seem to have made use of his powers there. The last touching on the continent was during the week ending 26 June; the first in England during the week ending 14 August (membrane 4).

28 Cf. also for the 1289 journey in France, but outside Aquitaine, what was said in the previous note.

29 Edward III landed at Antwerp on 16 July 1338; he left the continent on 20

February 1340: T. F. Tout in W. Hunt and Reginald L. Poole, *The political history of England*, III, pp. 335, 344. 'Les Itinéraires d'Edouard III d'Angleterre pendant ses expéditions en France', given by Jean Lemoine in an appendix to his edition of Richard Lescot's *Chronique* (Soc. de l'hist. de France), are altogether inadequate.

30 'Mémoire touchant l'usage d'écrire sur des tablettes de cire', *Mém. Acad. Inscriptions*, 20, 1753, p. 307: 'on y marquoit le nom, la qualité et le pays des personnes auxquelles elles [les aumônes] se faisoient: *ce qui mérite d'être observé dans le détail*'.

31 The Renaud de Roye tablets are published in the *Recueil des Historiens de France*, 22, pp. 545–65; the references that follow are to this volume. The tablets are difficult to read, and for some of the items relating to the touch the editors were unable to read the place of origin; these items will not be included below. I have compared this edition with the ancient copy of the tablets of 1307 contained in Bibl. Nat. MS. lat. 9026.

32 554 d. : 'Domicella Johanna de Torre, patiens morbum regium, ibi tunc, LX s. per Vivianum'. For the functions of Vivien, cf. ibid. 511 j, 538 f, 543 e.

33 560 k.; 557 h; 553 k.

34 558 b; 559 b; 558 b.

35 La Souterraine (Creuse): 557 e; La Marche (?), 557 h; Toulouse and Toulousain: 554 c, 558 l; Bigorre: 561 a; Bourgogne: 558 l; Nantes: 557 c; Guingamp: 557 c; Montpellier: 558 c; Bordeaux: 553 k. For the political or feudal situation of these towns, reference can be made once and for all to A. Longnon, *La Formation de l'unité française*, 1922. The sum paid to Sister Agnes, a Franciscan nun, is abnormally high—twelve pounds—a figure that only occurs again for each of the four Lombards and inhabitants of Navarre who came to receive the royal touch shortly before (553 j). Might the explanation be that the royal government was keen to attract sick persons from among the king of England's subjects by the allurement of handsome alms-giving? (Cf. above p. 178, for the policy towards the Spaniards in the sixteenth century.)

36 561 a : 'Guillelmus de Alba in Bigorra, paciens morbum regis, ibi tunc, xx s. per Petrum de Carnoto'. The identification of *Alba* with Hauban (Hautes-Pyrénées, cant. Bagnères de Bigorre) is only conjectural; moreover, it is of little importance, since the regional locality is given with certainty by the word *Bigorra*.

37 Above, n. 20. In 1344—the date of the treaty of Bradwardine—Frenchmen, in the eyes of a loyal adherent of the Plantagenets, might be considered subjects of Edward III; but the Germans remained undeniably foreigners.

38 This is the title of F. Kern's well-known book, *Die Anfänge der französischen Ausdehnungpolitik bis zum Jahr 1308*, Tübingen, 1910.

39 Metz: 558 b; Lorraine: 553 k; Lausanne: 554 d; Savoy: 551 g; Tarascon: 554 b. For Metz and the Capetian diplomacy, cf. Kern, loc. cit., pp. 172, 144. It will be observed that the sums given to foreigners, although sometimes fairly high, come down in other cases as low as 20 sous, the minimum, and no doubt the normal, figure for alms at the royal touch.

40 Navarre: 522 c, 553 j, 554 a; Spain: 553 m, 554 c, 557 c, 559 e ('Maria de Garda in Esturia, paciens morbum regis, . . . apud Longum Pontem');

Lombardy: 553 j and lat. 9026, p. 13 of the tablets: ' . . de Lombardia paciens morbum regium' (omitted in the edition); Milan: 560 a; Parma: 551 h; Piacenza: 560 f; *Johannes de Verona*, 558 d; Venice: 553 f; Romagna: 558 h, 560 h; Bologna: 553 m; Tuscany: 554 c; Urbino: 557 k; 'Gando' near Perugia: 560 k.

41 *Purg.*, XX, 43 ff.

42 560 k: 'Frater Gregorius de Gando prope Perusium, ordinis sancti Augustini, paciens morbum regis . . .'; 553 m: 'Clara de Bononia Crassa et Maria de Hispania, patientes morbum regium . . .' (The comma placed by the editor between Bononia and Crassa should of course be removed.)

43 Cf. Ives de St-Denis, *Histor. de France*, XXI, pp. 202, 205; Wenck, *Philipp der Schöne*, p. 67, n. 2.

44 P. Dupuy, *Histoire du differend d'entre le pape Boniface VIII et Philippe le Bel*, 1655, p. 519: 'apertaque miracula Deus infirmis, Deus per manus eius ministrat'. For the date of the memoir, cf. R. Holtzmann, *Wilhelm von Nogaret*, Fribourg, 1890, p. 200; Georges Lizerand, *Clément V et Philippe IV le Bel* (thesis, Paris), 1910, p. 209.

45 The text of Fortescue, quoted below, n. 46; medical texts, p. 68; various texts (theology, political philosophy), pp. 77 ff.

46 *De titulo Edwardi comitis Marchie*, c.X, in *The works of Sir John Fortescue . . . now first collected by* Thomas Lord Clermont—forming vol. 1 of *Sir John Fortescue, knight, his life, works and family history*, London, 1869 ('printed for private distribution'; a copy in the British Museum), p. 70*: 'virtute cujus debitae sibi unctionis per mundissimorum suarum manuum contactum labe aliquâ utpote sanguine homicidii et fame luxuriae incontaminatarum, languentes morbo regio, de quibus medici expertissimi desperarunt, usque in hodiernum diem optatam Domino conferente recipiunt sospitatem ad Dei omnipotentis laudem, de cujus gratia venit gratia sanitatum, ad videntium et assistentium fidelitatis ad ipsum regem constantiam et sui indubitatissimi tituli, Domino approbante, confirmationem'. For the continuation of the passage, see above p. 130. Cf. by the same author, another document of the same period, the *Defensio juris domus Lancastriae* (ed. Clermont, p. 508; a passage likewise published by Freind, *The History of Physick*, 5th ed., II, 1758, p. [32], and Crawfurd, *King's Evil*, p. 45 (cf. below, Book 2, Ch. II, n. 37). Fortescue lists among the royal gifts refused to queens the healing of sufferers from scrofula. This passage from the *Defensio* appears translated almost word for word in a third treatise, still in the same period: *Of the title of the House of York* (ed. Clermont, p. 498; Crawfurd, loc. cit., p. 46). For the life of Fortescue and the chronology of his works, see C. Plummer, Introduction to his edition of the treatise *On the governance of England*, Oxford, 1885.

47 The exact amount was 22⅔ grains, at least up to the eighteenth year of the reign; the grain is equivalent to 0·0648 gr. Later on the denier declined progressively to eighteen grains: E. Hawkins, *The silver coins of England*, 3rd ed. (revised R. L. Kenyon), London, 1887, p. 207.

48 The exact amount, eighty grains: R. L. Kenyon, *The gold coins of England*, London, 1884, p. 89. The weight given is for Henry VIII's reign; but it was no doubt approximately the same for Henry VII. For all that relates to the

monetary history of the royal touch under the Tudors, see Farquhar, 'Royal Charities', I.

49 Farquhar, I, p. 84. I am simplifying somewhat when I say 'the same gold piece', for the title of the coin varied at that time, and was to vary subsequently, but that is really of no importance here.

50 For the denier, see *Statute of Labourers*, of 1350, *Statutes*, I, p. 311; 'et que nul preigne en temps de sarcler ou feyns faire for que j. d. le jor'; I think *feyns faire* should be translated by *faner* (toss), because of its close association with *sarcler*, and especially because in the following items the wages for those who reap meadows are set out, and they are naturally higher : 5 d. the acre or 5d. a day. For the 'angel', see Farquhar, I, p. 73.

51 Below, Book 2, Ch. V, n. 3. Under Louis XII, by virtue of the decree of 19 November 1507, the *grand blanc*, which was worth twelve deniers of Tours, weighed a little less than 2·85 grammes; likewise under Francis I up to 1519. From 1519 to 1539 the *blanc* would make a little less than 2·66 grammes; from 1540 to 1547, the douzain (deniers of Tours) a little more than 2·68 grammes. Cf. A. Blanchet and A. Dieudonné, *Manuel de numismatique francaise*, II, pp. 308, 314.

52 The Lyons edition, 1510, in the chapter 'De scrophulis et glandulis': 'et vocantur scrophule . . . et etiam morbus regis quia reges hunc morbum curant'. Fearing that this sentence might have been introduced at a later stage, I made a point of going back to one of the ancient MSS. in the *Compendium*, MS. 173 in the Bibl. de Vendôme, which is of the thirteenth century, and the sentence is there all right (fol. 122a). As regards the date of the treatise, it can be established as follows. Speaking of eye diseases, Gilbert mentions 'collirium quod feci Bertranno filio domini H. de Jubileto' (Vendôme MS., fol. 94b, p. 137 of the Lyons edition). The family of Giblet (Djebaïl) was one of the great seignorial families in the Holy Land, whose genealogy will be found in Du Cange, *Les Familles d'Outremer*, edit., E. G. Rey (*Documents inédits*), 1869, p. 325; the person in question can be none other than Bertrand II, the son of Hugo. Bertrand took part in the 1217 crusade, and that same year appeared as witness to a deed. Hugo died in 1232. This passage was pointed out by Littré, *Histoire littéraire*, 21, p. 394. M. J. Payne, 'English Medicine in the Anglo-Norman Period', *British Medical Journal*, 1904, 2, p. 1283, rejects it as an interpolation. Nothing short of an exhaustive study of the MSS. would enable one to produce a definitive solution to the question; yet I must point out that the Vendôme MS. does contain the contentious passage. Moreover, Payne dates Gilbert's activities round about the year 1200. He accepts the tradition—though there is no testimony to it before the seventeenth century—that he was physician to the Archbishop of Canterbury, Hubert Walter. But what confidence can one place in such a late verbal testimony unsupported by any ancient documentary reference? I have not been able to see H. E. Henderson, *Gilbertus Anglicus* (published posthumously for private distribution by the Cleveland Medical Library Association, Cleveland, Ohio, 1918, referred to by Lynn Thorndike, *A History of magic and experimental science*, II, London, 1923, p. 478, n. 1; but Thorndike's note on Gilbert does not add any exact information on the problem of the date.

53 *Lilium Medicinae*, 1550 ed., pars I, p. 85; the *Lilium* was written about 1305.

54 *Collectio Salernitana*, II, Naples, 1853, p. 597; the attribution to French authors is quite probable, but not certain; cf. Gurlt, *Geschichte der Chirurgie*, I, p. 703.

55 J. L. Pagel, *Leben, Lehre und Leistungen des Heinrich von Mondeville, Theil I, Die Chirurgie des H. von M.*, Berlin 1892 (text first edited in *Archiv für klinische Chirurgie*, 40 and 41), Tract. II, *Notabilia introductoria*, p. 135: 'Et sicut praedictum est, quod Salvator noster, Dominus Jhesus Christus, officium cyrurgicum propriis manibus exercendo voluit cyrurgicos honorare, ita et eodem modo Princeps Serenissimus, Francorum rex, ipsos et eorum status honorat, qui curat scrophulas solo tactu . . . ' Cf. Tract III, doctr. II, cap. IV, p. 470. These two passages are missing in the French translation (in which the whole of the third treatise is lacking, and the prologue to the second is only present in a very summary form): *La Chirurgie de maître Henri de Mondeville*, ed. A. Bos, 2 vols, 1897–8 (Soc. des anciens textes). For Henri de Mondeville's dates, see a note in Wenck, *Philipp der Schöne*, p. 16, n. 4.

56 'La Chirurgie de maître Jehan Yperman', ed. Broeckx, *Annales académ. archéolog. Belgique*, 20, 1863, p. 259. 'Van des conincs evele sal men jou nou segghen her hebben vele lieden ghelove ane den coninc van Vranckerike dat hem God macht heeft ghegheven scrouffelen te ghenesene die loepen ende dat alle met sin begripe van der hant ende dese lieden ghenesen vele bi hore ghelove ende onder wilen ghenesen si niet'. I owe the translation of this passage to my colleague in Brussels, M. Ganshof. For Jean Yperman, see the introduction by Broeckx; he was in charge of the medical service in the Ypres army during the war against Count Louis in 1325 (p. 134). Cf. Gurlt *Geschichte der Chirurgie*, II, p. 137.

57 Tract. II, doct. I, cap. IV; latin text: *Chirurgia magna Guidonis de Gauliaco*, Lyons, 1535, p. 79; French text ed. E. Nicaise, 1890, p. 127.

58 *Praxis medica, rosa anglica dicta*, Book II, at the § entitled: 'Curatio scrophularum . . .' ed. of 1492, no place or date, p. 54 v.

59 *Breviarum Bartholomaei*, B.M. Harleian MS. 3, fol. 41, col. 1 (already quoted, Crawfurd, *King's Evil*, p. 42). I do not know why Lanfrank, who gives a chapter in his *Science of Cirurgie* (*Early English Texts*, O.S. 102, III, II, 13) to the subject of scrofula, does not refer to the healing power of kings. Perhaps he was copying an older author who made no mention of it.

60 *Compendium medicinae practicae*, lib. II, cap. V, Lyons ed., 1586, p. A 54 v. and ff.

61 As far as I know, the first doctor from outside France or England who mentioned it and appeared to believe in it was the Italian Geronimo Mercuriale, in his *De morbis puerorum*, which came out for the first time in 1583: 1588 ed., Venice, p. 35. Then another Italian, Fabrizio d'Acquapendente, one of the founders of scientific anatomy, in his *Pentateuchus*, first published in 1592 (quoted by Gurlt, *Geschichte der Chirurgie*, II, p. 451).

62 Loc. cit.: 'Finaliter oportet recurrere ad manum chirurgicam . . . et si non, vadamus ad reges'. John Mirfield uses similar expressions.

63 Loc. cit.: 'Et si ista non sufficiant, vadat ad Regem, ut ab eo tangatur atque benedicatur: quia iste vocatur morbus regius; et valet tactus nobilissimi et

serenissimi regis anglicorum. Ultimo tamen si ista non sufficiunt tradatur cirurgico.'

64 It would be quite absurd to claim to give even a very summary bibliography here of the Gregorian movement. Recent works have been conveniently summarized by J. P. Whitney, 'Gregory VII', *Eng. Historical Review*, 1919, p. 129. For the history of political doctrines during this period, the most recent comprehensive work is R. W. and A. J. Carlyle, *A history of mediaeval political theory in the West*, III and IV, Edinburgh and London, 1915 and 1922. I admit that I got very little from E. Bernheim, *Mittelalterliche Zeitanschauungen in ihrem Einfluss auf Politik und Geschichtsschreibung*, I, Tübingen, 1918; on the other hand it is always worth while referring to F. Kern, *Gottesgnadentum*.

65 *Ad Gebehardum liber*, chap. xxx (*Monumenta Germaniae, Libelli de lite*, I, p. 365: 'Neque enim populus ideo eum super se exaltat, ut liberam in se exercendae tyrannidis facultatem concedat, sed ut a tyrannide ceterorum et improbitate defendat. Atqui, cum ille, qui pro coercendis pravis, probis defendendis eligitur, pravitatem in se fovere, bonos conterere, tyrannidem, quam debuit propulsare, in subiectos ceperit ipse crudelissime exercere, nonne clarum est, merito illum a concessa dignitate cadere, populum ab eius dominio et subiectione liberum existere, cum pactum, pro quo constitutus est, constet illum prius irrupisse? . . . Ut enim de rebus vilioribus exemplum trahamus, si quis alicui digna mercede porcos suos pascendos committeret ipsumque postmodo eos non pascere, sed furari, mactare et perdere cognosceret, nonne, promissa mercede etiam sibi retenta, a porcis pascendis cum contumelia illum amoveret?' For Manegold see, among others, A. Fliche, 'Les Théories germaniques de la souveraineté à la fin du XIe siècle', *Revue historique*, 125, 1917, pp. 41 ff., and R. W. and A. J. Carlyle, op. cit.

66 P. Jaffé, *Gregorii VII registrum* (*Bibliotheca rerum Germanicarum*, II), VIII, 21, pp. 453 ff., esp. p. 457: 'Quis nesciat reges et duces ab iis habuisse principium qui, Deum ignorantes, superbia, rapinis, perfidia, homicidiis, postremo universis pene sceleribus, mundi principe, diabolo videlicet, agitante, super pares, scilicet homines, dominari caeca cupidine et intolerabili praesumptione affectarunt.' For the inferiority of the king as compared with the exorcist, p. 459: 'Meminisse etiam debet fraternitas tua: quia maior potestas exorcistae conceditur, cum spiritualis imperator ad abiciendos demones constituitur, quam alicui laicorum causa saecularis dominationis tribui possit.' For the priest, p. 460, in particular: 'Et quod maximum est in christiana religione, quis eorum valet proprio ore corpus et sanguinem Domini conficere?' The words 'spirituales imperatores ad abjiciendos daemones' are still to be found today in one of the prayers prescribed by the Roman Pontifical for the ordination of an exorcist. It is an ancient form of words: see for instance the various *ordines* collected by Dom Martene, *De antiquis ecclesiae ritibus*, Bassano ed., 1788, fol., II, pp. 30 ff. As regards the question whether Gregory VII really attributed a diabolical origin to the civil power, it has often been discussed; see particularly the interesting discussion by Canon Cauchie (*Revue d'histoire ecclésiastique*, V (1904), pp. 588–97), attempting to reconcile the different pronouncements of Gregory VII on this subject, which varied considerably, it must be admitted,

according to whether the pope had reasons for being agreeable or disagreeable to such and such a temporal sovereign. Mgr Cauchie concludes (p. 593): 'there is no contradiction in saying: (1) in actual fact, this power asserts itself in a diabolical manner; (2) in principle, and in spite of this original vice, it must be considered as willed or allowed by God'. Does not this amount to saying that Gregory VII considered that nothing in this world is done, even by the devil, without God's permission—in other words that he was not a Manichean?—a point which would be easily agreed. In short, there is no doubt that he did see something diabolic about the origin of royalty. This is likewise the meaning of the famous reply of Wazon, Bishop of Liège—a Gregorian before his time—to the Emperor Henry III about a comparison between the royal and the priestly unction, to the effect that the latter was created ad *vivificandum*, whereas the former was ad *mortificandum*: *Anselmi Gesta Episcop. Leodensium* in *Monum German.*, SS., VII, p. 229.

67 Loc. cit., p. 462: 'Namque, ut de apostolis et martyribus taceamus, quis imperatorum vel regum aeque ut beatus Martinus, Antonius et Benedictus miraculis claruit? Quis enim imperator aut rex mortuos suscitavit, leprosos mundavit, cecos illuminavit? Ecce Constantinum piae memoriae imperatorem, Theodosium et Honorium, Carolum et Lodoicum, iustitiae amatores, christianae religionis propagatores, ecclesiarum defensores, sancta quidem ecclesia laudat et veneratur; non tamen eos fulsisse tanta miraculorum gloria indicat.'

68 See, e.g., St Thomas Aquinas, *Summa Theologiae*, II, 2, q. 178, a. 2.

69 Quoted Book 1, Ch. I, n. 33.

70 Ed. Luard (Rolls Series), no. cxxiv, p. 350. It may likewise be observed that Giraldus Cambrensis, writing in the time of Philip Augustus his *De principis instructione*, in a sense so favourable to the Capetian dynasty, does not give any place in it to the royal miracle.

71 *De vita sua*, I, c. VII, ed. G. Bourgin (Collection de textes pour servir à l'étude et l'ens. de l'histoire), p. 20.

72 He was Chancellor to Archbishop Richard, who succeeded Thomas à Becket in the see of Canterbury, and his policy seems to have been very different from his predecessor's. Cf. J. Armitage Robinson, *Somerset historical essays*, 1921, p. 108.

73 It is right to add that, as far as I can see, the silence observed by authors of fictional works seems to have been prolonged beyond the moment when, as we shall presently see, the ostracism we have been speaking about ceased, even in very strict ecclesiastical circles, to surround the whole subject of the royal miracle. Not that any romantic work in the Middle Ages, as far as I know, ever used the theme of the royal touch for scrofula. Perhaps this abstinence, which is after all rather strange, is to be explained by the routine habits of the romance writers, who, as the Middle Ages drew towards an end, did little more than repeat the themes handed down from earlier ages. I hasten to point out, moreover, that my explorations on this point have less reason to claim completeness than on any other; besides, I have not found the same help for the literature of the later centuries as for the first epoch of the Middle Ages. My study of the latter, and of certain adventurous

romances, has been greatly assisted by some German dissertations which have proved most useful as a source of references. Here is a list of them: A. Euler, *Das Königtum im altfranzösischen Epos* (Ausg. u. Abh. 65), Marburg, 1886; O. Geissler, *Religion und Aberglaube in den mittelenglischen Versromanzen*, Halle, 1908; M. Hallauer, *Das wunderbare Element in den Chansons de Geste*, Basle, 1918; O. Kühn, *Medizinisches aus der altfranzösischen Dichtung* (Abh. zur Gesch. der Medizin, 8), Breslau, 1904; F. Laue, *Über Krankenbehandlung und Heilkunde in der Literatur des alten Frankreichs*, Göttingen, 1904; F. Werner, *Königtum und Lehenswesen im französischen Nationalepos*.(Roman. Forsch. 25), 1908. From a hint in Funck-Bretano, *Le Roi*, p. 177, n. 4, it might be gathered that the *Mystère de St-Remy*, preserved in a fifteenth century MS., Arsenal 3364, contains a passage relating to the touch; but this did not prove to be so: the *Mystère* only portrays the miracle of the Holy Phial.

74 One might be tempted to compare with the anonymous author, as a political theorist, the contemporary Frenchman Hugue de Fleury, whose *Tractatus de regia potestate et sacerdotali dignitate* is dedicated to Henry I of England; but in spite of the celebrated sentence in which Hugue compares the king to God the Father, and the bishop only to Christ (I, c. 3; *Monumenta Germaniae*, *Libelli de lite*, III, p. 468)—a sentence, moreover, which A. J. Carlyle (*A history of mediaeval political theory*, IV, p. 268) has shown to be no more than a bookish reminiscence—this author cannot be represented as an avowed partisan of the *regnum*. He belongs to the group which M. Luchaire, putting Hugue de Fleury side by side with Ive de Chartres, has rightly called the 'third party' in France (Lavisse, *Histoire de France*, II, 2, p. 219).

75 *Histor. de France*, 23, p. 597 c.: 'Dicebant autem aliqui qui eum visitabant quod hic erat morbus regius, id est lupus'.

76 *Histor. de France*, 23, p. 565, 26: 'morbus erat scrophularum, a quo rex Franciae tactu manuum suarum divinitus curat'. For this work and its author, see Paulin Paris, *Hist. littéraire*, 31, p. 65, and Leopold Delisle, *Mémoire sur le bienheureux Thomas de Biville*, St-Lô, 1912. In the French verse translation published by de Pontaumont, *Vie du B. Thomas Hélie de Biville*, Cherbourg, 1868, the miracles and consequently the passage we are concerned with are missing. A sermon in honour of St-Marcoul, probably of the thirteenth century, but impossible to date precisely, also uses the expression *morbus regius*: cf. below, Book 2, Ch. IV, n. 11. Du Cange, or rather the Benedictines completing du Cange's *Glossarium*, quotes in the article 'Scroellae' the following sentence, which they take from a Latin-French glossary in the Bibliothèque de St-Germain-des-Prés (I have reconstituted the text in exact conformity with the MS.): 'le Escroelle, une maladie qui vient ou col, c'est le mal le roy'. Thanks to some kind help from M. Antoine Thomas, I have been able to identify this glossary with Bibl. Nat. MS. lat. 13032; the sentence in question occurs in fol. 139 v.; this MS. is of the fourteenth century, and so considerably later than the documents referred to above. Later still are the Miracles de St-Fiacre, quoted by Carpentier in du Cange under 'Malum Regis': *AA. SS. Aug.*, VI, p. 618.

77 See above, Book 2, Ch. I, n. 11.

78 *Histor. de France*, 20, p. 20, c. xxxv: 'In tangendis infirmitatibus, quae vulgo scroalae vocantur, super quibus curandis Franciae regibus Dominus contulit gratiam singularem, pius Rex modum hunc praeter reges caeteros voluit observare. Cum enim alii reges praedecessores sui, tangendo solummodo locum morbi, verba ad hoc appropriata et consueta proferrent, quae quidem verba sancta sunt atque catholica, nec facere consuevissent aliquod signum crucis, ipse super consuetudinem aliorum hoc addidit, quod, dicendo verba super locum morbi, sanctae crucis signaculum imprimebat, ut sequens curatio virtuti crucis attribueretur potius quam regiae majestati.' The passage is reproduced by Guillaume de Nangis, ibid, p. 408.

79 Certain writers of the *ancien régime*, for example du Laurens, *De mirabili*, p. 17, and Raulin, *Panegyre*, p. 179, quote as a kind of semi-official recognition of the wonder-working gift attributed to the French kings a phrase from the Bull for the canonization of St-Louis, 'strumis beneficium liberationis impendit'; but this phrase (*Histor. de France*, 23, p. 159 d) is only applied, it stands to reason, to the miracles performed by the saint's body after the death of the king. No one could have ranked the healing of scrofula, a hereditary privilege of the French kings, among the proofs of Louis IX's sanctity, and there was no question of this in the Bull. It is natural enough, moreover, that people should have asked of St-Louis, after his death, among other healing miracles, that he should relieve an illness over which he had already had some power while alive. His relics have often been thought to have special virtue against the scrofula; cf. Jacobus Valdesius, *De dignitate regum regnorumque Hispaniae*, Granada, 1602 (relics at Poblet in Catalonia), and Cabanès, *Remèdes d'autrefois*, p. 40, n. 2.

80 Above, Book 2, Ch. I, n. 44.

81 M. Goldast, *Monarchia S. Romani Imperii*, Hanover, 1612, I, p. 49. The Latin original, ibid., II (published Amsterdam, 1631), p. 102; but I will quote directly from one of the manuscripts, Arch. Nat. JJ. 28, fol. 250: 'Secundo, hoc idem probant aperta miracula, universo orbi manifeste notoria et notorie manifesta. Unde Dominus Rex, de iusto titulo suo respondens, dicere potest illud Euangelicum quod respondit Dominus Ihesus contra calumpnias Judeorum: '*Si mihi non uultis credere, operibus credite.*' Sicut enim hereditario iure succedit patri filius in adoptionem regni, sic quasi hereditario iure succedit, faciente Deo, alter alteri in simili potestate huiusmodi miraculi faciendi.' On the work itself, see Richard Scholz, *Die Publizistik zur Zeit Philipps des Schönen und Bonifaz VIII* (*Kirchenrechtliche Abhandl. hgg. von U. Stutz*, 6–8), pp. 224 ff. Quite recently M. P. Fournier, in the *Bulletin du Jubilé*, pub. by the Comité français catholique pour la célébration du sixième centenaire de la mort de Dante Alighieri, p. 172 n. 1, has suggested, though without insisting upon it, the possibility that the *Quaestio* might well be by Plaisians. It is in fact unlikely that the author's anonymity will ever be removed.

82 *Histor. de France*, 22, p. 175, v. 198 ff.: 'Diex di ciel, li souverains peres,—Si grant bonne aventure donne—A quiconques a la couronne—De la terre ramenteue,—Qu'il fait, puis qu'il l'a receue—Tout son vivant miracles beles;—Car il guerist des escroeles—Tant seulement par y touchier,—Sans emplastres dessus couchier,—Ce qu'autres roys ne puent faire.'

83 Above, Book 2, Ch. I, n. 7.

84 Matthew 21:9.

85 Cf. Paul Fournier, 'La Monarchia de Dante et l'opinion française', Comité français catholique pour la célébration du sixième centenaire de la mort de Dante Alighieri, *Bulletin*, 1921, pp. 155 ff.

86 Bibl. Nat. lat. 16495, fol. 96 d. ff.; the sermon is in honour of St Nicolas, but the saint only makes a somewhat distant appearance in it. The debatable sentence is as follows: 'Quilibet heres Francie, ex quo inunctus et coronatus, habet specialem gratiam et virtutem a Deo quod tactu manus suae curat infirmos: propter quod habentes infirmitatem regiam veniunt ad regem de multis locis et terris diversis'; it is reproduced in the article by N. Valois on Guillaume de Sauqueville, *Histoire littéraire*, 34, pp. 298 ff., from which I have taken the information given above about the author and the date of the sermons.

87 There is a very plentiful literature on the subject of Tolomeo of Lucca, but no really exhaustive work. The majority of the useful works have been indicated and used by G. Mollat, *Étude critique sur les Vitae Paparum Avenionensium d'Étienne Baluze*, 1917, pp. 1 ff.; to which should be added the recent article by Martin Grabmann, 'La scuola tomistica italiana', *Rivista di filosofia neo-scolastica*, 15, 1923, of which IV is devoted to Tolomeo. It is still worth while referring to the essay by Karl Krüger, *Des Ptolomäus Lucensis Leben und Werke*, Göttingen, 1874; see likewise the introduction provided by M. Krammer to the edition quoted below, n. 88. For the rest, it will be sufficient to refer the reader to the references given by Mollat. The authors who have treated Tolomeo's political ideas, e.g. Albert Bazaillas, 'Étude sur le *De regimine principum*', *Rec. Académ. Sciences Belles Lettres et Arts de Tarn et Garonne*, 2nd series, 8, 1892, particularly pp. 136-43, and Jacques Zeiller, *L'Idée de l'État dans saint Thomas d'Aquin*, 1910, p. 161, do not seem to me generally to have paid enough attention to his relations with the Angevin party. For the relations of the Luccans with the House of Angevin, cf. Krammer, loc. cit., pp. xvi-xvii. Tolomeo calls Charles of Anjou 'rege nostro Karolo' in the *De regimine* IV, 8, and 'dominus noster rex Karolus' in the *Determinatio* (below, n. 88). In the *De regimine*, IV, 8, he insists on the perfect assimilation of the French with the native inhabitants in the kingdoms of Naples. Finally, the *Determinatio* has as its whole object the defence of Charles of Anjou's rights to be Papal Vicar of Tuscany, against Rudolf of Hapsburg and Pope Martin IV himself; see on this subject, besides the introduction to Krammer's edition, F. Kern, 'Die Reichsgewalt des deutschen Königs nach dem Interregnum', *Histor. Zeitschrift*, 106, 1911, pp. 71-4. For the episode cf. 1315, R. Davidsohn, *Forschungen zur Geschichte von Florenz*, 4, Berlin, 1908, p. 368.

88 Mario Krammer (ed.), Hanover and Leipzig, 1909 (*Fontes iuris germanici antiqui*), p. 39, c.xviii: 'Hoc etiam apparet in modernis principibus viris catolicis et ecclesiasticis, quod ex speciali divina influentia super eos, ex ampliori participatione Entis, singuliorem habent virtutem super populum egritudine laborantem, ut sunt reges Francie, dominus noster rex Karolus, et de rege Anglie fertur'. Cf. H. Grauert, 'Aus der kirchenpolitischen Literatur des 14. Jahrhunderts', *Histor. Jahrbuch*, 29, 1908, esp. pp. 502, 519.

Grauert thought the treaty was drawn up in 1300; the *rex Karolus* would then have been not Charles of Anjou, but his son Charles II; I prefer to hold to the date fixed by Krammer. There can no longer be any doubt that Tolomeo was the author of the *Determinatio* since Martin Grabmann, *Neues Archiv*, 37, 1912, p. 818, has discovered in another work by our author— the *Exaemeron*—a reference to this *libellus sive tractatus de iurisdictione Imperii et Summi Pontificis.*

89 *De regimine principum ad regem Cypri*, II, chap. 16; *Sancti Thomae Aquinatis . . . opera omnia*, Parma, 1864, p. 250, col. 1 and 2: 'Cujus sanctitatis etiam argumentem assumimus ex gestis Francorum de beati Remigii super Clodoveum regem primum Christianum inter reges Francorum, et delatione olei desuper per columbam; quo rex praefatus fuit inunctus et inumguntur posteri, signis et portentis ac variis curis apparentibus in eis ex unctione praedicta'. For the *De regimine*, see finally the excellent work by Martin Grabmann, *Die echten Schriften des hl. Thomas von Aquin*, Munich, 1920 (*Beitrage zur Gesch. der Philosophie des Mittelalters*, 22, 1–2), pp. 216 ff. The attribution of the continuation—which is certainly not by St Thomas—to Tolomeo is, if not certain, at least very probable; and I would add that when the passage referring to the royal miracle is put side by side with the more developed passage in the *Determinatio*, it seems to me to add another—and very strong—argument in favour of this thesis. The date of the continuation's composition is disputed; I would readily agree with the conclusions of A. Busson, *Sitzungsber. der phil.-hist. Klasse der k. Akademie Wien*, 88, 1877, p. 723.

90 For example Meurier, *De sacris unctionibus*, p. 261; Mauclerc, *De monarchia divina*, col. 1567; du Peyrat, *Histoire ecclésiastique de la Cour*, p. 806; Oroux, *Histoire ecclésiastique de la Cour*, I, p. 180.

91 Original in the archives of Rheims, metropolitan chapter section, Vauclerc, file 1, no. 4; ed. Dom Marlot, *Historia ecclesie Remensis*, II, p. 660 (French edition under the title *Histoire de la ville de Reims*, 4, Rheims, 1846, p. 631), and *Le Théâtre d'honneur*, p. 757 (partly). This chapter appears to have been unknown to E. Dupont, who in the *Notices et documents publiés par la Soc. de l'Hist. de France à l'occasion du cinquantième anniversaire de sa fondation*, 1884, pp. 187–218, has drawn up a list of charters 'with portraits of the grantor'. It is likewise lacking in the list of charters, the initials of which provide 'portraits' of Charles V, drawn up by L. Delisle, *Recherches sur la librairie de Charles V*, I, 1907, p. 61. I quote from the original: 'quando in sancta egregie civitatis Remensis ecclesia a Clodoveo, tunc Francorum rege, audita est gloriosissimi confessoris beati Remigii eiusdem clare urbis episcopi, predicacio, cui, dum ibidem prefatum regem cum suo populo baptizaret, Spiritus Sanctus seu angelus Dei in columbe specie, de Celo descendens, apparuit, portans et ministrans sibi ampulam sancti chrismatis liquore refertam de quo ipse Rex et omnes deinceps Francorum reges predecessores nostri in eorum et nos eciam in nostra consecracione et coronacione, Deo propicio, suscepimus unctionem, per quam ipsis regibus, diuina operante clemencia, virtus infunditur et gracia qua solo contactu manuum infirmos servant ab egritudine scrofularum, quod in personis innumeris per facti evidenciam constat esse probatum'.

92 Latin edition: Goldast, *Monarchia imperii*, I, Book I, chaps. 172, 173, pp. 128–9; French edition: J. L. Brunet, *Traitez des droictz et libertez de l'église gallicane*, fol. 1731, II, book I, chaps. 79, 80, pp. 81–2. The author of the *Songe du Verger*, moreover, reproduces Occam more or less textually (cf. below n. 104), as has been shown by Carl Müller *Zeitschrift für Kirchenrecht*, 14, 1879, p. 142, but with a not unimportant modification, to which we shall return later (see above, p. 129).

93 The 1531 ed., Paris, fol. a III v. After recalling unction and the miracle of the Holy Phial, Raoul addresses Charles V directly: 'Et ne tiengne vous ne autre que celle consecracion soit sans tres grant digne et noble mistere car par icelle voz devanciers et vous avez telle vertu et puissance qui vous est donnée et attribuée de dieu que vous faictes miracles en vostre vie telles, si grandes et si apertes que vous garissiez d'une tres horrible maladie qui s'appelle les escroelles de laquelle nul autre prince terrien ne peut garir fors vous'. This passage was reproduced by Guillebert de Metz in his *Description de Paris*, composed soon after 1434; Leroux de Lincy and L. M. Tisserand, *Paris et ses historiens* (*Hist. génér. de Paris*), 1867, p. 148.

94 C. E. Bulaeus (du Boulay), *Historia Universitatis Parisiensis*, Paris, 1668, 4, p. 408: 'ex sanctissima unctione spirituali, et divina, non humana, qua inungitur Rex ipse, propter quam sanctificatus est . . . et exinde curat morbos in signum sanctissimae unctionis'. For the author of this discourse, and the circumstances in which it was delivered, see R. Delachenal, *Histoire de Charles V*, 3, 1916, pp. 517 ff. (esp. 518, n. 5).

95 'Le Roi très chrétien', in *La France chrétienne dans l'histoire, ouvrage publié . . . sous la direction du R. P. Baudrillart*, 1896, pp. 317 ff. To the texts quoted by M. Valois may be added Jean Golein, in his treatise on consecration (below, Appendix IV, p. 276), and a passage in the little treatise by Étienne de Conty on French royalty. This is very little later than Charles V (cf. above, Book 2, Ch. I, n. 5), and is a faithful reflection of the theories current in the royal circle: Bibl. Nat. lat. 11730, fol. 32 v., col. 1: 'Romani pontifices omnes semper scripserunt et scribunt cotidie regi Francie *cristianissimo* (*sic*), quasi suppellativo in fide catholica, sed aliis regibus omnibus et principibus scribunt: tali regi *christiano*, in simplici positivo'. Valois has a clear understanding of all the work of propaganda that went on round Charles V: 'The throne was now surrounded by clerics who were skilled in discovering in the past the facts that were most calculated to exalt the prestige of royalty . . . Who were readier than they to affirm the sacred character of the monarchy? Who were readier to speak of the Holy Phial, or recall the celestial origin of the fleur-de-lis?' (p. 323).

96 Above, p. 134 and 136.

97 Léopold Delisle, *Recherches sur la librairie de Charles V*, II. *Inventaire général des livres ayant appartenu aux rois Charles V and Charles VI*, nos. 227–33, 226 and 59.

98 Above, Appendix IV, p. 282.

99 Delachenal, *Histoire de Charles V*, II, p. 369: 'Charles V, even before he became king, had . . . a very clear awareness of the power of public opinion'. For the movement against the nobility, a certain number of characteristic examples will be found brought together in this same book, I,

pp. 395 ff. It would not be very difficult to add others.

100 For the text of the preceding, I need only refer to Appendix IV, where the reader will find an analysis and long extracts from Jean Golein's treatise. It will be noted (p. 282) that Raoul de Presles is very definitely—though courteously—criticized.

101 See above, Book 2, Ch. I, n. 5. To these fifteenth-century authors who spoke of the royal touch may be added Nicolas de Larisvilla, in 'a treatise . . . on the dedication of the Church of St-Remy . . . in the year 1460', quoted by Marlot, *Le Théâtre d'honneur*, p. 758.

102 In front of Pius II, at Mantua, on 30 November 1459, d'Achery, *Spicilegium*, 1723, 3, p. 821, col. 2; cf. du Fresne de Beaucourt, *Histoire de Charles VII*, 6, p. 256. Before Sixtus IV, in 1478, de Maulde, *La Diplomatie au temps de Machiavel*, p. 60, n. 2; cf. J. Comblet, *Louis XI et le Saint Siège* (thesis, Nancy) 1903, p. 170. The first text expressly mentions the healing of scrofula; the second, 'miracles' accomplished by kings, without further details.

103 Arch. Nat. X 1 A.4834, fol. 141 (5 February 1493): 'Pareillement le roy n'est pas pur lay *quia non solum coronatur et inungitur, sicut ceteri, ymo consecratur;* y a plus, car, comme dit Jehan André in N(ovel)la *in* D(ecretales), *c*, licet, *ad solum tactum dicitur sanare languidos et egrotos* et par ce ne se fault esmerveiller s'il a droit de regale'. For the law suit cf. ibid., fol. 122 v. and the *Gallia Christiana*, 7, col. 155–6.

104 *Octo quaestiones super potestate ac dignitate papali*, quaest. V. cap. vii–ix; Goldast, *Monarchia S. Romani Imperii*, II, p. 372. (For the date of this work, see A. G. Little, *The Grey Friars in Oxford*, Oxford, 1892, p. 233.) The question debated is as follows: 'an rex hereditarie succedens ex hoc quod a persona ecclesiastica inungitur et consecratur et coronatur, gratiam consequatur doni spiritualis'. Among the reasons put forward in favour of an affirmative opinion is the following: 'Naturalis curatio aegritudinis corporalis est gratia Dei spiritualis. Quibusdam autem regibus, scilicet Franciae et Angliae, sicut fertur, per unctionem regalem confertur potestas curandi et sanandi specialiter scrophulas patientes. Ergo per huiusmodi unctionem rex consequitur gratiam doni spiritualis.' In conformity with the rules of scholastic discussion, Occam then gives the reasons for a negative conclusion, among which is the following: 'Ad secundum motivum respondetur, quod si reges Angliae et Franciae habent gratiam curandi de scrophulis, non habent potestatem propter unctionem regalem: quia multi alii reges, quamvis inunguntur, huiusmodi gratia non decorantur; sed sunt digni huiusmodi gratia propter aliam causam, que nec licet nec potest ab homine indicari'. Since the affirmative opinion wins the day in the subsequent development (chap. 10), there can be no doubt that this was Occam's own opinion. But it must be recognized that throughout this work, which is a tissue of propositions, counter-propositions, replies, counter-replies, etc., the author's own thought is extremely difficult to follow. One can well understand the horror inspired in the minds of men of the Renaissance period by Occam's methods of argumentation. The author of the *Songe du Verger* was inspired by Occam; cf. above, Book 2, Ch. I, n. 92, and p. 129.

105 'Collirium super hereses novas' in A. Scholz, *Unbekannte kirchenpolitische*

Streitschriften aus der Zeit Ludwigs des Bayern, Part II, Rome, 1914 (Bibl. des Kgl. Preuss. Instit. in Rom, 10), p. 509: 'Nec dicat hereticus quod reges Francie et Anglie gratiam curationis habere consueverant, quia hoc apocrifum enim vel sompnium . . . Item constat quod hec virtus curationis non est virtus corporis sed anime . . . sicut nec regnum, quod institutum est ad bene regendum, datur sanguini, sed vite . . .' For Alvarez and his works, see R. Scholz, *Unbekannte Streitschriften*, I (Bibliothek . . . Rom, 9) 1911, pp. 197 ff. (with bibliographical references). Alvarez did not always adopt the same attitude to the royal miracle: cf. above, p. 87.

106 Book VI. I quote from the text given by J. Quicherat, *Procès . . . de Jeanne d'Arc* (Soc. de l'hist. de France), 4, pp. 514–15 (for the pilgrimage of Charles VII to Corbeny, to which this passage alludes, see above, p. 160): 'Mos enim Franciae regibus est, die quae coronationem sequitur, templum quoddam peregrinando petere, cui sanctus *Marchoul* praesidet, atque ibi aegrotos curare. Miraculum Galli vulgaverunt, morbum quemdam humano in gutture nasci, qui solo regis tactu et arcanis quibusdam curetur verbis; idque post coronationem in hoc templo fieri . . . quarta die peregrinatio facta est, in qua de curatione morborum nihil satis compertum habeo, quamvis Gallici omnia illa credant fieri miraculose.'

107 Above, Book 2, Ch. I, n. 20.

108 Joannis Andreae, *J.C. Bononiensis, In sextum Decretalium librum Novella Commentaria*, Venice, 1581, lib. III, tit. IV, *De praebendis et dignitatibus*, cap. ii, fol. 94 v.; an exposition of the reasons why, as the French maintain, the kings of France and England have certain rights of ecclesiastical collation: 'Item ad solum manus tactum certos infirmos sanare dicuntur'. J. André died in 1348; cf. above, n. 102. Felino Sandei (1444–1503), *Commentaria in V libros Decretalium*, Basle, 1567, lib. II, tit. XX, cap. lii, p. 823: the author explains that for a saint to be canonized, not only must his miracles be proved, but 'sanctimonia vitae': 'quia multi non sancti faciunt miracula, aut vi verborum, ut consecratio eucharistiae, aut vi parentelae, ut Rex Franciae, vel illi de domo sancti Pauli arte magica'. For the 'family' of St Paul, Italian magicians who claimed to be descended from the apostle to the Gentiles, see above, p. 171 and Book 2, Ch. IV, n. 145. For Sandei's theory, cf. also below, pp. 235–6.

109 Above, Introduction, n. 3.

110 De Maulde, *Les Origines de la Révolution française*, pp. 26–7 (27 December 1478).

111 Elphinstone, the future Bishop of Aberdeen, was sent by James III in 1479 to Louis XI. His speech is reproduced (perhaps with some retouching) by Hector Boetius, *Murthlacencium et Aberdonensium episcoporum vitae*, ed. J. Moir (New Spalding Club), Aberdeen, 1894, p. 73 (the first edition of the *Lives* is dated 1522).

112 See above Appendix II, no. 1 (for the miniature representing the miracle by St Edward), and no. 2 (for the Mont St-Michel window).

113 *Histor. de France*, 22, p. 175, lines 204 ff.: cf. above, Book 2, Ch. I, n. 82. In the same way Jean Golein (see p. 280) considers the French king to possess 'ceste prerogative sur touz autres roys quels qu'ils soient'; the king of England was at that time the enemy.

114 Text quoted above, Book 2, Ch. I, n. 53. In the passage reproduced above, note 20, Thomas Bradwardine likewise recognizes, although an Englishman, the miraculous power of the French dynasty; but writing in 1344, he no doubt considered his master, Edward III, as the legitimate heir of the Capetians, as well as of the Plantagenets—which detracts somewhat from his impartiality.

115 P.H.B.P. (Jérôme Bignon), *De l'Excellence des roys et du royaume de France*, 1610, p. 510; Besian Arroy, *Questions décidées*, 1634, pp. 40–1. There is no mention of this tradition—evidently altogether spurious—in the work of a Danish scholar, C. Barfoed, on the healing of illnesses by the touch: *Haands-Paalaeggelse*, Copenhagen, 1914.

116 The power of healing jaundice is recognized as belonging to the kings of Hungary by the Jesuit Melchior Inchofer, *Annales ecclesiastici regni Hungariae*, 1797 ed. III, Presburg, pp. 288–9 (as well as the power of healing— like the English kings(?)—poisonous bites); the first edition came out in 1644. There is testimony to the same tradition in France in du Laurens, *De mirabili*, p. 31; Mathieu, *Histoire de Louis XI*, p. 472 (followed by du Peyrat, *Histoire ecclésiastique*, p. 793; Balthasar de Riez, *L'Incomparable piété des tres chrestiens rois de France*, 1672, 2, pp. 151–2); and on Spanish soil by Armacanus (Jansenius), *Mars Gallicus*, p. 69; it is obvious, moreover, that these authors are copying from one another. The passage quoted can be read in *Bibliothèque raisonée*, 16, 1 (Amsterdam, 1736), p. 153 (review by Mathias Bel, *Notitia Hungariae novae*). For the word *morbus regius*, see above, Book 1, Ch. II, n. 16.

117 XXIV, 9, ed. Förstemann, 3, pp. 15–16; 'Aber Wunder ist es (dass ich dieses auch sage, dass ich gewiss bericht bin), dass grosser Fürsten und Herrn Arznei, die sie selbs geben und appliciren, kräftig und heilsam sind, sonst nichts wirkte, wenns ein Medicus gäbe. Also höre ich, dass beide Kurfürsten zu Sachsen etc., Herzog Friedrich und Herzog Johanns, haben ein Augenwasser, das hilft, wem sie es geben, es komme die Ursach der Augenweh aus Hitze oder aus Kälte. Ein Medicus dürfte es nicht wagen noch geben. Also in Theologia, da den Leuten geistlich gerathen wird, hat ein Prediger mehr Gnade, betrübte Gewissen zu trösten und lehren, denn ein ander.' The edition of the *Tischreden* by Förstemann reproduces the edition *princeps* given by Aurifaber to Eisleben in 1566. Now as is well known, Aurifaber's text is always a little subject to caution. Unfortunately in the critical edition of his works, called the Weimar edition, the *Tischreden* are still incomplete; and the absence of an index makes any research work almost impossible in the volumes that have already come out.

118 E. S. Cyprianus, *Catalogus codicum manuscriptorum bibliothecae Gothanae*, 1714, p. 22, nos. lxxii–lxxiv.

119 Felicis Fabri *Monachi Ulmensis Historiae Suevorum*, lib. I, c. xv, in Goldast, *Rerum Suevicarum Scriptores*, Ulm, 1727, p. 60: 'Legimus enim in Chronicis Comitum de Habspurg, quod tantum donum gratis datum habeant, ut quicunque strumosus aut gutture globosus de manu alicuius Comitis de Habspurg potum acceperit, mox sanum, aptum et gracile guttur reportabit quod sepe visum est in valle Albrechztaal in Alsatia superiori, in qua sunt homines strumosi naturaliter, qui passim praedicto modo sanabantur, dum

vallis adhuc esset illorum Comitum vel Austriae Ducum. Insuper notorium est, et sepe probatum, quod dum quis balbutiens est, vel impeditioris linguae, si ab uno Principe de praemissis sine alio quocunque suffragio osculum acceperit, officium loquendi disertissime aetati suae congruum mox patenter obtinebit.' For the author, see Max Haeussler, *Felix Fabri aus Ulm und seine Stellung zum geistlichen Leben seiner Zeit* (*Beiträge zur Kulturgeschichte des Mittelalters*, 15), 1914.

120 O. Redlich, *Rudolf von Habsburg*, Innsbruck, 1903, p. 87; T. Nartz, *Le Val de Villé*, Strasbourg, 1887, p. 17; *Das Reichsland Elsass-Lothringen*, 3, pp. 1191–2.

121 The tradition according to which the Hapsburgs possessed the power to heal the scrofulous—denied by Camerarius in *Operae horarum subcisivarum*, 1650, p. 145—recurs in Armacanus [Jansenius], *Mars Gallicus*, 1636, p. 69; and with the Jesuit Melchior Inchofer, *Annales ecclesiastici regni Hungariae*, ed. 1797, 3, p. 288. Raulin, *Panégyre*, p. 176, thinks they 'have cured men of goitres or swollen throats'.

122 *Speculum regum*, ed. R. Scholz, *Unbekannte kirchenpolitische Streitschriften*, 2, p. 517: 'Reges Francie et Anglie habere dicuntur virtutem; et reges devoti Yspanie, a quibus descendis, habere dicuntur virtutem super energuminos et super quibusdam egritudinibus laborantes, sicut vidi, cum essem puer, in avo tuo, inclito domino rege Sancio, qui me nutriebat, quod a muliere demoniaca ipsum vituperante tenentem pedem super guttur eius et legentem in quodam libelo ab ea demonem expulsit et curatam reliquit'.

123 It would take too long, and be tedious to the reader, to quote all the seventeenth-century authors who mentioned the tradition relating to the healing of demoniacs by the kings of Castile. It will be enough to refer to Gutierrez, *Opusculum de Fascino*, 1653, p. 153 and to Gaspar a Reies, *Elysius*, 1670, pp. 162, 342, which both provide an abundance of references. The same tradition crops up in France in Albon, *De la Maiesté royalle*, Lyon, 1575, p. 29 v., in du Laurens, *De mirabili*, p. 31, and in various other authors who were obviously inspired by this last writer.

124 Gutierrez, *Opusculum de fascino*, 1653, p. 155–6: 'vana eius est arguties, ab actu negative ad potentiam, quasi diceret Deus non produxit creaturas possibiles, imo non producet, ergo non est illarum productiuus, haec illatio undique falsa est, sed Reges nostri humili majestate ducti illius virtutis exercitio non intendunt, omne huiuscemodi ius sacris Sacerdotibus relinquentes. Tum quia minus, quam exteri, his nouitatibus Hispani delectamur.' I only know dom Sebastien de Soto's work *De monialium clausura licite reseranda ob morbos* through the refutation contained in Gutierrez.

125 The above-mentioned enquiry contained in the memoir of a Canon of Majorca, Antoni de Busquets, has been studied by M. Aguilo in the *Calendari Català pera l'any 1902*, a publication directed by M. Joan B. Batle. I have unfortunately not been able to procure this work, and I only know the translation of the passage relating to the scrofula given by M. Batista y Roca, *Notes and Queries*, 1917, p. 481. For posthumous miracles, and the cult of don Carlos, see G. Desdevises du Désert, *Don Carlos d'Aragon, prince de Viane*, 1889, pp. 396 ff. A letter from Louis XI in the edition of the Société de l'histoire de France, 2, no. XIII. There is an interesting testimony

to the relics of Poblet in the account given by a French traveller, Barthélemy Joly when he visited the monastery in 1604, *Revue hispanique*, 20, 1909, p. 500. According to J. Valdesius, *De dignitate regum regnorumque Hispaniae*, 1602, at Poblet people venerated an arm of St-Louis which was also supposed to heal the scrofula. Was there perhaps some confusion between the powers attributed to these two relics?

126 For example, J. Valdesius, *De dignitate regum regnorumque Hispaniae*, Granada, 1602, p. 140; Armacanus (Jansenius), *Mars Gallicus*, p. 69; Gaspar a Reies, *Elysius*, p. 275 (which all attribute an Aragonese origin to this power); Gutierrez, *Opusculum de fascino*, p. 153. These authors all refer to P. A. Beuter, *Cronica generale d'Hispagna*. I have not been any more successful than M. Batista in finding the passage this writer had in mind.

127 Above, p. 179.

128 Above, p. 76.

BOOK 2   CHAPTER II   *The second miracle of English royalty*

1 *Liber Quotidianus contrarotulatoris garderobae* (Soc. of Antiquaries of London), London, 1787, Glossary, p. 365; Hubert Hall, *The antiquities and curiosities of the Exchequer*, 2nd ed., London, 1898, p. 43.

2 Migne, *P.L.*, vol. 147, col. 51: 'Adoratio omnium ita fiat, ut uniuscuiusque venter in terra haereat; dum enim juxta Augustinum in psalmo XLIII genuflectitur, adhuc restat quod humilietur; qui autem sic humiliatur et totus in terra haereat, nihil in eo amplius humilitatis restat.' For this rite see J. D. Chambers, *Divine worship in England in the thirteenth and fourteenth centuries*, London, 1877, Appendix, p. 31, and E. K. Chambers, *The Mediaeval Stage*, 2, p. 17, n. 3 (bibliography).

3 Lat. 5716, fol. 63; reproduced in Joinville, ed. N. de Wailly, 1874, p. 2.

4 J. A. H. Murray, *A New English Dictionary*, under the word 'Creep' (the oldest documentary evidence about the year 1200).

5 Household Ordinance of York, June 1323: the best edition in T. F. Tout, *The place of the reign of Edward II in English History*, Manchester, 1914, p. 317: 'Item le roi doit offrer de certein le jour de graunde venderdy a crouce Vs., queux il est acustumez recivre divers lui a le mene le chapeleyne, a faire ent anulx a doner pur medicine as divers gentz, et a rementre autre Vs.' For the accounts, which give us the best description of the rite, see above, p. 250. Cf. Murray, loc. cit., under 'cramp-ring'.

6 Jacobus Valdesius, *De dignitate regum regnorumque Hispaniae*, Granada, 1602, p. 140.

7 Twysden, *Historiae anglicanae scriptores*, X, col. 409; Migne, *P.L.*, vol. 195, col. 769.

8 *Analecta Bollandiana*, 1923, pp. 58 ff.

9 A certain number of works of art have been indicated by John Dart, *Westmonasterium*, I, London, fol. 1742, p. 51, and by Waterton, 'On a remarkable incident', pp. 105 ff. (the miniature of the thirteenth century reproduced by Waterton opp. p. 103 has also been reproduced more recently by Hubert Hall, *Court Life under the Plantagenets*, London, 1902, pl. VII).

Without making any claim to completeness, we can add to their list: (1) a stained glass window in the church at Ludlow, (mentioned by W. Jones, *Finger-Lore*, p. 118, n. 1); (2) a china tile in the Chapter House of Westminster Abbey, reproduced by Kunz, *Rings for the finger*, p. 342; (3) two tapestries from the early thirteenth century (?), now lost, made for Westminster Abbey (Notes and documents relating to Westminster Abbey, no. 2: *The history of Westminster Abbey by John Flete*, ed. J. A. Robinson, Cambridge, 1909, pp. 28-9; (4) in France, a thirteenth-century stained glass window in Amiens Cathedral (G. Durand, *Monographie de la cathédrale d'Amiens*, I, p. 550). There is in the library of Cambridge University, under the classification Ee III 59, a thirteenth-century MS. containing a poem in French, the *Estoire de Seint Aedward le Rei*, dedicated by its author to Queen Eleanor, the wife of Henry III. Three miniatures, already referred to by Waterton and summarily described by Luard, *Lives of Edward the Confessor*, p. 16, are devoted to the legend of the ring. Another, from the same MS., reproduced by Crawfurd in 'Cramp-rings', pl. 39, represents the sick persons approaching the saint's reliquary. On the reliquary are two statuettes, one of the king holding the ring, and one of St John as a pilgrim. I don't know whether this little painting can be considered as an exact representation of the reliquary given by Henry III to Westminster and melted down under Henry VIII. For other works of art that are now lost, devoted to the same legend, see also the following note.

10 Order of Henry III: John Stow, *A survey of the Cities of London and Westminster*, I, London, 1720, p. 69. For Edward II, Dart, loc. cit.

11 This at least is what John Flete affirms in his *History of Westminster Abbey*, ed. J. A. Robinson (Notes and Documents relating to Westminster Abbey, 2), 71. True, Flete is writing rather late in time; he was a monk at Westminster from 1420 to 1425, but the tradition he echoes has nothing at all improbable about it. It agrees with the evidence of Osbert of Clare, who, writing in 1139, noted that Edward was buried with his ring: *Analecta Bollandiana* 1923, p. 122, line 1.

12 *Mirk's Festial*, ed. T. Erbe (Early English Text Society, Extra Series, 96), p. 149: 'Then whoso lust to have this preuet sothe, go he to Westminstyr; and ther he may se the same ryng that was seuen yere yn paradys'. For the author, see the most recent work, Gordon Hall Gerould, *Saints' Legends*, Boston and New York, 1916, pp. 184 ff.

13 Polydorus Virgilius, *Historia Anglica*, in 8 books, Leyden ed., 1651, p. 187; the same theory is met in the seventeenth century in Richard Smith, *Florum historiae ecclesiasticae gentis Anglorum libri septem*, 1654, p. 230; and in Nicolas Harpsfield, *Historia Anglorum ecclesiastica*, Douai, 1612, p. 219, quoted by Crawfurd, 'Cramp-rings', p. 179. Modern historians have thought they saw a kind of confirmation of it in one of the popular names for epilepsy, known in the Middle Ages, for reasons we cannot discover, as the mal-St-Jean (Laurence Joubert, *La Premiere et Seconde Partie des erreurs populaires touchant la medicine*, 1587, 2nd part, p. 162; Guillaume du Val *Historia monogramma*, 1643, p. 24; H. Günter, *Legenden-Studien*, Cologne, 1906, p. 124, n. 1; M. Höfler, *Deutsches Krankheitsnamenbuch*, Munich, 1899, under the words 'Krankheit', 'Sucht', 'Tanz'). But why was epilepsy given this

name in the first place? And which St John gave it this name? We are really in complete ignorance, though we are well aware that sometimes St John the Evangelist, and sometimes John the Baptist, were invoked against the disease. At Amiens, John the Baptist's head, kept in the Cathedral since 1206, was an object of pilgrimage much visited by the epileptic; cf. O. Thorel, 'Le Mal Monseigneur Saint-Jean Baptiste au XVIᵉ siècle à Amiens' (*Bullet. trimestriel Soc. antiquaires Picardie*), 1922, p. 474. According to Antoine Mizauld (*Memorabilium . . . Centuriae IX*, Cologne, 1572, *cent.* V, 11), St John's Day in the summer—the festival of John the *Baptist*—was particularly favourable for the healing of epileptics. Perhaps, as Günter suggests, loc. cit., the word mal-St-Jean originated from a comparison in the common mind between the disordered gestures of epileptics and the ritual dances of St John the Baptist's Day. Later on, the very word suggested the idea of attributing to the saint, whose label the illness bore, a special power of healing it. Then, by a perfectly natural mistake, the virtues ascribed to the Baptist were transferred to the Apostle who bore the same name—an example of the fairly frequent confusion between saints of the same name. It was in this way that St Hubert of Bretigny ended, by analogy with St Hubert of Liège, by also being considered a healer of rabies (H. Gaidoz, *La Rage et St Hubert*, Bibliotheca mythica, 1887, p. 173). All this, of course, can be no more than conjecture, and this little hagiological problem remains far from clear. But after all, its solution is of no great importance to us here. The comparison between the popular name for epilepsy and the episode in the legend of the Confessor which brings St John into the picture does not appear to have been made before the nineteenth century (cf. Waterton, 'On a remarkable incident', p. 107, where it appears very tentatively, and more boldly in Crawfurd, 'Cramp-rings', p. 166); but it should not be viewed as more than an ingenious theory held by over-erudite scholars, and by no means a popular idea.

14 For the magical and medical power of the rings, cf. besides the works of C. F. Kunz and W. Jones quoted in the Bibliography, V: *Archaeologia*, 21, 1827, pp. 119 ff.; *Archaeological Journal*, 3, 1846, p. 357; 4, 1847, p. 78; *Notes and Queries*, 4th Series, 6, 1870, p. 394; 8th Series, 9, 1896, p. 357 and 10, 1896, p. 10; Pettigrew, *On superstitions connected with the history and practice of medicine*, p. 61; O. Geissler, *Religion und Aberglaube in den mittelenglischen Versromanzen*, pp. 67 ff.

15 *Procès de condamnation*, ed. P. Champion, I, 1920, p. 13 (interrogation of 1 March): 'Item dicit quod nunquam sanavit quamcumque personam de aliquo anulorum suorum'.

16 Gotschalc Hollen, *Preceptorium divine legis*, Nuremberg, 1497, p. 25 v. (on the subject of healing epilepsy): 'Hoc genus demoniorum non ejicitur nisi in jejunio et oratione'; A. Franz, *Die kirchlichen Benediktionen*, 2, pp. 501, 503. Cf. the English prayer quoted p. 106.

17 *Germania*, 1879, p. 74; cf. A. Franz, *Die kirchlichen Benediktionen*, II, p. 507.

18 Coffin-nails or metal ornaments: W. G. Black, *Folk-Medicine* (Publications of the Folklore Society, 12), London, 1883, p. 175; J. C. Atkinson, *Cleveland Glossary*, 1878 (quoted by Murray, *A New English Dictionary*, under the word 'cramp-ring'); A. Wuttke, *Der deutsche Volksaberglaube*, 2nd ed. 1869,

p. 334. For nails on which a man has hanged himself: Grimm, *Deutsche Mythologie*, 4th ed., 2, p. 978.

19 J. Brand, *Popular Antiquities*, 1870 ed., 3, pp. 254 ff. (The first edition came out in 1777; the later editions were completed from the manuscripts of the author, who died in 1806.) For another practice of the same type, see Black, loc. cit., pp. 174–5 (the county of Northampton). Here is yet another prescription kindly sent me by J. Herbert, of the British Museum; the reader will note the collection taken at the church door, a feature to be compared with the practices concerning the 'sacrament-rings' referred to on p. 97. I will give the actual words of my kind correspondent: 'From 1881 until his death in 1885 my father was Rector of Northlew in Devonshire, a village about 9 miles west of Okehampton. During that time (I think in 1884) my mother wrote me a description of what had happened on the previous Sunday: At the end of the morning service a girl stood at the church door and collected 29 pennies, one from each of 29 young men. She gave these to a 30th young man in exchange for a half-crown, and took the half-crown to a local 'White Witch' (a farmer's wife who kept a small shop in the village), who was to return it to her eventually in the form of a silver ring, as a sovereign remedy for her fits.'

20 *S. Bernardi Senensis . . . Opera*, Venice, 1745, 1, p. 42a, 'Quadragesimale de religione christiana': 'Contra malum gramphii portant annulos fusos dum legitur Passio Christi, dies et horas contra Apostolum observantes'.

21 B.M. MS. Arundel, 276, fol. 23 v.; quoted for the first time, but with an inaccurate reference, which has since then always been repeated, by Stevenson, 'On cramp-rings', p. 49 (*Gentleman's Magazine Library*, p. 41): 'For the Crampe . . . Tak and ger gedir on Gude Friday, at fyfe parisch kirkes, fife of the first penyes that is offerd at the crose and say v. pater noster in the worschip of fife wondes, and bare thaim on the v. dais, and say ilk a day als meki on the same wyse; and than gar mak a ryng ther of withowten alay of other metel, and writ within *Jasper*, *Bastasar*, *Attrapa*, and writ withouten *Jhc Nazarenus;* and sithen tak it fra the goldsmyth apon a Fridai, and say v. pater noster als thou did be fore and vse it alway aftirward.' Thanks to the kindness of J. Herbert of the British Museum, who was good enough to collate the MS. for me, I have been able to produce a more accurate version here than the one hitherto published.

22 Cf. for the Magi, Jones, *Finger-ring lore*, p. 137, and esp. pp. 147 ff.; for the five wounds ibid., p. 137 (inscription from a ring found in Coventry Park).

23 Above, p. 97.

24 J. Labarte, *Inventaire de mobilier de Charles V roi de France* (*Documents inédits*), 1870, no. 524.

25 In the same way forms of words taken from the Passion were considered efficacious against the pains of torture: Edmund le Blant, 'De l'Ancienne Croyance à des moyens secrets de défier la torture', *Mém. Acad. Inscriptions*, 34, 1, p. 292. In Flanders at the beginning of the seventeenth century children born on a Good Friday had the reputation of being born healers (Delrio, *Disquisitionum magicarum*, I, cap. III, qu. IV, p. 57); in France in the seventeenth century the seventh sons, who were considered specially able to heal scrofula, preferred to exercise their powers on a Friday (p. 175,

and Book 2, Ch. IV, n. 161); the same in Ireland, even at the present time (*Dublin University Magazine*, 1879, p. 218).

26 The rings are known by the name of 'sacrament-rings'. See Black, *Folk-medicine*, p. 174 (a Cornish custom, according to which the silver piece coming from the offerings must first be redeemed for thirty pence obtained by begging at the church door—silent begging, for it was forbidden to ask for alms explicitly—then, once obtained, it was still the object of a supplementary sanctificatory rite. The sick person who wore it had to go three times round the Communion table); and p. 175; *Notes and Queries*, 2nd series, I, p. 331; C. J. S. Thompson, *Royal cramp and other medycinable rings*, p. 10.

27 *Traité des Superstitions*, p. 439; cf. 4th ed., under the title of *Traité des superstitions qui regardent les sacremens*, 1777, I, p. 448.

28 An analysis of MS. 932 in the library of the town of St-Gall, p. 553, in A. Franz, *Die kirchlichen Benediktionen*, 2, p. 502.

29 Above, Book 2, Ch. II, n. 5.

30 At least the Public Record Office does not possess any copy of it in the series 'Household and Wardrobe' of the Exchequer Accounts.

31 The reader will find the accounts of Edward I which I have been able to break down enumerated below, Appendix I, n. 15, and n. 17; those of Edward II, n. 24.

32 For this affair, see above, pp. 137 ff.

33 For all these relations of the saints, see in particular J. B. Thiers, *Traité des superstitions*, 4th ed., I, pp. 438–48; for the relations of St Hubert, in particular, H. Gaidoz, *La Rage et St Hubert*, pp. 112 ff, and above p. 215. For the relations of St Paul, cf. the text of Felino Sandei above, Book 2, Ch. I, n. 108, and Pomponazzi, *De naturalium effectuum causis*, Basle, 1567, p. 48; for those of St Catherine, above, p. 171. For the text relating to St Paul and the snake-bite, see Acts 28: 3–6.

34 Royal Household Counter-roll, 13 February–27 June, forty-third year of the reign (1369), Public Record Office, Exchequer Accounts, 396, 11, fol. 122 v.: 'In consimilibus oblacionibus domine regine factis adorando crucem in precio quinque solidorum argenti in capella sua ibidem eodem die V s. In denariis solutis pro eisdem oblacionibus reassumptis pro anulis medicinalibus inde faciendis V s.'

35 Above, Book 2, Ch. I, n. 20.

36 For Mary Tudor, this is clearly brought out by the very text of her missal, in the passage concerning the cramp rings,—above, p. 105; for Mary, James II's daughter, and for Victoria, see the documents relating to their coronations: L. G. W. Legg, *English Coronation Records*, pp. 328 and 370; for Elizabeth and Anne I do not know of any direct evidence, but there seems no reason why, in the case of the first, the precedent of Mary Tudor should not have been followed, and in the case of the second, that of the other Mary. The fact that anointing on the hands was explicitly forbidden for the simple wives of kings is clearly brought out in the various English consecration rituals: Legg, loc. cit., pp. 101, 177, 235, 266–7, 310.

37 The text, already published by J. Freind, *The history of Physick*, 5th ed., 2, 1758, p. [32], is given by Crawfurd, *King's Evil*, p. 45, according to the MS.

in the B.M. Cotton (Claud, A. VIII ?). But Crawfurd is wrong in thinking that the *Defensio juris domus Lancastriae* has never been published. It was printed, if not actually published, by Lord Clermont, in his edition of Fortescue's works (cf. above Book 2, Ch. I, n. 46), pp. 505 ff. The passage that concerns us is on p. 508. In this edition, it offers some variants from Crawfurd's text, which seems to me better, and which I reproduce here: 'Item aurum et argentum sacris unctis manibus Regum Angliae in die Parascevae, divinorum tempore, (quemadmodum Reges Angliae annuatim facere solent), tactum devote et oblatum, spasmaticos et caducos curant: quemadmodum per annulos ex dicto auro seu argento factos et digitis huiusmodi morbidorum impositos, multis in mundi partibus crebro usu expertum est. Quae gratia Reginis non confertur, cum ipsae in manibus non ungantur.' The same argument is reproduced, in almost the same form, in a little English treatise: *Of the title of the House of York*, written by Fortescue about the same period: Crawfurd, p. 46; Lord Clermont, p. 498. It may be mentioned that, in France likewise under Charles V, Jean Golein considered the fact that a woman could not heal scrofula an argument in favour of succession by the male line; above, p. 281.

38 Appendix I, p. 251.

39 To my knowledge, there are in existence at least three manuscripts of this ceremonial: (1) Bibl. Nat. ang. 29, which appears to date from the thirteenth year of Henry VIII's reign (fol. 1 v.); the text dealing with the cramp rings in fol. 14 v.; the passage relating to the cramp rings was published from this MS. in the *Gentleman's Magazine*, 1834, I, p. 48 (*Gentleman's Magazine Library*, III, p. 39), by Crawfurd, 'Cramp-rings', p. 167; (2) a MS from about the year 1500, coming from the collection of Anstis, Garter King of Arms, and kept in the Duke of Northumberland Collection; the passage on the cramp rings was published from this MS. by T. Percy, *The regulations and establishment of the household of Henry Algernon Percy, the fifth Earl of Northumberland*, London, 1827 (reprint), p. 436, and from Percy by Maskell, *Monumenta ritualia*, 2nd ed., 3, p. 390, n. 1, as well as by the *Gentleman's Magazine*, 1774, p. 247 (*Gentleman's Magazine Library*, III, p. 38); (3) a MS. preserved as no. 7 at College of Arms, London, dating from the first half of the sixteenth century: cf. Farquhar, 'Royal Charities', I, p. 67, n. 6 and p. 81, n. 1 (and a personal communication from Miss Farquhar). I have collated the text given by Dr Crawfurd with that of the Bibl. Nat. MS., and found it correct (but note that the words in brackets in line 5 were added by Dr Crawfurd).

40 See Appendix II, no. 19.

41 The meaning of this act of redemption had been forgotten to such an extent under Mary Tudor that, if one may believe the account given by the Venetian Faitta (quoted below), the queen used to consecrate on Good Friday, as well as the rings specially made for the ceremony by the Royal Treasury, any other rings that might be handed to her for this purpose belonging to private persons, to whom they were no doubt given back once the rite had been performed. The fact perhaps explains, as C. J. S. Thompson suggests in *Royal cramp and other medycinable rings*, p. 9, that certain texts from the fifteenth century onwards mention cramp rings set with a precious stone. If we are

to understand by cramp rings, rings blessed by the king, one can only interpret these as obviously rings that had been lent for this purpose by private persons; but as nothing in the documents tells us whether these were 'royal' cramp rings, it is also possible that we are dealing here with some kind of magical rings, thought to be effective against the cramp.

42 In Mary Tudor's missal, preserved today in the library of Westminster Cathedral, cf. Appendix II, no. 6. The cramp rings liturgy given by this missal has been several times published, in particular: Gilbert Burnett, *The history of the reformation*, ed. Pocock, V, London, 1865, p. 445; Wilkins, *Concilia Magnae Britanniae et Hibernaie*, 4, fol. 1737, p. 103; S. Pegge, *Curialia Miscellanea*, London, 1818, p. 164; Crawfurd, 'Cramp-rings', p. 182. For the English translation of this liturgy, dating no doubt from James II's reign, see below, Book 2, Ch. VI, n. 15.

43 *Calendar of State Papers, Venice*, VI, 1, no. 473, p. 436. Faitta was Cardinal Pole's secretary; he saw Mary bless the rings on 4 April 1556.

44 'Omnipotens sempiterne Deus, qui . . . quos ad regalis sublimitatis fastigium extulisti, insignioribus gratiis ornatos, donorumque tuorum organa atque canales esse voluisti, ut sicut per te regnant aliisque praesunt, ita te authore reliquis prosint, et tua in populum beneficia conferant' (Crawfurd, pp. 182–3); 'Deus . . . hos annulos propitius benedicere et sanctificare digneris: ut omnes qui eos gestabunt sint immunes ab omnibus Satanae insidiis, sint armati virtute coelestis defensionis, nec eos infestet vel nervorum contractio, vel comitialis morbi pericula' (ibid., p. 183). '. . . facessat omnis superstitio, procul absit diabolicae fraudis suspicio' (ibid., same page); 'Sanctifica Domine annulos istos, et rore tuae benedictionis benignus asperge, ac manuum nostrarum confricatione, quas, olei sacra infusione externa, sanctificare dignatus es pro ministerii nostri modo, consecra, ut quod natura metalli praestare non possit, gratiae tuae magnitudine efficiatur' (ibid., p. 184).

BOOK 2   CHAPTER III   *The sacred and miraculous aspects of royalty*

1 *Summa gloria de Apostolico et Augusto; Monumenta Germaniae, Libelli de lite*, vol. 3, c. 9, p. 69: *Quod rex sit laicus* 'Aut enim rex est laicus aut clericus. Sed si non est laicus, tunc est clericus. Et si est clericus, tunc aut est ostiarius aut lector aut exorcista aut acolithus aut subdiaconus aut diaconus aut presbyter. Si de his gradibus non est, tunc clericus non est. Porro si nec laicus nec clericus est, tunc monachus est. Sed monachus eum excusat uxor et gladius.' Cf. also c. 28, p. 78. The personality of Honorius, who was a prolific writer, remains—in spite of all research—fairly enigmatic; but he was undoubtedly a German (see in particular J. A. Endres, *Honorius Augustodunensis, Beitrag zur Geschichte des geistigen Lebens im 12. Jahrhundert*, Kempten and Munich, 1902).

2 Cf. below, n. 14, 50 and 53. The reader will find some ingenious, but rather exaggerated, remarks on this subject in Thurston, *The Coronation Ceremonial*, p. 36, quoted in the following note. For the difficulties there were in

arriving at a legal definition of the status of clerk, cf. R. Génestal, *Le Privilegium fori en France du Décret de Gratien à la fin du XIVᵉ siècle* (Bibl. École Hautes Études, Sc. religieuses, 35).

3 Certain Anglican authors, foremost among whom is L. G. W. Legg, have insisted most vigorously and sometimes with some exaggeration upon the quasi-sacerdotal character of mediaeval royalty; and with the avowedly religious and apologetic intention: 'It seemed', wrote Legg in 1902 in the *Church Times*, 'that it might be a useful thing if it were shown that, so far from the claims of the King to govern the Church beginning with Henry the Eighth, his rights began much earlier . . . And with this, that the king was a minister of the Church, consecrated to this special office by the Church itself.' This provoked an attempted refutation, equally transparent in its purpose, by an English Jesuit, Fr. H. Thurston, *The Coronation Ceremonial*, 2nd ed., London, 1911. This is an able and penetrating piece of argument, sound enough in its attack upon the opposite school of thought, but much too absolute in its denials and in my opinion, farther in the end from the truth than Legg's thesis. It is interesting, incidentally, for the historian to note that these ancient quarrels still have a certain life in them today!

4 Among the origins of this conception of priestly royalty, so familiar to the Middle Ages, should we also include Roman influences? The Christian Emperors from Gratian onwards, in 382, had renounced the old pagan title *pontifex maximus*; but at least up till the fifth century they were still given the name of priest in certain forms of official veneration (on these facts cf. J. B. Sägmüller, *Lehrbuch des katholischen Kirchenrechts*, 3rd ed., I, Freiburg, 1914, pp. 51–2): 'ἀρχιερεῖ βασιλεῖ [πολλὰ τὰ ἔτη]' exclaimed the Fathers of the Synod of Constantinople in the year 444 in their official acclamations. Likewise in 451 the Council of Chalcedon: 'τῷ ἱερεῖ τῷ, βασιλεῖ' (Mansi, *Concilia*, 6, col. 733 and 7, col. 177). A little later, Pope Leo the Great was to write to the Emperor Leo I: 'sacerdotalem namque et apostolicum tuae pietatis animum' (Migne, *P.L.*, vol. 54, ep. CLVI, col. 1131). But these texts were not taken up by the great Latin canonical compilations, and do not seem to have been quoted or even known by Western writers in the Middle Ages; the same is true of the famous passage in Eusebius where Constantine calls himself 'τῶν ἐκτὸς . . . ἐπίσκοπος' (cf. below, Book 2, Ch. V, n. 111). Only later on—in the seventeenth century—were these ancient memories destined to recover some force, thanks to the revival of learning; cf. above, p. 198. On the other hand, it is clear from a passage in Guillaume Durand that certain jurists, in order to prove the sacerdotal character attributed to the Emperor, were wont to make much of a text borrowed from the Roman juricical compilations, *Rationale divinorum officiorum*, II, 8 (Lyons ed., 1584, p. 56 v.): 'Quidam etiam dicunt ut not. ff. de rerum diuisio l. sancta quod fit presbyter, iuxta illud, Cuius merito qui nos sacerdotes appellat, Imperator etiam pontifex dictus est, prout in tractatu de Episcopo dicetur' (cf. ibid., I, II, p. 62: 'Unde et Romani Imperatores pontifices dicebantur'). The passage referred to is Ulpian, *Dig.* I, i, 1 and really applies not to the Emperors, but to the laywers.

5 *Anselmi Gesta Episcop. Leod.*, c. 66; *Monumenta Germaniae* SS., VII, p. 229–30 : 'Imperator vero, utpote qui eiusmodi homo esset, qui sibi super

episcopos potestatem nimis carnaliter, ne dicam ambiciose, quereret usurpare : "Ego vero, inquit, similiter sacro oleo, data mihi prae caeteris imperandi potestate, sum perunctus". Quem contra antistes veritatis zelo iustitiaeque fervore vehementer accensus, talibus breviter instruendum esse censuit : "Alia, inquiens, est et longe a sacerdotali differens vestra haec quam asseritis unctio, quia per eam vos ad mortificandum, nos auctore Deo ad vivificandum ornati sumus, unde quantum vita morte praestantior, tantum nostra vestra unctione sine dubio est excellentior.' For the facts, see E. Steindorff, *Jahrbuch des deutschen Reichs unter Heinrich III*, 2, pp. 50-1.

6 *Summa gloria*, c.9; 'Sed garruli fortasse tumido fastu contendunt regem non esse de numero laicorum, cum unctus sit oleo sacerdotum'.

7 *De controversia inter Hildebrandum et Heinricum imperatorem; Libelli de Lite*, I, p. 467: 'Unde dicunt nulli laico umquam aliquid de ecclesiasticis disponendi facultatem esse concessam, quamvis rex a numero laicorum merito in huiusmodi separetur, cum oleo consecrationis inunctus sacerdotalis ministerii particeps esse cognoscitur'. For other quotations borrowed from polemical writers of the same party, and for refutations by their opponents, see Heinrich Böhmer, *Kirche und Staat in England und der Normandie*, p. 235; Kern, *Gottesgnadentum*, p. 86, n. 152; cf. also the language put into the mouth of Henry V's entourage by a chronicler of the papal party: 'Quid referam, quosdam comites eius . . . eum regem pariter et summum sacerdotem . . . praedicasse'. Laurentius, *Gesta episcop. Virdunensium; Monumenta Germapiae SS.*, XVIII, 502.

8 *Monumenta Germaniae, Libelli de lite*, III, p. 677: 'Quare non est appellandus laicus, quia Christus Domini est . . . '

9 *Vie de Louis le Gros*, xiv, ed. A. Molinier (Collection de textes pour servir à l'étude . . . de l'hist.), p. 40: 'abjectoque secularis militie gladio, ecclesiastico ad vindictam malefactorum accingens'. Cf., in the same order of ideas, ibid., xviii, p. 62: 'partem Dei, cujus ad vivificandum portat rex imaginem, implorant'. I don't know whether we should regard the first passage as an allusion to the celebrated allegory of the two swords, taken from Luke 22:38, from which the partisans of papal power and the defenders of the temporal power both in their turn drew opposing arguments. Even in Suger's time, Geoffroi de Vendôme, anticipating St Bernard, had used it: cf. Paul Gennrich, *Die Staats-und Kirchenlehre Johanns von Salisbury*, Gotha, 1894, p. 154, n. 1, and E. Jordan, 'Dante et St Bernard', *Bulletin*, Comité catholique français pour le centenaire de Dante, 1922, pp. 277, 278.

10 A. Luchaire, *Études sur les actes de Louis VII*, 1885, no. 119 (add to the editions mentioned by Luchaire the one by R. de Lasteyrie, *Cartulaire de Paris* (*Histoire Générale de Paris*), no. 302, which is now the best): 'Scimus quod ex auctoritate Veteris Testamenti, etiam nostris temporibus, ex ecclesiastica institutione soli reges et sacerdotes sacri crismatis unctione consecrantur. Decet autem et qui, soli pre ceteris omnibus sacrosancta crismatis linitione consociati, ad regendum Dei populum perficiuntur, sibi ipsis et subditis suis tam temporalia quam spiritualia subministrando provideant, et providendo invicem subministrent'. We might wonder whether it would not be better to translate *sacerdotes* by bishops, since chrism—in the strict sense of the word—is an episcopal privilege, not a priestly one (cf.

above, p. 116). But in documents of this period *chrism* sometimes has the simple meaning of holy oil. It is as well to keep the natural translation—priests—while not forgetting that in the minds of Louis VII's clerks, it was bishops in particular who were considered the natural allies of kings; moreover, the decree itself was made out in favour of a bishop. One can compare with Louis VII's preamble what Otto de Friesing a few years later wrote about Frederick Barbarossa's consecration; on the same day as the Emperor had been consecrated, in the same church and by the same bishops as he, the bishop elect of Munster had been consecrated: 'ut revera summus rex et sacerdos presenti iocunditati hoc quasi prognostico interesse crederetur, qua in una aecclesia una dies duarum personarum, quae solae novi ac veteris instrumenti institutione sacramentaliter unguntur et christi Domini rite dicuntur, vidit unctionem'. (*Gesta Friderici*, 2, c.3; *Scriptor. rer. germ. ad usum scholarum*, 3rd ed., p. 105). Finally, an analogous idea is expressed in the liturgical formula common to French and German consecration rites: 'Accipe coronam regni, quae . . . episcoporum . . . manibus capiti tuo imponitur . . . et per hanc te participem ministerii nostri non ignores, ita ut, sicut nos in interioribus pastores rectoresque animarum intelligimur, tu quoque in exterioribus verus Dei cultor . . . semper appareas . . . ' (Waitz, *Die Formeln der Deutschen Königs- und der Römischen Kaiserskrönung*, Göttingen, 1872, pp. 42, 74, 82; and with some variants, Dewick, *The coronation book of Charles V of France* (Henry Bradshaw Soc., 16), London, 1899, col. 36).

11 *Histoire des Institutions monarchiques*, 2nd ed., 1890, I, p. 42. In the same work, I, p. 41, Luchaire quotes an edict of Henry I for the Church in Paris (F. Soehnée, *Catalogue des actes de Henry I*, Biblioth. École Hautes Études, p. 161, no. 29), where it would seem to be a question of the 'divine ministry' of royalty; but on closer examination the words 'divinum ministerium' in the preamble to this edict are found to refer to the divine ministry of generosity (towards the churches).

12 For these facts see Luchaire in *L'Histoire de France*, Lavisse, III, 1, p. 5, and Vacandard, *Saint Bernard*, n. d., II, p. 183.

13 *Epistolae*, ed. Luard (Rolls Series), 124, p. 351; cf. L. G. W. Legg, *English Coronation Records*, p. 67: 'Hec tamen unccionis prerogativa nullo modo regiam dignitatem prefert aut etiam equiparat sacerdotali aut potestatem tribuit alicuius sacerdotalis officii'.

14 *Summa Decretorum*, XXII, qu. 5, c. 22: 'Si opponatur de iuramento fidelitatis quod hodie episcopi faciunt imperatori, respondeatur non omnia, que consuetudo habet, canones permittere. Vel dicatur imperatorem non omnino laicum esse, quam per sacram unctionem constat consecratum esse'; ed., J. F. v. Schulte, Giessen, 1892, p. 360; ed. H. Singer, Paderborn, 1902, p. 403.

15 Saxo Grammaticus, ed. A. Holder, p. 539: 'prouinciarum reges'.

16 For the dukes of Normandy, Benedict of Peterborough, *Gesta Henrici regis*, ed. Stubbs, Rolls Series, II, p. 73 (Richard Coeur de Lion, on 20 July 1189, takes from the altar of Notre-Dame de Rouen, in the presence of the Archbishop, prelates and barons, 'gladium ducatus Normanniae'); Matthew Paris, *Chronica majora*, ed. Luard, Rolls Series, II, p. 454, and *Historia*

Anglorum, ed. Madden, Rolls Series, II, p. 79 (Jean Lackland, 25 April 1199: sword and crown); much later, evidence relating to the enthronement of Charles of France, Louis XI's brother, in H. Stein, *Charles de France, frère de Louis XI*, 1921, p. 146, (ring, sword and banner); a ritual known only from two seventeenth-century copies in the Arch. communales of Rouen (De-lachenal, *Histoire de Charles V*, I, p. 137, n. 1), published by Duchesne, *Historiae Normannorum Scriptores*, 1619, p. 1050, and Martene, *De antiquis Ecclesiae ritibus*, II, col. 853 (ring and sword). For the dukes of Aquitaine we possess an *ordo ad benedicendum*, which was—unfortunately—only drawn up at the beginning of the thirteenth century by the precentor Elie of Limoges, and therefore cannot be considered a very reliable document as regards ancient uses; the insignia are the ring (said to have belonged to Ste-Valérie), the crown ('circulum aureum'), the banner, the sword and the spurs (*Histor. de France*, 12, p. 451). See also—outside France proper—for Dauphiné, R. Delachenal, *Histoire de Charles V*, I, p. 40. Guillaume Durand's *Pontifical* (Bibl. Nat. MS. lat. 733, fol. 57), contains a rubric: *De benedictione principis siue comitis palatini*; there is nothing but a form of blessing, obviously borrowed from the imperial consecration ritual (ibid., fol. 50 v.), and perfectly commonplace; there is no mention, of course, of the anointing.

17 Moreover, unction was considered by the kings as such an important prerogative that the dynasties with whom it was not traditional often tried to acquire the privilege. In the thirteenth century at the latest the idea took root that this needed authorization by the pope—an authorization obtained by the kings of Navarre in 1257, and the Scottish kings in 1329, after long solicitation. Thus in the end the papacy discovered, at least in certain countries, a source of influence in the old rite. In 1204, Innocent III himself anointed Peter II of Aragon, who had come to Rome to make himself a vassal of the Holy See; this was the first Aragonese anointing. Cf. above p. 262 and Appendix III, n. 1.

18 In terms of post-scholastic theology, no distinction was made between the sacraments and the *sacramentalia*. There is a very clear explanation of this subject in G. L. Hahn, *Die Lehre von den Sakramenten in ihrer geschichtlichen Entwicklung innerhalb der abendländischen Kirche bis zum Concil von Trient*, Breslau, 1864, esp. p. 104.

19 Ives de Chartres, Ep. CXIV (*Histor. de France*, XV, p. 145); Peter Damian, *Sermo* LXIX, Migne, *P.L.*, vol. 144, col. 897 ff., and *Liber gratissimus*, c. x (*Monumenta Germaniae, Libelli de lite*, I, p. 31); Thomas à Becket, letter to Henry II, *Materials for the History of Th. B.*, Rolls Series, V, no. CLIV, p. 280. Cf. Peter of Blois, texts quoted above, Book 1, Ch. I, n. 25, and below, n. 25; Hugue de Rouen, quoted by Hahn, loc. cit., p. 104; Otto de Freising, *Gesta Friderici*, II, c. iii (*Scriptor. rer. Germ.*, 3rd ed., p. 104: 'dum finito unctionis sacramento diadema sibi imponeretur'). A good discussion of the question in Kern, *Gottesgnadentum*, p. 78; cf. p. 87, n. 154.

20 The text quoted above, n. 13: 'unccionis sacramentum'.

21 Baronius-Raynaldus, ed. Theiner, XXII (1257, no. 57 and 1260, no. 18). Cf. Potthast, *Regesta*, II, nos. 17054 and 17947. But for the attitude of John XXII in 1318, see above, p. 138.

22 *Histoire littéraire*, 26, p. 122.

23 *De catechizandis rudibus*, c. xxvi (Migne, *P.L.*, vol. 40, col. 344): 'signacula quidem rerum divinarum esse visibilia, sed res ipsas invisibiles in eis honorari'.

24 I Samuel 10:6.

25 Wipo, *Gesta Chuonradi*, c. iii, ed. H. Bresslau, *Scr. rer. Germ. in usum scholarum*, 3rd ed., p. 23; Peter of Blois, ep. 10, Migne, *P.L.*, vol. 207, col. 29; in both cases the words of the Bible serve as a theme for advice or reproaches. Alexander IV, Bull of 6 October 1260: Baronius-Raynaldus, ed. Theiner, XXII, 1260, no. 18; Potthast, *Regesta*, no. 17947.

26 Text quoted above, n. 13 (ed. Luard, p. 350): 'regalis inunccio signum est prerogative suscepcionis septiformis doni sacratissimi pneumatis'.

27 Appendix IV, p. 278. Jean Golein gives a moralizing turn to his thought in the following sentence, but somewhat restricts its application: The royal dignity, he says, must surely enjoy the same privileges as the religious order, for it carries with it much more 'anxiety and troubles'.

28 Cf. Appendix III, p. 273.

29 *De idolatria politica et legitimo principis cultu commentarius*, p. 73. For this work see below, Book 2, Ch. V, n. 124.

30 Cf. J. W. Legg, 'The sacring of the English Kings', *Archaeological Journal*, 51, 1894, p. 33, and Woolley, *Coronation rites*, p. 193.

31 *Corpus Iuris Canonici*, ed. Friedberg, II, col. 132-3 (*Decretal*, I, tit. XV): 'Refert autem inter pontificis et principis unctionem, quia caput pontificis chrismate consecratur, brachium vero principis oleo delinitur, ut ostendatur, quanta sit differentia inter auctoritatem pontificis et principis potestatem'; cf. Kern, *Gottesgnadentum*, p. 115; the same theory is reproduced in the Bull of Alexander IV for the anointing of the kings of Bohemia in 1260 (Baronius-Raynaldus, ed. Theiner, XXII, 1260, no. 18; Potthast, no. 17947). Guillaume Durand, *Rationale*, I, c. viii, Lyons ed., 1584; since the introduction of the New law, royal unction 'a capite ad brachium est translata, ut princeps a tempore Christi non ungatur in capite sed in brachio siue in humero vel in armo'; for the anointing of the bishop on the head, cf. 40 v. In the *ordo* for the coronation of kings, in conformity with the canonical prescriptions, given by G. Durand in his *Pontifical* (Bibl. Nat. MS. lat. 733), we read as follows (fol. 54 v.): 'Post hec metropolitanus inungit in modum crucis cum oleo exorcisato de[x]trum illius brachium et inter scapulas'.

32 Woolley, *Coronation rites*, p. 68, 71, 104; H. Schreuer, *Über altfranzösische Krönungsordnungen*, pp. 39, 48; Legg, *Coronation records*, p. xxxv. Unction on the head disappeared quite soon from the imperial consecration ritual (Kern, p. 115, n. 207), but survived in the ceremonial for consecrating the King of the Romans as sovereign of Germany (Schreuer, *Die rechtlichen Grundgedanken*, p. 82, n. 3, and Woolley, p. 122). Cardinal Henry of Susa— known in canonical literature by his title of Hostiensis—notes in his *Summa aurea*, written between 1250 and 1261, lib. I, c.xv (Lyons ed., 1588, fol. 41 v.), that in spite of Innocent III's prescriptions and the official texts of the Roman pontifical, 'sed et consuetudo antiqua circa hoc obseruatur, nam supradictorum Regum Franciae et Angliae capita inunguntur'.

33 The Bulls of Innocent I and Alexander IV, and Guillaume Durand's text, quoted above, n. 31; cf. J. Fluck, *Katholische Liturgie*, I, Giessen, 1853, pp. 311, 322; Vacant and Mangenot, *Dictionnaire de théologie catholique*, under 'Chrème'. Already in the twelfth century we read in the little poem known as 'De anulo et baculo versus' (*Monumenta Germaniae histor.*, *Libelli de lite*, III, p. 726, line 9): 'Presulis est autem sacra *crismatis* unctio . . .' For the French use, attested by numerous texts, see e.g. Dewick, *The Coronation Book of Charles V of France* (H. Bradshaw Soc., 16), col. 8, 25 ff. (with the chrism was mixed a drop of oil from the Holy Phial). For the English use, Legg, *Coronation records*, p. xxxv.

34 For these facts, refer to A. Diemand, *Das Ceremoniell der Kaiserkrönungen*; Histor. Abh. von Th. Heigel und H. Grauert, 4, Munich, 1894, p. 65 n. 3 and 74, and esp. to E. Eichmann, 'Die Ordines der Kaiserkrönung', *Zeitschr. der sav. Stiftung für Rechtsgesch*, *Kan. Abt*, 1912, *passim*. Whatever Diemand may say, there is nothing to prove that the custom of receiving the Emperor in the Chapterhouse of St Peter's, Rome, was in imitation of the custom by which he was required to be a member of the Chapter of Aix-la-Chapelle; the Aix canon would seem rather to be an imitation of the Roman one; cf. Beissel, 'Der Aachener Königsstuhl', *Zeitschrift des Aachener Geschichtsvereins*, 9, 1887, p. 23 (useful for the facts quoted, rather than for their interpretation). I should add at this point that I have not been able to see the recent work by Eva Sperling, *Studien zur Geschichte der Kaiserkrönung und Weihe*, Stuttgart, 1918.

35 Eichmann, loc. cit., pp. 39, 42 (*ordo* of the imperial coronation, 'third period'). In his memoir Eichmann has well brought out the significance of the status of canon attributed to the Emperor; but he does not seem to me to have attached enough importance to the imperial diaconate.

36 *Rationale*, II, 8, 1584 ed., p. 56 v.: 'Canon † Adriani Papae lxiij distinct. Valentinianus in fine videtur innuere, quod Imperator debet ordinem subdiaconatus habere, ubi dicitur, Adiutor et defensor tuus, ut meum ordinem decet, semper existam, sed non est ita. gerit tamen illud officium, quoniam in die ordinationis sue, receptus est primum in canonicum, a canonicis sancti Petri, ministrat domino papae in missa in officio subdiaconatus, parando calicem et huiusmodi faciendo.' The question refers to *Decret. Grat.*, Dist. LXIII, c. iii; but it is erroneous in the sense that the canon in question is really an extract from the *Historia tripartita*; it is in c. ii that Pope Hadrian II is mentioned.

37 John Cantacuzenus, *Histor.* lib. I, cap. xli (Migne, *Patrologia Graeca*, vol. 153, col. 281, cf. for the Communion 288) and Codinus, *De officiis Constantinopolitanis*, c. xvii (*P.G.*, vol. 157, col. 109; cf. for the Communion col. 111), make the Emperor into a δεποτάτος (cf. Brightman, *Journal of Theological Studies*, 2, 1901, p. 390, n. 1); Simon of Salonika, *De sacro templo*, c. cxliii (*P.G.*, vol. 155, col. 352) makes him—as far as Communion is concerned—a deacon.

38 For Charles IV, R. Delachenal, *Histoire de Charles V*, I, 1909, p. 278, n. 1 (the miniature quoted is now reproduced in vol. IV of the *Chronique de Jean II et Charles V*, ed. Delachenal, Soc. de l'hist. de France, pl. xxxii). For Sigismund, *Chronique du Religieux de Saint-Denys*, ed. L. Bellaguet

(*Documents inédits*), V, p. 470. There is the following passage in the pontifical ceremonial of Pierre Amelii (1370–5) on the subject of the papal Christmas Mass: 'Si imperator vel rex sit in curia hac nocte, sacrista et clerici praesentant sibi librum legendarum, in quo debet legere quintam lectionem, et eum honeste instruunt de ceremoniis observandis in petendo benedictionem, in levando ensem cum vagina, et extrahendo, ipsum vibrando . . . ' (Mabillon, *Museum italicum*, 2, 1689, p. 325). On the other hand, there is no doubt that we should regard as pure fancy the following affirmation, reproduced by Martene, *De antiquis Ecclesiae ritibus*, 1, II, c. ix, ed. Bassano, 1788, 2, p. 213, 'ex codice Bigotiano', with no other indication of date or origin: at the Mass said at the entry of the Emperor into Rome after his election 'l'empereur doit dire l'evangile, et le roy de Cecile l'epistre. Mais si le roy de France s'y trouve, il le doit dire devant lui.'

39 H. Schreuer, *Über altfranzösische Krönungsordnungen*, Weimar, 1909, (reprinted separately and revised by the *Zeitschrift der Savigny-Stiftung*, G. A., 1909), pp. 38, 46; E. S. Dewick, *The Coronation Book of Charles V of France*, col. 8; Jean Golein, Appendix IV, p. 278. I think we should once again remind ourselves that in default of any really critical classification of the *ordines* of the French consecration rite (H. Schreuer's work not having gone much beyond the printed sources), we cannot really say anything more than vague uncertainties about the ritual of this ceremony.

40 For the gloves, see Dewick, loc. cit., col. 32: 'Postea si uoluerit rex cirotecas subtiles induere sicut faciunt episcopi dum consecrantur'; cf. the note, col. 82, Prayers : 'Christe perunge hunc regem in regimen unde unxisti sacerdotes . . .' 'Deus electorum . . . Iterumque sacerdotem aaron'; 'Accipe coronam . . . ' (with the formula 'per hanc te participem ministerii nostri non ignores'), ibid., col. 29, 36. The gloves seem to have been introduced in early times into the ceremonial in answer to a specifically ritual need; they served to protect the chrism from all profanation after the hands had been anointed: cf. Dewick, loc. cit., and esp. Jean Golein, above, p. 278. But the use of gloves at once suggested a similarity with the episcopal dress. It should be noted that Jean Golein, who as a general rule avoids too much insistence upon the priestly character of royalty, is unaware of this similarity, or passes it over in silence.

41 B.M. Cotton Nero C IX, fol. 173, quoted by Legg, *Coronation Records*, p. 40, n. 4.

42 General information about the history and doctrine of Communion in Vacant and Mangenot, *Dictionnaire de théologie catholique*, under the article 'Communion'. For Communion in both kinds by the Emperors, A. Diemand, *Das Ceremoniell der Kaiserkrönungen*, p. 93, n. 2. Pius IV, with a kind of condescension for the Lutheran sympathies of Maximilian II, allowed him the right to partake of the chalice (cf. J. Schlecht, *Histor. Jahrbuch*, 14, 1893, p. 1), but we do not know whether this gave rise to a return to the ancient use of which we have evidence in Leopold II's reign. For France, Clement VI's Bulls of 1344 in favour of Philip VI, his wife the Queen, the Duke of Normandy and the Duchess, in Baronius-Raynaldus, *Annales*, ed. Theiner, XXV, and analysed—except the one relating to the Duke, which is published in its entirety. It would seem likely that they all had the same

tenor. No doubt it was through a slip that Mabillon, *Museum Italicum*, II, 1689, p. lxij, affirms that the same privilege was granted at the same time to the Duke of Burgundy. The Bull in favour of the Duke of Normandy—and in all probability the others too—likewise contains the authorization: 'ut quae sacra sunt, praeterquam corpus Dominicum, quod per alios quam per sacerdotes tractari non convenit, tangere quoties opportunum fuerit . . . valeas'. For Communion in both kinds at the coronation of Charles V; Dewick, *The coronation book of Charles V of France*, col. 43, and (for the queen) 49; cf. col. 87. For the change that took place under Henry IV, du Peyrat, *Histoire ecclésiastique de la Cour*, pp. 727–9. Du Peyrat only attributes this to 'the inadvertence of those who were at first in control of his chapel after his conversion'; I prefer to assume the motive suggested above; for the use of the following century, cf. Oroux, *Histoire ecclésiastique de la Cour*, I, p. 253, n. (1). According to a Catholic theologian of the second half of the sixteenth century, Gasparus Cassalius, *De caena et calice Domini*, Venice, 1563, c. ii, quoted by Henriquez, *Summa Theologiae Moralis*, Mainz, 1613, lib. VIII, c. xliv, § 7, notes n and o, the French king only made use of this privilege at his consecration and at the hour of his death. If this information is accurate, it proves without a doubt that even before Henry IV's time the fear of seeming to make concessions to Protestantism had led to the reduction of this cultural privilege. It is strange that the ceremonial for royal Communion contained in MS. 2734 of the Bibl. Mazarine, dating from the seventeenth century and probably from Louis XIII's reign, should envisage communion in both kinds. This was very likely nothing more than a reproduction of an older ceremonial. This text has been published by Franklin, *La Vie privée, les médecins*, p. 300; but it is missing from the similar MS. preserved in the Bibl. Nat. as MS. fr. 4321; cf. below, Book 2, Ch. V, n. 145. The dissertation by Gabriel Kehler, *Christianissimi regis Galliae Communionem sub utraque . . .* Wittenberg, 1686, is a Protestant pamphlet of little interest. I have not been able to see J. F. Mayer, *Christianissimi regis Galliae communio sub utraque*, Wittenberg, same date. In England, there is no trace of the kings having received Communion in both kinds before the Reformation: Legg, *Coronation records*, p. lxi. For pictorial documents referring to the king of France receiving Communion in both kinds, see Appendix II, nos. 2 and 3, and Dewick, *The coronation book*, pl. 28.

43 Ferdinand Kattenbusch, *Lehrbuch der vergleichenden Confessionskunde*, I, 1892, pp. 388, 498, and above, n. 37.

44 For the text of Jean Golein, see Appendix IV, p. 279; for the interpretation of Communion in both kinds as given in the seventeenth century, see above, p. 198.

45 Lines 340 and 3066. I quote from the edition by J. Bédier.

46 For Turpin, see esp. lines 1876 ff. This passage was already written by the time I was able to become acquainted with the book by P. Boissonnade, *Du Nouveau sur la Chanson de Roland*, 1923. The comparison with Manasses of Rheims also occurred to Boissonnade (p. 327). I must be careful to add that I only mean a simple comparison, and am not attempting to represent Turpin as a kind of political pseudonym for Manasseh. The *Chanson de Roland* is not a novel with a hidden meaning! But how can Boissonnade write that the

author of the *Chanson* 'professes the ideas of an adherent of the Gregorian or theocratic reforms'? (p. 444; cf. on the person of Charlemagne, interpreted as 'the ideal sovereign of the great theocracy dreamt by Gregory VII', p. 312). Lines 3094 and 373, quoted in support of this thesis, only prove that 'Turold' knew Charlemagne to have been on good terms with the popes. As for l. 2998, which is also quoted in support, it shows that our poet considered St Peter to be a great saint: but who ever doubted it? If one wanted to follow up the idea of the king-priest in literature—which is no part of our present purpose—material would no doubt be found in the Grail cycle, which is so charged with archaic and pre-Christian elements.

47 The rhymed version in the Châteauroux and Venice VII MSS. W. Foerster, *Altfranzösische Bibliothek*, VI, str. 31 (l. 340); for l. 3066, str. 288. It might well seem that this absolution given by an emperor would only have been slightly shocking to the most orthodox minds of the time; for up to the Counter-Reformation there was a very widespread custom—only contested very late in the day by theologians, and then very hesitantly—of allowing laymen to administer confession in cases of urgency. Joinville has told us how, in an hour of peril, 'messire Gui d'Ibelin' made his confession to him: 'et je li dis: "Je vous asol de tel pooir que Diex m'a donnei."' (c. lxx; ed. of the Soc. de l'Hist. de France, pp. 125-6); cf. Georg Gromer, *Die Laienbeicht im Mittelalter* (*Veröffentlich. aus dem Kirchenhistor. Seminar München*, 3, 7), Munich, 1909, and C. J. Merk, *Anschauungen über die Lehre . . . der Kirche in altfranzösischen Heldenepos* (*Zeitschr. für Romanische Philologie*, suppl. vol. 41), p. 120. But these confessions received and absolutions given —with certain reservations: 'de tel pooir que Diex m'a donnei'—in a moment of urgent need, when no priest was at hand, could not be compared with Charlemagne's gesture, performed in the midst of an army which tradition represents as well supplied with clergy.

48 *Chronique*, § 184, ed. Delaborde (Soc. de l'Hist. de France), I, p. 273: 'His dictis, petierunt milites a rege benedictionem, qui, manu elevata, oravit eis a Domino benedictionem . . .'

49 Cf. H. Francois-Delaborde, *Receuil des actes de Philippe-Auguste*, I, pp. xxx–xxxi. In a comprehensive study of French royalty, there would of course be occasion to insist on the probably very great influence exercised by the Carolingian tradition and the literature relating to Charlemagne on our kings and their entourage; but here I can only touch on this point in passing, to return to it perhaps later in another place.

50 *Apparatus in librum Sextum*, lib. III, tit. IV: *De praebendis*, c. ii, *Licet*; Bibl. Nat. lat. 16901, fol. 66 v.: 'Item reges, qui inuncti sunt, partem (?) laici meri obtinere non videtur, sed excedere eandem'. For Cardinal Le Moine, cf. R. Scholz, *Die Publizistik zur Zeit Philipps des Schönen*, pp. 194 ff.

51 *Tractatus de officio regis*, ed. A. W. Pollard and C. Sayle, London, 1887 (*Wyclif's Latin Works*, edited by the Wyclif Society, 10), pp. 10-11: 'Ex istis patet quod regia potestas, que est ordo in ecclesia . . .' The *Tractatus*, which appeared a few months after the Great Schism, was written at a moment when this event was as yet far from having produced its eventual consequences in doctrine.

52 Above, pp. 280–2, 281, 278.

53 Lib. III, tit. 2; 1525 ed., London, p. 92 v., 'nonobstante quod rex unctus non sit mere persona laica, sed mixta secundum quosdam'.

54 *Opera omnia*, Leyden, 1604, ep. 137: 'Ideo autem Regnum sacerdotale esse debere Dominus adstruit, quia propter sacram chrismatis unctionem Reges in christiana religione ad similitudinem Sacerdotum sancti esse debent . . .'

55 P. Pithou, *Preuves des libertez de l'eglise gallicane*, II, 1639, p. 995.

56 Above, Book 2, Ch. I, n. 103.

57 A pleading by Framberge on behalf of Master Pierre de Croisay, the petitioner, against Cardinal d'Estouteville, the defendant: 14 July 1477; Arch. Nat. X 1 A 4818, fol. 258 v. ff: 'Sed ponis ex institucione canonica subsequente, que non excludit regem sacratissimum unctione sacra miraculose et celitus missa, qui tanquam persona sacrata capax est rerum spiritualium large accipiendo . . . . Et jaçoit ce que par les droiz canons on veuille dire que *interdicta est administracio spiritualium laicys*, c'est a entendre *de mere laicis, et non de personis sacratis et sublimibus qui ecclesie temporalitates obtulerunt in habundancia* . . .' And further on in the same folio: 'regi, qui est sacrata persona'. My attention was drawn to this text by R. Delachenal, *Histoire des avocats au Parlement de Paris*, 1885, p. 204.

58 'Mémoire addressé à Charles VII', in Noël Valois, *Histoire de la Pragmatique Sanction*, 1906, p. 216: 'And as head, and principal person in the Church . . . '; a discourse upon the dispute between the kings of France and England, quoted by Godefroy, *Ceremonial*, p. 77: 'The king of France, once consecrated, is an ecclesiastical person'; remonstrance to Charles VII, Ibid., and J. Juvénal des Ursins, *Histoire de Charles VI*, ed. Godefroy, 1653, *Annotations*, p. 628: 'Au regard de vous, mon Souverain Seigneur, vous n'estes pas simplement personne laye, mais Prelat, Ecclesiastique, le premier en vostre Royaume qui soit apres le Pape, le bras dextre de l'Eglise'.

59 Bibl. Nat. MS. fr. 1029, fol. 90 a; a Latin translation in the *Opera*, 1606 ed., fol. *Pars IV*, col. 644; cf. E. Bourret, *Essai historique et critique sur les sermons français de Gerson*, 1858, pp. 56 ff., 87 n. 1.

60 Cf. Grassaille, *Regalium Franciae iura omnia*, lib. ii, p. 17; P. Pithou, *Preuves*, p. 13; R. Hubert, *Antiquitez historiques de l'eglise royale de Saint Aignon d'Orléans*, Orléans, 1661, pp. 83 ff.; E. R. Vaucelle, *La Collégiale de Saint-Martin de Tours, des origines à l'avènement des Valois* (Bullet. et Mém. Soc. Archéol. Tours, Mém. 46), pp. 80–1. According to Vaucelle, Charles VII put forward to the Council of Basle his title as Abbot of St-Martin (p. 81, n. 2, no references).

61 For Lyndwood's ideas, cf. F. W. Maitland, *Roman Canon Law in the Church of England*, London, 1898, pp. 1 ff.

62 Panormitanus, *Super tertio decretalium*, Lyons, 1546, a commentary on tit. XXX, *De decimis*, c. xxi, fol. 154 v.: 'Quarto, nota quod laica etiam reges non possunt aliquid donare de iure ecclesiastico nec possunt possidere jus spirituale. Ex quo infertur quod reges sunt puri laici: ita quod per coronationem et unctionem nullum ordinem ecclesiasticum recipiunt.' For Panormitanus' doctrine at this time, see his gloss upon Book I of the *Decretals*, VI, 4, (1546 ed., fol. 119 v.) where, talking of those who—

wrongly, as he thought—consider the oath required of metropolitans by the Pope as unlawful, because not prescribed by the Councils, he declares: 'romana ecclesia prestat autoritatem conciliis et per ejus autoritatem robur accipiunt, et in conciliis semper excipit ejus autoritas'. Later on, at the Council of Basle,—largely, it would seem, for political reasons—he changed his attitude. See the notice on him in the *Realencyclopädie für protestantische Theologie*, under the word 'Panormitanus', where his biography is given. Panormitanus is often quoted and opposed by the French partisans of the quasi-sacerdotal character of kings, for instance Arnoul Ruzé in the passage mentioned below, Book 2, Ch. V, n. 103.

63 On the other hand, these archaic conceptions seem to be more or less absent from the *Defensor Pacis* of Jean de Jandun and Marsilius of Padua, whose outlook is much more rationalist.

64 Hincmar, above, Book 1, Ch. II, n. 42, Ratherius of Verona, *Praeloquium* IV, 2 (Migne, *P.L.*, vol. 136, col. 249); Hugh of Saint-Victor, *De sacramentis*, II, pars II, cap. 4 (*P.L.*, vol. 176, col. 418); John of Salisbury, *Policraticus*, IV, 3, ed. C. C. J. Webb, Oxford, 1909, I, pp. 240–1; *Innocent* III, reply to the envoys from Philip of Swabia in 1202, *P.L.*, vol. 216, col. 1012: 'Minor est autem qui ungitur quam qui ungit et dignior est ungens quam unctus'; Egidio Colonna, *De ecclesiastica sive de summi pontificis potestate*, c. iv, ed. Oxilio-Boffito, *Un tratto inedito di Egidio Colonna*, Florence, 1908, p. 14. These names are of course merely quoted as examples: cf. E. Jordan, *Nouv. Rev. historique du Droit*, 1921, p. 370. The text from the Epistle to the Hebrews, 7:7, is quoted by Hugh of St Victor, John of Salisbury and Colonna.

65 The legend is reproduced in Manfred's manifesto to the Romans, 24 May 1265: *Monumenta Germaniae, Constitutiones*, II, p. 564, lines 39 ff., the text to be corrected by the indications given in Hampe, *Neues Archiv*, 1911, p. 237. On this manifesto's probable redactor—Peter of Prezza—see Eugen Müller, 'Peter von Prezza', *Heidelberger Abh. zur mittleren und neueren Gesch.*, vol. 37; cf. also E. Jordan, *Rev. histor. du droit*, 1922, p. 349.

66 *De investigatione Antichristi*, I, 40; ed. F. Scheibel-Berger, Linz, 1875, p. 85: 'apparet reges ac duces per sacerdotum benedictionem non creari sed ex divina ordinatione per humanam electionem et acclamationem creatis, ut praedictum est, sacerdotes Domini benedicunt, ut officium, ad quod divina ordinatione assumpti sunt, sacerdotali benedictione prosequente congruentius exequantur'. Cf. 'De quarta vigilia noctis', *Oesterreichische Vierteljahrsschrift für katholische Theologie*, 1871, I, p. 593: 'Sicut enim primus Adam primo de limo terrae legitur formatus et postea, Deo insufflante illi spiraculum vitae, animatus atque animantibus cunctis ad dominandum praelatus; sic imperator vel rex primo est a populo vel exercitu creandus tanquam de limo terrae, ac postea principibus vel omnibus vel melioribus in eius principatu coadunatis per benedictionem sacerdotalem quasi per spiraculum vitae animandus, vivificandus et sanctificandus est'. Cf. W. Ribbeck, 'Gerhoh von Reichersberg und seine Ideen über das Verhältniss zwischen Staat und Kirche', *Forsch. z. deutschen Geschichte*, 24, 1884, pp. 3 ff. The cautious neutral position taken up by Gerhoh and its variant forms have caused him to be treated—perhaps a little over-severely—as a 'sehr

unklarer Kopf' by a recent historian; see Schmidlin, *Archiv. für katholisches Kirchenrecht*, 24, 1904, p. 45.

67 Johannes Parisiensis, *De potestate regum et papali*, c. xix, in Goldast, *Monarchia*, II, p. 133 (cf. R. Scholz, *Die Publizistik*, p. 329); *Somnium Viridarii*, I, chaps. 166, 171, 174 and 179 (Goldast, *Monarchia*, I, pp. 126-8, 129-36, with direct borrowings from Occam, *Octo Quaestiones*, V-VII, Goldast, II, pp. 369-78); Gerson, *De potestate Ecclesiastica et laica*, q. II, cap. ix-xi, 1606 ed., Pars I, col. 841 ff (which contains this definition of consecration: 'illud est solum solemnitatis, et non potestatis'). For the same theory in modern times, see above, p. 201.

68 For the attitude of the French monarchy, cf. Schreuer, *Die rechtlichen Grundgedanken*, pp. 92 ff., esp. 99 ff. For the calculation of the length of reigns in France, Schreuer, loc. cit., p. 95 (the interest of this problem appears not to have been noticed by Giry; it would deserve following up more closely); in England, J. E. W. Wallis, *English regnal years and titles* (Helps for students of history), London, 1921, p. 20; it should be added that the association of the heir presumptive with the throne, which was prac-tised in particular and very consistently by the Capetian monarchy, made the custom of calculating the years of the reign from the consecration fairly harmless over a long time, since the son's consecration took place during his father's lifetime. For the cry: 'The king is dead, long live the king', see R. Delachenal, *Histoire de Charles V*, III, 1916, p. 21; for the ceremony at Charles VI's death, *Chronique d'Enguerran de Monstrelet*, ed. Douët-d'Arcq (Soc. de l'hist. de France), IV, p. 123; cf. Petit-Dutaillis, *Rev. historique*, 125, 1917, p. 115, n. 1. Of course as far as the imperial dignity was concerned, the question presented itself rather differently. Up to the end of the Middle Ages—to be precise, up to Maximilian I (1508)—there was no Emperor not crowned by the Pope; but the German theory had for a long time held that 'the King of the Romans', if regularly elected, had a right—even without the imperial title—to rule over the Empire. Cf. the following note; and see esp. F. Kern, 'Die Reichsgewalt des deutschen Königs nach dem Inter-regnum', *Histor. Zeitschr.*, 106, 1911; K. G. Hugelmann, 'Die Wirkungen der Kaiserweihe nach dem Sachsenspiegel', in his 'Kanonistische Streif-zügen durch den Sachsenspiegel, *Zeitschr. der Sav.-Stiftung, Kanon. Abt.*, 9, 1919 and the note by U. Stutz, following on from this article.

69 *Propositiones Henrici regis; Monumenta Germaniae, Constitutiones*, V, p. 411, c. 4: 'Quia quanquam homines intelligentes sciant, quod ex quo dictus rex legitime electus et per dictum papam approbatus habere debeat administrationem in imperio, acsi esset coronatus, tamen quidam querentes nocere et zizaniam seminare, suggerunt simplicibus, quod non est ei obediendum, donec fuerit coronatus'. Cf. E. Jordan, *Rev. histor. du droit*, 1922, p. 376.

70 A letter from three Angevin noblemen (17 July 1429), Quicherat, *Procès de Jeanne d'Arc*, V, p. 128; cf. p. 129.

71 *Hist. de France*, 21, p. 661: 'Tibi dixeram diu ante quod quando Ecclesia papa careret, et regnum Franciae rege et regina, et Imperium imperatore, quod tunc esset tibi vitae terminus constitutus. Et haec vides adimpleta. Ille enim quem tu regem Franciae reputas non est unctus adhuc nec

coronatus et ante hoc non debet rex nominari.' Cf. G. Péré, *Le Sacre et le couronnement des rois de France*, p. 100.

72 Quicherat, *Procès de Jeanne d'Arc*, IV, p. 513: 'negantque [Galli] verum esse regem qui hoc oleo non sit delibutus'.

73 For the *Great Chronicles* and Froissart, cf. R. Delachenal, *Histoire de Charles V*, III, pp. 22, 25. For the taking of the title by Charles VII, see de Beaucourt, *Histoire de Charles VII*, II, 1882, p. 55 and n. 2. In England at the end of the twelfth century the so-called *Chronicle* of Benedict of Peterborough (ed. Stubbs, Rolls Series, II, pp. 71–82), was pedantically careful only to give Richard Coeur de Lion the title of count (of Poitiers) after his father's death, then after his ducal consecration at Rouen the title of Duke (of Normandy) and only after his royal consecration the title of king.

74 Farquhar, 'Royal Charities', IV, p. 172 (for Charles II and James II; James II followed the usage of his Protestant predecessors).

75 See above, Book 2, Chapter IV. For the case of Henry IV—which proves nothing about earlier usage—above, p. 201.

76 See the passage quoted above, Book 2, Ch. I, note 92; for Occam, cf. Book 2, Ch. I, note 104.

77 Above, p. 105.

78 *Charisma*, Ch. X, quoted by Crawfurd, *King's Evil*, p. 70; see also the *Epistola dedicatoria*, p. [9].

79 Fortescue, *De titulo Edwardi comitis Marchie*, cap. x; cf. above, Book 2, Ch. I, n. 46, and also, on the importance of unction recognized by our author in connection with the cramp rings, p. 104. Jean Golein, Appendix IV, p. 278 and 280.

80 Such at any rate was the primitive version; later, from the end of the tenth century, there was sometimes a tendency to substitute an angel for the dove: Adso, *Vita S. Bercharii*, Migne, *P.L.*, vol. 137, col. 675; *Chronique de Morigny*, Book II, c. xv, ed. L. Mirot (Collection de textes pour l'étude . . . de l'hist.), p. 60; Guillaume le Breton, *Philippide*, line 200; Étienne de Conty, Bibl. Nat. MS. lat. 11730, fol. 31 v. (cf. above, Book 2, Ch. I, n. 5); cf. Dom Marlot, *Histoire de la ville, cité et université de Reims*, II, p. 48, n. 1. The conciliatory spirits were inclined to say: an angel in the form of a dove: Philippe Mouskes, *Chronique*, ed. Reiffenberg (*Coll. des chron. belges*), 11. 432–4.

81 *Vita Remigii*, ed. Krusch (*Monumenta Germaniae Histor., Scriptor. rer. merov.*, III), c. 15, p. 297. The record of the ceremony of 869 was inserted by Hincmar in the official annals of the Kingdom of Western France, known as the *Annales Bertiniani*: ed. Waitz (*Scriptores rer. germanic.*), p. 104 and *Capitularia* (*Monumenta Germaniae, Hist.*), II, p. 340; for the facts themselves, cf. R. Parisot, *Le royaume de Lorraine sous les Carolingiens*, 1899 (thesis, Nancy), pp. 343 ff. There is a rather vague allusion to the miracles supposed to have marked the baptism of Clovis in the spurious privilege granted by Pope Hormisdas which Hincmar inserted as early as 870 in his *Capitula* against Hincmar of Laon; *P.L.*, vol. 126, col. 338; cf. Jaffé-Wattenbach, *Regesta*, no. 866. On Hincmar, the reader need only refer to the two works by Carl von Noorden, *Hinkmar, Erzbischof von Reims*, Bonn, 1863 and Heinrich Schrörs, with the same title, Freiburg, 1884; cf. also

B. Krusch, 'Reimser-Remigius Fälschungen', *Neues Archiv*, 20, 1895, esp. pp. 529–30, and E. Lesne, *La hiérarchie épiscopale . . . depuis la réforme de saint Boniface jusqu'à la mort de Hincmar* (Mém. et travaux publiés par des professeurs des fac. catholiques de Lille, 1), Lille and Paris, 1905. This is not the place to give a complete bibliography of the Holy Phial; but it may be noted in passing that it is always worth consulting, besides the work by Chiflet, *De ampulla remensi*, 1651, the commentary by Suysken, *AA.SS.*, Oct. I, pp. 83–9.

82 As J. Weiszäcker wrote in 1858: 'in such cases, the first story is the most suspicious': 'Hinkmar und Pseudo-Isidor', *Zeitschr. für die histor. Theologie*, 1858, III, p. 417.

83 On the accusations made by Nicholas I, see Lesne, *Hiérarchie épiscoplae*, p. 242, n. 3. For once, it would seem that the charges made against Hincmar were not altogether just. But there were numerous other well-known deceptions of which Hincmar was guilty, as for instance the famous spurious Bull of Pope Hormisdas; cf. also the facts brought forward by Hampe, 'Zum Streite Hinkmars mit Ebo von Reims', *Neues Archiv*, 23, 1897, and Lesne, *Hiérarchie*, p. 247, n. 3. The points put forward by M. Krusch, *Neues Archiv*, 20, p. 564 are passionately severe; but it is rather piquant to see the great Catholic historian Godefroy Kurth, Krusch's great opponent, protest energetically that 'whatever M. Krusch may say, he has never set out to guarantee Hincmar's truthfulness' (*Études franques*, 2, 1919, p. 237); the fact is that his 'truthfulness' is strictly indefensible.

84 *De ampulla remensi*, p. 70; cf. p. 68.

85 See the articles 'Colombe' and 'Colombe eucharistique' in Cabrol, *Dictionnaire d'archéologie chrétienne*. There is of course nothing to be deduced from the fact that in the eighteenth century—and for a long time before, no doubt —the Holy Phial was preserved at Rheims in a dove-shaped reliquary, for this reliquary might have been devised in this form later on in order to recall the legend: cf. Lacatte-Joltrois, *Recherches historiques sur la Sainte Ampoule*, Rheims, 1825, p. 18, and the lithograph at the beginning of the volume. We can only make conjectures as to the form of the reliquary at the period when the legend originated. In Hincmar's time there used to be on display at Rheims at least one other object said to have belonged to St-Rémi —a chalice bearing a metrical inscription: *Vita Remigii*, c. ii, p. 262. In an interesting article entitled 'Le Baptême de Christ et la Sainte Ampoule' *Bullet. Acad. royale archéologie de Belgique*, 1922, M. Marcel Laurent has pointed out that from the ninth century onwards, a new feature appears in some of the representations of Christ's baptism: the dove is carrying a phial in its beak. M. Laurent thinks that this supplementary detail, added to the traditional iconography, originates in the Rheims legend of the Holy Phial; and by a kind of counter-effect, the baptism of Christ was then pictured along the lines of that of Clovis. One could equally well imagine it working the other way round: the phial, and likewise the dove, might well have been suggested to the imagination of the faithful or the clerics by the sight of some work of art which depicted the Saviour's baptism. Unfortunately, our oldest evidence of the legend and the oldest iconographical document known to us depicting the dove descending above Jordan with a phial in its mouth—in

this case, an ivory of the ninth century—are approximately contemporary. Unless there should be some new discovery, the question of knowing in which direction the influence worked must remain unsolved.

86 There is a list of the places of consecration and the consecrating prelates in R. Holtzmann, *Französische Verfassungsgeschichte*, Munich and Berlin, 1919, pp. 114-19 (751-1179), 180 (1223-1429) and 312 (1461-1775). Urban II's Bull: Jaffé-Wattenbach, *Regesta*, no. 5415 (25 Dec. 1089). Louis VI's consecration: A. Luchaire, *Louis VI le Gros*, no. 57; for Henry IV's, above, p. 193. It will be noticed that Urban II's Bull confers equally upon the Archbishops of Rheims the exclusive right of placing the crown upon the king's head whenever they might be present at one of these solemnities, when—in accordance with the custom of those days—the king appeared wearing his crown.

87 This legend was attested for the first time, it would seem, by Philippe Mouskes, *Chronique* (Collect. des chron. belges), lines 24221 ff; and by a note written in a thirteenth-century hand on one of the leaves of Bibl. Nat. MS. lat. 13578, published by Hauréau, *Notices et extraits de quelques manuscrits*, II, 1891, p. 272; it crops up again in Froissart, II, § 173, and Étienne de Conty, lat. 11730, fol. 31 v., col. 1. One may well wonder whether there is not already an allusion to this belief in Nicolas de Bray, *Gesta Ludovici VIII, Hist. de France*, 17, p. 313, where l. 58 is certainly corrupt.

88 Robert Blondel, *Oratio historialis* (composed in 1449), chap. 43, 110, in *Oeuvres*, ed. A. Héron (Soc. de l'hist. de la Normandie), I, p. 275, and the French translation, ibid., p. 461; B. Chassanaeus (Chasseneux), *Catalogus gloriae mundi*, Frankfurt, 1586 (the first ed. 1579), pars V, consideratio 30, p. 142.

89 René de Ceriziers, *Les Heureux Commencemens de la France chrestienne*, 1633, pp. 188-9; Ceriziers incidentally rejects this belief as well as the preceding one.

90 Jean Golein, Appendix IV, p. 277. In every country we get evidence of respect for the consecrating oil, mingled with terror, the manifestations of which are somewhat suggestive of the practices classed by ethnographers under the conception of *taboo*: cf. Legg, *Coronation Records*, p. xxxix; but in France especially the miraculous character of chrism led the doctors to refine upon these prescriptions: Jean Golein even goes as far as asserting that the king, like a Bible 'Nazarite' (cf. Judges, 13:5), must never allow the head that has been touched by holy unction to be shorn, but must all his life, for the same reason, wear a 'coiffe' (see above, p. 279).

91 (No pig will benefit or gain a penny from selling unction.) *La Vie de Saint Rémi, poème du XIIIᵉ siècle, par Richier*, ed. W. N. Bolderston, London, 1912 (very inadequately edited), lines 8145 ff. In Charles V's reign, Jean Golein, who had perhaps read Richier, two copies of which existed in the royal library (cf. Paul Meyer, *Notices et Extraits des Manuscrits*, 25, I, p. 117), uses analogous expressions; see Appendix IV, p. 276.

92 There is a whole literature from the *ancien régime* bearing upon the history of the fleur-de-lis. It will be sufficient, from our point of view, to call attention to the following three works or memoirs: J. J. Chifletius, *Lilium francicum*, Antwerp, 1658; Sainte-Marthe, *Traité historique des armes de*

France, 1683 (the passage referring to the lilies is reproduced in Leber, *Collect. des meilleures dissertations*, 13, pp. 198 ff). de Foncemagne, *De l'Origine des armoiries en général, et en particulier celles de nos rois* (Mém. Acad. Inscriptions, 20) and Leber, 13, pp. 169 ff. As to modern works, the notes provided by P. Meyer in his edition of the *Débat des hérauts d'armes de France et d'Angleterre* (Soc. Anc. Textes), 1877, at § 34 of the French debate, and at § 30 of the English reply, and esp. Max Prinet, 'Les Variations du nombre des fleurs de lis dans les armes de France', *Bullet. monumental.*, 75, 1911, pp. 482 ff. The brochure by J. van Malderghem, *Les Fleurs de lis de l'ancienne monarchie française*, 1894 (extracted from the *Annales de la soc. d'Archéologie de Bruxelles*, 8), does not study the legend that interests us here. The memoir by Renaud, 'Origine des fleurs de lis dans les armoiries royales de France', *Annales de la Soc. histor. et archéolog de Château-Thierry*, 1890, p. 145, is the kind of work that is only worth mentioning in order to spare scholars the trouble of reading it.

93 L. Delisle, *Catalogue des actes de Philippe-Auguste*, Introduction, p. lxxxix.

94 *De principis instructione*, Dist. III, cap. xxx, ed. in the Rolls Series, 8, pp. 320–1. For the lion of the Guelphs and of Otto IV—the loser at Bouvines—see esp. Erich Gritzner, *Symbole und Wappen des alten deutschen Reiches* (Leipziger Studien aus dem Gebiete der Geschichte, 8, 3), p. 40.

95 *Le Chapel:* ed. Piaget, *Romania*, 27, 1898; 'le Dict', as yet unpublished; I have consulted Bibl. Nat. MS. lat. 4120, fol. 148, cf. Prinet, loc. cit., p. 482.

96 It is of course perfectly clear that the famous war-cry is much earlier than the fourteenth century; it is testified to for the first time in the form Mont-joie (*Meum Gaudium*) by Orderic Vital, in the year 1119: XII, 12; ed. Le Prévost (Soc. de l'hist. de France), IV, p. 341. Its origin, however, remains a mystery.

97 Bibl. Nat. MS. lat. 14663, fol. 35–36 v. The MS. is a collection of various historic texts from different hands compiled about the middle of the four-teenth century, no doubt at St-Victor (fol. 13, 14); extracts from the preface added by Raoul de Presles to *The City of God* lie side by side with our poem, (fol. 38 and v.). The fact that the poem was edited at Joyenval is brought out by numerous passages in the text itself, and particularly the beginning of the final quatrain: 'Zelator tocuis boni fundavit Bartholomeus—locum quo sumus coloni . . .' For Montjoie, near Conflans, see Abbé Lebeuf, *Histoire de la ville et de tout le diocèse de Paris*, ed. J. Bourbon, II, 1883, p. 87. For the Montjoies in general, in particular A. Baudoin, 'Montjoie Saint-Denis', *Mém. Acad. Sciences Toulouse* 7th series, 5, pp. 157 ff. One might be tempted to explain the localization of the fleur-de-lis legend at Joyenval by icono-graphical reasons, namely an interpretation given to the armorial bearings of the abbey—which perhaps as a royal concession—bore the fleur-de-lis. But in order to give some likelihood to this hypothesis, one would have to prove that these armorial bearings had that form before the very earliest evidence about the legend occurs; and, in the present state of our informa-tion, this would seem to be impossible. The fleur-de-lis are found on an abbatial counter-seal in 1364; but they are not present on the commu-nity's seal in 1243 (Douët d'Arcq, *Collection de sceaux*, 3, no. 8776, and 8250).

98 1531 ed., fol. a IIII; the king who is Clovis' adversary is called Caudat (an allusion to the popular legend which attributed a tail to Englishmen: *caudati Anglici*?); cf. Guillebert de Metz, ed. Leroux de Lincy, p. 149.

99 Jean Golein, Appendix IV, p. 278 (but cf. Appendix IV, n. 16); de Conty, lat. 11730, fol. 31 v. col. 2 (a particularly well-developed account, containing a mention of the angel's appearance to St-Denis: 'in castro quod gallice vocatur Montjoie, quod castrum distat a civitate Parisiensi per sex leucas vel circiter'); Gerson (?) *Carmen optativum ut Lilia crescant*, *Opera*, 1606, ed., Pars II, col. 768; Jean Corbechon, a translation of Bartholomew the Englishman's *De proprietatibus rerum*, Lyons ed., about 1485 (Sorbonne Library), book XVII, cap. cx; the passage in mind is of course an addition to Bartholomew's text; cf. C. V. Langlois, *La Connaissance de la nature et du monde au moyen âge*, 1911, p. 122, n. 3 (the reader will find in M. Langlois' notice on Bartholomew the Englishman the bibliography relating to J. Corbechon); *Songe du Verger*, I, c. 86, cf. c. 36 (Brunet, *Traitez*, pp. 82, 31); Latin text, I, c. 173 (Goldast, I, p. 129). For the annotations to Jean Golein's MS., which are probably not by the hand of Charles V, but might have been dictated by him to some scribe or other, see above, p. 276.

100 Claude Fauchet, *Origines des chevaliers, armoiries et héraux*, Book I, chap. II: *Oeuvres*, 1610, p. 513 recto and verso. The iconographical hypothesis was taken up by Sainte-Marthe; see C. Leber, loc. cit., p. 200.

101 Rudolf Brotanek, 'Die englischen Maskenspiele,' *Wiener Beiträge zur englischen Philologie*, 15, 1902, pp. 317 ff.; cf. p. 12 (the hermit of Joyenval; toads).

102 B.M. Add. MS. 18850; cf. George F. Warner, *Illuminated manuscripts in the British Museum*, 3rd series, 1903.

103 A tapestry depicting the history of the fleur-de-lis is mentioned by Jean de Haynin in his description of the nuptial festivities for the marriage of Charles le Téméraire to Margaret of York: *Les Mémoires de Messire Jean, seigneur de Haynin*, ed. R. Chalon (Soc. bibliophiles belges), I, Mons, 1842, p. 108. Chiflet, *Lilium francicum*, p. 32, has reproduced in an engraving a fragment of another tapestry (which used in his time to be at the Palais de Bruxelles), showing Clovis—supposedly about to depart for the wars against the Alamans—followed by a standard bearing the emblem of the three toads; the pen drawing from which the plate was engraved has been preserved in the Plantin Museum at Antwerp, no. 56; it is attributed to J. van Werden. Cf. also above, in the 'Additions and Corrections', p. 287.

104 Rather exceptionally, the origin of the fleur-de-lis was attributed to Charlemagne; it was said to have been brought down to him by an angel from heaven. The legend is related in this form by the English writer Nicholas Upton, who had taken part in the siege of Orléans in 1428: *De studio militari*, lib. III, London, 1654, p. 109; cf. also *Magistri Johannis de Bado Aureo tractatus de armis*, published at the same time as Upton and under the same cover by E. Bissaeus, who moreover considers it as likewise written by Upton under a pseudonym. This form of the tradition does not seem to have been very successful. Upton seems to refer it back to Froissart, but I can find nothing of the kind in his works.

105 On the oriflamme, nothing better has yet been written than the essay by

du Cange, *De la Bannière de Saint Denys et de l'oriflamme; Glossarium*, ed. Henschel, VII, pp. 71 ff. Modern literature on the subject is in general more plentiful than really helpful: but see Gustave Desjardins, *Recherches sur les drapeaux français*, 1874, pp. 1–13, 126–9. It goes without saying that I am only concerned here with the legendary history of the oriflamme.

106 Charter of Louis VI (1124) in favour of St-Denis. J. Tardif, *Monuments historiques*, no. 391 (Luchaire, *Louis VI*, no. 348): Suger, *Vie de Louis le Gros*, ed. A. Molinier (Collect. de textes pour servir à l'étude . . . de l'histoire), c. xxvi, p. 102. For the use of standards possessed by churches, see an interesting document, *Miracles de Saint Benoit*, V, 2, ed. E. de Certain (Soc. de l'hist. de France), p. 193 (relating to the *milices de paix* in Berry).

107 This is the opinion expounded by Guillaume Guiart, *Branche des royaux lignages*, in Buchon, *Collection des chroniques*, VII, lines 1151 ff. (year 1190). It will be noted that, according to Guiart, the French kings should only raise the oriflamme when they are to do battle against 'Turs ou Païens', or 'faus crestiens condampnés'; for other wars, they may use a banner resembling the oriflamme, but which is not the authentic oriflamme (lines 1180 ff.). Indeed, there were at St-Denis in Raoul de Presles' day (preface to the *City of God*, 1531 ed., fol. a II) two similar banners 'dont l'une estoit appellée la banniere Charlemaine . . . Et est ce que l'on appelle proprement l'oriflamme.' Cf. also J. Golein, above, p. 279, according to whom the kings would have a new pseudo-oriflamme made for each campaign. It is from Guiart that I take the words 'cendal rouge.'

108 Lines 3093 ff.; cf. the commentary by J. Bédier, *Légendes épiques*, II, 1908, pp. 229 ff. For the mosaic, P. Lauer, *Le Palais du Latran*, 1911, (thesis, Paris), pp. 105 ff. For the oriflamme currently considered as the *signum regis Karolis*, the *vexillum Karoli Magni*, cf. Gervase of Canterbury, *Chronica* (Rolls Series), I, p. 309, a. 1184; Richer de Senones, *Gesta Senoniensis eccl.*, III, c. 15, *Monumenta Germaniae*, SS., XXV, p. 295.

109 Raoul de Presles, preface to the translation of the *City of God*, 1531 ed., fol. a III v.; cf. Guillebert de Metz, ed. Leroux de Lincy, pp. 149–50. Lancelot, *Mémoire sur la vie et les ouvrages de Raoul de Presles* (Mémoires Acad. Inscriptions, 13, 1740), p. 627, quotes from Raoul a *Discours sur l'oriflamme* that is unknown to me, in which he likewise attributed the origin of the oriflamme to Charlemagne, to whom it was said to have been transmitted by St-Denis (loc. cit., p. 629); Jean Golein, Appendix IV, p. 279. The formation of the oriflamme legend coincides with the introduction into the consecration ceremonial of a blessing of this standard; this liturgical text appears for the first time, it seems, in a pontifical at Sens, Martene, *De antiquis Ecclesiae ritibus*, Rouen, 1702, III, p. 221, then in the *Coronation Book of Charles V of France*, ed. Dewick, p. 50; in B.M. Add. MS. 32097, likewise contemporary with Charles V (quoted by U. Chevalier, *Bibl. liturgique*, VII, p. 32, n. 2); in Jean Golein, above, p. 279; cf. the miniature reproduced by Montfaucon, *Monumens de la monarchie française*, III, pl. 3, and those of the *Coronation Book*, pl. 38, and of Bibl. Nat. MS. fr. 437 containing the work of Jean Golein (see below, Appendix IV, n. 19).

110 See for example the treatise *des Droiz de la Couronne* composed in 1459 or 1460, which will be quoted below, n. III; the *Débat des hérauts d'armes de*

France et d'Angleterre, written between 1453 and 1461, ed. L. Pannier and P. Meyer (Soc. des anc. textes), 1877, § 34, p. 12. It would certainly seem that the same theory is reflected in the rather vague language used by Charles VII's ambassadors to Pius II; below, n. 111. See also, later on, R. Gaguin, *Rerum gallicarum Annales*, lib. I, cap. 3, 1527 ed., Frankfurt, p. 8. It was through a similar confusion—though in the reverse direction—that the invention of the fleurs-de-lis was sometimes attributed to Charlemagne: above, n. 104.

111 D'Achery, *Spicilegium*, 1723, III, p. 821, col. 2; for the fleurs-de-lis, cf. the speech of Louis XI's envoys to the Pope in 1478 in de Maulde, *La Diplomatie au temps de Machiavel*, p. 60, n. 2. 'Les armes des fleurs de lis avec l'auriflambe et la saincte ampoule', all three sent by God to Clovis, are likewise mentioned in the little treatise *des Droiz de la Couronne de France* (composed in 1459 or 1460), which is incidentally nothing but a translation —though it often presents perceptible deviations from the original—of the *Oratio historialis* of Robert Blondel; the Latin text is less precise: 'celestia regni insignia et ampulam' (*Oeuvres de Robert Blondel*, ed. A. Héron, pp. 402, 232).

112 The consecration *ordo* known as Louis VIII's; ed. H. Schreuer, *Über altfranzösische Krönungsordnungen*, p. 39: 'Regem qui solus inter universos Reges terrae hoc glorioso praefulget Privilegio, ut oleo coelitus misso singulariter inungatur'.

113 *Chronica majora*, ed., Luard (Rolls Series), V, p. 480, a. 1254: 'Dominus rex Francorum, qui terrestrium rex regum est, tum propter ejus caelestem inunctionem, tum propter sui potestatem et militiae eminentiam'; ibid, p. 606 (1257): 'Archiepiscopus Remenensis qui regem Francorum caelesti consecrat crismate, quapropter rex Francorum regum censetur dignissimus'. As we saw above, Tolomeo of Lucca also boasted of the royal French unction.

114 What follows is in accordance with the Bull of John XXII, Avignon, 4 June 1318, the most complete text of which has been given by L. G. W. Legg, *English Coronation Records*, no. X. But Legg is wrong in thinking that it has never been published: it already exists—a large part of it—in Baronius-Raynaldus, *Annales*, John XXII, year 4, no. 20. The Dominican, who had been sent by the King of England, is simply designated in the Bull as 'fratris N., ordinis praedicatorum nostri penitentarii'; he should clearly be identified with Nicolas of Stratton, a former provincial of England, and since 12 Feb. 1313 Penitentiary of the diocese of Winchester, cf. C. F. R. Palmer, 'Fasti ordinis fratrum praedicatorum', *Archaeological Journal*, 35, 1878, p. 147.

115 M. Kern, *Gottesgnadentum*, p. 118, n. 214, writes on the subject of John XXII's Bull: 'Es wurde also nicht an eine Einwirkung auf die öffentliche Meinung, sondern an eine ganz reale Zauberwirkung des Oels durch physischen Influx gedacht'. We can agree that Edward II may well have believed in this kind of 'magic' action; but it seems clear enough from the Pope's refusal that the king was also seeking for a public and open ceremony, capable of having an effect on 'popular opinion'. For the usual tone adopted by the Pope towards sovereigns, cf. N. Valois, *Histoire littéraire*, 34, p. 481.

116 We may well wonder whether Edward II did not seek to imitate the Capetian traditions in another respect too. As far as I can see, it was in his reign that

there was the first mention of 'chevage', an annual amount paid by the English kings to St Thomas of Canterbury's shrine (Royal Household Counter-roll, 8 June–31 Jan.; year 9: E.A. 376, 7, fol. 5 verso; the Household Ordinance of York of June 1323, in Tout, *The place of the reign of Edward II*, p. 317; for the following reigns, cf. *Liber Niger Domus Regis Edw. IV*, p. 23; and Farquhar, 'Royal Charities', I, p. 85); might this not be a simple copy of the 'chevage' paid by the French kings to St Denis, probably as vassals of the Abbey, and so since the time of Philip I or Louis VI? For French usage, see H. F. Delaborde, 'Pourquoi Saint Louis faisait acte de servage à Saint Denis, *Bullet. soc. antiqu.*, 1897, pp. 254–7 and also Charlemagne's spurious edict., *Momunenta Germaniae, Dipl. Karol.*, no. 286, to which Delaborde does not appear to have paid attention, though it is our oldest evidence of this strange and interesting rite. This edict is at the moment being studied in the *Histor. Jahrbuch* by Max Buchner, but I have so far only been able to see the first part of it (vol. 42, 1922, pp. 12 ff.).

117 For the consecration of Henry IV, cf. J. H. Ramsay, *Lancaster and York*, Oxford, 1892, I, pp. 4–5 and the notes. The official account spread by the royal government was given in great detail by the *Annales Henrici Quarti Regis Angliae* ed. J. H. Riley, in the *Chronica Monasterii S. Albani: Johannis de Trokelowe . . . Chronica et Annales* (Rolls Series), pp. 297 ff. The 'cédule' written by St Thomas, said to have been discovered with the phial, is reproduced in the *Annales* and likewise in France by the Religieux de Saint-Denys, ed. L. Bellaguet, (*Documents inédits*), II, p. 726; Legg, *Coronation Records*, no. XV, has published it according to two MSS. in the Bodleian Library, Ashmole 59 and 1393, both of the fifteenth century. Cf. also *Eulogium Historiarum*, ed. F. S. Haydon (Rolls Series), III, p. 380; Thomas of Walsingham, *Historia anglicana*, ed. H. T. Riley (Rolls Series), II, p. 239. A point of detail of no particular importance: in the new account the Poitiers church in which the phial was kept for a long time is dedicated to St Gregory, and no longer to St George. In his *Annales d'Aquitaine* (1644 ed., Poitiers, p. 146), Jean Bouchet relates the history of St Thomas' oil; he even knows the name of the monk of St Cyprian's, Poitiers, to whom the saint had given the phial—Babilonius!

118 Woolley, *Coronation Rites*, p. 173. Cf. Fortescue, *De titulo Edwardi comitis Marchie*, ed. Clermont, cap. X, p. 70*.

119 The oldest document on the biblical origin of the stone of Scone seems to be Rishanger, *Chronica*, ed. H. T. Riley (Rolls Series), p. 135, year 1292; see also p. 263 (1296). According to the monk of Malmesbury (?) who wrote a *Life of Edward II* (*Chronicles of the reigns of Edward I and Edward II*, ed. Stubbs, Rolls Series, II, p. 277), it was said to have been brought to Scotland by Scotia, the daughter of Pharaoh. Cf. the study by William F. Skene, *The Coronation Stone*, Edinburgh, 1869. On the Tara Stone—or *Lia Fa'il*—see John Rhys, *Lecture on the origin and growth of religion as illustrated by Celtic Heathendom*, London and Edinburgh, 1888, pp. 205–7, and Loth, *Comptes rendus Acad. Inscriptions*, 1917, p. 28. I must leave on one side here, in this study of legendary history, everything not concerned with French and English royalty. For the carbuncles on the German imperial crown and the miraculous traditions connected with it, cf. K. Burdach, *Walther von der*

Vogelweide, Leipzig, 1900, pp. 253 ff., 315 ff., and the memoir, which seems distinctly adventurous, by F. Kampers, 'Der Waise', *Histor. Jahrbuch*, 39, 1919, pp. 432–86.

120 There is already this suggestion in Giraldus Cambrensis, *De principis institutione*, Dist. I, cap. xx and Dist. III, cap. xxx, ed. Rolls Series, VIII, pp. 141 and 319; and later, the very significant bantering tone of the German cleric who, about Philip III's time, composed the *Notitia Saeculi*, ed. Wilhelm, *Mitteil. des Instituts für österreichische Geschichtsforschung*, 19, 1898, p. 667.

121 *Histor. de France*, 23, p. 127, l. 100.

122 Appendix IV, p. 277, l. 4; cf. ibid. l. 8 and p. 280, l. 41.

123 *Histoire Littéraire*, 30, p. 453: 'Ex illustri prosapia oriundo domino Philippo'; p. 400: 'Magnifico principi, suo domino speciali, domino Roberto'. Wenck, *Philipp der Schöne*, p. 5, n. 2: 'Ex regia ac sanctissima prosapia oriundo, suo domino speciali, domino Philippo'.

124 Ed. Bolderston, lines 46 ff: the text had already been published in *Notices et extraits*, 35, i, p. 118: 'Et ce doit donner remenbrance—As Francois d'anmer la coronne—Dont sor teil onciòn coronne—Sains Remis son fil et son roi—
. . . Autresi doit estre aourée—Com nus haus corsains par raison;—Et qui por si juste occoison—Morroit com por li garder,—Au droit Dieu dire et esgarder—Croi je qu'il devroit estre saus,—S'il n'estoit en creance faus,—Ou de teil pechié entechiés—Qu'il fust ja a danner jugiés.'

125 Decrees of the Council of Limoges: Migne, *P.L.*, vol. 142, col. 1400: words attributed to a bishop addressing a knight, who, on the orders of Duke Sancho of Gascony, and on pain of death if disobedient, had slain his lord: 'Debueras pro seniore tuo mortem suscipere, antequam illi manus aliquo modo inferres, et martyr Dei pro tali fide fieres'; Cf. J. Flach, *Les Origines de l'ancienne France*, III, p. 58, n. 3,—*Li romans de Garin le Loherain*, ed. P. Paris (*Romans des douze pairs de France*, 3), II, p. 88: 'Crois font sor aus, qu'il erent droit martir,—Por lor seignor orent esté ocis'. It is obvious that we should have to distinguish on this point between the different *chansons de geste*, some of them dominated by respect for personal loyalty, and exploiting as literary motifs the cases of conscience raised by the vassal's moral code, and others—represented to perfection by *Roland*—steeped in sentiments of a rather different kind, especially the crusading spirit and a certain monarchical and national loyalty. Although it perhaps partly obeyed the dictates of literary inspiration—witness for instance the Virgilian echoes in the very expression 'douce France'—it was none the less, it would seem, profoundly sincere. It is also worth noting that Roland is as much the vassal as the subject of Charlemagne: cf. lines 1010 ff. All this, which is an extremely delicate matter, can only be suggested in passing, and may perhaps be taken up again elsewhere.

126 *La Monarchie constitutionelle en France*; *Réforme intellectuelle et morale*, pp. 251–2. Incidentally, Renan seems to exaggerate the exceptional position of the French monarchy; the legendary development was much more active in France than elsewhere, and as a consequence, the monarchical religion; but the idea of sacred royalty was universally present in the Middle Ages.

127 Guillaume le Breton, *Philippide*, I, XII, lines 613 ff. (in line 619, the corpse

is treated outright as 'sancto corpore'); Ives de Saint-Denis in Duchesne, *Scriptores*, V, p. 260; A. Cartellieri, *Philipp II August*, IV 2, Leipzig, 1922 (an extract from the Latin annals of St-Denis, Bibl. Mazarine, MS. 2017). A chapel was built between Mantes and St-Denis in order to commemorate the miracles. I am leaving on one side certain miraculous manifestations which in the king's lifetime were thought to have been evidence of divine protection in his wars: Rigaud, § 29 and 61—for it may very well be a question here of simple literary ornament invented by the chronicler—such as a vision of no particular interest relating to the king's death (cf. Guillaume le Breton, ed. Delaborde, Soc. de l'hist. de France, II, p. 377 n. 2).

128 For the bibliography of this belief, I would refer the reader to the Bibliography, p. 436; I have been able to add some fresh texts to the much more numerous ones already collected before my research, and to bring together certain texts which up till now have only been studied independently of one another.

129 *Richars li Biaus*, ed. W. Foerster, Vienna, 1874, lines 663 ff. (in this and the following notes the references are to the passages relating to the 'royal cross' we shall be considering later); the poem belongs to the second half of the thirteenth century; there is a convenient analysis by R. Koehler, *Rev. critique*, III, 2, 1868, p. 412.

130 In the poem of *Florent et Octavian : Hist. littéraire*, 31, p. 304.

131 Ibid., p. 332.

132 *Macaire*, ed. Guessard, line 1434; Jean d'Outremeuse, *Le myreur des histors*, ed. A. Borgnet (Acad. royale de Belgique, collection des doc. inédits), 2, p. 51.

133 The references brought together by A. Stimming, *Die festländische Fassung von Bueve de Hantone, Fassung I* (Gesellsch. für roman. Literatur, 25), p. 408, n. on l. 708; and *Fassung II*, vol. II (ibid. 41), p. 213, n. on lines 1312–1315.

134 *Parise la Duchesse*, ed. Guessard and Larchey (Les anciens poètes de la France), 1860, lines 825 and 1171.

135 *Le livre de Baudoyn, comte de Flandre*, Brussels, 1836, pp. 152, 172, 173.

136 In the poem known by the name of *Charles le Chauve : Hist. littéraire*, 26, pp. 101–2.

137 In the Chanson 'Lion de Bourges' (unpublished): cf. H. Wilhelmi, *Studien über die Chanson de Lion de Bourges*, Marburg, 1894, R. Krickmeyer, *Weitere Studien zur Chanson de Lion de Bourges*, part I, Greifswald, 1905, pp. 8, 9, 25, 29. For the 'literature', consisting essentially of essays produced by the Greifswald 'Seminary' on the subject of this interminable chivalrous romance, see the bibliography by Karl Zipp, *Die Clarisse-Episode des Lion de Bourges*, Greifswald, 1912.

138 *Bueve de Hantone*, the continental version, ed. Stimming, 2nd version, line 5598.

139 *Richars li Biaus*, line 670.

140 It may likewise be observed that in *Parise la Duchesse*, Hugue, who carries the 'croiz roial', although he is only the son of a Duke, will at the end of the poem become King of Hungary. The only exception I can find to this rule is in the 'Chanson de Lion de Bourges', where Lion, at the end of the poem, does not become a king, but disappears mysteriously to the land of the fairies. True,

his sons wear crowns; the poet no doubt thought that this father of kings, who was only prevented by this fairyland adventure from ending up on a throne, had nevertheless been destined for royalty.

141 *Bueve de Hantone*, ed. Stimming—the continental version—2nd version, line 1314 ('il ert' = il sera).

142 G. Paris, *Histoire poétique de Charlemagne*, 1905, p. 393.

143 *I Reali di Francia, di Andrea da Barberino*, ed. Vandelli (*Collezione di opere inedite o rare*), II, 2, Book II, c. I, pp. 4–5. For the word *niello*, cf. A. Thomas, 'Le Signe royal', p. 281, n. 3. Other references to the Italian adventure romances—imitated from the French—in Pio Rajna, *Le origine dell'epopea*, pp. 294–5.

144 Walter W. Skeat, *The lay of Havelock the Dane*, Oxford, 1902, lines 602, 1262, 2139. For the poem, apart from Skeat's introduction, Harald E. Heymann, *Studies in the Havelock tale*, Upsala, 1903. In the English lay, the cross is added as a mark of recognition to a singular physical peculiarity which all the versions—French and English—agree in giving to Havelock: whenever he is asleep, a flame spreading a delectable scent comes out of his mouth.

145 Wolfdietrich, B. I, Str. 140: A. Amelung and O. Jaenicke, *Deutsches Heldenbuch*, III, 1, Berlin, 1871, p. 188. For the date of this version, see H. Paul, Grundriss II, 1, 2nd ed. 251. It is amusing to note that Hermann Schneider, treating of this passage in his voluminous work entitled *Die Gedichte und die Sage von Wolfdietrich*, Munich, 1913, p. 278, entirely ignores the fact that 'royal' crosses of this kind could be attributed, even in Germany, to historical persons; on the other hand, M. Grauert, in his useful article 'Zur deutschen Kaisersage', *Histor. Jahrbuch*, 1892, only knows of the royal sign as a matter for political prophecies, and is completely unaware of its literary uses, either in France or in Germany.

146 Str. 143–7: ed. E. Martin and R. Schröder, *Sammlung germanis. Hilfsmittel*, 2, pp. 17–18.

147 *Oeuvres*, ed. Coussemaker, 1872, p. 286.

148 'Le "signe royal" et le secret de Jeanne d'Arc', *Rev. histor.* 103; I have borrowed several expressions from A. Thomas' lively analysis.

149 Here is another text, relating likewise to Charles VII, in which there is perhaps an allusion to the royal sign, though its interpretation remains extremely dubious. In his *Oratio historialis*, composed in 1449, Robert Blondel had written, on the subject of the consecration at Rheims, 'insignia regalia miraculose assumpsisti' (cap. xliii, 110, *Oeuvres*, ed. A. Héron, I, p. 275), which should no doubt be understood to refer to the handing over of the royal insignia: crown, ring, etc. This work was translated into French in 1459 or 1460, under the title *Des Droiz de la couronne de France*; and the passage in question is rendered as follows (ibid. p. 761): 'illecque receustes vous par miracle divin les enseignes roialles dont vous estes merchié'. *Merchier* means to mark, and the *enseigne* is the very word, as we have seen, that the good Jean Batiffol used to designate the fleur-de-lis imprinted on the bodies of true kings. It is difficult to avoid the impression that the author of the translation had been acquainted with a tradition according to which Charles VII showed the miraculous sign, perhaps only after his consecration.

150 According to the evidence of the contemporary chronicler Pierre de Zwittau, *Chronicon Aulae Regiae*, 2, c. xii: *Die Königsaaler Geschichtsquellen*, ed. J. Loserth, *Fontes rerum austriacarum*, 1, vol. VIII, p. 424. For Frederick, see F. X. Wegele, *Friedrich der Friedige*, Nördlingen, 1878; cf. H. Grauert, 'Zur deutschen Kaisersage', pp. 112 ff., and Eugen Müller, *Peter von Prezza*, esp. pp. 81 ff.

151 *Historia Suevorum*, I, c. xv, in Goldast, *Rerum Suevicarum Scriptores*, p. 60: 'et fama publica est, quamvis scriptum non inuenerim, quod praefati Comites de Habspurg ab utero matris suae crucem auream in dorso habeant hoc est, pilos candidos ut aurum in modo crucis protractos'. For Felix Fabri, cf. above, Book 2, Ch. I, n. 119.

152 A tradition garnered by the Protestant minister Abraham Buchholzer, *Index Chronologicus*, Görlitz, 1599, p. 504 (quoted in Camerarius, *Opera horarum subcisivarum*, 1650 ed., p. 146, and Grauert, 'Zur deutschen Kaisersage', p. 135, n. 2); Johannes Rosinus, *Exempla pietatis illustris*, Jena, 1602, p. V 3 (according to Buchholzer); Georg Fabricius, *Saxoniae illustratae libri novem: libri duo posteriores*, Leipzig [1606], Book VIII, p. 33. In a little mystico–political treatise, preserved today in the library at Colmar, composed no doubt in the early years of the sixteenth century, by an Alsatian or Swabian reformer, the author announces the advent of a *König vom Schwarzwalde*—also called the emperor Frederick—the future saviour of Germany, who shall wear a golden cross on his chest; but whatever Richard Schröder may say in *Die deutsche Kaisersage*, Heidelberg, 1891, pp. 14–15, this cross would seem to be present not as a bodily sign, but as a simple emblem adopted by the 'roi de la Forêt Noire' as head of the brotherhood of St Michael: H. Haupt, 'Ein Oberrheinischer Revolutionär aus dem Zeitalter Kaiser Maximilians I', Westdeutsche Zeitschr. Ergänzungsh., 8, 1893, p. 209.

153 Camerarius, *Operae horarum subcisivarum*, 1650 ed., p. 145; Philip Kammerer died in 1624.

154 By way of exception, the Wolfdietrich cross is red, as in the French tradition: 'ein rotez kriuzelin'.

155 Lance of the Σπαρτοί: the references are brought together in Preller, *Griechische Mythologie*, 4th ed. revised by C. Robert, II, i, pp. 109, n. 7, 947, n. 5; I borrow from Julian, *Oratio*, II, 81C, the expression τοῦ γένους τὰ γνωρίσματα. Anchor of the Seleucids : Justin, XV, 4; Appian, *Syrica*, 56; Ausonius, *Oratio urbium nobilium*, lines 24 ff. (*Monumenta Germaniae Histor. AA.*, V, 2, p. 99); for the coins, see E. Babelon, *Catalogue des monnaies grecques de la Bibliothèque Nationale, Rois de Syrie*, Introd. pp. vii, viii; for the Delos vases, *Bulletin de correspondance hellénique*, 35, 1911, p. 434, n. 1. Julian (loc. cit) and Gregory of Nazianzen, epist. xxxviii (Migne, *P.G.*, vol. 37, col. 80) also quote, as a family sign, the shoulder of the Pelopides. I am much indebted for this passage to my colleague and friend Pierre Roussel. Cf. also A. Thomas, *Le Signe royal*, p. 283 (according to a communication sent me by Max Prinet).

156 Ed. Pauthier, I, 1865, ch. xxii, p. 40.

157 The Theatine Father Cristoforo di Castelli—speaking of King Alexander of Iberia—quoted by H. Yule in his edition of Marco Polo, London, 1875,

I, pp. 54–5; it is to the passage in Fr. Castelli that I owe the collation with the verse in Isaiah which I shall use later on. According to this missionary, the subjects of the king of Iberia attributed to their sovereigns another and stronger peculiarity: their ribs were all in one piece.

158 Above, p. 171.

159 Such at least is the text of the Vulgate. That of the introit of the Christmas Mass presents an unimportant variant: 'cujus imperium super humerum ejus'. For the Hebrew text, and the meaning to be attached to it, see B. Duhm, *Das Buch Jesaia* (Göttinger Handkommentar zum Alten Testament), 3rd ed., 1914, p. 66; for interpretation through the symbolism of the cross, St. Jerome, *Commentarium in Isaiam*, Migne, *P.L.*, vol. 24, col. 130; Walafrid Strabo, *Glossa ordinaria*, ibid., vol. 113, col. 1248; Hugues de St-Cher, *In libros prophetarum; Opera*, IV, Venice, 1703, fol. 25 v. . . . etc. Diemand, *Ceremoniell der Kaiserkrönungen*, p. 76, connects the royal sign with unction performed on the king's back 'in modum crucis'; but unction, as far as I can see, was ordinarily performed between the two shoulders, whereas the royal cross, more often than not, appears on the (right) shoulder.

160 For the final avatars of the royal sign in France, see above, p. 172.

161 'Selon la coutume, comme en témoigne l'écrit, le lion ne doit [jamais] manger un enfant de roi, mais le doit, au contraire protéger et respecter.' A large number of texts, French, English and Italian, relating to this superstition about lions have been collected by E. Kölbing in an article of the *Englische Studien*, 16, 1892, the only reproach against which I have to make is its title, which is calculated rather to conceal than reveal its contents: 'Zu Shakespeare, *King Henry IV*, Part I, Act I. 4'. I do not think it is necessary here to produce the references given by Kölbing. It may be observed that in the French lay of Havelock the Dane (two Anglo–Norman versions are reproduced in Gaimar, *Estorie des Engles*, ed. Duffus-Hardy and C. T. Martin, Rolls Series, 1888, lines 429 ff. of the *Lai* on its own, 235 of the version inserted in the work of Gaimar), Argentille, Havelock's wife, sees in a dream some lions kneeling before her husband (who had, as we know, been promised a royal lot); likewise in *Florent et Octavian*, a lion spares and then takes as his master Octavian, a royal child (*Histoire littéraire*, 36, p. 306). I have not been able to find anything about this superstition in the Bestiaries or in various books of natural science. I have consulted: Albert the Great, *De animalibus*, Bartholomew the Englishman, *De proprietatibus rerum*, Vincent of Beauvais, *Speculum naturale*. I do not know whether there is a trace of it in the literature written in German: O. Batereau, *Die Tiere in der mittelhochdeutschen Literatur*, diss. Leipzig, 1900, does not mention it.

162 Line 2549. Compare the legend—attested as early as the ninth century—of the combat between Pepin and the lion: G. Paris, *Histoire poétique de Charlemagne*, p. 223.

163 Above, p. 1; Kölbing has omitted to mention this text.

164 The rules relating to the ordeal: F. Liebermann, *Die Gesetze der Angelsachsen*, Halle, 1898, I, p. 386. My attention was drawn to this passage by the interesting article by Heinrich Böhmer, 'Die Entstehung des Zölibates', *Geschichtliche Studien Albert Hauck . . . dargebracht*, Leipzig, 1916. Böhmer has well brought out the importance of certain popular ideas, on a really

'primitive' mental level, in the struggle for celibacy during the Gregorian period; but, like more than one Protestant author, he does not seem to appreciate at its full value the power of these quasi-magical conceptions on the notion of chastity already entrenched in the Christian circles where it originated. The Middle Ages was the time when it definitely triumphed, for that was the period when the popular religion exercised the greatest effect upon the more learned religion. The part played by laymen in the battle against married priests is well enough known. I need only recall at this point—apart from the Milanese *Pataria*—the significant title of the opuscule by Sigebert of Gembloux: *Epistola cuiusdam adversus laicorum in presbyteros conjugatos calumniam*. It was especially in lay circles that the idea must have grown up that sacraments performed by married priests were invalid (cf. e.g. *Vita Norberti*, C.II, *SS.*, XII, p. 681). Certain imprudent declarations by the papacy might well have appeared to favour this notion; but it is well known that Catholic theology as a whole has always firmly refused to make the validity of a sacrament depend on the worthiness or unworthiness of the priest.

BOOK 2   CHAPTER IV   *Some confused beliefs*

1 For the whole of this chapter I have drawn heavily upon the archives in the Priory at Corbeny forming part of the records of St-Rémi preserved at Rheims in a section of the Departmental Archives of the Marne in this town. All the details of files given as references in these notes must then be understood—in default of any other details—as referring to the Rheims archives, St-Rémi records. The classification of this material was drawn up in the eighteenth century, and is rather peculiar: the Abbey archives first of all put on one side what they judged to be the most important documents, grouping them under a certain number of files with a continuous numbering system. As for the documents they thought uninteresting—often in our eyes the most valuable—they formed them into subsidiary files, each tacked on at the end of one of the preceding ones, and given the same number, but labelled 'information'. Thus—to give only one example—you will often see below a reference, along with the file number 223, to 'file 223 (information)'. I need hardly add how much my task has been lightened by the enthusiastic help of the archivist, M. G. Robert.

2 *Marcoul* is the true French form of the name; I shall use it here, seeing that the cult of St-Marcoul had its chief centre, as we shall see, in the Laon district from the tenth century onwards. The Norman form is *Marcouf*; though it was often written and pronounced *Marcou*. Cf. below, n. 13. The form *Marcoulf*, sometimes found in the seventeenth century (e.g. file 223, no. 10, detailed account of the removal of relics on 17 April 1643) is evidently an imitation of the Latin name, of 'learned' origin.

3 The Manche *département*, canton of Montebourg. The oldest deed of precise date in which the name appears would seem to be a charter of Robert I, Archbishop of Rouen, which is to be placed between 1035 and 1037; published by F. Lot, *Études critiques sur l'abbaye de Saint-Wandrille*.

(Biblioth. Hautes Études, 104), 1913, p. 60; cf. ibid., p. 63. At St-Marcouf they still venerate today a miraculous fountain: A. de Caumont, 'La Fontaine St Marcouf', *Annuaire des cinq départements de la Normandie, publié par l'Assoc. Normande*, 27, 1861, p. 442.

4 For this life—life A—and the other life, slightly later—life B—that will come into the picture, I would refer the reader finally to the good critical study by Baedorf, *Untersuchungen über Heiligenleben der westlichen Normandie*, where the necessary bibliographical details will be found. Cf. *Bibliographia hagiographica latina*, nos. 5266-7.

5 It also contains the names of a certain number of localities where the saint is believed to have passed. But they probably figure there, as in so many other writings of the kind, in order to link onto the legend of the monastery's patron saint the places where the monks had certain rights, or had staked certain claims.

6 This episode is known only through Wace, who reports it in his *Roman de Rou*, line 394 (ed. H. Andresen, Heilbronn, 1877, vol. I), no doubt following annals that have now disappeared. He attributes the pillage and burning of the abbey to Hasting and Björn, cf. G. Koerting, *Über die Quellen des Roman de Rou*, Leipzig, 1867, p. 21. The lines 'A Saint Marculf en la riviere— Riche abeie ert a pleneire' raise an incidental difficulty, for there is no river at St-Marcouf; no doubt Wace was guilty of some geographical confusion, more or less required by the exigencies of the rhyme. W. Vogel, 'Die Normannen und das frankische Reich', *Heidelb. Abh. zur mittleren und neueren Gesch.*, 14, p. 387, gives no other proof of the destruction of Nant than the edict of Charles the Simple establishing the refugee monks at Corbeny. He appears to be ignorant of the passage in the *Roman de Rou*.

7 An edict of Charles the Simple of 22 Feb. 906: *Histor. de France*, 9, p. 501. The monastery, moreover, was placed under the patronage of St Peter: the custom of the time required that religious establishments should in principle have apostles or extremely famous saints as their patrons. Later on, St-Marcoul completely ousted St Peter; cf. *St-Pierre* des Fossés, which then became *St-Maur* des Fossés, etc.

8 On what precedes, see the edicts of Charles the Simple of 19 April 907 and 14 Feb. 917, *Histor. de France*, 9, pp. 504, 530; Flodoard, *Annales*, ed. Lauer (Soc. pour l'étude et l'ens. de l'histoire), year 938, p. 69, and *Historia ecclesie Remensis*, IV, c. xxvi, reproduced in Lauer, op. cit., p. 188; edicts by Lothair in the *Recueil des actes de Lothaire et de Louis V*, ed. Halphen and Lot (*Chartes et Diplômes*), nos. III and IV; A. Eckel, *Charles le Simple* (Bibl. École Hautes Études, f. 127), pp. 30, 232. Corbeny was still of notable military importance in the sixteenth century; fortifications were constructed there in 1574; file 199, no. 2. Besides, one can well remember the part played by the Corbeny-Craonne positions in the 1914-18 war. The Priory church—demolished in 1819—still had some quite important ruins visible before the war, cf. Ledouble, *Notice sur Corbeny*, p. 164; but they have completely disappeared today, as M. le curé of Corbeny was kind enough to inform me.

9 Mabillon, *AA. SS. ord. S. Bened.*, IV, 2, p. 525 and *AA. SS. maii*, VII, p. 533.

10 E. A. Pigeon, *Histoire de la Cathédrale de Coutances*, Coutances, 1876, pp. 218-20; for the episode of the huntsman, *AA. SS. maii*, I, p. 76 (life A) and p. 80 (life B).

11 Published under the rather inaccurate title of *Miracula circa annum MLXXV Corbiniaci patrata*, by Mabillon, *AA. SS. ord. S. Bened.*, IV, 2, p. 525, and, according to him, *AA. SS. maii*, VII, p. 531. Mabillon had used a MS. belonging to St-Vincent of Laon which I have not been able to find; he also refers to a MS. of St-Victor of Paris, which he inaccurately dates round about 1400; this is clearly the Latin MS. 15024 in the Bibl. Nationale (cf. *Catal. codic. hagiog.*, III, p. 299) which belongs to the thirteenth century; the sermon is also to be found in MS. 339 B in the Tours City Library, which goes back to the fourteenth century. The sentence (fol. 14 of the Latin 15034) is as follows: 'Nam illius infirmitatis sanande, quam regium morbum vocant, tanta ei gracia celesti dono accessit, ut non minus ex remotis ac barbaris quam ex vicinis nationibus ad eum egrotantium caterve perpetuo confluant.'

12 Chap. 38, ed. Ristelhuber, II, 1879, p. 311.

13 Certificates of healing of the seventeenth century, which we shall be considering later on (pp. 158 ff.) give us good examples of popular orthography; they often have the spelling *Marcou*. This is likewise the form given in the fifteenth century by the accounts in the church of St-Brice at Tournai (below, n. 49); see also the letters patent of Henry III (Sept. 1576) and of Louis XIII (8 Nov. 1610), file 199, nos. 3 and 6. For the nineteenth century, see the sentence in Beauceron patois transcribed in the *Gazette des Hôpitaux*, 1854, p. 498. For the part played by puns in the cult of the saints, consult H. Delehaye, *Les légendes hagiographiques*, Brussels, 1905, p. 54. The theory of the pun as the original basis of St-Marcoul's healing power has often been upheld, e.g. Anatole France, *Vie de Jeanne d'Arc*, I, p. 532; Laisnel de la Salle, *Croyances et légendes du centre de la France*, 2, 1875, p. 5 (cf. I, p. 179, n. 2) is the only author, it would seem, to have alluded to the word *mar*.

14 *AA. SS. maii*, I, p. 80, c. 21. This episode is also reported in one of the lives of St-Ouen, Life II (*Bibliotheca hagiographica latina*, no. 753), drawn up at Rouen in the middle of the ninth century. This raises a problem of relationship, and has given rise to some learned polemics: W. Levison, *Monum. Germ, SS., rerum merov.*, V, pp. 550-2, and following on from this Baedorf, *Untersuchungen über Heiligenleben*, p. 35, are of the opinion that the author of the second Life of St-Marcoul—life B—took his inspiration on this point from the Life of St-Ouen. M. Vacandard, *Analecta Bollandiana*, 20, 1901, p. 166 and *Vie de St-Ouen*, 1902, p. 211, n. 1, thinks on the other hand that the plagiarism should be ascribed to the *Vie* of St-Ouen, and that the *Vie* of St-Marcoul contains the original version. I would unhesitatingly support this second theory. The little story was clearly designed to affirm the possession by the monks of Nant of their patron's head; and it could only have been current, to begin with, in the abbey whose interests it served. It corresponds to a very frequent type of hagiographical legend; cf. an analogous feature in the life of Edward the Confessor by Osbert de Clare, *Analecta Bollandiana*, 41, 1923, p. 61, n. 1.

15 Either the St-Wandrille recension, or a recension—represented by a MS. in

Paris and a MS. in the Vatican—which would seem to originate in the dioceses of Bayeux, Avranches and Coutances, *AA. SS., November*, II, 1, p. [53].

16 Apart from St-Marcouf, Manche, cant. of Montebourg—the former Nant—there are St-Marcouf, Manche, commune of Pierreville, and St-Marcouf, Calvados, cant. of Isigny. Opposite to St Marcouf cant. Montebourg there are the islands of St-Marcouf, no doubt to be identified with the islands called *duo limones* mentioned in the Carolingian lives of the saint: cf. A. Benoist, *Mém. Soc. archéol. Valognes*, 3, 1882–4, p. 94.

17 E. A. Pigeon, *Histoire de la Cathédrale de Coutances*, pp. 184, 218, 221. For the breviaries, *Catal. codic. hagiogr. lat. in Bibl. Nat. Par.*, 3, p. 640; incidentally, the oldest is not earlier than the fourteenth century. It is worth noting that among the 350 liturgical MSS. examined by the Bollandistes at the Bibliothèque Nationale, these three Coutances breviaries were the only ones to contain the name of St-Marcoul.

18 For example, the following MSS. from the Library at Rheims, coming from religious establishments in the Rheims district (for further details of them, see the Catalogue; the oldest are of the twelfth century): 264, fol. 35; 312, fol. 160; 313, fol. 83 v.; 314, fol. 325; 346, fol. 51 v.; 347, fol. 3; 349, fol. 26; 1410, fol. 179; 'Martyrologe de l'église cathédrale de Reims (sec. moitié du XIIIᵉ siècle)', in U. Chevalier, *Bibliothèque liturgique*, 7, p. 39; *Codex Heriniensis* of the Martyrology of Usuard, Migne, *P.L.*, vol. 124, col. 11 (end of the eleventh century). The sole liturgical text of the Middle Ages relating to St-Marcoul collected by U. Chevalier in his *Repertorium hymnologicum* is one in prose of the fourteenth century, coming from a missal of St-Rémi of Rheims (no. 21164). At Laon the Proper of the Saints contained in two ordinaries belonging to the cathedral, from the early thirteenth century (U. Chevalier, *Bibliothèque liturgique*, 6), does not mention Marcoul.

19 Of course, even at Corbeny there must quite early on have been representations of the saint; but we have little information about them. The inventories of 1618 and 1642 (Ledouble, *Notice*, p. 121 and file 190 no. 10) mention a little silver statuette, used as a reliquary, but we have no idea of its date. The same is true of the statue which surmounted the high altar in 1642. The bas relief, known as the 'pierre de S. Marcoul', preserved up to the 1914–18 war in the village parish church, would not appear—from the drawings in Ledouble, p. 166, and Barthélemy, *Notice*, p. 261—to have been executed before the sixteenth century at the earliest. People have sometimes thought that a sixteenth-century statue in the archives at Rheims, which I was able to see, represents St-Marcoul; but there would seem to be no justification for this belief. For the saint's iconography at St-Riquier in Ponthieu and at Tournai, see above, pp. 156 and 164.

20 Cf. E. Langlois, *Table des noms propres de toute nature compris dans les chansons de geste imprimées*, 1904, and C. J. Merk, *Anschauungen uber die Lehre . . . der Kirche im altfranzösischen Heldenepos*, p. 316.

21 Book XXII, c. 11: 'Marculfus abbas Baiocacensis sanctitate claruit in Gallia'.

22 I have looked in vain for mention of St-Marcoul in Bernard Gui (*Notices et*

extraits des MSS., 27, 2, pp. 274 ff.), in the anonymous Latin collection of saints' lives of the mid-thirteenth century which Paul Meyer has tabulated (*Histoire littér.*, 33, p. 449), in the French collection studied by the same scholar (ibid., pp. 328 ff.), in the *Catalogus sanctorum* of Pierre de Natalibus (1321 ed.), in Pierre de Calo (*Analecta Bollandiana*, 29, 1910), in the *Légende Dorée*.

23 Bibl. Nat. MS. lat. 10525: Cf. Léopold Delisle, *Notice de douze livres royaux du XIIe et du XIVe siècles*, 1902, p. 105. Neither does St-Marcoul figure in the Latin MS. 1023 attributed to Philip the Fair, nor in the 'Très beau bréviaire' of Charles V (lat. 1052); cf. Delisle, loc. cit., pp. 57, 89; nor in the *Hours* of Charles VII (lat. 1370).

24 See S. Faroul, *De la Dignité des roys de France . . .* (the author was the dean and an official of Mantes) and M. A. Benoît, *Un Diplôme de Pierre Beschebien . . .* The date of the discovery of these so-called bodies of saints is given by Benoît (p. 45), perhaps in accordance with a MS. of the curé Chèvremont (end of the seventeenth century): 19 Oct. 1343; but it does not seem to have any serious documentary support, and is ignored by Faroul. The 1383 inventory is quoted by Benoît; the deed of translation (1451) by Faroul and Benoît. The former makes the following reference to the relics: 'Premierement, un grand repositoire de fust en maniere de chasse, auquel sont les ossements de trois corps saincts, que l'on dit pieça avoir esté treuvez au chemin de Rouen et apportez en ceste eglise de Mantes'. It is strange that André du Saussay, *Martyrologium gallicanum*, Paris, 1637, I, pp. 252–4, should not know—or pretend not to know—of any St-Marcoul relics except those at Mantes, and should pass over Corbeny in complete silence.

25 The *Apologie* of Dom Oudard Bourgeois, which appeared in 1638, is a reply to Faroul's book.

26 Report dated 6 June 1681, file 223 (information) no. 8, fol. 47.

27 Faroul, loc. cit., p. 223.

28 Sébillot, *Petite Légende dorée de la Haute-Bretagne*, 1897, p. 201.

29 L. Maître, 'Les Saints Guérisseurs et les pèlerinages de l'Armorique', *Rev. d'hist. de l'Église de France*, 1922, p. 309, n. 1.

30 Louis Texier, *Extraict et abrégé de la vie de Saint Marcoul, abbé*, 1648 (the cult is thus attested at least as early as the first half of the seventeenth century).

31 Blat, *Histoire du pèlerinage de Saint Marcoul*, p. 13.

32 J. Corblet, *Hagiographie du diocèse d'Amiens*, 4, 1874, p. 430.

33 Corblet, loc. cit., p. 433.

34 Corblet, *Mém. Soc. Antiquaires Picardie*, 2nd series, 10, 1865, p. 301.

35 Corblet, *Hagiographie du diocèse*, 4, p. 433.

36 Dancoisne, *Mém. Acad. Arras*, 2nd series, 9, 1879, p. 120 n. 3.

37 Louis Lallement, *Folk-lore et vieux souvenirs d'Argonne*, 1921, p. 40: the oldest documentary evidence quoted goes back to 1733.

38 *Revue de Champagne*, 16, 1883, p. 221.

39 Rodolphe de Warsage, *Le Calendrier populaire wallon*, Antwerp, 1920, nos. 817–19; and Jean Chalon, *Fétiches, idoles et amulettes*, I, Namur, 1920, p. 148.

40 Broc de Seganges, *Les Saints Patrons des corporations*, II, n.d., p. 505 (according to a pamphlet of 1748).

41 R. de Warsage, loc. cit., no. 1269.

42 J. Chalon, loc. cit.

43 E. van Heurck, *Les Drapelets de pèlerinage en Belgique*, pp. 124, 490; at Zellick, there is evidence of a 'drapelet' of 1698.

44 J. Chalon, loc. cit.

45 van Heurck, loc. cit., p. 473; the evidence goes back to 1685.

46 Evidence dated 1672; cf. below, n. 58. There is no relic of St-Marcoul mentioned by Gelenius, *De admiranda sacra et civili magnitudine Coloniae*, Cologne, 1645. When correcting the proofs, I realized that there should be added to this list the church of St-Jacques de Compiègne, where there is still a chapel dedicated to St-Marcoul; cf. Appendix II, no. 24.

47 Cf. what is said in the notes above about Saumur and Russé, St-Thomas en Argonne, Zellick and Wondelgem.

48 The martyrology is the *codex Centulensis* of Usard's *Martyrology*: Migne, *P.L.*, col. 124, col. 11. For the iconography—apart from the fresco referred to above, p. 163—mention should be made of a statue of the saint dating from the beginning of the sixteenth century: G. Durand in *La Picardie historique et monumentale*, 4, p. 284, and fig. 37; and a silver statuette, serving as a reliquary, destroyed in 1789, which I cannot precisely date: Corblet, *Hagiographie*, 4, p. 433.

49 Accounts of the church of St-Brice, 1408–69: 'A Jacquemart Blathon, machon, pour son sallaire d'avoir rassis en plonc le candeler de fier servant devant l'image de saint Marcou et, en ce faisant, fait trois traux au mur' (*Annales Soc. histor. Tournai*, 13, 1908, p. 185). In 1481–2 the accounts speak of an 'autel de saint Marcou'. (This is from a very kind communication from M. Hocquet, the city archivist of Tournai.)

50 Gautier, *Saint Marcoul*, p. 56. The cathedral at Angers and the church of St-Michel du Tertre would seem to have jointly venerated St-Marcoul.

51 Duplus, *Histoire et pèlerinage de Saint Marcoul*, p. 83. On Gissey [sur Ouche] there is a notice in the *Mémoires de la commission des antiquités de la Côte d'Or*, 1832–3, p. 157, but it does not contain any information about our saint.

52 L. Dancoisne, 'Les Médailles religieuses du Pas de Calais', *Mém. Acad. Arras*, 2nd series, 11, 1879, pp. 121–4. Dancoisne believes that in early times, when it was founded in the eleventh century, the church of Ste-Croix d'Arras was placed under the protection of St-Marcoul; but he gives no shadow of proof for this assertion, which does not seem to have any documentary support.

53 U. Chevalier, *Repertorium hymnologicum*, no. 21164; cf. above, n. 18. The collegiate church of St-Étienne at Troyes possessed in the seventeenth century certain relics of St-Marcoul, as is testified by N. des Guerrois, *La Saincteté chrétienne, contenant la vie, mort et miracles de plusieurs Saincts . . . dont les reliques sont au Diocese et Ville de Troyes*, Troyes, 1637, p. 296 v.

54 The theft had taken place at an unspecified time, probably towards the end of the sixteenth century. The detailed account of it was only recorded on 17

July 1637; it will be found in file 229, no. 9. It was incorrectly reproduced by Oudard Bourgeois, *Apologie*, p. 120 (O. Bourgeois writes 'Bué' instead of 'Bueil', as given in the authentic text). The whole head had at first been transferred to Bueil; Corbeny then recovered it, but the people of Bueil would seem to have kept a fragment of the skull: cf. Gautier, *Saint Marcoul*, p. 30.

55 *Notice sur la vie de S. Marcoul et sur son pèlerinage à Archelange*, p. 22. On the popularity of pilgrimages even nowadays in Burgundy, *Rev. des traditions populaires*, 2, 1887, p. 235.

56 Ledouble, *Notice*, p. 220 (reprod. opp. p. 208). The only medal of St-Marcoul possessed by the Cabinet des Médailles in the Bibl. Nat. is also of this type—a fact I have been able to verify through a mould kindly made for me by M. Jean Babelon, the Curator.

57 R. Toustain de Billy, *Histoire ecclésiastique du diocèse de Coutances* (Soc. de l'hist. de Normandie), 3, Rouen, 1886, p. 239.

58 Gautier, p. 29.

59 Cf. above, p. 175.

60 Daire, *Histoire de la ville d'Amiens*, 2, 1757, p. 192. The fraternity, who were founded as the result of a vow taken in a season of plague, had as its patrons St Roch, St Adrian, St Sebastian and St Marcoul. The founding of a fraternity does not of course prove the cult of the saint originated at the exact date when the fraternity was founded; cf. what is said below about Tournai, and add to it that at Wondelgem, where there is evidence of the cult from 1685, the fraternity was only founded in 1787; but a fact of this kind is incontrovertible proof that the cult had thrived.

61 Gautier, *Saint Marcoul*, p. 30.

62 Schépers, 'Le Pèlerinage de Saint Marcoul à Grez-Doiceau', van Heurck, *Les Drapelets de pèlerinage*, pp. 157 ff. A series of instructions for those patients who desired the help of St Marcoul were printed at Louvain in 1656; if they were indeed drawn up specially for the pilgrims to Grez-Doiceau— Van Heurck's remarks on this point are not very precise (p. 158)—the pilgrimage would then date from 1656 at the latest.

63 *AA. SS. maii*, I, p. 70 c.

64 It is attested for the first time in the accounts of 1673–1674 (information from M. Hocquet). On 27 May 1653 Childeric's tomb had been discovered in a piece of ground belonging to the Dean of St-Brice, and certain objects found in it were sent to Louis XIV. According to a local tradition, without any documentary support, the king of France, as a reward for this gift, sent the dean a relic of St-Marcoul; cf. the pious brochure entitled: *Abrégé de la vie de S. Marcou . . . honoré en l'église paroissiale de S. Brice à Tournai*, p. 3. Likewise at Rheims, where the cult of the saint had existed almost from time immemorial, it would seem to have taken on a new development in the seventeenth century. About 1650, a hospice was founded under his protection; and soon afterwards, a fraternity in his honour was set up in this same hospice; cf. Jadart, 'L'Hôpital Saint-Marcoul de Reims', *Travaux Acad. Reims*, 111, 1901–2, pp. 178, 192, n. 2.

65 Bibl. Nat., Cabinet des Estampes, Collection des Saints; reprod. in Landouzy, *Le Toucher des Ecrouelles*, p. 19.

66 See the *Dictionnaire topographique de l'Aisne*. Cf. the text of 1671 published by R. Durand, *Bulletin de la Soc. d'Hist. moderne*, p. 458 and the Letters Patent of Louis XIII, 8 Nov. 1610, file 199, no. 6.

67 For the corporations and the 'kings' of the mercers, see Pierre Vidal and Léon Duru, *Histoire de la corporation des marchands merciers . . . de la ville de Paris* [1911]: cf. E. Levasseur, *Histoire des classes ouvrières . . . avant 1789*, 2nd ed., 1900, I, pp. 612 ff.; A. Bourgeois, 'Les Métiers de Blois', *Soc. Sciences et lettres du Loir-et-Cher, Mém*, 13, 1892, pp. 172, 177; H. Hauser, *Ouvriers du temps passé*, 4th ed., 1913, pp. 168, 256. Numerous trades have had 'kings' at their head, in France and elsewhere; but this is not the place to attempt a bibliography of this strange form of language. We have a fair amount of documentary information about the mercers of Corbeny: a deed by Jean Robertet, representing the Grand Chamberlain, 21 Nov. 1527; file 221, no. 1, an agreement between the 'king' and the prior, 19 April 1531; ibid., no. 2 (de Barthélemy, *Notice*, p. 222, n. 1); a decree by the Privy Council of 26 Aug. 1542: Oudard Bourgeois, *Apologie*, p. 126; and some other documents from the end of the sixteenth century: file 221, nos. 3 and 4; Bourgeois, pp. 127 ff.; de Barthélemy, p. 222. The office certainly still existed in Bourgeois' time (1638). The seal is reproduced by Bourgeois on p. 146; and a specimen of it has been described by G. Soultrait, *Société de Sphragistique de Paris*, 2, 1852-3, p. 182; cf. ibid., p. 257.

68 See in file 195 (information) the 1495-6 accounts, fol. 12 v., 28 v.; 1541-2, pp. 30, 41; 1542-3, p. 31. None of these medals seems to have survived. The Seine, which has yielded up so many decorated leaden objects, has not produced one image of St-Marcoul (cf. A. Forgeais, *Collection de plombs historiés trouvés dans la Seine*, 2, 1863 and 4, 1965).

69 See the accounts quoted in the previous note. The first and most explicit simply speaks of 'boutillettes de grez en quoy ilz [the pilgrims] emportent du lavement'; but the booklet entitled *Avertissement à ceux qui viennent honorer . . .* (below, n. 70) is more specific: 'Les Malades . . . laveront leur mal avec l'eau qui se benit par l'immersion de la relique du Saint, et même en pourront user pour boire'. The regulations for pilgrims to Grez-Doiceau, inspired by those at Corbeny, still read as follows. 'On pourra toujours se procurer dans la dite église de l'eau bénite en l'honneur de Saint Marcoul, pour en boire, ou s'en laver les tumeurs ou les plaies': Schépers, 'Le Pèlerinage de Saint Marcoul à Grez-Doiceau', p. 179. For similar customs in other pilgrimages, see e.g. H. Gaidoz, *La Rage et St Hubert* (Bibliotheca Mythica, I), 1887, pp. 204 ff.

70 One of these booklets—of the seventeenth century, but undated—entitled: *Avertissement à ceux qui viennent honorer le glorieux Saint Marcoul, dans l'église du Prieuré de Corbeny au Diocèse de Laon*, is preserved in the Bibl. Nat. under the no. Lk⁷2444; another rather different one, entitled: *La Vie de Sainct Marcoul abbé et confesseur* and dated Rheims 1619, is to be found in the Rheims archives, St-Rémi, file 223. In 1673 a hospital for the pilgrims was established at Corbeny: file 224, no. 10.

71 Naturally, and in conformity with the general custom, the sick who by reason of their illness, their age, or any other cause were unable to journey to Corbeny could have a substitute in the person of a relation, a friend, or

even no doubt a hired pilgrim. The healing certificates we shall be considering later on contain fairly numerous examples of this practice. Others, who had been healed after dedicating themselves to the saint, only made a pilgrimage to Corbeny by way of thanksgiving; but this did not happen very often.

72 The reader will find the regulations entitled: *Les Ceremonies que l'on a acoustumé d'observer par ancienne tradition en la neufiesme qui se doibt observer au pelerinage de Saint Marcoul à Corbeny*, with annotations, in Latin, by Gifford, file 223 (information); it has no date, but an archivist of the eighteenth century has written at the top of the sheet: 1627. I have not been able to identify this Gifford. Opposite to the fourth article, in which the Prior orders the pilgrims to be present at the Offices and not to leave the precincts of Corbeny, there is the following annotation: 'Si respiciatur in eo perseverantia in bono opere, licet; alias non videtur carere superstitione'; opposite the fifth (which forbids touching any metal objects): 'Omnia ista sunt naturaliter agentia; ideo si sint noxia merito prohibentur'; opposite the sixth (forbidding certain foods): 'Idem ut supra, modo constat judicio medicorum tales cibos naturaliter esse noxios'; opposite the seventh (concerning substitutes, who are bound to fulfil the same observances as the pilgrims themselves: 'Hoc non videtur carere superstitione, quia non est ratio cur naturaliter noxia prohibeantur illi qui est sanus'. The regulation inscribed at the head of the Grez-Doiceau fraternity register in 1633 (cf. above, p. 159) does not contain the veto against touching any metal objects. By way of comparison, one can read the regulations concerning the conduct to be observed during the novena, which are still in use today in the pilgrimage to St-Hubert in the Ardennes: H. Gaidoz, *La Rage et Saint Hubert* (Bibliotheca Mythica), 1887, p. 69.

73 See the letter of one of these scrupulous persons, Louis Douzinel, of Arras, 21 Feb. 1657, file 223 (information), n. 7.

74 File 223 (information), no. 6. Oudard Bourgeois, *Apologie*, pp. 47 ff., analyses four certificates, the oldest of which refers to a healing effected in 1610.

75 File 223 (information), no. 7: *Bus*.

76 Numerous certificates—too many to be quoted—in file 223 (information).

77 A certificate by the curé of Saales, Bruche and Bourg, dated 31 Dec. 1705: file 223 (information), no. 8.

78 Remiremont, St-Clément near Lunéville, Val de St-Dié 1655, file 223 (information), no. 8.

79 Pithiviers: certificate dated 22 May 1719: file 223 (information), no. 7; Gisors, ibid., 12 July 1665; Rozoy-en-Brie, Grisy, Maintenon, Dreux (1655); ibid., no. 8; Paris, 9 May 1739, file 223, no. 11.

80 Jurques, diocese of Bayeux: 30 June 1665; file 223 (information), no. 7; a place situated between Les Andelys and Louviers, 1665 (ibidem).

81 Laval: 4 July 1665: file 223 (information), no. 7; Corné, diocese of Angers: 1665, ibid., no. 8.

82 A certificate drawn up by two doctors from Auray: file 223 (information), no. 7, 25 March 1669.

83 Places in the diocese of Nevers and Langres, Joigny près Auxerre, 1655: file 223 (information), no. 8; Sancerre, 11 June 1669, ibid., no. 11.

84 Vorly, diocese of Bourges: certificate dated 30 March 1669; file 223 (information), no. 7; Nassigny, same diocese, 1655, ibid., no. 8.

85 Jaro (?), near Cusé, diocese of Clermont, 1655: file 223 (information), no. 8.

86 Charlieu 'en Lionnois', Dammartin (diocese of Lyons): 1655, file 223 (information), no. 8.

87 'Bourg-le-Namur, six leagues from Grenoble, in the Piedmont direction': file 223 (information), no. 7.

88 Schépers, 'Le pèlerinage de Saint-Marcoul à Grez-Doiceau', p. 179.

89 At Amiens, in 1581, St-Marcoul is found associated with three great saints considered as protectors against the plague—St Roch, St Adrian and St Sebastian: above, n. 60.

90 O. Bourgeois, Apologie, p. 60; Marlot, Théâtre d'honneur, p. 718. This is also the theme of the Gallia Christiana, IX, col. 248. Some even said: Charles the Simple (the small collection of material on St-Marcoul put together after Louis XV's consecration: file 223 (information)). The effigy of St Louis on the mercers' fraternity seal even gave rise to the idea that this prince had been its founder: O. Bourgeois, p. 63; Gallia, loc. cit.; AA. SS., maii, I, p. 70. G. Ledouble, Notice, goes as far as to write (p. 116) that St-Louis 'écrivit son nom, Louis de Poissy, en tête du registre de l'association'. Through a rather amusing confusion, people came to imagine that the kings of France, rather than the 'kings' of the mercers, had been the first members of this pious association (see the certificate of A. Baillet, 24 Sept. 1632, above, p. 175).

91 Report of the enquiry into the theft of St-Marcoul's head (18 July 1637): Bourgeois, Apologie, pp. 123–4 (cf. above, n. 54).

92 File 190b, no. 2; an account from the end of the fifteenth century, showing the use of the sums of money received by the prior 'pour la repparation des clochers et pavillon du roy'. For documentary evidence of the royal pilgrimages, see Appendix V.

93 Appendix V, p. 283.

94 Ed. Vallet de Viriville, 1859, chap. 59, p. 323.

95 For the Chronique de la Pucelle, see the preceding note; Jean Chartier, Chronique de Charles VII, ed. Vallet de Viriville, 1858, I, chap. 48, p. 97; the other texts, Quicherat, Procès de Jeanne d'Arc (Soc. de l'hist. de France), IV, pp. 187, 433, 514; V, p. 67.

96 Ed. Goubaud and P. A. Lemoisne (Soc. de l'hist. de France), I, p. 170. Cf. Grassaille, Regalium Franciae iura, p. 65, which is cautious in its verdict: 'Alij dicunt, quod hanc potestatem capiunt in visitatione corporis beati Marcolphi, quam post coronationem facere consueverunt Reges'.

97 Hubertus Thomas Leodius, Annalium de vita illustrissimi principis Friderici II . . ., 1624 ed., Frankfurt, p. 97; for H. Thomas' inaccuracies, see below, Book 2, Chapter V, n. 1.

98 For the royal touch given by Charles VIII: Godefroy, Ceremonial, I, p. 208; by Louis XII: Alms register, Arch. Nat., KK. 77, fol. 124 v.; by Henry II: below, Book 2, Chapter V, n. 10; by Louis XIII: Godefroy, p. 457 (860 sick persons), and J. Héroard, Journal, 1868, II, p. 32 ('neuf cents et tant'); by Louis XV and Louis XVI: above, pp. 223 and 224. The fact that Louis XII did not touch any sick persons before the ceremony at Corbeny emerges

from an examination of his alms register, quoted above; the whole literature of the royal miracle in the seventeenth century agrees in general that there was this waiting period.

99 The preceding account follows the contemporary version published by Godefroy, *Ceremonial*, I, pp. 184 ff. Cf. the 'Mémoires de Sieur Fouquart, procureur syndic de la ville de Reims', *Revue des soc. savantes*, 2nd series, 6, 1861 2nd week, pp. 100, 102; for the part played by G. Coquillart, see a note by Rathery, ibid., p. 98, n. 2.

100 'O Marculphe tuis medicaris cum scrofulosis—Quos redigis peregre partibus incolumes—Morbigeras scrofulas Franchorum rex patienti—Posse pari fruitur (te tribuente) medicus—Miraculis igitur qui tantis sepe coruscas—Astriferum merear sanus adire palum.' Cf. Appendix II, no. 20.

101 Bibl. Nat., lat. 1429, fol. 108–12. For this very famous MS., the reader need only refer to the notice by Léopold Delisle, *Annuaire-Bulletin de la Soc. de l'hist. de France*, 1900, p. 120.

102 For these works of art, see Appendix II, nos. 14, 15, 16, 20, 21, 22, 23; cf. Plate 2. The same theme recurs at Grez-Doiceau, in a statuette and a picture whose dates I do not know. There are also, of course, representations of St-Marcoul of the ordinary abbot type in which the king does not appear: e.g. the images in the Falaise fraternity and in that of the Carmelites of Place Maubert quoted above, n. 65, and below, n. 163. An engraving of the seventeenth century preserved in the Collect. des Saints in the Cabinet des Estampes (reproduced by Landouzy, *Le Toucher des Ecrouelles*, unnumbered). Two engravings of the same period coming from pilgrim booklets are reproduced ibid., pp. 21, 31; an engraving in [Bourgoing de Villefore] *Les Vies des SS. Pères des déserts d'Occident*, I, 1708, opp. p. 170, likewise in the Cabinet des Estampes, Collection des Saints and Bibliothèque Ste-Geneviève, coll. Guénebault, cartoon 24, no. 5108 (here, St-Marcoul, in company with two other hermits, is represented as an anchorite and not as an abbot); a devotional image of the seventeenth century representing the saint tempted by the devil disguised as a woman: Coll. Guénebault, cartoon 24, no. 5102 (kindly communicated to me by C. Mortet). It is nonetheless true that the really characteristic attribute of the saint, as soon as one rises above the most commonplace hagiographical iconography, is to be accompanied by the king of France. St-Marcoul is not mentioned by A. M. Pachinger in his two works: 'Über Krankheitspatrone und Heiligenbildern' and 'Über Krankheitspatrone auf Medaillen', *Archiv. für Gesch. der Medizin*, 2, 1908–9 and 3, 1909–10.

103 Forcatel, *De Gallorum imperio*, pp. 128 ff.; du Laurens, *De mirabili*, pp. 14–15; du Peyrat, *Histoire ecclésiastique de la Cour*, p. 807. Cf. also Mauclerc, *De monarchia divina*, 1622, col. 1567. The author who has perhaps been the most deliberate in attributing the healing power to St-Marcoul's intercession is Robert Ceneau, *Gallica historia*, fol. 1557, p. 110. For the attitude of the sixteenth- and seventeenth-century writers towards unction considered as the source of the royal miracle, see above, p. 201.

104 *Apologie*, p. 65; cf. p. 9. The same conciliatory theory recurs in Marlot, *Théâtre d'honneur*, pp. 717 ff.; cf. above, p. 167.

105 File 223 (information), no. 7; certificate issued 25 March 1669 by two doctors from Auray for a scrofulous patient who had been healed 'au retour d'estre touché de sa Majesté tres Chrestienne et du pèlerinage de St Marcoul'. File 223, no. 11: certificate issued 29 April 1658 by the curé of Neufchâtel, near Menneville (no doubt Neuchâtel-sur-Aisne, Aisne, and Menneville, same canton); the sick woman had been touched by Louis XIV the day after his consecration 'en sorte que peu de temps après par l'intercession de St. Marcou, auquel elle avait faict prière, elle aurait receu du soulagement'; but subsequently the disease came on again, she returned to Corbeny, did her novena, and was completely cured. See also the certificate quoted below, n. 107.

106 Schépers, 'Le Pèlerinage de Saint-Marcoul à Grez-Doiceau', p. 181.

107 File 223 (information), no. 7.

108 Benedict XIV, *Opera omnia*, Venice, 1788: *De servorum Dei beatificatione et beatorum canonizatione*, Book IV, pars I, cap. iii, c. 21, p. 17: 'Ad aliud quoddam genus referendum est illud, quod modo a Nobis subnectitur, ad privilegium videlicet Regum Galliae strumas sanandi: illud quippe non hereditario jure, aut innata virtute obtinetur, sed Gratia ipsa gratis data, aut cum Clodoveus Clotildis uxoris precibus permotus Christo nomen dedit, aut cum Sanctus Marculphus ipsam pro Regibus omnibus Galliarum a Deo impetravit'.

109 *Théâtre d'honneur*, p. 718; the phrase recurs in Regnault, *Dissertation*, p. 15.

110 *Apologie*, p. 9.

111 It is true that according to a theory apparently fathered by Carte in his *General History of England*, 1747, I, IV, § 42 (cf. Law Hussey, 'On the cure of scrofulous diseases', p. 208, n. 9; Crawfurd, *King's Evil*, p. 17), the English kings touched for scrofula in a room of the Palace of Westminster called the St-Marcoul Chamber. In actual fact the *Rotuli Parliamentorum* several times mention a room in this palace called the *Marcolf* or *Marcholf Chamber* (cf. the Index, p. 986), for the first time in 1344 (II, p. 147a), and the last in 1483 (VI, p. 238a). But there is no evidence that the kings ever touched anyone in it. This room was generally used as a sessions-room for the commission of the examiners of petitions, composed of not more than ten members, and must have been of very small dimensions. It does not seem at all likely that it could have been used for the very large groups attending the royal healings. Besides, it must be noted that although mentioned seventy-three times in the *Rotuli*, this room always appears under the name *Marcolf* (or *Marcholf*) *Chamber*, and never *St Marcolf*, which would have been quite contrary to the ordinary custom of the time if it had really derived its name from a saint. No doubt the *Marcolf* after whom it was named was an entirely secular person, very different from the Abbot of Nant. One might think—though this is pure hypothesis—of the facetious Marculfus whose conversations with the good king Solomon were the joy of the mediaeval public (cf. among others G. Paris, *La littérature française au moyen âge*, § 103); may there not have been on the walls of the room some painting depicting these amusing conversations? Moreover, it would seem that St-Marcoul never enjoyed great popularity in England, which is all the less surprising in that even on the Continent his cult only spread, as we know, to a large extent after the Reformation. He does not figure either in the

Sanctilogium Angliae of John of Tynemouth (d. about 1348) (C. Horstmann, *Nova legenda Angliae*, I, Oxford, 1901, p. ix), or in the *Martiloge in englyshe* of Richard Whytford (1526). There is no sign that any English church was ever dedicated to him; cf. Frances Arnold-Forster, *Studies in church dedications*, 3, 1899.

112 This expression recurs in particular again and again in the certificates of healing preserved in the archives at Rheims.

113 On this point the reader may be referred to W. H. Roscher, 'Die Sieben-und Neunzahl im Kultus und Mythus der Griechen', *Abh. der phil.-histor. Klasse der kgl. sächsischen Gesellsch. der Wissensch.*, 24, I, 1904. Cf. also Petri Bungi Bergomatis, *Numerorum mysteria*, Paris, 1618, pp. 282 ff.; and F. von Adrian, 'Die Siebenzahl im Geistesleben der Völker', *Mitteil. der anthropol. Gesellschaft in Wien*, 31, 1901.

114 W. Henderson, *Notes on the Folk-lore of the Northern Counties of England*, 2nd ed. (Publications of the Folk-lore Society, II), London, 1879, p. 306 (the fact is quoted from a communication by Professor Marecco). According to F. von Adrian, *Die Siebenzahl*, p. 252, the seventh sons or daughters are sometimes held to be devils, in the same way that demons were thought to come out of the seventh egg of a black hen, or from the eggs laid by a seven-year-old hen.

115 *Revue des traditions populaires*, 9, 1894, p. 112, no. 17 (at Mentone). The popular conception, which explains the attribution sometimes of a favour-able, sometimes of an unfavourable character to the power of a seventh son, is well expressed in this saying by an English peasant woman, reported by Charlotte Sophia Burne, *Shropshire Folk-Lore*, London, 1885, p. 187: 'The seventh son'll always be different tille the others'.

116 Laisnel de la Salle, *Croyances et légendes du centre de la France*, 1875, II, p. 5.

117 Tiffaud, *L'Exercice illégal de la médecine dans le Bas-Poitou* (thesis, Paris), 1899, p. 31.

118 F. Liebrecht, *Zur Volkskunde*, Heilbronn, 1879, p. 346 (with references).

119 Theophilo Braga, *O Povo Portuguez*, II, Lisbon, 1885, p. 104.

120 Joseph Sirven, 'Les Saludadors' (1830), *Soc. agricole, scientifique et littéraire des Pyrénées-Orientales*, 14, 1864, pp. 116–18 (Catalonia and Roussillon).

121 The reader will find later on, quoted either in the text or in the notes, a certain number of ancient or modern testimonies to this superstition in France. I will confine myself here to pointing out those that I shall not have occasion to refer to later: Leonardus Vairus (L. Vairo), *De fascino libri tres*, Paris, 1583, lib. I, c. XI, p. 48 (the author, who is Italian, gives out this superstition as widespread 'in Gallia et Burgundia'; I am quoting, as the reader will see, from one of the French editions, the only one I have been able to consult. The book was translated into French under the title: *Trois Livres des charmes*, 1583, and may thus well have contributed to spreading this belief in our country); Thomas Platter, in his memoirs written down in 1604–5: tr. by L. Sieber, *Mémoire Soc. histoire Paris*, 23, 1898, p. 224; Petri Bungi, *numerorum mysteria*, 1618, p. 302 (seventh sons and seventh daugh-ters); de l'Ancre, *L'incrédulité et mescreance du sortilege . . .*, 1622, p. 157; Laisnel de la Salle, *Croyances et légendes du centre de la France*, 2, p. 5; Jaubert, *Glossaire du centre de la France*, 1864 (under the word 'Marcou');

M. A. Benoît, *Procès-verbaux soc. archéol. Eure-et-Loire*, 5, 1876, p. 55 (Beauce); Tiffaud, *L'Exercice illégal de la médecine dans le Bas-Poitou*, pp. 19, 31, 34, n. 2; Amélie Bosquet, *La Normandie romanesque et merveilleuse*, Rouen, 1845, p. 306 (seventh daughters); Paul Sébillot, 'Coutumes populaires de la Haute-Bretagne', *Les Littératures populaires de toutes les nations*, 22, p. 13; Paul Martellière, *Glossaire du Vendômois*, Orléans et Vendôme, 1893 (under the word 'Marcou').

122 M. Delrio, *Disquisitionum magicarum*, I, cap. III, q. IV, 1606 ed., vol. I, p. 57 (Flanders); E. Monseur, *Le Folklore wallon*, Brussels, 1892, p. 30, § 617 (Wallonia).

123 I am following the same rules for the references here as I did for France (see above n. 121). Some of the passages indicated also concern Scotland: *Diary of Walter Yonge Esqu.*, ed. G. Roberts (Camden Society, 41), London, 1848 (the journal is of 1607), p. 13; Crooke, *Body of man* (came out in 1615; I only know it through J. Murray, *A new English Dictionary*, under 'King's Evil'); John Bird, *Ostenta Carolina*, 1661, p. 77; Χειρεξοχη, 1665, p.2; Thiselton-Dyer, *Old English social life as told by the parish registers*, London, 1898, p. 77; W. G. Black, *Folk-medicine*, London, 1883, pp. 122, 137; W. Henderson, *Notes on the Folk-lore of the Northern Counties*, 2nd ed., pp. 304, 306; Henry Barnes, *Transactions of the Cumberland and Westmorland Antiquarian and Archaeological Society*, 13, 1895, p. 362; John Brand, *Popular Antiquities of Great Britain*, London, 1870, p. 233; Charlotte Sophia Burne, *Shropshire Folk-Lore*, London, 1885, pp. 186–8 (seventh son and seventh daughter); *Notes and Queries*, 5th series, 12, 1879, p. 466 (seventh daughter); *Folklore*, 1895, p. 205; 1896, p. 295 (seventh daughter); this last example shows that in Somerset the touch had to take place in two series of seven mornings, separated by seven days without any touch; in the same county, an even greater power was attributed to the seventh daughter of a seventh daughter; the sacred number is dominant throughout.

124 Robert Kirk, *Secret Commonwealth*, Edinburgh, 1815, p. 39 (the work was composed in 1691); J. G. Dalyell, *The darker superstitions of Scotland*, Edinburgh, 1834, p. 70; *Notes and Queries*, 6th series, 6, 1882, p. 306; *Folklore*, 1903, p. 371, n. 1 and 372–3; 1900, p. 448.

125 *Dublin University Magazine*, 4, 1879, p. 218; *Folklore*, 1908, p. 316. In county Donegal, as in Somerset, there is a refinement on the figure 7: the touch of the seventh son must be applied on *seven* successive mornings: *Folklore*, 1897, p. 15; in the same county the midwife who assists at the birth of a seventh son puts an object of her choice into his hand, and it is with objects made from this same substance that he must henceforth rub his patients in order to heal them: ibid., 1912, p. 473.

126 F. Sessions, 'Syrian Folklore; notes gathered on Mount Lebanon', *Folklore*, 9, 1898, p. 19.

127 *De occulta philosophia*, 2, c. iii, no date or place [1533], p. cviii. Cornelius Agrippa also mentions the seventh daughter.

128 Raoul de Presles, in the course of his translation, which we have already frequently quoted, of the *City of God*, treats—in the course of his exposition of Chap. 31 of Book XI—of the virtues of the number 7; but he does not mention the marvellous powers of the seventh son. Yet nothing can be

concluded from this silence, for he may very well have refused to treat of a popular superstition.

129 The use of sacred numbers, and in particular the number 7, was of course familiar to scholarly thought, and notably to theology, in the Middle Ages: the seven sacraments are the most famous, though not the only, example (cf. Hauck-Herzog, *Realencyclopädie der prot. Theologie*, under 'Siebenzahl'; but I only intend to speak here of *popular* superstitions.

130 Extracts from the case analysed in the *Calendar of State Papers, Domestic, Charles I*, 30 Sept. and 18 Nov. 1637, have been partially published by Green, 'On the cure by touch', pp. 81 ff. It should be added that ever since the birth of the child, his maternal grandfather had announced that he would work cures. But he did not begin to practise until after the yeoman Henry Poyntynge, who had read Lipton's book, had sent his niece along to him.

131 [T. Lupton], *A thousand notable things of sundry sortes*, London [1579], II, § 2, p. 25; cf. the *Dictionary of National Biography*, under the author's name.

132 Antonii Mizaldi, *Memorabilium, utilium ac iucundorum centuriae novem*, 1567, cent. 3, c. 66, p. 39 v.

133 J. B. Thiers (passage quoted below, n. 143), thinks they also cure 'des fièvres tierces ou quartes'. In Scotland they heal various diseases apart from scrofula: *Folklore*, 1903, p. 372. In Roussillon, where there is a mixture of French and Spanish influences, they heal both rabies—as in Catalonia—and scrofula, as in France: *Soc. agricole des Pyrénées–Orientales*, 14, 1864, p. 118. According to Thiers (4th ed., p. 443) the seventh sons used to cure 'chilblains in the heel'.

134 We have no evidence for Scotland during the period of its independence.

135 Above, pp. 209, 280.

136 A strange example of this kind is revealed by a correspondence analysed in *Calendar of State Papers, Domestic, Charles I*, 10 June, 20 Oct., 22 Oct. 1632.

137 For the two monarchies' attitude to these seventh sons, cf. above, pp. 208–9.

138 Mme de Sévigné: a letter to Count Gontaut, 18 May 1680 (dealing incidentally with a seventh daughter)—*Briefe der Prinzessin Elizabeth Charlotte von Orleans*, ed. W. Menzel (Biblioth. des literarischen Vereins in Stuttgart, 6), 1843, p. 407, cf. above, p. 207.

139 The Basle doctor Felix Platter, who studied at Montpellier from 1552 to 1557, met this individual there, a man of Poitou by birth: see F. Platter, *Praxeos . . . tomus tertius: de Vitiis*, I, c. iii, Basle, 1656; strangely enough this passage does not seem to be included in the earlier editions of the work. Platter does not mention the fact in his memories, on which see G. Lanson, *Hommes et livres*, Paris, 1895.

140 By 'L.C.D.G.', Aix, 1643; the author thinks that the seventh sons enjoy this gift only in France, if they are born of French ancestors (to the fourth generation), 'non concubinaires, bons catholiques et n'ayant point commis de meurtres'.

141 Cf. above, p. 174.

142 *Correspondence*, ed. C. Urbain et E. Levesque, VII, p. 47, no. 1197 (27 March 1695). This curious letter was kindly pointed out to me by M. l'abbé Duine.

143 Thiers, 4th ed., p. 442; Saint-Beuve, III, case 170, pp. 589 ff. Cf. the

similar attitude taken by Thiers and Jacques de Sainte-Beuve towards the superstitions flourishing in connection with the St Hubert pilgrimage: Gaidoz, *La Rage et Saint Hubert*, pp. 82 ff.

144 Menault, 'Du Marcoul; de la guérison des humeurs froides', *Gazette des hôpitaux*, 1854, p. 497; summarized in the *Moniteur Universel*, of 23 October.

145 Leonardus Vairus, *De fascino libri tres*, 2, c. xi, 1583 ed., p. 141; Théophile Raynaud, S.J., *De Stigmatismo sacro et prophano*, Sectio II, c. IV, in the *Opera*, Lyons, 1665, XIII, pp. 159–60; J. B. Thiers, *Traité des superstitions*, 4th ed. pp. 438–9 (the expressions between inverted commas are taken from this latter work).

146 T. Braga, *O Povo Portuguez*, II, p. 104 ('una cruz sobre a lingua'); J. Sirven *Soc. agricole Pyrénées Orientales*, 14, 1864, p. 116; 'Le vulgaire . . . assure qu'ils ont une marque distinctive au palais de la bouche comme une croix ou une fleur de lys'; as always in Roussillon, there is a mixture of influences; the cross is Spanish, the lily French; cf. above, n. 133.

147 The oldest evidence seems to be Raulin, *Panegyre . . . des fleurs de lys*, 1625, p. 178.

148 Fol. 1670, I, p. 181. E. Molinier, *Les Politiques chrestiennes*, 1621, 3, chap. iii, p. 310. writes, on the subject of families intended by God to exercise authority, whether royal or noble; 'Je dis que ceux qui descendent de telles maisons portent du ventre de leur mère, non comme ceux de nos vieux Romans la marque d'une ardente épée empreinte sur la cuisse, mais l'autorité d'un crédit héréditaire gravé dessus leur nom' (cf. Lacour-Gayet, *Education politique*, p. 353). This is clearly no more than a literary reminiscence. J. Barbier, in his treatise on *Les miraculeux Effects de la sacrée main des Roys de France*, which came out in 1618, mentions the lance (p. 38), a hereditary mark of the 'Spartes Thébains' and the anchor of the Seleucids (cf. above, p. 145): he does not appear to suspect that there has ever been a royal sign in France.

149 de Ceriziers, *Les Heureux Commencemens*, p. 194: [Regnault], *Dissertation historique*, p. 8.

150 This at least is what would seem to be the implications of a sentence written by Bossuet in the letter quoted above, n. 142: 'Le Roi ne touche plus ces sortes de gens [the seventh sons] que dans le cas qu'il touche les autres, c'est à dire dans *le* cas des écrouelles'. 'Ne touche *plus*': so the French kings did formerly have the habit of touching these seventh sons, even apart from 'cases of scrofula' . . .; it is annoying that no other text, as far as I know, enables us to give these rather enigmatic words an entirely certain interpretation.

151 E. Monseur, *Le Folklore wallon*, p. 30, § 617: 'Pour posséder le pouvoir de guérir . . . porter le nom de Louis et être le septième fils de la famille sont aussi deux prédispositions très grandes'. I think the two 'predispositions' were usually united in the same person.

152 Vairus, loc. cit., Raynaud, loc. cit. and *Naturalis Theologia*, Dist. IV, no. 317, in the *Opera*, V, p. 199; Thiers, loc. cit.

153 See above, n. 144. The sorcerer of Vovette used to hand out to his patients an image (probably of St-Marcoul) which had inscribed at the top: 'Le Roi te touche, Dieu te guérisse!' (ibid., p. 499); this was the form of words used

by the kings in later times when touching sick persons. Here then is another survival, in a rather distorted form, of this same order of beliefs. We read as follows in the *Revue des traditions populaires*, 9, 1894, p. 555, no. 4: in the Bocage Normand 'quand il y a sept filles dans une famille, la septième porte sur une partie quelconque du corps une *fleur de lis* et *touche du carreau*, c'est-à-dire qu'elle guérit les inflammations d'intestin chez les enfants'.

154 Du Laurens, *De mirabili*, p. 20; Favyn, *Histoire de Navarre*, p. 1059; de l'Ancre, *L'Incrédulité et mescreance du sortilege*, p. 161; Raulin, *Panegyre*, p. 178.

155 *AA. SS. maii*, V, pp. 171 ff. Cf. du Broc de Seganges, *Les saints patrons des corporations*, I, p. 391.

156 J. Sirven, *Soc. agricole des Pyrénées Orientales*, 14, 1864, pp. 116–18. The name *saludadors* was common in these regions to all magician-healers, J. B. Thiers applies it to the 'parents de Ste Catherine', who were not seventh sons (passage mentioned in n. 145).

157 The documents relative to the construction, and drawings, are in file 223. Cf. Barthélemy, *Notice historique sur le prieuré*, p. 235 (with an engraving). For dom O. Bourgeois, see the notice in the St-Rémi necrology, Rheims city library, MS. 348, fol. 14.

158 File 223 (information), no. 7 (1632). It is similar in essentials to the one by Antoine Baillet. Some differences are pointed out below.

159 'Nous, dom Odouard Bourgois, prieur du prieuré de Saint Marcoul de Corbenist en Vermendois du diocedz de Laon . . . Ayant veu, leu et examiné attentivement le proces et les attestations de la naissance du Reverend Pere frerre Anthoine Baillet, prestre religeux de l'order de Nostre Dame du Mont Carmel et profez du grand couvent des Perres Carmes de la place Maubertz de Paris, comme il est yssuz le septiesme filz malle sans aulcune interposition de fille . . . et attendu que ledit F. Anthoine Baillet est le septiesme filz malle et que le septiesme peult toucher et imposer sa main sur les pauvres affligés des escrouëlle, ainsi que le croi pieusement le vulguaire et nous ausy pareillement et que chacun l'experimente journellement . . . apres donc qu'il a visité par deulx divers fois l'eglise royalle de Saint Marcoul de Corbenist où reposent les relicque et sacré ossement de ce grand Sainct qui est imploré principallement pour le mal des escrouelles, et que, en son dernier voyage, il a faict sa neufvaine ainsi que les mallades et a observé de point en point et au myeulx qu'il lui a esté possible toutes ce qui est comandé de garder en la dicte neufvaine, et ausi c'est faict enregistrer au nombre des confrerre de la confrairie royalle, et, avant que toucher, oultre le proces et les attestations, il nous a faict voir son obbediance bien signée et scellée de son superiurre et datté du XVe septembre 1632 et le certificat et approbation des docteurs, bachelier, et anciens perre de son monastere comme il a tousjours vescu parmi eulx en tres bon religieux et en bon odeur et reputation . . . pour ceste cause nous lui avons permis et permettons autant que nous pouvons de toucher charitablement les malades des escrouelles en certains jours de l'année, scavoir aux jour et feste de Saint Marcoul qui est le premier jour de mai, et le septiesme jour de juillet qui est sa relation, et le second octobre sa translation, et le Vendredi, Saint et les Vendredi des Quatre Temps de l'année (Dieu veille que le tout soit a sa

375

gloire!) et ayant ainsi touché lesdict malade nous les renvoyer audit Corbenist pour ce faire enregistrer au nombre des confraire de la confrairie royalle de Saint Marcoul, erigée en ce lieu par nos rois de France dont ilz sont les premiers confrerre, pour y faire ou faire faire une neufvaine et le tout à la gloire de Dieu et de ce glorieux sainct.

En tesmoing de ce nous avons signée ces presentes et apposé le scel royal de la dite confrairie. Ce vingt quatriesme septembre mil six cent trent duelx.'

The certificate for Elie Louvet states explicitly that the seventh son heals 'par les prierres et merites du glorieux Sainct Marcoul, protecteur de la Couronne de France'.

160 'Charitablement et *sans sallaire*' says the certificate for E. Louvet, in more direct terms. The Vovette 'septennaire' would not take any money reward, either, but he used to receive ample presents in kind—a point in which he was no doubt following tradition.

161 E. Louvet's certificate only shows as authorized dates for the touching 'the Fridays in the four Ember Seasons, and Good Friday'.

162 For the attribution of this quality to the French kings—confused no doubt with the 'kings' of the mercers—cf. above, n. 90.

163 Removal of a vertebra of the saint for Anne of Austria on 17 April 1643; file 223, no. 10 (2 documents). A gift to the Carmelites of Place Maubert: a notice at the head of a volume containing certificates of healing; file 223 (information).

164 Bibl. Nat., Estampes Re 13, fol. 161; cf. Cahier *Caractéristiques des saints dans l'art populaire*, 1867, I, p. 264, n. 3 and Jean Gaston, *Les Images des confréries parisiennes avant la Révolution* (Soc. d'iconographie parisienne, 2, 1909), no. 34.

165 Such as the prohibition against eating 'de toutes têtes d'animaux . . . et aussi de celles de tous poissons'. The scrofula was considered as a disease of the head. Should we not see this prescription as originally related to sympathetic magic practices? The same veto is still imposed today in the brochure sold to pilgrims to the shrine of St-Marcoul at the hospice of Dinant; J. Chalon, *Fétiches, idoles et amulettes*, I, p. 148.

166 M. A. Benoît, *Procès verbaux soc. archéol Eure-et-Loir*, 5, 1876, p. 55, is the only one to mention the practice of giving the Christian name Marcoul to the seventh sons; but the use of *marcou* as a common name for them is vouched for by a large number of documents (see n. 167). It would seem probable that the common name originally went back to the baptismal name.

167 See among others the works of Laisnel de la Salle, Jaubert, Tiffaud and Martellière mentioned above, n. 121, and the article of Dr Menault mentioned in n. 144. We do not need to concern ourselves with the etymology of the word *marcou* as applied to healers given by Liebrecht, *Zur Volkskunde*, p. 347. In certain dialects or Romance patois—and notably Walloon—the word *marcou* has another and quite different sense: it means the cat, or rather the tom-cat, and this certainly seems to be a fairly ancient meaning; cf. Leduchat in his edition of A. Estienne, *Apologie pour Hérodote*, The Hague, 1735, III, p. 250, n. 1; the same in the *Dictionnaire étymologique* of Ménage, 1750 ed. under the word 'marcou' (quoting a *rondeau* by Jean Marot); L. Sainéan, 'La création métaphorique en français . . . le chat'

Beihefte zur Zeitschr. für romanische Philologie, 1, 1905, *passim* (see the table); J. Chalon, *Fétiches, idoles et amulettes*, II, p. 157. Should we suppose there was some relationship between St-Marcoul, the seventh sons, and the tom-cat? This was what Leduchat believed: '*Marcou*, moreover, is also the name of a cat, an animal whose fur is said to cause scrofula. Thus one *Marcou* cures the disease caused by another kind of *Marcou*'—a note quoted above in relation to H. Estienne. We should then have to suppose that the word had become a sort of common term for healers of scrofula, and had then, through a new shift of ideas, been secondarily applied to an animal thought to be capable of causing the same disease. But it would certainly seem that this over-ingenious explanation should be rejected. I have not seen anywhere else that the cat was thought to possess such a property, and I wonder whether Leduchat did not in fact attribute it, without any proof, in support of his own interpretation. The name *marcou* was certainly given to the cat, as suggested by Sainéan, through a kind of onomatopaeia originating in a vague imitation of the cat's purring. As for the idea— apparently rather favoured by Sainéan (p. 79)—that the seventh sons may have taken their name from the cat: well, after all that has been said above, it would not seem necessary to discuss it.

BOOK 2   CHAPTER V   *The royal miracle during the Wars of Religion and the absolute monarchy*

1 With modern times, we are confronted with a new category of source-material for the study of the healing rites; accounts of travels, and along with them guides for travellers. As a general rule, they are not altogether reliable documents. Many of them, no doubt, were drawn up after the event, and are based upon incomplete notes or distorted recollections, and so contain the most astonishing errors. It will be enough to give one or two examples. Abraham Gölnitz, *Ulysses belgico-gallicus*, Amsterdam, 1655, pp. 410 ff., gives a description of the French ceremony which appears to be partly based upon information from books, and partly pure invention. He affirms that on each occasion two sceptres are carried in before the king, one surmounted by the fleur-de-lis, the other by the hand of justice. In giving an account of his legation (1664), Cardinal Chigi makes the French king fast for three days before each royal touch. He represents him as kissing the sick (translation by E. Rodocanachi, *Rev. d'histoire diplomatique*, 1894, p. 271). Add to this the strange incapacity for accurate observation, which seems to afflict certain minds: Hubert Thomas of Liège visited France, where he saw Francis I giving the royal touch at Cognac, and England, where Henry VIII gave him cramp rings with his own hands (see below, n. 50). In general, he seems to be a man worthy of credence; but he nevertheless declares explicitly that the English kings do not touch for the scrofula: Hubertus Thomas Leodius, *Annalium de vita illustrissimi principis Frederici II*, Frankfurt, 1624, p. 98. Certain travel accounts, however, the work of particularly precise and fair-minded persons, are an exception; for instance, the one drawn up by the secretary to the Venetian ambassador Girolamo Lippomano, sent on a

mission to the Court of France in 1577: *Relations des ambassadeurs vénitiens*, ed. Tommaseo (*Documents inédits*) II; whenever I have been able to check them against other documents of certain accuracy, I have found his accounts entirely reliable.

2 For further details, see Appendix I, pp. 245 ff.

3 Each sick person received as a rule two *tournois sous* (as an exception (1) 31 Oct. 1502, 2 *carolus*, which according to Dieudonné, *Monnaies royales françaises*, 1916, p. 305, only made up twenty *tournois deniers*, though the total in money given by the alms-book is obviously inaccurate: Bibl. Nat. fr. 26108, fol. 302; (2) 14 Aug. 1507, two *sous* six *deniers*: KK 88, fol. 209 v.). Perhaps all the same the sick in Charles VIII's reign may have, for some time, received no more than one *tournois sou*; at least that is the impression given by an entry in the alms-book, KK 77, fol. 17 (14 Oct. 1497); but this entry ('A $\frac{\text{xx}}{\text{iiij}}$ xij malades des escrouelles . . . chacun xij d.t. pour eux ayder a vivre . . .) is so vaguely worded that it is uncertain whether it refers to alms distributed at the moment of the royal touch, or given to scrofula sufferers waiting upon his Majesty's good pleasure to heal them. On 28 March 1408, the last day that Charles VIII practised this rite, the sick received two *sous* each, as in the following reigns (KK 77, fol. 93).

4 According to KK 88. On 28 March 1498, Charles VIII had touched sixty persons: KK 77 fol. 93. Coming back to Corbeny from the consecration, Louis XII touched eighty: ibid., fol. 124 v.; during the month of October 1502, ninety-two (and not eighty-eight, as R. de Maulde wrongly states, *Les Origines*, p. 28); Bibl. Nat. fr. 26108, fol. 391-2.

5 According to KK 101, completed by the Bibl. Nat. fr. 6732; the register contains fairly numerous gaps—especially for the year 1529—so that one can arrive only at minimal figures; cf. above, p. 245. Some touching by Francis I is mentioned in the *Journal d'un bourgeois de Paris*, ed. V.-L. Bourrilly (Collect. de textes pour servir à l'étude . . . de l'histoire), p. 242 (Tours, 15 Aug. 1526) and in the *Chronique* published by Bourilly, as an Appendix to the preceding work, p. 421; cf. below, n. 26.

6 According to KK 137. Barthélemi de Faye d'Espeisse [B. Faius] in his polemical anti-protestant treatise entitled *Energumenicus*, 1571, p. 154, alludes to the role played by Amyot as almoner in the ceremony of the royal touch; this treatise, moreover, is dedicated to Amyot.

7 Henry II: KK 111, fol. 14, 35 v., 36, 37 v., 38 v., 39 v.; Charles IX: KK 137, fol. 56 v., 59 v., 63 v., 75, 88, 89, 94 (from which we have taken the quotation relating to the object of the special alms granted to the Spaniards), 97 v., 100 v., 108. Cf. the account of Girolamo Lippomano's journey, p. 54; the author says about the royal touch 'pare quasi cosa incredibile et miraculosa, ma pero tanto stimata per vera et secura in questo regno et in Spagna, dove piu che in ogni altro luogo del mondo questo male e peculiare'. Likewise Faius, *Energumenicus*, p. 155.

8 André du Chesne, *Les Antiquitez et recherches de la grandeur et maiesté des Roys de France*, 1609, p. 167, mentions '. . . le grand nombre de tels malades, qui vient encore tous les ans d'Espagne, pour se faire toucher à nostre pieux et religieux Roy; dont le Capitaine qui les conduisoit en

l'année 1602, rapporta attestion des Prelats d'Espagne, d'un grand nombre de gueris par l'attouchement de sa Maiesté'.

9 For the large number of Frenchmen settled in Spain, cf. Bodin, *République*, book V, § 1, 1579 ed., Lyons, p. 471, in an argument which ends with these words: 'de faict l'Espagne n'est quasi peuplée que de François'; for the movement in the opposite direction, the reader can consult J. Mathorez, 'Notes sur la pénétration des Espagnols en France du XIIᵉ au XVIIᵉ siècle', *Bulletin hispanique*, 24, 1922, p. 41 (it is really only a question of students). For a payment of 275 l.t. to a Spanish lady who had come to receive the royal touch: *Catal. des actes de François Iᵉʳ*, III, no. 7644 (21 Dec. 1534); to a Spanish lady who had come to have her daughter touched, ibid. VIII, no. 31036 (Jan. 1539). The popularity of the French miracle in Spain found an echo in a theologian, Louis of Granada, cf. below, n. 96.

10 KK 111, fol. 39 v.: 'Aus malades d'escrouelles Espaignolz et autres estrangers la somme de quarante sept livres dix solz tournois a eulx ordonnée par ledit sr. grant aumosnier pour leur aider a vivre et aller a St Marcoul attendre pour estre touchez.' The royal touching at Corbeny took place on 31 July 1547; references above, p. 284.

11 Charles VIII at Rome, 20 Jan. 1495: André de la Vigne, *Histoire du Voyage de Naples*, in Godefroy, *Histoire de Charles VIII*, 1684, p. 125; at Naples, 19 April, ibid., p. 145. Louis XII at Pavia, 19 Aug. 1502, at Genoa 1 Sept. following Godefroy, *Ceremonial françois*, I, pp. 700, 702; Francis I at Bologna, 15 Dec. 1515: *Journal de Jean Barillon*, ed. P. Vaissière (Soc. de l'hist. de France), I, p. 174; le Glay, *Négociations diplomatiques entre la France et l'Autriche (Documents inédits)* II, p. 88; Caelio Calcagnini, *Opera*, Basle, 1544, *Epistolicarum quaestionum*, book I, p. 7. For a seventeenth-century fresco representing the Bologna ceremony, cf. above, p. 205.

12 For the sceptics, see above p. 187; for the doctors, Book 2, Ch. I, n. 61.

13 A. Champollion-Figeac, *Captivité du roi François Iᵉʳ (Documents inédits)* 1847, p. 253, no. CXVI (18 July, 1525). Cf. M. Gachard, *Études et notices historiques*, I, 1890, p. 38.

14 Iani Lascaris Rhyndaceni, *Epigrammata*, Paris, 1544, p. 19 v.: 'Ergo manu admota sanat rex choeradas, estque—Captivus, superis gratus, ut ante fuit, —Iudicio tali, regum sanctissime, qui te—Arcent, inuisos suspicor esse deis'. These couplets were still often quoted in the seventeenth century, e.g. by du Laurens, *De mirabili*, pp. 21-2, du Peyrat, *Histoire ecclésiastique*, p. 817.

15 Commines, VI, c. vi, ed. Maindrot (Collection de textes pour servir à l'étude et l'ens. de l'histoire), II, 1903, p. 41: 'Quant les roys de France veulent toucher les mallades des escrouelles, ilz se confessent, et nostre roy n'y faillit jamais une foiz la sepmaine. Si les aultres ne le font, ilz font tres mal, car tousjours y a largement malades.' De Maulde, *Les origines*, p. 28, sees in this sentence an allusion to Louis XII. But Book VI of Commines' *Mémoires* was put together in Charles VIII's reign. Besides, the alms-book of Charles VIII, KK 77, indicates between 1 Oct. 1497 and the king's death (8 April 1498) only one certain royal touch, on 28 March 1498 (fol. 93)—a day, moreover, that does not coincide with any festival. To this may be added an obscure mention referring to 24 Oct. 1497 (fol. 17)—(cf. above, n. 3); in short, a very infrequent use of the royal healing power.

16 KK 101, fol. 273 v. and ff.

17 KK 101, fol. 68, April 1529: 'Au dessus dit aulmosnier pour bailler a ung mallades d'escrouelles que le Roi avoit guary sur les champs la somme de cinq solz tournoys'. We must add that persons of distinguished rank often enjoyed the favour of being touched on their own, away from the crowd; but these private touchings might take place on the same day as the general ceremony; see an example of this (for Henry IV) below, n. 89 (Thou's text).

18 26 May 1530, at Angoulême, in the course of the Court's travels to the south-west, the Grand Almoner distributed to eighty-seven sick persons suffering from scrofula two *tournois sous* a head 'affin de leur retirer sans plus retourner jusques a la feste de Penthecouste', KK 101, fol. 360 v. A further mention in similar terms, ibid., fol. 389.

19 Or the vigils of these feasts: sometimes both the vigil and the day itself.

20 KK 101, fol. 380 v.

21 KK 101, fol. 29 v., Aug. 1528: 'Au dessus dit aulmosnier pour baillier a maistre Claude Bourgeoys cirurgien du roy, qui avoit visité les mallades d'escrouelles, la somme de quarante ung solz tournoys'. Cf. the account of his journey by Girolamo Lippomano (quoted above, n. 1), p. 545: 'Prima che il re tocchi, alcuni medici e cerusichi vanno guardando minutamente le qualita del male; e se trovano alcuna persona che sia infetta d'altro male che dalle scrofole, la scacciano,' and Faius, *Energumenicus*, p. 155.

22 Appendix II, no. 3 and Plate 1. Cf. the remarks above, p. 83, on the stained glass window at Mont St-Michel.

23 Attested for the first time in the account of Girolamo Lippomano's journey, p. 545. In the seventeenth century there is a certain divergence in the evidence on the subject of this formula. Some texts give it in the following form, in which the subjunctive seems to introduce a semblance of doubt: 'Le Roi te touche, Dieu te guérisse' (or other similar expressions, likewise using the subjunctive). But such forms are only met with among authors of second-rate authority: in an obscure hagiographer, Louis Texier, *Extraict et abrégé de la vie de Saint Marcoul*, 1648, p. 6; in the absurd author of the *Traité curieux de la guérison des écrouelles . . . par l'attouchment des septen-naires*, Aix, 1643, p. 34; in Menin, *Traité historique et chronologique du sacre*, 1724, p. 328 and various others of the same stamp quoted by du Peyrat in his *Histoire ecclésiastique de la Cour*, p. 819; and especially in accounts of travel, well known to be nearly always of minimal value: Goelnitz, *Ulysses belgo-gallicus*, p. 143; Nemeiz, *Séjour de Paris*, Frankfurt, 1717, p. 191; a narrative by Count Gyldenstope, 1699 in *Archiv für Kulturgeschichte*, 1916, p. 411. Writers with better credentials are: du Laurens, *De mirabili*, p. 9; Favyn, *Histoire de Navarre*, p. 1057; de l'Ancre, p. 170; Barbier, p. 26; du Peyrat, p. 819; all unanimously give the formula in the indicative; so does the Ceremonial of the seventeenth century, ed. Franklin, *La vie privée. Les Médecins*, p. 304; cf. below, n. 145. Du Peyrat inveighs specifically against the authors who have seen fit to attribute the other formula to the king. There can thus be hardly any doubt about the official text; but a certain floating element in current tradition seems to have arisen. For Louis XV and his successors, above, p. 224. The 'and' connecting the two clauses seems to have dropped out quite soon.

24 I have not found anything related to the scrofula liturgy either in Charles VIII's *Hours* (Bibl. Nat. lat. 1370), or in those of Louis XII (lat. 1412), nor for the following century in the fine *Book of Hours* of Louis XIV (lat. 9476).

25 An account of Girolamo Lippomano's journey, p. 545: 'essendo gl'infermi accommodati per fila . . . il re li va toccando d'uno in uno . . .'

26 KK 101, fol. 34: 'A deus cens cinq mallades d'escrouelles touchez par ledit seigneur en l'eglise Nostre Dame de Paris le VIIIᵉ jour dudit moys la somme de vingt livres dix solz tournois'. The *Chronique*, published by V.-L. Bourrilly, following on his edition of the *Journal d'un bourgeois de Paris*, p. 421, mentions this ceremony ('plus de deux cens malades'). Further examples of the royal touch in churches: KK 88, fol. 142 v. (Grenoble), 147 (*Morant?*); K 101, fol. 273 v., 274 and v. (Joinville, Langres, *Torchastel*). Cf. Girolamo Lippomano's travel account, p. 545: 'essendo gl'infermi accommodati per fila o nel cortile regale, o in qualche gran chiesa'.

27 George Cavendish, *The Life of Cardinal Wolsey*, ed. S. W. Singer, Chiswick, 1825, I, p. 104.

28 KK 137, fol. 94; on that day, incidentally, and quite exceptionally, there were only fourteen sick persons touched.

29 Cf. below, p. 249 and Appendix I, n. 21.

30 The liturgy of Mary Tudor's time is contained in this sovereign's missal, preserved today in the library of the Catholic Cathedral of Westminster. It constantly mentions a king, but never a queen, and was therefore clearly not composed specially for Mary Tudor; one would imagine that it was already in use under Henry VIII, at least at the beginning of the reign—before the schism, or before its consequences had made themselves felt—and perhaps even earlier than Henry VIII. It was reprinted several times: see in particular Sparrow Simpson, 'On the forms of prayer', p. 295; Crawfurd, *King's Evil*, p. 60.

31 In 1686, the printer Henry Hills published 'by His Majesties Command' a small quarto book of 12 pp. containing *The Ceremonies us'd in the Time of King Henry VII for the Healing of Them that be Diseas'd with the King's Evil* (reprinted in *The literary museum*, London, 1702, p. 65); W. Maskell, *Monumenta ritualia Ecclesiae Anglicanae*, 2nd ed., III, p. 386, Crawfurd, *King's Evil*, p. 52. The text is of course in Latin; another volume published at the same time gave an English translation (reprinted in Crawfurd, ibid. p. 132). Thus we would appear to be in possession of the scrofula service in use under Henry VII. But should we consider the authenticity of this document to be beyond doubt? I would not venture to say so. It exactly reproduces the liturgy of Mary Tudor and Henry VIII's time (see the preceding note) and there is nothing suspect in that. But the conditions in which it was printed are slightly dubious. If James II ordered its publication, it was because—as we shall see—he was intent upon restoring the ancient Catholic forms for the royal touch. What could have been more natural in such a case than to try and link up with the last sovereign before the Reformation, who was moreover the direct ancestor of the Stuarts? One may well wonder whether the royal printer did not simply use a manuscript giving, perhaps anonymously, the Henry VIII or Mary Tudor service, and attribute it to Henry VII. As long as we have not discovered any MS. authenticating

the text handed in for publication to H. Hills, we must, while avoiding any direct argument for the spuriousness of the traditional form of this text, at any rate avoid accepting it as absolutely certain.

32 *Decretals*, Book 3, vol. XLI, 2 (according to the Synod of Seligenstadt of 1023): 'Quidam etiam laicorum et maxime matronae habent in consuetudine ut per singulos dies audiant evangelium, "in principio erat verbum . . ." et ideo sancitum est in eodem concilio ut ulterius hoc non fiat, nisi suo tempore'.

33 Appendix II, nos. 12 and 13, and Plate 4.

34 Appendix II, no. 1. This is mentioned by Miss Farquhar, I, p. 5.

35 The ancient formula: 'Per Crucem tuam salva nos Christe Redemptor': Farquhar, I, p. 70 (for a variant under Henry VII, ibid., p. 71). For the more modern one (taken from Psalm CXVII, 23: 'A Domino factum est istud, et est mirabile in nostris oculis', ibid., p. 96. It should be remembered that Miss Farquhar's work has definitely established the numismatic history of the English rite.

36 *Calendar of State Papers*, Venice, VI, 1, no. 473, pp. 436-7; cf. above, Book 2, Ch. II, note 43.

37 Tooker, *Charisma*, p. 105.

38 Browne's explanations on this subject reveal a considerable hesitation: *Adenochoiradelogia*, pp. 106-8, 139, 142, 148; cf. Wiseman, *Severall Chirurgical Treatises*, I, p. 396. For the superstition about the golden coin in the seventeenth century, see also *Relation en forme de journal du voyage et séjour que le sérénissime et très puissant prince Charles II roy de la Grande Bretagne a fait en Hollande*, The Hague, 1660, p. 77.

39 Cf. Browne, pp. 106, 148; Douglas, *Criterion*, p. 199.

40 Isbrandi de Diemerbroeck, *Opera omnia anatomica et medica*, Utrecht, 1683, *Observationes et curationes medicae centum*, Obs. 85, p. 108. This officer is even critical of the general belief; he believed that if indeed he should happen to lose his gold coin, nothing—not even a second royal touch—could prevent a relapse; it was generally believed that a second touch and a second coin carefully looked after this time would suffice to bring back the cure: cf. Browne, *Adenochoiradelogia*, p. 106. A gold coin was still being worn in 1723 by an old man—belonging evidently to the gentry—who had had it from Charles II: Farquhar, IV, p. 160 (according to a letter of Thomas Hearne, *Reliquiae Hearnianae*, 1857, II, p. 680).

41 Accounts of the churchwardens of Minchinhampton, *Archaeologia*, 35, 1853, pp. 448-52.

42 Quoted in Nicolas, *Privy Purse of Henry VIII*, p. 352: 'Amongst the Conway Papers (MSS.) there is an order for a proclamation, dated 13th May 1625 . . . that for the future all shall bring certificates from the minister etc. of the parish, for that many being healed, have disposed of their pieces of gold otherwise than was intended, and thereby fall into relapse'. It was a question of requiring certificates stating that the persons coming forward for the king's healing had not already been touched on a previous occasion: cf. below, n. 170.

43 Browne, *Adenochoiradelogia*, p. 93: 'were this not true and very commonly put in practice, without all question His Majesties touching Medals would not be so frequently seen and found in Gold-Smiths shops'. Cf. ibid. p. 139,

the story of the Russian merchant suffering from scrofula to whom an English lady brought a Charles I 'angel', and who was cured. For a case of a touch-piece being lent, see Farquhar, IV, p. 159.

44 At least in the isle of Lewis: William Henderson, *Notes on the Folklore of the Northern Counties of England and the Borders*, 2nd ed. (Publications of the Folklore Society, 2, London), 1879, p. 306; *Folklore*, 14, 1903, p. 371, note 1. Under Charles I, Boisgaudre, a French adventurer, the last of a series of seven sons, who used to touch for scrofula in a debtors' prison where he had been shut up, used to hang round his patients' necks a simple piece of paper with the inscription. 'In nomine Jesu Christi, ipse sanetur': *Calendar of State Papers, Domestic, Charles I*, 7 June 1632.

45 A superstition attested by Browne, pp. 106–7 (who is, incidentally, opposed to it).

46 For Lord and Lady Lisle, see the article 'Plantagenet (Arthur)' in the *Dictionary of National Biography*. Letters analysed in *Letters and Papers, Foreign and Domestic, Henry VIII*, 13, 1, nos. 903, 930, 954, 1022, 1105; 14, 1, nos. 32, 791, 838, 859, 923, 1082, 1145; 14, 2, no. 302. Cf. Hermentrude, *Cramp rings*; Crawfurd, 'Cramp-rings', pp. 175–6. The use of these rings to alleviate the pains of childbirth seems to be implied by the following passage in a letter from the Earl of Hertford to Lady Lisle, published by Hermentrude, loc. cit. and Crawfurd, p. 176: 'Hussy told me you were very desirous to have some cramp-rings against the time that you should be *brought a bedd* . . .'—the usual meaning of these last words being very well known. All the same I should add that the *D.N.B.* does not mention any children of Lady Lisle's born at Calais.

47 *Wills and Inventories from the registers of the Commissary of Bury St. Edmunds*, ed. S. Tymms (Camden Society), London, 1850, p. 41 (1463); p. 127 (1535); Maskell, *Monumenta ritualia*, 2nd ed. III, p. 384 (1516). It should indeed be added that these rings were simply called cramp rings, so that we cannot be absolutely certain that we are not dealing with some kind of magic rings held to be effective against the 'cramp'; yet it would seem that from this time onwards this term was applied for preference to the rings consecrated by the sovereign.

48 Thomas Magnus to Wolsey, 20 March 1526: *State Papers, Henry VIII*, IV, no. CLVII, p. 449; a fragment in J. Stevenson, 'On cramp-rings', p. 41 of the *Gentleman's Magazine Library*. Cf. a dispatch sent by Cromwell to Queen Margaret of Scotland, the daughter of Henry VII (14 May 1537): ibid, IV, 2, no. 317 and R. B. Merriman, *Life and Letters of Thomas Cromwell*, II, no. 185.

49 *Letters and Papers, Foreign and Domestic, Henry VIII*, XVIII, 1, no. 17 (7 Jan. 1543): Oliphaunt was only finally released on 1 July (ibid., no. 805); but as early as January the English government was negotiating with him and the other captive lords in order to obtain their support when they had been set free to return to Scotland (ibid., no. 37); it was probably not for his personal use that he received twelve gold and twenty-four silver cramp rings on 7 January.

50 Hubertus Thomas Leodius, *Annalium de vita illustrissimi principis Frederici II . . .*, 1624 ed., Frankfurt, p. 182: 'Discedenti autem mihi dono dedit . . .

sexaginta anulos aureos contra spasmum'. According to C. J. S. Thompson, *Royal cramp and other medycinable rings*, p. 7, there is a trace of this liberality in one of Henry VIII's accounts of the year 1533.

51 *Letters and Papers, Foreign and Domestic, Henry VIII*, XV, no. 480; R. B. Merriman, *Life and Letters of Thomas Cromwell*, II, no. 185; the letter from Thomas Cromwell published by Merriman (30 April 1530) is addressed to Bishop Gardiner, then ambassador in France; and the same Bishop Gardiner wrote to Nicholas Ridley in 1547 on the subject of the cramp rings: 'And yet, for such effect as they have wrought, when I was in France, I have been myself much honoured; and of all sorts entreated to have them, with offer of as much for them, as they were double worth' (letter mentioned below, n. 67; loc. cit., p. 501).

52 *Letters and Papers, Foreign and Domestic, Henry VIII*, II, 2, nos. 4228 and 4246; 20, 1, no. 542. The same in Mary's reign, when the Emperor was residing in Brussels belore his abdication: *Calendar of State Papers, Foreign, Mary:* 25 April, 26 April and 11 May 1555. On the other hand, Crawfurd would seem to be mistaken in thinking that he had read in W. Stirling's *The Cloister Life of Emperor Charles V*, London, 1853, that the Emperor possessed among his treasures some English cramp rings; I have not found a mention of anything except some magic rings as a remedy for haemorrhoids.

53 *Letters and Papers, Foreign and Domestic, Henry VIII*, XVIII, 1, no. 576.

54 Royal Household account book, in *Trevelyan Papers* (Camden Society), I, p. 150: 'to Alexander Grey, messenger, sente the vj-th day of Aprill [1529] to Rome with letters of great importance, at which tyme the Kinges cramp rings were sent'. Letter from Anne Boleyn to Gardiner, 4 April 1529: Gilbert Burnet *The history of the reformation*, ed. Pocock, V, 1865, p. 444.

55 *Letters and Papers, Foreign and domestic, Henry VIII*, II, 1, no. 584 (15 June 1515). For the sale of cramp rings even in England: Hubertus Thomas Leodius, loc. cit., p. 98: '[Rex Angliae] anulos aureos et argenteos quibusdam ceremoniis consecrat, quos dono dat, et *vendunt aurifabri*'.

56 *La vita di Benvenuto Cellini*, ed. A. J. Rusconi and A. Valeri, Rome, 1901, Book II, chap. I, p. 321: 'Al ditto resposi, che l'anello che Sua Eccellenzia [the Duke of Ferrara] m'aveva donato, era di valore d'un dieci scudi in circa, e che l'opera che io aveva fatta a Sua Eccellenzia valeva piu di ducento. Ma per mostrare a Sua Eccellenzia che io stimavo l'atto della sua gentilezza, che solo mi mandassi uno anello del granchio, di quelli che vengon d'Inghilterra che vagliono un carlino in circa: quello io lo terrei per memoria di Sua Eccellenzia in sin che io vivessi. . . .'

57 The fragment of a letter quoted, in translation, by Mrs Henry Cust, *Gentlemen Errant*, London, 1909, p. 357, n. 1. As Mrs Cust does not give any references, I have not been able to discover the letter in question; nevertheless I think I may use it, for I have been able to get other evidence of the reliability of Mrs Cust's testimony. The popularity of the cramp rings rite is moreover attested for Germany from the end of the fifteenth century by G. Hollen, *Preceptorium divinae legis*, Nuremberg, 1497, fol. 25 v., col. 1.

58 *Epistolae Guillelmi Budei*, quarto, Paris, 1520, p. 18 (Linacre to Budé, 10 June 1517); fol. 16 v. (Budé to Linacre, 10 July). Budé writes on the subject of the rings 'ὧν δὴ τοὺς πλείους ἤδη ταῖς τῶν φίλων καὶ συγγενῶν διενειμάμην

γυναιξί. παραδούς τε μεγαλοπρεπῶς καὶ ἐπομοσάμενος ἦ μὴν ἀλεξικάκους εἶναι καὶ νὴ Δία καὶ συκοφάντου γε δήγματος': 'I have distributed most of them to the wives of my relations and friends; I made a solemn present of them, assuring them that they would protect them against diseases and even against the tooth of envy.' The present consisted of one gold and eighteen silver rings.

59 *De mirabili*, p. 29: 'Reges Angliae . . . curavere comitialem morbum, datis annulis quos epileptici pro amuleto gestarent, quales hodie dicuntur extare nonnulli in thesauris plerisque Galliae'.

60 The first edition: *Claudii Ptolomaei Alexandrini geographicae enarrationis libri octo*, Lyons, Trechsel, atlas, 6th page v.: 'De Rege Galliae duo memoranda feruntur. Primum quod sit in Remensi ecclesia vas crismati perenni redundans, ad regis coronationem coelitus missum, quo Reges omnes liniuntur. Alterum, quod Rex ipse solo contactu strumas sive scrofulas curet. Vidi ipse Regem plurimos hoc langore correptos tangentem, an sanati fuissent non vidi.' The second edition, Lyons, Delaporte, 1541, atlas, 6th page v.; the last phrase (after 'tangentem') in the form 'pluresque senatos [*sic*] passim audivi'. I am indebted for this strange divergence to the 'Extrait d'une lettre de M. Des Maizeaux à M. De La Motte' which appeared in the *Bibliothèque raisonnée des ouvrages des savans de l'Europe*, III, 2, 1729, p. 179. For the two editions of Ptolemy—the second carefully expurgated—cf. Julien Baudrier, 'Michel Servet: ses relations avec les libraires et imprimeurs lyonnais', *Mélanges Emile Picot*, I, 1913, pp. 42, 50. The atlas is missing from the copy of the 2nd edition in the possession of the Bibliothèque Nationale; I consulted the copy in the British Museum.

61 For bibliographical information about the Italian naturalist school, usually known as the 'Paduan school', see above, pp. 235 ff., where there is also a detailed account of their attitude to the royal miracle; was it partly under their influence, I wonder, that the Venetian ambassador Constantine, at the court of Henry II, expressed a certain scepticism about the efficacy of the royal touch? See his account in the translation by Armand Baschet, *La Diplomatie vénitienne. Les princes de l'Europe au XVIᵉ siècle*, 1862, p. 436.

62 Lucien Romier, *Le Royaume de Catherine de Médicis*, II, 1922, p. 222.

63 For Luther, see above, p. 86; for Catherine of Schwarzbourg, p. 185.

64 Creeping to the cross was forbidden by the Grand Ordinance of 1549 proscribing the practices of worship as well as the beliefs of the old faith: G. Burnet, *The History of the Reformation*, ed. N. Pocock, IV, Oxford, 1865, p. 244, art. 9, and David Wilkins, *Concilia Magnae Britanniae*, 1737, IV, p. 32. In 1536 it was still among the ceremonies recommended by Convocation: Burnet, loc. cit., p. 284.

65 For the Edward VI accounts, which show him consecrating the rings, see below, Appendix I, n. 37. There is no certain evidence that he gave the royal touch; but it is scarcely conceivable that he should have maintained one of the two rites—the one most intimately linked with the ceremonies of the old cults, and the one to be abolished by Elizabeth—yet have rejected the other. For his attitude to the cramp-rings, see also above, p. 189. We do not know what liturgy was used for the royal touch during his reign, but one imagines that he probably modified the previous use in a Protestant direction.

We are likewise in the dark as to whether there had previously been changes under Henry VIII, after the schism; it does not indeed seem very probable, but it cannot be said to be absolutely impossible. We only know the Henry VIII service from its reproduction in Mary Tudor's missal (see above, n. 30). Mary evidently had it copied as it had been before the rupture with Rome; if there had been subsequent retouching, she certainly paid no attention to it. Hamon l'Estrange, writing in 1659 (*Alliance of Divine Offices*, p. 240), claims that Edward VI kept the sign of the cross, as Elizabeth was to do also; but such late testimony is of little worth. For the numismatic information— which likewise supports the idea that Edward VI did touch—see Farquhar, I, p. 92.

66 The text is quoted below, n. 81.

67 The letter is published in *The Works of Nicholas Ridley* (Parker Society), Cambridge, 1841, p. 495.

68 It was in 1548, not long after Ridley's sermon, that holy water—after much hesitation—was finally proscribed: see W. P. M. Kennedy, *Studies in Tudor History*, London, 1916, p. 99.

69 In the works of Tooker and Clowes on the royal touch (see above, p. 190) the cramp rings are never mentioned.

70 The Catholic English historian Richard Smith, who died in 1654, had preserved some cramp rings blessed by Mary Tudor (text quoted Book 2, Ch. VI, n. 7); likewise under Henry IV in France, certain people still preserved some of them carefully in their jewel-cases (du Laurens, testimony quoted n. 59). In seventeenth century English literature, and even in that of the eighteenth century, one still sometimes comes across a mention of the cramp rings (cf. C. J. S. Thompson, *Royal and other medycinable rings*, pp. 9–10); but is it a question of royal cramp rings, or rings rendered effective against the cramp by other magical practices? We cannot say. It is certain, moreover, that in James II's time the memory of the Good Friday rite was not altogether lost, and there certainly seems to have been a suggestion of reviving it among the king's entourage; see above, p. 219.

71 This fact has been frequently noted: e.g. Waterton, 'On a remarkable incident', pp. 112–13; Thompson, *Royal and other medycinable rings*, p. 10. The case rests, of course, essentially on the absence of any distinctive signs on the rings consecrated by royalty; on the other hand, the coins destined for the royal touch—not to mention the medals specially struck for this purpose since Charles II's day—are always recognizable by the hole pierced in them to take the ribbon. But if belief in the power of the royal cramp rings had persisted up to a period near enough to our own, it is probable that at least some rings of this kind would have come down to us with an authentic pedigree.

72 Later on, the idea grew up that Elizabeth had only resigned herself with some hesitation to touching the sick. Crawfurd, *King's Evil*, pp. 75–6, has effectively shown that this tradition rests without doubt upon a wrong interpretation of a passage from Tooker's *Charisma*.

73 The liturgy of Elizabeth's time is known to us through Tooker, *Charisma* (reproduced by Sparrow Simpson, 'On the forms of prayer', p. 298; translated in Crawfurd, *King's Evil* p. 72). Tooker gives it in Latin; but it is hard

to believe that it was really in use in this form. English had by then become the official language of the Church: surely the service for the royal touch would not have been an exception to this general rule. Besides, we know for certain that since James I's time it was indeed performed in English (below, n. 83). As already conjectured by Crawfurd, loc. cit., p. 71, and Farquhar, 'Royal Charities', I, p. 97, it is probable that Tooker, in publishing only the Latin text of this service, was simply concerned to preserve a certain linguistic harmony in his book; for the whole book is written in Latin, and a long English quotation would have been a blemish.

74 We must nevertheless admit that the few sets of figures we have of sick persons touched by Elizabeth are distinctly on the modest side: thirty-eight for the Good Friday before Tooker's book came out, 1597 or 1598 (Tooker, loc. cit., quoted by Crawfurd, *King's Evil*, p. 74); nine at Kenilworth on 18 July 1575 (contemporary account by Laneham, quoted in Farquhar, I, p. 70, n. 1, and *Shakespeare's England*, I, Oxford, 1917, p. 102). But no certain conclusions can be drawn from such scanty information.

75 *The discoverie of witchcraft*, ed. Brinsley Nicholson, London, 1886, Book 13, chap. IX, p. 247; on the subject of the healing power claimed by the French kings: 'But if the French kings use it no woorse than our Princesse doth, God will not be offended thereat; for hir majestie onelie useth godlie and divine praier, with some almes, and refereth the cure to God and to the physician'. It is remarkable that Scott should quote Pomponazzi, perhaps the most important of the Italian naturalist thinkers mentioned above. The first edition appeared in 1584.

76 John Howson, *A sermon preached at St. Maries in Oxford the 17 Day of November, 1602, in defence of the festivities of the Church of England and namely that of her Majesties Coronation*, 2nd ed., Oxford, 1603. Enumerating the graces granted by God to kings, Howson exclaims: 'Thirdly, they have gifts of healing incurable diseases, which is miraculous and above nature, so that when *Vespasian* was seen to perform such a cure the people concluded he should be Emperour, as Tacitus notes'. For this allusion to Roman history, cf. above, Book 1, Ch. II, n. 22.

77 For the exact title, see the bibliography. Polemics against the Catholics, pp. 90 ff. (notably pp. 91–2, the edifying story of a Catholic who had been healed by the royal touch and then realized that the excommunication was 'nullius plane . . . momenti'); against the Puritans, p. 109. The dedicatory letter is signed: 'Sacratissimae Maiestatis vestrae—humillimus capellanus—Guilielmus Tooker'.

78 For the exact title, see p. 430. It is likewise perhaps to Queen Elizabeth's time that we can assign the oldest English engraving representing the royal touch, see Appendix II, no. 7.

79 Cf. above, p. 199.

80 A letter from an anonymous informer to the Bishop of Camerino, nuncio in France (Jan. 1604). Arch. Vatican, Francia Nunzᵃ, vol. XLIX, fol. 22: copy in the Public Record Office, Roman transcripts, Gener. Series, Vol. 88, fol. 8 ff; extracts in Crawfurd, *King's Evil*, p. 82: 'E pero anco vero, che il Ré dal principio della sua entrata nel Regno d'Inghilterra desidero, e dimando queste tre cose . . . 2ᵃ di non toccare le scrofole, non volendosi vanamente

arrogare tal virtu et divinita di potere col suo tatto guarire le malatie . . .
intorno alle quali dimande fu'risposto dalli consiglieri, che non potea sua
Maesta senza suo gran pericolo e del Regno fuggir quelle cose'. See also a
letter from the Venetian envoy Scaramelli, *Calendar of State Papers, Venetian*, X, no. 69 (4 June 1603); a passage in the historian Arthur Wilson's *The
History of Great Britain, being the Life and Reign of James I*, 1653, p. 289
(quoted Farquhar, IV, p. 141); the account of a journey to the English Court
made in 1613 by Duke John Ernest of Saxe Weimar, published by von
Kundhardt, *Am Hofe König Jacobs I von England, Nord und Süd*, p. 109
(1904), p. 132. For James's religious sentiments, see the very acute observations of G. M. Trevelyan, *England under the Stuarts* (*A History of England*
ed. by C. Oman, VII), p. 79, and remember that he certainly seems to have
been the first sovereign to refuse to be consecrated with the miraculous oil
of St Thomas: above, p. 139. Perhaps we should suppose—though no document mentions this interpretation—that James's antipathy towards the rite
of the royal touch, arising from his Calvinistic convictions, was still further
increased by revulsion, natural enough in such a nervous constitution, at the
prospect of such an uninviting task.

81 An extract from an anonymous letter from London of 8 Oct. 1603: Arch.
Vatican, Inghilterra; copy in the Public Record Office, Roman Transcripts,
General Series, Vol. 87; Fragments in Crawfurd, *King's Evil*, p. 82: 'Il Re
s'abbia questi giorni intricato in quello ch'haveva di fare intorno di certa
usanza anticha delli Rè d'Inghilterra di sanare gl'infermi del morbo regio,
et cosi essendogli presentati detti infermi nella sua antecamera, fece prima
fare una predicha per un ministro calvinista sopra quel fatto, et poi lui
stesso disse che se trovava perplesso in quello ch'haveva di fare rispetto, che
dell'una parte non vedeva come potessero guarire l'infermi senza miracolo,
et già li miracoli erano cessati et non se facevano più: et cosi haveva paura di
commettere qualche superstitione; dell'altra parte essendo quella usanza
anticha et in beneficio delli suoi sudditi, se risolveva di provarlo, ma sola-
mente per via d'oratione la quale pregava a tutti volessero fare insiemi con
lui; et con questo toccava alli infermi. Vederemo presto l'effeto che seguitarà.
Si notava che quand'il Ré faceva il suo discorso spesse volte girava l'occhi
alli ministri Scozzesi che stavano appresso, com'aspettando la loro appro-
batione a quel che diceva, havendolo prima conferito con loro.'

82 Cf. Tooker, *Charisma*, p. 109.

83 The liturgy of James I's time is known to us from a broadside (a sheet printed
on one side only) preserved in the Library of the London Society of Antiquaries and published in Crawfurd, p. 85. It is identical with the Charles I
liturgy, which is well known thanks to its inclusion in the 1633 *Book of
Common Prayer*, and has been several times reproduced: Beckett, *A free and
impartial inquiry;* Sparrow Simpson, 'On the forms of prayer', p. 299; Crawfurd, p. 85. It is much the same as Elizabeth's; but among the directions
relating to the sovereign's gestures, the one referring to the sign of the cross
is no longer there. Various evidence collected by Crawfurd, p. 88, confirms
the conclusion on the subject of this modification of the ancient rite suggested
by an examination of the liturgy itself. There is one piece of discordant
testimony (quoted in the following note); but in face of the unanimity of the

other evidence, it can only be considered erroneous. There have been Catholics who claimed that James used to make the sign of the cross secretly (below, Book 2, Ch. VI, n. 8); but this is pure hearsay, intended to give an orthodox explanation for the cures the heretic king was held to have performed. For the disappearance of the cross from the *angels* (it was on the reverse side, on the mast of a vessel), and the suppression of the words in the formula 'A Domino factum est istud et est mirabile in oculis nobis': see Farquhar, I, p. 106–7; the author—wrongly, I should maintain—does not appear to attach any importance to this last modification.

84 A letter 'from Mr Povy to Sir Dudley Carleton' quoted (with an inaccurate reference) by Crawfurd, *King's Evil*, p. 84. According to Sir John Finett, who was Master of Ceremonies under Charles I, James made the sign of the cross over the Turkish child; but Sir John's memory no doubt played him false: *Finetti Philoxenis: some choice Observations of Sir John Finett, Knight, and Master of the Ceremonies to the two last Kings touching the Reception . . . of Forren Ambassadors*, London, 1656, p. 58. De l'Ancre, *La Mescreance du sortilège*, 1622, p. 165, reports that James I once touched the French Ambassador, the Marquis of Trenel, but I do not know what basis there is for this story. He touched at Lincoln, on 30 March and 1 April 1617, fifty and fifty-three sick persons respectively (John Nichols, *Progresses of James I*, III, pp. 263–4, quoted by Farquhar, I, p. 109). Prince Otto of Saxony saw him perform the rite in 1611: Feyerabend in *Die Grenzboten*, 1904, I, p. 705.

85 Lines quoted above, Book 1, Ch. I, n. 30.

86 *Oeuvres*, ed. Malgaigne, I, 1840, p. 352. This silence must have appeared all the more striking in that the medical literature of the time, with its inheritance from mediaeval literature, often mentioned the royal miracle: cf. in France, Jean Tagault, *De chirurgica institutione libri quinque*, 1543, Book I, chap. xiii, p. 93; Antoine Saporta (d. 1573), in his treatise *De tumoribus praeter naturam* (quoted in Gurlt, *Gesch. der Chirurgie*, 2, p. 677); in England, Andrew Boorde in his *Breviary of Health* which came out in 1547 (cf. Crawfurd p. 59); Thomas Gale, in his *Institution of a Chirurgian* of 1563 (quoted by Gurlt, *Gesch. der Chirurgie*, 3, p. 349); John Banister in his treatise *Of tumors above nature* (ibid., 3, p. 369). For the Italians, see above, Book 2, Ch. I, n. 61; cf. also what was said on p. 190 about Clowes and what is said on p. 194 about du Laurens; but for a similar case to that of Paré, see the following note.

87 *Premier Discours. Des miracles*, chap. xxxvi, § 4; 1602 ed., Rouen, p. 183. For the author, cf. H. Brémond, *Histoire littéraire du sentiment religieux en France*, I, 1916, pp. 18 ff., and Henri Busson, *Les Sources et le développement du Rationalisme dans la littérature française de la Renaissance* (thesis, Paris) 1922, p. 452. I don't know whether the doctor mentioned by Richeome should be identified with the 'Petrus de Crescentiis, Medicus Gallus', who— according to Le Brun (*Histoire critique des pratiques superstitieuses*, 2, p. 120 n.) who himself refers to Crusius (?), *De preeminentia*—would have denied the royal healings. We might equally think of Jacques Daleschamps (1513–88), to whom we owe a famous edition of Pliny (I have consulted the Lyons impression, fol. 1587, in which I did not find anything to our present purpose); it is a fact that Daleschamps, in chap. XXXV of his *Chirurgie françoise*,

Lyons, 1573, in which he treats of 'les Escroueles', is silent, just like Paré, about the royal miracle; but I do not see any evidence that he was a Protestant.

88 *De sacris unctionibus*, p. 262. (The book dates from 1593, but must have been put together in 1591, for it carries an appreciation by Jean Dadré, the penitentiary of Rouen, and by Jean Boucher, the pro-chancellor of Paris, dated 17 Oct. of that year.) J. J. Boissardus (d. 1602), *De divinatione et magiicis praestigiis*; Oppenheim, no date, p. 86, thinks that the 'admirable vertu' of healing came to an end under the sons of Henry II. There is another echo of the tradition relating to Henry III's lack of success in David Blondel, *Genealogiae francicae plenior assertio*, Amsterdam, 1654, I, fol. LXX*), which justifies the king by the example of St Paul, who, he says, was unable to heal Timothy. In actual fact, Henry III, as was to be expected, touched like his predecessors, and—we may well believe—with the same success; in particular he acted as a healer at Chartres in 1581, 1582, 1586 (J. B. Souchet, *Histoire de la ville et du diocèse de Chartres*, Public. Soc. Histor. Eure-et-Loir, 6, Chartres, 1873, pp. 110, 111, 128): and at Poitiers, 15 August 1577 (Cerf, 'Du Toucher des ecrouelles', p. 265).

89 L'Estoile, *Mémoires, Journaux*, ed. Brunet, IV, p. 204 (6 April 1594); J. A. Thuanus, *Histoira sui temporis*, Book CIX, vol. V, folio, 1620, p. 433, 'DLX egenis strumosis in area, ac circiter XX honestioris condicionis seorism ab aliis in conclavi'; Favyn, *Histoire de Navarre*, p. 1555.

90 Du Laurens, *De mirabili*, p. 5. Du Laurens declares that he once saw 1500 sick come before the king (p. 6); they were especially numerous at Pentecost. On Easter Day 1608 the king, according to his own testimony, touched 1200 sick: letter to the Marquise de Verneuil, 8 April, *Recueil des lettres missives de Henri IV*, ed. Berger de Xivrey (*Documents inédits*), VII, p. 510. The Basle doctor Thomas Platter saw Henry IV on 23 Dec. 1599 touch the sick at the Louvre: *Souvenirs*, trans. L. Sieber, *Mém. Soc. Hist. Paris*, 23, 1898, p. 222. Cf. also l'Estoile, 6 Jan. 1609.

91 See the letter to the Marquise de Verneuil quoted in the previous note.

92 Cap. ix: 'Mirabilem strumas sanandi vim Regibus Galliae concessam supra naturam esse, eamque non a Daemone. Vbi Daemones morbos inferre variis modis eosdemque sanare demonstratur.' Cap. x: 'Vim mirabilem strumas sanandi Galliae Regibus concessam, gratiam esse a Deo gratis datam concluditur.' For the exact title of the work, see the Bibliography.

93 Never, indeed, on its own, but in the new edition of 1628 of the *Oeuvres complètes*, in Latin, and in the four or five editions of these same works stretching from 1613 to 1646 and perhaps even 1661: see the article by E. Turner mentioned in the Bibliography, p. 429; Gui Patin's poetry is quoted there, on p. 416: 'Miranda sed dum Regis haec Laurentius—sermone docto prodit, et ortam polis—Aperire cunctis nititur potentiam—Dubium relinquit, sitne Rex illustrior—Isto libello, sit vel ipse doctior.'

94 Appendix II, no. 8 and Plate 3.

95 Notice likewise in the same legend the following sentence, where the propaganda intention stands out clearly enough, with a characteristic allusion to the re-establishment of interior peace. 'C'est pourquoy i'ay pensé que ce seroit fort à propos de mon deuoir, de tailler en cuivre ladite figure pour (en admirant la vertu diuine operer en nostre Roy) estre d'auantage incitez a

l'honorer, et luy rendre obeyssance pour l'union de la paix et concorde qu'il entretient en ce Royaume de France, et pour les commoditez qui nous en proviennent.'

96 There is a portrait of Henry IV by him still extant, and another of Louis XIII engraved as early as 1610: cf. E. Bénézit, *Dictionnaire des peintres, sculpteurs et dessinateurs de tous les temps et de tous les pays*, II.

97 Unfortunately, we do not possess any really satisfactory general work on the absolutist doctrines, not considered as a theory of social philosophy held by such and such an author, but rather as the expression of a movement of ideas or feelings common to a whole epoch. It goes without saying that the following summary indications make no pretensions towards filling this gap. In Figgis, *The divine right of kings*, and in Hitier, *La Doctrine de l'absolutisme*, we have nothing more than very rapid propositions which are far too theoretical. Cf. also—likewise in the same strictly juridical spirit—André Lemaire, *Les Lois fondamentales de la monarchie française d'après les théoriciens de l'ancien régime* (thesis, Paris), 1907. The book by Lacour-Gayet, *L'Éducation politique de Louis XIV*, gives a large amount of useful information not to be found elsewhere; but it skates over the real problems. It is also well worth while consulting Henri Sée, *Les Idées politiques en France au XVIᵉ siècle*, 1923. For propagandist royalist literature, there is a bibliography that is still of use today in the *Bibliotheca historica* by Struve, re-edited by J. G. Meusel, X, i, Leipzig, 1800, p. 179: *Scriptores de titulis, praerogativis, majestate et auctoritate Regum* [Franciae].

98 Perhaps, incidentally, the epochs most easily misunderstood are precisely those that one sees through a still living literary tradition. A work of art only maintains its life if each generation as it comes along puts something of itself into it; and in this way its meaning is gradually changed, until sometimes it has been twisted into the exact opposite, and ceases to give us information about the environment in which it originated. Brought up on the literature of the ancient world, the men of the eighteenth century nevertheless had a very imperfect understanding of antiquity. And we today occupy much the same position with regard to them as they did with regard to the Greeks and Romans.

99 *De Corpore Politico*, 2, VIII, 11 (ed. Molesworth, IV, 199).

100 *Aristippe, Discours septiesme*, 2nd ed., 1658, p. 221. For Balzac's political conceptions, the reader can consult J. Declareuil, 'Les Idées politiques de Guez de Balzac', *Revue du droit public*, 1907, p. 633.

101 The works of Ferrault, Raulin, and Grassaille are listed in the Bibliography, p. 429; the work by d'Albon in the Introduction, n. 5. Pierre Poisson, sieur de la Bodinière, *Traité de la Majesté Royale en France*, 1597; H. du Boys, *De l'origine et l'autorité des roys*, 1604; Louis Rolland, *De la Dignité du Roy ou est montré et prouvé que sa Majesté est seule et unique en terre vrayment Sacrée de Dieu et du Ciel*, 1623; Fr. Balthasar de Riez, a Capuchin preacher: *L'Incomparable Piété des très chrétiens rois de France et les admirables prerogatives qu'elle a méritées à Leurs Majestés, tant pour leur royaume en général que pour leurs personnes sacrées en particulier*, 2 vols, 1672–4; André du Chesne, *Les Antiquitez et recherches de la grandeur et maiesté des Roys de France*, 1609; Jérôme Bignon, *De l'Excellence des rois et du royaume de France*, 1610; the

same under the pseudonym of Théophile Dujay, *La Grandeur de nos roys et leur souveraine puissance*, 1615.

102 There are innumerable documents that could be quoted. We need only remind ourselves that Bossuet, in his *Politique tirée des propres paroles de l'Ecriture Sainte*, gives as the title of article II in Book Three: *L'autorité royale est sacrée*, and the Second Proposition in this article: *La personne des rois est sacrée.*

103 See the second chapter of Book II in his *Regalium Franciae iura omnia*, 1538. In his celebrated treatise on the *droit de régale* (*Tractatus juris regaliorum, Praefatio, Pars* III, *in Opera*, 1534, pp. 16–17), Arnold Ruzé is content in rather timid fashion to ascribe a 'mixed' status to the king, by virtue of which he would be 'considered a clerk': 'ratione illius mixturae censentur ut clerici'. On the other hand, on 16 Nov. 1500 'Lemaistre (speaking) for the king's procureur general' declared before the Parliament of Paris, in accordance with ancient principle: 'Nam licet nonnulli reges coronentur tantum alii coronentur et ungantur, ipse tamen rex Francie his consecracionem addit, adeo quod videatur non solum laicus, sed spiritualis', and in support of this thesis referred immediately after to spiritual patronage: Arch. Nat. X 1ª, 4842, fol. 47 v. (cf. Delachenal, *Histoire des avocats*, p. 204, n. 4).

104 *Gallica historia in duos dissecta tomos*, 1557, p. 110: 'Regia enim Francorum maiestas non prorsus laica dici debet. Primum quidem ex recepta coelitus unctione sacra: deinde ex coelesti privilegio curandi a scrophulis, a beato intercessore Marculpho impetrato: quo regni Francici successores in hunc usque diem fruuntur. Tertio iure regaliae magna ex parte spitituali in conferendis (ut passim cernere est) ecclesiasticis peculiari iure beneficiis.' On this author, consult A. Bernard, *De vita et operibus Roberti Cenalis* (thesis, Paris), 1901.

105 *Les Antiquitez et recherches*, p. 164; cf. Sée, loc. cit., p. 38, n. 3.

106 Paris, 1611, esp. pp. 220–2. Villette knew Jean Golein's treatise on consecration (cf. above, p. 276); he writes with some modification of the more prudent formula used by Golein about Communion in both kinds: '[le roi] communie sous les deux espèces, comme fait le Prestre, Et, dit le vieil Autheur, *Afin que le Roy de France sache sa dignité estre Presbiterale et Royale*'.

107 *Histoire ecclésiastique de la Cour*, p. 728. Cf. the account of Louis XIII's consecration, Godefroy, *Ceremonial*, p. 452: 'Il communia au précieux Corps et Sang de Nostre Seigneur sous les deux espèces du pain et du vin, après quoi on lui donna l'ablution comme aux Prestres pour montrer que sa dignité est Royale et Presbyterale'.

108 *L'Incomparable Piété des très chrétiens rois de France*, I, p. 12: '. . . icy nous pouvons et devons dire par occasion, que le sacre de nos rois n'est pas nécessaire pour leur asseurer leur droit sur la Couronne de France, lequel ils tirent de la naissance et de la succession. Mais que c'est une sainte cérémonie, qui attire sur eux des graces particulieres du Ciel, qui rend leurs personnes sacrées, et en quelque façon Sacerdotales. Aussi sont-ils vestus en cette action d'un habillement semblable à une tunique de nos Diacres et d'un manteau royal approchant de la ressemblance d'une Chappe, ou anciene Chasuble d'un Prestre.'

109 Quoted by Figgis, *Divine Right*, p. 256, n. 1. The author of the *Eikon* was

speaking seriously. It is curious that the same idea, let drop by way of jest, should have been uttered by Napoleon I when a prisoner on St Helena: 'You make your confession,' he said to Baron Gourgaud; 'Well, I am anointed—you can make your confession to me!' (General Gourgaud, *Saint-Hélène*, no date, II, p. 143).

110 *Oeuvres*, ed. Pardessus, 1819, I, p. 261. For the text of the Council and the other similar texts, cf. above, Book 2, Ch. III, n. 4.

111 Eusebius, IV, 24. E.-C. Babut, *Revue critique*, new series, 68, 1909, p. 261, thinks that Constantine meant: bishop of the pagans.

112 For example: B. de la Roche-Flavin, *Treize Livres des Parlemens de France*, 13, chap. xliv, § XIV, Bordeaux, 1617, p. 758: 'Evesque commun de France: qui est l'Eloge que le fragment des Conciles donne à l'Empereur Constantin'; d'Aguesseau, loc. cit. p. 261 ('évêque extérieur'). Even in the eighteenth century, a decree of the Council of 24 May 1766 (Isambert, *Recueil général*, 22, p. 452): 'évêque du dehors'.

113 *Basilikon Doron*, Book I, ed. MacIlwain (Harvard Political Classics, I), 1918, p. 12.

114 The third treatise *De la Souveraineté du Roy*, 1620, p.3: 'Le tout puissant . . . vous ayant estably son Vicaire au temporel de vostre Royaume, constitué comme un Dieu corporel pour estre respecté, servy, obéy de tous vos subjects . . . '

115 *Les Antiquitez et recherches*, p. 124; cf. p. 171.

116 A declaration by the Assembly of the Clergy, censuring two booklets entitled *Misteria Politica* and *Admonition de G.G.R. Theologien au Tres Chretien Roy de France et de Navarre Louis XIII*, both of which criticized the alliance between France and the protestant powers: *Mercure françois*, 11, 1626, p. 1072. The Bishop of Chartres then makes his thought more precise, but softens its form in respect of what might have been too shocking, as follows: 'Pourtant il s'ensuit que ceux qui sont appellez Dieux, le soient, non par essence, mais par participation, non par nature, mais par grace, non pour tousiours, mais pour un certain temps, comme estant les vrays Lieutenans du Dieu Tout-puissant, et qui par l'imitation de sa divine Majesté, representent icy bas son image'.

117 C. Moreau, *Bibliographie des mazarinades* (Soc. de l'hist. de France), II, no. 1684. For other characteristic quotations, see Lacour-Gayet, *L'Éducation politique de Louis XIV*, pp. 357–8. It is moreover to this work that I am indebted for the last three documentary quotations. Cf. also du Boys, *De l'Origine et autorité des roys*, 1604, p. 80 (to be compared with p. 37).

118 *Sermon sur les Devoirs des Rois* (2 April 1662), *Oeuvres oratoires*, ed. Lebarq, revised by C. Urbain and E. Levesque, IV, p. 362.

119 *Opera* (*Corpus Reformatorum*), 32, Psalm CX, col. 160; see a passage less favourable to the divine image of kings in *In Habacuc*, I, II, col. 506. Verses 6 and 7 of Psalm 82, quoted above, have embarrassed modern commentators, who have sometimes interpreted them as an irony directed against the kings of non-Jewish peoples who called themselves gods: cf. F. Baethgen, *Die Psalmen* (*Handkommentar zum alten Testament*, Göttingen,) 1897, p. 252.

120 *De la Maiesté royalle*, p. 6: 'le Prince par sa vertu, generosité, magnanimité, douceur et liberalité envers son peuple, surpasse tous les autres hommes de

tant, qu'à bon droit, et iuste raison plusieurs des anciens Philosophes l'ont estimé plus qu'homme, voyre estre Dieu. Et ceux qui de moins se sont fallis les ont (à raison de leurs perfections) dict et prononcé demi dieux.'

121 *Policraticus*, III, 10, ed. C. C. J. Webb, I, p. 203: 'Voces, quibus mentimur dominis, dum singularitatem honore multitudinis decoramur, natio haec invenit'; this refers, as will be seen, to the plural of majesty; but a little higher up John of Salisbury treats of the imperial apotheoses and adds (pp. 202–3): 'Tractum est hinc nomen quo principes uirtutum titulis et uerae fidei luce praesignes se diuos audeant nedum gaudeant appellari, ueteri quidam consuetudine etiam in vitio et aduersus fidem catholicam obtinente'.

122 Godfrey of Viterbo, *Speculum regum; Monum. Germ., SS*, XXII, p. 39, 1. 196: 'Nam Troianorum tu regna tenebis avorum—Filius illorum deus es de prole deorum'; cf. the euhemeristic explanation, p. 138, line 178 ff. Cf. also a little later on, in 1269, similar expressions in the *Adhortatio*, drawn up by an Italian partisan of the Hohenstaufen, the Peter of Prezza already mentioned above, Book 2, Ch. III, note 65: quoted by Grauert, *Histor. Jahrbuch*, 13, 1892, p. 121. *Des magisters Petrus de Ebulo liber ad honorem Augusti*, ed. Winckelmann, Leipzig, 1874, quotations collected on p. 82, n. 9 (there is another edition by G. B. Siragusa *Fonti per la storia d'Italia*, 1905). Applied as it was in this way to the Emperor, was it also sometimes applied to his arch-adversary the Pope? In the *Revue des sciences religieuses*, 2, 1922, p. 447, M. l'abbé Jean Rivière asks the question: 'Le pape est-il "Dieu" pour Innocent III?' and replies to it, of course, in the negative. But what he appears not to know is that the doctrinal error wrongly attributed to Innocent III figures among the superstitions with which the 'Anonymous writer from Passau' reproached his contemporaries in the year 1260: *Abhandl. der histor. Klasse der bayer. Akademie*, 13, 1, 1875, p. 245: 'Peregrinacioni derogant . . . qui dicunt quod Papa sit deus terrenus, maior homine, par angelis et quod non possit peccare, et quod sedes romana aut invenit sanctum aut reddit; quod sedes romana non possit errare . . . '

123 *De regimine principum*, Venice, 1498, Book I, pars I, cap. ix: 'quare cum regem deceat esse totum diuinum et semideum'. Cf. cap. VI: 'dictum est enim quod decet principem esse super hominem et totaliter diuinum'.

124 In 1615, a Parisian theologian, Jean Filesac, brought out a treatise *De idolatria politica et legitimo principis cultu commentarius*, the title of which seemed to promise an interesting discussion. Unfortunately this little treatise betrays a very indecisive line of thought. The author appears to be not at all favourable to the idea that unction confers a sacerdotal character on the king (p. 74), but does not openly controvert it; the king's subjects owe him the same 'culte' as a son does to his father. The reputation of Filesac for inconstancy was moreover well established among his contemporaries: he used to be called 'Monsieur le voici, le voilà' (P. Féret, *La Faculté de théologie de Paris, Époque moderne*, 4, 1906, p. 375). The use of the divine name as applied to temporal princes was criticized in the Middle Ages, e.g. by Charlemagne and by John of Salisbury (above, Book 1, Ch. II, n. 26, and above, n. 121).

125 Cf. the works of J. de la Servière, S.J., *De Jacobo I Angliae rege, cum Card. Roberto Bellarmino, super potestate cum regia tum pontificia disputante*, 1900—

'Une controverse au début du XVIIe siècle: Jacques Ier d'Angleterre et le cardinal Bellarmin' *Études*, vols. 94, 95, 96, 1903.

126 Fra Luys de Granada, *Segunda Parte de la introduction del symbolo de la fe*, Saragossa, 1583 (I have not been able to see the first edition, Antwerp, 1572), p. 171, § VIII: 'la virtud que los reyes de Francia tienen para sanar un mal contagioso, y incurabile, que es delos lamparones'.

127 Marlot, *Théâtre d'honneur*, p. 760, 5 Jan. 1547: 'Civitas Remensis, in qua Christianissimi Francorum Reges sibi coelitus missum Sanctae Unctionis, et curandorum languidorum munus, a pro tempore existente Archiepiscopo Remensi suscipiunt, et Diademate coronantur'.

128 It is interesting that Bernard de Girard de Haillan does not mention the royal touch, either in his treatise *De l'Estat et succez des affaires de France* (first ed., 1570; I consulted the 1611 ed.)—where he enumerates, at the beginning of Book IV, the 'prerogatives, droicts, dignitez et privileges' of kings—or, it would seem, in his *Histoire générale des rois de France*, 1576. It is true that the monarchy he prefers is a temperate and reasonable monarchy on which he theorizes without the slightest trace of mysticism.

129 Above, Book 2, Ch. IV, n. 150.

130 B. de Girard du Haillan, *De l'Estat et succez des affaires de France*, 1611 (1st ed., 1570), p. 624: 'le Roy ne laisse pas d'estre Roy, sans le couronnement et Sacre, qui sont ceremonies pleines de reverence, concernans seulement l'approbation publique, non l'essence de la souveraineté'. The same theory is put forward in Belleforest and de Belloy: G. Weill *Les Théories sur le pouvoir royal en France pendant les guerres de religion*, 1892 (thesis, Paris), pp. 186, 212. For the position of this problem at the beginning of Henry IV's reign, see especially the decisions of the Assembly of Clergy at Chartres in 1591, in Pierre Pithou, *Traitez des droitz et libertez de l'église gallicane*, p. 224, and the curious little work written in Jan. 1593 by Claude Fauchet, *Pour le Couronnement du Roy Henri IIII roy de France et de Navarre. Et que pour n'estre sacré, il ne laisse d'estre Roy et légitime Seigneur* (reproduced in the edition of the *Oeuvres*, 1610). For England cf. Figgis, *Divine Right*, p. 10, n. 1. On the importance attributed by the papacy to anointing in the eighteenth century, see a curious fact in connection with the Hapsburgs, Batiffol, *Leçons sur la messe*, 1920, p. 243.

131 Dom Oudard Bourgeois affirms that he made his novena to St-Marcoul in the chateau at St-Cloud, but his testimony is suspect; see above, p. 284. The common and semi-official view of the origin of the healing power is clearly explained in a seventeenth century ceremonial, ed. Franklin, *La Vie privée, Les Médecins*, p. 303 (cf. below, n. 145). 'La charité de nos Roys est grande en cette cérémonie en laquelle le Ciel les a obligez, en leur en baillant les privileges par dessus les autres Roys, *le jour de leur sacre*' (my italics).

132 The ambassadors of Charles VII to Pius II, in the speech mentioned above, p. 81 and Book 2, Ch. I, n. 102, express themselves as though they thought Clovis had already healed the scrofula; but it would seem that they were simply carried away by a fit of eloquence rather than alluding to a precise legendary belief.

133 See Berriat de Saint-Prix, *Vie de Cujas*, in the appendix to his *Histoire du*

droit romain, Paris, 1821, pp. 482 ff., where the saying by Papire Masson is quoted. Du Peyrat had already referred to it in connection with the legend that Clovis healed the scrofula in his *Histoire ecclésiastique de la Cour*, p. 802. There is a little about this author in G. Weill, *Les Théories sur le pouvoir royal en France pendant les guerres de religion*, p. 194. Kurt Glaser, 'Beiträge zur Geschichte der politischen Literatur Frankreichs in der zweiten Hälfte des 16. Jahrhunderts', *Zeitschrift für französische Sprache und Literatur*, 45, 1919, p. 31, only allows him a disparaging mention.

134 Two separate re-issues in 1580 and 1595, quite apart from the reprintings in the complete works: see the catalogue in the Bibliothèque Nationale.

135 *De Gallorum imperio*, p. 128.

136 According to Mézeray, *Histoire de France depuis Faramond jusqu'au règne de Louis le Juste*, 1685, Book VI, p. 9, the House of Montmorency claimed to go back to Lanicet. André Duchesne in his *Histoire généalogique de la maison de Montmorency*, 1624, and Desormeaux, *Histoire de la maison de Montmorenci*, 2nd ed., 5 vols, 1768, seem to be unaware of, or despise, this tradition, which is again reproduced by Menin, *Traité historique et chronologique du sacre*, 1724, p. 325.

137 *De sacris unctionibus*, p. 260.

138 For example: [Daniel de Priezac], *Vindiciae gallicae adversus Alexandrum Patricium Armacanum, theologum*, 1638, p. 61; Balthasar de Riez, *L'Incomparable Piété*, I, pp. 32–3, and II, p. 151; Oudard Bourgeois, *Apologie*, p. 9. Cf. also de l'Ancre, *L'Incrédulité et mescreance du sortilège*, 1622, p. 159. Among the historians, P. Mathieu, *Histoire de Louys XI*, 1610, p. 472, and —with some hesitation—Charron, *Histoire universelle*, Paris, 1621, chap. XCV, pp. 678–9. Charron writes with regard to Lanicet's history: 'un de mes amis m'a aussi assuré l'avoir leu a Rheims, dans un très ancien Manuscrit'. Dom Marlot, *Le Théâtre d'honneur*, p. 715, likewise alludes to this manuscript, whose existence nevertheless seems to me to be more than problematical.

139 Du Peyrat, *Histoire ecclésiastique de la Cour*, pp. 802 ff.; on his attempts to persuade du Laurens of the falsity of this legend, p. 805; cf. above, p. 15; S. Dupleix, *Histoire générale de France*, II, pp. 321–2. Mézeray's attitude (passage quoted, n. 136) is one of polite doubt.

140 *De mirabili*, pp. 10 ff. Cf. also Mauclerc, *De monarchia divina*, 1622, col. 1566.

141 Batista y Roca, *Touching for the King's Evil*, notes it in Esteban Garibay, *Compendio historial de las Chronicas y universal historia de todos los Reynos de Espana*, III, Barcelona, 1628, Book xxv, chap. XIX, p. 202.

142 P. 46, 4. For the work, which bears the certainly fictitious date of 1643, see Lacour-Gayet, *Éducation politique*, pp. 88 ff. For the title of saint as attributed to Clovis, cf. Jean Savaron, *De la Saincteté du roy Louys dit Clovis avec les preuves et auctoritez, et un abrégé de sa vie remplie de miracles*, 3rd ed., Lyons, 1622—where, incidentally, there is no mention of the royal touch.

143 In Book XXV; the child healed by Clovis is no longer Lanicet, but the son of the Burgundian Genobalde. In the 1673 edition, in which the arrangement of the books is modified, the episode is part of Book XIX.

144 Other princes besides Clovis, indeed, had found themselves being by chance credited with the honour of being the first healers of the scrofula; Charron, *Histoire universelle*, folio, 1621, p. 679, testifies to a tradition assigning this part to Charles Martel; the Spanish historian Anton Beuter, *Segunda Parte de la Coronica generale de Espana* . . . , Valencia, 1551, chap. L, fol. CXLIII, considers that the privilege of healing was conferred on St Louis when a prisoner during the Egyptian crusade, by the same angel who, according to a much older legend, enabled him to find his lost breviary. This seems also to be the theory of Louis of Granada, in the passage quoted above, n. 126.

145 There is a very precise description of the royal touch in du Peyrat, *Histoire ecclésiastique de la Cour*, p. 819, fully in agreement with that given at end of Henry IV's reign by du Laurens, *De mirabili*, p. 6. The Bibliothèque Nationale possesses—under the classification MS. fr. 4321—a *Recueil general des ceremonies qui ont esté observées en France et comme elles se doibvent observer*, dating from the seventeenth century (no doubt in Louis XIII's reign); on pp. 1 and 2 there is the 'Ceremonie a toucher les malades des escrouelles'. The same text has been published from MS. 2743 in the Mazarine, by Franklin, *La Vie privée*, *Les Médecins*, pp. 303 ff. Johann Christian Lünig in his *Theatrum ceremoniale historico–politicum*, II, p. 1015, gives a description of the French royal touch which does not contain any new information. For Louis XIII, there are numerous details and figures in the journal kept by his doctor Héroard, *Journal de Jean Héroard sur l'enfance et la jeunesse de Louis XIII*, ed. Soulié, and de Barthélemy, II, 1868; but this publication is unfortunately of a very fragmentary kind (see the following notes). For Louis XIV, there is useful information, though often inaccurate in its figures, in various memoirs, esp. the *Journal* of Dangeau and the *Mémoires* of the Marquis de Sourches, Provost of the Royal Household, and Provost Marshal of France (1681–1712), whose duties had led him to pay particular attention to the royal touch: ed. Cosnac and Bertrand, 13 vols, 1882 ff. The journals of the period also contain some interesting details: for instance, we know from the gazetteer Robinet that on Easter eve 1666 Louis XIV touched 800 sick persons: *Les Continuateurs de Loret*, ed. J. de Rothschild, 1881, I, p. 838. For iconographical information, see Appendix II.

146 Saint-Simon, *Mémoires*, ed. Boislisle, XXVIII, pp. 368–9: Louis XIV 'communioit toujours en collier de l'Orde, rabat et manteau, cinq fois l'année, le samedi saint à la Paroisse, les autres jours à la chapelle, qui étoient la veille de la Pentecôte, le jour de l'Assomption, et la grand messe après, la veille de la Toussaint et la veille de Noël . . . et à chaque fois il touchoit les malades'. In actual fact, there does not seem to have been such absolute regularity.

147 They are to be found at the Bibliothèque Nationale, in the series of the *Registres d'affiches et publications des jurés crieurs de la Ville de Paris*. Although this series—F.48 to 61—comprises 14 folio volumes, stretching from 1651 to 1745, it is only the first two volumes that contain the notices referring to the royal touch: in F.48, fol. 419, the one announcing the Easter ceremonies of 1655; in F.49, fol. 15, 35, 68, 101, 123, 147, 192, those which announce the All Saints' 1655 ceremonies, and those of 1 Jan., Easter and All Saints'

1656; for 1 Jan. and Easter 1657; and 1 Jan. 1658. They are all drawn up on the same model. Cf. Lecoq, *Empiriques, somnambules et rebouteurs*, p. 15. The custom of announcing in advance, through the offices of the Provost Marshal, the coming ceremonies 'par la ville de Paris, ou autre lieu où sa Majesté se trouve' is noted by du Peyrat, p. 819.

148 Héroard, *Journal*, II, p. 32: 'Il blémissoit un peu de travail et ne le voulut jamais faire paraître'; p. 76: 'il se trouve foible'.

149 An order by Henry IV, of 20 Oct. 1603, announcing that by reason of the 'malladie contagieuse' prevailing in certain towns and provinces there would be no royal touch on the following All Saints' Day, was published by J. J. Champollion-Figeac in *Le Palais de Fontainebleau*, 1866, p. 299.

150 Héroard, *Journal*, II, p. 237.

151 Héroard, *Journal*, II, pp. 59, 64, 76 (and Bibl. Nat., MS. fr. 4024); Héroard, MS. fr, 4026, fol. 294, 314 v., 341 v., 371 v.; Héroard, *Journal*, II, p. 120.

152 *Gazette de France*, 1701, p. 251

153 Dangeau, *Journal*, ed. Soulié, V, p. 348.

154 Ibid., XV, p. 432.

155 *De Galliae regum excellentia*, 1641, p. 27: 'Imperium non Pyrenaeorum jugis aut Alpium, non Rheni metis et Oceani circumscriptum, sed ultra naturae fines ac terminos, in aegritudinem ipsam et morbos, a quibus nulla Reges possunt imperia vindicare, propagatum acceperunt . . . Ita Galliae Regum arbitrio subiectam esse naturam'.

156 *Des Miraculeux Effects*, p. 25.

157 Héroard, MS. fr. 4026, fol. 341 v. (15 Aug. 1620): 'touched two sick Portuguese Jesuits'; A. Franco, *Synopsis annalium Societatis Jesu*, text quoted below, Book 3, n. 42 (the dates make it very unlikely that the Jesuit mentioned by Franco, who died in 1657, no doubt not many years after being touched, was one of the two people mentioned by Héroard in 1620).

158 See Appendix II, no. 11. For the part played by the Farnese and the support given them against the Papacy by France from 1658 onwards, see C. Gérin, *Louis XIV et le Saint Siège*, 2 vols., 1894. In 1667, Cardinal Farnese was put on the list of candidates for the tiara acceptable to the French king (ibid., II, p. 185).

159 Plentiful evidence on this point: e.g. Héroard, II, pp. 215, 233; du Laurens, p. 8; de l'ancre, p. 166: du Peyrat, p. 819; René Moreau, *De manu regia*, 1623, p. 19; a ceremonial published by Franklin, p. 305. Under Louis XIII, foreigners received larger alms than Frenchmen—a quarter of an *écu* instead of two *sols*: du Peyrat, p. 819; cf. Héroard, II, p. 33. Under Louis XIV, according to Oroux, *Histoire ecclésiastique de la Cour*, I, p. 184, note q, the value of alms in general (at least in money of account) had increased, but there was still a difference between foreigners and 'les naturels françois': 30 s. for the former, 15 for the latter. According to Bonaventure de Sorria, *Abrégé de la vie de la tres auguste et tres vertueuse princesse Marie-Thérèse d'Austriche reyne de France et de Navarre*, 1683, p. 88; this queen was said to have set up at Poissy a hospice 'pour y loger tous les malades qui venoient des païs eloignez' in order to receive the royal touch. But from the documents quoted by Octave Noël, *Histoire de la ville de Poissy*, Paris, 1869, pp. 254, 306 ff., it would certainly seem that the Poissy hospice was founded

for soldiers in the Achères camp 'and other soldiers passing through'. As in the past—at least in Louis XIII's time—the sick who arrived in advance of the appointed times for the royal touch were made to wait, and given some alms to support them meanwhile: du Peyrat, p. 819. For Spaniards touched by Louis XIV when his state of health prevented him from touching other sick persons, see: Sourches, *Mémoires*, IX, p. 259, XI, p. 153; for Spaniards and Italians touched under the same conditions, ibid., VII, p. 175.

160 The joke is to be found in a pamphlet by André Rivet: *Andreae Riveti Pictavi . . . Jesuita Vapulans, sive Castigatio Notarum Sylvestri Petrasanctae Romani, Loyolae Sectarii, in epistolam Petri Molinaei ad Balzacum . . .* , Leyden, 1635, chap. XIX, p. 388. For the polemics to which this little book owes its origin, cf. C. Sommervogel, *Bibliothèque de la Compagnie de Jésus*, article *Pietra-Santa*, VI, col. 740, no. 14. The amusing thing is that Morhof, *Princeps medicus* (Diss. academicae), p. 157, appears to have taken this joke quite seriously,

161 *De excellentia*, pp. 31 ff.

162 Francisco Marti y Viladamor, *Cataluna en Francia*, 1641 (cf. below, p. 431). At the front of the book there are two dedications: to Louis XIII and to Richelieu; the chapter on scrofula is followed by another about the legends of the fleur-de-lis and the oriflamme.

163 *Mars Gallicus*, 1636 ed., pp. 65 ff. To see in the miracle of scrofula-healing a proof that the French kings possess a more 'sublime' power than that of other kings would be 'fidei Christianae fides . . . evellere'; to be madder than the Hussites, for whom the legitimacy of an authority depended on the virtue of its possessors, but who at least did not go as far as to demand of them any extraordinary graces. God has caused asses to speak: 'An forte et asinis inter asinos tribues praerogativas alicujus potestatis?' *Mars Gallicus*, on which the reader can consult G. Hubault, *De politicis in Richelium lingua latina libellis* (thesis, Paris), St-Cloud, 1856, pp. 72 ff., was a reply to the book by Arroy quoted below, p. 429. It was quoted approvingly, and with an adoption of the Spanish point of view, by the famous doctor van Helmont, a native of Brussels: *De virtute magna verborum ac rerum; Opera omnia*, Frankfurt, 1707, p. 762, col. 2.

164 See the interesting little work by Joachim Christoph Nemeiz, *Séjour de Paris* (only the title is in French; the text is in German), Frankfurt, 1717, p. 191. Nemeiz had come to Paris in 1714 with the two sons of the Swedish general Count Stenbock, who were his pupils.

165 Pp. 69–73 (this work came out in 1618). For the author, see *France protestante*, 2nd ed., I, col. 797, and Jacques Pannier, *L'Eglise réformée de Paris sous Louis XIII* (thesis, Strasbourg), 1922, p. 501.

166 Cf. Amyraut, pp. 77–8.

167 *Briefe der Prinzessin Charlotte von Orleans an die Raugräfin Louise*, ed. W. Menzel (*Bibliothek des literarichen Vereins in Stuttgart*, VI), 1843, p. 407; 24 June 1719: 'Man meint hier auch dass der 7bente sohn die Ecruellen durch anrühren könte. Ich glaube aber dass Es Eben so Viel Krafft hatt alss der König In frankreich ahnrühren.'

168 Above, p. 224.

169 A certain number of proclamations have been published in Crawfurd, *King's*

Evil, pp. 163 ff., belonging to Charles I's reign (and one from Charles II's), fixing the dates for the royal touch, prohibiting sick persons from coming to the Court in times of epidemics, or at any rate regulating the conditions for the ceremony. Cf. *Calendar of State Papers, Domestic, Charles I*, under the dates 13 May, 18 June 1625; 17 June 1628; 6 April, 12 August 1630 (this last on p. 554 in the vol. relating to the years 1629–31); 25 March, 13 October, 8 November 1631; 20 June 1632; 11 April 1633; 20 April, 23 September, 14 December 1634; 28 July 1635; 3 September 1637.

170 Required, it would seem, for the first time by a proclamation of 13 May 1625, quoted above n. 42 (prescription renewed 18 June 1626: Crawfurd, p. 164), and remaining in force during the following reigns. Under Charles II it was laid down that each parish must keep a register: *Notes and Queries*, 3rd Series, I, 1862, p. 497. From this time onwards they have accordingly been very well preserved for us. Many of them have been indicated or published, esp. for Charles II's reign, see e.g. J. Charles Cox, *The Parish Registers of England*, London (The Antiquary's Books), 1910, p. 180; Pettigrew, *On superstitions connected with the history . . . of medicine*, p. 138; Thiselton-Dyer, *Social life as told by Parish Registers*, 1898, p. 79; Barnes in *Transactions of the Cumberland . . . Antiquarian Society*, 13, p. 352; Andrews, *The Doctor*, p. 15; *Notes and Queries*, 8th series, 8, 1895, p. 174; 10th series, 6, 1906, p. 345; Farquhar, III, pp. 97 ff. The abundance of this material is one more proof of the popularity of the royal touch. Of course, in England and in France, patients were subjected to a medical examination beforehand; and under Charles I the doctor on duty used to hand out to those he admitted metal discs which served as entrance-tickets: Farquhar, I, pp. 123 ff. No doubt the same procedure was followed under Charles II: Farquhar, II, pp. 124 ff.

171 *The boke of common prayer*, 1633, B.M. 3406, fol. 5. The service reappeared in the *Book of Common Prayer* from the Restoration onwards: 1662 ed. (B.M. C 83, e, 13); cf. already in Simpson, *A collection of articles . . . of the Church of England*, London, 1661, p. 223; and it kept its place in successive editions of the book even after the English kings had ceased to practise the miracle: below, Book 2, Ch. VI, n. 24. There is a description of the English rite, of no great interest, in J. G. Lünig, *Theatrum ceremoniale historico-politicum*, II, pp. 1043–7.

172 As in France, there existed, alongside the great ceremonies, private touching ceremonies for those whose rank prevented them from mixing with the common herd; and it was in this way, apparently, that Lord Poulett's daughter was healed, as we shall see later on.

173 An order quoted by G. Brunet, 'Notice sur les sculptures des monuments religieux du département de la Gironde', *Rev. archéol.*, 1st series, 12, 1, 1855, p. 170: 'en 1679, on y touchait [dans la chapelle St-Louis, en l'église St-Michel de Bordeaux] encore les malades atteints des écrouelles; une ordonnance de l'archevêque Henri de Sourdis, du 23 août de cette année, interdit cette pratique parce que "ce privilège de toucher tels malades est reservé à la personne sacrée de nostre roy très chrétien, et quand bien même il se trouveroit quelque personne qui eût ce don, elle ne le pourroit sans notre permission expresse par écrit"'. The last phrase shows that this pro-

hibition was not perhaps altogether absolute. As for the date 1679, it is certainly the result of a slip, since Henri de Sourdis was Archbishop of Bordeaux from 1629 to 18 June 1645, the date of his death. M. Brutails, archivist of the Gironde, has been kind enough to inform me that there does not seem to be any trace of this text in the archives of his *département*. We have no cause to be surprised at finding the Bordeaux 'touchers' exercising their art in a chapel; we shall see later on, and at the same period, a charlatan of the same stamp, the knight of St Hubert, obtaining leave from the diocesan authorities to touch for rabies in a Paris chapel.

174 In 1632, the Jacques Philippe Gaudre, or Boisgaudre, affair: *Calendar of State Papers, Domestic, Charles I*, 13 Jan. and 7 June 1632. In 1637, the Richard Leverett lawsuit (before the Court of the Star Chamber): Charles Goodall, *The Royal College of Physicians of London*, London, 1684, pp. 447 ff: *Calendar of State Papers, Domestic, Charles I*, 19 Sept. 1637; cf. Crawfurd, *King's Evil*, p. 95. Likewise in 1637, the affair of Gilbert of Prestleigh in Somerset: above, p. 169.

175 A letter (of 30 April 1631), published by Green, *On the Cure by Touch*, p. 80. Cf. *Calendar of State Papers, Domestic, Charles I*, of the same date. 'Ye returne of my sicke childe with so much amendment hath much revived a sick Father . . . I am much joyed that his Majesty was pleased to touch my poor child with his blessed hands, whereby, God's blessing accompanying that means, he hath given me a child which I had so little hope to keep, that I gave direction for her bones, doubting she would never be able to return, but she is come safely home and mends every day in her health; and ye sight of her gives me as often occasion to remember his Majestees gratious goodness towards her and me, and in all humilitye and thankfulness to aknowledge it.' For John Poulett, first Baron Poulett, see the *Dictionary of National Biography*.

176 For the title, see the Bibliography, p. 430. Of the illness called on p. 4 'that miraculous and supernatural evill', it is said on p. 6: 'all maladies may have a remedy by physick but ours, which proceeding from unknowne mysterious causes claime onely that supernaturall meanes of cure which is inherent in your sacred Majesty'. On the same page, the petitioners declare that they do not wish to be involved in the misfortunes and iniquities of the present time, 'having enough to reflect and consider our owne miseries'. On p. 8, they complain that they cannot approach the king 'so long as your Majestie resides at Oxford, invironed with so many legions of souldiers, who will be apt to hinder our accesse to your Court and Princely Person, which others that have formerly laboured with our Malady have so freely enjoyed at London'. On the same page: 'your palace at Whitehall, where we all wish your Majestie, as well for the cure of our affirmities, as for the recovery of the State, which hath languished of a tedious sicknesse since your Highnesse departure from thence, and can no more be cured of its infirmitie than wee, till your gracious returne thither'.

177 *Journal of the House of Lords*, IX, p. 6: a letter from the Commissioners in charge of the king, dated 9 Feb. 1647, new style. They announce that during the king's travels, both in Ripon and in Leeds, 'many diseased Persons came, bringing with them Ribbons and Gold, and were only touched, without any

other Ceremony'. They sent a copy of the declaration they had published to Leeds on 9 February: 'Whereas divers People do daily resort unto the Court, under Pretence of having the Evil; and whereas many of them are in Truth infected with other dangerous Diseases, and are therefore altogether unfit to come into the Presence of His Majesty'. For the zeal shown by the sick in seeking out the king during this journey, see also the testimony quoted by Farquhar, I, p. 119. Even before he was taken prisoner, and during the Civil War, Charles had run short of gold and had had to substitute silver for the alms given at the royal touch: Χειρεξοχη, p. 8; Wiseman, *A treatise of the King's Evil*, p. 247. From the passages in Browne quoted in the following note it is clear that the people who sought out Charles during his captivity in order to receive the royal touch used to bring either a gold or a silver coin; when the king provided the coin, it was of silver.

178 *Journal of the House of Commons*, V, dated 22 April 1647. The Chamber received 'a letter from the Commissioners from Holdenby of 20⁰ *Aprilis* 1647, concerning the Resort of great Numbers of People thither, to be Touched for the Healing'. A committee was set up to prepare 'a Declaration to be set forth to the People, concerning the Superstition of being Touched for the Healing of the King's Evil'. The commissioners are to 'take care that the Resort of People thither, to be touched for the Evil, may be prevented', and are to publish the declaration throughout the district. Cf. B. Whitelock, *Memorials of the English Affairs*, London, 1732, p. 244. I have not been able to find this proclamation: it does not form part of Lord Crawfurd's ample collection, catalogued by Robert Steele, *A bibliography of royal proclamations*, 1485–1714 (*Bibliotheca Lindesiana* V–VI). For the case of a child touched at Holmby: Browne, *Adenochoiradelogia*, p. 148; for other cases of persons touched by the king in captivity, see a later section: ibid, pp. 141–6. Cf. also ibid. p.163 and above, p. 216.

179 Page 4.

180 Browne, *Adenochoiradelogia*, pp. 109, 150 ff; it would seem to be implied by an anecdote reported on p. 150 that relics of this kind were kept and considered effective even by officers of the Parliamentary army, which is not after all impossible. Cf. the royalist pamphlets of 1649 and 1659 quoted in the *Gentleman's Magazine*, 81, 1811, p. 125 (reproduced in the *Gentleman's Magazine Library*, ed. G. L. Gomme, III, 1884, p. 171); Wiseman, *Severall Chirugical Treatises*, I, p. 195; Crawfurd, *King's Evil*, p. 101; Farquhar, 'Royal Charities', II, p. 107; W. G. Black, *Folk-Medicine*, p. 100.

181 Browne, p. 181.

182 Browne, *Adenochoiradelogia*, pp. 156 ff.; *Relation en forme de journal du voyage et séjour que le sérénissime et très puissant prince Charles II royale de Grande-Bretagne a fait en Hollande*, The Hague, 1660, p. 77.

183 Farquhar, II, pp. 103–4, on the testimony of the contemporary royalists Blount and Pepys; cf. Crawfurd, *King's Evil*, p. 102 (no references).

184 *Relation* (quoted above, n. 182), pp. 75, 77.

185 Pepys, *Diary* and *Mercurius Politicus*, both dated 23 June 1660, quoted in Farquhar, 'Royal Charities', II, p. 109; *Diary and Correspondence of John Evelyn*, ed. W. Bray, London, 1859. I, p. 357 (6 July 1660). Charles II's ritual was the same as his father's. It can be found in the *Book of Common*

Prayer: cf. above, n. 171; reproduced by Crawford, p. 114. A very detailed description in Evelyn, *Diary*, loc. cit.

186 W. S[ancroft], *A sermon preached at St Peter's Westminster on the first Sunday in Advent* . . . , London, 1660, p. 33: 'therefore let us hope well of the *healing* of the *Wounds of the Daughter of our People*, since they are under the Cure of *those* very *Hands*, upon which God hath entailed a *Miraculous Gift of Healing*, as it were on purpose to raise up our Hopes in some Confidence, that we shall ow one day to those *sacred Hands*, next under God, the healing of the *Church's* and the *People's* Evils, as well, as of the *King's*'.

187 Bird seems to consider Charles II's success to be so great that he will see the complete disappearance from his kingdom, for good and all, of both the scrofula and the *reckets*.

188 Dedicated to the Duke of York (the future James II). Χειρεξοχη should be translated: *Excellence of the Hand*.

189 Like the treatise by du Laurens, the *Adenochoiradelogia* contains a purely medical study of the scrofula. Only the third part, entitled *Charisma Basilikon*, is exclusively concerned with the royal touch.

190 Farquhar, II, pp. 134 ff.

191 P. 105.

192 The figures of the sick touched by Charles II come to us from two sources: (1) from Browne, who, in an appendix to his *Adenochoiradelogia*, pp. 197–9, gives (*a*) according to a register kept by Thomas Haynes, 'sergeant' of the Chapel Royal, the month-by-month figures from May 1660 to September 1664; (*b*) according to a register kept by Thomas Donkly, 'keeper of his Majesties closet' (a register preserved in the Chapel Royal), also giving the month-by-month figures from May 1667 to April 1682; (2) from the certificates relating to the medals supplied, which is discussed in Appendix I, p. 250. This second source is clearly the more reliable; for a good number of months one can compare the figures given by it with Browne's figures. There are some divergencies, now in one direction and now in another, but the majority of these can probably be explained either as copying errors on the part of Browne or his informer, or as printers' errors; but there is nothing here to produce any significant modification in the totals or the general level of the statistics. The indications given by me in the text are taken: (1) for the period May 1660 to Sept. 1664, from Browne (exact figure 23,801); (2) for the period 7 April 1669 to 14 May 1671, from the certificates, preserved in the Public Record Office; the reservation *at least* 6,666 is necessary because there are some gaps in our certificates (from 15 June to 4 July 1670; from 26 Feb. 1671 to 19 March) for which it is impossible to know whether they are there by chance or whether they indicate times when no touching took place; (3) for the period 12 Feb. 1684 to 1 Feb. 1685, likewise according to the certificates (with a single gap between 1 and 14 Jan. 1684). The total of the figures given by Browne for the two periods he deals with (that is, for the whole reign except for two periods, each of about 2½ years: 1 Oct. 1664 to 1 May 1667, and 1 May 1682 to 6 Feb. 1685) is 90,761 (cf. Farquhar, II, p. 132); hence my approximate figure for the complete reign—about 100,000. All the same, it is as well to remember that we are without one element that would complete the picture: in all probability,

certain sick persons, in spite of the constantly reiterated orders, used to present themselves several times for the royal touch. What proportion was represented by these backsliders? This is something we shall never know. For the eagerness shown on the days of the royal touch, cf. J. Evelyn, *Diary*, II, p. 205 (28 March 1684), quoted by Crawfurd, *King's Evil*, p. 107, n. 2.

193 Crawfurd, pp. 111–12.

194 Cobbett's *Complete Collection of State Trials*, X, pp. 147 ff. The accused, Rosewell by name, had been condemned by the jury on inadequate testimony, and was pardoned by the king. The government of Charles II's time was much less jealous of the king's miraculous healing prerogative than the government of Charles I had been. It is remarkable that Greatrakes (see above, p. 216) was never troubled by them. Cf. Crawfurd, *King's Evil*, p. 120.

195 Green, 'On the cure by Touch', pp. 89 ff., *Gentleman's Magazine*, vol. 81 1811, p. 125 (reproduced in the *Gentleman's Magazine Library*, ed. G. L. Gomme, III, London, 1884, p. 171).

196 T. B. Howell, *State Trials*, XI, Col. 1059.

BOOK 2   CHAPTER VI   *The decline and death of the royal touch*

1 Scaevola Sammarthanus, *Gallorum doctrina illustrium qui nostra patrumque memoria floruerunt elogia*, 1st ed., 1598. I saw the 1633 edition: *Scaevolae et Abelii Sammarthanorum . . . opera latina et gallica*, I, pp. 155–7 (the notice was certainly recast, if not more, after Henry IV's death). I quote Colletet's translation: Scevole de Sainte-Marthe, *Eloge des hommes illustres*, Paris, 1644, pp. 555 ff. On this work, see A. Hamon, *De Scaevolae Sammarthani vita et latine scriptis operibus* (thesis, Paris), 1901. Genealogies of the Bailleul in François Blanchard, *Les Présidents à mortier du Parlement de Paris*, 1647, p. 399, and Fr. Anselme, *Histoire généalogique de la maison royale de France*, II, 1712, p. 1534. Neither of them makes any mention of the miraculous gift of healing; no more does Fr. Pierre le Moine in his *Epistre panegyrique à Mgr. le Président de Bailleul*, following upon his *Le Ministre sans reproche*, 1645. It would seem to me not impossible that Nicholas II—explicitly mentioned by Sainte-Marthe as participating in the paternal gift—may later have ceased to practise it.

2 For the relations of the saints in general, see above, Book 2, Ch. II, n. 33 and p. 171. For those of St-Hubert, and more particularly Georges Hubert, the reader need only consult Henri Gaidoz, *La Rage et St Hubert*, pp. 112–19, where there is a bibliography. I have taken the details of the 1701 prospectus and the passage on the royal touch from le Brun, *Histoire critique des pratiques superstitieuses*, II, pp. 105 and 121. Tiffaud, *L'Exercice illégal de la médecine dans le Bas-Poitou*, 1899, p. 18, also indicates some descendants of St-Marcoul.

3 Du Laurens, *De mirabili*, p. 21; Favyn, p. 1058; du Peyrat, *Histoire ecclésiastique de la Cour*, *p.* 794; *Traité curieux de la guérison des écrouelles par l'attouchment des septennaires*, pp. 13, 21; Thiers, *Traité de superstitions*, p. 443. These authors often correct each other's mistakes (see e.g. du Peyrat, loc. cit.): a proof that they have not simply copied from one another. There was a tendency to relate the miraculous powers of this house to the relics

of the Magi, transported in Frederick Barbarossa's time from Milan to Cologne, and then said to have rested for a while at Aumont; also with a sacred fountain that was venerated in that same place. We may well suspect certain contaminations of belief like those which made St-Marcoul the patron saint of the royal miracle. K. Maurer, 'Die bestimmten Familien zugeschriebene besondere Heilkraft, *Zeitschrift des Vereins für Volkskunde*, 1896, p. 443, has studied some examples of families endowed by heredity with a healing power; but he assigns them to Sicily (cf. ibid, p. 337) and to the legends of Scandinavia. Thiers, loc. cit., p. 449, indicates 'la maison de Coutance dans le Vendômois', whose members were said to be able to heal 'les enfants de la maladie appelée le carreau, en les touchant'.

4 The necessary information, and a bibliography, will be found in the *Dictionary of National Biography;* see also Crawfurd, *King's Evil*, p. 143, and Farquhar, III, p. 102.

5 *Adenochoiradelogia*, pp. 133 ff. (with a letter testifying to the veracity of the anecdote, sent to Browne by the Warden of Winchester College).

6 Tooker, *Charisma*, p. 83; Browne, *Adenochoiradelogia*, p. 63; cf. above, p. 23.

7 On the question of cures performed by Elizabeth; the theory of Smitheus (Richard Smith), *Florum historiae ecclesiasticae gentis Anglorum libri septem*, Paris, 1654, Book III, cap. 19, sectio IV, p. 230, also brings in the influence of St Edward the Confessor; the queen healed 'non virtute propria . . . sed virtute Crucis et ad testandam pietatem S. Edwardi, cui succedebat in Throno Angliae'. Smith—who was Apostolic Vicar in England from 1625 to 1629—does not seem to admit any of the cures accomplished by Elizabeth's successors.

8 De l'Ancre, *L'Incrédulité et mescreance du sortilège*, 1622, p. 165, is an exception; he admits the cures performed by James I, but thinks that this king—secretly, no doubt—shapes his hand 'in the form of a cross'.

9 *Disquisitionum*, 1606 ed., pp. 60 ff.

10 Du Laurens, *De mirabili*, p. 19; du Peyrat, *Histoire ecclésiastique de la Cour*, pp. 796–801.

11 Loc. cit., p. 64: 'Sed ea cogimur dicere, vel fictitia, si non vere aegri: vel fieri physica aliqua vi emplastrorum, aut aliorum adhibitorum: vel ex pacto tacito vel expresso cum daemone'. For observations on persons presented for the royal touch and not healed, see p. 61; cf. above, pp. 238–9. The year when the first edition of the *Disquisitionum* appeared (1593) is that in which Henry IV was converted; at that time France could scarcely be considered to be under the rule of Catholic kings. Was del Rio, in his discussion of the scrofula, alluding to this difficulty? I cannot say, as I have not been able to see the edition previous to that of 1606, where (p. 65) there is the cautious formula 'De Franciae regibus; quorum adhuc nullus apertè haeresim professus fuit', reproduced in the subsequent editions.

12 The library of the 'Surgeon General' of the American Army in Washington possesses—among a collection of documents relating to the touch for scrofula—a small octavo brochure of 8 pp. entitled *The Ceremonies of blessing Cramp-Rings on Good Friday, used by the Catholick Kings of England*. I owe a copy of this document to the extreme kindness of Lieutenant-Colonel

F. H. Garrison, who had referred to it in his article entitled 'A relic of the King's Evil'; the same text will be found reproduced (1) according to a MS. by the *Literary Magazine*, 1792; (2) by W. Maskell, *Monumenta ritualia*, 2nd ed., III, p. 391. Maskell had used a MS. dated 1694, bound in with a copy of the *Ceremonies for the healing of them that be diseased with the King's Evil, used in the Time of King Henry VII*, printed in 1686 by the King's orders (cf. Sparrow-Simpson, 'On the forms of prayer', p. 289); (3) no doubt in accordance with Maskell by Crawfurd, 'Cramp-rings', p. 184. It is a faithful translation of the ancient liturgy, as prescribed by Mary Tudor's missal. The brochure preserved in Washington is dated 1694; it must therefore have been printed after James II's downfall (1688). But a note that appeared in *Notes and Queries*, 6th series, 8, 1883, p. 327, indicating the existence of this little work, intimates that it should be considered without doubt as a reprint: the first edition appears to have come out in 1686. This was the selfsame year in which the Royal Printer published by royal order the old scrofula liturgy (below, n. 15); the year, moreover, when James II attempted more and more to do without the services of the Anglican clergy for the ceremony of the royal touch. It seems, besides, that in Jacobite circles a rumour went round that the last of the Stuarts had blessed rings too: see on James II the letter of the Prince's secretary—which indeed denies the fact—quoted by Farquhar, IV, p. 169.

13 According to the certificates relating to the distribution of medals, preserved in the Public Record Office: see Appendix I, p. 250.

14 *The Diary of Dr Thomas Cartwright, bishop of Chester* (Camden Society, 22, 1843), pp. 74, 75.

15 All the testimony relating to James II's attitude will be found painstakingly collected and judiciously discussed by Farquhar, 'Royal Charities', III, pp. 103 ff. We do not in fact know the actual service used by James II. All we know is that in 1686 the Royal Printer published, by order, the old Catholic liturgy, attributed to Henry VIII and in two different volumes, one containing the Latin text (cf. above, Book 2, Ch. V, n. 31), the other an English translation of it; Crawfurd, *King's Evil*, p. 132. Moreover, a confidential letter from the Bishop of Carlisle dated 3 June 1686 (ed. Magrath, *The Flemings in Oxford*, II, Oxford Historical Society's Publications, 62, 1913, p. 159: quoted in Farquhar, III p. 104), contains the following words: 'Last week, his Majesty dismissed his Protestant Chaplains at Windsor from attending at ye Ceremony of Healing which was performed by his Romish Priests: ye service in Latin, as in Henry 7th time'—which appears to decide the question once and for all. For the scandal raised by the 'papist' forms of the service, cf. the testimony on the ceremony of the royal touch which took place in 1687 at Bath, collected by Green, *On the cure by Touch*, pp. 90-1.

16 In 1726 Sir Richard Blackmore, *Discourses on the Gout*, Preface, p. lxviij, considers the 'superstition' of the royal touch as a downright imposture of the papist priests.

17 *Gazette de France*, 23 April 1689, p. 188: 'De Londres le 28 avril 1689. Le 7 de ce mois le Prince d'Orange dina chez Mylord Newport. Il devoit ce jour la suivant l'usage ordinaire, faire la cérémonie de toucher les malades, et laver les pieds a plusieurs pauvres comme ont toujours fait les Roys légi-

times. Mais il déclara qu'il croyoit que ces cérémonies n'estoient pas exemtes de superstition; et il donna seulement ordre que les aumônes fussent distribuées aux pauvres selon la coûtume.' Cf. also Sir Richard Blackmore, *Discourses on the Gout*, Preface, p. lx; Rapin Thoyras, *Histoire d'Angleterre*, Book V, chap. relating to Edward the Confessor, The Hague, 1724 ed., vol. I, p. 446; Macaulay, *The History of England*, chap. XIV, Tauchnitz ed., I, pp. 145–6; Farquhar, 'Royal Charities', III pp. 118 ff.

18 Macaulay, loc. cit.

19 Oldmixon, *The History of England during the reigns of King William and Queen Mary, Queen Anne, King George I*, London, 1735 (inspired by the Whigs), p. 301. The royal touch began again in March or April 1703 at the latest: Farquhar, 'Royal Charities', IV, p. 143. It has often been recalled that Dr Johnson was touched by Queen Anne in his infancy: Boswell, *Life of Johnson*, ed. Ingpen, London, 1907, I, p. 12, cf. Farquhar, IV, p. 145, n. 1. A new ritual was introduced in this reign, with a shorter liturgy, and a considerably simplified ceremonial. The sick were now only brought once before the sovereign; each of them received the gold coin immediately after being touched: Crawfurd, *King's Evil*, p. 146 (which publishes the text of the service); Farquhar, 'Royal Charities', IV, p. 152. The Wellcome Historical Medical Museum in London possesses a magnet, coming from the family of John Roper, who was Deputy Cofferer to Queen Anne; this is said to have served this sovereign at the royal touch. In order to avoid direct contact with the sick, the queen was said to have held this magnet while making the healing gesture, and placed it between her fingers and the affected parts. Cf. Farquhar, IV, pp. 149 ff. (with a photograph); I also owe some useful information to the kindness of C. J. S. Thompson, Curator of this Museum. It is difficult, incidentally, to say what this tradition is worth. For the ring adorned with a ruby worn by Henry VIII when giving the royal touch in order to avoid contagion, it would seem: see Farquhar, p. 148.

20 *An ecclesiastical history of Great Britain*, ed. Barnham, I, London, 1840, p. 532 (first ed., 1708): 'King Edward the Confessor was the first that cured this distemper, and from him it has descended as an hereditary miracle upon all his successors. To dispute the matter of fact is to go to the excesses of scepticism, to deny our senses, and be incredulous even to ridiculousness.'

21 *Journal to Stella*, letter XXII (28 April 1711), ed. F. Ryland, p. 172.

22 See Appendix II, no. 17.

23 Green, 'On the cure by touch', p. 95.

24 In the English editions up to 1732; in the Latin editions up to 1759; see Farquhar, 'Royal Charities', IV, pp. 153 ff., the researches of which cancel out all previous work.

25 Robert Chambers, *History of the rebellion in Scotland in 1745–46*, 1828 ed., Edinburgh, I, p. 183. It was likewise related that George I, when asked by a lady for the royal touch, did not consent to touch her, but allowed her to touch him. We are not told whether she was cured: Crawfurd, p. 150.

26 James II in Paris and at Saint-Germain: Voltaire, *Siècle de Louis XIV*, chap. XV, ed. Garnier, XIV, p. 300; *Questions sur l'Encyclopédie*, art. 'Ecrouelles', ibid., XVIII, p. 469 (in the *Dictionnaire Philosophique*). James III in Paris, Farquhar, 'Royal Charities', IV, p. 161 (?); in Avignon, below, n. 29; in the

baths at Lucca, Farquhar, p. 170; in Rome, below, n. 27. For the numismatic documents, Farquhar, pp. 161 ff. James II was said to have performed posthumous miracles as a saint, but there is no healing of scrofula in the list of these (see G. du Bosq de Beaumont and M. Bernos, *La Cour des Stuarts à Saint-Germain en Laye*, 2nd ed., 1912, pp. 239 ff.); cf. also Farquhar, 'Royal Charities', III, p. 115, n. 1.

27 For the title, see Bibliography p. 9.

28 Reproduced in the *Gentleman's Magazine*, vol. 7 (1737), p. 495.

29 *A general History of England*, Book IV, § III, p. 291, n. 4. For the place where the royal touch took place, see Farquhar, IV, p. 167.

30 *Gentleman's Magazine*, vol. 18 (1748), pp. 13 ff., (the *Gentlemen's Magazine Library*, III, pp. 165 ff.); cf. Farquhar, 'Royal Charities', IV, p. 167, n. 1.

31 Robert Chambers, *History of the rebellion in Scotland in 1745–46*, 1828 ed., I, p. 184. James III had already touched in Scotland in 1716; Farquhar, 'Royal Charities', IV, p. 166.

32 It would even seem that his sister Mary (who had never been acknowledged by Charles II) practised the touch too: Crawfurd, p. 138.

33 The touch was practised by Charles Edward at Florence, Pisa and Albano in 1770 and 1786: Farquhar, 'Royal Charities', IV, p. 174. The numismatics of the touch under the exiled Stuarts have been studied by Farquhar with her usual care: IV, 161 ff.

34 Farquhar, IV, p. 177 (reproduction). It seems that perhaps in the period of the revolutionary wars 'Henry IX' may have had to fall back upon copper or pewter coins plated with silver: Farquhar, loc. cit., p. 180.

35 Chap. III, 1792 ed., p. 179. Voltaire writes in the *Questions sur l'Encylopédie* in the article on 'Ecrouelles', ed. Garnier, vol. XVIII, p. 470: 'Quand le roi d'Angleterre, Jacques II, fut reconduit de Rochester à Whitehall, [lors de sa première tentative de fuite, le 12 déc. 1688], on proposa de lui laisser faire quelques actes de royauté comme de toucher les écrouelles; il ne se présenta personne'. This anecdote is very unlikely, and should no doubt be rejected as a piece of pure calumny.

36 *Archaeologia*, 35, p. 452, note a. For the wearing of a coin in George I's time, cf. Farquhar, IV, p. 159.

37 Pettigrew, *On superstitions*, pp. 153–4. The St Louis pieces, pierced with a hole for hanging them round the neck or arm, were sometimes used in France as talismans against diseases: cf. le Blanc, *Traité historique des monnoyes*, Amsterdam, 1692, p. 176.

38 Farquhar, IV, p. 180 (and a personal communication from Farquhar).

39 Sheila Macdonald, 'Old-world survivals in Ross-shire', *Folklore*, 14, 1903.

40 Loc. cit., p. 372.

41 A printed account, published by the *Gazette de France*, Arch. Nat. K. 1714, no. 20.

42 Easter 1739: Luynes, *Mémoires*, ed. L. Dussieux and Soulié, II, 1860, p. 391; Barbier, *Journal*, ed. by the Soc. de l'Hist. de France, II, p. 224 ('cela a causé un grand scandale à Versailles et fait beaucoup de bruit à Paris'; indeed, Barbier reckons that 'nous sommes assez bien avec le pape pour que le fils aîné de l'Eglise eût une dispense pour faire ses Pâques, en quelque état qu'il fût, sans sacrilège et en sûreté de conscience'); the Marquis d'Argenson

Journal et Mémoires, ed. E. J. B. Rathery (Soc. de l'Hist. de France) II p. 126. Easter 1740, Luynes, III, p. 176. Christmas 1744, Luyens, VI, p. 193. This information given by P. de Nolhac, *Louis XIV et Marie Leczinska*, 1902, p. 196 (for 1378) is certainly wrong: cf. Luynes, II, p. 99. Louis XIV had already been refused absolution at Easter 1678 by Fr. de Champ, who was taking the place as confessor of Fr. de la Chaise, who was ill (Marquis de Sourches, *Mémoires*, I, p. 209, n. 2); the king probably did not do any touching at this feast.

43 Cf. above, p. 29.

44 Ed. Boislisle, XVII, pp. 74-5. Saint-Simon also believed—no doubt wrongly —that several of Madame de Soubise's children had died of scrofula. After the sentence about the would-be miracle—the one I could not pin down to a precise meaning—he writes as follows: 'the truth is that when they [the kings] touch the sick, it is just after they have made their Communion'.

45 *Questions sur l'Encyclopédie*, article on 'Ecrouelles' (ed. Garnier in the *Dictionnaire philosophique*, XVIII, p. 469), where there occurs on p. 470 the anecdote about François de Paule: 'Le saint ne guérit point le roi, le roi ne guérit point le saint'. *Essai sur les Moeurs*, Introduction xxiii, (vol. XI, pp. 96-7), where we read, apropos of William III's refusal: 'Si l'Angleterre éprouve jamais quelque grande révolution qui la replonge dans l'ignorance, alors elle aura des miracles tous les jours'; and chap. XLII, ibid., p. 365 from which comes the sentence quoted in the text above; it is missing from the first version of this chapter which came out in the *Mercure* of May 1746, pp. 29 ff. I have not been able to consult the genuine *editio princeps*, of 1756. The one of 1761, I, p. 322, contains the sentence in question—Letter to Frederick II of 7 July 1775 (anecdote about Louis XIV's mistress). Cf. also the manuscript notes known by the name of *Sottisier*, vol. XXXII, p. 492.

46 A printed account, published by the *Gazette de France*: Arch. Nat. K 1714, no. 21 (38); Voltaire to Frederick II, 7 July 1775. A picture representing Louis XVI at prayer before the shrine of St-Marcoul: Appendix II, no. 23.

47 For Louis XV, the account quoted above, n. 41 (p. 598). Cf. Regnault, *Dissertation*, p. 5. For Louis XVI, the account quoted above, n. 46 (p. 30); *Le Sacre et couronnement de Louis XVI, roi de France et de Navarre*, 1775, p. 79; [Alletz], *Ceremonial du sacre des rois de France*, 1775, p. 175. It will be observed that according to the account of the consecration of Louis XV and the various texts relating to that of Louis XVI, the order of the two phrases was likewise inverted: 'Dieu te guérisse, le roi te touche'. Clausel de Coussergues, *Du Sacre des rois de France*, 1825, gives an account of the consecration of Louis XIV which has the formula in the subjunctive (p. 697, cf. p. 150); but he does not give his source. For the official texts of the seventeenth century, cf. above, Book 2, Ch. V, n. 23. Charles X also used the subjunctive, which had become traditional; but it is clear that Landouzy, *Le Toucher des écrouelles*, pp. 11, 30, is wrong in attributing to him the initial use of it.

48 *Journal et Mémoires du marquis d' Argenson*, I, p. 47.

49 The letter from Rouillé d'Orfeuil, and Bertin's reply, Arch. de la Marne, C. 229; the first is published in Ledouble, *Notice sur Corbeny*, p. 211; I owe a copy of the second to the kindness of the Archivist of the *département*.

50 Certificates published by Cerf, *Du Toucher des écrouelles*, pp. 253 ff; and (with two corrections) by Ledouble, *Notice sur Corbeny*, p. 212; extreme dates: 26 Nov.–3 Dec. 1775. Neither of the two editors gives precise details of his sources: they would both seem to have drawn upon the archives of the Hospice St-Marcoul. All the same, the St-Marcoul deposit in the *Archives hospitalières* at Rheims, of which there is a copy in the Arch. Nat. F² I 1555, gives no indication of anything of the kind. The domiciles of the patients healed were Bucilly, in the *généralité* of Soissons (two cases), Condé-les-Herpy and Château-Porcien, in that of Châlons.

51 At first sight, it would seem natural to look for a solution to this enigma in the journals of the time. But none of those I have been able to see (the *Gazette de France* for the whole reign, and numerous samplings of the *Mercure* and the *Journal de Paris*) even mentions the performance of the royal touch, even for the period of the reign when it was still in all probability taking place. I have already pointed out above the kind of bashfulness men felt at that time about speaking of this rite, which was so calculated to shock 'the enlightened'. One might also consult Louis XVI's *Journal;* it was published for the period 1766–78 by the Comte de Beauchamp in 1902 (for private circulation only: I managed to see the copy in the Arch. Nat.); but there is no mention of the royal touch.

52 *Odes et Ballades*, 4th Ode, VII. The note (p. 322 in the edition of the *Oeuvres Complètes*, ed. Hetzel and Quentin) says: 'Tu es sacerdos in aeternum secundum ordinem Melchisédech. L'église appelle le roi *l'évêque du dehors;* à la messe du sacre, il communie sous les deux espèces.'

53 *Mémoires*, II, 1923, p. 65. In the appendix to vol. II, pp. 305–6, there is a note on the royal touch drawn up by Damas in 1853 after a visit of his at that time to Mgr Gousset, Archibishop of Rheims. We shall make use of this later on.

54 Léon Aubineau, p. 14 of the *Notice* quoted below, n. 56. We know that L. Aubineau has produced a by no means valueless criticism of the theories of Augustin Thierry.

55 9 Nov. 1825, p. 402.

56 For the part played by abbé Desgenettes, see Léon Aubineau, *Notice sur M. Desgenettes*, 1860, pp. 13–15 (reproduced in the *Notice Biographique* put by abbé G. Desfossés at the front of the *Oeuvres inédites de M. Charles-Eléonore Dufriche Desgenettes*, 1860, pp. 66–7). Cf. also Cahier, *Caractéristiques des saints*, 1867, I, p. 264. Petition by the inhabitants of Corbeny published by S. A. *L'hermite de Corbeny ou le sacre et le couronnement de Sa Majesté Charles X roi de France et de Navarre*, Laon, 1825, p. 167, and Ledouble, *Notice sur Corbeny*, p. 245.

57 The most complete contemporary accounts of the Hospice of St-Marcoul ceremony are to be found in the *Ami de la Religion*, 4 June and esp. 9 Nov. 1825, and in F. M. Miel, *Histoire du sacre de Charles X*, 1825, pp. 308 ff. (where we read, p. 312: 'Un des malades disait après la visite du roi que Sa Majesté était le premier médecin de son royaume'). See also, under 2 June, the *Constitutionnel*, the *Drapeau Blanc*, the *Quotidienne*, and the following two small works; *Précis de la cérémonie du sacre et du couronnement de S.M. Charles X*, Avignon, 1825, p. 78, and *Promenade à Reims ou journal des fêtes*

et cérémonies du sacre . . . par un témoin oculaire, 1825, p. 165; cf. Cerf, 'Du toucher', p. 281. On the Hôpital St-Marcoul (whose fine buildings, dating from the seventeenth century, and half ruined by bombardment, are today the home of the American Ambulance Corps), H. Jadard, 'L'hôpital Saint-Marcoul de Reims', *Travaux Acad. Reims*, III, 1901–2. Efforts were made in Rheims to take advantage of these events and revive the cult of St-Marcoul; a reprint was made of the *Petit Office* of the saint which had come out previously in 1773 (Biblioth. de la ville de Reims, R.170, *bis*). As to the formula pronounced by the king, the *Constitutionnel* writes that he gave the royal touch 'without once using the ancient form of words: *Le Roi te touche, Dieu te guérisse*'. But in view of the unanimous testimony of others who were there this would seem to be a mistake, pointed out already in the *Ami de la Religion* of 4 June 1825, p. 104, n. 1. For the number of sick persons, the various sources give slightly differing figures: 120 according to Baron de Damas, 121 according to F. M. Miel, about 130 according to the *Ami de la Religion* of 9 Nov. (p. 403), 130 according to Cerf (p. 283).

58 Below, Book 3, n. 35.
59 1860 ed., IV, p. 306.
60 2 June, *Correspondance particulière de Reims*. In the same number, *Extrait d'une autre lettre de Reims* in the same tone. Cf. the words put into Charles X's mouth by Miel, loc. cit., p. 312: 'The king said, I believe, as he left the sick persons: "My dear friends, I have brought you words of comfort: I wish with all my heart that you may be healed." '
61 *Oeuvres*, 1847 ed., II, p. 143.
62 *Du Toucher*, p. 280. Also in the same sense Père Marquigny, 'L'Attouchement du roi de France guérissait-il des écrouelles?', *Études*, 1868, and Abbé Lebouble in his *Notice sur Corbeny*, 1883, p. 215. In 1853, Mgr Gousset, Archbishop of Rheims, expressed his faith in the royal touch to Baron de Damas; but he did not consider that its effects were entirely miraculous: Damas, *Mémoires*, p. 305, and below, Book 3, n. 37.

BOOK 3   CHAPTER I   *A critical interpretation*

1 *Charisma*, p. 2: 'I shall presume, with hopes to offer, that there is no Christian so void of Religion and Devotion, as to deny the Gift of Healing: A Truth as clear as the Sun, continued and maintained by a continual Line of Christian Kings and Governors, fed and nourished with the same Christian Milk'.
2 [Mathieu], *Histoire de Louys XI roy de France*, folio, 1610, p. 472. The expression 'perpetual miracle' was taken up by du Peyrat, *Histoire ecclésiastique de la Cour*, p. 818; likewise by Balthasar de Riez, *L'Incomparable piété des très-chrétiens rois de France*, II, 1672, p. 151.
3 *L'Incrédulité et mescreance du sortilège*, p. 164: 'que s'il y avoit dans sa bague de guérison du pied d'élan, ou de la racine de Péonie, pourquoy attribuera-t-on à ce miracle, ce qui peut advenir par un agent naturel'.
4 For the works of Morhof, Zentgraff, Trinkhusius, see the Bibliography; for Peucer, below, n. 19.

5 For the complete title of Douglas's book—from which the quotation above is taken—see the Bibliography, p. 431. The work is dedicated to an anonymous sceptic, who is none other than Adam Smith. The supernatural interpretation of the royal miracle is rejected by him, as by Hume, in contemptuous terms: 'This solution might, perhaps, pass current in the Age of *Polydor Virgil*, in that of Mr *Tooker*, or in that of Mr *Wiseman*, but one who would account for them so, at this Time of Day, would be exposed, and deservedly so, to universal Ridicule' (p. 200). As for the miracles of the Deacon Paris, Hume had also referred to them in his *Essay*; this is about the only concrete example he mentions.

6 'Mirifica eventuum ludibria'; cf. below, n. 19.

7 *De papa*, c. 6: *English works of Wyclif*, ed. F. D. Matthew, *Early English Texts*, 1880, p. 469; cf. Bernard Lord Manning, *The people's faith in the time of Wyclif*, p. 82, n. 5, no. III.

8 *Disquisitionum*, p. 64; cf. above, Book 2, Ch. VI, n. 11.

9 Cf. above, p. 206.

10 Peucer seems to reject quite decisively the demon hypothesis; see the text quoted below, n. 19.

11 For the Italian naturalist school, see some useful information in J. R. Charbonnel, *La Pensée italienne au XVIe siècle et le courant libertin*, 1919; cf. also Henri Busson, *Les Sources et le développement du Rationalisme dans la littérature française de la Renaissance (1533–1601)*, 1922, pp. 29 ff., 231 ff.

12 The opinion of Junctinus is quoted by Morhof, *Princeps Medicus* (*Dissertationes Academicae*), p. 147. The only thing I know by this author—Franciscus Junctinus Florentinus—is a *Speculum Astrologiae*, 2 vols, Lyons, 1581, in which I have not come across anything on the subject of the royal miracle.

13 A passage from the *Contradicentium medicorum libri duo*, quoted many times, in particular by del Rio, *Disquisitionum*, 1624 ed., p. 27 (this indication is missing in the 1606 ed.), by du Peyrat, *Histoire ecclésiastique de la Cour*, p. 797, by Gaspard A. Reies, *Elysius jucundarum*, p. 275, though through lack of a proper table of contents I have not been able to find it. According to del Rio, loc. cit., Cardan had been 'dignum scutica Ioann. Brodaei, lib. 8 miscellan. c.10.' The only edition of Jean Brodeau's *Miscellaneorum* possessed by the Bibliothèque Nationale, Basle 1555, only contains six books.

14 Caelio Calcagnini, *Opera*, Basle, 1544, *Epistolicarum quaestionum*, liber I, p. 7: a letter to his nephew, Thomas Calcagnini: 'Quod Bononiae videris Franciscum Galliarum regem saliua tantum pollice in decussem allita strumis mederi, id quod gentilitium et peculiare Gallorum regibus praedicant: non est quod mireris, aut ulla te rapiat superstitio. Nam et saliuae humanae, ieiunae praesertim, ad multas maximasque aegritudines remedium inest.' Calcagnini (1479–1541) does not belong to the same group as Pomponazzi for instance, or Cardan, or to the same generation; but he was certainly a free thinker. He espoused the Copernican system, and Erasmus spoke of him in complimentary terms. On his career see Tiraboschi, *Storia della letteratura italiana*, VII, 3, Modena, 1792, pp. 870 ff. As for the idea of the curative power of saliva, it was a very ancient popular notion: cf. C. de Mensignac, *Recherches ethnographiques sur la salive et le crachat* (Extrait des bulletins de la Soc. anthropologique de Bordeaux et du Sud-Ouest, 1890,

vol. VI), Bordeaux, 1892; and Marignan, *Études sur la civilisation française*, II, *Le Culte des saints sous les Mérovingiens*, p. 190. In England the seventh sons used to moisten their fingers with saliva, sometimes before administering the healing touch: *Folklore*, 1895, p. 205. For the idea of a royal imposture, cf. del Rio's hypothesis about the secret 'plasters' used by the English kings: above, p. 218.

15 The text from Sandei, quoted above, Book 2, Ch. I, n. 108. Jacques Bonaud de Sauset, the work and the passage referred to in the Bibliography, p. 429. The miracle of the French kings is likewise considered as the effect of a 'vertus héréditaire' by the Italian Leonardo Vairo, who was not a rationalist: L. Vairus, *De fascino libri tres*, 1583, lib. I, c. XI, p. 48.

16 Petri Pomponatii Mantuam . . . *de naturalium effectuum Causis*, Basel ed., 1567, chap. IV, p. 43: 'Secundo modo hoc contingere posset, quoniam quemadmodum dictum est in suppositionibus, sicuti contingit aliquam esse herbam, vel lapidem, vel animal, aut aliud, quod proprietatem sanandi aliquam aegritudinem habeat . . . ita contingit aliquem hominem ex proprietate individuali habere talem virtutem'. And p. 48, in the enumeration of examples: 'Reges Gallorum nonne dicuntur strumas curasse'. On Pomponazzi and his attitude to the supernatural, see a penetrating passage in L. Blanchet, *Campanella*, 1922, pp. 208–9. It is interesting to note that when Campanella wanted to seem to be defending miracles against Pomponazzi—though in his heart of hearts he does not appear to have believed in them—he too chose, among other examples, that of the royal miracle: *De sensu rerum*, IV, c. 4, Frankfurt, 1620, pp. 270–1; cf. Blanchet, p. 218.

17 Julii Caesaris Vanini, *De admirandis Naturae Reginae Deaeque Mortalium Arcanis*, Paris, 1616, pp. 433, 441; the passage is indeed rather obscure, no doubt for a prudent reason, and interspersed with eulogies of the French kings.

18 Douglas also finds room for coincidence: 'in those Instances when Benefit was received, the Concurrence of the Cure with the Touch might have been quite accidental, while adequate Causes operated and brought about the Effect' (p. 202). Among contemporary authors, Ebstein, 'Heilkraft der Könige', p. 1106, thinks that the touch was really a kind of massage, and effective as such; but I have not thought it necessary to discuss this theory.

19 Peucer is inclined to consider belief in the wonder-working gift as a superstition, but does not pronounce between the various hypotheses put forward in his day to explain the cures: 'De incantationibus', in the *Commentarius de praecipuis divinationum generibus*, 1591 ed., Zerbst, p. 192: 'Regibus Franccicis aiunt familiare esse, strumis mederi aut sputi illitione, aut, absque hac, solo contactu, cum pronunciatione paucorum et solennium verborum: quam medicationem ut fieri, sine Diabolicis incantationibus manifestis, facile assentior: sic, vel ingenita vi aliqua, constare, quae a maioribus propagetur cum seminum natura, ut morbi propagantur, et similitudines corporum ac morum, vel singulari munere divino, quod consecratione regno ceu dedicatis [*sic*] contingat in certo communicatum loco, et abesse superstitionis omnis inanem persuasionem, quaeque haec sanciunt mirifica eventuum ludibria, non facile crediderim: etsi, de re non satis explorata, nihil temere affirmo.' As for the dissertations by Morhof and Zentgraff, they only have the value of

compilations, though as such they are of great worth, but they make no pretensions to originality of thought. Morhof's attitude is difficult to pin down; he seems to consider the healing power of kings as a supernatural grace granted by God (p. 155), but the conclusion is couched in slightly sceptical terms (p. 157). Zentgraff's sole object is to show that a natural explanation is possible, but he does not consider it his business to choose between the ones that had been put forward before his time. He seems to favour the idea of a kind of imposture (the kings smearing their hands with some kind of special balm), but does not insist upon it. He prudently concludes: 'Ita constat Pharaonis Magorum serpentes, quos Moses miraculose produxit, per causas naturales productos esse, etsi de modo productionis nondum sit res plane expedita.' (p. B² v).

20 For disturbance due to emotion or suggestion, see esp. J. Babinski, 'Démembrement de l'Hystérie traditionnelle, Pithiatisme', *Semaine médicale*, 29, 1909, pp. 3 ff. According to M. Gaidoz, it is a clinical confusion of the same kind which explains a certain number, at least, of the apparent cures of rabies observed among the St Hubert pilgrims. 'Les convulsions et les fureurs de la rage ressemblent à celles de diverses maladies nerveuses et mentales', *La Rage et Saint Hubert*, p. 103.

21 For example, Wiseman, *Severall Chirurgical Treatises*, I, p. 306; Heylin in his reply to Fuller, quoted below, n. 37, le Brun, *Histoire critique des pratiques superstitieuses*, II, p. 121. It is interesting to note that in 1853 Mgr Gousset, Archbishop of Rheims, a belated believer in the royal miracle, thought that 'de nos jours, des enfants sont plus facilement guéris' because one cannot be cured without faith (conversation reported by Baron de Damas, *Mémoires*, II, p. 306).

22 Cf. esp. Déjerine, *Seméiologie du système nerveux*, 1904, pp. 1110 ff.; J. Babinski, 'Démembrement de l'Hystérie traditionnelle', *Semaine médicale*, 1909; J. Babinski and J. Froment, *Hystérie, Pithiatisme et troubles nerveux d'ordre réflexe en Neurologie de guerre*, 2nd ed., 1918, pp. 73 ff.

23 This readiness to accept as real a miraculous action, even if persistently contradicted by experience, is constantly found among 'primitive' peoples, and is even perhaps one of the essential traits of the 'primitive' mentality. See an interesting example of this—among others—in L. Lévy-Bruhl, *La Mentalité primitive*, 1922, p. 343 (the Fiji islands).

24 Crawfurd, p. 109.

25 *Adenochoiradelogia*, p. 106. We know that in England from the time of Charles I a certificate was required of all patients to prove that they had not been touched before.

26 See Browne, p. 91, who of course contests this belief.

27 *Gazette des hôpitaux*, 1854, p. 498.

28 *Criterion*, pp. 201-2. Cf. in the *Mémoires* of Baron de Damas, vol. II, the note on the royal touch, p. 305: 'Not all are healed'.

29 *Disquisitionum*, p. 61 (cf. above, p. 218); according to Tooker, *Charisma*, p. 106, Cf. Browne, *Adenochoiradelogia*, p. 111.

30 *Les Miraculeux Effects*, pp. 70-3. Biblical references: Naaman the Syrian, Luke 4:27; the Pool of Bethesda, John 5:4.

31 *Some important points of primitive christianity maintained and defended in*

several sermons . . ., Oxford, 1816, p. 136. And p. 134 the argument about St Paul and the Apostles, who had received from Christ the gift of healing 'as not to be at their own absolute disposal, but to be dispensed by them, as the Giver should think fit'. See also the words of Regnault, *Dissertation historique*, 1722, p. 3: 'Je scay bien que tous les Malades ne sont pas guéris: aussi avoüons nous, que nos Rois n'ont pas plus de pouvoir que les Prophètes et les Apôtres, qui ne guérissoient pas tous les Malades qui imploriaent leur secours'.

32 *Adenochoiradelogia*, p. 111: 'Thus every unbelieving Man may rest satisfied, that without he brings Faith enough with him, and in him, that His Majesty hath Virtue enough in his Touch to Heal him, his expectation will not be answered'.

33 *Dissertation*, p. 4. Cf. the words of Mgr Gousset, Archbishop of Rheims, reported by Baron de Damas, *Mémoires*, II, p. 306: 'Ces guérisons doivent être considérées comme des grâces privilégiées . . . qui dependent en même temps et de la foi du roi qui touche et de la foi du malade qui est touché'. This is the same explanation as that given by the faithful adherents of St-Hubert d'Ardenne, and no doubt still given by them today, to explain why certain patients succumb to rabies, in spite of having made a pilgrimage to the saint's tomb: Gaidoz, *La Rage et Saint Hubert*, p. 88.

34 *AA. SS. aprilis*, I, p. 155, no. 36.

35 Five cases of healing were recorded in a report dated 8 Oct. 1825, drawn up in a double form: first, the testimony of the nuns from the Hospice St-Marcoul, then the testimony of a doctor, Dr Noel: *Ami de la Religion*, 9 Nov. 1825; reprod. by Cerf, 'Du Toucher des écrouelles', p. 246. In 1867, a nun—who incidentally had only entered the hospice in 1826—testified to three other cases known to her: Marquigny, *L'attouchement du roi de France guérissait-il des écrouelles?*, p. 389, n. 1. The five healings observed in 1825 were all concerned with children. Now adults as well had been touched, but were the sisters unable to follow them up? This would be a fresh reason for not considering the statistics to be in line with the usual proportions. In 1853, Baron de Damas, who had no knowledge of these five cases, wrote as follows: 'The Mother Superior of the Hospice thinks there were more healed, but that there was a failure to record them'. I don't know what L. Aubineau's authority is for stating that 'the first eleven persons touched by the king were cured'.

36 For Edward the Confessor, see the texts quoted above, Book I, Ch. I, n. 32. For Charles I, a fragment of Oudert's journal, quoted by Edward Walford, *Old and New London*, III, London, n. d., p. 352.

37 In his *Church History of Britain*, appearing in 1655, Fuller had expressed himself in rather lukewarm terms on the subject of the royal miracle (this was in Cromwell's time): 'Others ascribe it to the power of fancy and an exalted imagination' (fol. 145). On this point, as on many others, he was violently attacked by Peter Heylin, *Examen historicum or a discovery and examination of the mistakes . . . in some modern histories*, London, 1659. In an answer entitled *The appeal of injured Innocence*, London, 1659, Fuller replied in these terms: 'though I conceive fancy may much conduce, in *Adultis*, thereunto, yet I conceive it *partly Miraculous* . . . I say *partly*,

because a complete Miracle is done *presently* and *perfectly*, whereas this *cure* is generally advanced by Degree and some Dayes interposed'. As early as 1610, T. Morton—an Anglican and a good Royalist, but what would be called today a Low Churchman—in his work entitled *A catholike appeale for protestants*, London, p. 428, refused to consider the royal healings as properly speaking miraculous: (1) because not instantaneous; (2) because the royal touch was often followed by medical treatment. According to Baron de Dalmas (*Mémoires*, II, p. 306), Mgr Gousset, Archbishop of Rheims, also did not consider these healings as strictly miraculous, but for a different reason—namely, that in the fact of scrofula being cured there was nothing 'contrary to the general laws governing the world'. Baron de Dalmas moreover knew, from what the Archbishop had told him, that 'the healings are not instantaneous' (ibid., same page).

38 Text quoted by Crawfurd, *King's Evil*, p. 77.

39 Rheims archives, St-Rémi Section, file 223, inf. no. 7.

40 Rheims archives, St-Rémi section, file 223, no. 11, (29 Ap. 1658).

41 Crawfurd, p. 157. Our information about Lovel's end comes entirely from a letter addressed to the *General Evening Post* of 13 Jan. 1747 by a correspondent from Bristol who signs himself *Amicus Veritatis* (ed. *Gentleman's Magazine Library*, III, p. 167); a testimony that is in itself not particularly reliable, but is reinforced by the fact that it does not seem to have been denied by the Tories. For the Carte affair, see above, p. 221.

42 Antonius Franco, *Synopsis Annalium Societatis Jesu in Lusitania*, Augsburg, 1726, p. 319: ' . . . Michael Martinus, scholasticus, a longo morbo probatus est. Ad sanandas strumas in Galliam missus ut a Rege Christianissimo manu contingeretur, salvus in Lusitaniam rediit, sed alio malo lentae tabis consumptus.'

43 Crawfurd, pp. 122-3; on these confusions, cf. Ebstein, 'Die Heilkraft', p. 1104, n. 2. A dental abscess mistaken for a case of the 'King's Evil', and as such confided to the attentions of the seventh daughter of a seventh daughter, who—naturally—failed to effect a cure: see A. G. Fulcher, in *Folklore*, 7, 1896, pp. 295-6. We may note that the royal evil was considered—at least among the common people—to be rather hard to recognize; and this is proved by the strange diagnostic procedure indicated in a small collection of medical prescriptions of the eighteenth century, published by *Folklore*, 23, 1912, p. 494. It should incidentally be added that on occasions another treatment was sometimes added to the royal touch. Such at least was the case of the five little patients 'cured' by Charles X. The certificate from Dr Noel dated 8 Oct. 1825 says: 'I certify . . . that nothing but the usual treatment has been applied in this case' (Cerf, 'Du Toucher des écrouelles', p. 246). In such circumstances, to whom should the cure be ascribed? To the king, or to the 'usual treatment'? Cf. also above, n. 37—the remarks of Morton.

44 R. Carr, *Epistolae medicinales*, p. 154: 'Verbo itaque expediam quod sentio: Contactus regius potest esse (si olim fuit), proficuus; solet subinde esse irritus, nequit unquam esse nocivus'. Cf. Crawfurd, *King's Evil*, p. 78; esp. Ebstein, 'Die Heilkraft', p. 1106.

APPENDIX I   *The royal miracle in the French and English accounts*

1 For further details, see C.-V. Langlois, *Registres perdus des archives de la Chambre des Comptes de Paris; Notices et extraits*, XL, p. 1. Lenain de Tillemont (*Vie de Saint Louis*, ed. of the Soc. de l'Histoire de France, V, p. 301), had seen an account of Louis IX's marriage expenses in which 'il y a vingt livres pour les malades qui l'estoient venus trouver à Sens'; but were these scrofula sufferers who had come to seek the royal touch?

2 This is clearly brought out by the details of place of origin given by the Renaud de Roye tablets. They all refer either to foreign countries, or to distant parts of the French realm: cf. above, pp. 61 ff. If we came to the conclusion that all sufferers touched by the king received alms, it would follow that the royal miracle was only popular abroad, or at any rate outside the regions where the king's authority was most directly felt—a conclusion that would be, to say the least, extremely improbable.

3 Documents published in vols XXI and XXII of the *Recueil des Historiens de France* and studied by Borrelli de Serres, *Recherches sur divers services publics*, I, 1895, pp. 140-60, and II, 1904, pp. 69-76.

4 Documents published in *Histor. de France*, XXII, pp. 545-55 and 555-65. For the 1307 tablets, I have used the ancient copy in the MS. Latin 9026 in the Bibl. Nat. which is more complete on certain points than the published edition; cf. above, Book 2, Ch. I, n. 40. For Renaud de Roye, *Borrelli*, loc. cit., II, p. 75; for our tablets, ibid. pp. 72-3.

5 There is one exception: *Hist. de France*, loc. cit., 554B: 'Thomas Jolis, patiens morbum regium'; the place of origin has been omitted.

6 See the accounts published or analysed by L. Douët d'Arcq, *Comptes de l'hôtel des rois de France aux XIVe and XVe siècles*, (Soc. de l'hist. de France), 2 v., 1865.

7 The French MS. 11709 in the Bibl. Nat. contains—folios 147-159—a fragment of the Almonry regulations belonging to the fourteenth century. It does not contain any mention of the touch.

8 KK 111 is an artificial register, made up of various fragments bound up under the same cover. As is indicated by a note on the binding itself, it comes from the d'A. Monteil collection, although it has been omitted from the inventory of this collection contained in the *Tableau Méthodique des fonds* of 1871, col. b86. All the fragments contained in it are listed above (for they are all portions taken from alms-books) except the last one—fol. 54 —which appears to be the final leaf of an accounts-register, also probably coming from the Royal Almonry, which was sent to the Chamber of Accounts in Dec. 1489 (mentioning a sum of 20 *l.* paid on 14 Dec. 1489 to an usher of the Chamber 'commis a la recepte et payement des menuz necessitez d'icelle chambre). The alms-registers in the part devoted to expenses are not arranged within each month in strictly chronological order; first come the offerings, then the alms proper. On the other hand, each of these two chapters follows the order of the dates.

9 Box O¹ 750 in the Arch. Nat. contains documents relating to the Grand Almonry (Louis XVI's reign); there are no accounts in it, nor anything bearing upon the history of the royal touch. In Louis XVI's reign Oroux

seems still to have been able to see registers from Louis XIV's time where there were entries relating to the touch: *Histoire ecclésiastique de la Cour*, I, p. 184, note q.

10 I am especially thinking here of the fine work done by Prof. T. F. Tout, cf. below, n. 11.

11 I owe a great deal, of course, to T. F. Tout's book, *Chapters in the administrative history of mediaeval England: the Wardrobe, the Chamber and the Small Seals* (Publications of the University of Manchester: Historical Series, 34), 2 vols., 1920. Unfortunately this remarkable work only covers a fairly small part of the period I was forced to take into account; and the problems it deals with are not precisely the same as those which confronted me. Cf. also A. P. Newton, 'The King's Chamber under the early Tudors', *English Historical Review*, 1917. The bibliography of English financial history is given—at least as regards the Middle Ages—by C. Gross, *The sources and literature of English History*, 2nd ed., London, 1915. A large number of accounts have been used by Crawfurd and Farquhar in their research into the healing rites, but without any systematic study of them. Hilary Jenkinson has been kind enough to give me several items of information for this Appendix, and especially several corrections, which have been of the greatest service; but I must emphasize that he must in no way be held responsible for the mistakes I have probably made. If I had wanted to avoid all possibility of mistakes, I should have given up writing this present work, which I have had considerable difficulty in drawing up at such a distance from London; and I may even admit that I have several times actually been tempted to give up. In the end, I preferred to leave myself open to reproach —which would no doubt have very good reasons—rather than make use of documents without attempting any critical assessment of them. In spite of everything, I think I have been able to shed a little light upon a very obscure question, and I hope I may be forgiven for my rashness in return for the one or two useful pieces of information I have been able to provide.

12 The references are in accordance with the methods set out in the Foreword, p. xi. The figure in square brackets indicates the year of the reign; and in order to bring the years of the reign into line with our calendar, the little brochure by J. E. W. Wallis, *English regnal years and titles* (Society for promoting Christian Knowledge, Helps for Students of History, 40, London, 1921), will be found of considerable service. I have put an asterisk against the documents which have not yielded any information about the touch for scrofula. Limited as I have been for time, I have had to confine myself to what I could find in the Public Record Office, the British Museum MSS., and printed collections. This meant that from the start I had to resign myself to being incomplete. The two big London collections contain the major part by far of the financial archives from the old English monarchy; but there must be further gleanings to be made in other public and private collections. No complete inventory of the Royal Household Accounts has yet been made. Tout is quite right when he says (Chapter I, p. 48): 'The wide dispersion of the existing wardrobe accounts makes it very difficult to examine them systematically'.

13 I have looked at two expense accounts of Henry III's reign, Exchequer

Accounts *349,23 and *349,29, but they did not yield anything useful.

14 I have seen E.A. 350,23 [5]; 351,15 [12]; 352,18 [17]; *353,16 [21]; *361,21 [30].

15 I have seen P.R.O., Chancery Miscellanea, IV, 1 [6, only from 31 Jan. onwards]; *IV, 3 [14]; IV, 4 [18]; Exch. Treasury of Receipt, Misc. Books *202 [22–23]; B. M. Add. MSS. 7965 [25]; 35291 [28]; 8835 [32]. Add. MSS. *35292, which is a cash journal (*Jornale Garderobe de receptis et exitibus eiusdem*)—years 31–33—did not yield anything, nor did MS. Add. *37655 [34], which is of the same kind.

16 It was because of this ambiguity that I found myself led to consult a certain number of the Wardrobe accounts, in the narrower sense of the word, which naturally yielded no results. For Edward III, E.A. *384, 1 [2 and 3]; *388, 9 [11 and 12], both of them emanating from the Comptroller. For Richard II, *Archaeologia*, LXII, 2 (1911), p. 503 [16 and 17]. For Edward IV, B. M., MS. Harl. *4780. For Richard III, *Archaeologia*, I (1770), p. 361.

17 I have seen *Liber quotidianus contrarotulatoris garderobe* . . . , published by the Society of Antiquaries of London, London, 1787, 28; to be compared with B. M. Add. MS. 35291 quoted in n. 15 above; B. M. Add. MS. *7966A [29].

18 All the same there still exists among the Exchequer Accounts an alms account of Edward III: E.A. *394, 1 (which did not yield any information).

19 Cf. *Second Report of the royal commission on public records*, II, London, 1914, 2nd part, p. 172. The Royal Almonry collection does not at present contain any documents prior to 1723.

20 Cf. the work quoted in the preceding note, p. 69.

21 From the time of Edward III onwards—at the latest—there is an end to the practice of making the period correspond exactly with the king's reign year: its duration often varies, a sure sign that disorder was creeping into the financial administration.

22 The account for the 10th year of Edward II (8 July 1316–7 July 1317), known to me only through the description by T. Stapleton, *Archaeologia*, 26, 1836, pp. 319 ff., seems to have been in keeping with the older style.

23 E.g. B. M. Add. MS. 9951, Counter-roll (?) of Edward II for the 14th year of the reign (8 July 1320–7 July 1321), fol. 3 v.: 'Eidem [elemosinario] pro denariis per ipsum solutis lxxix infirmis benedictis ab ipso rege per diversas vices infra annum presentem predictum; videlicet cuilibet pauperi j d. : vj s. vij d.'

24 From Edward II's reign, as well as the article from the *Archaeologia* indicated in n. 22 above, I have seen: E.A. *376,7 [9; a counter-roll, remarkable both for the shortness of the period covered by it—from 31 Jan. to 9 June—and for the summary character of the various indications it contains]; B. M. Add. MS. 17362 [13; wardrobe account]; 9951 [14; counter-roll?]; in addition—and by mistake—an account of the personal expenses of the Comptroller, E.A. *376,13 [8 and 9]. For Edward III; B. M. MS. Cotton Nero C VIII, [years 8–11 : counter-roll]; E.A. 388, 5 [11–12; counter-roll]; P.R.O. Treasury of Receipt, Misc. Books, 203 [12–14 : wardrobe account]; E.A. *396, 11 [43: counter-roll]. In addition, for Edward II, B. M. Add. MS. *36763, expenses roll, from 8 July to 9 Oct. 1323, in short a kind of

cash-book for the Royal Household, on a day-to-day basis, but for each day showing simply the disbursements, office by office (including the Almonry), without precisely specifying their object.

25 Here is the list of accounts seen by me for the reigns subsequent to Edward III: Richard II, B. M. Add. MS. *35115 [16 ; counter-roll]; E.A. *403,10 [19; counter-roll]. Henry IV : E.A. *404,10 [2: roll; keeper of the wardrobe]; B. M. MS. Harl. *319 [8 : counter-roll; cf. *Archaeological Journal* 4, 1847 p. 78]. Henry V : E.A. *406,21 [1 : treasurer of the Royal Household]. Henry VI : E.A. 409,9 [20–21 : counter-roll]. Edward IV : E.A. *412,2 [6–7 : Keeper of the Great Wardrobe]. The Enrolled Accounts of the Exchequer do not provide any information, the Household expenses being merely indicated in summary form. I have consulted Exch. Enrolled Accounts, Wardrobe and Household, *5.

26 This arrangement can best be shown by an example. Here, taken entirely at random, is a day's entry in the Wardrobe accounts, 6th year of Edward IV. The day is 7 Oct. 1466; the king is staying at Greenwich: 'Dispensa : xxvij s. vj d. Buttillaria; cxv s. j. d. ob. Garderoba : xxxj s. xj d. ob. Coquira: vj l. xij s. iij d. Pullieria :lxj s. viij d. Scuttillaria: vj s. vj d. ob. Salsaria : ij s. iiij d. Aula et Camera : xviij s. ix d. Stabulum : xxix s. ix d. ob. Vadia : lxxvj s. x d. ob. *Elemosina* : iiij s. Summa : xxv l. vj s. ix d. ob.' E.A. 412, 2, fol. 5v.

27 For Henry VII, I have seen the counter-roll for year 8 : E.A. *413,9. For Henry VIII, the counter-roll for years 13 and 14: E.A. *419,6; the accounts of the Keeper of the Great Wardrobe, B. M. Add. MS. *35182 [23–24]. For Edward VI, the counter-roll E.A. *426,6 [2 and 3]. For Edward VI [6] and Mary [1], the Royal Household accounts, B. M. Add. MS. *35184. For Elizabeth, the account E.A. *421,11 [2] and the counter-roll E.A. *421,8 [1–3]. Cf. for Henry VIII the details given by Farquhar, 'Royal Charities', I, p. 73, n. 3.

28 For Henry VII, E.A. 415,3 [15–17] ; B. M. MS. Add. 21480 [20–21]; Samuel Bentley, *Excerpta historica*, London, 1831 (fragments of pay-books from extracts made from the originals by C. Ord; C. Ord's note-books are in the B. M. Add. MS. 7099). For Henry VIII, N. H. Nicolas, *The privy purse expenses of King Henry the Eighth from November MDXXIX to December MDXXXII*, London, 1827 (the book of Bryan Tuke, Treasurer of the Chamber, today in the B. M. MS. Add. 20030). See also various extracts from similar books, for Henry VIII, Edward VI, and Mary in the *Trevelyan Papers*, I and II (Camden Society), London, 1857 and 1863; cf. Farquhar, I, p. 82, n. 1. There is no mention of payments in respect of the royal touch, but an indication of numerous repayments made to the almoner for non-specified expenses in the *Boke of Payments* of Henry VII [21–24] and Henry VIII, P.R.O. Treasury of the Exchequer Misc. Books *214; nor is there anything on the royal touch in the pay-book of Henry VIII, B. M. Add. MS. *2182 [1–8]. I have likewise searched in vain in the cash-book of Edward VI [2 and 3], E.A. *426,6 and a rough-book from Elizabeth's time, E.A. *429,11. The accounts of the Tudor period have been examined most carefully by Farquhar; see, generally speaking, the information given by her, I, pp. 79, 81, 88 n. 3, 91 n. 4.

29 Nicolas, *Privy Purse Expenses*, p. 249 (31 Aug. 1549); the reference is to one

'master Hennage', whom we know from other sources to have been 'the Chief Gentleman of the Privy Chamber'.

30 For conscience's sake, but of course without success, I have consulted two counter-rolls of Charles II's time, P.R.O. Lord Steward's Dept. *1, 3 and 10.

31 For the numismatic history of the royal touch, cf. above, pp. 66 and 211.

32 These documents have been studied with the greatest care by Farquhar, II and III.

33 It seems to have been established by a series of decisions by the Treasury Board in the early months of 1668, and in particular on 2 March : cf. Farquhar, II, pp. 143 ff., esp. p. 149, bottom. The method is very clearly brought out, for instance, in the account of Baptist May, *Keeper of the Privy Purse*, of 12 Feb. 1668, and 25 March 1673: P.R.O. Pipe Office, Declared Accounts 2795.

34 Texts edited or analysed by F. H. Garrison, 'A relic of the King's Evil'; cf. Farquhar, II, p. 130 (facsimile), and for a correction to Garrison's text, III, pp. 117–18.

35 Exchequer of Receipts, Miscellaneous Books, E. 407, 85(1). I was led to this file by an indication contained in a note by G. Fothergill, *Notes and Queries*, 10th series, 4, 1905, p. 335. These documents go from April 1669 to December 1685; for the figures contained in them, cf. above, p. 336, Book 2, Ch. V, n. 192 and p. 219.

36 Leaving out, of course, the documents relating to the manufacture of the touch-pieces, which are in evidence up to the very end of the rite: cf. Farquhar, IV, p. 159.

37 In the notes above, 14–16 and 26–28, will be found an indication of the Royal Household Accounts I have been able to examine. Here is the list, reign by reign, of those that have yielded some information about the rite of the rings. It will be noted that from Edward III to Edward VI only the reign of Edward V is missing; and it could not have found a place there, for it was too short to include even one Good Friday; and the reign of Richard III, which only included two of them. Cf. above, p. 100 and Book 2, Ch. II, n. 30. The date between square brackets is that of the Good Friday when the rings were consecrated. Edward III: B. M. MS. Cotton Nero C VIII, fol. 202 [14 April 1335], fol. 205 [29 March 1336], fol. 206 v. [18 April 1337], (the first two articles reproduced in Stevenson, 'On Cramp rings', p. 49; *Gentleman's Magazine Library*, p. 40; all three in Crawfurd, pp. 169–70); E.A. 388,5 [10 April 1338]; P.R.O. Treasury of Receipt, Misc. Books, 203, fol. 150 [26 March 1339], and fol. 153 [14 April 1340]; E.A. 396,11, fol. 12 [30 March 1369]; 'Account Book of John of Ypres' [12 April 1370], reproduced in Crawfurd, p. 170. Richard II : B. M. MS. Add. 35115, fol. 33 v. [4 April 1393] ; E.A. 403,10, fol. 36 [31 March 1396] (reproduced in Crawfurd, p. 170). Henry IV : B. M. MS. Harl. 319, fol. 39 [25 March 1407] (reproduced *British Archaeological Journal*, 4, 1847, p. 78). Henry V : E.A. 406,21, fol. 37 [21 April 1413]. Henry VI : E.A. 409, 9, fol. 32 [30 March 1442]. Edward IV : E.A. 412, 2, fol. 31 [27 March 1467] (for 15 April 1468, quotation without references in Crawfurd, p. 171). Henry VII : E.A. 413,9, fol. 31. [5 April 1493]. Henry VIII : B. M. Add. MS. 35182, fol. 31v. [11

April 1533]. Edward VI : E.A. 426, 1, fol. 19 [8 April 1547]; B. M. Add. MS. 35184, fol. 31 v. [31 March 1553]. In comparing this list with that of the accounts that have been broken down, it can be seen that, without any apparent reason, some of the Wardrobe accounts do not mention the expenses incurred for the rite of the rings: a fresh example of these anomalies to which all historians must be resigned in advance when they are using the administrative documents of the Middle Ages.

38 Examples: Edward III's reign, 14 April 1335: 'In oblacionibus domini regis ad crucem de Gneyth, die Paraceues, in capella sua infra manerium de Clipstone, in precio duorum florenciorum de Fflorentia, xiiij die aprilis, vj s. viij d.; et in denariis quos posuit pro dictis florenciis reasumptis pro anulis inde faciendis, ibidem, eodem die, vj s. Summa xij s. vjjj d.' B. M. MS. Cotton Nero C. VIII, fol. 202, publ. Stevenson, 'On Cramp-rings', p. 49, (*Gentleman's Magazine Library*, p. 40); Crawfurd, p. 169, Henry V's reign, 21 April 1413: 'In oblacionibus domini regis factis adorando crucem in die Parasceues in ecclesia fratrum de Langley, videlicet in tribus nobilibus auri et quinque solidis argenti xxv s. In denariis solutis decano Capelle pro eisdem denariis reassumptis pro anulis medicinalibus inde faciendis xxv s.' E.A. 406,21, fol. 19. It will be noted, in the text referring to Edward III, that there is a very slight difference in value between the two successive payments, which can easily be explained: the need to carry out the first payment in good coin led to the use of foreign coinages, whose value could not be brought to a round sum in terms of national money of account.

39 Henry VI, 30 March 1442: 'In oblacionibus domini Regis factis ad orandam crucem die Parasceues in Auro et argento pro Anulis medicinalibus inde fiendis xxv s.' E.A. 409,9, fol. 32 v. Similar formulae : E.A. 412,2, fol. 31 (Edward IV); 413,9, fol. 31 (Henry VII).

40 Henry VIII, 29 March 1532: 'In oblacionibus domini Regis factis in adorando crucem die Parasche(ues) et pro redempcione, anulis medicinalibus inde fiendis, aurum et argentum, infra tempus huius compoti xxv s.' B. M. Add. MS. 35182, fol. 31 v. The formula in E.A. 426, 1, fol. 18 (Edward VI: 8 April 1547) is likewise rather unsatisfactorily expressed: 'In oblacionibus domini Regis secundum antiquam consuetudinem et ordinem pro adhorando crusem die Parascheues et pro rede[m]ptione Anulorum Medicinalium inde fiendum [*sic*] aurum et argentum, infra tempus huius computi xxxv s. (*a probable mistake for* xxv s.)'. It is repeated almost textually by Add. MS. 35184, fol. 31 v. (Edward VI: 31 March 1553).

41 E.A. 396, 11, fol. 12.

42 Above, p. 104.

43 For Edward IV, Privy Seal Account, quoted Crawfurd, 'Cramp-rings', p. 171; cf. *Liber Niger Domus Regis* in *A Collection of ordinances and regulations for the government of the Royal Household* London (Soc. of Antiquaries), 1790. p. 23 (payment to the 'jewel-house'). Henry VII : W. Campbell, *Materials for a history of the reign of Henry VII* (Rolls-Series), II, p. 142. Henry VIII : pay-book for the Royal Household, B. M. Add. MS. 2181, year 2, 19 April 1511 ; *Letters and Papers, Foreign and Domestic*, Henry VIII, XV, no. 862; XVIII, 1, no. 436; 2, no. 231, pp. 125, 127. Under Henry VIII —from 1542 onwards at the latest—the expenses arising from the rite of the

medicinal rings were charged against the Augmentations fund, which was fed by the income accruing from the confiscated religious establishments (for these funds, see F. A. Gasquet, *Henry VIII and the English Monasteries*, II, 6th ed., 1895, p. 9). Mary Tudor : (J. Nichols), *Illustrations of the manners and expenses of antient times in England*, London, 1797, *New Years' Gifts presented to Queen Mary*, p. 27.

APPENDIX II *Notes on the iconography*

1 Cf. also above, nos. 14, 15 and 16.

APPENDIX III *The beginnings of royal unction and consecration*

1 The first of the kings of Aragon to be anointed certainly seems to have been Peter II, who received it from the hands of Pope Innocent III himself, on 11 Nov. 1204; cf. G. de Blanca, *Coronaciones de los serenissimos reyes de Aragon*, Saragossa, 1641, pp. 1 ff.

2 Cf. on the wearing of the crown in the Visigothic kingdom, Felix Dahn, *Die Könige der Germanen*, Leipzig, 1885, IV, pp. 530–1.

3 I only know the work of P. G. Preobrazensky on Theophanes (in Russian) through the review by E. W. Brooks, *Byzant. Zeitschrift*, 22, 1913, pp. 154–5. The author considers as interpolations the passages that are not common to both our Greek MSS. of the *Chronographia* and the Latin translation by Anastasius. There would therefore be no doubt about the passage relating to unction.

4 C.XII *Monum.*, pp. 23–4: 'Duodecimo sermone sanximus, ut in ordinatione regum nullus permittat pravorum praevalere assensum, sed legitime reges a sacerdotibus et senioribus populi eligantur, et non de adulterio vel incaestu procreati: quia sicut nostris temporibus ad sacerdotium secundum canones adulter pervenire non potest, sic nec christus Domini esse valet, et rex totius regni, et heres patrie, qui ex legitimo non fuerit connubio generatus'. The same decisions had been taken earlier on by a Council held in the kingdom of Northumbria, in the presence of one of the papal legates. The decrees of the two Councils tallied point by point; but in Northumbria—no doubt because there was no suitable occasion—there does not seem at that moment to have been any royal unction.

5 For a shortened redaction of this life, for a long time believed to be earlier than Adaman, but in reality no more than a résumé of the self-same work by the Abbot of Iona, see G. Brüning, 'Adamnans Vita Columbae', *Zeitschrift für celtische Philologie*, 11, 1916.

6 In the same way the English king Edgar, who was only consecrated after he had reigned sixteen years (cf. above, p. 269), wore the crown well before the coronation proper. The *Vita Oswaldi* (in J. Raine, *The historians of the Church of York* (Rolls Series), I, p. 437), shows him entering the church on the day of the ceremony, wearing the crown, then placing the insignia upon the altar, and finally having it placed upon his head, after receiving unction, by Archbishop Dunstan.

7 It may be as well to point out that the article by W. Fischer, 'Eine Kaiser-krönung in Byzantion', *Zeitchr. für allg. Geschichte*, 4, 1887, is only an uninteresting paraphrase of the description by John Cantacuzenus quoted above.

8 Sickel, loc. cit., p. 547, n. 80, in order to prove the antiquity of unction in Byzantium, cites an Armenian text of the 10th century (*Histoire d'Arménie* by John Katholikos, c.17, tr. Saint-Martin, p. 135) which shows the king of Armenia being both anointed and crowned in one ceremony; according to him, Armenia could only have borrowed this rite from Byzantium. I am too ignorant of the East to be able to discuss the meaning of this text taken by itself, or to examine whether Armenian unction may really have been only an imitation of Byzantine usage. In any case it seems to me difficult to have anything to set against the silence of Constantine Porphyrogenitus.

9 Ἀντὶ δὲ τοῦ χριομένου ἐλαίου τοῖς βασιλεῦσι καὶ τοῖς ἀεχιερεῦσι, κατὰ τὸν παλαιὸν νόμον, εἶπον ἀρκεῖν τοῖς ἀεχιερεῦσι τὸ ἐπικείμενον ξυγὸν τοῦ Εὐαγγελίου τῷ τραχήλῳ αὐτῶν, καὶ δι᾽ ἐπικλήσεως τοῦ ἁγίου πνεύματος σφραγῖδα τοῦ χειροτονοῦντος.

APPENDIX IV   *Extract from Jean Golein's Treatise on Consecration*

1 *The Coronation Book of Charles V of France*, ed. E. S. Dewick 1899 (Bradshaw Soc., XVI).

2 *Le Racional des divins offices*, Paris, 1503.

3 *Les Raisons de l'office et ceremonies qui se font en l'Eglise catholique, apostolique et romaine, ensemble les raisons des ceremonies du sacre de nos Roys de France, et les douze Marques uniques de leur Royauté Céleste, par dessus tous les Roys de Monde*, 1611. 'Ian Goulain' is expressly quoted in the dedication (to the Queen Mother). For the consecration, see. pp. 211–50; esp. reference to Jean Golein on p. 220.

4 But because of a fault in numbering, fol. 56 follows directly after fol. 54. The treatise on the consecration is enriched by three miniatures: the anointing of the king (44 v.), and of the queen (50); and the blessing of the oriflamme (51 v.).

5 The rubric is borrowed from the printed edition; there is no rubric in the MS.

6 MS. ccclx; in actual fact, 19 May 1364, Trinity Sunday. This first sentence, incorrectly constructed, stops short. It is found in this form—with the variant 'la benoite Sainte Trinité'—in the MS. fr. 176, which comes from the library of the Duc de Berry (fol. 26).

7 *Sic*; cf. further on, p. 277. But further on still, pp. 281 and 282, Jean Golein calls his king 'Charles le Quint'.

8 2 Peter I: 17.

9 Psalm XLIV:8: 'oleo laetitiae prae consortibus suis'.

10 This interesting detail does not appear to have been mentioned by the chronicles.

11 The church of St-Denis, built by the Canons in the 10th century outside the Cathedral precincts as they then existed (Marlot, *Histoire de Reims*, II, p.

689); the Chapelle St-Nicolas in the chief hospital; cf. *The Coronation Book*, ed. Dewick, col. 7 and Godefroy, *Ceremonial*, p. 247.

12 I have not discovered anything bearing upon this tradition.

13 The *mal Saint-Rémi* is the plague; cf. L. Dubroc de Seganges, *Les Saints patrons des corporations*, II, p. 303; I do not know the anecdote to which Jean Golein is referring here: cf. above, p. 130.

14 Earlier on (fol. 47, col. 1), Jean Golein has already alluded to an oath of allegiance made by Alexander the Great to the High Priest of Jerusalem.

15 This is the statue that was thought later on to represent Philip of Valois; I hope to publish a note on this subject in another place.

16 In the text of Jean Golein himself—later on, p. 279—the origin of the fleurs de lis is attributed to the hermit of Joyenval; cf. above, p. 134.

17 *De praecepto et dispensatione*, XVII, 54, (Migne, *P.L.*, vol. 182, col. 889): 'Audire et hoc vultis a me, unde inter caetera paenitentiae instituta monasterialis disciplina meruerit hanc praerogativam, ut secundum baptisma nuncupetur'.

18 It would be a good thing to verify the accuracy of this iconographical rule in detail; at first sight, it does not seem to me to have been very rigorously applied.

19 That is to say, the *bannière fleurdelisée*; the miniature on the same folio, however, represents the blessing of the oriflamme. The text of the blessing is given in Dom Martene, *De antiquis ecclesiae ritibus*, III, p. 221, and Dewick, *Coronation Book*, p. 50, (where the miniature, pl. 38, likewise shows the oriflamme).

20 In actual fact, Turpin had simply been buried at Rheims, in his cathedral (Flodoard, *Historia Remensis ecclesie*, II, 17; *Monumenta*, SS., XIII, p. 465); but how could legend have been content to give him such a commonplace burial? His tomb was shown in more than one place: in the church of St-Romain de Blaye, alongside Roland and Oliver, according to the *Chanson de Roland* (line 3961); at Vienne, in accordance with the so-called letter from Pope Calixtus II, which forms the preface of the famous *Historia Karoli Magni et Rotholandi* which was circulated under the name of Turpin himself (the pseudo-Turpin); ed. F. Castets (Publications de la Soc. pour l'étude des langues romanes, VII), p. 65. As far as I know, Jean Golein is the only author who expressly assigns him the old Roman cemetery of the Aliscamps as a resting place; but the *Karlamagnussaga* (German tr. in *Romanische Studien*, hgg. by Böhmer, III, p. 348), had already placed the tomb of the twelve peers in that spot; and it was natural enough that the valiant prelate, who was said to have died at Roncevaux, should be associated with his companions in arms.

21 This tradition is not mentioned by Arturo Graf, *Roma nella memoria e nelle immaginazioni del Medio Evo*, II, Turin, 1883, in the few pages (pp. 453 ff.) devoted to the eagle.

22 I Timothy 5:17.

23 Romans 11:13.

24 The so-called Athanasian Creed (H. Denzinger, *Enchiridion Symbolorum*, 12th ed., Freiburg, 1913, p. 19: 'aequalis Patri secundum divinitatem, minor Patre secundum humanitatem'.

25 Psalm LXXXV:10: 'Quoniam magnus es tu, et faciens mirabilia; tu es Deus solus'; Psalm LXXI:18: 'Benedictus Dominus Deus Israel, qui facit mirabilia solus'; Psalm CXXXV:4: 'qui facit mirabilia magna solus'.

26 Jean Golein seems to be referring here to the fourth book of the treatise *De Consideratione*, addressed by St Bernard to Pope Eugenius III. But the quotation indicated by him is not to be found there, and I have not succeeded in finding it anywhere else in St Bernard's works.

27 Cf. above, Book 2, Ch. I, n. 93.

28 A device taken from the Easter Lauds, which had figured since the time of St Louis on most of the French gold coins: cf. G. Froehner, *Annuaire de la Soc. française de numismatique*, 1889, p. 45. Jean Golein has already quoted it previously, fol. 45, col. 2.

29 The reference is to the *Otia imperialia* by Gervase de Tilbury, composed for the Emperor Otto IV.

Bibliography

Two categories of bibliographical references will be found below. Those references, by far the fewest, which constitute section I, concern a certain number of works about royalty in general or French or English royalty in particular, which will be quoted frequently in the course of my narrative. Their only purpose is to facilitate reference. I have in no way aimed at providing in this respect a bibliography—even a *select* bibliography—which is exhaustive. I have shown for each book or memoir, where appropriate, pages which particularly concern miracle-working royalty.

The secondary category—section II onwards—bears more precisely on the power of healing and, in section VII, on that other form of belief in the miraculous nature of royalty, the superstition of the royal birthmark. I have made these references as complete as possible, but they are, however, not absolutely complete. By this limitation I do not mean only to cover unintentional omissions, which I must undoubtedly have made. I have intentionally left out some obscure journal articles which seemed too insignificant to merit mention. With a subject which has always offered too much attraction to those amateurs who are drawn to historical 'curiosities' not to have tempted from time to time, notably in England, authors who are more intrepid or naïve than competent, such pruning was essential. I have taken great care in carrying it out. I have remembered that in the course of my research a short note, the substance of which had no bearing on my subject, often gave me a valuable reference. When the sources are so scattered, the most inexperienced worker must be welcome when he adds an unpublished text to the collection. I would add that the excellent articles published by Miss H. Farquhar under the title 'Royal Charities' (see section IV, 3) have rendered useless all that had been written before on the numismatics of the English touch. They have enabled me to eliminate several older works which would have uselessly cluttered up my lists.

I have included in this bibliography, apart from works specially devoted to miraculous powers or to the royal birthmark, a large number of books or articles which, while they deal with more general subjects, on occasion give useful information on one or other of these two manifestations of the same idea: each time I indicate the pages to consult. Works of this kind are not always the least valuable. Of course, I have omitted everything which was only simple allusion to facts already well known from other sources, without fresh insight.

427

I have put an asterisk against some works of which only the titles are known to me. I am concerned to point them out to researchers who may perhaps be able to find them in collections to which I have not had access.

The order followed within each subdivision is, basically, alphabetical under authors (or under titles where the works are anonymous). I have made an exception only in section III, where works published before the beginning of the nineteenth century on the subject of the king's evil are listed. There I have adopted chronological order. I thought this would provide a more faithful picture of the development of a literature, the evolution of which concerns in the highest degree the history of belief in royal miracles.

I *General works on kingship*

JOHN NEVILLE FIGGIS, *The divine right of kings*, Cambridge, 1914.

J. G. FRAZER, *The Golden Bough*, 12 vols, London, 1922. Part I, *The magic art and the evolution of Kings*, I, pp. 368–71; Part II, *Taboo and the perils of the soul*, p. 134.

J. G. FRAZER, *Lectures on the early history of Kingship*, London, 1905, especially p. 126.

FRANTZ FUNCK-BRENTANO, *L'Ancienne France, Le Roi*, Paris, 1912, especially pp. 176–81.

J. HITIER, 'La doctrine de l'absolutisme', *Annales de l'Université de Grenoble*, 15, 1903.

FRITZ KERN, *Gottesgnadentum und Widerstandsrecht im früheren Mittelalter: Zur Entwicklungsgeschichte der Monarchie*, Leipzig, 1914 (and see my review in *Revue Historique*, 138, 1921, p. 247.

G. LACOUR-GAYET, *L'Éducation politique de Louis XIV*, Paris, 1898.

HANS SCHREUER, *Die rechtlichen Grundgedanken der französischen Königskrönung*, Weimar, 1911.

II *The healing power of kings: bibliographies*

ULYSSE CHEVALIER, *Topobibliographie*, I, 1894–9 under 'Écrouelles' (see also under 'Corbeny' and in the *Biobibliographie*, II, 2nd ed., 1907, under 'Marcoul, St'.

Index Catalogue of the Surgeon General's Office, U.S. Army, 12, Washington, 1891, under 'Scrofula', pp. 793 ff. and especially pp. 805 ff.; 2nd series, 15, 1910, p. 347.

ALPHONSE PAULY, *Bibliographie des sciences médicales*, Paris, 1874, col. 1092–4.

JULIUS ROSENBAUM, *Addimenta ad Lud. Choulant Bibliothecam medico-historicam*, Halle, 1842–7, I, p. 43 and II, pp. 63–4.

III *The touch for scrofula: works before the nineteenth century*

1 French works

VINCENTIUS (CIGAULD), *Allegationes super bello ytalico*, Paris, 1512, last chapter, p. 39 v. Reprinted in V. Cigauld, *Opus laudabile et aureum* (1516).

JOHANNES FERRALDUS (J. FERRAULT), *Insignia peculiaria christianissimi Francorum regni, numero viginti seu totidem illustrissimae Francorum coronae prerogativae ac preeminentiae*, Paris, 1520; 'Ius quartum', pp. 45–7.

JACQUES BONAUD DE SAUSET, *Panegyricus ad Franciam Franciaeque regem*, appendix in Joannes de Terra Rubea, *Contra rebelles suorum regum* (three treatises edited by Bonaud himself), Lyon, 1526, p. 110 v.

CAROLUS DEGRASSALIUS (C. DE GRASSAILLE), *Regalium Franciae jura omnia*, Lyon, 1538, Book I, pp. 62–5.

BARTHOLOMEUS FAIUS (B. FAYE D'ESPEISSE), *Energumenicus*, Paris, 1571, pp. 154–6.

H. MORUS (MEURIER), *De sacris unctionibus libri tres*, Paris, 1593, pp. 260–2.

STEPHANUS FORCATULUS (ETIENNE FORCATEL), *De Gallorum imperio et philosophia libri VII*, Lyon, 1595, pp. 128–32.

ANDREAS LAURENTIUS (A. DU LAURENS), *De mirabili strumas sanandi vi solis Galliae Regibus Christianissimis divinitus concessa*, Paris, 1609. For editions and translations of this work and for a life of its author, see E. Turner, 'Bibliographie d'André du Laurens . . . avec quelques remarques sur sa biographie', *Gazette hebdomadaire de médecine et de chirurgie*, 27, 1880, pp. 329, 381, 413.

ANDRE FAVYN, *Histoire de Navarre*, Paris, 1612, pp. 1055–63.

I. BARBIER, *Les miraculeux effects de la sacrée main des Roys de France Tres-Chrestiens: pour la guarison des Malades et conversion des Heretiques*, Paris, 1618.

P. DE L'ANCRE, *L'incredulité et mescreance du sortilege plainement convaincue*, Paris, 1622, pp. 156–73.

MICHAEL MAULERUS (M. MAUCLERC), *De monarchia divina, ecclesiastica et seculari christiana, deque sancta inter ecclesiasticam et secularem illam coniuratione, amico respectu, honoreque reciproco, in ordine ad aeternam non omissa temporali felicitatem*, Paris, 1622, Book 7, chapter 10, col. 1565–9.

HIPPOLYTE RAULIN, *Panegyre orthodoxe, mystérieux et prophetique sur l'antiquité, dignité, noblesse et splendeur des fleurs de lys*, Paris, 1625, pp. 116–80.

RENÉ DE CERIZIERS, S. J., *Les heureux commencemens de la France chrestienne sous l'apostre de nos roys S. Remy*, Rheims, 1633, pp. 190–206.

BESIAN ARROY, *Questions décidées, sur la Justice des Armes des Rois de France, sur les Alliances avec les heretiques ou infidelles et sur la conduite de la Conscience des gens de guerre*, Paris, 1634, pp. 39–46.

(DANIEL DE PRIEZAC), *Vindiciae gallicae adversus Alexandrum Patricium Armacanum, theologicum*, Paris, 1638, pp. 60–5.

LOUIS MAIMBOURG, S. J., *De Galliae regum excellentia, ad illud D. Gregorii Magni: quanto caeteros homines Regia dignitas antecedit; tanto caeterarum gentium Regna Regni Francici culmen excedit, Panegyricus in solemnibus Rhotomag. gymnasii comitiis . . . dictus XIII Kal. Decembr. anno 1640*, Rouen, 1641, pp. 26–34.

DOM GUILLAUME MARLOT, *Le Theatre d'honneur et de magnificence préparé au sacre des roys*, Rheims, 1643, 2nd ed. 1654, pp. 710–24 and 757–60.

GUILLAUME DU PEYRAT, *L'histoire ecclesiastique de la Cour ou les antiquitez et recherches de la chapelle et oratoire du Roy de France*, Paris, 1645, pp. 793–819.

THEODORE and DENYS GODEFROY, *Le ceremonial françois*, 2 vols, Paris, 1649.

JEAN BAPTISTE THIERS, *Traité des superstitions*, Paris, 1679, pp. 424–41 (chapter 36); 4th edition under the title *Traité des superstitions qui regardent les sacremens*, I, 1777, pp. 431–62 (Book 6, chapter 4).

MENIN, *Traité historique et chronologique du sacre et couronnement des rois et reines de France*, 2nd edition, Amsterdam, 1724 (1st edition 1723), pp. 323–9.

(REGNAULT, canon of St-Symphorien at Rheims), *Dissertation historique touchant le pouvoir accordé aux Rois de France de guerir des Escroüelles, accompagné* (sic) *de preuves touchant la verité de la sainte Ampoule*: following the *Histoire des sacres de nos rois* by the same author, Rheims, 1722.

PIERRE LE BRUN, *Histoire critique des pratiques superstitieuses*, new edition of 1750, pp. 112–35.

OROUX, *Histoire ecclésiastique de la cour de France*, Paris, 1776, pp. 180–4.

(The work by RENÉ MOREAU, *De manu Regia, oratio panegyrica et inauguralis habita in collegio Cameracensi regio*, Paris, 1623, mentioned by Rosenbaum (I, p. 43) and Pauly (col. 1092) on the subject of the touch, is really a panegyric of Louis XIII and mentions the touch only in passing (p. 5 and especially pp. 18–19.)

2   English works

WILLIAM TOOKER, *Charisma sive donum sanationis seu explicatio totius quaestionis de mirabilium sanitatum gratia, in qua praecipue agitur de solenni et sacra curatione strumae, cui Reges Angliae rite inaugurati divinitus medicati sunt et quam serenissima Elizabetha, Angliae, Franciae et Hiberniae Regina, ex coelesti gratia sibi concessa, Applicatione manuum suarum, et contactu morbidarum partium, non sine Religiosis ceremoniis et precibus, cum admirabili et faelici successu in dies sanat*, London, 1597.

WILLIAM CLOWES, *A right frutefull and approved treatise for the artificiall cure of that malady called in Latin, Struma, and in English, the Evill, cured by Kynges and Queenes of England*, London, 1602.

To the Kings most Excellent Majesty The Humble Petition Of divers hundreds Of the Kings poore Subjects, Afflicted with that grievous Infirmitie Called the Kings Evill. Of which by his Majesties absence they have no possibility of being cured, wanting all meanes to gain accesse to his Majesty, by reason of His abode at Oxford; London, *Printed for John Wilkinson, Feb. 20, Anno Dom.* 1643, 8 pp. British Museum Thomason Tracts E 90 (6). The title page is reproduced by C. Cox, *The parish registers of England*, London (The Antiquary's Books), 1910, p. 181.

JOHN BIRD, *Ostenta Carolina, or the late Calamities of England with the authors of them. The great happiness and happy government of K. Charles II ensuing, miraculously foreshewn by the Finger of God in two wonderful diseases, the Rekets and Kings-evil. Wherein is also proved, I that the reckets after a while shall seize in no more children but vanish by means of K. Charles II, II that K. Charles II is the last of Kings which shall so heal the Kings-evil*, London, 1661.

Χειρεξοχη. *The Excellency or Handywork of the Royal Hand*, London, 1665.

RICHARD WISEMAN, *Severall Chirurgical Treatises*: Book 4, *A treatise of the King's Evil*, Chapter 1, 'Of the cure of the Evil by the King's touch', 1st edition, London, 1676; 6th edition, 1734, I, pp. 392–7.

J. BROWNE, *Adenochoiradelogia; or an anatomick-chirurgical treatise of gandules and strumaes, or king's evil swellings; together with the royal gift of healing, or cure thereof by contact or imposition of hands, performed for above* 640 *years by our kings of England, continued with their admirable effects and miraculous events; and concluded with many wonderful examples of cures by their sacred touch*, London, 1684. Part 3, entitled *Charisma Basilikon or the Royal Gift of Healing Strumaes or Kings-Evil*, is devoted to the royal miracle. It is paginated separately and unless indicated otherwise all my references are to it.

RICHARD CARR, *Epistolae medicinales variis occasionibus conscriptae*, London, 1691, ep. 14, pp. 152–8.

A letter from a gentleman at Rome to his friend in London, giving an account of some very surprising Cures in the King's Evil by the Touch; lately effected in the Neighbourhood of that City . . . Translated of the Italian, London, 1721.

WILLIAM BECKETT, *A free and impartial inquiry into the antiquity and efficacy of touching for the cure of the King's evil . . . Now first published in order to a compleat confutation of that supposed supernatural power lately justified in a pamphlet, intituled A letter from a gentleman at Rome to his friend in London . . .*, London, 1722.

RICHARD BLACKMORE, *Discourses on the Gout, a Rheumatism and the King's Evil*, London, 1726.

(SAMUEL WERENFELS), *Occasional thoughts on the power of curing for the king's-evil ascribed to the kings of England*, London, 1748. This forms Part 2 (with separate title and pagination) of the brochure entitled *A Dissertation upon super-stition in natural things*, London, 1748.

*JOHN BADGER, *Cases of Cures of the King's Evil perfected by the royal touch*, London, 1748 (indicated in *Notes and Queries*, 3rd series, I (1862), p. 258, but apparently missing from the B.M.)

(JOHN DOUGLAS), *The Criterion or Miracles examined with a view to expose the pretensions of Pagans and Papists to compare the Miraculous Powers recorded in the New Testament with those said to subsist in Later Times, and to shew the great and material Difference between them in Point of Evidence: from whence it will appear that the former must be True, and the latter may be false*, London, 1754, pp. 191–205.

3 Works by authors other than French and English

MARTIN DELRIO, S.J., *Disquisitionum magicarum libri sex*, Lib. I, cap. 3, qu. iv, Mainz, 1606, I, pp. 57–65 (I have not seen the first edition, Mainz, 1593). A number of points are developed in the 1624 edition, Mainz, pp. 24–7.

O. WIESELGREEN, ' "The King's Evil", Zwei gleichzeitige Berichte' *Archiv für Kulturgeschichte*, 12, 1916, pp. 410–11 (accounts by the Swedish travellers Rosenhane—to London in 1629—and Gyldenstolpe—to Versailles in 1699).

ALEXANDER PATRICIUS ARMACANUS (JANSENIUS), *Mars Gallicus seu de justitia armorum et foederum regis Galliae libri duo: editio novissima*, 2nd edition, no place, 1636, Book I, chap. 13, pp. 65–72 (the first edition, 1635).

DR FRANCISCO MARTY Y VILADAMOR, *Cataluna en Francia Castilla sin Cataluna y Francia contra Castilla. Panegyrico glorioso al christianissimo monarca Luis XIII el Iusto*, Barcelona, 1641, chapter 11, pp. 81–4.

PHILIPPUS CAMERARIUS, *Operae horarum subcisivarum sive meditationes historicae; Centuria tertia*, chap. 42, 'De peculiaribus donis Regum et Principum nonnullorum sanandi aegrotos et peculiaribus eorum notis', Frankfurt, 1644, pp. 143–6. This is the earliest of the editions I was able to consult. The first edition of the *Centuria tertia* was published at Frankfurt in 1609 (cf. Meusel, *Bibliotheca historica*, I, 2, Leipzig, 1784, p. 338). The book which had great success was reprinted and translated numerous times. French translation by S(imon) G(oulard): *Le Troisiesme volume des meditations historiques de M. Philippe Camerarius*, Lyon, 1610, pp. 171–5 (with additions).

JOHANNES JACOBUS CHIFLETIUS (J. J. CHIFLET), *De ampulla Remensi nova et accurata disquisitio*, Antwerp, 1651, (especially pp. 57–8).

JOANNIS LAZARI GUTIERRII (J. L. GUTIERREZ), *Opusculum de Fascino*, Lyon, 1653, pp. 153–6.

*G. TRINKHUSIUS, *De curatione regum per contactum*, Jena, 1667 (mentioned in Rosenbaum, *Addimenta*, II, p. 64).

GASPAR A REIES, *Elysius jucundarum quaestionum campus*, Frankfurt am Main, 1670, qu. 24 and 28.

DANIEL GEORGIUS MORHOVIUS (MORHOF), *Princeps medicus*, Rostock, 1665 (48 pp.). Reprinted in D. G. Morhofi, *Dissertationes academicae*, Hamburg, 1699.

JOHANNES JOACHIMUS ZENTGRAFF, *Disputatio prior de tactu Regis Franciae, quo strumis laborantes restituuntur*, Wittenberg, 1667 (16 pp.); *Disputatio posterior de tactu Regis Franciae*, Wittenberg, 1667 (16 pp.).

JOHANN CHRISTIAN LUENIG, *Theatrum ceremoniale historico-politicum*, II, Leipzig, 1720, pp. 1015 and 1043–7.

*S. P. HILSCHER, *De cura strumarum contactu regio facta*, Jena, 1730.

In connection with the touch or at least with the healing power of kings, ROSENBAUM (*Addimenta*, II, p. 64) mentions Mich. Bernh. Valentin, *De herniis arcano regis Galliarum absque sectione curandis*, Giessen, 1697. We can identify this with Zentgraff, *Disputatio VI: De nova herniarum cura* included in the *Polychresta exotica* of Michael Bernhardus Valentinus, Frankfurt, 1700. The subject is a cure for hernia called 'le secret du Roy', a simple cure with a name destined to catch the imagination of the people but with no connection whatsoever with the royal miracle.

IV   *The touch for scrofula: works after 1800*

1   General

CHR. BARFOED, *Haands Paalaeggelse* (Medicinsk-Historiske Smaaskriften ved Vilhelm Maar, 8), Copenhagen, 1914.

JOSEPH M. BATISTA Y ROCA, 'Touching for the King's Evil', *Notes and Queries*, 12th series, III, 1917, pp. 480–2.

*J. R. BILLINGS, 'The King's Touch for Scrofula', *Proceedings of Charaka Club, New York*, II.

PAULUS CASSEL, *Le roi te touche*, Berlin, 1864 (*2nd edition, Berlin, 1878).

A. CHÉREAU and A. DELAMBRE, *Dictionnaire encyclopédique des sciences médicales*, vol. 32, 1885, article on 'Écrouelles', pp. 481–6.

L. CHOULANT, 'Die Heilung der Skrofeln durch Königshand', *Denkschrift zur Feier der fünfzigjährigen Amtsführung . . . J. A. W. Hedenus . . . hgg. von der Gesellschaft für Natur- und Heilkunde in Dresden*, Dresden, 1833.

RAYMOND CRAWFURD, *The King's Evil*, Oxford, 1911.

EBSTEIN, 'Die Heilkraft der Könige', *Deutsche mediz. Wochenschrift*, 1908, I, pp. 1104–7.

EBSTEIN, 'Zur Geschichte der Krankenbehandlung durch Handauflegung und verwandte Manipulation', *Janus*, 1910, pp. 220–8 and 1911, pp. 99–101.

E. GURLT, *Geschichte der Chirurgie und ihrer Ausübung*, 3 vols, Berlin, I, pp. 104, 108, 110; II, pp. 139, 871; III, p. 570.

L. LANDOUZY, *Le Toucher des Ecrouelles, L'Hôpital Saint-Marcoul. Le Mal du Roi*, 1907 (printed for the Association française pour l'Avancement des sciences; a development of a shorter article in the *Presse Médicale*, 10 May 1905).

*M. A. STARR, 'The king's evil and its relation to psychotherapy', *Medical Record*, New York, 1917 and 1918.

2   Works on the French ceremony

E. BRISSAUD, 'Le mal du roi', *Gazette hebdomadaire de médecine et de chirurgie*, 22, 1885, pp. 481–92.

Dr CABANÈS, *Remèdes d'autrefois*, 2nd series, 1913, pp. 5–74.

Abbé CERF, 'Du toucher des écrouelles par les rois de France', *Travaux Acad. Reims*, 43, 1865–6, pp. 224–88.

ALFRED FRANKLIN, 'Les rois de France et les écrouelles', *Nouvelle Iconographie de la Salpêtrière*, 4, 1891, pp. 161–6. The article is reprinted in A. Franklin, *La vie privée d'autrefois, Les médecins*, Paris, 1892, pp. 254–68.

A. JAL, *Dictionnaire critique de biographie et d'histoire* under the word 'Écrouelles', 2nd edition, 1872, pp. 522–3.

C. LEBER, *Des cérémonies du sacre*, Paris, 1825, pp. 447–61 and 523–4.

A. LECOCQ, *Empiriques, somnambules et rebouteurs beaucerons*, Chartres, 1862, pp. 11–19.

E. MARQUIGNY, 'L'attouchement du roi de France guérissait-il des écrouelles?', *Études religieuses, historiques et littéraires*, 4th series, I, 1868, pp. 374–90.

GIOVANNI MARTINOTTI, 'Re taumaturghi: Francesco I a Bologna nel 1515', *L'Illustrazione Medica Italiana*, 4, 1922, pp. 134–7.

R. DE MAULDE-LA-CLAVIÈRE, *Les origines de la Révolution française au commencement du XVIe siècle*, Paris, 1889, pp. 26–8.

R. DE MAULDE-LA-CLAVIÈRE, *La diplomatie au temps de Machiavel*, Paris, 1892, I, pp. 52, 60 (reissued in 1893 under the title *Histoire de Louis XII, Deuxième partie: La diplomatie, I*).

ROSHEM, 'Les écrouelles, leur étiologie, leur traitement vers 1690', *Paris Médical*, 13, 17 March 1923, 'variétés', pp. vi-x.

KARL WENCK, *Philipp der Schöne von Frankreich, seine Persönlichkeit und das Urteil der Zeitgenossen*, Marburg, 1905, pp. 54–7.

3   Works on the English ceremony

WILLIAM ANDREWS, *The doctor in history, literature, folklore etc.*, Hull and London, 1896, pp. 8–23.

H. FRANÇOIS-DELABORDE, 'Du toucher des écrouelles par les rois d'Angleterre', *Mélanges d'histoire offerts a M. Ch. Bémont*, Paris, 1913. The article 'Le toucher des écrouelles par les rois d'Angleterre' by the same author in *Bulletin soc. antiquaires de France*, 1913, pp. 86–8 is a kind of résumé of that in *Mélanges*.

HELEN FARQUHAR, 'Royal Charities', *British Numismatic Journal*, 12, 1916, pp. 39–135; 13, 1917, pp. 95–163; 14, 1918, pp. 89–120; 15, 1919, pp. 141–84.

KARL FEYERABEND, 'Bilder aus der englischen Kulturgeschichte, I, Die königliche Gabe', *Die Grenzboten*, 1904, I, pp. 703–14 and 763–73.

FIELDING H. GARRISON, 'A Relic of the King's Evil in the Surgeon General's Library (Washington D.C.)', *Proceedings of the Royal Society of Medicine*, 7, 1914, *Section of the History of Medicine*, pp. 227–34 (A résumé of this article has appeared in German under the title of 'Medizinisch-historisch Denkmäler des Königsübels in der Medizinischen Bibliothek des Kriegsministeriums zu Washington', *Archiv für die Geschichte der Naturwissenschaften und der Technik*, 6, 1913, pp. 113–16).

EMANUEL GREEN, 'On the Cure by Touch, with some Notes on some Cases in Somerset', *Proceedings of the Bath Natural History and Antiquarian Field Club*, 5 (No. 2, 1883), pp. 79–98.

EDWARD LAW HUSSEY, 'On the cure of scrofulous diseases attributed to the royal touch', *Archaeological Journal*, 10, 1853, pp. 187–211; cf. ibid., p. 337.

THOMAS LATHBURY, *A History of the convocation of the Church of England*, 2nd edition, London, 1853, pp. 428–39.

W. E. H. LECKY, *History of England in the Eighteenth Century*, London, 1892, I, pp. 84–90.

CORNELIUS NICHOLLS, 'On the obsolete custom of touching for the King's Evil', *Home Counties Magazine*, 14, 1912, pp. 112–22.

THOMAS J. PETTIGREW, *On superstitions connected with the history and practice of medicine and surgery*, London, 1844, pp. 117–54.

'The royal cure for the King's Evil', *British Medical Journal*, 1899, II, pp. 1182–4; cf. ibid., p. 1234.

W. SPARROW SIMPSON, 'On the forms of prayer recited "at the healing" or touching for the King's Evil', *Journal of the British Archaeological Association*, 1871, pp. 282–307.

ARCHIBALD J. STEPHENS, *The book of common prayer with notes legal and historical*, London (Ecclesiastical History Society), 1850, II, pp. 990–1005.

V   *The healing rings*

(*Note :* several of the works in III and IV have information on the healing rings).

RAYMOND CRAWFURD, 'The blessing of cramp-rings. A chapter in the history of the treatment of epilepsy', *Studies in the history and method of science*, edited by Charles Singer, Oxford, 1917, I, pp. 165–87.

GEORG F. KUNZ, *Rings for the finger, from the earliest known times to the present*, Philadelphia and London, 1917, pp. 336 ff.

HERMENTRUDE, 'Cramp rings', *Notes and Queries*, 5th series, 9, 1878, p. 514.

WILLIAM JONES, *Finger-ring lore*, 2nd edition, London, 1890, pp. 522–6 (largely derived from Waterton, below).

J. STEVENSON, 'On cramp-rings', *Gentleman's Magazine*, 1834, I, pp. 48–50; reprinted in the *Gentleman's Magazine Library*, G. L. Gomme, Vol. 3, *Popular Superstitions*, London, 1884, pp. 39–42.

C. J. S. THOMPSON, *Royal cramp and other medycinable rings*, London, 1921, 10 pp.

EDMUND WATERTON, 'On a remarkable incident in the life of St Edward the Confessor, with Notices of Royal Cramp-Rings', *Archaeological Journal*, 21, 1864, pp. 103–13.

VI   *St-Marcoul and the pilgrimage to Corbeny*

BALTHASAR BAEDORF, *Untersuchungen über Heiligenleben der westlichen Normandie*, Bonn, 1913, pp. 24–42.

E. DE BARTHÉLEMY, 'Notice historique sur le prieuré Saint-Marcoul de Corbeny', *Société academique des science, arts . . . de Saint-Quentin*, 3rd series, 13, 1874–5, pp. 198–299.

M. A. BENOIT, 'Un diplôme de Pierre Beschebien, évêque de Chartres: les reliques de Saint Marcoul', *Procès-verbaux, Société archéologique Eure-et-Loir*, 5, 1876, pp. 44–55.

BLAT, *Histoire du pèlerinage de Saint Marcoul à Corbeny*, 2nd edition, Corbeny, 1853.

OUDARD BOURGEOIS, *Apologie pour le pèlerinage de nos roys à Corbeny au tombeau de S. Marcoul, abbé de Nanteuil, contre la nouvelle opinion de Monsieur Faroul, licencié aux droits, doyen et official de Mantes*, Rheims, 1638 (In his *Notice historique sur le prieuré Saint-Marcoul*, E. de Barthélemy writes (p. 210), 'Oudard Bourgeois publia un second ouvrage la même année: *Traité des droits, privileges et immunités de l'église et monastère de Corbeny*.' I have not been able to lay my hands on this book which is not in the Bibliothèque Nationale. Has not a confusion arisen in de Barthélemy's mind? Like me, Ledouble (*Notice sur Corbeny*, p. 131) has looked for the *Traité* and failed to find it.

H. M. DUPLUS, *Histoire et pèlerinage de Saint-Marcoul*, Dijon, 1856.

SIMON FAROUL, *De la dignité des roys de France et du privilege que Dieu leur a donné de guarir les escroüelles : ensemble la vie de saint Marcoul abbé de Nanteuil*, Paris, 1633.

CHARLES GAUTHIER, *Saint Marcoul ou Marculphe abbé de Nanteuil, sa vie, ses reliques, son culte . . .*, Angers, 1899.

EMILE H. VAN HEURCK, *Les drapelets de pèlerinage en Belgique et dans les pays voisins. Contribution à l'iconographie et à l'histoire des pèlerinages*, Antwerp, 1922.

Abbé LEDOUBLE, *Notice sur Corbeny, son prieuré et le pèlerinage à Saint Marcoul*, Soissons, 1883.

LE POULLE, *Notice sur Corbeny, son prieuré et le pèlerinage de Saint-Marcoul*, Soissons, 1883.

Notice sur la vie de Saint Marcoul et sur son pèlerinage à Archelange, Cîteaux, 1879.

C. J. SCHÉPERS, 'Le pèlerinage de Saint-Marcoul à Grez-Doiceau (canton de Wavre)', *Wallonia*, 7, 1899, pp. 177–83.

LOUIS TEXIER, *Extraict et abrégé de la vie de S. Marcoul Abbé*, Saumur, 1648, 8pp (following *Discours touchant la fondation de la chapelle Nostre-Dame de Guarison à Russé*).

VII *The royal birthmark*

(*Note:* Camerarius, *Operae horarum subcisivarum*, mentioned above, should be added to this list as an ancient source).

OTTO GEISSLER, *Religion und Aberglaube in den mittelenglischen Versromanzen*, Halle, 1908, pp. 73–4.

H. GRAUERT, 'Zur deutschen Kaisersage', *Histor. Jahrbuch*, 13, 1892, pp. 122, 135–6.

FERDINAND LOT, 'La croix des royaux de France', *Romania*, 20, 1891, pp. 278–81 (with a note by Gaston Paris).

PIO RAJNA, *Le origini dell'epopea francese*, Florence, 1884, chapter 12, pp. 294–9.

ANTOINE THOMAS, 'Le "signe royal" et le secret de Jeanne d'Arc', *Revue Historique*, 103, 1910, pp. 278–82.

Index